# FiNANCiAL ACCOUNTiNG

*PRINCIPLES AND ISSUES—SECOND EDITION*

## Michael H. Granof

*Graduate School of Business*
*University of Texas at Austin*

PRENTICE-HALL, INC., Englewood Cliffs, NJ 07632

*Library of Congress Cataloging in Publication Data*

Granof, Michael H
    Financial accounting.

    Includes index.
    1.  Accounting.  I.  Title.
HF5635.G772  1980        657        79-20101
ISBN  0-13-314153-5

Editorial/production supervision
and interior design by **Esther S. Koehn**
Cover by **Miriam Recio**
Manufacturing buyer: **Edmund W. Leone**

Printed in the United States of America

10  9  8  7  6  5  4  3  2  1

Prentice-Hall International, Inc., *London*
Prentice-Hall of Australia Pty. Limited, *Sydney*
Prentice-Hall of Canada, Ltd., *Toronto*
Prentice-Hall of India Private Limited, *New Delhi*
Prentice-Hall of Japan, Inc., *Tokyo*
Prentice-Hall of Southeast Asia Pte. Ltd., *Singapore*
Whitehall Books Limited, Wellington, *New Zealand*

# Contents

*Preface*                                                                    ix

**1** *Introduction*                                                          1

Accounting: A Dynamic Discipline / Objectives of
Accounting / Standards and Nonstandards / The Accounting
Profession / Summary

**2** *A Look at Financial Statements*                                       25

The Balance Sheet / The Income Statement / The Balance
Sheet—A More Detailed Examination / The Income
Statement—A Closer Look / The Statement of Retained
Earnings / The Statement of Changes in Financial Position /
A Financial Report Illustrated / Measures of Financial
Performance / Summary

## 3  *The Recording Process*   **73**

Ledger Accounts / Debits and Credits / Journal Entries /
Revenues and Expenses / Closing Entries / Overview /
The Complete Accounting Cycle Demonstrated / Summary

## 4  *Accruing Revenues and Expenses*   **121**

The Accrual Concept / Periodic Adjusting Entries / Year-End
Adjustments—An Example / Errors and Omissions / Cost of Goods
Sold / Product vs. Period Costs / Basic Books of Accounting /
Summary

## 5  *Revenues and Expenses*   **169**

Statement of the Problem / Impact upon Related Accounts /
Guidelines for Revenue Recognition / Recognition at Time
of Sale / Recognition During Production / Recognition at Completion
of Production / Recognition upon Collection of Cash / Analysis of
Transactions / Revenue Recognition—Selected Industry Problems /
Revenue and Expense Recognition—An Overview / Timing of Expenses /
Arm's-length Transactions / Monetary Unit / The Going Concern /
Conservatism / Summary

## 6  *Valuation of Assets:*
## *Cash and Marketable Securities*   **211**

### Part I: Valuation of Assets

Historical Cost / Market Values / Value to User / Compound
Interest and Value of Cash Receipts / Discounted Cash Flow
as a Means of Determining the Value of Assets / Summary
of Part I

### Part II: Cash and Marketable Securities

Cash / Marketable Securities / Valuation of Marketable
Securities—An Alternative Approach / Summary of Part II

**7** *Receivables and Payables*   245

Receivables–An Overview / Uncollectible Accounts Receivable /
Methods of Estimating Uncollectibles / Industry Example: Real
Estate Investment Trusts / Sales Returns / Cash Discounts /
Promissory Notes / Notes with Interest Included in Face Value /
Noninterest-Bearing Notes / Industry Example: Retail Land
Sales Companies / Receivables and Revenue in Practice: The
Franchise Industry / Payroll Transactions / Summary

**8** *Inventories and Cost of Goods Sold*   285

Accounting for Quantities on Hand / Objectives / Costs
Included in Inventory / Flows of Costs / Specific Identification /
First In, First Out / Weighted Average / Last In, First Out / The
Rationale for LIFO / LIFO–Some Reservations / LIFO–Its Recent
Popularity / Retail Inventory Method / Lower of Cost or Market
Rule / Proposed Alternative: Use of Current Values / Summary

**9** *Long-Lived Assets
and the Allocation of Their Costs*   321

Issues of Valuation / Advantages of Historical Costs / Issues
of Ownership / Cost of Plant Assets / The Distinction Between
Maintenance or Repairs and Betterments / Depreciation /
Depreciation Based on Productivity / Retirement of Fixed
Assets / Trade-ins / Determination of Useful Life / Natural
Resources and Depletion / Intangible assets / Summary

**10** *Liabilities and Related Expenses*   365

Bonds / The Nature of Bonds / Determination of Discount or
Premium / Recording the Sale of Bonds / Nature of Premium
or Discount / Recording the Payment of Interest / End-of-Year
Accruals / Straight-Line Amortization / Redemption of Bonds /
Interpreting Gains and Losses on Redemptions / Leases /
Accounting for Income Taxes / Investment Tax Credit /
Pensions / Summary

**11** *Transactions Between a Firm and Its Owners* **407**

Proprietorships and Partnerships / Corporations /
Corporations vs. Partnerships: The Distinctions in Perspective /
Distinctive Features of Partnership Accounting / Corporate
Capital Accounts / Common Stock: Characteristics and Rights of
Shareholders / Preferred Stock: Characteristics and Rights of
Shareholders / Formation of a Corporation—Issuance of Common
Stock / Issuance of Additional Shares / Issurance of Preferred
Stock / Transactions in a Corporation's Own Shares / Is Interest
Really an Expense? / Financial Statements: Proprietary vs. Entity
View of a Company / Accounting for Nonprofit Organizations /
Summary

**12** *Special Problems of Measuring and Reporting Dividends and Earnings* **449**

Retained Earnings and Cash Dividends / Dividends in Kind /
Stock Splits / Stock Dividends / When Is a Loss a Loss? /
Appropriations of Retained Earnings / Employee Stock
Options / Income Statement: All-inclusive vs. Current Operating
Performance / Extraordinary Items / Earnings Per Share /
Interim Financial Reports / Summary

**13** *Intercorporate Investments and Earnings* **485**

Level of Influence / Degree of Influence / Cost Method /
Equity Method / Cost and Equity Methods Compared /
Consolidated Reports / Principles of Consolidation—
Balance Sheet / Principles of Consolidation—Income Statement /
Instant Earnings / Pooling of Interests / Summary

**14** *Statement of Changes in Financial Position* 529

Changes in Working Capital / The Statement of Changes in
Financial Position: A Report on Long-Term Financial and Investment
Activity / Changes in Components of Working Capital / Earnings as
a Source of Working Capital / Capital Stock and Related Accounts /
Noncurrent Assets / Noncurrent Debt / Preparation of Funds
Statement—an Example / Statement of Changes in Financial Position
on a Cash Flow Basis / Summary

**15** *Financial Statements:*
*The Perspective of the Analyst* 577

Corporate Personality / Quality of Earnings / Ratio and
Percentage Analysis / Footnotes / Other Required Disclosures /
Summary

**16** *Accounting for Increases in Prices and Values* 623

Historical Costs: Adjusting for Changes in the Level of Prices /
An Alternative Approach to Accounting—Current Values / Ac-
counting Alternatives—Do They Make a Difference? / Concluding
Comment

*Appendix* 665

Table 1: Future Value of $1 / Table 2: Present Value of $1 /
Table 3: Future Value of an Annuity of $1 in Arrears / Table 4:
Present Value of an Annuity of $1 in Arrears

*Index* 675

# Preface

The objective of the revised edition of this text is the same as that of the first edition. It is to present an introduction to financial accounting in practice and in theory. The text aims to provide students with an understanding of basic accounting principles as well as with an appreciation of the significant issues currently facing the accounting profession.

The distinguishing feature of this text is that it presents accounting as a dynamic and sometimes controversial discipline, not as a dogmatic set of rules or even principles. It points out the limitations of, as well as the rationale for, current practice. It challenges the reader not only to understand what is being done today, but also to become aware of why continually changing circumstances require constant reevaluation of specific accounting methods.

The author believes that professors of accounting are prone to underestimating the intellectual abilities of their students to cope with fundamental accounting issues. Even the seemingly complex questions that are begin debated today—if presented in a clear and straightforward manner—can readily be understood and appreciated by students in a first or second course in accounting.

The text focuses on the historical cost "model" of accounting—

that on which conventional accounting is based—in order to make certain that the reader has a thorough knowledge and understanding of the profession as it is practiced today. However, integrated throughout the text are discussions of alternative approaches, including fair market and discounted cash flow valuation methods. The alternative approaches are introduced because they serve to highlight the strengths and limitations of current practices and they enable students to view current procedures from several different perspectives.

By introducing students to accounting controversies at the very start of their careers—indeed, on the first page of the text—the author assumes two risks. The first is that they will be confused by the differences between current and proposed practices. They should be on guard, therefore, to distinguish those sections of the text that describe "what is" from those that discuss "what might be." The second is that readers will be left with the impression that most businesses select certain accounting practices solely because they permit the presentation of financial data in the most favorable and self-serving light. These risks have been taken to expose students to the availability of alternative methods and to make students aware of the often conflicting objectives that the accountant is attempting to reconcile. It is to be hoped that readers will thereby be able to appreciate both the problems and challenges the profession faces and to put its shortcomings in proper perspective.

The revised edition contains new or expanded materials on a number of issues which have taken on greater import since the publication of the first edition. Among them are foreign currency translation, oil and gas accounting, and replacement cost accounting. A brief discussion of the features of nonprofit accounting has also been added. Several sections of the text have been rewritten in an effort to make them clearer.

A few topics that were covered in the first edition have been omitted from the second. Among them are compensating balances and prior period adjustments. They are no less important today than they were several years ago. Inasmuch as those issues which are included in the text can only be viewed as *examples* of questions facing the profession, preference has generally been given to those which seem to be of greater current concern.

Each chapter (except for the first) contains an exercise for review which addresses one or two key topics covered in the text. (Solutions to these exercises appear at the end of chapters.) By asking a series of leading questions it is intended to draw the student toward a greater understanding of the material discussed.

As in the previous edition, some of the problems at the conclusion of each chapter are intended to demonstrate the rationale for particular practices, others show their limitations. Many are designed to be provocative and to highlight current issues. There are several problems with alternative solutions, each of which may be defensible. The student should not be satisfied with an answer merely because it results in a journal entry or financial report that is "in balance." Instead he or she should carefully weigh the implications of the particular methods used to account for the transaction in question and consider whether an alternative approach might not lead to financial reports that are more appropriate in the circumstances.

A student guide that sets forth in outline form the key points presented in the textbook is available for purchase. Additional illustrations, exercises and problems—most of which address fundamental accounting concepts and practices—and a glossary of words and phrases are provided. (Solutions are given for the exercises and problems.) This student guide has been prepared by Thomas G. Evans, Charles Inman, and the author of the text in recognition of the fact that for most students the accounting process represents a new way of classifying, recording, and summarizing financial events. Once the fundamental principles and practices have been mastered the study of accounting becomes relatively easy.

### Acknowledgments

I am indebted to numerous individuals for their assistance in writing and preparing the revised edition of this text.

Robin Hatami of the University of Texas worked closely with me in editing the manuscript, preparing the problems, compiling an index and proofreading the galleys. His advice was as welcome as it was sound.

The following reviewers made exceedingly useful comments and suggestions: Thomas G. Evans, University of South Carolina; Robert N. Freeman, University of California at Berkeley; Lawrence Kessler, Duke University; Mohamed Onsi, Syracuse University.

M. H. G.
*Austin, Texas*

# 1

# Introduction

## Accounting: A Dynamic Discipline

Accounting involves the collection, summarization, and reporting of financial information. It is a dynamic discipline in which new principles and procedures are constantly evolving. The objective of this text is to enable the reader to acquire a reasonably sophisticated understanding of financial accounting. It aims to provide the reader with an overview of basic accounting principles as well as a familiarity with the significant issues currently facing the accounting profession. The theme of the book is that there are very few accounting principles which are not subject to challenge. It is essential that the student understand not only how accounting is currently practiced and why it is so practiced but also, and most significantly, which the possible alternatives are.

Accountants are concerned with the description of economic events, with the *measurement* of economic values, and with the determination of periodic changes in such economic values. A brief example can be used to demonstrate the difficulty of establishing precise rules of measurement that can be unanimously agreed upon. The illustration involves concepts and terminology that will be defined or explained in subsequent chapters; a layman's understanding of them should suffice, however, to appreciate why a number of basic accounting issues remain unresolved.

Home Heating Oil, Inc. was organized on January 1, 1980. On that date the company sold to individual investors shares of common stock for $1 million cash. The objective of the company was to purchase heating oil from a refinery and to resell and deliver it to residential customers. Upon its formation the company purchased storage tanks, delivery trucks, and other equipment at a total cost of $1 million. The useful life of such *fixed assets* was estimated at 10 years.

The following additional events took place during the company's first year of operations:

> The company purchased 4 million gallons of heating oil at a total cost of $2.4 million (an average cost of $.60 per gallon).
> The company sold 3.6 million gallons of oil at a price of $.70 per gallon. Total sales revenue was, therefore $2.52 million, and at the end of the year the firm had in inventory (i.e., goods available for sale) the 400,000 gallons that had not yet been sold.

Total operating costs for the year, including labor, advertising, selling, and administrative costs, were $200,000.

The question at issue is how much profit did the firm earn during its first year of operations. Income, or profit, is a measure of change in "well-offness." How much "better off" was the firm at the end of the year than it was at the beginning?

Profit is commonly computed by deducting from sales or other revenues the expenses incurred in the production of such revenues. Thus, for the first year of operations,

| | | |
|---|---:|---:|
| Sales revenue (3.6 million gal @ $.70 per gal) | | $2,520,000 |
| Less: Costs applicable to revenues: | | |
| Cost of goods sold (3.6 million gal @ $.60 per gal) | $2,160,000 | |
| Other operating expenses | 200,000 | |
| Depreciation ($1 million ÷ 10 years) | 100,000 | 2,460,000 |
| Income | | $   60,000 |

Sales revenue for the year was $2.52 million. Cost of the heating oil *purchased* (at an *average* price of $.60 per gallon) was $2.4 million, but of the 4 million gallons purchased only 3.6 million gallons, or 90 percent of those purchased, were actually sold. Hence the cost of the oil actually sold was 90 percent of $2.4 million, or $2,160,000. Cost of the remaining 400,000 gallons that were being held in inventory awaiting sale cannot be considered an expense of the first year of operations since the oil has not yet been used and can be assumed to retain its original value.

Operating expenses of the period were $200,000. In addition, the company purchased fixed assets at a cost of $1 million. But the entire purchase price of such fixed assets cannot be considered to be an expense only of the first year of operations. The assets have a 10-year life; they will serve to benefit 10 accounting periods. The cost must be spread over, or *allocated* to, each of the 10 periods. Hence depreciation for the period was $1 million ÷ 10 = $100,000.

The implication of the "bottom line" of the income statement is that Home Heating Oil, Inc. and collectively its stockholders were $60,000 better off at the end of the first year of operations than they were at the beginning. The computation of net income was governed by "generally accepted accounting principles"—those currently followed by the large majority of accountants and their clients.

But is the company really $60,000 better off at the end of the year than it was at the beginning? Consider some alternative approaches to determining the income of the company. Suppose that the "going" or "market" price for the fixed assets which the company had purchased on January 1 for $1 million had, by year end, increased to $1,150,000. Should $150,000 be added to the revenues ("revenue from appreciation of fixed assets") to reflect the increase in value (thus increasing income to $210,000)? Or should the increase in market value be ignored? Under conventional accounting procedures (for reasons to be indicated shortly) the increase in the value of the fixed assets *would not,* in fact, be reported in financial reports to be made available to stockholders, creditors, or the general public. But many accountants argue that conventional procedures should be modified so that gains from appreciation are given recognition in accounting reports.

Suppose also that, of the 4 million gallons of heating oil that were purchased at a total cost of $2.4 million, the first 3.6 million were purchased at a price of $.59 per gallon (a total cost of $2,124,000) and the last 400,000 gallons were purchased at a price of $.69 per gallon (a total cost of $276,000). Should the cost of the 3.6 million gallons sold be computed using the *weighted average* price of oil purchased during the year ($.60, as in the earlier computation), or should it be assumed that the oil that was purchased first was sold first? If the latter assumption is made, then the cost of goods sold would not be $2,160,000 as previously calculated. Instead it would be 3.6 million gallons times $.59 per gallon: $2,124,000. Since the cost of goods sold would then be $36,000 less than before, income would be $36,000 greater: $96,000.

Alternatively, since all oil purchased was mixed together in the same tank, is it less logical to assume that the oil purchased *last* was sold first? Cost of goods sold would then be 400,000 times $.69 per gallon + 3.2 million times $.59 per gallon—a total of $2,164,000 (as compared with $2,160,000)—and income would be $4,000 *less* than that originally computed. Conventional practice would permit the company to make any one of the three assumptions regarding the flow of costs; it could assume that the goods sold were purchased at an "average" price, the first price, or the last price.

Suppose additionally that in the course of the company's first year of operations inflation was a major problem in the country and that the general consumer price level increased by 10 percent. Was the income of the company still $60,000? Were the shareholders of the company really $60,000 better off at the end of the accounting period than they were at the beginning? When they initially purchased the common sock of Home Heating Oil, Inc. they surrendered $1 million of purchasing power. If after one year they were able to sell the stock for $1,060,000—original investment plus the "income" of the period—they would clearly be worse off at the end of the period than they were at the beginning, for it would take $1.1 million to purchase the goods and services that previously could have been obtained for $1 million. Should the financial statements of the company take into account the loss of purchasing power? Traditional practice would ignore the loss of purchasing power, but a large number of accountants believe that the company should prepare two sets of financial statements: one which takes into account the impact of inflation and one which does not.

The objective of this oversimplified example is to dispel at the very beginning of this text any notion that the study of accounting is merely a matter of learning to apply existing rules and procedures. Unfortunately, there are few definitive answers to questions asked of accountants. The discipline of accounting is alive with issues that are currently—and likely to remain forever—unresolved. In reading and studying this text, the student should strive not only to understand and be able to apply what is currently being done in practice but also to be able to evaluate available alternatives in light of the objectives of financial reporting.

## Objectives of Accounting

Accounting aims to provide information to facilitate a number of key functions. Among them are

1. *Allocating the scarce resources of our society.* Under any form of economic arrangement, be it capitalism or socialism, decisions as to where capital should be invested are made on the basis of information contained in financial statements. In a free enterprise system, private investors make determinations as to the stock of companies they purchase largely on the basis of data contained in periodic reports of earnings. Bankers and other suppliers of funds study financial reports before making loan decisions. Government agencies decide whom to tax and whom to subsidize on the basis of financial reports. The decisions of labor unions as to how much of a wage increase to seek are strongly influenced by reports of profit or loss.

2. *Managing and directing the resources within an organization.* Profit and nonprofit entities alike rely upon accounting information to assure that they maintain effective control over both their human and material resources and to make certain that within their organizations they allocate such resources to the products, subunits, or functions where they can be most productive.

3. *Reporting on the custodianship of resources under the command of individuals or organizations.* Individuals, acting either as investors or merely as citizens, entrust resources to professional managers and governmental officials. They expect such managers or officials to provide them with periodic reports by which their performance in office can be evaluated.

Accounting focuses on the *measurement and communication* of a wide range of financial data. Accountants provide the information required to make decisions as to where to allocate financial resources, and once such decisions are made they provide the data necessary to effectively control such resources. Periodically, as the management process is being carried out, accountants "report the score"—they provide information by which the results of prior decisions can be evaluated.

Viewed from a slightly different perspective, accounting aims to enable investors, creditors, and other users of financial statements to determine the future earning power of an enterprise. Decisions made today can affect only the future, not the past. Those who seek information from financial statements are primarily concerned with how well the enterprise will perform in the years approaching rather than those gone by. Will the enterprise be able to satisfy its obligations to those to whom it is indebted? Will it be able to satisfy the wage demands of its employees? Will it be able to provide adequate returns to its owners?

What will occur in the future, however, can best be predicted by what has taken place in the past. The competence of management in administering the enterprise in the years to come can most readily be forecast by examining the record of prior years. The ability of a firm to generate revenues in years ahead depends in large measure on resources acquired in periods behind. Accounting, while it necessarily reports on events of the past, does so to facilitate decisions that will affect the future.

## Standards and Nonstandards

**relevancy**   If information provided by the accountant is to be useful, then, above all, it must be *relevant*—it must bear upon or be associated directly with the decisions it is designed to facilitate. Unfortunately, what is relevant for one group of financial statement users may not be relevant for another. As a result there is no such thing as "all-purpose" financial statements. Data that may be useful for one type of decision may be useless—or highly misleading—for another. A brief example may illustrate this conflict.

The MNO Company manufactures a single product in a plant that it rents. In a given year it produces and sells to its regular customers 1,000 units at a cost of $300 per unit, determined as follows:

| | |
|---|---:|
| Fixed costs: rent, executive salaries, heat, power, administrative costs, etc. | $100,000 |
| Variable costs: labor and materials ($200 per unit produced × 1,000 units) | 200,000 |
| Total costs | $300,000 |
| Number of units produced and sold | ÷ 1,000 units |
| Cost per unit | $    300 |

The plant is not currently operating at capacity. The federal government has offered to buy 500 units of the product at a price of $250 each. If the company were to accept the offer, its sales to its regular customers would remain unchanged. Should the company sign the contract to sell to the government, even though the selling price is below "cost?"

From the standpoint of an executive of the company, the *relevant* cost to be considered would be $200 per unit, rather than the $300 previously computed. The fixed costs of $100,000 will, of course, remain unchanged whether or not the company accepts the offer of the government. The only additional costs the company would have to incur are the variable costs. If the company accepted the offer of the government, it would earn additional revenue of 500 units times $250 per unit—$125,000—and incur additional costs of 500 units times $200—$100,000. Thus, it would be $25,000 better off by accepting the offer.

If the company accepted the offer, then the average cost of each unit produced would be

| | |
|---|---:|
| Fixed costs: rent, executive salaries, heat, power, administrative costs, etc. | $100,000 |
| Variable costs: $200 per unit produced × 1,500 units (the new level of production) | 300,000 |
| Total costs | $400,000 |
| Number of units produced | ÷ 1,500 |
| Average cost per unit | $ 267 |

The average cost per unit would be the relevant cost for the determination of overall income. But for a decision as to whether or not to accept the offer of the government, the relevant cost would be the *incremental* or *marginal* cost—the cost of producing the additional units required for the government contract.

**objectivity**    Accounting information should, ideally, be *objective* and *verifiable.* Qualified individuals working independently of one another should be able, upon examination of the same data or records, to derive similar measures or reach similar conclusions. Insofar as possible information contained in financial reports should not depend on the subjective judgments of the individual accountant who prepared it.

Herein lies a catch. Information that is most objective may not be relevant to many decisions, and that which is most relevant may not be objective. A few illustrations will serve to highlight the conflict.

1. Should a corporation value land at *historical cost* or *fair market value*? The most objective amount would be *historical cost*—that which the company

paid for the land. Such amount is readily verifiable. But of what relevance is it? The company may have bought such land decades ago, and the historical cost provides no indication of what it can be sold for today. Yet any amount other than historical cost—e.g., present market value—would necessarily involve estimates or appraisals and hence be less objective. *Conventional accounting reports are based on historical costs.* Increases in market values are *not,* as a rule, given accounting recognition. Some accountants maintain, however, that assets should be carried at the amounts for which they could be sold. Their position will be evaluated in the course of the chapters that follow.

2. Should a firm's statement of annual income reflect as earned revenue the potential selling price of goods that the company has produced but not yet sold? Or, alternatively should the firm defer recognition of such revenue until it has actually sold the items, or even until it has actually collected the full selling price in cash? Income is often said to result from the entire process of production and sale, and since the firm is *usually* able to sell what it produces, financial statements in which income has been reported as soon as goods have been produced would be most relevant for most decision purposes. But such statements would be considerably less objective than those in which profit recognition is delayed until the goods have been formally sold—and hence a firm sales price has been established—or until cash has actually been collected and the full amount to be received is known with certainty.

3. Should a company's income statement include as current pension expenses, only amounts actually paid to retired workers or amounts that will eventually have to be paid to present employees as well? A company provides its employees with retirement benefits. The liability for the pensions is incurred during the productive years of the employees. The actual cash payment, however, does not have to be made until an employee retires and the actual amount to be paid may depend on the number of years the employee survives after his retirement. Such amount cannot be determined with certainty until after the employee dies. Should the company report an estimate of the pension expense as the employee "earns" the right to his pension (the most relevant time), or should it wait until it actually disburses the cash (when the expense can be objectively determined)?

One of the central themes of this text is that a great many accounting issues can be attributable to the conflict between the objectives of relevance and objectivity. Accountants are continually faced with situations in which they must trade the realization of one goal for that of the other.

**uniformity** Accounting practices should be uniform both within and among corporations or other organizations. Ideally, financial reports of one enterprise should be readily comparable with those of another. In practice, the goal of comparability has not yet been achieved. Such failure can be ascribed to at least two causes. First, until recently both the professional accounting societies and the government agencies responsible for establishing accounting principles and maintaining accounting standards have allowed individual companies a relatively free hand in selecting among alternative accounting practices. Even today, for example, some firms within the same industry will assume that goods purchased first are sold first, while others will assume that goods purchased last are sold first. Second, the task of prescribing uniform principles that would be appropriate for all companies—or even those within a specific industry—is one that is easier to write about than to accomplish. In the last several decades the range and complexity of business transactions have increased enormously. Accounting procedures designed to account for one type of transaction may be highly inappropriate for a slightly different transaction or even an identical transaction that takes place under slightly differing circumstances. For example, a dividend check received by a company that owns a 1 percent interest in the firm that declared the dividend could justifiably be accounted for differently from one received by a company that owns a 99 percent interest in the same firm; the latter company is likely to control the dividend policy of the firm whereas the former is not.

**consistency**  For a reader to compare performance in one period with that in another, financial statements must be based on accounting practices that are consistent over time. Thus, although different firms may make differing assumptions pertaining to the flow of goods, the same firm would ordinarily be expected to base its financial reports on the same assumptions from one year to the next. "A foolish consistency," Emerson pointed out, however, "is the hobgoblin of little minds." In an era of a rapidly changing business environment, accounting practice must necessarily change also. Hence, over a number of years, some degree of consistency must be sacrificed in order for accounting to achieve its other objectives.

**non-standards**  Laymen place far greater faith in financial statements than is generally warranted. It is essential, therefore, that the limitations of financial statements be clearly understood.

1. Financial statements are *not accurate* (i.e., precise). This is as true if amounts are carried out to the penny as if they are rounded off to the hundreds or, in the case of many published reports, to the thousands of dollars. Accounting statements are necessarily based on estimates; estimates are inherently inaccurate. In an earlier example it was indicated that the useful life of the fixed assets purchased was 10 years. However, is it possible to predict with any degree of precision how long an asset will last? Why not 9 years, or even 15? If in the example useful life were estimated to be 8 years instead of

10, then depreciation charges would have increased from $100,000 per year to $125,000. Net income would have decreased from $60,000 to $35,000—a reduction of over 41 percent!

2. Financial data *cannot be used as the sole measure of managerial accomplishment.* Financial statements of private enterprises generally focus on *profit* or *income.* But profit is by no means a comprehensive measure of performance. Profit tells only a small part of the annual story of a business. Profit for a period of one year can readily be manipulated in order to make an enterprise "look good." To the extent that a manager knows that he will be evaluated on the basis of income for a given single year he can readily increase *reported* profit by postponing maintenance and nonessential repairs, cutting back on advertising and research and development costs, and reducing the quality of products or services. The negative impact of such actions is unlikely to be reflected in reported profits until subsequent years.

But profit, even over a longer period of time, may be only a poor indication of management performance. Profit, after all, can be influenced by factors over which a manager has little control. In the 1970s, for example, some oil companies reported unusually high earnings. Yet because of the sudden increase in worldwide oil prices those years, the managers of a number of individual oil companies would have had to have been thoroughly incompetent not to have led their firms to record earnings. At the same time, managers in firms which were unable to obtain needed petroleum supplies, except at extraordinarily high costs, may have suffered declines in income which could not practically have been avoided. As long as profits are influenced to a considerable extent by forces beyond management control (and such forces do not exert equal pressures on all firms alike—not even those within a given industry) net income by itself may be an inappropriate criterion for management evaluation.

Moreover, managers have goals in addition to that of maximizing profit. (Indeed, some writers have suggested that executives in major corporations do not even attempt to maximize profits; instead they seek to achieve "satisfactory" levels of earnings.) Many managers would include among their goals improving the environment surrounding company plants; increasing the economic, social, physical, and mental well-being of employees; and increasing the number of minority employees on the corporate payroll. Accountants do not purport that the extent to which such objectives have been achieved is given recognition in conventional financial statements.

3. Financial statements are *not neutral.* It is often said that accounting information must be unbiased—that accountants should be disinterested umpires who "call 'em like they see 'em." Accountants may indeed attempt to use an unbiased measuring device when reporting on economic events. But value judgments enter into the measurement process as accountants determine *what* to measure. Accountants measure income as conventionally defined: revenues less expenses. But they include in their measurements only *selected* revenues and expenses. They do not, for example, include in their financial reports costs of "externalities," such as water or air pollution, employee injuries, or discrimina-

tory hiring practices. Similarly, they fail to give recognition to the benefits received by their efforts to clean up the environment, improve community welfare, and eliminate safety hazards. Indeed several firms, on an experimental basis, have prepared "social" income statements and balance sheets which are based on nonconventional judgments as to what revenues and costs should be measured and reported upon.

4. The primary criterion by which the adequacy of financial statements should be judged is *not* whether they minimize the tax liability of the reporting business entity. In the course of this text, numerous alternative accounting procedures will be presented and evaluated. The merits of the alternatives will normally be considered in terms of their objectivity and their relevance to the users of the financial information. Sometimes, unfortunately, a company's choice among alternatives is motivated primarily by income tax considerations, and as a consequence its financial reports are both less objective and less useful to stockholders and potential investors than they might otherwise be.

That is not to say that an accountant should not assist his client in arranging his financial affairs in such a manner as to pay the least amount of taxes legally permissible. Judge Learned Hand has pointed out

> Over and over again courts have said that there is nothing sinister in so arranging one's affairs as to keep taxes as low as possible. Everyone does so, rich and poor; and all do right, for nobody owes any public duty to pay more than the law demands.

But accounting reports filed with the Internal Revenue Service are not generally relevant for decisions that investors, creditors, employees, or managers must make. Taxable income as reported to the Internal Revenue Service is computed in accord with specific provisions of the tax codes and regulations. Such provisions are *not* necessarily consistent with "generally accepted" accounting principles. In general (though with a number of exceptions) a company is permitted to follow differing accounting principles in determining taxable income than in calculating income to be reported to the general public. Some companies do, in fact, maintain supplementary accounting records or even "sets of books." Such a practice is neither illegal nor unethical; it is simply reflective of different information needs of different decision makers.

## *The Accounting Profession*

**a brief background**   Accountants are employed by *public* accounting firms, corporations, and private business enterprises as well as by government and other nonprofit organizations. The term *accountants* is often used to designate persons who provide a wide range of services—from clerks who perform routine clerical functions to corporate vice-presidents who make major financial decisions.

Most commonly, however, the professional accountant is associated with the practice of public accounting. The public accountant who has satisfied various state-imposed education and experience requirements and has demonstrated technical competence on a nationally administered examination is recognized as a *certified public accountant* (CPA). In most states a CPA must have earned a bachelor's degree; must have completed a specified number of courses in accounting and related disciplines such as business law, finance, and economics; and must have been employed as an independent auditor, under the supervision of another CPA, for at least one to three years.

Although modern accounting can trace its roots to 1494, when an Italian monk named Fr. Luca Paciolo described a "double-entry" accounting procedure that forms the basis for accounting practice today, public accounting as a profession is relatively new. The development of the profession was spurred primarily by new forms of economic activity associated with the Industrial Revolution. Many of the significant developments in the early stages of the profession's growth can be traced to Great Britain. By the latter half of the eighteenth century, small associations of professional accountants began to develop. In the early part of the twentieth century, the momentum for growth and innovation shifted to the United States. Since 1900, the number of public accountants in the United States has grown exponentially.

Ask a layman what certified public accountants do, and he is more than likely to refer immediately to income taxes. In truth, the profession is associated with three primary functions: auditing, management advisory services, as well as tax services. It is the auditing function that is unique to, and most characteristic of, the public accounting profession.

## auditing and financial reporting

The purpose of the audit function is to lend credibility to financial reports. Persons who rely upon such reports want assurance that they "present fairly" the results of the economic activities that they purport to describe.

SEC

Regulatory agencies such as the Securities and Exchange Commission and the New York Stock Exchange require that publicly held corporations under their jurisdiction have an *independent* party—a CPA—*attest* to, or vouch for, the fairness of the financial statements the companies issue to their stockholders. Similarly, banks, insurance companies, and other investors and lenders of funds also demand that financial statements on which they intend to rely be audited or attested to by CPAs.

In performing the attest function, the CPA is concerned with *external* financial statements—those given to users outside of the company being reported upon. The division of the accounting discipline dealing with external reports is known as *financial accounting. Internal* financial reports, on the other hand, are those given to managers within a firm to facilitate planning and control. Since such reports are directed to specific users they can be tailor-made to provide information most relevant to the decisions at hand. The division of accounting dealing with internal reports is known as *managerial* accounting. Managerial accounting is ordinarily studied in a second-semester accounting course.

Although the CPA firm is *not* assigned the responsibility of preparing external financial reports—*corporate management* is so charged—its influence over them is predominant. The CPA firm does not, of course, verify each of the transactions underlying the financial statements. In a large corporation the number of transactions in a year would make that an impossible task. The firm does, however, review the accounting systems used to accumulate and summarize the underlying data, tests a substantial number of transactions (especially those involving large dollar amounts), and, most importantly, makes certain that the financial statements have been prepared in conformity with generally accepted accounting principles. The end product of the independent CPA's examination is the auditor's report or opinion on the financial statements. Typically, it might appear as shown in Exhibit 1-1. Alternatively, if the auditors have been unable to obtain sufficient evidential matter on which to base an opinion, or if they take exception to the information as presented, they might disclaim an opinion, qualify their opinion, or even express an "adverse" opinion—i.e., "In our opinion the aforementioned consolidated financial statements *do not* fairly present the financial position. . . ."

## EXHIBIT 1-1

**Report of
Certified Public Accountants**

Arthur Young & Company
Certified Public Accountants

The Board of Directors and Shareholders
Koppers Company, Inc.

We have examined the consolidated financial statements of Koppers Company, Inc. and subsidiaries listed in the accompanying Index to Financial Statements. Our examinations were made in accordance with generally accepted auditing standards and, accordingly, included such tests of the accounting records and such other auditing procedures as we considered necessary in the circumstances.

In our opinion, the financial statements listed in the accompanying Index to Financial Statements present fairly the consolidated financial position of Koppers Company, Inc. and subsidiaries at December 31, 1977 and 1976 and the consolidated results of its operations and changes in its financial position for the years then ended in conformity with generally accepted accounting principles applied on a consistent basis during the period.

*Arthur Young & Company*

Pittsburgh, Pennsylvania
January 24, 1978

In recent years the accounting profession has been severely criticized for its alleged failure to conscientiously fulfill its audit responsibilities. To a great extent such criticism has been the result of a number of corporate bankruptcies, frauds, and illegal or unethical practices. It has been charged that the financial reports of the companies were false and misleading in that they failed to reveal deteriorating financial conditions, misappropriations of funds by high-level corporate officials, or illegal payments to foreign officials. In many of the cases, the auditors were accused of either allowing their clients to employ inappropriate accounting principles or misapplying acceptable accounting principles. In a number of widely publicized cases, auditors have been successfully sued by stockholders who suffered losses attributable to their reliance upon the financial reports, and in other cases auditors have been charged with criminal fraud for actions associated with statements that were allegedly false and misleading. In a number of instances the financial reports in question were said to have artificially inflated company earnings and correspondingly overstated the values of assets or understated the values of liabilities. A key objective of this text is to explore the difficulties faced by management and auditors in selecting among and applying "generally accepted accounting principles" and to highlight resulting limitations of financial reports.

**generally accepted accounting principles**

What are "generally accepted accounting principles?" Who decides what is, and what should be, generally accepted? To a large extent what is generally accepted is what has been done over a large number of years. Hence, tradition and widespread use are major determinants of what is generally accepted.

But in an effort to make practice more uniform, as well as to eliminate obvious abuses in financial reporting, the accounting profession, private industry, and government have created specific organizations to promulgate accounting principles and standards. Two such groups are the *Financial Accounting Standards Board* (FASB) and the *Securities and Exchange Commission* (SEC).

The Financial Accounting Standards Board began operations in 1973. The board consists of seven full-time members, who are drawn from industry, the accounting profession, and government. Its function is to develop accounting principles. The board is appointed by an independent board of trustees, whose members, in turn, are nominated by the American Institute of Certified Public Accountants (AICPA) as well as by several other private organizations concerned with financial reporting. As problems in financial reporting come to its attention, the board, with the assistance of a full-time research staff, examines the relevant considerations. After a lengthy process during which it issues preliminary proposals and receives comments from interested parties, it issues "Statements of Financial Accounting Standards." Such statements must be adhered to by all CPAs in their determination of whether the financial reports of their clients are in conformity with generally accepted accounting principles.

Prior to the formation of the Financial Accounting Standards Board, the task of developing accounting principles was assigned to the *Accounting Principles Board* (APB), which was a board appointed by the AICPA. During its life span of 14 years (1959 to 1973) the APB issued 31 "opinions" which accountants are required to follow. The board was dissolved and replaced by the FASB primarily as the result of criticism that it was too slow in reacting to reported abuses; that its members, many of whom were partners of large CPA firms, were overly influenced by pressures brought by their clients; and that its research capability was inadequate.

The authority of the Securities and Exchange Commission to regulate financial reporting derives from the Securities Act of 1933, the Securities Exchange Act of 1934, and the Public Utility Holding Company Act of 1935. In past years, the SEC, an independent agency of the federal government, has elected to allow responsibility for the establishment of accounting principles to rest in the private sector, specifically with the AICPA and the FASB. In the face of criticism that the authoritative organizations in the private sector have been insufficiently sensitive to the interests of the public at large, the SEC has, in recent years, played an increasingly active role in the promulgation of accounting principles. The pronouncements of the SEC are issued either as amendments to *Regulation S-X,* a document that prescribes the form and content of financial reports to be submitted to the SEC, or as *Accounting Series Releases,* statements that indicate the current positions of the agency on matters of financial reporting. Seldom are the pronouncements of the SEC in direct conflict with those of the FASB, but there can be little question that the FASB takes into account the views of the SEC in formulating its own statements of accounting principles.

The Financial Accounting Standards Board represents what some observers believe to be the final opportunity for the private sector to play the key role in establishing accounting principles. In 1977 and 1978 the accounting profession was scrutinized by two congressional committees, and the reports of these committees were exceedingly critical of the practices of individual CPA firms as well as of the performance of the rule-making organizations. In response to these reports, the profession instituted a number of reforms designed to elevate the quality of its services to the public. Nevertheless, some congressional critics have continued to press for the transfer of regulatory authority from the AICPA and the FASB to the SEC and other governmental agencies.

**tax services**   For many corporations the effective tax rate on income, taking into account federal income taxes as well as state and local taxes, is over 50 percent. For individuals the tax rate on income over a specified amount may be as high as 80 percent. It is critical that a manager give careful consideration to the tax implications of his decisions. Indeed, it is essential that he calculate the tax impact before entering into a transaction, while he still has an opportunity to alter its terms in a way such that the tax burden can be minimized. Accountants serve their clients by advising them how to minimize their tax liability in advance of a business undertaking (tax planning) and by assisting them in filing their periodic tax returns.

**management advisory services**

Most CPAs serve as financial advisors to their clients. Large CPA firms have separate management consulting divisions which provide a wide range of services to both industry and government. Although most consulting engagements are directly related to the accounting and reporting systems of their clients (a large number, for example, involve installation of data processing equipment), some are in such diverse fields as marketing, pensions and insurance, and production management. Smaller CPA firms often provide day-to-day business advice to their clients; some establish the accounting systems used by their clients and maintain a close watch over them to make certain that they are operating as planned.

In recent years the consulting activities of many firms, especially the larger ones, have come under fire for being incompatible with the primary function of CPAs, that of attesting to financial reports. Critics assert that CPAs who provide consulting services cannot be sufficiently independent of their clients to provide unbiased audit services. They question, for example, whether a CPA who has advised a client on means of increasing income, and has seen such advice followed *unsuccessfully,* could be sufficiently objective in auditing the financial reports that reflect the results of his own poor advice. CPAs respond that they have developed professional guidelines which minimize the possibility of bias and that the benefits of consulting services to their clients—and hence to society —far outweigh the risk of diminished independence.

**accountants in industry**

Many accountants are employed by private business enterprises. Normally they work in financial areas of their companies, but they hold a number of diverse positions. Among those commonly held by accountants are financial vice-president; treasurer, controller (the difference between treasurer and controller functions varies from firm to firm, but in general the treasurer is more concerned with relationships between the firm and bankers, stockholders, and creditors and the controller with internal control and performance evaluation); internal auditor; budget analyst; tax accountant; electronic data processing supervisor. Moreover, many chief executive officers are accountants. Current or former heads of General Electric, Chrysler, General Motors, Ford, and ITT are accountants.

**accountants in nonprofit organizations**

Government and other nonprofit (or, more properly, not for profit) organizations are unconcerned with the computation of net income; they are interested in public service, not profit. Yet financial budgets, accounting controls, and quantitative measures of performance are as necessary in nonprofit as in profit-making organizations. Unfortunately many nonprofit organizations have been slow in realizing the importance of adequate accounting systems and reports. Today, however, they are attempting to make rapid reforms in the area of financial management, and as a result job opportunities in such organizations are abundant.

Nonprofit accounting is an especially challenging field. Administrators of nonprofit organizations require the same types of information as their counterparts in private industry to carry out effectively the functions of management. On a day-to-day basis, problems of planning, controlling, and evaluating performance in nonprofit organizations are remarkably similar to those in industry. The manager of a government-owned electric power company must make the same types of decisions as does one in a private utility. Supervisors of motor pools, mail rooms, clerical departments, and maintenance staffs in government are equally as concerned with reducing costs and increasing output as are those who hold similar positions in private industry.

Accounting in the public sector can be distinguished from that in the private sector by the absence of profit as a primary measure of organizational performance. In the private sector, accountants focus on profit as an indicator of how much better off a company is at the end of an accounting period than it was at the start. In the public sector, managers are not interested in how much better off an organization is; instead they are concerned with how much service or benefit it has provided to the community in relation to costs incurred. Unfortunately, such benefits and costs may be exceedingly difficult to identify, let alone measure.

Suppose, for example, that a state official requested information that would enable him to determine which of two school districts, each of which received the same amount of funds, was more effectively managed. What data should the accountant provide him with? There are numerous possibilities: number of students attending schools, number of graduates, number of graduates who were able to find jobs, average reading level of students at various grade levels, average change in reading level over a period of several years, etc. None of the measures, either individually or cumulatively, is likely to be a satisfactory indicator of administrative performance. Accountants, experienced in the art of measurement, can play a major role in helping organizations to more clearly define their objectives and appraise the progress they have made in achieving them.

The U.S. General Accounting Office (GAO), the "watchdog of Congress," as well as state and local audit agencies are actively engaged in evaluating the efficiency and effectiveness of governmental programs. The GAO, whose staff is comprised largely of persons with accounting backgrounds, has recently issued reports that are seemingly unrelated to accounting. Among the titles are "Problems of the Upward Bound Program in Preparing Disadvantaged Students for a Postsecondary Education," "Issues Related to Foreign Sources of Oil for the United States," and "More Intensive Reforestation and Timber Stand Improvement Programs Could Help Meet Timber Demand."

## Summary

The primary purpose of this introductory chapter has been to dispel any notion that an understanding of accounting involves little more than a familiarity with the more widely adhered to practices and procedures. The chapter has placed considerable emphasis on the limitations of accounting reports: they are not based on universally accepted principles; they are not "accurate," in that they are a function of numerous estimates and judgmental determinations; they cannot be used as the sole measure of managerial accomplishment; they are not neutral; they cannot always serve as a basis for comparing financial position or income of one company to that of another. The decision to stress the negative was made at some risk; a student may be misled into questioning whether the efforts required to understand such a seemingly limited discipline are commensurate with the benefits to be derived.

The intent of the approach was to emphasize the dynamic nature of accounting. Accounting information serves a variety of functions and is used by parties with different interests and goals. As a consequence, there can never be any single "correct" means of reporting upon an economic event or quantifying an economic value. The principles upon which a particular accounting report is based must necessarily represent compromises among the various objectives (sometimes conflicting) of financial reporting. The balance among objectives that is appropriate for one company at a particular time may be inappropriate either for a different company or for the same company at some other time.

In Chapter 2 we shall present an overview of financial reports and shall examine the underlying structure upon which the discipline of accounting is built.

## Questions

**review
and
discussion**

1. On January 15, 1980, the controller (the chief accounting officer) of the Highland Hills Corp. reported to the president that company income for the previous year was $1.5 million. Two months later, after conducting an examination of the company's books and records, Scott and Co., Certified Public Accountants, determined that the company had earned only $900,000. Upon receiving the report of the CPAs, the president declared that he was going either to fire his controller or to engage a new CPA firm. "One of the two," he commented, "must be either dishonest or incompetent." Do you agree?

2. The financial vice-president of a corporation recently urged that all amounts in the firm's annual report to stockholders be "rounded" to the nearest

*not neces info precise required*

thousand dollars. "It is misleading," he said, "to give stockholders a report in which all figures are carried out to the last penny." Explain what the financial vice-president most likely had in mind by his comment.

3. The Mid-Western Gas and Electric Co. recently submitted statements of income to stockholders, to the Internal Revenue Service, and to the Federal Power Commission. In no two of the reports was net income the same, even though the period covered by the reports was identical. Release of all three reports was approved by the firm's certified public accountants. How is it possible for all three reports to be "correct"?

4. In preparing a financial statement to accompany his loan application to a local bank, Glen Ellison was uncertain as to whether he should report his home as having a value of $25,000 or $60,000. Ellison purchased his house 25 years ago at a price of $25,000; similar homes in his neighborhood have recently been sold for between $55,000 and $65,000. Which amount do you think would be more useful to the bank? Which amount is more objective?

5. The accounting reports of one company are unlikely to be readily comparable with those of another. Why has it not been considered feasible to develop a set of accounting rules by which all companies must abide?

6. "A corporation's annual report to stockholders, if correctly prepared, is an unbiased indicator of its performance during the period covered by the report." Do you agree?

7. In the early stages of the development of the accounting profession, independent auditors would "certify" to the "accuracy" of a company's financial statements. Today, independent certified public accountants express an "opinion" that the company's financial statements "present fairly" the firm's financial position and results of its operations. Why do you suppose CPAs are reluctant to "certify" to the "accuracy" of a company's financial statements?

8. What role does the Financial Accounting Standards Board play in the development of accounting standards? What role does the Securities and Exchange Commission play?

9. What three primary services do CPA firms render to their clients? Why are such services sometimes thought to be in conflict with one another?

10. Wilbur Wood is concerned about his prospects for reelection as mayor of the town of Wippakinetta. Mayor Wood had promised the citizens of Wippakinetta that as long as he was in charge of fiscal affairs, the town would never run a deficit—i.e., that expenditures would never exceed revenues. Yet in 1980 the town did, in fact, report a deficit of $450,000. The deficit was attributable entirely to the fleet of nine busses purchased by the city. The city purchased and paid for the nine busses in November 1980. At the time the city ordered the busses it had met all requirements for a federal transportation grant for the full cost of the vehicles. As the result of a bureaucratic snarl, payment of the grant was delayed until the following year.

The city accounting system requires that revenues be recognized only upon actual receipt of cash and that expenses be recorded upon cash payment.

a. What deficiencies do you see in Wippakinetta's accounting system? What revisions would you suggest?

b. Suppose alternatively that the city did not receive a federal grant to pay for the busses. It is the policy of the city to pay cash (not to borrow) for transportation vehicles and equipment. The useful life of the busses is approximately five years. In those years in which new busses must be acquired reported municipal expenditures are substantially greater than in those years in which they need not. As a consequence, some citizens believe that the operating efficiency of the city is less in the years in which busses are replaced than in others. Do you believe that the city is really less efficient by virtue of its acquisition of new busses? How might the financial reporting practices of the city be changed so as to reduce the confusion on the part of some of its citizens?

11. Critics of traditional financial accounting have asserted that financial reports are biased in that they fail to account for certain "social" benefits provided and costs incurred. They recommend that corporations prepare and distribute a "socioeconomic operating statement." The statement might take the following form:

| | | |
|---|---|---|
| Social benefits | | |
| Improvement in the environment | $xxxx | |
| Minority hiring program | xxxx | |
| Day-care center | xxxx | |
| Staff services donated to hospitals | xxxx | $xxxx |
| | | |
| Social costs | | |
| Damage to the environment | $xxxx | |
| Work-related injuries and illness | xxxx | |
| Failure to install recommended | | |
| safety equipment | xxxx | xxxx |
| | | |
| Social surplus (deficit) for | | |
| the year | | $xxxx |

Comment on the proposed financial report in terms of the dual accounting goals of relevancy and objectivity.

## Problems

1. *There is no such thing as "correct" cost. Alternative computations of cost facilitate different types of decisions.*

   Artcraft, Inc. manufactures costume jewelry rings. The firm has three employees, each of whom earns $10,000 per year. It rents its plant and equipment at a cost of $10,000. Materials used in the production of the rings cost $4 per ring.

The company has been manufacturing 5,000 rings per year. It has sold them for $15 each.

The company was recently approached by the manager of a large department store. He offered to purchase 1,000 rings at a cost of $7 per ring. If the company were to accept the offer, its other sales would be unaffected. Since the company has not been operating at capacity, it would not have to add additional employees, space or equipment.

a. Determine the average cost of a ring at an operating level of 5,000 rings.

b. Determine the average cost of a ring if the offer of the department store were to be accepted and the company were to increase volume to 6,000 rings per year.

c. Should the company accept the offer? Determine income at the present operating level and again at the new operating level if the company were to accept the offer.

d. What is the *relevant* cost to be considered in making the decision whether to accept the offer?

2. *Financial statements are based on estimates. The impact of the estimates on reported earnings may be substantial.*

TransAmerica Airlines owns and operates 10 passenger jet planes. Each plane had cost the Airlines $6 million. The company's income statement for 1980 reported the following:

| | | |
|---|---:|---:|
| Revenue from passenger fares | | $30,000,000 |
| Operating expenses (including salaries, maintenance costs, terminal expenses, etc.) | $22,000,000 | |
| Depreciation of planes | 5,000,000 | 27,000,000 |
| Income before taxes | | $ 3,000,000 |

Each plane has an estimated useful life of 12 years. The $5 million depreciation charge was calculated by dividing the cost of each plane ($6 million) by its useful life (12 years). The result ($500,000) was multiplied by the number of planes owned (10).

a. Suppose that the useful life of each plane was 8 years rather than 12 years. Determine income before taxes for 1980. By what percent is income less than that computed above?

b. Suppose that the useful life of each plane was 15 years. Determine income before taxes for 1980. By what percent is income greater than that originally computed?

c. It is sometimes said that accountants must be concerned that financial statements are accurate to the penny. Based on your computations, do you agree?

3. *It is not always obvious when a company is "better off" by virtue of its production and sales efforts.*

The Quick-Cut Lawnmower Co. began operations in January 1980. In its first month of operations the company manufactured 200 lawnmowers at a cost of $60 each. Although it completed all 200 mowers by the end of the month, it had not yet sold any of the mowers.

In February the company produced 300 mowers. It sold and delivered to customers both the 200 mowers manufactured in January and the 300 mowers manufactured in February. Selling price of the mowers was $100 each.

a. Determine income for January and for February.

b. Assume instead that on January 2 the company signed a noncancellable contract to sell 500 mowers at $100 each to a major chain of department stores. The contract called for delivery in February. The company completed but did not deliver 200 of the mowers by January 31. It completed the remainder and delivered all 500 by February 28. Determine income for each of the two months.

4. *The most relevant information may not always be the most objective.*

The president and sole owner of the Blue Mountain Brewery asked his CPA to audit (i.e., to express his opinion on the fairness of) the financial statements of his company. The audited financial statements had been requested by a local bank in order to facilitate review of the company's application for a loan.

The controller of the company, who had actually prepared the statements, included among the firm's assets "Land—$3,000,000." According to the controller, the land was reported at a value of $3 million since the company had recently received offers of approximately that amount from several potential purchasers.

After reviewing the land account, the CPA told the president that he could not express the usual "unqualified" opinion on the financial statements so long as land was valued at $3 million. Instead, he would have to express an "adverse" opinion (i.e., "the financial statements do *not* fairly present. . .") unless the land were valued at $150,000, the amount the company had actually paid for it.

The president was dumbfounded. The land, he told the CPA, was purchased in 1921 and was located in the downtown section of a major city.

a. At what amount do you think the land should be recorded? Explain. Which amount is likely to be the more relevant to the local banker? Which amount is the more objective?

b. Which amount should be reported if the statements are to be prepared in accord with "generally accepted accounting principles."

5. *Sometimes it is easy to assign specific costs to specific items sold; sometimes it is more difficult. Choice of method used to determine cost affects the determination of reported income.*

The De Kalp Used Car Co. purchased four cars in the month of June and sold three cars. Purchase prices and sale prices are as follows:

|  | *Purchase Price* | *Sale Price* |
|---|---|---|
| Car 1 | $600 | $1,000 |
| Car 2 | 700 | 1,100 |
| Car 3 | 800 | 1,200 |
| Car 4 | 900 | — |

The Natural Foods Grocery Store purchased 300 pounds of sugar in the month of June and sold 200 pounds. The sugar is not prepackaged. Instead, as the sugar is purchased it is added to a single barrel; as it is sold, it is scooped out and given to the customer in a paper bag. During June 100 pounds of sugar were purchased on each of three separate dates. Purchase prices, in sequence, were $.60, $.70, and $.80 per pound. All sugar was sold at $1.00 per pound.

Determine the income of the two merchants for the month of June. (Ignore other costs not indicated.)

Are there other assumptions that you might have made regarding the cost of the goods actually sold? Would income remain the same?

6. *Accounting reports that are suitable for making a long-term investment decision may not be appropriate for deciding whether to discontinue a product line.*

John Williams sells greeting cards. Operating out of a garage that he rents for $1,000 per year, he purchases greeting cards from a wholesaler and distributes them door to door. In 1980 he sold 1,000 boxes of cards at $3 per box. The cost of the cards from the wholesaler was $1 per box.

In 1981 Williams decided to expand his product line to include candy. In that year he sold 300 boxes of candy for $5 per box. The candy cost him $4 per box. By making efficient use of his garage, he found that he was able to store his inventory of cards in one-half the garage; thus he could use the other half for his candy. His sales of cards neither benefited nor suffered as the result of the new product. Sales in 1981 were the same as in 1980.

At the conclusion of 1981 Williams had to decide whether to continue selling candy or to return to selling cards only. His friend, Fulton, an occasional accountant, prepared the following report for him:

| | | |
|---|---:|---:|
| Sales of candy (300 boxes @ $5) | | $1,500 |
| Less costs: | | |
|   Cost of candy sold (300 boxes @ $4) | $1,200 | |
|   Rent (½ of $1,000) | 500 | 1,700 |
|     Net loss on sale of candy | | ($ 200) |

On the basis of the report Williams decided to abandon his line of candy.
a. Do you think he made the correct decision? Explain.
b. Prepare a report comparing the total earnings of Williams in 1980 with those in 1981. How do you reconcile the apparent contradiction between your report and that of Fulton?

7. *Higher reported earnings for a particular year can sometimes be achieved by actions that do not serve the long-run interests of the enterprise.*

Don Watson, president of a construction corporation, was concerned about the poor performance of his company in the first 11 months of the year. If the company continued at its present pace, reported profits for the year would be down $20,000 from those of the previous year. Thinking of ways to increase reported earnings, the president hit upon what he considered to be an ingenious scheme: Two years earlier the company had purchased a crane at a cost of $100,000. Since the crane was now 2 years old and had an estimated useful life of 10 years, it was currently reported on the company's books at eight-tenths of $100,000: $80,000. Prices of cranes had increased substantially in the last 2 years, and the crane could be sold for $120,000. The president suggested that the company sell the crane for $120,000 and thereby realize a gain on the sale of $40,000 ($120,000 less the book value of $80,000). Of course, the company would have to buy a new crane—and new cranes were currently selling for $160,000— but the cost of the new crane could be spread out over its useful life of 10 years. In future years, the president realized, "depreciation" charges would increase from $10,000 on the old crane ($100,000 divided by 10) to $16,000 on the new ($160,000 divided by 10), but in the current year, the company would report a gain of $40,000. Hence reported income would go from $20,000 less than that in the previous year to $20,000 greater.

a. The scheme of the president is, in fact, consistent with generally accepted accounting principles. Do you think, however, that the company would really be $40,000 better off if it sold the old crane and purchased a new one than if it held on to the old one? Comment.

b. Would the scheme of the president be in the best interest of the stock-holders "in the long run?"

c. Assume that generally accepted accounting principles requires that "fixed assets," such as the crane, be reported on corporate books at the price at which it could currently be sold—i.e., $120,000. Would the scheme of the president accomplish its desired results? Why do you suppose generally accepted accounting principles do not require that such assets be valued at the prices at which they could be sold?

# 2

# A Look at Financial Statements

Accountants report on the results of operations and on the current status of a business enterprise by means of two basic financial statements, the *balance sheet* and the *income statement.* Because of inherent limitations in the balance sheet and income statement, the two basic statements are supplemented in corporate annual reports by a third statement, the *statement of changes in financial position,* and by footnotes which explain and amplify the reported numerical data. Most reports contain a fourth statement, the *statement of changes in retained earnings.* This chapter explains the concepts that underlie each of these statements.

## The Balance Sheet

The balance sheet reports the status of the enterprise at a *specific point in time.* It describes the enterprise *as of* the close of business on a specific date. In contrast, the income statement reports the history of a business for a period of time, e.g., income for the month of June, income for the year ended December 31, 1980.

The balance sheet, or *statement of financial position* (as it is less frequently but more descriptively called), indicates the financial resources (assets) available to the firm to carry out its economic activities as well as the claims against such resources. These resources may be either *tangible* (of a physical nature) such as buildings, equipment, land, and motor vehicles or *intangible* (characterized by legal rights) such as amounts owed by customers (accounts receivable), patents, and bank deposits. They represent *future* benefits or service potentials.

The claims against the enterprise are referred to as *equities* (meaning "rights to or claims against"). There are two primary categories of equities: *liabilities* and *owners' equity.*

Liabilities are the claims against the business by creditors. They are amounts to be paid in the *future.* They include amounts owed to employees, suppliers, banks, bondholders, and government agencies. Owners' equity represents the "residual" interests of the owners. It includes the amounts that they contributed to the business either at the time of formation or when additional funds were needed for expansion as well as the earnings accumulated over the years. Owners' equity may be viewed as the resources that would be left over

26

for the owners if the business were to be dissolved and all the creditors were to be paid.

*Assets:* Economic resources of an enterprise that are recognized and measured in conformity with generally accepted accounting principles; future benefits or service potentials.

*Liabilities:* Economic obligations of an enterprise that are recognized and measured in conformity with generally accepted accounting principles; obligations to pay definite or reasonably certain amounts at a time in the future.

*Owners' equity:* The interest of owners in an enterprise; its assets less its liabilities.

An abbreviated balance sheet is indicated in Exhibit 2-1.

*EXHIBIT 2-1*

**The Austin Company**
**Balance Sheet as of June 30, 1981**

| *Assets* | | *Liabilities and Owners' Equity* | |
|---|---|---|---|
| Cash | $ 15,000 | Liabilities | |
| Accounts receivable | 80,000 | Accounts payable | $ 90,000 |
| Merchandise inventory | 60,000 | Wages payable | 20,000 |
| Equipment | 110,000 | Bonds payable | 250,000 |
| Buildings | 330,000 | | |
| Patents and copyrights | 25,000 | Total liabilities | $360,000 |
| | | Owners' equity | 260,000 |
| Total assets | $620,000 | Total equities | $620,000 |

As illustrated, the equities, i.e., the claims against the assets, including the residual interest of the owners, *must* be equal to the assets themselves. Thus, in general form,

$$\text{Assets} = \text{Claims against the assets}$$

or

$$\text{Assets} = \text{Equities}$$

In a slightly more specific form,

$$\text{Assets} = \text{Claims of outsiders} + \text{Claims of owners}$$

or

$$\text{Assets} = \text{Liabilities} + \text{Owners' equity}$$

In Exhibit 2-1

$$\$620,000 = \$360,000 + \$260,000.$$

The basic accounting equation, assets = liabilities + owners' equity, serves as the foundation for the *double-entry* record-keeping process on which modern accounting is based. Any *transaction* (financial event) which increases (decreases) the left-hand side of the equation (assets) must, by definition of the terms of the equation, increase (decrease) the right side of the equation (the claims against such assets) by an identical amount.

Consider, for example, several transactions in which an enterprise might engage. The titles beneath the amounts indicate the specific accounts (types of assets or equities) that would be affected.

| | Assets | = | Liabilities | + | Owners' Equity |
|---|---|---|---|---|---|
| Owners contribute $100,000 cash to form a business. | +$100,000 (cash) | = | | | +$100,000 (contri- bution of own- ers) |
| *(The owners have an interest of $100,000 in the assets.)* | | | | | |
| The new firm borrows $50,000 from a bank. | +$ 50,000 (cash) | = | +$50,000 (notes payable) | | |
| *(The claim of the lender against the firms assets is reduced by $3,000.)* | | | | | |
| The firm purchases equipment for $10,000, giving a note for the full amount. | +$ 10,000 (equipment) | = | +$10,000 (notes payable) | | |
| *(The seller of equipment has a claim of $10,000 against the assets.)* | | | | | |
| The firm purchases supplies for $8,000 cash. | +$ 8,000 (supplies) −$ 8,000 (cash) | | | | |
| *(Some transactions may affect only one side of the equation.)* | | | | | |
| The firm pays $3,000 of the amount it borrowed from the bank. | −$ 3,000 (cash) | = | −$ 3,000 (notes payable) | | |
| *(The lender has a claim of $3,000 against firm's assets.)* | | | | | |
| The firm purchases merchandise inventory for $15,000; it pays $5,000 cash and receives the remaining $10,000 of goods "on account." | +$ 15,000 (merchandise inventory) −$ 5,000 (cash) | = | +$10,000 (accounts payable) | | |

*(One transaction may affect more than two accounts; note that the liability account affected is referred to as "accounts payable" rather than "notes payable" since no formal written note was presented to the supplier.)*

|  | Assets | = | Liabilities | + | Owners' Equity |
|---|---|---|---|---|---|
| The firm sells merchandise which originally cost $15,000 for $20,000 cash. | +$ 20,000 (cash) −$ 15,000 (merchandise inventory) | = |  | + | $ 5,000 (retained earnings) |

*(As the result of this transaction the firm has "earned" $5,000. The firm gave up assets of $15,000 in exchange for those of $20,000. As a result, the claims of the owners against the business are $5,000 greater than they were previously. The owners' equity account affected is commonly referred to as retained earnings when the enterprise is a corporation or as owners' capital, e.g., J. Smith, capital, if the firm is a partnership or proprietorship.)*

The basic accounting equation can be expressed in a slightly altered form:

Assets − Liabilities = Owners' equity.

This equation is equivalent to the one previously illustrated, but the latter expression, by isolating owners' equity on one side of the equation, focuses more directly on the interests of the owners of the business. As a general rule the equity of the owners will increase as the result of two types of events:

1. The owners make a direct contribution to the firm. Such contribution is almost always made in return for the right to share in the profits of the firm. If the firm is a corporation, evidence of an ownership interest is provided by a stock certificate indicating the number of "shares" of stock owned. If the firm is a partnership, then the partnership agreement indicates the proportionate interest in the enterprise of each of the owners.
2. The firm earns income. The net assets (assets less liabilities) of the firm will be greater than they were previously; hence the residual interest of the owners will also be greater.

Conversely, the equity of the owners will decrease as the result of two opposite types of events:

1. The owners make withdrawals from the firm. The firm pays out a portion of its assets to the owners. In a corporation, such withdrawals are known as *dividends.* The effect is to reduce the assets of the firm and to reduce the remaining equity of the owners—that is, to reduce the size of the asset pool in which the owners are entitled to share.
2. The company incurs a loss. The net assets (assets less liabilities) of the firm are reduced; hence the residual interest of the owners is also reduced.

# The Income Statement

The accounting equation and the balance sheet indicate net assets (assets less liabilities) and the owners' claims against such net assets at a given *point* in time. The income statement, on the other hand, indicates changes in owners' equity (and thus changes in net assets) over a given *period* of time resulting from the operations of the business, *excluding* contributions or withdrawals on the part of the owners. (Such changes are indicated in the statement of changes in owners' equity.) The income statement indicates the revenues of the period and the expenses incurred in earning such revenues.

*Revenues* are the inflows of cash or other assets attributable to the goods or services provided by the enterprise. Most commonly, revenues result from the sale of the company's product or service, but they could also result from interest earned on loans to outsiders, dividends received on shares of stock of other companies, royalties earned on patents or licenses, or rent earned from properties owned.

*Expenses* are the outflows of cash or other assets attributable to the profit-directed activities of an enterprise. Expenses are a measure of the effort exerted on the part of the enterprise in its attempt to "realize" (to obtain) revenues.

An income statement, in condensed form, is illustrated in Exhibit 2-2.

EXHIBIT 2-2

**The Austin Company**
**Income Statement for the Year Ended June 30, 1981**

| | | | |
|---|---|---|---|
| Revenue from sales | | | $120,000 |
| Cost of merchandise sold | $70,000 | | |
| Wages and salaries | 15,000 | | |
| Advertising | 3,000 | | |
| Rent | 4,000 | $92,000 | |
| Taxes | | 12,000 | 104,000 |
| Net income | | | $ 16,000 |

Contrast the manner in which the date appears on the income statement with the way it does on the balance sheet. The income statement is *for the year ended* June 30, 1981—it describes what has happened over a one-year period. The balance sheet is *as of* June 30, 1981—it describes the business as of a particular moment in time.

The relationship between the balance sheet and the income statement can be explained with reference to a household bathtub filled with water. The water in the bathtub is comparable to the owners' equity—or, alternatively, to the net assets (assets less liabilities)—of the firm. In describing the level of water in the tub one could say that at a given moment the tub contains $x$ gallons of water. Similarly, one could describe a firm as having a particular level of net assets. Indeed, the balance sheet of a firm does exactly that. It indicates, and describes, the level of assets, of liabilities, and of the difference between the two—owners' equity.

Suppose, however, that water is entering the tub through the faucets and at the same time it is leaving through the drain. It would still be possible—and indeed necessary if comprehensive information is to be presented—to describe the level of water in the tub. One could say, for example, that at 11:03 p.m. there were 10 gallons of water in the tub. But such information would hardly constitute a very complete description of activity in the tub. Also needed would be a description of the rate at which the water level is rising or falling. More complete information might be as follows: Water is entering the tub at the *rate* of 3 gallons per minute; it is leaving at the rate of 2 gallons per minute; hence it is rising at the *rate* of 1 gallon per minute.

So also with the firm. Information is required as to the rate at which the equity of the owners is increasing or decreasing. The water entering the tub might be compared to revenues; the water leaving, to expenses; and the difference between the two, to income. Thus it might be said that assets are entering the firm at the *rate* of $3 million per year (i.e., revenues for the year are $3 million), that assets are leaving the firm at the *rate* of $2 million per year (i.e.,

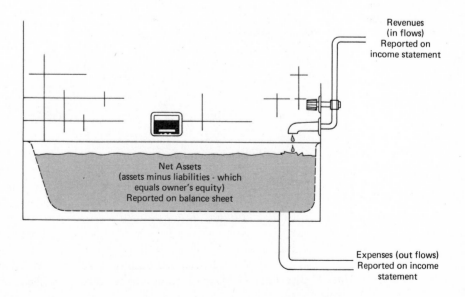

expenses for the year are $2 million), and that the change in net assets (owners' equity) for the year is $1 million (i.e., income for the year is $1 million).

If the amount of water in the bathtub at 11:03 p.m. were 10 gallons and it were increasing at the rate of 1 gallon per minute, then the amount at the end of the minute would be 11 gallons. The beginning amount plus the net amount added during the period would equal the ending amount.

So too with the firm. If the owners' equity at January 1, 1981, were $10 million and income for the year were $1 million, then owners' equity at the end of the year would be $11 million.

The balance sheet indicates the equity that the owners have in the firm at any given *point* in time. Such point of time is usually the end of a month or the end of a year. The balance sheet also indicates the assets and the liabilities which result in the particular level of owners' equity.

The income statement indicates the *rate* at which the equity of the owners is changing. It reveals the revenues, the expenses, and the resultant income for the period. Assuming that no assets or liabilities entered or left the firm from other sources (e.g., the owners neither contributed nor withdrew assets), then owners' equity at the beginning of the period per the balance sheet plus income for the period (per the income statement) must equal owners' equity at the end of the period (per the new balance sheet):

> Owners' equity, beginning of period
> + (−) Income (or loss) for the period
> + (−) Additional contributions (or withdrawals)
>     of owners during the period
> _____
> = Owners' equity, end of period

The owners' equity of the Austin Company as of June 30, 1981 was $260,000. If during the following year, that ending June 30, 1982, the company had income of $25,000 and paid dividends of (that is, the owners withdrew) $19,000, then owners' equity as of June 30, 1982 would be $266,000:

| Owner's Equity 6/30/81 | + | Income | − | Dividends | = | Owners' Equity 6/30/82 |
|---|---|---|---|---|---|---|
| $260,000 | | $25,000 | | $19,000 | | $266,000 |

### The Balance Sheet—A More Detailed Examination

Exhibits 2-3 through 2-6 illustrate the financial statements of the Mercury Truck Manufacturing Corporation for the year 1981. The balance sheet in Exhibit 2-3 is divided not only into the major categories of assets, liabilities, and owners' (stockholders') equity but several subcategories or accounts as well.

EXHIBIT 2-3

## Mercury Truck Manufacturing Corp.
### Statement of Position as of December 31, 1981

#### Assets

| | | |
|---|---:|---:|
| **Current assets** | | |
| Cash | | $ 1,042,954 |
| Marketable securities | | 380,000 |
| Accounts receivable | $9,083,414 | |
| Less allowance for doubtful accounts | 100,000 | 8,983,414 |
| Inventories | | 10,958,103 |
| Prepaid expenses | | 331,115 |
| Total current assets | | $21,695,586 |
| **Noncurrent assets** | | |
| Property, plant, and equipment | | |
| Land | $ 918,649 | |
| Buildings | $4,805,401 | |
| Less accumulated depreciation | 1,207,021 | 3,598,380 |
| Machinery and equipment | $9,835,027 | |
| Less accumulated depreciation | 2,414,042 | 7,420,985 |
| Net property, plant, and equipment | | $11,938,014 |
| **Investment and other assets** | | |
| Investment in subsidiary | | $ 6,244,395 |
| Notes receivable | | 3,682,487 |
| Unamortized organization costs | | 1,000 |
| Patents and trademarks | | 34,000 |
| Total investment and other assets | | $ 9,961,882 |
| Total noncurrent assets | | $21,899,896 |
| Total assets | | $43,595,482 |

#### Liabilities and Stockholders' Equity

| | |
|---|---:|
| **Current liabilities** | |
| Accounts payable | $ 5,515,469 |
| Notes payable | 4,152,249 |
| Salaries and wages payable | 1,938,795 |
| Taxes payable | 1,662,171 |
| Interest payable | 82,157 |
| Total current liabilities | $13,350,841 |
| **Noncurrent liabilities** | |
| Advances from customers | $ 87,218 |
| Notes payable | 3,057,679 |
| Bonds payable | 10,048,075 |
| Total noncurrent liabilities | $13,192,972 |
| Total liabilities | $26,543,813 |
| **Stockholders' equity** | |
| Preferred stock ($100 par value) | $ 96,655 |
| Common stock ($1 par value, 625,773 shares issued and outstanding) | 625,773 |
| Retained earnings | 16,329,241 |
| Total stockholders' equity | $17,051,669 |
| Total liabilities and stockholders' equity | $43,595,482 |

**current assets** *Current assets* include cash and such other assets that will either be transformed into cash or will be sold or consumed within one year or within the *normal operating cycle* of the business if longer than one year. For most businesses the normal operating cycle is one year, but for some (such as those in the tobacco or distilling industries where the products must be stored for a period of several years) it may be a longer period. *Cash* includes not only currency but savings bank or commercial bank deposits as well. When it is said that a company disburses "cash" there is no necessary implication that it is making a payment in currency. The term could readily (and most commonly does) apply to payments by check.

*Marketable securities* include shares of stock and other securities held by the firm as short-term investments. Such securities are ordinarily reported at original cost, unless there has been a drop in the price at which they are selling in the open market; in such case they are reported at the (lower) market value. Primarily because of the accountant's tendency to be conservative in asset valuation and revenue realization, increases in market value are almost never given accounting recognition, however.

*Accounts receivable*—the amounts due from customers—represent those amounts that *can* be expected to be collected within the normal operating cycle (those that cannot are included among noncurrent assets). Deducted from accounts receivable is an *allowance for doubtful accounts*—an estimate of the amounts owed to the company that will be uncollectible. Thus, the net amount of accounts receivable represents not the total amount owed to the firm but only the amount that it estimates will actually be collectible.

*Inventories* include both items available for sale to customers and raw materials, parts, and supplies to be used in production. Inventories are ordinarily reported at original cost of either purchase or production, but in the event that the cost of replacing such items has declined, then the inventories may be "written down" to reflect the decline in value. As with marketable securities, increases in value are not ordinarily given similar accounting recognition.

*Prepaid expenses* represent services or rights to services purchased but not yet consumed. As they are consumed they will be "charged off" as actual expenses. A firm might, for example, purchase a one-year insurance policy for $120 ($10 per month). At the time of purchase it would record the policy as a current asset, prepaid insurance—$120. Each month it would reduce the asset by one-twelfth of the original amount ($10) and would charge insurance expense with the same amount. Thus, after eight months, the balance in the prepaid insurance account would be only $40 (four months remaining times $10 per month). Other common prepaid expense accounts are prepaid interest, prepaid advertising, and prepaid rent. Prepaid expenses are one type of *deferred charge*—outlays made in one period to benefit future periods.

*Noncurrent* assets are those assets that *cannot* be expected to be sold or consumed within a normal operating cycle of the business. Noncurrent assets are usually considered to be *long-lived* assets, and plant assets in particular are often referred to as *fixed* assets.

*Property, plant, and equipment* are recorded on the balance sheet at original cost. Deducted from each of the assets, other than land, is *accumulated depreciation*—an allowance to reflect the fact that the assets are being "consumed" over time, by wear and tear as well as by technological obsolescence.

Depreciation is the process of allocating (spreading) the cost of an asset over its useful life. Depreciation on each individual asset or group of similar assets is computed separately, and the total amount accumulated is a function of the original cost, age, and expected useful life of the asset. No depreciation is provided for land since it is not consumed over time and seldom declines in utility.

*Investments and other assets* include amounts owed to the company by outsiders that are not due for at least either one year or one business cycle if greater than one year and amounts that the company has invested in other companies. If, for example, a company owns 30 percent of another company, such interest would ordinarily be included among investments and other assets. An interest in another company, however, may be classified as either "marketable securities," a current asset, or as "investments in subsidiaries," a noncurrent asset. The decision as to how the interest should be classified depends to a large extent on the *intent* of the company's management. If it intends to maintain its interest for a relatively long period of time and views ownership as a long-term investment, then the amounts owned should be classified as a noncurrent asset. If, on the other hand, the company purchases the interest with the intention of selling it as soon as additional cash might be needed (for example, if it purchases a few hundred shares of General Motors' stock as a temporary investment with no intention of exercising significant control over the company), then the amount owned should be classified as marketable securities, a current asset.

*Deferred charges* such as prepaid expenses may also be included among noncurrent assets. If, for example, a company purchased an insurance policy or a license that had more than a one-year life, then the percentage of original cost representing the unexpired portion of such insurance policy or license would be included among noncurrent assets.

Some deferred charges represent outlays that will benefit future accounting periods but for which both the number of such periods and the value of the benefits are exceedingly difficult to measure. Consider the costs incurred to organize a corporation: the legal fees required to draw up the documents of incorporation, the costs of printing the shares of stock to be issued, and the fees paid to the state upon filing for a corporate charter. Such costs—like those of buildings and equipment—were incurred to benefit the business over a long period of time. Just as income of a single year of operations would be understated if the entire cost of a building were charged as an expense at the time it was purchased, income would also be distorted if the costs of organizing the corporation were charged off in a single year. As a result, organizational costs are frequently reported as assets of the company, and each year a portion of such costs are *amortized* (i.e., "depreciated") and charged off as an expense.

Deferred charges representing benefits which will accrue to the firm over a long period of time in the future are often a source of confusion to stockholders. Deferred charges, unlike most other assets, are intangible and frequently have no market value. Amounts spent as organizational costs, for example, cannot readily be transferred to any other business entity; they cannot be sold to outsiders. How, then, can such amounts be considered assets?

The question must be answered in terms of the nature of all assets. Assets can be defined as future services to be received in money or benefits convertible into money. They can readily be viewed as "bundles of services" available for use or sale by a particular entity. The determination of service potential is made with respect to the business entity issuing the financial reports—not with respect to the world at large.

In accordance with currently employed practices of valuation (alternative practices will be discussed in subsequent chapters), assets are measured and recorded at the time they are acquired at the price paid for them. As their service potential declines over time (e.g., as the assets are consumed) the reported value is reduced *proportionately* through the process of depreciation or amortization. If one-third of the services has been consumed, then the asset is reported at two-thirds its original cost. As long as the asset is not intended for sale to outsiders, market value seldom enters into the determination of the amount at which an asset is reported. Indeed, an automobile owned by a business might be reported at an amount either greater or less than the price at which similar used cars are being traded.

The outlay for organizational costs will benefit many accounting periods. To the extent that it has "future service potential"—the corporation would not exist without it—it can properly be considered an asset. Even though it may have no value to outsiders, it should still be reported on the balance sheet at initial cost less that fraction of cost representing services already consumed.

**current liabilities**   Liabilities are also categorized as either current or noncurrent. *Current liabilities* are those expected to be satisfied out of current assets (or through the creation of other current liabilities) or to be satisfied within a relatively short period of time, usually one year or one operating cycle of the business if greater than one year. Most common categories of current liabilities are amounts owed to employees for wages and salaries; to suppliers for services, supplies, and raw materials purchased (conventionally called trade accounts, or simply accounts payable); to the government for taxes (taxes payable); and to banks or other lenders for amounts borrowed (notes payable) and for interest on such amounts (interest payable) that is payable within one year or one business cycle if greater than one year.

**noncurrent liabilities**

Noncurrent liabilities include all other amounts owed. They include long-term (for a period greater than one year) notes as well as bonds. Bonds are similar to long-term notes but differ in that the promise to pay is usually included in a more formal legal instrument and in that the term of the loan is often longer. The same bond or note may be classified as both a current and a noncurrent liability. The portion that is due within one year would be considered current; the portion due beyond one year would be noncurrent.

Just as amounts that a company pays in advance to receive goods or services in the future are considered to be assets of the company, so too are amounts that others pay to the company for goods and services to be provided by the company considered to be liabilities of the company. Suppose, for example, that TWA sells a ticket for a trip the traveler intends to take a month after his purchase. At the time of sale the airline receives an asset (cash or accounts receivable) equal to the price of the ticket. At the time of sale it incurs an obligation to provide services (i.e., one airline trip) to the customer. To be sure, the obligation is not a liability in the usual sense, in that the airline has no monetary debt outstanding to the customer. But it is an obligation nonetheless. Such amounts are reported among the liabilities and may be labeled as appropriate: "advances from customers," "revenues received but not yet earned," or, less descriptively but more generally, "deferred credits." They are classified as current if the obligation is likely to be satisfied within one year; otherwise they are classified as noncurrent.

**"nonassets and non-liabilites"**

Not all amounts that a firm will have to pay to others if it continues in business are recorded as liabilities, nor are all amounts that it can be expected to receive recorded as assets. If a firm signs a three-year contract with a new president, for example, and promises to pay him $100,000 per year, the firm may be legally liable for the full $300,000 as long as the new president is willing to provide the required services. The firm would not, however, record the full amount as a liability. Only as the president "earns" his salary—i.e., as he performs his side of the bargain—would the firm record as a liability amounts earned but not paid. Similarly accounted for is a transaction in which a firm borrows $1,000 from a bank at a 12 percent rate of interest and gives the bank a one-year note.

At the end of the one-year period, the firm will owe the bank $1,120—the principal of $1,000 plus interest of $120. At the time the note is signed, however, the only liability that would be recorded is the $1,000 actually borrowed. Each month, as the company has use of the borrowed funds, an additional $10 interest for one month will be recorded as a liability. The bank, for its part, would record as an asset a note for $1,000. It, too, would recognize an asset "interest receivable," only as it earns the interest revenue with the passage of time.

In general, assets and liabilities arising out of "executory" contracts (those contingent upon the mutual performance of the two sides to the contract) are recorded only to the extent that one of the parties has fulfilled its contractual obligations. The reason for such limited accounting recognition of assets and liabilities will become considerably clearer as the relationship between balance sheet and income statement accounts is discussed more fully in subsequent chapters.

**owners' equity**

The stockholders' equity section of the corporate balance sheet is divided into at least two main subsections. The first indicates the *capital contributed by shareholders*—either at the time the corporation was formed or when additional shares of stock were issued in the course of the corporation's existence. Corporations may issue several different types of stock.

*Common stock* generally gives its owners the right to vote for members of the corporation's board of directors as well as on numerous other corporate matters and the right to share in corporate profits whenever dividends are declared by the board of directors.

*Preferred stock,* on the other hand, generally does *not* carry voting rights, but it does ordinarily guarantee the owner that he will receive dividends of at least a minimum amount each year. The dividend rate is fixed at the time the stock is issued.

Often shares of both common and preferred stock are arbitrarily assigned a *par* or *stated* value (e.g., $100 per share). Such values have some legal, but little economic, significance, and shares are commonly issued for amounts above or below these arbitrarily assigned values. Amounts that the company receives above the par values of the shares are categorized as *additional paid-in capital* or *capital in excess of par* and those below (almost always for preferred stock) as a *discount* on the shares issued.

The second subsection, *retained earnings,* indicates the accumulated earnings of the business. Retained earnings will be commented on in greater detail later in this chapter.

If the firm is not a corporation, that is, if it is a *sole proprietorship* (a firm owned by a single individual) or a *partnership* (a firm owned by two or more parties), then the owners' equity section of the balance sheet may take a somewhat different form. Since such enterprises do not issue stock and are not bound by many of the legal restrictions that apply to firms that do, it is generally most useful to readers of the financial reports to indicate the entire equity of each of the owners in a single separate account. The owners' equity section of the Mercury Truck Manufacturing Corp., if it were owned by two partners, W. King and F. Prince, might appear as follows:

|  |  |
|---|---|
| Partners' capital | |
| W. King, capital | $ 9,525,347 |
| F. Prince, capital | 7,526,322 |
| Total partners' capital | $17,051,669 |

### The Income Statement—A Closer Look

Statements of income are presented in a variety of formats, but virtually all are based on the fundamental relationship

$$\text{Revenues} - \text{Expenses} = \text{Net income}$$

Although the income statement illustrated in Exhibit 2-4 is that of a manufacturing corporation, there are no costs of either labor or raw materials listed among the expenses. The company would, of course, maintain separate accounts for labor, materials and other factors of production, but to avoid inundating the reader with detail such costs are grouped together in one account, *cost of goods sold.* Cost of goods sold may not represent the actual costs of labor, material, and other factors to production incurred during the reporting period. Adjustment must be made for those costs applicable to goods that may have been produced but not yet sold (i.e., retained in inventory) and those goods that have been sold but were produced in prior periods.

Occasionally firms engage in transactions or are affected by events that are highly unusual and are unlikely to be repeated. Examples of such events might be losses from natural disasters or from governmental expropriation of a company's plant in another country. Unless such gains or losses are segregated from income derived from the normal operations of the firm, the income statement will not serve as a meaningful instrument of comparison among financial performances of various years. Moreover, the income of the year in which such events or transactions occurred will provide little insight into earnings potential for the future. As a consequence, such *extraordinary items*—those which are exceptional in nature and infrequent in occurrence—are reported separately in the income statement. And since these events are likely to have a major impact on the income taxes of the firm, the applicable taxes are also reported separately.

EXHIBIT 2-4

**Mercury Truck Manufacturing Corp.**
**Statement of Income for Year Ended December 31, 1981**

| | |
|---|---:|
| Revenues | |
| Sales | $32,904,468 |
| Rents received from equipment leased | 3,464,491 |
| Miscellaneous revenues | 1,209,975 |
| Total revenues | $37,578,934 |
| Expenses | |
| Cost of goods sold | 28,691,473 |
| Selling and administrative expenses | 2,319,231 |
| Depreciation expense | 1,704,621 |
| Property taxes and other taxes not based on income | 823,347 |
| Interest expense | 1,221,896 |
| Total expenses | $34,760,568 |
| Income before taxes and extraordinary items | 2,818,366 |
| Taxes on income | 1,245,000 |
| Income after taxes, but before extraordinary items | $ 1,573,366 |
| Extraordinary gain—amount received upon settlement of legal action  $576,923 | |
| Less applicable taxes  276,923 | 300,000 |
| Net income | $ 1,873,366 |

## The Statement of Retained Earnings

The statement of retained earnings (Exhibit 2-5) serves as the link between the income statement and the balance sheet. The basic accounting equation can readily be expanded as follows:

> Assets – Liabilities = Capital contributed by owners + Retained earnings.

Retained earnings represent the sum of the earnings of the accounting periods that the company has been in existence less the amounts paid as dividends to stockholders. The retained earnings per the balance sheet at the beginning of the period (which of course must be identical to those at the end of the previous period), plus the income for that period per the income statement, less any dividends declared during the period, equals the retained earnings at the end of the period:

*EXHIBIT 2-5*

**Mercury Truck Manufacturing Corp.**
**Statement of Retained Earnings**
**for the Year Ended December 31, 1981**

| | |
|---|---:|
| Balance at January 1, 1981 | $15,210,861 |
| Net income for the year | 1,873,366 |
| | $17,084,227 |
| Less cash dividends ($1.21 per share outstanding at time of declaration) | 754,986 |
| Balance at December 31, 1981 | $16,329,241 |

> Retained earnings, balance at beginning of year + Income – Dividends declared
> = Retained earnings, balance at end of year

**retained earnings contrasted with assets** The statement of retained earnings, by indicating both dividends declared during the year and the income for the year, provides a reconciliation of the retained earnings at the beginning of the year with those at the end. Retained earnings, it cannot be overemphasized, *do not* represent tangible resources of the firm. Earnings *per se* cannot be distributed to stockholders; earnings cannot be used to purchase goods or services. Only cash or other assets are generally accepted in exchange for other goods or services. Retained earnings represent nothing more than a *claim* against the assets of the enterprise—the claims of the owners attributable to the income earned by the firm over the course of one or more years. Although assets must be equal to the claims against those assets (claims of owners as well as creditors), *there is generally no specific relationship between particular assets and particular claims.*

**dividends** *Dividends* are distributions of the assets of the enterprise to its owners. The asset distributed most often is cash, but it could, in fact, be any asset of the firm. As the assets of the firm are reduced upon distribution to the owners, so also are the claims of the owners against such assets. Assume, for example, that several individuals contribute a total of $1,000 to form a corporation. During the first year of operations the firm earns $200. Its position, at the end of the first year, as indicated by the accounting equation might appear as follows:

Assets = Liabilities + Capital contributed by owners + Retained earnings
$1,200 = $0 + $1,000 + $200

If the firm declared and paid a dividend of $100, then the position of the company after the $100 in assets had been distributed would appear as

Assets = Liabilities + Capital contributed by owners + Retained earnings
$1,100 =      $0     +              $1,000              +        $100

The statement of retained earnings is not included in the financial reports of all corporations. Some companies indicate the dividends distributed to shareholders directly beneath the net income figure on the income statement and omit the reconciliation between beginning-of-year and end-of-year retained earnings. Others include the reconciliation as an addendum to the income statement. Moreover, if during the year there are significant changes in any of the other owners' equity accounts (e.g., if additional amounts of stock are sold), then the statement of changes in retained earnings is sometimes expanded to include such changes and retitled "statement of changes in owners' equity."

## The Statement of Changes in Financial Position

The statement of changes in financial position has only recently (1972, per a decision of the Accounting Principles Board) become a required component of published corporate reports, equal in status to the balance sheet and the income statement. Until then, relatively few companies included a statement of changes in financial position in their annual reports. The statement of changes in financial position is illustrated in Exhibit 2-6.

The statement of changes in financial position is most commonly used to indicate changes during the year in the companies' *working capital* position. Working capital, often used interchangeably with the term *funds,* refers to the difference between the *current assets* (cash, accounts receivable, inventory, etc.) and the *current liabilities* (wages payable, accounts payable, etc.) of the firm. The working capital position of a company is an indication of its *liquidity* —its ability to meet current debts as they come due. Current assets, other than prepaid expenses, can normally be expected to be transformed into cash within a year. They can thereby be used to satisfy the firm's current liabilities, which, by definition, will come due within a year. Prepaid expenses make unnecessary the cash disbursements which might otherwise have to be made.

**profitability vs. liquidity**   The statement of changes in financial position indicates both the sources and applications of working capital—how a company acquired working capital and what it did with it. Its importance can readily be illustrated by a question relating, perhaps, to an extreme situation: Is it possible for a company to be highly profitable (as reported on its income statement) and still be on the brink

*EXHIBIT 2-6*

**Mercury Truck Manufacturing Corp.**
**Statement of Changes in Financial Position**
**for the Year Ended December 31, 1981**

| | | |
|---|---:|---:|
| Sources of working capital | | |
| Operations | | |
|   Net earnings | $1,873,366 | |
|   Add: Operating expenses deducted in the determination of net earnings that did not require the use of working capital | 1,704,621 | $3,577,987 |
| Issue of common stock | | 4,960,519 |
| Amounts borrowed from bank | | 1,000,000 |
|     Total sources of working capital | | $9,538,506 |
| Applications of working capital | | |
|   Cash dividends paid to stockholders | | $ 754,986 |
|   Purchases of property, plant, and equipment (less disposals) | | 3,011,819 |
|   Increases in investments and other assets | | 254,735 |
|   Portion of long-term debt reclassified as a current liability | | 2,307,656 |
|     Total applications of working capital | | $6,329,196 |
|     Net increase in working capital for the year | | $3,209,310 |

of bankruptcy because of a deficiency of liquid assets? The answer, of course, is a resounding, and all too frequent, yes.

Consider the case, for example, of a small electronics company. Encouraged by the great demand for its products and the resultant high profits, it decides to expand its operations. It applies all available cash toward the purchase of new manufacturing equipment and, in addition, borrows heavily to finance the expansion. Orders continue to increase as anticipated, but there is a substantial delay among the time an order is received, when the product is manufactured, and when the cash is collected. In the meantime, obligations which the firm incurs come due, leaving the company with insufficient cash, or assets which could readily be transformed into cash, to meet its current debts. Creditors, who may themselves be caught in a "cash squeeze," may be unable or unwilling to give the company additional time to generate the necessary cash to meet its obligations. Consequently, the firm may have to default on its debts and be placed under the financial supervision of a court-appointed trustee of bankruptcy.

The income statement is a severely deficient indicator of a firm's ability to generate cash to pay bills, finance expansion, or pay dividends, since transactions may be recorded as revenues and expenses long before or after they result in inflows or outflows of cash or other components of working capital. The purchase of an item of equipment may result in a cash outflow in the year in which it is purchased, but it would not result in an expense on the income statement of the same amount. Rather, the purchase price would be charged as an expense (i.e., depreciated) over the useful life of the equipment. To remedy the deficiencies of the income statement in this regard, the statement of changes in financial position has been made an integral part of the financial report. Focusing on changes in both cash and other accounts which are either "near" cash (other current assets) or which will require the disbursement of cash in the near future (current liabilities) provides a more complete picture of the firm's financial health.

There are considerable variations among firms in both the format and the substance of the statement of changes in financial position. Some firms elect to report changes in working capital. Others, however, choose to indicate changes in cash or cash plus selected other current assets, such as accounts receivable or marketable securities that can most readily be transformed into cash. The statement of changes in financial position will be discussed in detail in Chapter 14.

## A Financial Report Illustrated

Exhibit 2-7 contains excerpts of the 1977 financial report of Koppers Company, a diversified manufacturing company. The statements illustrated were taken from the annual report of the corporation.

Contained in Exhibit 2-7 are the four statements described previously as well as a statement of accounting policies and several additional "footnotes." The complete annual report presents a great deal of additional financial information: a review of financial operations by the firm's chief financial officer, a summary of operating results by business segment, and a statement of financial highlights of the last 10 years.

The annual report of Koppers Company is in accordance with requirements of the Securities and Exchange Commission, sent to all stockholders, and made available to the general public. The SEC also requires that corporations under its jurisdiction file with the commission (and make available to stockholders at their specific request) a more detailed report of financial operations. This report, called a 10-K report, should always be examined carefully by any party intending to engage in serious financial analyses of a firm's financial position. 10-K reports of firms whose shares are traded on the New York or American stock exchange markets are available on microfiche at the libraries of many business schools and at the larger offices of many brokerage firms.

The financial statements of the Koppers Company are atypical of those of most firms in that each of the statements contains explanations of the various account titles. Moreover, the dollar amounts are shown to the left of the

EXHIBIT 2-7

**Consolidated Statement of Income**

| Years ended December 31,<br>1977 | 1976 | Koppers Company, Inc. and Subsidiaries | | Explanations |
|---|---|---|---|---|
| ($ Thousands, except<br>per share figures) | | | | |
| **$1,355,689** | $1,189,233 | Net sales | 1 | **1.** TOTAL RECEIVED, OR RE-CEIVABLE, FROM CUSTOMERS. |
| | | Operating expenses (Notes 5, 7 and 8): | 2 | **2.** Costs directly related to operations. |
| **1,064,349** | 919,954 | Cost of sales | 3 | **3.** Wages, salaries, pensions, raw materials, transportation, fuel, and various supplies and services. |
| **40,681** | 35,957 | Depreciation and depletion | 4 | |
| **26,213** | 22,150 | Taxes, other than income taxes | 5 | **4.** This portion of the original cost of machinery, plants, etc. has been allocated against the year's income. |
| **110,269** | 107,307 | Selling, research, general and administrative expenses | 6 | |
| **1,241,512** | 1,085,368 | | | **5.** Social Security and unemployment benefits taxes, state and local franchise taxes and real estate taxes. |
| **114,177** | 103,865 | Operating profit | | |
| | | Other income: | 7 | **6.** Pensions, research activities, salesmen's compensation, advertising, officers' salaries and general corporate expenses. |
| **212** | 5,165 | Dividends from ARCO/Polymers, Inc. (Note 1) | 8 | |
| **3,569** | 3,854 | Profit on sales of capital assets | 9 | **7.** Included in the operating income of business segments, on page 32, although not resulting directly from the operations of those lines. |
| **2,232** | 2,922 | Equity in earnings of affiliates (dividends received: 1977—$786; 1976—$1,739) | 10 | |
| **3,295** | 3,161 | Miscellaneous | | **8.** From Koppers investment in ARCO/Polymers. |
| **9,308** | 15,102 | | | |
| **123,485** | 118,967 | Income before interest expense and provision for income taxes | | **9.** Profit or loss on the sales of equipment, facilities, etc. no longer needed in operations. |
| | | Interest expense: | 11 | **10.** Represents Koppers portion of earnings of companies in which it has 20%-50% ownership interest. |
| **9,643** | 9,952 | Term debt (Note 6) | | |
| **842** | 1,084 | Other | | **11.** Cost of borrowed funds. |
| **10,485** | 11,036 | | | |
| **113,000** | 107,931 | Income before provision for income taxes | | **12.** Total state and foreign, as well as Federal, income taxes. |
| **46,801** | 41,090 | Provision for income taxes (Note 9) | 12 | |
| **$ 66,199** | $ 66,841 | Net income for the year | 13 | **13.** This was earned for shareholders. In 1977 $0.6 million in dividends was paid to preferred shareholders, $23.6 million to common shareholders. The remainder was reinvested in Koppers operations. |
| **24,886** | 24,809 | Average number of shares of common stock outstanding during year (in thousands) | | |
| **$2.64** | $2.67 | Earnings per share of common stock | | |

(See accompanying statement of accounting policies and notes to financial statements.)

account titles; conventionally they are presented at the right. It is because of these "irregularities" that the report of the Koppers Company was selected for illustration in this text. The statements provide an opportunity to make the point that financial reports must be designed to provide information in a way that is readily understandable by those who rely upon them. Traditional forms of presentation may not necessarily be the most effective. The study of accounting, therefore, must focus on underlying concepts and issues as opposed to only conventional procedures and practices.

# EXHIBIT 2-7 (Cont.)

## Consolidated Balance Sheet

### ASSETS

| December 31, 1977 | 1976 | Koppers Company, Inc. and Subsidiaries | | Explanations |
|---|---|---|---|---|
| ($ Thousands, except per share figures) | | | | |
| | | Current assets: | 1 | **1. KOPPERS OWNED:** |
| $ 27,788 | $ 57,489 | Cash, including short-term investments of $20,593 in 1977 and $53,467 in 1976 | 2 | **2.** Primarily kept in bank accounts for normal business use or in short-term notes. |
| | | Accounts receivable: | 3 | **3.** Amounts owed to Company by customers and others. |
| — | 6,657 | Due from ARCO/Polymers, Inc. (Note 1) | | |
| 233,148 | 196,273 | Trade, less allowance for doubtful accounts of $3,321 in 1977 and $3,595 in 1976 (Note 2) | | **4.** Goods being used in the process of manufacturing, or being held for sale, including materials and supplies used. |
| | | Inventories (Note 3): | 4 | |
| 79,861 | 78,315 | Product | | **5.** Amounts paid in advance for services to be rendered in the future, such as insurance premiums, property taxes and rents. |
| 48,277 | 45,441 | Work in process | | |
| 40,605 | 33,798 | Raw materials and supplies | | |
| 9,270 | 9,077 | Prepaid expenses | 5 | |
| 438,949 | 427,050 | Total current assets | 6 | **6.** Likely to be converted into cash in due course of business, usually within one year. |
| | | Investments: | 7 | **7.** Represents ownership in other companies. |
| — | 8,818 | Common stock of ARCO/Polymers, Inc., at cost (Note 1) | | |
| 16,689 | 15,153 | Affiliated companies, at equity (Note 4) | | **8.** The unexpended portion of funds borrowed for Woodward coke plant expansion; being held by a trustee. |
| 3,895 | 1,845 | Affiliated and other, at cost | | |
| 20,584 | 25,816 | | | **9.** The original amount paid for Company-owned buildings, machinery and equipment. |
| 1,400 | 1,400 | Less allowance for decline in value | | |
| 19,184 | 24,416 | | | **10.** Accumulation of the portion of the original amount paid for fixed assets that has been allocated to operating costs since the assets were purchased. |
| 5,315 | 1,158 | Notes and accounts receivable due after one year | | |
| 18,991 | — | Funds held for capital expenditures (Note 6) | 8 | |
| | | Fixed assets, at cost: | 9 | |
| 70,282 | 68,397 | Buildings | | **11.** Cost of properties having exhaustible resources, such as timber and stone, reduced for resources used in the past. |
| 531,662 | 453,868 | Machinery and equipment | | |
| 601,944 | 522,265 | | | **12.** The total net cost assigned to everything Koppers owns. |
| 289,067 | 256,369 | Less accumulated depreciation | 10 | |
| 312,877 | 265,896 | | | |
| 31,020 | 25,318 | Depletable properties, less accumulated depletion | 11 | |
| 15,866 | 13,982 | Land | | |
| 359,763 | 305,196 | | | |
| ◂ 7,380 | 3,790 | Intangible assets, net of amortization | | |
| 2,318 | 1,747 | Deferred charges | | |
| $851,900 | $763,357 | | 12 | |

(See accompanying statement of accounting policies and notes to financial statements.)

---

Significantly, all the statements are described as being *consolidated*. This term indicates that the parent company, Koppers Company, owns a majority interest (more than 50 percent of outstanding shares of common stock) in one or more subsidiary companies and that the financial statements of such subsidiary companies are combined with those of the parent. It is common for large companies to be composed of several smaller companies, with a majority interest in the smaller companies held by the parent firm. Although each of the firms may be a distinct legal entity, shareholders of the parent also own,

EXHIBIT 2-7 (Cont.)

**Consolidated Balance Sheet**

**LIABILITIES**

| December 31, 1977 | 1976 | Koppers Company, Inc. and Subsidiaries | | Explanations |
|---|---|---|---|---|
| ($ Thousands, except per share figures) | | | | |
| | | Current liabilities: | 1 | **1. KOPPERS OWED:** The ordinary course of business requires the assumption of debts. |
| $ 9,499 | $ 6,112 | Accrued income taxes | 2 | |
| 9,260 | 6,167 | Other taxes | 2 | **2.** Owed, but not required to be paid at year end. |
| 81,960 | 63,359 | Accounts payable, principally trade | 3 | **3.** Due to suppliers for goods and services. |
| 19,921 | 18,035 | Accrued pensions (Note 5) | 4 | |
| 37,246 | 35,612 | Other accruals | 4 | **4.** Anticipated expenses, primarily for pensions and compensation. |
| 35,371 | 25,394 | Advance payments received on contracts | 5 | **5.** For services and products paid for by customers, which Koppers will provide in the near future. |
| 12,981 | 10,697 | Debt due within one year, including short-term borrowings of $5,283 in 1977 and $3,768 in 1976 (Note 6) | | |
| 206,238 | 165,376 | Total current liabilities | 6 | **6.** Payable within one year; the Company's current assets at year-end 1977 covered these liabilities by a current ratio of 2.13-to-1. |
| 137,509 | 143,156 | Term debt, due after one year (Note 6) | 7 | **7.** Borrowings used to expand Koppers income-producing base. Shareholders benefit as this added capital generates earnings in excess of interest costs on the debt. |
| 8,710 | 7,659 | Deferred compensation (Note 8) | | |
| 30,552 | 22,747 | Deferred income taxes | 8 | |
| 383,009 | 338,938 | Total liabilities | | **8.** Differences in accounting rules and tax regulations result in certain income and expenses in financial reports that are not included in tax reports in the same year. This total represents the taxes on the difference that will be paid in future years. |

**SHAREHOLDERS' EQUITY**

| | | | | |
|---|---|---|---|---|
| 15,000 | 15,000 | Cumulative preferred stock, $100 par value; authorized 300,000 shares; issued and outstanding 150,000 shares, 4% series: | | **9.** The total common shareholders' ownership in Koppers. Equal to $18.17 for each share of common stock outstanding at the end of 1977, versus $16.47 at the end of 1976. |
| — | — | Preference stock, no par value; authorized 1,000,000 shares; issued—none | | |
| 31,223 | 31,074 | Common stock, $1.25 par value; authorized 40,000,000 shares; issued and outstanding 24,978,090 shares in 1977 and 24,859,240 shares in 1976 | | |
| 78,080 | 75,706 | Capital in excess of par value | | |
| 344,588 | 302,639 | Earnings retained in the business (Notes 4 and 6) | | |
| 453,891 | 409,419 | Common shareholders' equity | 9 | |
| 468,891 | 424,419 | Total preferred and common shareholders' equity | | |
| $851,900 | $763,357 | | | |

(See accompanying statement of accounting policies and notes to financial statements.)

albeit indirectly, controlling interest in the subsidiaries. Since stockholders are generally more interested in the financial performance of their interest as a whole, rather than that of the individual components, the several reports of the individual companies are consolidated into a single report.

The several footnotes to the financial statements contain an extensive amount of supplementary and explanatory information. Although footnotes should never contradict the information contained in the main sections of the financial reports, the sophisticated analyst is aware that disclosures made in the

EXHIBIT 2-7 *(Cont.)*

**Consolidated Statement of Changes in Financial Position**

| Years ended December 31, | | Koppers Company, Inc. and Subsidiaries | | Explanations |
|---|---|---|---|---|
| **1977** | 1976 | | | |
| ($ Thousands) | | | | **1.** WHERE THE FUNDS CAME FROM: |
| | | Source of funds: | 1 | |
| | | Operations: | | **2.** From line 13 of Income Statement on page 41. |
| **$ 66,199** | $ 66,841 | Net income | 2 | |
| **40,681** | 35,957 | Depreciation and depletion | 3 | **3.** This operating cost does not require the payment of funds, which are retained for use in the business. |
| **8,856** | 2,598 | Deferred income taxes and other expenses | 4 | |
| **(1,446)** | (1,183) | Equity in earnings of affiliated companies, less dividends received | | **4.** Taxes and other expenses not paid currently. Available for use in operations until the time when payment becomes due. |
| **114,290** | 104,213 | Funds provided from operations | | |
| **32,363** | 18,069 | Term debt issued | 5 | |
| **8,818** | 23,764 | Redemption of investment in ARCO/Polymers, Inc. | 6 | **5.** Borrowings explained on page 36. |
| **2,523** | 9,516 | Common stock issued | 7 | **6.** Redemption of investment in ARCO/Polymers stock. |
| **3,548** | 6,885 | Book value of fixed assets and other noncurrent assets disposed of or sold | 8 | |
| **161,542** | 162,447 | | 9 | **7.** Negotiated value of companies acquired in exchange for shares of common stock, plus value of shares contributed to Employees Stock Ownership Plan trust as determined by Federal tax regulations. |
| | | Disposition of funds: | 10 | |
| **104,522** | 90,639 | Capital investments | 11 | |
| **38,010** | 7,469 | Term debt retired | 12 | |
| **24,250** | 20,240 | Dividends paid | 13 | **8.** Disposal of equipment, facilities, etc. no longer needed in operations. |
| **18,991** | — | Funds held for capital expenditures | 14 | **9.** Total of all cash generated from all sources. |
| **4,732** | 1,214 | Other | | |
| **190,505** | 119,562 | | | **10.** WHERE THE FUNDS WENT: |
| **$ (28,963)** | $ 42,885 | Increase (decrease) in working capital | 15 | **11.** Capital investments to provide further growth. |
| | | Changes in components of working capital: | 16 | **12.** Repayment of debt. |
| | | Increase in current assets: | | **13.** Return to common and preferred shareholders. |
| **$ (29,701)** | $ 34,080 | Cash and short-term investments | | |
| **30,218** | 20,931 | Accounts receivable | | **14.** The unexpended portion of funds borrowed for Woodward coke plant expansion; being held by a trustee. |
| **11,189** | 1,943 | Inventories | | |
| **193** | 662 | Prepaid expenses | | |
| **11,899** | 57,616 | | | **15.** Amount derived by subtracting funds paid out from funds generated. |
| | | Increase (decrease) in current liabilities: | | **16.** Here is what working capital consisted of at year end. |
| **3,387** | (3,074) | Accrued income taxes | | |
| **3,093** | (265) | Other taxes | | |
| **18,601** | 6,646 | Accounts payable | | |
| **1,886** | 4,766 | Accrued pensions | | |
| **1,634** | 7,359 | Other accruals | | |
| **9,977** | (6,069) | Advance payments received on contracts | | |
| **2,284** | 5,368 | Debt due within one year, including short-term borrowings | | |
| **40,862** | 14,731 | | | |
| **$ (28,963)** | $ 42,885 | Increase (decrease) in working capital | | |

(See accompanying statement of accounting policies and notes to financial statements.)

footnotes can add considerably to the picture of corporate financial health painted by the basic statements themselves. Footnotes not only indicate the accounting policies adopted by the company (and often the dollar effect of having selected one alternative as opposed to another) but also provide additional support for selected amounts reported in the body of the financial report. In addition, they disclose pending legal actions against the company,

EXHIBIT 2-7 (Cont.)

**Consolidated Statement of Shareholders' Equity**

| Koppers Company, Inc. and Subsidiaries | | | | ($ Thousands, except per share figures) | |
| --- | --- | --- | --- | --- | --- |
| Years ended December 31, 1977 and 1976 | Cumulative Preferred Stock | Common Stock | Capital In Excess of Par Value | Earnings Retained in the Business | Total Preferred and Common Shareholders' Equity |
| **Balance at January 1, 1976** | $15,000 | $30,304 | $72,949 | $250,049 | $368,302 |
| Net income for the year 1976 | — | — | — | 66,841 | 66,841 |
| Cash dividends paid: | | | | | |
| On preferred stock, $4.00 per share | — | — | — | (600) | (600) |
| On common stock, 80¢ per share | — | — | — | (19,640) | (19,640) |
| Common stock issued during 1976: | | | | | |
| 80,000 shares for acquisitions accounted for as purchases | — | 100 | 1,705 | — | 1,805 |
| 536,094 shares for acquisition accounted for as a pooling | — | 670 | 1,052 | 5,989 | 7,711 |
| **Balance at December 31, 1976** | 15,000 | 31,074 | 75,706 | 302,639 | 424,419 |
| Net income for the year 1977 | — | — | — | 66,199 | 66,199 |
| Cash dividends paid: | | | | | |
| On preferred stock, $4.00 per share | — | — | — | (600) | (600) |
| On common stock, 95¢ per share | — | — | — | (23,650) | (23,650) |
| Common stock issued during 1977: | | | | | |
| 92,448 additional shares for acquisition accounted for as a purchase in 1975 | — | 116 | 1,859 | — | 1,975 |
| 26,402 shares contributed to Employee Stock Ownership Plan trust | — | 33 | 515 | — | 548 |
| **Balance at December 31, 1977** | $15,000 | $31,223 | $78,080 | $344,588 | $468,891 |

(See accompanying statement of accounting policies and notes to financial statements.)

## Statement of Accounting Policies
Koppers Company, Inc. and Subsidiaries

The major accounting policies of the Company are set forth below. The word "Company" as used in this report includes consolidated entities as well as Koppers Company, Inc.

### Principles of Consolidation
The consolidated statements include the accounts of the Company and all of its subsidiaries. All intercompany transactions have been eliminated.

### Inventories
Inventories are valued at the lower of cost or market. Cost for substantially all domestic inventories of Koppers Company, Inc. is determined by the LIFO (last-in, first-out) method. At December 31, 1977 and 1976, the current cost of inventories valued under the LIFO method (approximately 69% and 71%, respectively, of total inventories) exceeded the LIFO value by $55,007,000 and $49,217,000, respectively. Cost for the remainder of the inventories represents average costs or standard costs which approximate actual on the first-in, first-out basis. Market is replacement cost for raw materials and net realizable value for work-in-process and finished goods.

### Investments
Companies owned 50% or less but more than 20% are accounted for on the equity method except for certain foreign investments accounted for at cost because of repatriation regulations.

### Fixed Assets
Buildings, machinery and equipment are depreciated on the straight-line method over their useful lives. All ordinary maintenance and repair expenses are charged to operations. Extraordinary repairs, which materially extend the life of property, are generally charged to accumulated depreciation. Timber and mineral properties are depleted on the basis of units produced.

When land, standing timber or property units are sold, the difference between selling price and cost, after recognition of accumulated depreciation and depletion, is reflected in Other income.

### Intangible Assets
Patent costs are amortized over the lives of the patents. The excess of purchase price over net asset value of businesses acquired is amortized over the estimated useful lives of such assets not exceeding 40 years.

### Long-Term Contracts
Sales and income on long-term construction contracts are accounted for on the percentage-of-completion basis; losses are recognized as soon as they are determined.

### Pension Plans
The Company has pension plans covering substantially all employees. The Company provides for amortization of unfunded prior service costs over periods up to 40 years and pays provisions for pension expense into trust funds annually.

### Income Taxes
Benefits from investment tax credit are reflected currently in income.

*EXHIBIT 2-7 (Cont.)*

## Notes to Financial Statements

December 31, 1977 and 1976
Koppers Company, Inc. and Subsidiaries

### 1. Investment in ARCO/Polymers, Inc.

On January 1, 1974, the Sinclair-Koppers partnership was reorganized with the Company receiving securities of ARCO/Polymers. These securities were redeemed during the period 1974 through 1977.

• • • • •

### 3. Inventories

Product inventories, including work-in-process, used in the calculation of cost of sales before deducting progress billings amounted to $134,180,000, $129,643,000 and $131,922,000 at December 31, 1977, 1976 and 1975, respectively.

• • • • •

### 4. Investments in Affiliated Companies, at Equity

Consolidated earnings retained in the business included $11,991,000 in 1977 and $10,578,000 in 1976 representing the Company's equity in undistributed retained earnings of affiliated companies less deferred taxes.

• • • • •

### 7. Commitments and Contingencies

The Company has entered into various lease agreements covering buildings, machinery and equipment, and land.

The future minimum lease payments required under noncancelable leases with remaining terms of more than one year were as follows:

| | |
|---|---:|
| 1978 | $ 5,848,000 |
| 1979 | 4,648,000 |
| 1980 | 3,979,000 |
| 1981 | 2,066,000 |
| 1982 | 1,614,000 |
| 1983 and later | 10,338,000 |
| | $28,493,000 |

The Company entered into no leases after December 31, 1976 that could be considered capital leases under the criteria of Financial Accounting Standards Board State-ment No. 13. As permitted under Statement No. 13, the Company has not retroactively applied the criteria of this Statement to leases existing at December 31, 1976. Had the Company done so, capitalization of leases would have increased the following items in the financial statements by the amounts shown:

| | 1977 | 1976 |
|---|---:|---:|
| Fixed assets | $16,239,000 | $17,225,000 |
| Liabilities | $11,512,000 | $13,570,000 |
| Net income | $  564,000 | $  502,000 |

Debts issued by municipal authorities and guaranteed by the Company are not considered lease agreements even though the legal form of the transactions is a lease. Such obligations are classified as term debt.

• • • • •

### 9. Income Taxes

Income tax expense has the following components:

| | Years Ending December 31, | |
|---|---:|---:|
| | 1977 | 1976 |
| Federal: | | |
|   Current | $31,627,000 | $29,911,000 |
|   Deferred | 5,236,000 | (216,000) |
| | 36,863,000 | 29,695,000 |
| State | 5,696,000 | 6,090,000 |
| Foreign: | | |
|   Current | 3,420,000 | 3,311,000 |
|   Deferred | 822,000 | 1,994,000 |
| | 4,242,000 | 5,305,000 |
| Total | $46,801,000 | $41,090,000 |

Deferred taxes for the years ended December 31, 1977 and 1976 resulted from the factors shown in Table 2, below.

The differences between the statutory and effective income tax rates for the years ended December 31, 1977 and 1976 are as shown in Table 3, below.

### Table 2. Deferred Taxes

| December 31, | 1977 | 1976 |
|---|---:|---:|
| Excess of tax over book depreciation | $7,080,000 | $1,355,000 |
| Reversal of prior provisions related to inventory costing adjustments | (450,000) | (450,000) |
| Difference in book and tax income recognition methods on contracts of foreign subsidiary | (772,000) | 772,000 |
| Other—net | 200,000 | 101,000 |
| | $6,058,000 | $1,778,000 |

### Table 3. Differences Between Statutory and Effective Income Tax Rates

| December 31, | 1977 | 1976 |
|---|---:|---:|
| Statutory tax rate: | | |
|   Federal | 48.0% | 48.0% |
|   State, net of Federal tax benefit | 2.6% | 2.9% |
| Investment tax credit | (4.5%) | (5.5%) |
| Nontaxable earnings of Domestic International Sales Corporation | (1.3%) | (1.6%) |
| Effect of lower statutory tax rate applicable to dividends received from an affiliated company | (0.2%) | (2.5%) |
| Effect of lower statutory tax rate applicable to capital gain income | (0.5%) | (0.9%) |
| Other—net | (2.7%) | (2.3%) |
| | 41.4% | 38.1% |

**Selected Footnotes**

EXHIBIT 2-7 (Cont.)

### 9. Income Taxes (Cont.)

The provisions for income taxes for the years 1977 and 1976 have been reduced by $5,506,000 and $5,932,000, respectively, for investment tax credit.

At December 31, 1977 and 1976, consolidated earnings retained in the business included approximately $15,300,000 and $12,300,000, respectively, on which Federal income tax has not been provided since the Company has reinvested such earnings and intends to continue such investment permanently in export activities and foreign corporations.

. . . . .

### 13. Replacement Costs (Unaudited)

Koppers management has consistently recognized that financial statements in the Company's reports to shareholders, which are based on historical costs, do not reflect the effects of inflation. It should be realized, however, that there are limitations upon the usefulness of the replacement cost information that follows. The required information is not precise and does not give a complete or balanced presentation of the impact of inflation. It does not necessarily reflect management's intent to replace existing inventory or productive facilities. Neither does it reflect any operating cost savings that can result from replacement of existing production facilities with assets of improved technology or of higher productivity.

Management strongly concurs with the SEC's intention that the following replacement cost data not be used to indicate the effect of inflation upon the Company's net income. Simplistic use of the data to restate net income could be greatly misleading. Because of the many unresolved conceptual problems involved, the Company has not attempted to quantify the total impact of inflation. Further, consideration of the following replacement cost information alone does not recognize the customary relationship between cost changes and changes in selling price to maintain profit margins. Competitive conditions permitting, the Company expects to modify its future selling prices to recognize cost changes.

**Table 5. Replacement Cost Information**

| ($ Thousands) | 1977 | | 1976 | |
| --- | --- | --- | --- | --- |
| | Historical Cost From Balance Sheet | Estimated Replacement Cost | Historical Cost From Balance Sheet | Estimated Replacement Cost |
| Inventory | $ 168,743 | $ 232,754 | $157,554 | $ 214,000 |
| Cost of Sales (excluding depreciation) | $1,064,349 | $1,066,131 | $919,954 | $ 921,000 |
| Productive Capacity | | | | |
| Machinery, Equipment and Buildings | $ 601,944 | $1,241,000 | $522,265 | $1,092,000 |
| Less accumulated depreciation | 289,067 | 774,000 | 256,369 | 687,000 |
| | $ 312,877 | $ 467,000 | $265,896 | $ 405,000 |
| Depreciation Expense | $ 40,136 | $ 87,000 | $ 35,198 | $ 75,000 |

**Table 6. Replacement Cost Information**

| ($ Thousands) | 1977 | | 1976 | |
| --- | --- | --- | --- | --- |
| | Fixed Assets | Accumulated Depreciation and Depletion | Fixed Assets | Accumulated Depreciation and Depletion |
| Totals as shown in the accompanying Consolidated Financial Statements | $659,671 | $299,908 | $570,552 | $265,355 |
| Less amounts for which replacement cost data have not been provided: | | | | |
| Mineral reserves | 19,365 | 2,720 | 13,063 | 2,016 |
| Depletable timber properties | 22,496 | 8,121 | 21,242 | 6,970 |
| Land at cost | 15,866 | — | 13,982 | — |
| Historical amounts for which replacement cost data have been provided | $601,944 | $289,067 | $522,265 | $256,369 |

**Selected Footnotes (cont.)**

potential changes in financial structure (e.g., proposed bond or stock issues), and events that take place subsequent to the end of the year being reported upon that may have an impact on the future earning ability of the company.

## Measures of Financial Performance

Familiarity with some widely used measures of financial performance may enable the reader to better understand the rationale behind several accounting principles and procedures to be discussed in subsequent chapters. To the extent that corporations believe that such measures are of primary concern to stockholders, creditors, or other readers of financial reports, both the corporations and their accountants may (unfortunately) evaluate accounting alternatives in light of their impact upon such measures, rather than on the basis of more meaningful criteria such as relevance and objectivity.

**earnings per share**  Some analytically significant financial indicators are explicitly reported in the body of the financial statements; others are displayed in supplementary reports accompanying the basic financial statements or must be derived by the analyst himself. One important indicator that is reported in the financial statements themselves—generally directly beneath net income—is *earnings per share* (EPS). Earnings (or income) per share is computed by dividing net income available to common shareholders by the average number of shares of common stock outstanding during the period (with adjustment for additional shares that the company expects to issue in the future). It is of significance not only because it enables individual stockholders to compute readily their share of total corporate earnings by multiplying EPS by number of shares owned but also because it facilitates comparisons of corporate performance among years in which there were a greater or lesser number of shares outstanding.

Koppers had earnings per share of $2.64 in 1977—net income available to common stockholders of $65,599,000 divided by 24,886,000 shares of common stock outstanding.*

**price/earnings ratio**  A short analytical step from earnings per share is the *price/earnings ratio*. The price/earnings (P/E) ratio compares earnings per share with the price per share at which the common stock of the company is selling on the open market.

*From reported income of $66,199,000 was deducted $600,000 in dividends paid to preferred stockholders, which is not available to common stockholders. The rationale for this deduction will be provided in Chapter 12 as part of a more detailed discussion of earnings per share.

Since such price fluctuates from hour to hour, such ratio is constantly changing, and it is not therefore reported in corporate annual reports.

At the close of business on December 31, 1977, the market price of Koppers' common stock was quoted on the New York Stock Exchange at 22 3/4 ($22.75 per share). The P/E ratio, based on 1977 earnings was $22.75/$2.64—approximately 8.6 times. The importance of the P/E ratio to investors is indicated by the fact that *The Wall Street Journal,* as well as many other financial periodicals, incorporate P/E ratios into their daily stock market quotations.

**return on investment**

Perhaps the measure of corporate performance that is most relevant to investors is *return on investment.* Return on investment relates the earnings of the enterprise to the resources provided by the owners of that business. The resources provided by the owners are measured by the equity of the owners—which, of course, is equivalent to net assets (i.e., assets less liabilities). Thus,

$$\text{Return on investment (ROI)} = \frac{\text{Net income}}{\text{Owners' equity}}$$

The balance sheet of Koppers Company indicates that the total investment of the stockholders at the end of 1977 was $468,891,000. This figure includes the original amounts contributed by the stockholders as well as the retained earnings. The income statement reveals that income of the company was $66,199,000. Hence,

$$\text{Return on investment} = \frac{\$66,199,000}{\$468,891,000^*} = 14.1\%$$

For the year 1977 the stockholders of Koppers Company received a return of approximately 14 percent. This percentage return is greater than they could have obtained by placing their funds in a savings institution, but, of course, it was achieved only at substantially greater risk.

**current ratio**

Another widely used measure of financial health is the *current ratio.* The current ratio provides an insight into the ability of the enterprise to meet its short-term debts. As such it is especially meaningful to parties considering whether to ex-

---

*Preferably, owners' equity should be computed by calculating the average owners' equity during the year. Such refinement, as well as others to be discussed in Chapter 15, is ignored for the sake of simplicity at this stage of the text.

tend credit to the firm. The current ratio compares current assets to current liabilities; that is, it relates cash and the assets that are most likely to be transformed into cash within a single business cycle to the debts that will fall due within that period.

$$\text{Current ratio} = \frac{\text{Current assets}}{\text{Current liabilities}}$$

The current ratio for Koppers Company as of December 31, 1977, based on data provided in the balance sheet, is

$$\text{Current ratio} = \frac{438{,}949{,}000}{206{,}238{,}000} = 2.13$$

In most industries, a current ratio of 2.0 is a sign of reasonable financial health. Koppers Company appears, therefore, to have sufficient working capital (current assets minus current liabilites) on hand to meet its obligations as they come due in the forthcoming year.

Additional techniques of financial analysis will be described in Chapter 15. At that time a number of caveats will be issued pertaining to possible misleading conclusions that are often drawn from the various widely used financial measures.

**importance of comparisons**   Financial statements provide an insight into a company's past operating performance and future earnings potential, that is perhaps unmatched by that which could be obtained from any other sources. But the picture presented has meaning only when the reader is able to put it into proper perspective. He must be able to examine the financial data with reference to financial position and results of operations of both previous years and of other companies in the same or a related industry. No set of dollar amounts, ratios, or other indicators of financial health have meaning in and of themselves. They are of significance only when compared with similar indicators of the same company in other years and of other companies in the same or related industries. Toward this end, the annual report of Koppers Company contains comparable financial data for the year immediately prior to that being reported upon as well as a statistical summary for a nine-year period.

The financial statements of Koppers, it should be noticed, are "rounded" to the nearest thousand dollars. The practice of rounding serves to highlight the fact that financial statements are not precise; they are necessarily based on a number of estimates and judgmental determinations. Although such estimates and judgmental determinations unquestionably permit a degree of subjectivity to enter into the financial statements, and perhaps make them less comparable with those of other firms, they serve at the same time to make them more relevant for most decisions that they will be used to facilitate.

Additional techniques of financial analysis will be alluded to throughout the text and will be discussed specifically in Chapter 15.

### Summary

In this chapter we have presented an overview of the three primary financial statements—the balance sheet (statement of financial position), the income statement, and the statement of changes in financial position—as well as a secondary statement, the statement of changes in retained earnings. The chapter was intended to familiarize the reader with the purposes of each statement, with its underlying nature, with its basic format, and with the terminology conventionally employed.

The key to accounting as it is currently practiced is the fundamental accounting equation: assets – liabilities = owners' equity. This equation serves as the basis for analyzing and recording all accounting events. In the following chapter we shall illustrate in greater detail the means by which transactions are given accounting recognition.

*exercise for review and self-testing*

(The solutions to this exercise—and similar exercises in other chapters—will be found following the last problem in the chapter.)

1. A businessman forms a corporation. He contributes to the enterprise $100,000 cash. To provide evidence of his investment, the corporation issues to him 10,000 shares of common stock, assigning to each share a par value of $10.
   a. What are the total assets of the corporation immediately after it has been formed?
   b. What are the total equities of the corporation? That is, what are the total claims, by either the owner or by outsiders, against these assets?

2. The corporation borrows $50,000 from a bank.
   a. What are the new total assets of the corporation?
   b. What are the total claims against these assets? Of these total claims (equities), how much are claims of outsiders (liabilities); how much are claims of the owner?

3. The company acquires an automobile for $10,000 cash.
   a. What are the total assets of the corporation?
   b. What are the corporation's liabilities; its owners' equity?

4. The company acquires 300 units of inventory at a cost of $5 per unit. The purchase is made "on account," with the firm promising to pay for the goods within 30 days.
   a. What are the total assets of the corporation now?
   b. What are the corporation's liabilities; its owners' equity?

5. The firm sells 100 of the units of inventory for $7 per unit. The purchasers pay cash.
   a. What are the total assets of the corporation?
   b. What are the corporation's liabilities; its owners' equity?

6. By how much has the equity of the owner increased since he made his initial contribution of cash? How much "better off" is the corporation (and thus its owner) since the owner made such contribution? What was the "income" of the corporation during the period in which the transactions took place?

## Questions

**review and discussion**

1. Explain why the balance sheet of a firm might be dated "*As of* December 31, 1981" but the income statement dated "*For the Year Ended* December 31, 1981."

2. What is meant by owners' equity? Why is owners' equity not necessarily indicative of the amount of cash that would be returned to the owners if the assets of a business were to be sold and the creditors paid the amounts owed to them?

3. A bookkeeper recently totaled up the recorded assets of a firm and found that they came to $1,398,576. The total liabilities came to $600,000 and the total owners' equity to $800,000. Are such totals possible in the context of the double-entry bookkeeping process if no error has been made? Suppose instead that assets were equal to liabilities plus owners' equity. Do such totals assure that no accounting errors have been made?

4. Which of the following events would usually be accorded accounting recognition on the books of United Electric Co.?
   1. The firm signs a three-year contract with its union.
   2. The firm issues 1,000 additional shares of common stock.
   3. The president of United sells 3,000 shares of United Electric Co. stock from his personal holdings to a close friend.
   4. The passage of another year has reduced the remaining useful life of plant and equipment.
   5. The wholesale price of copper wire has *increased.* United Electric Co. has 100,000 feet of copper wire in inventory.
   6. The wholesale price of copper wire has *decreased.* United Electric Co. has 100,000 feet of copper wire in inventory.

5. Included among a firm's noncurrent assets are "unamortized corporate

organizational costs, $25,000." What is meant by such an asset? Is it possible to sell such an asset? If not, why is it considered an asset?

6. The same firm has recorded among its current liabilities "advances from customers, $3,000." Why is such amount a liability? What impact did receipt of the $3,000 have on the accounting equation?

7. A company reported substantial earnings for the last several years, yet it is about to file for bankruptcy. How is such a situation possible?

8. A firm recently received a check from a customer for $10,000, yet it did not record such amount as "revenue." What are two possible reasons for its not doing so?

9. A firm recently purchased equipment for $80,000 yet did not record an expense. Why not? Will the amount paid ever be reported as an expense? When?

10. What is meant by a *current asset?* How is it possible that shares of the common stock of XYZ Company owned by one company may be recorded as a current asset but those owned by another may be recorded as a noncurrent asset?

11. What is meant by *preferred stock?* What preferences do preferred stockholders have over common stockholders? What rights do common stockholders have that preferred stockholders generally do not have?

12. What are *extraordinary items?* Why are they reported on the income statement apart from ordinary operating revenues and expenses?

13. Is it possible for a firm to have a substantial balance in retained earnings and still be unable to declare a cash dividend? Why?

## *Problems*

1. *Balance sheet accounts indicate the value assigned to resources or obligations as of a particular point in time. Income statement accounts provide information on inflows and outflows of resources during a particular period of time.*

   Some accounts are conventionally reported on the balance sheet; others are reported on the income statement. For each of the accounts indicated below, specify whether they would ordinarily be reported on the income statement or on the balance sheet.

   1. Sales revenue –   *Inc St.*
   2. Accounts receivable – *Bal Sh.*
   3. Insurance expense – *I. St*
   4. Prepaid insurance– *current asset – Bal Sh, – is expense at end of 1 year*
   5. Inventories – *A – Bal Sh*
   6. Cost of goods sold – *Inv.– Bal Sh. Inc St.– Expense*
   7. Depreciation expense – *Inc. St.   dr*
   8. Accumulated depreciation – *Bal Sh.   cr*
   9. Interest expense– *Inc St.*
   10. Notes payable – *Bal Sh.*

   *adjusting entry* {7, 8

11. Retained earnings   *— B.S. — party OE*
12. Investment in subsidiary — *B.S.   asset*

*close*

2. *All transactions serve to increase or decrease the balances in some combination of asset, liability and owners' equity accounts.*

For each of the following transactions, indicate whether assets (A), liabilities (L) or owners' equity (OE) would increase (+) or decrease (–). The first transaction is illustrated for you.

1. A corporation issues common stock in exchange for cash. (A+; OE +)
2. It issues preferred stock in exchange for a building. *— rather than cash*
3. It purchases inventory, giving the seller a 30-day note for the amount of the merchandise.   *L*
4. It collects from a customer the amount the customer owed on goods purchased several months earlier.
5. It exchanges shares of preferred stock for shares of common stock.
6. It repays bondholders by issuing to them shares of common stock.
7. It declares and pays a dividend to stockholders, thereby distributing assets of the company (cash) to the owners.
8. It returns to a manufacturer defective merchandise for credit on its account.
9. It receives from a customer defective merchandise and reduces the balance owed by the customer.

3. *Assets must equal liabilities plus owners' equity.*

The balances that follow were taken from the December 31, 1981 balance sheet of a corporation. Arrange a sheet of paper into three columns, each corresponding to a term in the accounting equation:

Assets = Liabilities + Owners' Equity

Place each of the balances in the appropriate column. Total each of the columns to make certain that the equation is in balance.

| | |
|---|---:|
| Marketable securities | $ 20,000 |
| Common stock | 100,000 |
| Buildings and equipment | 300,000 |
| Bonds payable | 250,000 |
| Accounts receivable | 90,000 |
| Prepaid rent | 15,000 |
| Preferred stock | 50,000 |
| Inventories | 80,000 |
| Taxes payable | 25,000 |
| Advances from customers | 3,000 |
| Accounts payable | 17,000 |
| Interest payable | 8,000 |
| Organization costs | 12,000 |
| Retained earnings | 64,000 |

4. *Retained earnings may be derived from other balance sheet accounts.*
From the following accounts, taken from the books and records of the

Finch Company on December 31, 1981, prepare both an income statement and a balance sheet. Derive the amount of retained earnings.

| | |
|---|---:|
| Cash | $15,000 |
| Accounts payable | 12,000 |
| Building and equipment | 90,000 |
| Cost of goods sold | 60,000 |
| Notes payable | 5,000 |
| Wages and salaries payable | 3,000 |
| Preferred stock | 20,000 |
| Common stock | 50,000 |
| Marketable securities | 18,000 |
| Inventory | 22,000 |
| Sales revenue | 88,000 |
| Tax expense | 3,000 |
| Taxes payable | 1,000 |
| Rent expense | 4,000 |
| Prepaid rent | 1,000 |
| Retained earnings | ? |

5. *Owners' equity equals assets minus liabilities.*
   *Owners' equity is affected by income (or loss), capital contributions, and capital withdrawals (dividends).*

   Fill in the missing amounts. Assume that there were no capital contributions by owners during 1980.

| | (a) | (b) | (c) |
|---|---:|---:|---:|
| Assets, December 31, 1980 | $100,000 | $50,000 | ? |
| Liabilities, December 31, 1980 | 25,000 | 10,000 | $20,000 |
| Owners' equity, *January* 1, 1980. | 60,000 | ? | 80,000 |
| Income, 1980 | 80,000 | 8,000 | 5,000 |
| Dividends paid 1980 | ? | 4,000 | 10,000 |

   (*Hint:* First compute owners' equity as of December 31, 1980.)

6. *Corporate performance may be evaluated by relating income to the investment of the owners, which may be expressed in terms of "book" or "market" values.*

   A company has assets of $3 million and liabilities of $2 million. There are 100,000 shares of common stock outstanding. Net income for the year was $150,000. The common stock of the company is being traded on a major stock exchange at $30 per share. Compute the return on investment (ROI) and the price/earnings ratio.

7. *Account titles generally provide an indication of whether the account represents a "stock" (and is thereby reported on the balance sheet) or a "flow" (and is thereby reported on the income statement).*

   From the following account balances, taken from the books and records of the Julie Company as of December 31, 1981, prepare an income statement and a balance sheet. Title and date the statements as appropriate, and, insofar as the information permits, separate assets and liabilities into current and noncurrent classifications.

| | |
|---|---:|
| Cash | $18,000 |
| A. Julie, capital | 51,600 |
| Sales | 75,000 |
| Cost of goods sold | 52,000 |
| Prepaid insurance | 1,000 |
| Advances from customers | 3,000 |
| Patents | 8,000 |
| Depreciation expense | 2,500 |
| Insurance expense | 2,000 |
| Interest revenue | 500 |
| Interest expense | 900 |
| Prepaid interest | 200 |
| Interest payable | 600 |
| Accounts receivable | 10,000 |
| Inventory | 9,000 |
| Rent expense | 6,000 |
| Advertising expense | 5,000 |
| Notes payable (due in three years) | 8,000 |
| Buildings and equipment | 26,000 |
| Notes receivable | 10,000 |
| Accounts payable | 19,000 |

8. *In the absence of additional contributions by owners, owners' equity is increased by earnings and decreased by dividends or losses.*

The Gail Company was organized as a partnership on January 2, 1981. Each of its two owners contributed $10,000 in cash to start the business. After one year of operations the company had on hand the following assets: cash, $18,000; accounts receivable, $3,000; inventory available for sale, $10,000; furniture and fixtures, $25,000.

The company owed suppliers (i.e., accounts payable) $8,000 and had notes outstanding to a bank (due in 1984) of $16,000.
a. Prepare a balance sheet as of December 31, 1981.
b. Assuming that the owners neither made additional contributions of capital to the business nor made any withdrawals, compute income for 1981.
c. Assume instead that during the year the owners withdrew $4,000 from the business. Compute income for 1981.

9. *The beginning balance in an account plus increases and minus decreases in that account during a period equals the ending balance.*

The table following is a condensed balance sheet of the Withington Corporation as of December 31, 1980. On a sheet of paper, copy the account titles and the initial balances. Leave room for seven additional columns of figures. Label six of the columns Transaction 1, 2, 3, etc., and the seventh column "Balance at 1/31/81."

The following six transactions took place in January. Indicate the effect that each would have on the balance sheet. Summarize the effects of the six transactions on the December 31, 1980 balance by adding across the rows and indicating the new balance in the column marked "Balance at 1/31/81."

## WITHINGTON CORPORATION

| | Balance 12/31/80 | 1 | 2 | Transactions 3 | 4 | 5 | 6 | Balance 1/31/81 |
|---|---|---|---|---|---|---|---|---|
| Cash | $ 40,000 | | | | | | | |
| Accounts receivable | 25,000 | | | | | | | |
| Inventory | 57,000 | +8,000 | | | | | | |
| Prepaid rent | 2,000 | | | | | | | |
| Equipment | 85,000 | | | | | | | |
| Building | 200,000 | | | | | | | |
| | $409,000 | | | | | | | |
| Accounts payable | $ 19,000 | +8,000 | | | | | | |
| Wages payable | 4,000 | | | | | | | |
| Notes payable | 38,000 | | | | | | | |
| Bonds payable | 150,000 | | | | | | | |
| Common stock | 45,000 | | | | | | | |
| Retained earnings | 153,000 | | | | | | | |
| | $409,000 | | | | | | | |

1. The company purchases inventory on account, $8,000. (Transaction 1 is done for you.)
2. The company purchases equipment for $12,000, giving the seller a two-year note.
3. The company pays its employees the $4,000 owed.
4. The company declares and pays a dividend of $20,000.
5. The company reaches an agreement with its bondholders. In exchange for their bonds, they agree to accept shares of common stock that have a market value of $150,000.
6. The company collects $5,000 that was owed by its customers.

10. *The balance sheet is nothing more than a detailed expression of the accounting equation.*

Arrange a sheet of paper into three columns, each corresponding to a term in the accounting equation:

Assets = Liabilities + Owners' Equity

Indicate the impact that each of the following transactions would have on

the accounting equation. Suggest titles for the specific accounts that would
be affected.

1. Whitman and Farrel form a corporation. The corporation issues 1,000
   shares of common stock and sells 500 shares to each of the founders
   for $3 per share.
2. The corporation borrows $3,000 from a bank, giving the bank a one-
   year note.
3. The corporation purchases furniture and fixtures for $5,000. The com-
   pany pays $1,000 cash and gives a six-month note for the balance.
4. The corporation rents a building. It pays, in advance, the first month's
   rent of $700.
5. The corporation purchases office supplies for $400 cash.
6. The corporation purchases inventory for future sale to customers for
   $1,200 cash.

Compute the "balance" in each of the accounts. Summarize the balances
in the form of a balance sheet.

11. *Working capital (current assets less current liabilities) in adequate amounts
   provides assurance that a firm is able to meet its obligations as they come
   due. It is important that all transactions be analyzed in terms of their
   impact upon working capital.*

   For each of the transactions described, indicate the effect that it will have
   upon current assets, current liabilities, and working capital. State whether
   current assets, current liabilities, and working capital will increase, decrease, or remain the same, and specify the accounts that will be affected.
   Indicate also any accounts, other than current assets or current liabilities,
   that will be affected. Transaction 1 is done for you as an illustration.

   1. A company purchases equipment for $7,000 cash.

| Transaction no. | Current Assets | Current Liabilities | Working Capital | Other Accounts |
|---|---|---|---|---|
| 1 | Cash –$7,000 | No effect | –$7,000 | Equipment +$7,000 |

   2. It borrows $3,000 and issues a 60-day note.
   3. It borrows $5,000 and issues a three-year note.
   4. It purchases inventory for $1,000 and promises to pay within 30 days.
   5. It purchases inventory for $600 cash.
   6. It purchases a building for $100,000 and issues 10-year bonds for the
      same amount.
   7. It repays a five-year note for $1,790.
   8. It sells, for $100, goods carried in inventory that were recorded at
      their original cost of $80. The purchaser agrees to pay within 60
      days. (Analyze this transaction in two steps: the increase in the asset
      received, and the decrease in the asset surrendered.)
   9. It sells, for $600 cash, land that it had recorded on its books for the
      same amount.

10. It records first-year depreciation on a building that originally cost $100,000 and that has a 20-year life. (That is, the company determines that one-twentieth of the services to be provided by the building have already been consumed.)

12. *Many balance sheet accounts have a direct relationship to those on the income statement.*

a. The 1/1/81 balance sheet of a firm reported "prepaid insurance, $1,200." During the course of the year 1981 the firm purchased an additional $1,400 of insurance. The income statement of the firm for the year indicated that insurance expense for the year was $1,300 (i.e., that $1,300 of insurance had been "used up"). How much "prepaid insurance" should be reported on the 12/31/81 balance sheet?

b. The balance sheet of 1/1/81 also reported "prepaid rent, $200." During the course of the year the firm made rent payments of $800. Since the monthly rent on the premises occupied is $100 per month, rent expense per the income statement was $1,200. How much "rent liability" (or "accrued rent payable," as it is often called) should be reported on the 12/31/81 balance sheet?

c. The balance sheet of 1/1/81 reported "interest liability" of $200 representing two months' interest on a note outstanding. During the year the firm made interest payments of $1,100. The year-end balance sheet reported "interest liability" of $300. How much "interest expense" should be reported on the 1981 income statement?

d. As of 1/1/81 the firm had inventory on hand of $3,000. At the end of the year the inventory on hand was $2,000. During the year the firm purchased new merchandise of $20,000. What was the cost of the merchandise sold during the year?

e. Assume instead that the firm had inventory on hand at the beginning of the year of $1,000. During the year it sold merchandise that had originally cost $18,000. At the end of the year it had inventory on hand of $3,000. How much inventory did it purchase during the year?

13. *Retained earnings must not be associated with cash or any other specific assets.*

As of December 31, 1981, the balance sheet of the Morgan Co. appeared as follows:

| | |
|---|---:|
| Cash | $ 85,000 |
| Other current assets | 75,000 |
| Other assets, including buildings, land, and equipment | 670,000 |
| Total assets | $830,000 |
| Liabilities | $220,000 |
| Common stock (10,000 issued and outstanding) | 10,000 |
| Retained earnings $\longrightarrow$ | 600,000 |
| Total equities | $830,000 |

In 1981 the company had earnings of $40,000. Since there were 10,000 shares of common stock outstanding (par value per share, $1.00) earnings per share were $4. In 1981 the company declared no dividends since the directors claimed funds were needed for expansion.

Shortly after the close of the year, the president of the company received a letter from a stockholder protesting the company's refusal to declare a dividend. The letter said in part,

> When I studied accounting "retained earnings" were called "surplus." No amount of name changing can obscure the fact that the company has $600,000 available for distribution to stockholders.

a. How would you respond to the angry stockholder? Does the company have $600,000 available for distribution to stockholders?

b. Suppose the company did decide to declare a dividend of $60 per share ($600,000). What effect would such dividend likely have on corporate operations?

c. Does the balance sheet provide assurance that the company could, in fact, declare a dividend of $60 per share even if it wanted to? Why?

d. Suppose that instead of earnings of $40,000 the company had a loss of $10,000. The company nevertheless declared a dividend of $2.00 per share. A disgruntled stockholder questioned the decision and wrote to the president:

> Dividends are supposed to be distributions of earnings. How is it possible to pay a dividend in a year in which there were no earnings?

How would you respond to his question?

14. *Alternative borrowing arrangements have different effects upon the current ratio.*

The balance sheet of the First Corporation as of December 31, 1981, appears on the following page.

a. Compute the current ratio as of December 31, 1981.

b. Suppose that the company were to borrow an additional $50,000 and give the bank a six-month note. How would that affect the current ratio?

c. Suppose instead that the company were to borrow $50,000 and give a note payable in full at the end of two years. How would that affect the current ratio?

d. Suppose instead that the company were to issue bonds for $200,000 and use the proceeds to purchase a new plant? How would that affect the current ratio?

**First Corporation**
**Balance Sheet**
**December 31, 1981**

| *Assets* | | *Liabilities and owners' equity* | |
|---|---|---|---|
| Current assets | | Current liabilities | |
| Cash | $ 10,000 | Accounts payable | $ 30,000 |
| Accounts receivable | 20,000 | Notes payable | 20,000 |
| Note receivable | 50,000 | | |
| Marketable securities | 15,000 | | $ 50,000 |
| Inventories | 5,000 | | |
| | | Noncurrent liabilities | |
| | $100,000 | Bonds payable | $100,000 |
| Noncurrent assets | | Owners' equity | |
| Plant and equipment | $120,000 | Common stock | $200,000 |
| Land | 70,000 | Retained earnings | 20,000 |
| Investment in subsidiaries | 80,000 | | $220,000 |
| | $270,000 | | |
| | | Total liabilities and | |
| Total assets | $370,000 | owners' equity | $370,000 |

15. *Alternative financing arrangements may have substantially different effects on the accounting equation as well as on earnings per share.*

    The following information relates to the Emerson Corp.:

    | | |
    |---|---|
    | Total assets, 12/31/81 | $1,000,000 |
    | Total liabilities, 12/31/81 | 200,000 |
    | Total owners' equity, 12/31/81 | 800,000 |
    | Net income 1981 | 100,000 |
    | Number of shares of common stock outstanding | 10,000 |

    a. Determine earnings per share for 1981.
    b. The Emerson Corp. is currently negotiating to purchase a new manufacturing facility. The present owner of the plant is asking $200,000 for his facility. Emerson Corp. estimates that the increased capacity of the new plant would add $30,000 annually to its income. But in order to purchase the plant it would have to borrow the $200,000. It estimates that it could issue long-term bonds at an annual interest rate of 11 percent (i.e., $22,000 per year).

(1) If the company were to purchase the plant and borrow the necessary funds, what effect would the purchase (excluding effects on earnings) have on "the accounting equation"?

(2) What effect would it have on earnings per share (assuming that income would otherwise have been the same as in 1981)? Ignore income tax considerations.

c. Assume instead that the president of Emerson is considering an alternative means of purchasing the new plant. Instead of offering the present owner of the plant $200,000 in cash, he would offer him common stock of the Emerson Corp. that has a present market value of $200,000. The common stock of the Emerson Corp. is currently being traded on a major stock exchange at $100 per share. The Emerson Corp. would issue 2,000 new shares of common stock. Obviously, the company would no longer have to issue the bonds.

(1) What effect would the alternative purchase plan have on the accounting equation?

(2) If you were a present stockholder of Emerson Corp. concerned primarily with earnings per share, would you prefer the original purchase plan or the alternative proposal? Why?

**16.** *The balance sheet is closely related to the income statement.*

The balance sheets and income statements of the Ames Corp. for the years 1978 through 1981 are indicated in the table following. Also indicated are dividends paid during those years. Some critical figures, however, have been omitted. You are to provide the missing figures. The Ames Corp. began operations on January 1, 1978.

|  | 1978 | 1979 | 1980 | 1981 |
|---|---|---|---|---|
| | | Balance sheet—December 31 | | |
| | | *Assets* | | |
| Cash | $100 | $200 | $ ? | $300 |
| Accounts receivable | 200 | 100 | 300 | 100 |
| Inventory | 350 | ? | 100 | 100 |
| Building and equipment | 600 | 900 | 800 | 400 |
| | | *Liabilities and owners' equity* | | |
| Accounts payable | $200 | $100 | $200 | $300 |
| Notes payable | ? | 600 | 300 | 100 |
| Common stock | 200 | 200 | 200 | 300 |
| Retained earnings | 100 | 400 | ? | ? |
| | | Income statement | | |
| Sales | $ ? | $1,000 | $ ? | $1,200 |
| Cost of goods sold and other operating expenses | 500 | ? | 600 | ? |
| Net income | ? | ? | 400 | 300 |
| Dividends paid | $ 0 | $ 150 | $200 | $ ? |

**17.** *Not all financial events give rise to assets or liabilities. Sometimes, assets or liabilities resulting from contractual arrangements are recognized only upon the performance of either of the parties to the contract.*

Indicate the nature (i.e., descriptive account title) of the assets and liabilities (if any) that would receive accounting recognition on the books of the Utica Company as a result of the following events or transactions:

1. The Utica Co. employs six men to perform routine maintenance work at a rate of $5 per hour. The men work a total of 200 hours. They have not yet been paid.
2. The company signs a three-year contract with a security company. The company will provide guard service for the company at a cost of $200 per month.
3. The security company performs one month's services as promised.
4. The company orders machinery and equipment at a cost of $10,000.
5. The machinery and equipment previously ordered is received and installed as agreed upon by the manufacturer.
6. A customer orders 300 units of the company's product at a price of $2 per unit.
7. Utica Co. ships the merchandise previously ordered.
8. Utica Co. borrows $40,000 at an interest rate of 10 percent per year. The company gives the bank a four-year note.
9. One year elapses, and the company has paid the bank neither principal nor interest on the note.
10. The company guarantees to repair any defective products. During the year it sells 10,000 units of product. It estimates from previous experience that 5 percent of such units will be returned for repair work. It estimates also that the cost of such repairs will be $1 per unit.

**18.** *The statement of changes in financial position accounts for the increase or decrease in working capital (current assets minus current liabilities) during a period.*

The balance sheets following are of the Todd Company as of December 31, 1980 and 1981. Also provided is information pertaining to financial events that took place during 1981.

*Additional information:*

1. The company had income in 1981 of $37,000. Working capital provided by operations was actually $52,000, since $15,000 of the expenses deducted from revenues did not involve an outlay of current assets or an increase in current liabilities—i.e., depreciation expense involved a reduction in buildings and equipment (a noncurrent asset).
2. The company purchased equipment (for cash) at a cost of $35,000.
3. The company sold a parcel of land that had cost $10,000 for $10,000 (cash).
4. The company borrowed from the bank an additional $15,000 and agreed to repay the entire loan in five years.
5. Owners of the company made cash withdrawals totaling $12,000.
   *Required:*
   a. Compute working capital as of December 31, 1980.
   b. Compute working capital as of December 31, 1981.

c. Compute the increase or decrease in working capital during the year 1981.

d. Based on the additional information, prepare a statement of changes in financial position in which you account for all increases (sources of) and decreases (applications of) in working capital. Be certain that the net increase or decrease in working capital is equal to the amount computed in part c. Use the following format.

Sources of working capital:

Applications of working capital:

Net increase (decrease) in working capital for the year:

|  | December 31, 1980 | December 31, 1981 |
|---|---|---|
| *Assets* | | |
| Current assets | | |
| Cash | $ 30,000 | $ 20,000 |
| Accounts receivable | 40,000 | 70,000 |
| Inventory | 39,000 | 44,000 |
| Prepaid rent | 5,000 | 5,000 |
| | $114,000 | $139,000 |
| Noncurrent assets | | |
| Land | $ 50,000 | $ 40,000 |
| Building | 160,000 | 150,000 |
| Equipment | 15,000 | 45,000 |
| | $225,000 | $235,000 |
| Total assets | $339,000 | $374,000 |
| *Liabilities and owners' equity* | | |
| Current liabilities | | |
| Accounts payable | $ 71,000 | $ 68,000 |
| Wages payable | 5,000 | 4,000 |
| Interest payable | 3,000 | 2,000 |
| | $ 79,000 | $ 74,000 |
| Noncurrent liabilities | | |
| Notes payable | $ 60,000 | $ 75,000 |
| Owners' equity | 200,000 | 225,000 |
| Total liabilities and owners' equity | $339,000 | .$374,000 |

19. *Some transactions affect the composition of net assets (assets less liabilities) without affecting the level of net assets. Others serve to increase or decrease the level of net assets—and thereby result in an increase or decrease in owners' equity.*

As you might have done in Question 9, arrange a sheet of paper into three columns, each corresponding to a term in the accounting equation. Indicate the impact that each of the following transactions would have on the accounting equation. Suggest titles for each of the specific accounts that would be affected.

1. Petrified Products, Inc. purchases furniture and fixtures for $30,000, giving a five-year note.
2. The company purchases "on account" merchandise inventory for $15,000.
3. The firm, realizing that it had purchased an excessive amount of furniture, sells a portion of it. It sells for $3,000 cash furniture that had initially cost $3,000.
4. The firm sells an additional amount of furniture. It sells for $5,000 cash furniture that had initially cost $2,000. (Has the "level" of net assets increased as the result of this transaction?)
5. The firm sells for $800 "on account" merchandise inventory that had been purchased for $600.
6. The firm purchases supplies for $300 on account.
7. The firm uses supplies that had originally cost $200.
8. The firm collects $600 of the amount owed to it by customers.
9. The firm pays one month's rent in advance, $400.
10. At the end of one month, the firm wishes to give accounting recognition to the fact that it had occupied the rented premises for the one month paid for in advance.

20. *Even to those who are not experts in accounting, financial statements provide a great deal of information.*

Refer to the financial statements of Koppers Company contained in Exhibit 2–7.

1. The company had record sales in 1977.
   a. Did it also have record earnings?
   b. Did the cost of goods sold (cost of sales) increase more in proportion to sales or less?
   c. Why do you suspect that interest expense on term debt decreased in 1977? (To which balance sheet account might you look for an explanation?)
   d. What percentage of its income (before taxes) was the company required to pay as income taxes in 1977 and 1976? Does the annual report provide an explanation for the increase in the effective tax rate?
   e. Why did the firm's dividends received from ARCO/Polymers, Inc. decline in 1977? Can you verify your explanation with reference to the balance sheet?
2. The company had record total assets as of December 31, 1977.
   a. Did the firm's current ratio improve between December 31, 1976 and December 31, 1977?

b. Did the firm issue additional shares of common stock in 1977? (Verify your answer with reference to the consolidated statement of shareholders' equity and the consolidated statement of changes in financial position.)

c. Were the customers of Koppers indebted to the firm for more or less as of December 31, 1977 than as of December 31, 1976? Was the amount of the trade receivables greater or less in relation to the net sales of the firm?

d. As of December 31, 1976 the firm reported retained earnings of $344,588,000. Do you think that the firm could, if it elected, pay a dividend of that amount and still continue to operate?

21. *The resources of a firm can be valued on differing bases.*

Refer to the financial statements of Koppers Company.

a. According to the firm's balance sheet, what is the total value of inventory on hand?

b. How much would it cost to replace such inventory at current market prices? (*Hint:* See footnotes.)

c. Do you think that either of these two values is indicative of the amount for which the inventory could be sold?

d. According to the firm's balance sheet, what is the net value (cost less accumulated depreciation) of available buildings, equipment, and machinery?

e. What would it cost to replace those items?

f. Determine the percentage by which replacement cost exceeds "historical" cost. Comment on any limitations on the usefulness of the balance sheet to facilitate investment decisions that might be suggested by your comparisons of historical and replacement costs.

22. *Values assigned in financial statements may differ from those assigned by "the market."*

a. Refer to the financial statements of Koppers Company and determine the total value of the equity of the common shareholders as of December 31, 1977.

b. The stock market price per share of Koppers Company stock on December 31, 1977 was $22.75. Taking into account the total number of shares issued and outstanding on that date (see the balance sheet), determine the total "market" value of the equity of the stockholders.

c. Propose a reason why market value exceeds "book" value.

*solutions to exercise for review and self-testing*

1. a. Assets = $100,000
   b. Equities = $100,000

2. a. Assets = 150,000
   b. Total equities = $150,000; those of owner = $100,000; those of outsiders = $50,000

3. a. Assets = $150,000 (This transaction serves to decrease "cash" and increase "fixed assets"—automobile.)
   b. Liabilities = $50,000; owners' equity = $100,000

**4.** a. Assets = $151,500

   b. Liabilities = $51,500; owners' equity = $100,000

**5.** a. Assets = $151,700 ($151,500 per above, plus $700 cash received upon sale, minus $500 of goods surrendered.)

   b. Liabilities = $51,500; owners' equity = $100,200 (The "level" of assets increased by $200 as a consequence of the sale of 100 units. Liabilities remained unchanged but the equity of the owner must have increased by $200.)

**6.** Owners' equity has increased by $200; income of the corporation was $200.

# 3

## The Recording Process

The accounting system is a model of logic and order. This chapter will serve to introduce the *accounting cycle*—the procedures that lead from the initial recognition of a financial event to the preparation of financial statements. The practices that are described are the conventional ones; they can be employed efficiently and effectively by most organizations. But there is nothing sacrosanct about them. In fact, many firms, particularly those that make use of sophisticated computers, have modified them to suit their own particular needs. An understanding of the fundamental accounting cycle, however, is crucial to an appreciation of the relationships among the various accounts—particularly among balance sheet accounts and the associated income statement accounts.

## Ledger Accounts

The basic accounting equation—assets = liabilities + owners' equity—or the slightly expanded equation—assets = liabilities + capital contributed by owners + retained earnings—serves as the basis for all accounting transactions. Conceivably, all financial events that affect a business and are deemed worthy of accounting recognition could be recorded in a single ledger (or book of accounts), derived from the basic equation. Changes in assets would be indicated on the left-hand side of the page; changes in liabilities or owners' equity would be indicated on the right.

*example*

1. The CDE Company issues capital stock for $25,000 cash. (An asset, cash, is increased; owners' equity, common stock, is increased.)
2. The company purchases furniture and fixtures for $10,000 on account. (An asset, furniture and fixtures, is increased; a liability, accounts payable, is increased.)
3. The company purchases merchandise for $7,000 cash. (An asset, merchandise, is increased; an asset, cash, is decreased.)
4. The company pays $5,000 of the amount it owes on account. (An asset, cash, is decreased; a liability, accounts payable, is decreased.)

**CDE Company**
**"General Ledger"**

| Assets | | Liabilities and Owners' Equity | |
|---|---|---|---|
| 1. Cash (asset +) | +$25,000 | 1. Common stock (owners' equity +) | +$25,000 |
| 2. Furniture and fixtures (asset +) | + 10,000 | 2. Accounts payable (liability +) | + 10,000 |
| 3. Merchandise (asset +) | + 7,000 | | |
| Cash (asset –) | – 7,000 | | |
| 4. Cash (asset –) | – 5,000 | 4. Accounts payable (liability –) | – 5,000 |
| | $30,000 | | $30,000 |

The ledger indicates that after the fourth transaction the firm has assets of $30,000 and liabilities and owners' equity of the same amount. The ledger reveals that the accounts are "in balance" (they would have to be unless an error was made), and it indicates the total assets and the total liabilities and owners' equity. But by itself it provides little information that would be useful to either management or owners. Since each side of the ledger page combines changes in a great variety of accounts, the balance in any particular account is not readily available. To find the amount of cash on hand, for example, it would be necessary to search the entire page (or entire book insofar as there were numerous transactions) for all entries affecting cash. How much more convenient it would be if a separate page were provided for each account. Thus,

**CDE Company**
**General Ledger**

| Assets | | | Liabilities and Owners' Equity | | |
|---|---|---|---|---|---|
| | Cash | | | Accounts payable | |
| (1) 25,000 | (3) 7,000 | | (4) 5,000 | (2) 10,000 | |
| | (4) 5,000 | | | | |
| | Furniture and fixtures | | | Common stock | |
| (2) 10,000 | | | | (1) 25,000 | |
| | Merchandise | | | | |
| (3) 7,000 | | | | | |

In the illustration each of the "T"'s represents (for instructional purposes) a separate page in the ledger or book of accounts. Thus, there is a separate page or "T account" for cash, furniture and fixtures, accounts payable, etc.

*An increase* in an *asset* account is recorded on the *left* side of the ledger page or T account; a *decrease* in an asset account is recorded on the *right* side.

Conversely, an *increase* in a *liability* or *owners' equity* account is recorded on the *right* side of the ledger page or T account; a *decrease* in a *liability or owners' equity* account is recorded on the *left* side.

The balance in an account at any particular time can be determined by subtracting the amounts recorded on one side from those recorded on the other. The convention of recording increases in assets on the left side of the account and increases in liabilities and owners' equity on the right may be related directly to the accounting equation (assets = liabilities + owners' equity) in which assets appear to the left of the equal sign and liabilities and owners' equity to the right.

## Debits and Credits

In accounting terminology, any entry to the left side of an account is referred to as a debit and any entry to the right side as a *credit*. The term *charge* is often used interchangeably with *debit*.

Debits are used to signify *increases in assets* or *decreases in liabilities or owners' equity*.

Credits are used to represent *decreases in assets* or *increases in liabilities or owners' equity*.

If a company purchases merchandise for cash, the accountant would *debit* the merchandise account and *credit* the cash account. At any given point in time it would ordinarily be expected that asset accounts would show a *debit* balance (that is, the entries on the left side of the account would exceed in dollar amount those on the right) and liabilities and owners' equity accounts would show a *credit* balance.

Debits and credits are often a source of confusion to an individual who has had dealings with either a bank or a department store. Should a person deposit funds in the bank, the bank would ordinarily *credit* his account. Should he withdraw funds or "bounce" a check, the bank might send him a *debit* (debt) memo. Similarly, when a person returns merchandise to a store, the store credits his account; it advises him that his liability to the store has been reduced. Does it not appear that *credits* are associated with increases in assets and *debits* with increases in liabilities? Bear in mind, however, that both the bank and the department store maintain their records from their own points of view, not those of their customers. Thus, when a customer deposits money in the bank, the liability of the bank to the customer is increased. Hence, the bank *credits* his account on its books. (If the customer maintained a set of books, then he would *debit* his account, "cash in bank," to reflect the debt of the bank to him.) Similarly, when the department store accepts returned merchandise from a customer the accounts receivable of the store have been decreased; thus the store *credits* the account on its books that represents the amount owed by the customer.

## Journal Entries

Each T account represents a separate page in a book of accounts. Such a book is often referred to as a *general ledger.* Since a transaction normally affects two or more accounts, each transaction necessitates entries on two or more pages. No one page will contain a complete record of the transaction; at best it will indicate only one-half of the transaction. To maintain a comprehensive history of all transactions that affect the various accounts, accountants conventionally maintain a *journal*—a book which serves as the source of many of the entries to the various accounts. The purchase of merchandise for cash ($7,000) necessitates that a debit entry be made in the merchandise account and a credit entry be made in the cash account. The journal is a convenient place to indicate both accounts affected by the transaction. At the time of purchase, the accountant would record the following in the journal:

|  |  |  |
|---|---|---|
| Debit: | Merchandise | $7,000 |
| Credit: | Cash | $7,000 |

More commonly, the words debit and credit are omitted from the entry, and the accountant indicates a debit or credit by placement of the account title and the amounts. The account to be debited is placed along the left-hand margin, and that to be credited is indented slightly. Similarly, the amount to be debited is shown slightly to the left of that to be credited. A brief explanation is often indicated beneath the entry, and the entry is numbered or lettered to facilitate referencing. Thus,

**(1)**

| | | |
|---|---|---|
| Merchandise | $7,000 | |
|     Cash | | $7,000 |

**To record the purchase of merchandise.**

The amounts indicated in the journal would be posted to or recorded in the appropriate ledger account either at the time the transaction is recorded in the journal or, if more convenient, after a number of transactions have been recorded.

Some simple transactions can be used to illustrate the relationship between entries in the journal and those in the various ledger accounts. In this and in several subsequent examples the nature of the account (asset, liability, owners' equity) and whether it has increased (+) or decreased (–) will sometimes be indicated in parentheses next to each journal entry. Mr. B. Heller decides to establish a television repair service. He signs a lease on a small store.

1. He takes $10,000 of his personal funds and deposits them in a checking account in the name of "Heller TV Repair Service."
2. He purchases tools and test equipment for $5,000. He gives a two-year note for the full amount.
3. He purchases parts for $3,000. He pays $2,000 cash and receives 30 day's credit for the balance.
4. He pays rent in advance for the first three months, $200 per month.

### Required Journal Entries

#### (1)

| | | |
|---|---|---|
| Cash in bank (asset +) | $10,000 | |
| B. Heller, invested capital | | |
| (owners' equity +) | | $10,000 |

**To record the initial contribution of cash.**

#### (2)

| | | |
|---|---|---|
| Tools and equipment (asset +) | $5,000 | |
| Notes payable (liability +) | | $5,000 |

**To record the purchase of tools and equipment.**

#### (3)

| | | |
|---|---|---|
| Parts inventory (asset +) | $3,000 | |
| Cash (asset –) | | $2,000 |
| Accounts payable (liability +) | | 1,000 |

**To record the purchase of the parts.** (Note that a journal entry can combine more than one debit or credit.The account "notes payable" is used to record a liability when a written note is given by the borrower. When short-term trade credit is accepted the liability is recorded as an "account payable.")

#### (4)

| | | |
|---|---|---|
| Prepaid rent (asset +) | $600 | |
| Cash (asset –) | | $600 |

**To record the rent paid in advance.** ("Prepaid rent" represents the right to use the store for three months. It is a current asset—one that will be "written off" or *amortized* as it expires over the three-month period.)

The journal entries would be *posted* to the various ledger accounts:

| *Assets* | | | | *Liabilities + Owners' Equity* | |
|---|---|---|---|---|---|

| Cash in bank | | | | Accounts payable | B. Heller, invested capital |
|---|---|---|---|---|---|
| (1)  10,000 | (3) | 2,000 | | (3)  1,000 | (1) 10,000 |
| | (4) | 600 | | | |
| 7400 | | | | | |

| Tools and equipment *NC* | | Notes payable *NC* | |
|---|---|---|---|
| (2)  5,000 | | (2)  5,000 | |

| Parts inventory |
|---|
| (3)  3,000 |

| Prepaid rent |
|---|
| (4)    600 |

*C  current*
*NC  noncurrent*

If it were decided to prepare a balance sheet, after the four transactions had been journalized and posted, then it would be necessary to determine and summarize the balances in each account. The balance in each account can readily be calculated by subtracting the total credits from the total debits. Thus, the balance in the cash in bank account is $10,000 minus the sum of $2,000 and $600: $7,400.

The balance sheet separates current from noncurrent assets and liabilities. In the example, the note payable is classified as a noncurrent liability since it will not be due for over one year. Similarly, the tools and equipment are classified as noncurrent assets, because they are expected to have a useful life greater than one year. Prepaid rent, the parts inventory, and the cash in bank are all expected either to be used up or to "turn over" (be replaced by like assets) within a one-year period, so they are classified as current assets.

**Heller TV Repair Service**
**Balance Sheet as of December 31, 1981**

| *Assets* | | | *Liabilities and Owners' Equity* | | |
|---|---|---|---|---|---|
| Current assets | | | Current liabilities | | |
| Cash in bank | $7,400 | | accounts payable | $1,000 | |
| Parts inventory | 3,000 | | Noncurrent liabilities | | |
| Prepaid rent | 600 | $11,000 | Notes payable | 5,000 | $ 6,000 |
| Noncurrent assets | | | Owners' equity | | |
| Tools and | | | B. Heller, | | |
|   equipment | | 5,000 |   invested capital | | 10,000 |
| | | | Total liabilities and | | |
| Total assets | | $16,000 |   owners' equity | | $16,000 |

An additional example may serve to illustrate the accounting treatment afforded other types of financial events. The Universal Sales Corporation is organized on June 1, 1981. The following events occur during the first month of operation:

*Date*

---

6/1 The company issues 10,000 shares of stock to its two cofounders for a price of $50 per share. The stock has a par value of $10 per share. The purchasers make payment in cash.

**(1)**

| | |
|---|---|
| Cash (asset +) | $500,000 |
| Common stock, par value (owners' equity +) | $100,000 |
| Common stock, additional paid-in capital (owner's equity +) | 400,000 |

To record the sale of common stock.

6/1 The firm, for $100,000, issues long-term bonds—6 percent debentures (no security provided), interest payable semiannually, principal payable in year 2013.

**(2)**

| | |
|---|---|
| Cash (asset +) | $100,000 |
| Bonds payable (liability +) | $100,000 |

To record the issue of long-term bonds. (The liability only for the principal, not the interest is recorded at this time.)

6/2 The company purchases a building for $300,000. It gives a down payment of $100,000 and a 10-year note for the balance.

**(3)**

| | |
|---|---|
| Building (asset +) | $300,000 |
| Cash (asset–) | $100,000 |
| Notes payable (liability +) | 200,000 |

To record the purchase of the building.

6/3 The company purchases equipment for $100,000 and incurs installation and transportation costs of $20,000. The equipment is purchased "on sale." The salesman informs the purchaser that it normally sells for $130,000.

**(4)**

| | |
|---|---|
| Equipment (asset +) | $120,000 |
| Cash (asset –) | $120,000 |

To record the purchase of equipment. (Note that the installation and transportation costs are necessary to bring the equipment to a *serviceable* condition; hence they are added to the cost of the equipment. The alleged discount of $30,000 is ignored. Except in highly unusual circumstances, an asset is recorded at the amount which is actually to be paid as long as the transaction is "at arm's length" —that is, between two independent parties. Such amount represents the fair market values of the assets both received and surrendered by the purchaser.)

*Date*

6/27 The firm decides to rent out a portion of its building. The company acquires a lessee, and a five-year lease is signed. Rent is to be $1,000 per month, and three months' rent is paid in advance. Occupancy is to begin July 1.

**(5)**

Cash (asset +)     $3,000
    Rent received in advance (liability +)     $3,000
**To record three months' rent received in advance.**
(The company has received the cash. It is still obligated to provide services to the lessee. "Rent received in advance" can be viewed as "value of rental services yet to be furnished.")

6/28 The company receives an invoice (a bill) from its attorneys—$5,000—for services performed in connection with drawing the corporate charter and issuing common stock.

**(6)**

Organization costs
    (asset +)     $5,000
      Accounts payable
      (liability +)     $5,000
**To record the costs of organizing the corporation.**
(The organization costs,—like the cost of equipment and the prepaid rent, were incurred in order to benefit future accounting periods. Although they are "intangible"—they cannot be seen or felt—they are nevertheless *assets* of the company. Accounts payable, rather than cash, has been credited, because the company has not yet paid the invoice.)

6/28 The company hires J. Pringle as president. The two parties sign a two-year employment contract requiring the firm to compensate Pringle at a salary of $35,000 per year.

**No entry is required.**
Although the firm seemingly has incurred a liability of $70,000, the president has not yet performed any services for the company. As indicated previously, accountants generally record liabilities resulting from contracts only to the extent that services have been performed or cash has been paid. Thus, after Pringle has been employed for one month, the company will, at that time, record a liability of one-twelfth of $35,000, or $2,917.

6/28 The company purchases merchandise for $60,000. The company is granted a "trade discount" (available to all commercial customers) of 10%.

**(7)**

Merchandise inventory
    (asset +)     $54,000
      Accounts payable
      (liability +)     $54,000
**To record the purchase of merchandise.**
(The firm will be required to pay $54,000; that is the "fair market" value of both the goods received and the consideration to be paid.)

*Date*

---

6/28 The firm purchases 100 shares of General Motors stock as a temporary investment. Cost per share is $61.

**(8)**
Marketable securities
(asset +)                    $6,100
    Cash (asset –)                    $6,100
**To record the purchase of 100 shares of General Motors stock.**

6/29 The company pays $5,000 of the amount it owes to its supplier.

**(9)**
Accounts payable
(liability –)                    $5,000
    Cash (asset –)                    $5,000
**To record the payment to the supplier.**

6/29 The company returns merchandise that is defective to the supplier. The merchandise cost $7,000 after taking into account the discount. The supplier gives the company credit for the merchandise returned.

**(10)**
Accounts payable
(liability –)                    $7,000
    Merchandise inventory (asset –)                    $7,000
**To record the return of merchandise.**

6/30 The company learns through *The Wall Street Journal* that the market price of its General Motors stock has increased to $64 per share.

No entry is necessary.

Increases in the market value of assets generally are not recorded—in large measure because of the accountant's preference toward conservative expressions of value.

6/30 The market price of the General Motors stock declines to $61 per share. The company sells 50 shares.

**(11)**
Cash (asset +)                    $3,050
    Marketable securities
    (asset –)                    $3,050
**To record the sale of 50 shares of General Motors stock.**
(The stock was sold at original cost; hence there was no gain or loss on the sale.)

---

As before, the journal entries must be posted to ledger or T accounts so that the balances in the accounts can be summarized in a statement of position. To facilitate the process of summarizing the end-of-period balances, double lines have been drawn beneath the recorded debits and credits. The difference between the sums of the debits and credits has been indicated on the appropriate side of the T account. Such amount represents not only the balance at the close of one accounting period but also the balance at the beginning of the next accounting period. For example, if $374,950 is the cash balance at the end of June 1981, it must also be the balance at the beginning of July 1981. Thus, the same account—the same ledger sheet—that was used in June could also be used in July. The entries for the latter year would simply be recorded beneath the end-of-old-year (beginning-of-new-year) balances.

|  | Assets |  |  |  | Liabilities and Owners' Equity |  |  |
|---|---|---|---|---|---|---|---|

### Assets

**Cash** ↑ C

| (1) | 500,000 | (3) | 100,000 |
|---|---|---|---|
| (2) | 100,000 | (4) | 120,000 |
| (5) | 3,000 | (8) | 6,100 |
| (11) | 3,050 | (9) | 5,000 |
| | 374,950 | | |

**Organization costs** NC

| (6) | 5,000 | | |
|---|---|---|---|
| | 5,000 | | |

**Equipment** NC

| (4) | 120,000 | | |
|---|---|---|---|
| | 120,000 | | |

**Merchandise inventory** C

| (7) | 54,000 | (10) | 7,000 |
|---|---|---|---|
| | 47,000 | | |

**Building** NC

| (3) | 300,000 | | |
|---|---|---|---|
| | 300,000 | | |

**Marketable securities** C

| (8) | 6,100 | (11) | 3,050 |
|---|---|---|---|
| | 3,050 | | |

### Liabilities and Owners' Equity

**Accounts payable** ↑ C

| (9) | 5,000 | (6) | 5,000 |
|---|---|---|---|
| (10) | 7,000 | (7) | 54,000 |
| | | | 47,000 |

**Bonds payable** NC

| | | (2) | 100,000 |
|---|---|---|---|
| | | | 100,000 |

**Rent received in advance** C

| | | (5) | 3,000 |
|---|---|---|---|
| | | | 3,000 |

**Notes payable** NC

| | | (3) | 200,000 |
|---|---|---|---|
| | | | 200,000 |

**Common stock, par value**

| | | (1) | 100,000 |
|---|---|---|---|
| | | | 100,000 |

**Common stock, additional paid-in capital**

| | | (1) | 400,000 |
|---|---|---|---|
| | | | 400,000 |

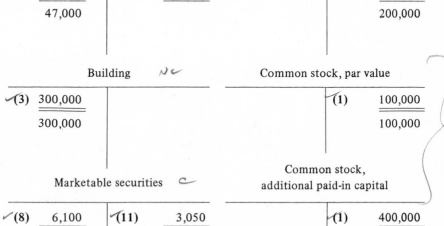

**Universal Sales Corporation**
**Balance Sheet as of June 30, 1981**

| *Assets* | | | *Liabilities and Owners' Equity* | | |
|---|---|---|---|---|---|
| Current assets | | | Current liabilities | | |
| Cash | $374,950 | | Accounts | | |
| Marketable | | | payable | $ 47,000 | |
| securities | 3,050 | | Rent received | | |
| Merchandise | | | in advance | 3,000 | $ 50,000 |
| inventory | 47,000 | $425,000 | | | |
| | | | Noncurrent liabilities | | |
| Noncurrent assets | | | Notes payable | $200,000 | |
| Building | $300,000 | | Bonds payable | 100,000 | 300,000 |
| Equipment | 120,000 | | | | |
| Organization | | | Total liabilities | | $350,000 |
| costs | 5,000 | 425,000 | | | |
| | | | Owners' equity | | |
| | | | Common stock, par | | |
| | | | value $10, | | |
| | | | 10,000 shares | | |
| | | | issued and | | |
| | | | outstanding | $100,000 | |
| | | | Common stock, | | |
| | | | additional | | |
| | | | paid-in | | |
| | | | capital | 400,000 | 500,000 |
| | | | Total liabilities | | |
| | | | and owners' | | |
| Total assets | | $850,000 | equity | | $850,000 |

## Revenues and Expenses

Up to this point in the chapter, the illustrated transactions, with few exceptions, involved only exchanges among asset and liability accounts. Goods or services were received in exchange for other assets or for the firm's promise to pay in the future. Increases or decreases in liability accounts were offset by concurrent increases or decreases in asset accounts. As a result, the level of *net* assets—that is, assets less liabilities (which is equal, by definition, to owners' equity)—remained the same. To refer back to the bathtub analogy used in the previous chapter, the level of water in the tub never changed as a consequence of the transactions illustrated. The only time owners' equity did change was when owners made their initial investment in the business.

Since the differences between assets and liabilities stayed constant once the owners made their initial contribution to form their companies, the subsequent transactions could not possibly have left them any better or worse off than they were at the very start of business. There were no inflows or outflows of net assets to the business, no revenues, and no expenses and hence no profits or earnings that could be retained in the business.

How does the accountant record those transactions that do, in fact, result in increases or decreases in the equity of the owners of a business? Assuming that the firm has not previously incurred losses which have reduced the equity of of the owners below their original contribution, any transaction in which assets received or liabilities reduced are greater than assets surrendered or liabilities incurred must increase the earnings being retained by the firm. Take, for example, a merchandise transaction. A firm sells for $100 goods that it had previously purchased for $70. The firm receives an asset of $100; it surrenders an asset of $70. Assets have increased by $30, so the owners of the business are $30 better off than they were previously. Income as the result of the transaction is $30, and hence retained earnings must have increased by $30.

To view the transaction in two steps: The receipt of cash resulted in an increase of $100 in both cash and retained earnings. An appropriate journal entry would be

**(1)**

| | |
|---|---|
| Cash (asset +) | $100 |
|    Retained earnings | |
|      (owner's equity +) | $100 |

The transfer of goods to the new owners resulted in a decrease in both merchandise and retained earnings:

**(2)**

| | |
|---|---|
| Retained earnings | |
|    (owners' equity −) | $70 |
|      Merchandise inventory | |
|        (asset −) | $70 |

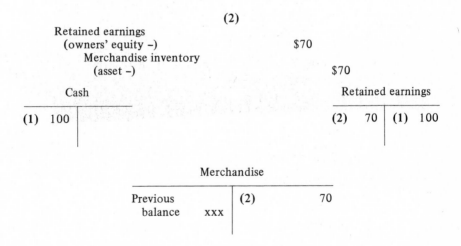

As a consequence of the transaction, it could be said that the firm had *revenues* of $100 and *expenses* of $70.

*Revenue:* The *inflow* of assets into the firm as a result of production or delivery of goods or rendering of services.

*Expense:* The *outflow* of assets in the course of the profit-directed activities of the firm.

*Income:* The *excess* of revenues over expenses.

A series of simple transactions can further illustrate the relationships among revenues, expenses, and retained earnings.

An entrepreneur establishes Booksellers, Inc. to sell books door to door. The firm issues 1,000 shares of common stock (par value $1) in exchange for $10,000 cash.

**(1)**

| | | |
|---|---|---|
| Cash (asset +) | $10,000 | |
| Common stock (owner's equity +) | | $10,000 |

**To record the issuance of common stock.**

The firm purchases advertising circulars at a cost of $500, paid in cash. A firm's assets and the claims (by owner) against the assets increase.

**(2)**

| | | |
|---|---|---|
| Advertising circulars (asset +) | $500 | |
| Cash (asset –) | | $500 |

**To record purchase of advertising circulars.** This transaction involves only an exchange of one asset for another. It affects neither the level of net assets (assets minus liabilities) nor the equity of the owner.

The firm distributes the circulars.

**(3)**

| | | |
|---|---|---|
| Retained earnings (owner's equity –; advertising expense) | $500 | |
| Advertising circulars (asset –) | | $500 |

**To record the distribution of advertising circulars.** This transaction results in a reduction in an asset without an offsetting decrease in another asset or an increase in a liability. Therefore, it serves to reduce the equity of the owner (i.e., retained earnings).

The firm leases an office and pays one month's rent in advance, $200.

**(4)**

| | | |
|---|---|---|
| Prepaid rent (asset +) | $200 | |
| Cash (asset –) | | $200 |

**To record payment of rent in advance.** An asset, prepaid rent, is received in exchange for another asset, cash.

The firm gives accounting recognition to the use of the office for one month.

**(5)**

| | | |
|---|---|---|
| Retained earnings (owner's equity –; | | |
| rent expense) | $200 | |
| Prepaid rent (asset –) | | $200 |

**To record occupancy of office for one month.** The level of net assets is reduced; hence the equity of the owner is reduced.

The firm purchases an automobile for $7,200 cash. It estimates the useful life of the car to be two years (24 months).

**(6)**

| | | |
|---|---|---|
| Automobile (asset +) | $7,200 | |
| Cash (asset –) | | $7,200 |

**To record purchase of the automobile.** One asset is exchanged for another.

The firm gives recognition to the use of the auto for one month.   $\frac{3600}{12} = 300/mo$

**(7)**

| | | |
|---|---|---|
| Retained earnings (owner's equity –; | | |
| depreciation expense) | $300 | |
| Automobile | | $300 |

**To record the use (depreciation) of the automobile for one month.** The asset was expected to provide services for 24 months. One-twenty-fourth of its service potential has now been consumed. The equity of the owner has correspondingly been reduced by the value of the services consumed. (It is conventional for an "allowance for depreciation" rather than the asset itself to be credited for the amount of depreciation charged, but an explanation of such "contra accounts" will be deferred to the next chapter.)

The firm purchases for sale to customers 400 books at $5 per book.

**(8)**

| | | |
|---|---|---|
| Merchandise inventory (asset +) | $2,000 | |
| Cash (asset –) | | $2,000 |

**To record purchase of merchandise inventory.** Once again, one asset is exchanged for another.

The firm sells the 400 books for $8 each.

**(9)**

| | | |
|---|---|---|
| Cash (asset +) | $3,200 | |
| Retained earnings (owner's equity +; | | |
| sales revenues) | | $3,200 |

**To record sale of books.** As a consequence of this first part of the sales transaction—that in which recognition is given to the revenues earned—the assets of the firm are increased; so too is the equity of the owner.

**(10)**

Retained earnings (owner's equity –;
    cost of goods sold)                           $2,000
        Merchandise inventory (asset –)                  $2,000

**To record the cost of books sold.** As a result of the second part of the transaction—that in which recognition is given to the cost of the merchandise sold—an asset is reduced; so too is the equity of the owner. The entire transaction (entries **9** and **10**) leaves the firm with $1,200 of additional assets and its owner with $1,200 of additional claims against the assets.

The firm incurs utility costs of $100 and pays them in cash.

**(11)**

Retained earnings (owners' equity –;
    utility expense)                              $100
        Cash                                       $100

**To record utility costs.** Each of the previous expenses have been recorded in two steps. First, an asset (i.e., advertising circulars, prepaid rent, automobile, merchandise inventory) was acquired; then it was consumed. An initial entry involved an exchange of one asset for another; a second involved a reduction in an asset and a corresponding reduction in retained earnings. This transaction, however, was recorded in a single step. Conceptually, this transaction is not different from the others. For *bookkeeping convenience*—motivated in large measure by the somewhat brief interval between the moment when electricity, gas, or water is received by a firm and when it is actually consumed—the cost of the utility services was never placed even temporarily in a "storage" (asset) account. Instead, the assets of the firm, as well as the equity of the owner, were presumed to have been reduced at the time the utility costs were first given accounting recognition.

The journal entries can be posted to T accounts. To highlight the impact of the transactions on the equity of the owner, a brief explanation is included beside each of the entries to the retained earnings account.

At the conclusion of the first month of operations, the position of the company can be reported as follows:

**Booksellers, Inc.**
**Balance Sheet as of the End of the First Month**

| *Assets* | | *Liabilities and Owners' Equity* | |
|---|---|---|---|
| Cash | $ 3,200 | Common stock | $10,000 |
| Automobile | 6,900 | Retained earnings | 100 |
| Total assets | $10,100 | Total equities | $10,100 |

|  | *Assets* |  |  |  | *Liabilities and Owner's Equity* |  |
|---|---|---|---|---|---|---|

| | Cash ↑ | | | | Common stock ↑ | |
|---|---|---|---|---|---|---|
| (1) | 10,000 | (2) | 500 | | (1) | 10,000 |
| (9) | 3,200 | (4) | 200 | | | ———— |
| | | (6) | 7,200 | | | 10,000 |
| | | (8) | 2,000 | | | |
| | | (11) | 100 | | | |
| | ———— | | | | | |
| | 3,200 | | | | | |

| | Advertising circulars | | | | Retained earnings ↑ | |
|---|---|---|---|---|---|---|
| (2) | 500 | (3) | 500 | Advertis- (3) 500 | (9) 3,200 Sales revenue | |

Rent ex- (5) 200
pense

Depreci- (7) 300
ation ex-
pense

*put in full amount, later take care of CGS*

| | Prepaid rent | | |
|---|---|---|---|
| (4) | 200 | (5) | 200 |

Cost of (10) 2,000
goods
sold

Utility (11) 100
ex-
pense

———— 100

| | Automobile | | |
|---|---|---|---|
| (6) | 7,200 | (7) | 300 |
| | 6,900 | | |

| | Merchandise inventory | | |
|---|---|---|---|
| (8) | 2,000 | (10) | 2,000 |

Because retained earnings are now $100, it is apparent that the equity of the entrepreneur has increased by that amount and that the earnings of the one-month period were also $100. The firm is $100 "better off" at the end of the first month than it was at the beginning. Income for the period is therefore $100.

If the owners of a business make no withdrawals from their firm, then income can be determined by subtracting retained earnings at the beginning of the period from those at the end. But both owners and managers of a business need far more information than income alone. They need to know *how* that income was derived: What were the sources of revenue? What were the expenses? In the example at hand, a statement of income can readily be derived from the entries in the retained earnings account:

**Booksellers, Inc.**

**Statement of Income for the First Month of Operation**

| | | |
|---|---:|---:|
| Sales revenue | | $3,200 |
| Less: Expenses | | |
| Cost of goods sold | $2,000 | |
| Advertising | 500 | |
| Rent | 200 | |
| Depreciation | 300 | |
| Utilities | 100 | 3,100 |
| Income | | $  100 |

Suppose, however, that there were not six entries that affected retained earnings but that instead there were several hundred. The task at the end of the accounting period of classifying the various entries into a manageable number of revenue and expense categories and of summarizing them into an income statement would be enormous. Would it not make more sense to divide the retained earnings account into several subaccounts, each of which would represent a particular type of revenue or expense?

The retained earnings subaccounts would have but one purpose. They would be used to accumulate data necessary to prepare the periodic statements of income. As soon as the last business day of an accounting period were complete and all entries to subaccounts had been made, the balances in those accounts would be transferred to the overall retained earnings account. The subaccounts could be viewed as serving a very temporary function. They would be used to accumulate, by category, the revenues earned and the expenses incurred for one accounting period only. Seldom do users of financial statements demand knowledge of total revenues and expenses, by category, since the inception of the company, because such information would bear upon few decisions that they are required to make. Instead they want the information on a period-by-period basis. As a result, each subaccount—the revenue and expense accounts —would be terminated—closed—at the end of each accounting period. New revenue and expense accounts would be established for the next accounting period.

|  | *Retained earnings* | | = |
|---|---|---|---|

| Advertising expense | **(3)** 500 | **(9)** 3,200 | Sales revenue |
| Rent expense | **(5)** 200 | | |
| Depreciation expense | **(7)** 300 | | |
| Cost of goods sold | **(10)** 2,000 | | |
| Utility expense | **(11)** 100 | | |

*Retained earnings*

**Advertising expense**

**(3)** 500

**Sales revenue**

**(9)** 3,200

**Rent expense**

**(5)** 200

**Depreciation expense**

**(7)** 300

**Cost of goods sold**

**(10)** 2,000

**Utility expense**

**(11)** 100

---

Returning to the accounts of Booksellers, Inc., the revised journal entries (including only those that affected retained earnings) would appear as

**(3)**

| Advertising expense | $500 | |
| Advertising circulars | | $500 |

**To record the distribution of advertising circulars.**

**(5)**

| | | |
|---|---|---|
| Rent expense | $200 | |
| Prepaid rent | | $200 |

**To record occupancy of office for one month.**

**(7)**

| | | |
|---|---|---|
| Depreciation expense | $300 | |
| Automobile | | $300 |

**To record the use (depreciation) of the automobile for one month.**

**(9)**

| | | |
|---|---|---|
| Cash | $3,200 | |
| Sales revenue | | $3,200 |

**To record sales of books.**

**(10)**

| | | |
|---|---|---|
| Cost of goods sold | $2,000 | |
| Merchandise inventory | | $2,000 |

**To record the cost of the books sold.**

**(11)**

| | | |
|---|---|---|
| Utility expense | $100 | |
| Cash | | $100 |

**To record utility costs.**

## Closing Entries

At the end of the accounting period the balances in the revenue and expense accounts would be transferred to the overall retained earnings account. Normally, revenue accounts would have a credit balance; expense accounts would have a debit balance.

The transfer can be made by two simple journal entries. First, a journal entry is made in which each revenue account is debited with an amount equal to the balance in the account, and retained earnings is credited with the total of such amounts. Second, a similar journal is made in which each expense account is credited with the balance in the account and retained earnings is debited. If the company had a profit, then the net effect of the two entries would be to increase the balance in retained earnings, and if a loss, then to decrease the balance.

*Entries to "Close" Revenue and Expense Accounts*

### Closing Entry 1

| | | |
|---|---|---|
| Sales revenue | $3,200 | |
|    Retained earnings | | $3,200 |
| **To close revenue account** | | |

### Closing Entry 2

| | | |
|---|---|---|
| Retained earnings | $3,100 | |
|    Cost of goods sold | | $2,000 |
|    Advertising expense | | 500 |
|    Rent expense | | 200 |
|    Depreciation expense | | 300 |
|    Utility expense | | 100 |
| **To close expense accounts** | | |

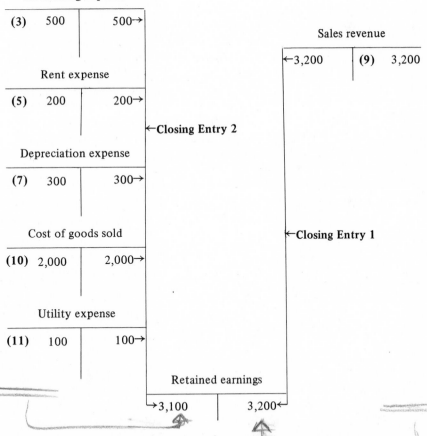

After the closing entries have been made and posted to the individual revenue and expense accounts, the balances in those accounts must be zero. The company, would then be ready to open new revenue and expense accounts (subaccounts of retained earnings) to accumulate data for the statement of income for the following accounting period.

It must be emphasized that only the revenue and expense accounts need be "closed" at year end. The balance in the Booksellers, Inc. *cash* account was $3,200 at the end of the first month of operations. It will necessarily be $3,200 at the beginning of the second month. Asset and liability accounts describe the position of a business at a given point of time. Revenue and expense accounts describe inflows and outflows per a given period of time (a week, a month, a year). Once that period of time has elapsed, new accounts must be established to meter the flows of the next accounting period.

## Overview

The reader should take special note of the approach to revenues and expenses taken in the previous illustration. At the start of the example, whenever there was a transaction that resulted in an increase or decrease in the *level* of net assets, the retained earnings account was either debited or credited. Subsequently, however, the entries were revised. Instead of a debit or credit being made directly to retained earnings, it was made to a revenue or expense account. Then, at the end of the accounting period, the balances in the various revenue and expense accounts were transferred, via a closing entry, to retained earnings.

This approach was taken to emphasize the relationship between revenue and expense accounts and retained earnings. Revenue and expense accounts are but temporary "subaccounts" of retained earnings, the "parent" account. At the conclusion of an accounting period they are closed out and their balances are transferred to the parent account.

In practice, revenue and expense accounts are, in fact, maintained. But, in making entries to or analyzing such accounts, one should bear in mind that they are nothing more than subaccounts of retained earnings; an entry to a revenue or expense account serves to increase or decrease retained earnings and thus the equity of the owners.

## The Complete Accounting Cycle Demonstrated

To demonstrate the complete accounting cycle for an accounting period, we shall assume that Daniel's Den, Inc., a restaurant and night club, has been in business for one month. Its financial position as of June 30, 1981, is described by a balance sheet taken as of that date.

Most firms complete an accounting cycle once a year. That is, once a year they close their books, prepare a complete set of financial statements, and open new revenue and expense accounts. There is no conceptual reason, however, why a firm cannot complete an accounting cycle more frequently than once a year. For purposes of illustration it may be assumed that Daniel's Den, Inc. closes its books at the end of each month.

It is clear from the owners' equity section that the company is organized as a corporation, since only corporations and not partnerships or proprietorships have stockholders.

### Daniel's Den, Inc.
### Statement of Position at June 30, 1981

*Assets*

| | | |
|---|---:|---:|
| Current assets | | |
| Cash in bank | $ 6,530 | |
| Inventory of beverages | 3,000 | |
| Inventory of food | 300 | |
| Inventory of supplies | 1,500 | |
| Prepaid rent | 1,400 | $12,730 |
| Noncurrent assets | | |
| Furniture and fixtures | $ 5,900 | |
| Kitchen equipment | 11,800 | 17,700 |
| Total assets | | $30,430 |

*Liabilities and Owners' Equity*

| | | |
|---|---:|---:|
| Current liabilities | | |
| Accounts payable | | $ 3,750 |
| Noncurrent liabilities | | |
| Notes payable | | 7,500 |
| Total liabilities | | $11,250 |
| Owners' equity | | |
| Common stock | | $17,000 |
| Retained earnings | | 2,180 |
| Total owners' equity | | $19,180 |
| Total liabilities and owners' equity | | $30,430 |

It is also obvious from the owners' equity section that the corporation earned a profit during its first month of operations. This is indicated by the positive balance in the retained earnings account. There is, however, no way to be sure *how much* profit was earned during the first month. The firm earned at least $2,180, but it may have earned considerably more than that. If the company decided to distribute the earnings to its shareholders in the form of a cash dividend, then the balance in the retained earnings account would be equal to the first-month earnings of the company less the dividends paid to stockholders. In paying the dividends to stockholders the firm would have recorded the following (or similar) journal entry:

> Retained earnings (owners' equity –)        xxxxx
>     Cash (asset –)                                         xxxxx
> **To record the declaration and payment of a dividend.**

The distribution of the cash would have reduced both the assets and the retained earnings.

Assume that the events reported below take place during the month of July 1981. Many of the transactions are summaries of several individual transactions—for example, the sales indicated were by no means made to a single customer in a single evening.

1. The club purchases glassware and other supplies on account for $500.

**(1)**
Inventory of supplies        $500
    Accounts payable                 $500
**To record the purchase, on account, of supplies.**

2. Advertising costs for the month amount to $1,300. As of the end of the month, the bill for the advertising has not yet been paid.

**(2)**
Advertising expense        $1,300
    Accounts payable                 $1,300
**To record advertising costs.**

3. Utilities expense for the month amounts to $150. The entire amount is paid in cash.

**(3)**
Utility expense                $150
    Cash                                   $150
**To record the cost of utilities.**

4. The club pays the salaries of bartenders, waiters, and kitchen employees a total of $4,000.

**(4)**
Salary expense                $4,000
    Cash                                   $4,000
**To record the cost of employee salaries.**

5. The club purchases, for inventory, beverages (cost $4,000) and food (cost $1,000). The purchases are made "on account."

**(5)**
Inventory of beverages        $4,000
Inventory of food                1,000
    Accounts payable                 $5,000
**To record the purchase, on account, of beverages and food.**

6. The club makes payments of $4,500 to creditors from whom it had purchased goods or services on account.

**(6)**

| | | |
|---|---|---|
| Accounts payable | $4,500 | |
| Cash | | $4,500 |

**To record payments to suppliers and other creditors.**

7. Sales of beverages for the month total $15,000; those of food $3,000.

**(7)**

| | | |
|---|---|---|
| Cash | $18,000 | |
| Sales revenue, food | | $ 3,000 |
| Sales revenue, beverages | | 15,000 |

**To record sales of food and drink.**

8. The club rents its premises for $700 per month. Upon signing the lease on June 1, the company paid three months' rent in advance. The amount paid was recorded in an asset account, prepaid rent. No rent payments were made during the month of July, but the firm must give accounting recognition to the use of the premises.

**(8)**

| | | |
|---|---|---|
| Rent expense | $700 | |
| Prepaid rent | | $700 |

**To record the cost of rent for the month of July and the corresponding reduction of the asset, prepaid rent.**

9. The note payable indicated on the June 30 balance sheet bears interest at the rate of 12% per year. Interest is payable monthly but at the month's end the company had not yet made its July payment. The firm must give accounting recognition to the expense of using borrowed funds for one month.

**(9)**

| | | |
|---|---|---|
| Interest expense | $75 | |
| Interest payable | | $75 |

**To record the cost of using borrowed funds for the month of July: one-twelfth of 12% of $7,500.**

10. The club estimates that both the furniture and fixtures and the kitchen equipment have a useful life of 5 years (60 months). The furniture and fixtures originally cost $6,000; the kitchen equipment cost $12,000 (the difference between original cost and the amount shown on the balance sheet represents depreciation recorded for the first month of operation). The firm must give accounting recognition to the pro-rata cost of the equipment for one month.

**(10a)**

| | | |
|---|---|---|
| Depreciation expense | $100 | |
| Furniture & fixtures | | $100 |

**(10b)**

| | | |
|---|---|---|
| Depreciation expense | $200 | |
| Kitchen equipment | | $200 |

**To record depreciation (one-sixtieth of original cost) for the month of July.** (The entries could, of course, have been combined into one.)

11. An inventory taken at the month's end indicates the following balance of beverages, food, and supplies to be on hand:

| Beverages | $1,000 |
| Food | 100 |
| Supplies | 900 |

Since the accounts indicate the balances on hand at the beginning of the month and the purchases during the month (see entries 1 and 5), the amounts sold or used during the month can readily be derived (assuming, of course, no theft or other misuse) using the procedure that follows:

**(11)**

| | |
| --- | --- |
| Cost of beverages sold (expense) | $6,000 |
| Cost of food sold (expense) | 1,200 |
| Cost of supplies used (expense) | 1,100 |
| Inventory of beverages | $6,000 |
| Inventory of food | 1,200 |
| Inventory of supplies | 1,100 |

**To record the cost of the sale or use of beverages, food, and supplies and to reduce the balance in the beverage, food, and supplies inventory accounts to those indicated by the physical count.**

| | *Beverages* | *Food* | *Supplies* |
| --- | --- | --- | --- |
| Balance on hand, July 1 | $3,000 | $ 300 | $1,500 |
| Add: Purchases in July | 4,000 | 1,000 | 500 |
| Amounts available for sale or use | $7,000 | $1,300 | $2,000 |
| Less: Balance on hand, July 31 | 1,000 | 100 | 900 |
| Amount sold or used in July | $6,000 | $1,200 | $1,100 |

After the journal entries have been posted to the individual accounts, it is possible to take a *trial balance* of the accounts. A trial balance is nothing more than a complete listing of the balances in each of the accounts. Naturally, the total debit balances must be exactly equal to the total credit balances. If they are not, an error has been made, and the accountant or bookkeeper must review the individual accounts and retrace each of the postings back to the journal entries.

Unfortunately, the equality of total debit balances to total credit balances is only a necessary condition for the accounts to be in order; it is by no means a sufficient condition. For even if in the trial balance total debit balances are equal to total credit balances, the financial records may still be in error. Transactions may have been recorded using incorrect dollar amounts or may not have been recorded at all; journal entries may have been posted to improper ledger accounts.

A trial balance may be taken at any time. One taken before the closing entries (those which transfer the balances in the revenue and expense accounts to retained earnings) are made is referred to as a *preclosing* trial balance; one taken after the closing entries have been made is called a *postclosing* trial balance.

## Preclosing Ledger Accounts

| Assets | = | Liabilities | + | Owners' Equity (including revenues and expenses of the period) |
|---|---|---|---|---|

### Assets

**Cash in bank**

| | | | |
|---|---|---|---|
| Bal. 7/1 | 6,530 | (3) | 150 |
| (7) | 18,000 | (4) | 4,000 |
| | | (6) | 4,500 |
| Bal. 8/1 | 15,880 | | |

**Inventory of supplies**

| | | | |
|---|---|---|---|
| Bal. 7/1 | 1,500 | (11) | 1,100 |
| (1) | 500 | | |
| Bal. 8/1 | 900 | | |

**Furniture and fixtures**

| | | | |
|---|---|---|---|
| Bal. 7/1 | 5,900 | (10a) | 100 |
| Bal. 8/1 | 5,800 | | |

**Inventory of food**

| | | | |
|---|---|---|---|
| Bal. 7/1 | 300 | (11) | 1,200 |
| (5) | 1,000 | | |
| Bal. 8/1 | 100 | | |

**Inventory of beverages**

| | | | |
|---|---|---|---|
| Bal. 7/1 | 3,000 | (11) | 6,000 |
| (5) | 4,000 | | |
| Bal. 8/1 | 1,000 | | |

**Kitchen equipment**

| | | | |
|---|---|---|---|
| Bal. 7/1 | 11,800 | (10b) | 200 |
| Bal. 8/1 | 11,600 | | |

**Prepaid rent**

| | | | |
|---|---|---|---|
| Bal. 7/1 | 1,400 | (8) | 700 |
| Bal. 8/1 | 700 | | |

### Liabilities

**Accounts payable**

| | | | |
|---|---|---|---|
| (6) | 4,500 | Bal. 7/1 | 3,750 |
| | | (1) | 500 |
| | | (2) | 1,300 |
| | | (5) | 5,000 |
| | | Bal. 8/1 | 6,050 |

**Notes payable**

| | | |
|---|---|---|
| | Bal. 7/1 | 7,500 |
| | Bal. 8/1 | 7,500 |

**Interest payable**

| | | |
|---|---|---|
| (9) | | 75 |
| Bal. 8/1 | | 75 |

### Owners' Equity

**Common stock**

| | | |
|---|---|---|
| | Bal. 7/1 | 17,000 |
| | Bal. 8/1 | 17,000 |

**Retained earnings**

| | | |
|---|---|---|
| | Bal. 7/1 | 2,180 |

**Sales revenue, beverages**

| | | |
|---|---|---|
| | (7) | 15,000 |

**Sales revenue, food**

| | | |
|---|---|---|
| | (7) | 3,000 |

**Advertising expense**

| | |
|---|---|
| (2) | 1,300 |

**Salary expense**

| | |
|---|---|
| (4) | 4,000 |

**Utility expense**

| | |
|---|---|
| (3) | 150 |

**Rent expense**

| | |
|---|---|
| (8) | 700 |

**Depreciation expense**

| | |
|---|---|
| (10a) | 100 |
| (10b) | 200 |
| | 300 |

**Interest expense**

| | |
|---|---|
| (9) | 75 |

**Cost of beverages sold**

| | |
|---|---|
| (11) | 6,000 |

**Cost of food sold**

| | |
|---|---|
| (11) | 1,200 |

**Cost of supplies used**

| | |
|---|---|
| (11) | 1,100 |

By identifying the revenue and expense accounts from a preclosing trial balance, see below, a statement of income may be prepared.

**Daniel's Den, Inc.**
**Preclosing Trial Balance as of July 31, 1981**

| | Debit Balances | Credit Balances |
|---|---|---|
| Cash in bank | $15,880 | |
| Inventory of beverages | 1,000 | |
| Inventory of food | 100 | |
| Inventory of supplies | 900 | |
| Prepaid rent | 700 | |
| Furniture and fixtures | 5,800 | |
| Kitchen equipment | 11,600 | |
| Accounts payable | | $ 6,050 |
| Interest payable | | 75 |
| Notes payable | | 7,500 |
| Capital received from stockholders | | 17,000 |
| Retained earnings | *from previous period* | 2,180 |
| Sales revenue, beverages | | 15,000 |
| Sales revenue, food | | 3,000 |
| Advertising expense | 1,300 | |
| Utility expense | 150 | |
| Salary expense | 4,000 | |
| Rent expense | 700 | |
| Depreciation expense | 300 | |
| Interest expense | 75 | |
| Cost of beverages sold | 6,000 | |
| Cost of food sold | 1,200 | |
| Cost of supplies used | 1,100 | |
| | $50,805 | $50,805 |

**Daniel's Den, Inc.**
**Statement of Income for the Month Ending July 31, 1981**

| | | |
|---|---|---|
| Revenues | | |
| From sales of beverages | $15,000 | |
| From sales of food | 3,000 | $18,000 |
| Expenses | | |
| Advertising expense | 1,300 | |
| Utility expense | 150 | |
| Salary expense | 4,000 | |
| Depreciation expense | 300 | |
| Rent expense | 700 | |
| Interest expense | 75 | |
| Cost of beverages sold | 6,000 | |
| Cost of food sold | 1,200 | |
| Cost of supplies used | 1,100 | 14,825 |
| Net income | | $ 3,175 |

The preclosing trial balance could also be used to prepare a balance sheet except for the fact that one account would not be current. *The balance in the retained earnings account would represent that of the previous period.* Until the closing entries have been made, earnings of the current period would not have been added to retained earnings.

It makes sense, therefore, to make first the closing entries and then to prepare the balance sheet from the postclosing trial balance. The postclosing trial balance would give effect to the closing entries and would therefore exclude revenue and expense accounts. It would include only those accounts required to prepare the balance sheet.

The entries necessary to close the revenue and expense accounts can also be prepared from the data contained in the preclosing trial balance.

---

### Closing Entry 1

| | *dr* | *cr* |
|---|---|---|
| Sales revenue, beverages | $15,000 | |
| Sales revenue, food | 3,000 | |
| Retained earnings | | $18,000 |

**To close revenue accounts.**

### Closing Entry 2

| | | |
|---|---|---|
| Retained earnings | $14,825 | |
| Advertising expense | | $ 1,300 |
| Utility expense | | 150 |
| Salary expense | | 4,000 |
| Depreciation expense | | 300 |
| Rent expense | | 700 |
| Interest expense | | 75 |
| Cost of beverages sold | | 6,000 |
| Cost of food sold | | 1,200 |
| Cost of supplies used | | 1,100 |

*reduction in ret'nd earnings*

**To close expense accounts.**

---

Once the closing entries have been made and posted to the appropriate ledger accounts (only those affected by the closing entries are shown on the next page), then the balances in all revenue and expense accounts would be zero. Their balances would have been transferred to retained earnings. In this example, $18,000 of revenues (per closing entry 1) and $14,825 of expenses (per closing entry 2) have been transferred. The net amount of the transfer is $3,175—income for the period.

## Selected Ledger Accounts
### (Postclosing—Revenues, Expenses, and Retained Earnings)

| | Rent expense | | | | | Depreciation expense | | |
|---|---|---|---|---|---|---|---|---|
| (8) | 700 | (C2) | 700 | (10a) | 100 | (C2) | 300 | |
| | | | | (10b) | 200 | | | |

| | Interest expense | | | | Advertising expense | | |
|---|---|---|---|---|---|---|---|
| (9) | 75 | (C2) | 75 | (2) | 1,300 | (C2) | 1,300 |

| | Utility expense | | | | Salary expense | | |
|---|---|---|---|---|---|---|---|
| (3) | 150 | (C2) | 150 | (4) | 4,000 | (C2) | 4,000 |

| | Cost of beverages sold | | | | Cost of food sold | | |
|---|---|---|---|---|---|---|---|
| (11) | 6,000 | (C2) | 6,000 | (11) | 1,200 | (C2) | 1,200 |

| | Cost of supplies used | | | | Sales revenue, beverages | | |
|---|---|---|---|---|---|---|---|
| (11) | 1,100 | (C2) | 1,100 | (C1) | 15,000 | (7) | 15,000 |

| | Retained earnings | | | | Sales revenue, food | | |
|---|---|---|---|---|---|---|---|
| (C2) | 14,825 | Bal. 7/1 | 2,180 | (C1) | 3,000 | (7) | 3,000 |
| | | (C1) | 18,000 | | | | |
| | | Bal. 8/1 | 5,355 | | | | |

A postclosing trial balance can be taken from the remaining accounts, those that have not been closed. These would be the owners' equity accounts—including retained earnings account, which have been adjusted by the closing entries—as well as the asset and liability accounts.

**Daniel's Den, Inc.**
**Postclosing Trial Balance as of July 31, 1981**

|  | | *Debit Balances* | *Credit Balances* |
|---|---|---|---|
| C | Cash in bank | $15,880 | |
| C | Inventory of beverages | 1,000 | |
| C | Inventory of food | 100 | |
| C | Inventory of supplies | 900 | |
| C | Prepaid rent | 700 | |
| NC | Furniture and fixtures | 5,800 | |
| NC | Kitchen equipment | 11,600 | |
| C | Accounts payable | | $ 6,050 |
| C | Interest payable | | 75 |
| NC | Notes payable | | 7,500 |
| Own. Eq. | Common stock | | 17,000 |
| | Retained earnings | | 5,355 |
| | | $35,980 | $35,980 |

The postclosing trial balance includes only balance sheet accounts. The income statement accounts have been closed to retained earnings. They have been "zeroed" out, ready to meter the flows of the next accounting period. By contrast, the balances that remain and are reported in the postclosing trial balance will be carried forward to serve as the opening balances of the accounting period that follows. By properly classifying each of the accounts in the post-closing trial balance into groups of assets (current and noncurrent), liabilities (current and noncurrent), and equities, a balance sheet (also called a statement of position) can be prepared. Once this has been done (see next page) the recording process has completed a full cycle: a new accounting year can now begin.

**Daniel's Den, Inc.**
**Statement of Position as of July 31, 1981**

*Assets*

| | | |
|---|---|---|
| Current assets | | |
| Cash in bank | $15,880 | |
| Inventory of beverages | 1,000 | |
| Inventory of food | 100 | |
| Inventory of supplies | 900 | |
| Prepaid rent | 700 | $18,580 |
| | | |
| Noncurrent assets | | |
| Furniture and fixtures | 5,800 | |
| Kitchen equipment | 11,600 | 17,400 |
| | | |
| Total assets | | $35,980 |

*Liabilities and Owners' Equity*

| | | |
|---|---|---|
| Current liabilities | | |
| Accounts payable | $ 6,050 | |
| Interest payable | 75 | $ 6,125 |
| | | |
| Noncurrent liabilities | | |
| Notes payable | | 7,500 |
| | | |
| Total liabilities | | $13,625 |
| | | |
| Owners' equity | | |
| Common stock | | $17,000 |
| Retained earnings | | 5,355 |
| | | |
| Total owners' equity | | $22,355 |
| | | |
| Total liabilities and owners' equity | | $35,980 |

## Summary

The accounting equation, assets = liabilities + owners' equity, serves as the basis for recording all transactions worthy of accounting recognition and for maintaining the basic books of account. The fundamental accounting cycle may be summarized in eight steps:

1. Transactions are recorded in journals in the form of journal entries.
2. The component parts of the journal entries (the individual debits and credits) are posted to (recorded in) appropriate ledger accounts.

3. At the end of the accounting period the balance in each ledger account is determined by computing the difference between the total debit entries and the total credit entries (taking into account the opening balance).
4. The balances in the various accounts are summarized in the form of a preclosing trial balance. The sum of the accounts that have debit balances must equal the sum of the accounts with credit balances; otherwise an error has been made.
5. Based on the balances in the revenue and expense accounts of the preclosing trial balance, an income statement is prepared.
6. Journal entries are made to "close" the revenue and expense accounts— that is, to transfer the balances in those accounts to retained earnings.
7. Once the closing entries have been made, the revenue and expense accounts would have zero balances. The balances in the remaining accounts are summarized in the form of a postclosing trial balance.
8. Based on the postclosing trial balance, a balance sheet is prepared.

In Chapter 4, the explanation of the accounting cycle will be refined to take into account additional types of transactions and financial events.

*exercise for review and self-testing*

a. A trucking service company purchases, on account, 1,000 gallons of gasoline at $.80 per gallon. Indicate the effect of the transaction on each of the terms of the basic accounting equation, expressed as assets – liabilities = owners' equity.

b. The company uses 200 of those gallons. Determine the effect on each of the terms of the accounting equation.

c. The firm provides delivery services for a customer and bills the customer $2,000. Determine the effect on each of the terms of the accounting equation.

d. Compute the net effect of the latter two transactions on owners' equity (and, more specifically, on retained earnings).

e. Prepare journal entries to record the purchase and use of the 200 gallons of gasoline and the provision of delivery services. Rather than debiting or crediting retained earnings directly, make use of appropriate revenue or expense accounts.

f. Assume that these were the only transactions having an effect on the revenue and expense accounts that you used in the journal entries. Prepare two additional journal entries to "close" the accounts.

g. Determine the net effect on retained earnings of the journal entries that you have made. Is it consistent with your response to part d?

h. Determine the amounts by which each of the asset and liability accounts increased as a result of your journal entries. Does the increase in net assets equal the change in retained earnings?

    i. Should the asset and liability accounts also be "closed" to a parent account? If not, why not?

## Questions

1. What is a debit? What is a credit?

2. How do you account for the fact that when a customer returns merchandise to a department store he is given *credit*—an increase in a liability or a decrease in an asset—on his account when it would appear as if his liability to the store has been decreased?

3. "All accounting transactions can be recorded directly to balance sheet accounts. There is no real reason to maintain income statement accounts." Do you agree? Explain.

4. What is the purpose of *closing entries*? Why must revenue and expense accounts have a zero balance at the start of each accounting period? Why aren't balance sheet accounts "closed" at the end of each accounting period?

5. If, prior to the end of an accounting period (before closing entries have been made), one were to take a trial balance of all *balance sheet* accounts (assets, liabilities, owners' equity), the debits would probably not equal the credits. Why not?

6. What differences, if any, are there in accounting for corporations as opposed to partnerships or proprietorships (single-owner businesses)?

7. The retained earnings account is generally one of the least active on the balance sheet. What types of transactions or financial events generally require an entry directly to the retained earnings account?

8. A company purchases merchandise listed in a catalog at a price of $50,000. The company is allowed a discount of 20 percent ($10,000) but incurs shipping costs of $2,000, taxes and duties of $500, and insurance of $750. At what value should the goods be recorded on the books of the company? What general rule governs the values at which assets, such as merchandise inventory or plant equipment, should be initially recorded?

9. (1) If at the end of an accounting period the trial balance is not in balance (the debits do not equal the credits), then an accounting error has been made. (2) If at the end of an accounting period the trial balance is in balance, then an accounting error has not been made. Do you agree with either or both of these statements? Explain.

10. What accounting recognition would be given to each of the following financial events on the books of International Electric Co.?

    1. International Electric Co. owns 3,000 shares of Ford Motor Co. common stock. In the course of a year, the market price of the stock increases from $50 per share to $60.

    2. International Electric Co. has outstanding 20,000 shares of its own

common stock. In the course of a year, the market price of the stock increases from $45 per share to $50.

3. William Barefield sells 100 shares of International Electric Co. to Jack Abelson for $45 per share.

## *Problems*

1. *Financial accounting requires an understanding of only nine basic types of transactions.*

   An accounting transaction, when analyzed in terms of the basic accounting equation, can have only nine possible effects, summarized as follows. Analyze each of the financial events listed, and indicate by letter which of the nine effects is best described. Base your answer on the assumption that each transaction is being entered directly into position statement accounts (i.e., bypassing the income statement), but indicate which of the transactions would, in fact, ordinarily be reported on the income statement.

   1. Collection of an account receivable.
   2. Purchase of merchandise on account.
   3. Sale of merchandise on account.
   4. Recognition of the cost of goods that have been sold.
   5. Declaration (but not payment) of a dividend.
   6. Payment of a dividend that had been previously declared.
   7. Recognition of one year's depreciation on a company-owned truck.
   8. Payment of one month's rent on a truck that the company leases from a "rent-a-truck" agency.
   9. Issuance of 1,000 shares of the company's own common stock in exchange for forgiveness on a $100,000 note payable.
   10. Exchange of 1,000 shares of common stock for 2,000 shares of preferred stock.

      a. Asset +; asset –.
      b. Asset +; liability +.
      c. Asset +. stockholders' equity +.
      d. Asset –; liability –.
      e. Asset –; stockholders' equity –.
      f. Liability +; liability –.
      g. Liability –; stockholders' equity +.
      h. Liability +. stockholders' equity –.
      i. Stockholders' equity +. stockhoders' equity –.

2. *A familiarity with the "mechanics" of accounting can serve to facilitate an understanding of its underlying concepts, principles and issues.*

   Complete the following table by specifying whether each of the accounts would ordinarily be increased or decreased by a debit and a credit. The first one is done for you as an example.

|  | A debit *would serve to increase/decrease the account* | A credit *would serve to increase/decrease the account* |
|---|---|---|
| 1. Cash | increase | decrease |
| 2. Interest payable | | |
| 3. Interest receivable | | |
| 4. Interest revenue | | |
| 5. Interest expense | | |
| 6. Marketable securities | | |
| 7. Common stock | | |
| 8. Retained earnings | | |

3. *A preclosing trial balance summarizes the balances in all ledger accounts; only some of the accounts, however, are affected by year-end closing entries.*

Indicated in the table is the December 31, 1981 *preclosing* trial balance of the Boston Company. Prepare required year-end closing entries. What was the company's income for the year?

|  | Debits | Credits |
|---|---|---|
| Cash | $10,000 | |
| Accounts receivable | 12,000 | |
| Inventory | 5,000 | |
| Supplies | 1,000 | |
| Prepaid rent | 800 | |
| Accounts payable | | $ 3,000 |
| Accrued interest payable | | 200 |
| Notes payable | | 2,000 |
| Common stock | | 1,000 |
| Retained earnings | | 23,600 |
| Sales revenue | | 48,000 |
| Cost of goods sold | 35,000 | |
| Supplies expense | 4,000 | |
| Rent expense | 9,600 | |
| Interest expense | 400 | |
|  | $77,800 | $77,800 |

4. *Not all of the financial events described in this problem require financial recognition, but those that do, affect only balance sheet accounts.*

Prepare journal entries (as necessary) to reflect the following financial events pertaining to the Edinburg Corporation in the month of June 1981.

1. The company issues $300,000 in long-term bonds. The bonds provide for the payment of interest twice each year at an annual rate of 8 percent. The bonds are payable 10 years from date of issue.

2. The company purchases a new typewriter. Normal selling price of the typewriter is $400, but because the machine is on sale, the company pays cash of only $320.

3. The company signs a contract with the Watchdog Security Service to provide guard service for the period July 1, 1981 to June 30, 1982. The contract calls for payment of $2,000 per month, payable 15 days after the close of the month in which the service is provided.
4. The firm receives a check for $5,000 from one of its customers for payment on merchandise that was delivered in January. The amount owed is included among the company's accounts receivable.
5. The firm purchases 100 shares of Exxon common stock for $84 per share as a short-term investment.
6. *The Wall Street Journal* reports that the price of Exxon stock has increased to $88 per share.
7. The company purchases manufacturing equipment for $86,000. The company pays cash of $20,000 and gives a three-year note for the balance. In addition, the company incurs costs (paid in cash) of $2,000 to install the equipment.
8. The company issues 10,000 shares of its common stock for $12 per share. The common stock has a par value of $10 per share.
9. The company pays $600 rent on its office space. The rent is applicable to the month of May and had previously been recorded as a liability, "accrued rent payable."
10. The company returns to the manufacturer raw materials that it deems defective. The company had been billed $900 for such materials and had recorded the amount as a liability.

5. *Revenues and expenses result in an increase or decrease in net assets (assets minus liabilities) as well as in owners' equity.*

If the basic accounting equation is expressed in the form assets − liabilities = owners' equity, then which of the following transactions serve to increase or decrease the right side (owners' equity) of the equation? Which transactions would represent revenues or expenses as opposed to only changes in asset and liability accounts?
1. A firm purchases fuel oil for cash.
2. It purchases fuel oil on account.
3. It uses the fuel oil previously purchased.
4. It pays for the fuel oil previously purchased on account.
5. It receives and pays the electric bill; no previous accounting recognition has been given to electric costs.
6. It provides services for a customer and bills him.
7. It collects the amount previously billed.
8. It borrows an amount from a bank.
9. It repays the amount borrowed.
10. It gives accounting recognition to interest on the amount borrowed and makes the interest payment.

6. *In analyzing these transactions be sure to distinguish those that affect only asset and liability accounts from those that involve revenue and expense accounts.*

Prepare journal entries to reflect the following transactions. Be certain to indicate the nature of each account affected.
1. A company purchases supplies for $500 cash.

2. The company uses $300 of the supplies.
3. The company purchases merchandise for $3,000 on account.
4. The company pays $1,500 of the $3,000 owed to suppliers.
5. The company sells for $4,000, on account, merchandise that had initially cost $3,000. (Two entries are required.)
6. The company collects $4,000 from its customers.
7. It borrows $10,000 at 6 percent annual interest.
8. The company pays one year's interest.
9. The company purchases for cash a machine for $6,000. The machine has an estimated useful life of three years.
10. The company gives accounting recognition to the use of the machine for one year.

7. *After completing this exercise, consider why, when a firm returns merchandise, it receives "credit" on its account.*

Prepare journal entries to reflect the following events on the books of both Wholesale, Inc. and Retail, Inc.
1. Wholesale, Inc. sells, for $5,000 on account to Retail, Inc., merchandise that had cost Wholesale, Inc. $4,000.
2. Upon discovering that some of the merchandise did not meet its specifications, Retail, Inc. returns it to Wholesale, Inc. The returned merchandise had been sold to Retail for $1,000 and had cost Wholesale $800.
3. Retail, Inc. pays the balance due on its account.

8. *A balance sheet prepared from a preclosing trial balance will not balance.*

The preclosing trial balance of Frost, Inc. as of December 31, 1981 is as follows:

|  | Debits | Credits |
|---|---|---|
| Cash | $ 3,000 | |
| Accounts receivable | 5,000 | |
| Other assets | 12,000 | |
| Accounts payable | | $ 5,000 |
| Other liabilities | | 2,000 |
| Capital contributed by stockholders | | 4,000 |
| Retained earnings | | 6,000 |
| Sales revenue | | 25,000 |
| Cost of goods sold | 18.000 | |
| Other expenses | 4,000 | |
|  | $42,000 | $42,000 |

a. If, from the trial balance, you were to prepare an income statement and a balance sheet, which accounts would have to be adjusted? Why?
b. Prepare an income statement.
c. Make the necessary closing entries.
d. Prepare a balance sheet, taking into account the effect of the closing entries.

9. *The basic accounting can be expanded so as to highlight the relationships among the various balance sheet accounts and revenues, expenses, and dividends.*

Arrange a piece of paper in columns with the following headings, each of which corresponds to a term in the accounting equation:

Assets = liabilities + Contributed capital + Retained earnings, 1/1
+ Revenues – Expenses – Dividends

a. Indicate the effect of each of the following events or other items of information on the accounting equation.
   1. As of 1/1 a firm reported assets of $200,000, liabilities of $100,000, contributed capital of $10,000, and retained earnings of $90,000.
   2. The firm purchased merchandise, on account, for $80,000.
   3. It issued additional common stock for $40,000 cash.
   4. It borrowed $10,000.
   5. It made sales of $98,000, all of which were for cash.
   6. The cost of merchandise sold was $50,000.
   7. It incurred interest costs, which were paid in cash, of $7,000.
   8. Taxes assessed for the period, payable the following period, were $11,000.
   9. It declared and paid dividends of $4,000.
b. Determine, by summing the columns, the financial position of the firm at the end of the accounting period as well as the revenues, expenses, and dividends of the period.
c. Compute income for the period.
d. Determine the end-of-period balance in retained earnings assuming that the balance as of 1/1 is adjusted to give effect to the revenues, expenses, and dividends of the period.

10. *Owners' equity increases whenever net assets (assets minus liabilities) increase, and decreases whenever net assets decrease.*

Indicate the effect (if any) that each of the several transactions described as follows would have on owners' equity (after closing entries have been made):
1. The firm sold for $100 merchandise that had cost $80.
2. The firm purchased merchandise for $2,000.
3. The firm purchased a truck for $12,000 cash.
4. The firm purchased and used $300 of supplies.
5. The firm paid its advertising agency $600 for ads that had been run (and had been given accounting recognition) the previous month.
6. The firm received $750 in dividends on 1,000 shares of XYZ Co. stock that it owns.
7. The firm paid $45 interest on $1,000 that it had previously borrowed from a local bank.

11. *Because of the logical relationships inherent in an accounting system, a great deal of information can be derived from a little.*

Given the following data about a company over a period of three years, determine the missing amounts.

|                                      | 1981    | 1982    | 1983    |
|--------------------------------------|---------|---------|---------|
| Retained earnings, 1/1               | $1,000  | $5,000  | $   ?   |
| Revenues for the year                | 8,000   | ?       | ?       |
| Expenses for the year                | ?       | 5,000   | 8,000   |
| Income for the year                  | 6,000   | ?       | 4,000   |
| Dividends declared during the year   | ?       | 2,000   | 3,000   |
| Retained earnings, 12/31             | 5,000   | 7,000   | ?       |

12. *Entries to revenue and expense accounts can be viewed as entries to retained earnings.*

    Assume that a company maintains only four accounts: (1) assets, (2), liabilities, (3) invested capital, and (4) retained earnings. The following transactions occurred during its first month of operations:

    1. The owners of the company contributed a total of $100,000 to establish the business.
    2. The company issues bonds for $50,000; that is, it borrowed $50,000.
    3. The company purchased equipment, $60,000, giving the seller a note for the full amount.
    4. The company purchased merchandise for cash, $40,000.
    5. The company had sales of $30,000. Cash sales were $25,000, and those on account, $5,000.
    6. The company paid $2,000 rent for the current month.
    7. The company paid one month's interest on the bonds, $250.
    8. The company recognized one month's depreciation on the equipment purchased. The estimated useful life of the equipment is 60 months.
    9. The company paid insurance premiums for two months—the current month and the following month—$300 per month.
    10. The company collected $2,000 of the accounts receivable from customers.
    11. The company learned that $500 of the amount owed by customers would not be collectible owing to the bankruptcy of one customer.
    12. The company determined that of the merchandise purchased $22,000 remained on hand, unsold, at the end of the month.

    a. Establish T accounts for each of the four accounts. Prepare a journal entry to record each of the transactions, and post the entries to the appropriate T accounts. Compute end-of-month balances in each account.
    b. Determine income for the month.
    c. Suppose that the company had paid a dividend of $2,000 to its owners. How would that affect the balance in the retained earnings account? How would it affect income for the month?

13. *Some errors affect only the income statement or the balance sheet; those that affect both are naturally considered to be more serious.*

    A bookkeeper made several errors as described below. For each, indicate whether, for the period in which they were made, they would cause a misstatement, of (1) the balance sheet only, (2) the income statement only, or (3) both the balance sheet and the income statement.

1. Failed to record a sale of $300, on account, to a customer.
2. Failed to record the collection of $200 owed by a customer for a purchase he had made several weeks earlier.
3. Incorrectly recorded the issuance of 1,000 shares of common stock at $2 per share; made the following journal entry:

| Cash | $2,000 | |
|------|--------|--------|
| Marketable securities | | $2,000 |

4. Recorded the purchase of a new carburetor for a company-owned vehicle as an addition to fixed assets rather than as a repair.
5. Recorded funds given to a salesman to entertain customers as a miscellaneous expense rather than a sales expense.
6. Failed to record the purchase of a new truck.
7. Failed to record depreciation on a company-owned car.
8. Incorrectly counted merchandise inventory on hand at year end.
9. Failed to record repayment of the company's loan from a bank.
10. Failed to record payment of interest on the same loan.

14. *A balance sheet may not balance until a certain key account has been updated.*

Arrange a sheet of paper as indicated in the table. Leave room for additional accounts that might be required. The first column indicates balances as of January 1.

| Account | Balance 1/1 | Transactions in January Dr. | Cr. | Income Statement for January Dr. | Cr. | Balance Sheet 1/31 Dr. | Cr. |
|---------|-------------|------|------|------|------|------|------|
| Cash | $20,000 | | | | | | |
| Accounts receivable | 50,000 | | | | | | |
| Merchandise inventory | 15,000 | | | | | | |
| Fixed assets | 60,000 | | | | | | |
| Accounts payable | 30,000 | | | | | | |
| Notes payable | 25,000 | | | | | | |
| Common stock | 2,000 | | | | | | |
| Retained earnings | 88,000 | | | | | | |

a. Record the effect of the transactions described, all of which occurred in the month of January, in columns 2 and 3. Indicate the month-end balances in the accounts in columns 4 through 7 as appropriate. Record the total of each column.

1. Sales for the month, all on credit, were $70,000.
2. Collections from customers totaled $80,000.

    3. Purchases of merchandise intended for sale were $45,000. All purchases were "on account."

    4. Goods on hand at the month's end totaled $5,000.

    5. Other operating expenses were $15,000. They were paid in cash.

    6. Depreciation expense, in addition to other operating expenses, was based on an estimated useful life of five years (60 months) for all fixed assets. (Assume fixed assets were all purchased on 1/1.)

  b. Why doesn't the balance sheet balance after all transactions have been posted?

  c. Prepare a journal entry to close accounts as necessary.

15. *Most firms close their books once a year. Financial statements, however, can be prepared at any time and for any time period. The balance sheet and the income statement may be derived from a preclosing rather than a postclosing trial balance. Retained earnings, however, must be adjusted for the income or loss of the period.*

    Typewriter Rental Service, Inc. began operations on January 1, 1981. During its first month of operations, the following events took place:

    1. The company issued 200 shares of common stock at $100 per share.

    2. The company rented a store for $200 per month. It paid the first month's rent.

    3. The company purchased 20 typewriters at a price of $500 each. The company paid cash of $4,000 and promised to pay the balance within 60 days.

    4. The company purchased, on account, supplies for $500.

    5. The company rented the typewriters. Total revenues for the month were $800. Of this amount $200 was collected in cash.

    6. The company paid $150 cash to cover other operating expenses.

    7. A count at month end indicated that $450 of supplies remained on hand.

    8. At month end the company gave accounting recognition to the depreciation of 1 month on its typewriters. The useful life of the typewriters is estimated at 36 months.

  a. Prepare journal entries to recognize the above transactions.

  b. Post the journal entries to T accounts.

  c. Prepare a preclosing trial balance.

  d. Prepare an income statement and a statement of position (balance sheet).

16. *Retained earnings may be affected not only by revenues, expenses, and dividends but by "extraordinary" gains and losses and prior period adjustments as well. In evaluating extraordinary gains and losses and prior period adjustments, first consider their impact upon assets and liabilities. The effect on retained earnings should then become relatively clear.*

    The Bastrop Co. had a balance in retained earnings as of January 1, 1981, of $2.5 million. The following financial events, which affected the company, occurred in 1981.

1. The firm had operating revenues of $3.8 million and operating expenses of $2.6 million.
2. The company suffered an extraordinary loss, not included in operating expenses, of $600,000, attributable to the expropriation of foreign properties.
3. In January 1981 the company paid dividends of $3 per share on 100,000 shares of common stock outstanding. The dividend had been declared in December 1980 and had been properly accounted for at that time.
4. The market price of the company's common stock was $60 per share on January 1, 1981. On December 31, 1981, it was $55 per share.
5. In June 1981 the company issued 10,000 additional shares of common stock. The stock had a par value of $1 per share and was issued at a price of $58 per share.
6. In July 1981 the company settled a claim against the Internal Revenue Service. The Internal Revenue Service returned to the company $1.5 million in previously paid taxes, which the company contended were improperly assessed. The company had recorded the $1.5 million as an expense in 1978. It accounted for the $1.5 million as a "prior period adjustment" (i.e., a correction of income reported in 1978).
7. In December 1981 the company declared a common stock dividend of $4 per share on 110,000 shares outstanding and a preferred stock dividend of $1 per share on 200,000 shares outstanding.

a. Indicate the impact of each event on *retained* earnings.
b. Determine the December 31, 1981 balance in retained earnings.

**17.** *It is useful to distinguish between sales revenue and cash collections.*

The following problem is based on an actual case:

Boscoble Auto Parts began operations in mid-1979. According to the records maintained by the proprietor, sales for 1980, the first full year of operation, were $98,000. The cost of goods sold was $55,000, and other operating expenses were $23,000. In light of the fact that he believed that business had been profitable in 1980, the proprietor could not understand why he was having difficulty making timely payments on his outstanding bills. He engaged an accountant in order to obtain financial guidance.

Inquiry by the accountant revealed that the company made sales both for cash and on credit. At the end of each day the proprietor recorded the day's "sales" in a book he called a "sales journal." The single figure recorded each day was a sum of the sales for cash, the sales for credit, and the subsequent cash collections on previous sales for credit.

Further investigation revealed that at the beginning of 1980 the company had accounts receivable of $8,000 from customers; at the end of 1980 the amount receivable from customers had increased to $10,000. During 1980, $22,000 had been collected from customers who had made purchases on credit.

a. What was the primary deficiency in the accounting system of Boscoble Auto Parts?

b. Determine total cash sales and total credit sales. By how much were 1980 sales overstated? Assuming that the amount paid to the state for collections of sales taxes was based on the amount recorded in the sales journal, how much of a refund from the state should the proprietor request? The sales tax rate is 5 percent.

c. What was the true income (loss) of the firm during 1980?

18. *Many firms do not maintain ongoing records of the cost of the goods they sell. Instead, they determine such cost from data on purchases during the period and beginning and ending inventory balances. In an emergency, the historical relationship between selling prices and costs of merchandise sold can serve as the basis of an estimate of any required information that might be unavailable.*

The D. J. Book Co. keeps accurate records of all sales. Each time a customer purchases a book, the sale is rung up on the cash register. At the end of each day, the total sales per the cash register tape is recorded in a "sales journal." Sales for the year can be computed simply by summing the amounts recorded in the sales journal. The company also keeps an accurate tally of the cost of all books which it purchases from its suppliers. It does not, however, keep any day-to-day records of the cost of the books which it sells.

On December 31, 1980, a count of books on hand revealed that the company had an inventory of books that had cost $85,000. A similar count on December 31, 1981, indicated an inventory of $63,000. During 1981 the company had purchased from suppliers books that cost a total of $324,000. Total sales for the year, per the sales journal, were $415,000.

a. Determine the cost of the goods sold during the year.

b. Suppose that in the following year a fire destroyed the store and its inventory on June 30, 1982. Accounting records, which were kept in a different building, indicated that sales for the year up to that point were $250,000. Purchases from suppliers to that date were $180,000. The company follows a policy of "marking up" all books by 20 percent. That is, if it purchases a book for $5, it would sell such a book for $6. What would you estimate to be the cost of the inventory lost in the fire?

19. *This problem serves to review the accounting cycle.*

Upon receiving a gift of $4,000, J. Keats decides to enter the copy business. During the first month of operations, the following events took place:

1. Keats places the entire $4,000 in a bank account in the name of "Fast-Copy Co."

2. He signs a three-year lease on a store. Rent is to be at the rate of $400 per month. Keats pays three months' rent at the time he signs the lease, $400 for the current month and $800 in advance.

3. He purchases furniture and fixtures for $1,500. He pays $500 at the time of purchase and promises to pay the balance within 60 days.

4. He signs a rental agreement with a manufacturer of copy equipment.

The agreement stipulates that Keats will pay $200 per month plus $.02 for each copy made.

5. He places advertisements in the local newspapers. The cost of the ads is $600, payable in cash.
6. He purchases paper and other supplies for $800 on account.
7. He makes his first copies for customers. He sells 30,000 copies at $.05 each. Customers pay cash for all copies.
8. He takes an end-of-month inventory and finds $200 of supplies on hand.
9. He withdraws $200 from the business to meet personal expenses.
10. He pays the amount due the manufacturer of the copy equipment for the first month's operations.
11. He gives accounting recognition to the use of the furniture and fixtures for one month. The furniture and fixtures have an estimated useful life of five years.

a. Prepare journal entries to record the transactions of the first month of operations.
b. Post them to T accounts.
c. Prepare an income statement for the month.
d. Prepare any closing entries that would be necessary *if* the books were to be closed at the end of the month (ordinarily books would be closed only at the end of a full accounting period, usually one year).
e. Prepare a statement of position (a balance sheet).

 20. *This problem serves not only to review the accounting cycle but also to highlight a key deficiency of income as a measure of financial strength.*

 The stockholders of Regal Gifts, Inc. were extremely gratified to receive an income statement from management. It revealed that in its first year of operations, the company, which operates a gift shop, had earnings that far exceeded original expectations. Two months after receipt of the income statement, the company was forced to declare bankruptcy. The following information summarizes the major financial events of the company's first year of operations:

1. Stockholders purchased 1,000 shares of common stock at a price of $100 per share.
2. The company leased a store in a shopping center. Monthly rent was $1,000. During the year rent payments of $12,000 were made.
3. The company purchased furniture and fixtures for the store at a cost of $30,000. The company paid cash of $20,000 and gave a one-year note for the balance. The estimated useful life of the furniture and fixtures is 10 years.
4. In the course of the year the company purchased at a cost of $240,000 merchandise intended for sale. The company paid $210,000 cash for the merchandise; as of year end the balance was owed.
5. The company had sales of $240,000. Sales were made for both cash and credit. As of year end, the company had outstanding receivables from customers of $40,000.

6. The company paid salaries of $40,000.
7. The company incurred and paid other operating costs of $15,000.
8. As of year end, the company had $90,000 of merchandise still on hand.

a. Prepare journal entries to reflect the financial events of the company's first year of operations.
b. Prepare an income statement and a balance sheet.
c. Prepare an analysis of the cash account. Indicate the sources of cash and how it was used.
d. Explain why the company may have been forced to declare bankruptcy.

*solutions to
exercise for
review and
self-testing*

a. Assets (fuel inventory) would increase by $800.
   Liabilities (accounts payable) would increase by $800.
   Owners' equity would not change.
b. Assets (fuel inventory) would decrease by $160.
   Liabilities would not change.
   Owners' equity would decrease by $160.
c. Assets (accounts receivable) would increase by $2,000.
   Liabilities would not change.
   Owners' equity would increase by $2,000.
d. Owners' equity (in this case retained earnings) would increase by $1,840 ($2,000 – 160).

e. 
| | | |
|---|---|---|
| Fuel inventory (asset +) | $800 | |
|     Accounts payable (liability +) | | $800 |

**To record purchase of fuel.**

| | | |
|---|---|---|
| Fuel expense (owners' equity –) | $160 | |
|     Fuel inventory (asset –) | | $160 |

**To record use of fuel.**

| | | |
|---|---|---|
| Accounts receivable (asset +) | $2,000 | |
|     Delivery revenue (owners' equity +) | | $2,000 |

**To record delivery services provided.**

f. 
| | | |
|---|---|---|
| Retained earnings (owners' equity –) | $160 | |
|     Fuel expense (owners' equity +) | | $160 |

**To close expense account.**

| | | |
|---|---|---|
| Delivery revenue (owners' equity +) | $2,000 | |
|     Retained earnings (owners' equity +) | | $2,000 |

**To close revenue account.**

g. The net effect of the journal entries is to increase retained earnings by $1,840, an amount equal to that determined in d.

h. Increase in assets:

| | | |
|---|---|---|
| Fuel inventory (+$800, –$160) | $ 640 | |
| Accounts receivable | 2,000 | $2,640 |
| Less increase in liability: | | |
| Accounts payable | | 800 |
| Increase in net assets | | $1,840 |

The increase in net assets is equal to the increase in retained earnings.

i.  No. There is no need to transfer the balances in asset and liability accounts to "parent" accounts. Moreover, the balances at the end of an accounting period must remain for the start of the next accounting period. Unlike revenue and expense accounts, asset and liability accounts do not have to be "zeroed out" to accumulate new information each accounting period.

# 4

# Accruing Revenues and Expenses

The primary objective of this chapter is to examine the accrual concept and to see what its impact is upon the recording process. An overview of the basic books of account will also be presented.

## The Accrual Concept

Central to modern-day accounting is the notion that revenues and expenses should be reported on an accrual basis. The effects of transactions and other financial events on the assets and liabilities of an enterprise should be accorded accounting recognition at the time that they have their primary economic impact, *not necessarily when cash is received or disbursed*. Revenues should be assigned to that period in which they are *earned*. Revenues are said to be *realized* at that point when they are earned. Costs are charged as expenses in the period in which they provide their expected services in an effort to generate revenues.

Under the accrual concept, costs which are intended to provide future services are *capitalized*—i.e., recorded as assets (bundles of "prepaid" expenses) —until such time as the services are actually provided. Such services might be provided before or after the related cash disbursement. The services to be provided by office supplies are, at the time the supplies are purchased, recorded as an asset, "supplies inventory." The cost of the supplies is not recorded as an expense until the supplies are actually consumed. The supplies could be consumed either before or after the supplies are paid for.

Similarly, the cost of services provided by an office clerk is generally recorded as an expense during the period in which the firm benefits from his services even though his paycheck may be delivered in a subsequent (or even a previous) accounting period.

Revenues are most commonly recognized when the company sells its goods (point of sale is ordinarily considered to be when goods are delivered and title passes to the purchaser) or performs its promised services. As with expenses, the criterion for recognition is not transfer of cash, which can occur either in prior or subsequent accounting periods.

Several series of events and the appropriate journal entries can be used to illustrate the accrual concept.

*example 1*    A company purchases supplies but does not pay for them until after they are consumed.

**(a)**

| 1/3/81 | Supplies inventory (asset +) | $300 | |
| | Accounts payable (liability +) | | $300 |

**To record the purchase of $300 of supplies on account.** (No expense is charged.)

**(b)**

| 2/5/81 | Supplies expense (expense +) | $200 | |
| | Supplies inventory (asset –) | | $200 |

**To record the use of $200 of the supplies previously purchased.**

**(c)**

| 3/2/81 | Accounts payable (liability –) | $300 | |
| | Cash (asset –) | | $300 |

**To record payment of the $300 owed for the supplies.** (No expense is charged.)

The expense is charged when the supplies are *consumed*—not when the supplies are received or when they were paid for. The use of the supplies is the critical economic event.

Occasionally a term such as *supplies* is used to refer to both an asset, "supplies in inventory," and an expense, "supplies expense." Accountants allow themselves considerable flexibility in the titles that they ascribe to accounts. To avoid confusion, however, titles that clearly indicate the nature of the account should always be employed.

*example 2*    A company benefits from the services of salaried employees in one accounting period but does not pay them until the next.

Salaries are paid each Tuesday for the week ending the previous Friday.

*has occurred*

**(a)**

| 12/31/80 | Salaries expense (expense +) | $14,000 | |
| (Friday) | Accrued salaries payable | | |
| | (liability +) | | $14,000 |

**To record one week's salaries.**

**(b)**

| 1/4/81 | Accrued salaries payable (liability –) | $14,000 | |
| (Tuesday) | Cash (asset –) | | $14,000 |

**To record payment of $14,000 owed for salaries.**

The expense is charged in the accounting period in which the work is performed—regardless of when cash payment is actually made.

*example 3*     A firm receives payment in one accounting period for merchandise that it will deliver to a customer in a subsequent accounting period.

**(a)**

| 1/15/81 | Cash (asset +) | $25,000 | |
|---|---|---|---|
| | Advances from customers | | |
| | (liability +) | | $25,000 |

*liability since has claim to service*

**To record advance payment from a customer for merchandise to be delivered in the following period.**

**(b)**

| 2/20/81 | Advances from customers (liability -) | $25,000 | |
|---|---|---|---|
| | Sales revenue (revenue +) | | $25,000 |

**To record the delivery of merchandise to the customer.**

**(c)**

| 2/20/81 | Cost of goods sold (expense +) | $18,000 | |
|---|---|---|---|
| | Merchandise inventory (asset -) | | $18,000 |

**To record the cost of the goods delivered to the customer as part of the sales transaction recorded in entry (b).**

The significant event in a merchandise transaction is most frequently (though not necessarily) considered to be the transfer of goods (and title) to the customer. It is at the time of transfer, therefore, that both sales revenue and the related cost of the goods sold should be recognized.

*example 4*     A company delivers merchandise in one period but receives payment in a subsequent period.

**(a)**

| 2/25/81 | Accounts receivable (asset +) | $46,000 | |
|---|---|---|---|
| | Sales revenue (revenue +) | | $46,000 |

**To record the delivery of merchandise to a customer.**

*4 entries*

**(b)**

| 2/25/81 | Cost of goods sold (expense +) | $33,000 | |
|---|---|---|---|
| | Merchandise inventory (asset -) | | $33,000 |

**To record the cost of the goods delivered to the customer as part of the sales transaction recorded in entry (a).**

**(c)**

3/11/81    Cash (asset +)                                        $46,000
                    Accounts receivable (asset –)                              $46,000
**To record the receipt of the amount previously billed.**

As in the previous example, both revenue and the related expense are re-corded at the time the merchandise is delivered to the customer—not when the cash payment is received.

*example 5*    A company declares (announces its intention to pay) a dividend in one accounting period but does not pay it until the next period. For example, on November 28, 1979 a company declares a dividend of $1.00 per share payable to stockholders on January 15 of the following year; there are 50,000 shares of stock outstanding.

*reduction on Ret. Earnings*

**(a)**

11/28/79    Dividends (cannot properly be classified as
                    revenue, expense, asset, or liability; they
                    represent a reduction of owners' equity
                    owing to a distribution of assets to stock-
                    holders)                                              $50,000
                    Dividends payable (liability +)                         $50,000
**To record the declaration of the dividend.**

**(b)**

1/15/80    Dividends payable (liability –)                        $50,000
                    Cash (asset –)                                              $50,000
**To record the payment of the dividend.**

On December 31, 1979 when year-end financial statements are prepared the "dividends" account (like revenue and expense accounts) would be "closed" to retained earnings:

*directly affects Ret'nd Earng*

12/31/79    Retained earnings                                    $50,000
                    Dividends                                                  $50,000
**To close the dividend account.**

As a consequence, the dividend will have its critical impact on the finan-cial statements (i.e., will result in the decrease of owners' equity) in the year in which it is declared, rather than when it is actually paid. It is upon declara-tion of the dividend that the company establishes its obligation to distribute assets to stockholders.

## Periodic Adjusting Entries

**adjusting for continuous processes**

Some expenses are incurred and some revenues are earned on a continuous basis. Buildings, for example, depreciate over time. Rent, insurance, and interest expenses are also incurred as a function of time. Similarly, electricity and heating costs are often incurred without interruption. Revenues, such as interest revenue, rent revenue, and insurance premium revenue (from the standpoint of an insurance company), are also continuously being earned. To the extent that the accrual concept requires that accounting recognition be given to expenses as they are incurred and to revenues as they are earned, a firm's bookkeeper would have to be making entries around the clock to keep the accounting records current.

Although the accrual concept need not be adhered to with a vengeance, it is important that the financial records be updated periodically, and it is essential, if misleading reports are not to be presented, that an enterprise give recognition to ongoing revenues and expenses whenever financial reports are to be issued. In practice, it is common for firms to make updating journal entries monthly, quarterly, or, at a minimum, annually.

Several *updating* entries are indicated in the examples that follow. Common to all is the fact that the credits to revenues or the debits to expenses are made regardless of whether or not there has been a receipt or disbursement of cash.

*example 1*

On January 1 a firm borrows $3,000 for two months at an annual rate of interest of 12 percent.

| 1/1/81 | Cash (asset +) | $3,000 | |
| | Notes payable (liability +) | | $3,000 |

**To record the receipt of cash and the corresponding liability.**

| 1/31/81 | Interest expense (expense +) | $30 | |
| | Accrued interest payable (liability +) | | $30 |

**To record both interest expense for one month and the corresponding liability.** The term "accrued" is frequently used to reflect the fact that the related expense or revenue has been earned or incurred but the asset or liability is not yet *legally* receivable or due.

| 2/28/81 | Interest expense (expense +) | $30 | |
| | Accrued interest payable (liability +) | | $30 |

**To record the interest expense for the second month.**

| 2/28/81 | Accrued interest payable (liability –) | $ 60 | |
| | Notes payable (liability –) | 3,000 | |
| | Cash (asset –) | | $3,060 |

**To record the subsequent payment of both the interest and the principal due.**

126

In this example *interest expense* was debited at the end of each month—and the liability to make the required payments was credited—to give accounting recognition to the continuous accrual of the cost of using borrowed funds.

The two entries of 2/28 could have readily been combined as follow:

| 2/28/81 | Interest expense (expense +) | $   30 | |
| | Accrued interest payable (liability -) | 30 | |
| | Notes payable (liability -) | 3,000 | |
| | Cash (asset -) | | $3,060 |

**To record payment of note and related interest.**

*example 2*  On June 15 Left Bank Properties, Inc. leases a residential house to a tenant. Rent is $400 per month, and the lease is for a one-year period beginning July 1. One month's rent is paid in advance. Subsequent payments are to be made each month.

| 6/15/80 | Cash (asset +) | $400 | |
| | Unearned rent (liability +) | | $400 |

**To record both the receipt of one month's rent in advance and the corresponding "liability"—in this instance a "deferred credit" or obligation to provide services to the tenent. "Unearned rent" is similar to "advances from customers."**

| 7/31/80 | Unearned rent (liability -) | $400 | |
| | Rent revenues (revenue +) | | $400 |

**To give accounting recognition to both the revenue earned in July and the satisfaction of the related liability.**

| 8/31/80 | Rent receivable (asset +) | $400 | |
| | Rental revenues (revenue +) | | $400 |

**To give accounting recognition to the revenue earned in August.** (Assume that the tenant has failed to make his required payment for August.)

| 9/31/80 | Cash (asset +) | $1,200 | |
| | Rent receivable (asset -) | | $400 |
| | Rental revenue (revenue +) | | 400 |
| | Unearned rent (liability +) | | 400 |

**To record $1,200 cash received from tenant.** The amount received represents rent for August, which was due the previous month; rent for September, which is currently due; and rent for October, paid in advance.

*example 3*  On January 2, 1979 a firm purchases a bookkeeping machine for $10,000. The estimated useful life of the machine is five years, after which it will have negligible scrap or resale value.

1/2/79    Office equipment (asset +)                              $10,000
                     Cash (asset -)                                   $10,000
**To record the purchase of the machine.**

12/31/79    Depreciation expense (expense +)                $2,000
                     Office equipment—accumulated
                        depreciation (contra asset +)               $2,000
**To record depreciation for the first year.** An identical entry would be made at the end of each of the following four years.

In Example 3, it was necessary, at the end of the first accounting period, to give accounting recognition to the fact that the "bundle of future services" represented by the asset, office equipment, had been depleted by one year's use. The credit in the journal entry was not made directly to "office equipment"; instead it was made to "office equipment—accumulated depreciation." The latter account is known as a *contra* (meaning against or opposite) or *offset* account, and its balance is always reported directly beneath that of the account with which it is associated. If the contra account is associated with an asset account, then the asset account would always have a debit balance, and the contra account would always have a credit balance. The asset account would indicate the original cost of the equipment; the contra account would indicate the expired portion of the cost. The difference between the two would reflect the unexpired cost (i.e., its *book value*). At the end of the *second* year of operation, the office equipment and the related contra account would appear as follows:

| Office equipment | | Office equipment, accumulated depreciation | |
|---|---|---|---|
| 1/1/79  10,000 | | 12/31/79  2,000 | |
| | | 12/31/80  2,000 | |

The two accounts would be reported on the balance sheet as follows:

Office equipment                $10,000
Less: Accumulated depreciation    4,000    $6,000

The periodic credits could have been made directly to the office equipment account. Use of the contra account, however, provides additional information: the original cost of the equipment as well as the portion of the cost that has expired to date.

Should the assets be removed from the books, it would also be necessary to remove the related accumulated depreciation from the contra account. Assume, for example, that immediately after the second year the office equipment described above was sold for $7,000. The book value at the time of sale was $6,000—the original cost of $10,000 less accumulated depreciation of $4,000. Hence there was a gain on the sale of $1,000. The following journal entry would therefore be appropriate:

| | | |
|---|---|---|
| Cash (asset +) | $7,000 | |
| Office equipment—accumulated depreciation (contra asset –) | 4,000 | |
| Office equipment (asset –) | | $10,000 |
| Gain on sale of equipment (revenue +) | | 1,000 |

**To record the sale of office equipment.**

The expression "allowance for" depreciation is often used in place of "accumulated" depreciation.

**other entries to update the accounts**

Periodically, additional adjustments to the financial records must be made. These adjustments stem primarily from the willingness of business enterprises and their accountants to permit out-of-date information to remain in the accounts in order to obtain a measure of bookkeeping convenience. There is no harm in such practice—as long as necessary adjustments are made prior to the preparation of financial statements derived from the accounts.

Suppose that at the beginning of an accounting period a company has on hand $1,000 in supplies. During the accounting period the company purchases for cash $4,000 of supplies and consumes $2,000. The correct ending balance in the supplies account would therefore be $3,000; supplies expense for the period would be $2,000 (the amount consumed).

| | | |
|---|---|---|
| Balance, supplies inventory, 1/1 | $1,000 | |
| Purchases, 1/1–12/31 | 4,000 | $5,000 |
| Supplies used (expense), 1/1–12/31 | | 2,000 |
| Balance, supplies inventory, 12/31 | | $3,000 |

The most direct means of accounting for supplies would be to increment the supplies inventory account each time supplies were purchased and to relieve the account each time supplies were withdrawn and presumably used. Thus,

(a)

*Various Dates*

| | | |
|---|---|---|
| Supplies inventory | $4,000 | |
| Cash | | $4,000 |

**To record the purchase of supplies.** (If the $4,000 of supplies represents the sum of several purchases, then similar journal entries would be made for each purchase.)

**(b)**

*Various Dates*

| | |
|---|---|
| Supplies expense | $2,000 |
| Supplies inventory | $2,000 |

**To record the use of $2,000 of supplies.**

At the end of the year the accounts would appear as follows:

| Supplies inventory | | | | Supplies expense | |
|---|---|---|---|---|---|
| Bal. 1/1 | 1,000 | (b) var. | 2,000 | (b) var. | 2,000 |
| (a) var. | 4,000 | dates | | dates | |
| dates | | | | | |

| | Cash | | |
|---|---|---|---|
| Bal. 1/1 | xxx | (a) var. | 4,000 |
| | | dates | |

The accounts correctly reflect the fact that ending inventory is $3,000 and supplies expense for the period was $2,000. No adjusting entries are required. It is necessary only to "close" the supplies expense account. But insofar as supplies are withdrawn in small amounts at frequent intervals, record keeping in the course of the year may tend to become burdensome since a separate entry must be made for each purchase and each withdrawal.

Alternatively, a company can avoid making an accounting entry each time supplies are *withdrawn* from the storeroom. Instead of recording both the purchase and the use of supplies, it would record only the purchase. In the course of the year, the supplies inventory account would only be debited—never credited. At the end of the year, however, the firm would take a *physical inventory* (count) to determine the actual amount of supplies on hand. The company would assume that all supplies purchased plus those on hand at the beginning of the year must have been used during the year if they are not physically present at the conclusion of the year. It would adjust the accounts by crediting inventory with the amount required to reduce supplies inventory to reflect the inventory actually on hand and by debiting supplies expense with the same amount —the amount presumably used during the year. Thus,

**(a)**

*Various Dates*

| | |
|---|---|
| Supplies inventory | $4,000 |
| Cash | $4,000 |

**To record the purchase of supplies throughout the year.**

At the end of the year, prior to the physical inventory count, the accounts would show the following:

| Supplies inventory | | | Supplies expense | | Cash | |
| --- | --- | --- | --- | --- | --- | --- |
| Bal. 1/1 | 1,000 | | | | xxx | (a) var. 4,000 |
| (a) var. | 4,000 | | | | | dates |
| dates | | 2,000 | | | | |

3,000

If a physical count at year end reveals supplies on hand of $3,000, then $2,000 of supplies ($5,000 per the accounts less $3,000 on hand) must have been consumed. The appropriate adjusting journal entry would be

**(b)**

| 12/31 | Supplies expense | $2,000 | |
| --- | --- | --- | --- |
| | Supplies inventory | | $2,000 |

**To adjust the accounts at year end to reflect the physical count of supplies.**

| Supplies inventory | | | | Supplies expense | |
| --- | --- | --- | --- | --- | --- |
| Bal. 1/1 | 1,000 | (b) 12/31 | 2,000 | (b) 12/31  2,000 | |
| (a) var. | 4,000 | | | | |
| dates | | | | | |

Once the adjusting entries have been posted, the account balances would be identical to those derived from the procedure illustrated previously. The former approach is often referred to as a *perpetual* method, since the inventory account is always reflective of the actual quantity on hand, and the latter approach as a *periodic* method, since periodic counts are necessary to bring the inventory account up to date.

The same results could also be obtained by a third procedure, which is also widely used. A company, instead of charging (debiting) all purchases of supplies to supplies inventory, could charge them to supplies expense. Then, as it would do if it followed the second procedure, it would take a year-end count of supplies on hand. To adjust the inventory account to reflect the actual inventory on hand, the balance in the supplies inventory account (which would represent supplies on hand at the *beginning* of the year) would be debited (increased) *or* credited (decreased) with the amount required to bring it up or down to the quantity indicated by the physical count. The corresponding credit or debit would be made to supplies expense. If more supplies were purchased than were actually used, then the amount in the supplies expense account would have to be reduced (credited); if more were used than purchased (i.e., beginning inventory reduced), then supplies expense would have to be increased (debited).

**(a)**

*Various Dates*

| | Supplies expense | $4,000 | |
| --- | --- | --- | --- |
| | Cash | | $4,000 |

**To record the *purchase* of supplies.**

At the end of the year, prior to adjusting entries, the accounts would appear as follows:

| Supplies inventory | | Supplies expense | |
|---|---|---|---|
| Bal. 1/1   1,000 | | (a) var.   4,000 | |
| | | dates | |

| | Cash | |
|---|---|---|
| xxx | (a) var.   4,000 | |
| | dates | |

If the physical count at year end revealed that $3,000 of supplies were on hand, then supplies inventory would be understated by $2,000. Correspondingly, supplies expense would be overstated by that same amount. The required adjusting entry would therefore be

(b)

| 12/31 | Supplies inventory | $2,000 | |
|---|---|---|---|
| |     Supplies expense | | $2,000 |

**To adjust the inventory and expense accounts for the excess of the physical count over the balance in the inventory account.**

| Supplies inventory | | Supplies expense | |
|---|---|---|---|
| Bal. 1/1   1,000 | | (a)   4,000 | (b)   2,000 |
| (b)      2,000 | | var. | 12/31 |
| 12/31 | | dates | |

The adjusted balances would, of course, be in accord with those derived by the other two methods.

The three alternatives are of significance for two primary reasons. First, they are illustrative of the flexibility of the double-entry system. Identical events can be accounted for in a variety of ways. If a firm deems it too inconvenient or costly to keep its books and records perpetually up to date—that is, to record immediately every financial event that is worthy of accounting recognition—it can readily make periodic adjustments whenever current information is needed.

Second, the three alternatives are demonstrative of the intrinsic relationships between balance sheet and income statement accounts. For almost all income statement (*flow*) accounts there are corresponding balance sheet (*storage*) accounts. Among the expenses, cost of goods sold is related to inventory; interest expense is related to either prepaid interest (an asset) or accrued interest payable (a liability). Depreciation is related to fixed assets such as buildings or equipment. Similarly, among the revenues, sales revenue is related to either accounts receivable or to "unearned" or "deferred" revenue (e.g., airline tickets sold but services not yet provided); rent revenue is related to either rent receivable or to "unearned" rent (i.e., rent received in advance).

**a warning**   In making either updating or adjusting entries, neophyte accountants are often unsure of the accounts to be adjusted. Although it may be obvious that one account must be corrected, they are unsure of the corresponding half of the entry. There is a temptation, in the face of uncertainty, to debit or credit either "cash" or "retained earnings." In fact, neither is likely to be affected by periodic adjustments. "Cash" needs to be debited or credited only upon the actual receipt or disbursement of cash. Indeed, unless the student can actually envision a transfer of cash—by check, in currency, or by notification of credits or charges by the bank—he can be reasonably certain that it is not "cash" that should be debited or credited. Similarly, retained earnings in the ordinary course of business are affected directly by only two types of events: the declaration of a dividend and the posting of year-end closing entries. Most updating or adjusting entries affect either an asset or liability account and its related revenue or expense account.

## Year-End Adjustments—An Example

Exhibit 4-1 indicates the December 31, 1981 trial balance of the Altoona Appliance Company, a retail store, before year-end adjustments have been made. Available to the accountant in charge of preparing annual financial statements is the additional information described below which requires accounting recognition.

**unexpired insurance**   The prepaid insurance indicated on the trial balance represents the unexpired portion of a three-year policy purchased in 1980. No insurance expense ($2,000 per year) has yet been charged for 1981.

**(a)**

| | | |
|---|---|---|
| Insurance expense | $2,000 | |
| Prepaid insurance | | $2,000 |

**To record the expiration of one-third of a three-year policy.**

**depreciation**   The company charges depreciation semiannually, June 30 and December 31. The building, which originally cost $45,000, is being depreciated over a 30-year period; furniture and fixtures, which originally cost $4,700, are being depreciated over a 10-year period. Depreciation charges for a full year would be $1,500 and $470, respectively—for a half-year, $750 and $235.*

## EXHIBIT 4-1

**Altoona Appliance Company**
**Trial Balance**
**December 31, 1981**

| | Debits | Credits |
|---|---|---|
| Cash | $ 10,500 | |
| Accounts receivable | 43,750 | |
| Allowance for uncollectible accounts | | $ 4,500 |
| Merchandise inventory | 65,200 | |
| Prepaid insurance | 4,000 | |
| Supplies inventory | 500 | |
| Land | 10,000 | |
| Building | 45,000 | |
| Accumulated depreciation, building | | 11,000 |
| Furniture and fixtures | 4,700 | |
| Accumulated depreciation, furniture and fixtures | | 1,410 |
| Notes receivable | 2,000 | |
| Accounts payable | | 17,000 |
| Sales taxes payable | | 200 |
| Advances from customers | | 500 |
| Dividends payable | | 1,200 |
| Common stock | | 25,000 |
| Retained earnings | | 87,365 |
| Sales revenue | | 330,200 |
| Gain on sale of furniture and fixtures | | 1,200 |
| Cost of goods sold | 217,900 | |
| Wages and salaries | 56,700 | |
| Delivery and shipping charges | 3,350 | |
| Depreciation expense | 1,285 | |
| Property taxes | 180 | |
| Supplies expense | 940 | |
| Other expenses | 3,570 | |
| Income taxes | 10,000 | |
| | $479,575 | $479,575 |

*Note that the amount to be charged for the second half of the year is less than that charged for the first ($1,285 per "depreciation expense" on the trial balance). As indicated by the account "gain on sale of furniture and fixtures," some fixed assets must have been sold during the year.

**(b)**

| | | |
|---|---|---|
| Depreciation expense | $985 | |
| Accumulated depreciation, building | | $750 |
| Accumulated depreciation, furniture and fixtures | | $235 |

**To record depreciation for one-half year.**

**interest earned**   The note receivable, $2,000, is a one-year note and was received from a customer on November 1, 1981. The note bears a rate of interest of 12 percent. Interest is payable at the expiration of the note. Accounting recognition must, however, be given to interest earned in the two months in 1981 during which the company held the note. Interest earned would be two-twelfths of 12 percent of $2,000–$40.

**(c)**

| | | |
|---|---|---|
| Accrued interest receivable | $40 | |
| Interest revenue | | $40 |

**To record the interest earned but not yet collected.**

**property taxes**   The company makes property tax payments once a year, on January 31. Total taxes payable on January 31, 1982 will be $2,280. Accounting recognition must be given to that portion—eleven-twelfths—of the total amount payable applicable to the current year. Tax expense for 1981, to be added to the expense applicable to January 1981 which was recorded when the previous tax bill was paid, is, therefore, $2,090.

11/12 % 2280

**(d)**

| | | |
|---|---|---|
| Property taxes (expense) | $2,090 | |
| Accrued property taxes payable | | $2,090 |

**To record the portion of property taxes due in 1982 applicable to 1981.**

**supplies**   A physical count indicated supplies on hand of $300. Supplies purchased during the year were charged entirely to supplies expense. The supplies inventory account must be credited by $200 to reflect the difference between the current balance in the account ($500 per the trial balance) and actual supplies in stock.

500 | 200
300

**(e)**

| | | |
|---|---|---|
| Supplies expense | $200 | |
| Supplies inventory | | $200 |

**To adjust the accounts to reflect the physical count of supplies on hand.**

**wages and salaries** The company pays its employees every two weeks. At year end employees had worked four days for which they will not be paid until the first payday of the new year. Wages and salaries applicable to the four-day period totaled $1,090.

**(f)**

| | |
|---|---|
| Wages and salaries (expense) | $1,090 |
|     Accrued wages and salaries payable | $1,090 |

**To record wages and salaries earned by employees but not yet paid.**

**inventory shortage** The company maintains its merchandise inventory on a *perpetual* basis. Each time an item is sold an entry is made in which merchandise inventory is relieved of the cost of the item sold, and cost of goods sold is charged for the same amount. Thus, at year end, the amount recorded in the accounts should be in agreement with that actually on hand. However, an actual count of merchandise on hand revealed an unexplained shortage of $600. The shortage, of course, requires accounting recognition.

**(g)**

| | |
|---|---|
| Inventory shortage (expense) | $600 |
|     Merchandise inventory | $600 |

**To adjust the accounts to reflect the physical count of merchandise on hand.**

**income taxes** Based on a preliminary computation, income taxes (both state and federal) for the year will total $15,500. To date, the company has, in compliance with the law, made payments, based on quarterly reports of earnings, of $10,000. The company now estimates that additional payments of $5,500 will be required. Although such payments need not be made until March 15, 1982, they represent an expense of the current year, 1981.

**(h)**

| | |
|---|---|
| Income taxes (expense) | $5,500 |
|     Accrued income taxes payable | $5,500 |

**To record additional income tax expense based on preliminary computation.**

Exhibit 4–2 depicts the affected accounts of the company after the above transactions have been posted. Exhibit 4–3 depicts a trial balance derived from the adjusted accounts; Exhibit 4–4 illustrates the income statement and balance sheet developed from the adjusted trial balance. Notice, however, that the retained earnings indicated on the balance sheet are those per the adjusted trial balance *plus* income for the year. Until the closing entries are prepared and posted, the balance in the retained earnings account indicates only the beginning balance, less any dividends declared during the year that might have served to reduce retained earnings directly.

The closing entries transfer amounts in the revenue and expense accounts to their *parent* account, retained earnings. Conceptually, they cannot be made until after the income statement has been prepared; otherwise the balances in all revenue and expense accounts would be zero.

## EXHIBIT 4-2

**General Ledger Accounts (Only Those Affected by Adjusting Entries)**

Accrued interested receivable

| (c) | 40 | |
|-----|----|--|
| | (40) | |

Prepaid insurance

| Bal. | 4,000 | (a) | 2,000 |
|------|-------|-----|-------|
| | (2,000) | | |

Supplies inventory

| Bal. | 500 | (e) | 200 |
|------|-----|-----|-----|
| | (300) | | |

Merchandise inventory

| Bal. | 65,200 | (g) | 600 |
|------|--------|-----|-----|
| (64,600) | | | |

Accumulated depreciation, building

| | | Bal. | 11,000 |
|--|--|------|--------|
| | | (b) | 750 |
| | | | (11,750) |

Accumulated depreciation, furniture and fixtures

| | | Bal. | 1,410 |
|--|--|------|-------|
| | | (b) | 235 |
| | | | (1,645) |

EXHIBIT 4-2 (cont.)

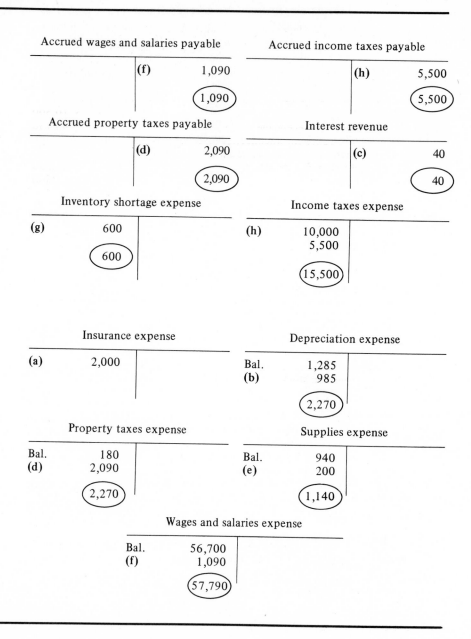

Accrued wages and salaries payable

| | |
|---|---|
| (f) | 1,090 |
| | (1,090) |

Accrued income taxes payable

| | |
|---|---|
| (h) | 5,500 |
| | (5,500) |

Accrued property taxes payable

| | |
|---|---|
| (d) | 2,090 |
| | (2,090) |

Interest revenue

| | |
|---|---|
| (c) | 40 |
| | (40) |

Inventory shortage expense

| | |
|---|---|
| (g) | 600 |
| (600) | |

Income taxes expense

| | |
|---|---|
| (h) | 10,000 |
| | 5,500 |
| (15,500) | |

Insurance expense

| | |
|---|---|
| (a) | 2,000 |

Depreciation expense

| | |
|---|---|
| Bal. | 1,285 |
| (b) | 985 |
| (2,270) | |

Property taxes expense

| | |
|---|---|
| Bal. | 180 |
| (d) | 2,090 |
| (2,270) | |

Supplies expense

| | |
|---|---|
| Bal. | 940 |
| (e) | 200 |
| (1,140) | |

Wages and salaries expense

| | |
|---|---|
| Bal. | 56,700 |
| (f) | 1,090 |
| (57,790) | |

EXHIBIT 4-3

**Altoona Appliance Company**
**Adjusted Trial Balance**
**December 31, 1981**

| | Debits | Credits |
|---|---|---|
| Cash | $ 10,500 | |
| Accounts receivable | 43,750 | |
| Allowance for uncollectible accounts | | $ 4,500 |
| Accrued interest receivable | 40 | |
| Merchandise inventory | 64,600 | |
| Prepaid insurance | 2,000 | |
| Supplies inventory | 300 | |
| Land | 10,000 | |
| Building | 45,000 | |
| Accumulated depreciation, building | | 11,750 |
| Furniture and fixtures | 4,700 | |
| Accumulated depreciation, furniture and fixtures | | 1,645 |
| Notes receivable | 2,000 | |
| Accounts payable | | 17,000 |
| Sales taxes payable | | 200 |
| Advances from customers | | 500 |
| Accrued property taxes payable | | 2,090 |
| Accrued wages and salaries payable | | 1,090 |
| Accrued income taxes payable | | 5,500 |
| Dividends payable | | 1,200 |
| Common stock | | 25,000 |
| Retained earnings | | 87,365 |
| Sales revenue | | 330,200 |
| Interest revenue | | 40 |
| Gain on sale of furniture and fixtures | | 1,200 |
| Cost of goods sold | 217,900 | |
| Wages and salaries expense | 57,790 | |
| Delivery shipping charges | 3,350 | |
| Depreciation expense | 2,270 | |
| Property taxes | 2,270 | |
| Supplies expense | 1,140 | |
| Insurance expense | 2,000 | |
| Inventory shortage | 600 | |
| Income taxes expense | 15,500 | |
| Other expenses | 3,570 | |
| | $489,280 | $489,280 |

# EXHIBIT 4-4

**Altoona Appliance Company**

## Income Statement
### for the Year Ended December 31, 1981

| | | |
|---|---:|---:|
| Revenues | | |
| Sales | | $330,200 |
| Interest | | 40 |
| Gain on sale of furniture and fixtures | | 1,200 |
| Total revenue | | $331,440 |
| Expenses | | |
| Cost of goods sold | 217,900 | |
| Wages and salaries expense | 57,790 | |
| Delivery and shipping charges | 3,350 | |
| Depreciation expense | 2,270 | |
| Property tax expense | 2,270 | |
| Supplies expense | 1,140 | |
| Insurance expense | 2,000 | |
| Inventory shortage expense | 600 | |
| Other expenses | 3,570 | |
| Total expenses | | 290,890 |
| Income before taxes | | $ 40,550 |
| Income taxes | | 15,500 |
| Net income | | $ 25,050 |

## Balance Sheet December 31, 1981

### Assets

| | | |
|---|---:|---:|
| Current assets | | |
| Cash | | $ 10,500 |
| Accounts receivable | $43,750 | |
| Less: Allowance for bad debts | 4,500 | 39,250 |
| Accrued interest receivable | | 40 |
| Merchandise inventory | | 64,600 |
| Supplies inventory | | 300 |
| Prepaid insurance | | 2,000 |
| Total current assets | | $116,690 |
| Noncurrent assets | | |
| Land | | $ 10,000 |
| Building | $45,000 | |
| Less: Accumulated depreciation | 11,750 | 33,250 |
| Furniture and fixtures | 4,700 | |
| Less: Accumulated depreciation | 1,645 | 3,055 |
| Notes receivable | | 2,000 |
| Total noncurrent assets | | $ 48,305 |
| Total assets | | $164,995 |

### Liabilities and Stockholders' Equity

| | | |
|---|---:|---:|
| Current liabilities | | |
| Accounts payable | | $ 17,000 |
| Sales tax payable | | 200 |
| Advances from customers | | 500 |
| Accrued property taxes payable | | 2,090 |
| Accrued wages and salaries payable | | 1,090 |
| Accrued income taxes payable | | 5,500 |
| Dividends payable | | 1,200 |
| Total liabilities | | $ 27,580 |
| Stockholders' equity | | |
| Common stock | | $ 25,000 |
| Retained earnings | | 112,415 |
| Total stockholders' equity | | $137,415 |
| Total liabilities and stockholders' equity | | $164,995 |

Appropriate closing entries for the Altoona Appliance Company would be

| | | |
|---|---|---|
| Sales revenue | $330,200 | |
| Gain on sale of furniture and fixtures | 1,200 | |
| Interest revenue | 40 | |
| Retained earnings | | $331,440 |

**To close the revenue accounts.**

| | | |
|---|---|---|
| Retained earnings | $306,390 | |
| Cost of goods sold | | $217,900 |
| Wages and salaries | | 57,790 |
| Delivery and shipping charges | | 3,350 |
| Depreciation | | 2,270 |
| Property taxes | | 2,270 |
| Supplies expense | | 1,140 |
| Other expenses | | 3,570 |
| Income taxes | | 15,500 |
| Inventory shortage | | 600 |
| Insurance expense | | 2,000 |

**To close the expense accounts.**

A trial balance struck after the closing entries had been posted would, of course, be composed entirely of balance sheet accounts.

## Errors and Omissions

Accountants do, unfortunately, make errors. An examination of some common types of errors and their impact on financial reports provides additional insight into the accounting process.

Some errors are readily detectable. If an entry to a journal is made in which the debits do not equal the credits, or if incorrect amounts are posted to the ledger accounts, then when a trial balance is struck the sum of the general ledger debits may not equal the sum of the credits.

Other errors, most particularly those related to updating or adjusting entries, are less readily detectable and are likely to impact upon both balance sheet and income statement accounts. Many such errors are, however, *self-correcting* over time. They will automatically be eliminated either upon the liquidation of the offending asset or liability or when other routine adjustments to the accounts are made. Unfortunately, though, the errors may affect the financial reports of one or more intervening accounting periods, and for parties who relied upon the erroneous statements all that ends well may not, in fact, *be* well.

Consider a firm that maintains its inventory records on a periodic basis.

The firm physically counts merchandise on hand at the end of each fiscal year. During the year it maintains accurate records of all purchases. In determining the cost of goods sold for the year, it computes goods available for sale (beginning inventory plus purchases during the year) and subtracts goods that remained unsold at the end of the year (ending inventory). If beginning inventory were $3,000, purchases were $30,000, and ending inventory were $6,000, then cost of goods sold during the year would be $27,000:

| | | |
|---|---|---|
| Beginning inventory | $ 3,000 | |
| Purchases | 30,000 | $33,000 |
| Ending inventory | | (6,000) |
| Cost of goods sold | | $27,000 |

If in the following year, purchases were $35,000 and ending inventory were $2,000, then cost of goods sold would be $39,000:

| | | |
|---|---|---|
| Beginning inventory (same as ending inventory of previous year) | $ 6,000 | |
| Purchases | 35,000 | $41,000 |
| Ending inventory | | 2,000 |
| Cost of goods sold | | $39,000 |

Suppose, however, that at the end of the first year the firm miscounted its inventory. Instead of $6,000, the firm counted goods on hand of $5,000. As a result of the miscount, cost of goods sold during the first year would have been reported as $28,000—*overstated* by $1,000. In the second year, the *beginning inventory* would have been understated by $1,000. As a result, cost of goods sold for the second year (assuming a correct count at the end of the second year) would have been reported at $38,000—*understated* by $1,000.

| | Year 1 | | Year 2 | |
|---|---|---|---|---|
| Beginning inventory | $ 3,000 | | $ 5,000 *under* | |
| Purchases | 30,000 | $33,000 | 35,000 | $40,000 |
| Ending inventory | | *under* (5,000) | | (2,000) |
| Cost of goods sold | *over* | $28,000 | *under* | $38,000 |

Cost of goods sold—and thus income—would be correctly stated for the two-year period combined but incorrectly stated for each of the two individual periods.

Both current assets (inventory) and retained earnings would be in error after the first year, but correct after the second.

Consider also a firm that received a two-year, $1,000 note in June 1979. The note carried an interest rate of 14 percent. Interest was receivable annually each June; the principal, in its entirety, was due from the borrower at the expiration of the note in June 1981.

If the firm made proper adjusting entries, then revenue from the note would be $70 in 1979 (six months' interest), $140 in 1980 (one year's interest), and $70 in 1981 (six months' interest)—regardless of when cash payments were received. Suppose, however, that the firm neglected to "accrue" interest at the end of 1979 and instead recognized revenue only upon the receipt of cash. For the year ended 1979, revenues, current assets (accrued interest receivable), and retained earnings each would be understated by $70. For the year ended 1980, revenues would be correctly stated, as the firm would have recorded $140 interest revenue upon the receipt of the cash interest payment. However, since the cash payment represented interest for the period June 1979 to June 1980, current assets, and thus retained earnings, would still be understated by $70—the interest for the period June 1980 to December 1980. For the year ended 1981, however, revenues would be *overstated* by $70, as the entire cash interest payment of $140 would be recorded as revenue. Current assets (accrued interest receivable would be zero) however, would now be correctly stated; so, too, would retained earnings.

Although in the *long run* many errors may be self-correcting, a primary purpose of accounting is to report changes in the welfare of an enterprise in the course of specific, relatively short periods of time. Accountants are not permitted the luxury of allowing the passage of the years to compensate for their errors and omissions.

## Cost of Goods Sold

It has been previously pointed out that, in accordance with the accrual concept, costs are *capitalized* as assets until the intended services are actually provided. But what are such services, and when are they provided? In a business enterprise costs are incurred in order to generate revenues. Hence costs should be recognized as expenses at the same time that the benefits that they produce are recognized as revenues. In other words, costs should be *matched* with revenues.

In a retail sales operation the major cost incurred in the generation of revenue is that of the goods to be sold. As the goods to be sold are received, their cost is *stored* in an asset account, "merchandise inventory." Only when they are actually sold, and when sales revenue is recognized, is the cost of the goods sold charged as an expense. At the time of sale (or if a periodic inventory method is followed, then at least in the period of sale) the following entry is made:

| | |
|---|---|
| Cost of goods sold (expense) | xxxx |
| Merchandise inventory (asset) | xxxx |

It follows that in a manufacturing operation all costs of producing the goods intended for sale should also be stored as assets until the goods are actually sold. This means that not only should costs of raw materials be capitalized as assets, but so too must costs of labor, maintenance, machines used (i.e., depreciation), and all other costs that can readily be identified with the production process.

When raw materials are purchased, their cost is charged initially to an asset account, "raw materials." As they are placed in production, their cost is transferred to "work in process," another asset account, and when the goods are completed their cost is transferred to "finished goods," also an asset account.

This is also true with labor. Although labor, unlike raw materials, cannot be physically stored, the *cost* of labor, like the cost of raw materials, *can* be stored in an asset *account*. Labor costs are conventionally recorded initially in an asset account, "labor," and then transferred immediately (since labor cannot be physically stored) to "work in process." The labor account, although perhaps unnecessary since the costs are transferred immediately to work in process, is ordinarily maintained inasmuch as it facilitates cost control by providing management with a record of labor costs incurred.

So also with other manufacturing costs. Even that portion of manufacturing equipment considered to be consumed in the accounting period must be capitalized as part of the cost of the goods produced. The equipment serves to benefit the periods in which the goods that it has been used to produce are actually sold. Costs of using up the equipment (i.e., depreciation) must be added to work in process (an asset account) and thereby included in the cost of the finished goods. They will be charged as an expense (as part of cost of goods sold) when the finished goods are actually sold.

The manufacturing cycle is depicted graphically in Exhibit 4–5. The key point that the exhibit illustrates is that cost of goods sold represents a conglomerate of several different types of costs. All such costs, even those of services that contribute to the value of the product but that cannot be physically stored (labor and utility costs, for example) are accumulated and retained in asset accounts (such as factory labor, work in process, and finished goods) until the time of sale. Upon sale, when the goods are transferred to a customer, an asset account (finished goods) is reduced (credited) by the cost to manufacture the goods sold and an expense (cost of goods sold) is increased (debited).

*EXHIBIT 4-5*

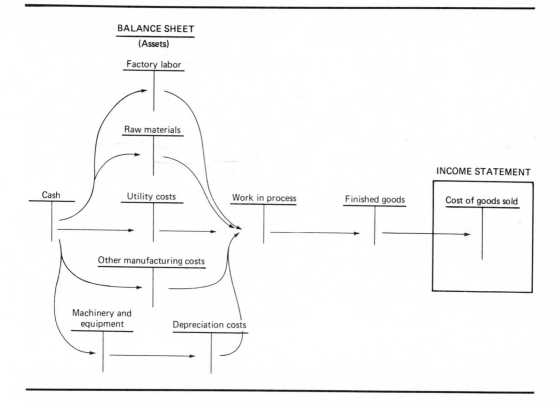

## Product vs. Period Costs

**principle of matching**

Accountants make frequent reference to a *principle of matching*—one that provides that insofar as practical all costs should be associated with particular revenues and recorded as expenses in the same periods in which the related revenues are given accounting recognition. Costs that are associated with revenues to be recognized in the future are to be maintained in asset accounts until such time as recognition is accorded the revenues and the costs can properly be charged as expenses.

Expenses have been defined as the goods or services consumed in the creation of revenues. Indeed, *all* expenses are incurred in the hope of generating revenues. If the accountant's objective of determining periodic income is to be best served, then all costs incurred by the firm should be capitalized as assets —i.e., charged initially to "work in process" or otherwise added to the cost of goods held in inventory—and recorded as expenses only as the goods are actually sold. Costs of borrowing necessary funds (interest), administering the home office, and selling the products contribute as much to the generation of revenue as those of manufacturing products. Logically, such costs should also be added to the cost of goods manufactured.

In practice, however, many types of costs are not capitalized as assets. Instead they are charged as expenses in the period in which they incur, regardless of when the products are sold. The logical inconsistency of capitalizing some costs but not others has by no means been lost upon accountants. They have yielded to practical exigencies, however. It is simply too difficult to associate meaningfully—to match—certain expenses with specific revenues.

Consider, for example, costs of administration—the salaries of officers, secretaries, computer operators, and accountants; the fees paid to outside attorneys and auditors; the costs of renting office space and equipment. If a firm manufactured numerous types of products, it would be difficult, to say the least, to *allocate* such costs to specific products. Or consider sales costs. A salesman might make numerous calls on customers before he receives an order. Is it possible, in any meaningful way, to associate costs of the unsuccessful calls with specific revenues to be generated in the future? Or take interest costs. Funds borrowed benefit the entire company. Can the costs of borrowing be reasonably identified with sales of specific products?

**conventions**   In an effort to reduce the need to make knotty allocation decisions, accountants have adopted certain conventions as to which types of costs should be added to the cost of the product and which should be charged off as expenses in the period in which they are incurred. Although there is by no means universal agreement on the conventions, as a general rule, *direct* manufacturing costs, such as factory labor and raw materials, are always charged to the product (i.e., included in "work in process"). So are several types of *indirect* costs such as depreciation on manufacturing equipment, factory utility costs, rent on the factory building, and salaries of employees who are directly concerned with manufacturing operations. On the other hand, costs of selling, advertising and promotion, interest, employee health and recreational facilities, most taxes, and most other "home office" costs are ordinarily considered to be *period* costs, which are charged as expenses as incurred.

The widely followed conventions do not, by any means, eliminate the need to allocate common costs to specific products. *Factory overhead* costs (those which cannot readily be identified with specific products), such as supervision, utilities, maintenance, and rent, must still be assigned on the basis of the best judgment of accountants. And, as a consequence of the conventions, seemingly similar types of costs are sometimes accorded different accounting treatment. Depreciation on tables or chairs in a factory is considered to be a product cost; that on table or chairs in the home office is considered to be a period cost; salaries of accounting clerks who are concerned specifically with factory-related accounts are included among product costs; those of accounting clerks who deal with other types of accounts are included as period costs.

**impact on financial statements**  In evaluating whether to include a specific cost as a product or a period cost, one relevant question must always be raised: What would be the impact on both the income statement and the balance sheet of alternative classifications?

If within a given accounting period the enterprise sells the *same* number of goods that it produces (assuming no change in per unit costs from one period to the next), then it makes no difference whether a cost is classified as a product or a period cost. Suppose, for example, the salary of an accounting clerk were $12,000 in a given year. During the year the firm produces and sells 12,000 units. If the salary were considered a period cost, then $12,000 would be reported as an expense among "administrative" expenses; if it were considered a product cost, then $12,000 would first be capitalized as "work in process," then transferred to "finished goods inventory" and finally reported as an expense, in the same period, "cost of goods sold."

If the enterprise sells *fewer* goods than it produces, then reported expenses would be *greater* if the costs were categorized as period cost than if they were treated as product costs. Assume the same firm produces 12,000 units but sells only 10,000 units. If the $12,000 salary of the accounting clerk were classified as a period cost, then the full $12,000 would be charged off as an expense. If, however, it were classified as a product cost, then $1 ($12,000 divided by the number of units produced) would be added to the cost of each unit produced. Since 10,000 units were sold, only $10,000 would be included among costs of goods sold. The remaining $2,000 would be *stored* on the balance sheet, included in "finished goods inventory." Hence current assets, specifically inventory, would be $2,000 greater than if the salary were accounted for as a period cost.

If the enterprise sells more goods than it produces, then the reverse would be true. Reported expenses would be less if certain costs were treated as period rather than as product costs. Assume that in the following year the firm produces 12,000 units but sells 14,000 units, taking the additional 2,000 units from inventory. If the accounting clerk's salary were treated as a period cost, then, as previously, the $12,000 would be reported as an expense. But if it were treated as a product cost, $14,000 of salary costs would be charged off as expense—$1 per unit produced and sold in the current period (12,000 units) plus $1 per unit of the goods sold in the current period but produced in the previous period (2,000 units).

## Basic Books of Account

The basic accounting information processing system is simple and straightforward. Relatively few books and records need be maintained or prepared—

regardless of the size of the business enterprise and irrespective of whether or not the system will be manually or electronically maintained.

The fundamental means of giving accounting recognition to financial events or transactions is the journal entry. Journal entries, as their name implies, are transcribed in journals. Journals are nothing more than books appropriately ruled and designed to facilitate two-sided entries of the type illustrated throughout the text. Journal entries are ordinarily prepared from source documents, such as invoices (bills), payment vouchers (internal documents authorizing disbusements), receiving or shipping reports, remittance advices (documents indicating the receipt of cash), and credit memoranda (documents authorizing that a customer be given credit for merchandise damaged or returned, or special allowances or discounts to which he may be entitled).

Journal entires are *posted* to the *general ledger,* a book in which the current status of all balance sheet and income statement accounts are maintained. General ledger accounts are represented in this text by T accounts. Posting involves nothing more than transcribing the entries from the journals to the appropriate accounts.

**special journals**

Although conceptually there is need for only a single or *general* journal in which to record transactions, in practice, most firms find that record keeping is facilitated by several supplementary, often called special, journals. Since a firm may enter into numerous transactions which affect identical accounts, it is relatively easy to combine such transactions into a single journal entry and periodically make but one entry into the accounts affected. Supplementary journals enable the firm to do just that. Most firms, for example, maintain a sales journal. The sales journal may be designed as follows:

**Sales Journal**

| Date | Purchaser | Sales (Cr) | Cash (Dr) | Accounts receivable (Dr) |
|------|-----------|------------|-----------|--------------------------|
|      |           |            |           |                          |
|      |           |            |           |                          |
|      |           |            |           |                          |

As each sale is made, the accounting clerk enters the name of the customer to whom the sale was made; enters the amount of the sale in the column "Sales (Credit)"; the amount of cash received, if any, in the column "Cash (Debit)"; and enters the difference between the amount of sale and the amount of cash received in the column "Accounts Receivable (Debit)." At the end of each month, the columns would be totaled. Then either the following entry would be made in the general journal or the amounts posted would be directed to the appropriate general ledger accounts:

| | | |
|---|---|---|
| Cash | xxxx | |
| Accounts receivable | xxxx | |
| Sales | | xxxx |

Similarly, a firm might maintain a *cash receipts book* and a *cash disbursements book,* both of which are also supplementary journals. One column would indicate the amount of cash received or disbursed; other columns would be reserved for the accounts that would most frequently represent the corresponding side of the journal entry. As with the sales journal, the columns would be periodically totaled and either a single summary entry would be made in the general journal or the totals would be posted directly to the general ledger accounts affected.

**subsidiary ledgers**  A firm almost always finds it necessary to keep records of each customer from whom it holds a receivable, each fixed asset owned, and each supplier to whom it is indebted. But it would obviously necessitate a general ledger of massive proportions if separate accounts were maintained for each customer, supplier, or fixed asset. Instead, most firms maintain, in the general ledger, *control accounts* that summarize the numerous individual accounts. Control accounts might be maintained for accounts receivable, accounts payable, and fixed assets, among others. The individual accounts would be maintained in *subsidiary ledgers.* Obviously the sum of the balances in a subsidiary ledger must equal the balance in the general ledger control account for which the subsidiary ledger provides support. Each time an entry is made to the general ledger control account, one or more entries which sum to the amount debited or credited to the control account must be made to the subsidiary accounts.

Suppose, for example, that in the course of a month a firm makes sales, all on account, to a number of different customers. In the general ledger the firm would debit accounts receivable for the total amount of the sales. In the accounts receivable subsidiary ledger—which might be a file of cards, one for each customer—the firm would debit the individual accounts of the various customers for the amount of each sale. As the customers paid the balance in their accounts, the firm would credit accounts receivable in the general ledger for the total amount collected within a period and credit the individual accounts for the amount of each remittance.

Insofar as an enterprise maintains a computerized accounting system, the journals or ledgers may not take the precise form illustrated. They would, however, serve the same function and be designed to accommodate the same information.

## Summary

The primary purpose of this chapter has been to explain the accrual concept and to demonstrate some of its many ramifications for accounting practice. The accrual concept requires that the effect of transactions and other financial events on the assets and liabilities of an enterprise be accorded accounting recognition at the time they have their primary economic impact, not necessarily when cash is received or disbursed. Revenues should be assigned to the periods in which they are earned. Costs should be matched to the revenues that they serve to generate and should be charged as expenses in the periods in which accounting recognition is given to such revenues.

The services associated with a cost may be both acquired and paid for in periods other than those in which the revenues to which they must be matched are given accounting recognition. The services provided by supplies, for example, may be acquired (purchased) in one period, consumed in a second, and paid for in a third. The double-entry accounting system provides that costs applicable to services that will benefit future periods may be *stored* in asset accounts and charged as expenses only as the revenues with which they are associated are recognized. Similarly, the obligation for the payment may be maintained in a liability account until such time as the required cash disbursement is actually made.

In order that a measure of bookkeeping convenience may be achieved, accounting records are not always kept up to date. Sometimes, as in the case of supplies, it is more convenient to record the use of supplies periodically rather than each time supplies are consumed. Or, as in the case of rent or interest revenue, the benefits received accrue over time; it would be physically impractical to update the books on an around-the-clock basis. As a consequence, firms must periodically bring the records to a current status by means of updating and adjusting entries.

The manner in which costs are accounted for in a manufacturing operation is another manifestation of the accrual concept and the related principle of matching. All manufacturing costs are maintained in asset accounts (e.g., raw materials, labor, work in process, finished goods) until that period in which they can properly be matched to revenues from the sale of the product and charged as expenses (cost of goods sold).

Conventionally, not all costs are matched directly with specific revenues. The relationships between some costs and revenues are sufficiently indirect that accountants have surrendered to practical exigencies and make no attempt to match certain costs with particular revenues. These costs, often referred to as *period* costs, are charged as expenses in the periods in which they are incurred, regardless of the amount of revenues recognized in that particular period.

A secondary objective of this chapter has been to provide an overview of the major types of books and records maintained by most business enterprises. Firms conventionally maintain two basic books of account: the general journal and the general ledger. Transactions are recorded in the general journal; they are then posted to the accounts that they affect, which are maintained in the general ledger. To facilitate the processing of large numbers of transactions and the maintenance of large numbers of accounts, most firms employ additional journals and ledgers to support and supplement entries in the general journals and ledgers. These are referred to as specialized or subsidiary journals and ledgers.

In the following chapter we shall expand upon the accrual concept and consider the issue of the most appropriate means of recognizing revenue.

*exercise for review and self-testing*  Global Real Estate leases an office building to a corporate tenant for $300,000 per month. As of January 1, 1981, the tenant had paid two months' rent in advance. The firm included among its liabilities "Unearned rent, $600,000."

a. Assuming that the tenant occupied the apartment for 12 months in 1981, how much rent revenue should the firm recognize during the year? Does it matter how much cash the firm collected from the tenant?

b. Prepare a journal entry that the firm should make at the end of January assuming that it received from the tenant no cash during the month.

c. Suppose instead that during 1981 Global Real Estate received a total of $2,400,000 from its tenant. Each time cash was collected, the firm made an entry in the following form:

| | | |
|---|---|---|
| Cash | xxx | |
|     Rent revenue | | xxx |

It made no other entries with respect to rent.
   (1) How much rent revenue should properly have been recognized during the year? By how much is rent revenue understated?
   (2) At year end, what should be the balance in "Unearned rent"?
   (3) What should be the balance in "Rent receivable"?
   (4) Prepare a journal entry to adjust and update the accounts.

d. The firm contracted with a maintenance company to perform cleaning services at a monthly cost of $120,000. At year end, what amounts should the firm report in its income statement account, "Cleaning expense" and its related balance sheet account, either "Cleaning costs payable" or "Prepaid cleaning costs" if it actually made cash payments of
   1. $ 80,000
   2. $140,000
The maintenance company performed its services throughout the entire year.

e. What generalizations can be made with respect to the relationship among services provided or received, revenue or expense accounts, asset or liability accounts, and cash received or disbursed?

## Questions

**review and discussion**

1. What is meant by the accrual method of accounting? How does it differ from the cash method?

2. What are adjusting entries? Why are they necessary?

3. What are *contra accounts?* Why are they used? Where are they reported on the balance sheet?

4. A company charges all purchases of merchandise intended for sale to "cost of goods sold." Is such practice acceptable? What year-end adjusting entry would be necessary to "correct" the accounts?

5. A bookkeeper incorrectly charges a prepayment of January 1980 rent made on December 28, 1979 to "rent expense." What would be the impact of such error on the financial statements of the year ended December 1979 and that ended December 1980?

6. A manager of a manufacturing company noticed that the account "labor cost was included in the general ledger among the asset accounts. In view of the fact that he was unable to visually inspect labor costs he wondered how they could possibly be considered to be an asset. How would you answer him?"

7. What is meant by the *matching principle?* If a company were to recognize revenue upon the collection of cash from the customer rather than upon the delivery of goods, when would you recommend that the cost of the goods sold be charged as an expense?

8. Distinguish between product costs and period costs. How would you defend the position of accountants who claim that depreciation can sometimes be considered a product cost and sometimes a period cost?

9. Suppose that in a particular accounting period a company sells the same number of goods that it produces. Would it make any difference insofar as net income is concerned if depreciation on office equipment used in the factory were considered a product or a period cost? What if the company sells only a portion of the goods that it produces?

10. Give an example of a subsidiary ledger. Why do companies maintain subsidiary ledgers rather than include all accounts in the general ledger?

11. What is meant by a specialized journal? Give examples of several commonly used specialized journals. Why do companies maintain specialized journals?

12. An accountant attempted to prepare both an income statement and a balance sheet from an adjusted trial balance. Closing entries had not yet been made. He was unable, however, to get his balance sheet to balance. Assets exceed liabilities plus owners' equity by an amount exactly equal to income for the year. Which account is most likely in error? Why?

## Problems

1. *Expenses must be given accounting recognition even if invoices have not yet been received.*

As you are getting ready to prepare year-end financial statements you learn that your company has not yet received invoices (bills) for services it received in December. The company estimates that in January it will receive invoices as follows:

| | |
|---|---:|
| From the telephone company | $130 |
| From the gas and electric company | 327 |
| From the outside maintenance service | 100 |

a. Prepare any journal entries that you would consider necessary.
b. Suppose you failed to make such journal entries. What effect would such failure have on income of the year, income of the following year, and current liabilities?

2. *All costs must be divided between the income statement and the balance sheet.*

A firm made the following payments during its first year of operation:

| | |
|---|---:|
| For rent | $12,000 |
| For interest | 8,000 |
| For advertising | 3,000 |
| For manufacturing products | 96,000 |

The firm's accountant has determined that the following amounts should properly be reported as expenses:

| | |
|---|---:|
| Rent expense | $10,000 |
| Interest expense | 7,000 |
| Advertising expense | 6,000 |
| Cost of goods sold | 80,000 |

Determine the amounts that should be reported in balance sheet accounts that correspond to each of the reported expenses.

3. *Costs may be accounted for by three alternatives.*

The December 31, 1981 balance sheet of a company reported accrued interest payable of $3,000 in connection with bonds outstanding of $100,000. Interest, at a rate of 12 percent, is payable semiannually on April 1 and October 1.

Prepare all required journal entries for the next year, including year-end adjusting entries, assuming that cash payments are made when due, if alternatively

1. The company makes appropriate *accrual* entries every three months.
2. The company debits "interest expense" with the full amount of each cash payment.
3. The company debits "accrued interest payable" with the full amount of each cash payment.

4. *Alternative accounting practices can lead to the same results as long as proper end-of-year adjustments are made.*

   Three companies each account for insurance costs differently. Each began the year with a balance of $400 in prepaid insurance costs, which represented two months of insurance remaining on a one-year policy. Upon the expiration of the policy, each renewed for another year, paying $3,600 in cash. The general ledgers of the three companies reported the following balances as of year end, prior to adjustment.

   |  | Company A | Company B | Company C |
   |---|---|---|---|
   | Prepaid insurance | $ 400 | $4,000 | $ 600 |
   | Insurance expense | 3,600 | 0 | 3,400 |

   a. Explain how each of the companies accounts for insurance costs.
   b. Determine the "correct" amounts that should be reported as "Prepaid insurance" and "Insurance expense."
   c. Prepare the adjusting entries, if any, that should be made by each of the firms.

5. *Cost of goods sold is a conglomerate of all costs associated with the manufacture of a product. Convention often determines whether a particular type of cost is to be considered as being associated with the manufacture of a product or with the other activities engaged in by a firm.*

   During March a company incurred the following costs, all of which were related directly to the manufacture of its product:

   | | |
   |---|---|
   | Raw materials | $100,000 |
   | Factory labor | 200,000 |
   | Utility costs for factory | 4,000 |
   | Depreciation on factory equipment | 10,000 |
   | Rent on factory building | 50,000 |

   The company started and completed 10,000 units of product. There was no opening inventory.

   a. How much cost should have been added during the month to "Work in process"?
   b. How much cost should have been transferred to "Finished goods"?
   c. Assume that the company sold 8,000 units. What amount should it report as "Cost of goods sold"? What amount as "Finished goods inventory"?
   d. Assume that at the end of the month the company discovered that it had failed to record the wages of two secretaries. One was employed in the office of the factory, the other in the office of the marketing department. Each was paid $1,500. Comment on how the omission would affect cost of goods sold and finished goods inventory.

6. *Consider the relationship, if any, between revenue earned and cash collected.*

A company holds from a customer a note receivable of $100,000. Interest is payable each month at a rate of 12 percent per year ($1,000 per month). For each of the following independent situations indicate the amounts that the firm should report on its December 31, 1981 financial statements for (1) interest revenue, (2) interest receivable, and (3) unearned interest.

1. The balance in interest receivable as of January 1, 1981 was $2,000. The company collects $12,000 in interest payments.
2. The balance in interest receivable as of January 1, 1981 was $2,000. The company collects $14,000 in interest payments.
3. The balance in interest receivable as of January 1, 1981 was $2,000. The company collects $15,000 in interest payments.
4. The balance in unearned interest (interest paid by the borrower in advance) as of January 1, 1981 was $3,000. The company collects $9,000 in interest payments.
5. The balance in unearned interest as of January 1, 1981 was $3,000. The company collects $8,000 in interest payments.

7. *Costs must be matched with revenues.*

During the first three years of its existence, Bravo Company's manufacturing costs, end-of-year inventories, and sales were as follows:

| Year | Manufacturing Costs | End-of-Year Inventories | Sales |
|------|--------------------|------------------------|-------|
| 1 | $80,000 | $ 80,000 | None |
| 2 | 90,000 | 130,000 | $ 60,000 |
| 3 | 30,000 | None | 250,000 |

Ignoring all other costs and revenues, determine the income of Bravo Company for each of the three years.

8. *The significant economic (and therefore accounting) event is the declaration of a dividend, not the payment. Which event will serve to reduce retained earnings?*

On December 13, 1981, the board of directors of a company declared a dividend of $.75 per share of common stock. The dividend will be payable on January 18, 1982, to the "stockholders of record" (i.e., to those who owned the stock on a particular date) of January 10, 1982. The company has 100,000 shares of common stock outstanding.

a. Prepare an appropriate journal entry to record the declaration of the dividend.
b. Prepare an appropriate closing entry as of December 31, 1981.
c. Prepare an appropriate journal entry to record payment of the dividend.

9. *Does choice of accounting method affect total reported earnings over the life of an enterprise?*

Suppose that a company was organized on January 1, 1970. In each of the next 10 years it had sales of $100,000; the costs of the goods sold were $80,000 per year. In each year, the company collected in cash 75 percent of the sales of that year plus 25 percent of the sales of the previous year. Similarly, in each year the company paid in cash 75 percent of the costs incurred in that year plus 25 percent of the costs incurred in the previous year. The company ceased operations at the end of year 10. It remained in business in year 11 only to collect outstanding receivables and to liquidate remaining debts.

  a. Assuming that the company maintained its accounts on an *accrual* basis, compute total income for the 11-year period. Determine income for each of the 11 individual years.

  b. Assume instead that the company maintained its accounts on a cash basis—i.e., recognized revenues and expenses as cash was received or disbursed. Determine total income for the 11-year period as well as income for each of the 11 individual years.

10. *This exercise reviews the basic entries required to account for depreciable assets.*

  Prepare journal entries to record the following events:
  1. A company purchases two trucks, each for $15,000 cash. The estimated useful life of a truck is five years, after which it has negligible scrap or resale value.
  2. The company records first-year depreciation on the trucks.
  3. At the beginning of the second year, the company sells one of the trucks for $13,000 cash.
  4. The company records second-year depreciation on the remaining truck.
  5. At the beginning of the third year, the company sells the second truck for $8,000 cash.

11. *Should a dance studio recognize revenue when it signs a contract and collects cash or when it provides its services? Which is the more significant economic event?*

  Foxtrot Dance Studio offers customers a "One Year Learn to Dance Special." Customers pay $120 at the time they sign a contract and are entitled to four lessons per month for one year.

  In November, 10 customers signed contracts and paid "tuition" for the series of lessons. In December, each of the customers took four lessons.

  a. Prepare a journal entry to record the sales of the contracts and the collection of the cash.

  b. Prepare any entries that would be appropriate when the customers took their first four lessons in December. (Ignore expenses incurred in connection with the lessons.)

  c. Prepare any *closing* entries that might be necessary at December 31.

12. *Firms do not have to give instantaneous accounting recognition to all economic events (including the passage of time), but prior to preparing financial statements they must bring the books up to date.*

  In each of the following *independent* situations, prepare any necessary journal entries that would be required either to adjust a company's books or to bring them up to date in order to prepare year-end (December 31) financial statements. Assume that closing entries have not yet been made.

1. Property taxes, which amount to $15,000 annually, are payable on the last day of the city's fiscal year, which ends April 30. No property tax accruals have yet been made.
2. Employees are paid each Monday for wages earned during the previous week. December 31 falls on a Wednesday. Weekly payroll (for a five-day work week) is $3,000.
3. As heating oil was purchased it was debited to "fuel expense." As of the end of the year, heating oil which had cost $300 was still on hand.
4. On March 1, the company purchased a one-year fire insurance policy at a cost of $3,600 paid in cash. The entire cost of the policy was charged to "insurance expense."
5. The company is on a periodic inventory basis. After taking year-end inventory and making appropriate adjustments to its accounts it discovered that $400 of inventory was incorrectly omitted from the count.
6. The company is on a periodic inventory basis. After taking year-end inventory and making appropriate adjustments to its accounts it discovered that goods which had cost $1,000 had just recently been purchased. No accounting recognition, however, had been given to either the purchase or the corresponding liability for payment. (Note that since the adjustment to the accounts resulting from the physical inventory count had already been made, the inventory account is *properly* stated.)
7. The company ran an advertisement in the December 30th edition of the local newspaper. The company has not yet received a bill for such advertisement or given it any other accounting recognition. The cost of the advertisement was $250.
8. The company is on a periodic inventory basis. After taking year-end inventory and making appropriate adjustments to its accounts it discovered that a purchase of equipment was incorrectly debited to "inventory" rather than to "equipment." The cost of the equipment was $2,100. (The *physical* count was correctly taken.)
9. On June 1 the company borrowed $10,000 from a bank. It paid the entire interest for one year ($1,200) in advance at the time it signed the note. The advance payment of interest was properly recorded, but no entries pertaining to the interest have been made since the date of payment.
10. On November 1 customers placed orders for merchandise with a selling price of $15,000. The customers paid in advance, and their payment was properly recorded. The goods were delivered on December 29, but no accounting recognition has been given to the delivery. The company uses a periodic inventory method, and the goods were not included in the December 31 inventory count.

**13.** *Incorrect journal entries can subsequently be corrected.*

As you were about to prepare year-end financial statements, the journal entries indicated below, which were made by an inexperienced bookkeeper, came to your attention. You are to make the journal entries that would be required to correct the errors. (*Hint:* First determine the entry that should

have been made; then determine the most efficient means of eliminating
the incorrect, and adding the correct, amounts.)

1. A customer made a payment to reduce the balance in his account.

| | | |
|---|---|---|
| Cash | $75 | |
| Sales revenue | | $75 |

2. The company sold for $300 a machine that had originally cost $400
when purchased three years earlier. Accumulated depreciation on the
asset amounted to $200.

| | | |
|---|---|---|
| Cash | $300 | |
| Sales revenue | | $300 |

3. In January the company paid rent for the previous December. Before
preparing the year-end financial statements as of December 31 the
company had correctly accrued rent for December.

| | | |
|---|---|---|
| Rent expense | $500 | |
| Cash | | $500 |

4. The company charged depreciation of one year on equipment that had
cost $6,000 and had a useful life of three years with no salvage value.

| | | |
|---|---|---|
| Allowance for depreciation | $2,000 | |
| Depreciation expense | | $2,000 |

5. The company paid a bill received from its advertising agency for an ad
that it had run the previous year. The company had properly accounted
for the ad at the time it was run.

| | | |
|---|---|---|
| Advertising expense | $675 | |
| Cash | | $675 |

6. The company paid $130 to Cooks Auto Service for repairs to one of its
trucks. It had given no previous accounting recognition to the repair
costs.

| | | |
|---|---|---|
| Fixed assets, autos and trucks | $130 | |
| Accounts receivable | | $130 |

14. *The effects of classifying a cost as a product rather than a period cost will
depend upon the relationship between number of units produced and
number of units sold.*

The president of a corporation is uncertain as to whether certain administrative, transportation, and depreciation costs should be classified as *product*

or *period* costs. Such costs average approximately $120,000 per year. He asks your advice as to the significance over the next two years of his decision. Labor and material costs are estimated at $6 per unit. Selling price of the product is $10 per unit.

a. Suppose that in both year 1 and year 2 the company expects to produce and sell 40,000 units per year. What would be the resulting differences in (1) income, (2) ending inventory, and (3) retained earnings for (or after) each of the two years if the company classified the costs as period rather than product costs?

b. Suppose instead that the company expected in year 1 to produce 40,000 units but sell only 30,000 units and in year 2 to produce 30,000 units and sell 40,000 units. What would be the resultant differences in (1) income, (2) ending inventory, and (3) retained earnings for (or after) each of the two years if the company classified the costs as period rather than product costs?

15. *Many companies charge (debit) an account called "Purchases" for all acquisitions of merchandise inventory (instead of debiting "Merchandise inventory"). This practice is acceptable but requires that an adjusting entry be made at year end to eliminate the balance in the purchases account.*

Examination of a company's general ledger as of the end of the year reveals the following account balances (both debit balances) pertaining to merchandise inventory:

| | |
|---|---|
| Inventory | $100,000 |
| Purchases | 600,000 |

Upon inquiry, you learn that the balance in inventory represents that at the *beginning* of the year. No entries were made to that account during the year. All purchases during the year were debited to "Purchases." You also learn that a physical count at the end of the year revealed goods on hand of $60,000.

What adjusting entry would you propose assuming that you want to eliminate the balance in the purchases account, to have the inventory account reflect the correct balance of goods on hand at year end, and to have a cost of goods sold account reveal the cost of merchandise sold during the year?

16. *A company can report a profit yet still experience a reduction in cash.*

Comparative balance sheets for Black's Men's Shop for the years 1981 and 1982 are presented in the table following. Also presented is an income statement for 1982. All sales were recorded initially as charge sales. All purchases of merchandise were made "on account."

a. Compute the amount of cash collectons made in 1982 as a result of either current year or prior year sales. Be sure to relate sales to accounts receivable (that is, accounts receivable, 12/31/81 + sales − cash collections = accounts receivable, 12/31/82).

b. Compute the amount of cash disbursed in connection with each of the expenses. Be especially careful in computing cash expended, if any, in connection with purchases of inventory and with depreciaton. (*Hint:* Compute first the amount of goods actually purchased.) Be sure to relate each expense to a corresponding asset or liability account (e.g., rent expense to prepaid rent; cost of goods sold to inventory).

c. Does the difference between cash received and cash disbursed equal the difference between cash on hand at the beginning of 1982 and cash on hand at the end? (If not, review your computations.)

d. Comment on why net income cannot be used as a measure of cash received or disbursed.

### Black's Men's Shop
### Balance Sheet

|  | *12/31/81* |  | *12/31/82* |  |
|---|---|---|---|---|
| Cash |  | $ 4,000 |  | $ 3,800 |
| Accounts receivable |  | 28,000 |  | 44,000 |
| Prepaid rent |  | 1,000 |  | – |
| Inventory |  | 17,000 |  | 14,000 |
| Fixed assets | $20,000 |  | $20,000 |  |
| Less: Accumulated depreciation | 4,000 | 16,000 | 8,000 | 12,000 |
| Total assets |  | $66,000 |  | $73,800 |
| Accounts payable |  | $ 2,000 |  | $ 4,000 |
| Accrued salaries payable |  | 3,500 |  | 1,000 |
| Accrued interest payable |  | 200 |  | 100 |
| Accrued rent payable |  | – |  | 2,000 |
| Notes payable |  | 4,800 |  | 4,800 |
| H. Black, capital |  | 55,500 |  | 61,900 |
| Total liabilities and owners' equity |  | $66,000 |  | $73,800 |

### Income Statement
### for the Year Ended 12/31/82

| Sales |  | $220,000 |
|---|---|---|
| Cost of goods sold |  | 130,000 |
| Gross margin |  | $ 90,000 |
| Other expenses: |  |  |
| Salaries | $67,000 |  |
| Interest | 600 |  |
| Rent | 12,000 |  |
| Depreciation | 4,000 | 83,600 |
| Net income |  | $ 6,400 |

17. *Under conventional accounting practices, the greater the number of units produced, the less the cost per unit—and the less the reported cost of goods sold.*

    The Prettyman Doll Co. requires $2 of raw materials and $4 of factory labor to produce each doll. In addition the company estimates that depreciation costs on the factory building and equipment as well as other *fixed* factory costs total $40,000 per year. ("Fixed" factory costs, although considered product costs, do not vary with number of units produced. They would be the same regardless of whether the company produced 10,000 or 50,000 dolls per year.) Sales price per doll is $10.

    a. In both 1981 and 1982 the company produced 20,000 dolls and sold 20,000 dolls. Compute the manufacturing cost per doll. Determine also gross margin (sales less cost of goods sold) for each of the two periods.

    b. Assume instead that in 1981 the company produced 30,000 dolls but sold 20,000 dolls; in 1982 the company produced 10,000 dolls and sold 20,000 dolls. Determine the manufacturing cost per doll in each of the two years. Compute the amount that should be reported as "finished goods inventory" at the end of 1981. Determine also the gross margin for each of the two years.

    c. Suppose the company planned to issue additional capital stock in January 1982. The company controller thought it important that the firm impress potential purchasers with a significant growth in earnings. Based on the above analysis, what steps might the company have taken in 1981 to give the *appearance* of improved performance?

18. *This is a challenging exercise that requires an understanding of the flow of costs in a manufacturing operation.*

    The following table gives information taken from the ledger accounts of the Wright Manufacturing Co. The figures reported are the total amounts debited or credited to the various accounts during the year 1981. The figures do *not* represent ending balances and do *not* include beginning balances. Some amounts have been omitted. Based on your knowledge of the accounting flow in a manufacturing operation, you are to fill in the missing amounts. That is, you are to determine which accounts are normally

|  | Debits | Credits |
|---|---|---|
| Allowance for depreciation (factory) | $    0 | $ 17,000 |
| Depreciation cost (factory) | ? | ? |
| Raw materials inventory | ? | 95,000 |
| Factory labor cost | 107,000 | 107,000 |
| Work in process | ? | ? |
| Finished goods | 212,000 | ? |
| Cost of goods sold | 197,000 | 0 |
| Factory wages payable | 105,000 | ? |
| Accounts payable[a] | 85,000 | 110,000 |

[a]Includes only amounts owed in connection with purchases of raw materials.

associated with debits or credits to other accounts. (For example, by knowing the amount *credited* to accounts payable, you can determine the amount *debited* to raw materials inventory.) No closing entries have yet been made.

19. *Ability to evaluate the effect of errors on the income statement and the balance sheet is persuasive evidence of understanding the double-entry bookkeeping system.*

On December 31, at the end of the 1979 annual accounting period, a book-keeper made the following errors:

1. He failed to record $90 of accrued salaries.
2. A portion of the company's warehouse was rented on December 1, 1979 at $150 per month to a tenant who paid his December, January, and February rents in advance. The bookkeeper did not make an adjustment for the unearned rent on December 31, which had been credited on receipt to the "rent revenue" account.
3. Through an oversight the bookkeeper failed to record $245 of depreciation on store equipment. The equipment had a useful life of an additional five years. Depreciation was properly recorded in 1980, and no equipment was sold in 1980.
4. The bookkeeper failed to accrue one-half year's interest on a note receivable. The $1,000 note was received on July 1, 1978, and was due on June 30, 1980. Interest was at the rate of 6 percent per year, payable each year on June 30.
5. The bookkeeper made an error in adding the amounts on the year-end inventory sheets which caused a $75 understatement in the merchandise inventory. (Inventory on December 31, 1980, was properly stated.)
6. On January 2, 1979, the company purchased a two-year fire insurance policy for $800. The bookkeeper charged the entire amount to "insurance expense."
7. On December 31, 1979, the company declared a dividend of $6,000 payable on January 15, 1980. The bookkeeper failed to record the declaration.
8. The company owned 1,000 shares of General Motors common stock. On December 20, the company received notification from Gooder and Co., the firm's stockbroker, that General Motors had declared and paid a dividend of $1.20 per share. Since Gooder and Co. holds in its own name the shares owned by the company, it credited the company's account for $1,200. The bookkeeper first recorded the dividend in January 1980 when the cash was forwarded to the company.

Under the assumption that none of the errors was explicitly discovered and corrected in 1980 but that some of the errors would automatically be corrected if normal accounting procedures were followed, indicate the effect of each error on the financial statements. In each case, indicate the amount of the overstatement or understatement the error would cause in the assets, liabilities, owners' equity, revenues, expenses, and net income.

If the error would have no effect on an item, then so state. The first one is done for you as an example.

| | 1979 Income Statement | | | December 31, 1979 Balance Sheet | | | 1980 Income Statement | | |
|---|---|---|---|---|---|---|---|---|---|
| *Error* | *Revenues* | *Expense* | *Net income* | *Assets* | *Liabilities* | *Owners' equity* | *Revenues* | *Expense* | *Net income* |
| 1 | None | Under $90 | Over $90 | None | Under $90 | Over $90 | None | Over $90 | Under $90 |

**20.** *This problem provides a review of the accounting cycle from unadjusted trial balance to financial statements.*

The following table gives the unadjusted trial balance of the Coronet Company as of December 31, 1980 as well as selected other information.

**The Coronet Company**
**Unadjusted Trial Balance**
**12/31/80**

| | | |
|---|---|---|
| Cash | $ 3,000 | |
| Accounts receivable | 5,000 | |
| Merchandise inventory | 155,000 | |
| Prepaid rent | 1,500 | |
| Furniture and fixtures | 15,000 | |
| Accumulated depreciation | | $ 6,000 |
| Accounts payable | | 9,000 |
| Notes payable | | 6,000 |
| Sales revenue | | 220,000 |
| Selling expenses | 55,000 | |
| General expenses | 18.000 | |
| Interest expense | 800 | |
| Tax expense | 3,500 | |
| Capital received from stockholders | | 6,000 |
| Retained earnings | | 9,800 |
| | $256,800 | $256,800 |

*Other information:*

1. Interest on the note, at a rate of 12 percent, is due semiannually, April 30 and October 31.
2. Useful life of the furniture and fixtures is five years with no salvage value. No depreciation has yet been recorded for the year.
3. The company employs a periodic inventory system. A physical count at year end indicates merchandise on hand of $24,000.
4. The company last paid its rent on December 1. Such payment was intended to cover the month of December. (Rent expense is included among "general expenses"; the payment was properly recorded.)

Beg
Punch

Says are used
75 more than are did

End.     75 under

5. On December 31, the board of directors declared a cash dividend, payable January 12, of $4,000.

6. $700 of advertising costs were incorrectly charged to "general expenses" rather than "selling expenses."

7. Estimated taxes for the year are $8,500. Of these only $3,500 have yet been paid.

a. Prepare all necessary updating or adjusting entries.
b. Post such entries to T accounts.
c. Prepare a year-end income statement, balance sheet, and statement of changes in retained earnings.

21. *The accounting cycle in manufacturing firms is no different from that in other types of enterprises, but it is especially important that period costs be distinguished from product costs.*

The Highbridge Products Co. began operations on January 1, 1981. The following events took place in January:

1. On January 2 the owners of the company contributed $25,000 in cash to start the business.

2. The company borrowed $10,000 from a local bank. It agreed to make annual interest payments at a rate of 12 percent and to repay the loan in its entirety at the end of three years.

3. The company rented manufacturing and office space. It paid three months' rent in advance. Rent is $400 per month.

4. The company purchased manufacturing equipment at a cost of $35,000 and office furniture and equipment at a cost of $4,800. Both purchases were made on account.

5. The firm purchased raw materials at a cost of $7,000 cash. Of these, raw materials that cost $6,000 were placed in production (added to work in process).

6. The firm hired and paid in cash factory workers, $6,000, and office workers, $1,500. The costs of the factory wages were added to work in process; the costs of the office workers were considered to be period costs and thereby charged directly to an expense account.

7. Factory maintenance costs incurred during the month were $450; factory utility costs were $600. Neither costs have yet been paid. Both were added to work in process.

8. The company recorded depreciation for the month: manufacturing equipment, $1,000; office equipment and furniture, $100. The depreciation costs on the manufacturing equipment were added to work in process; those on the office equipment and furniture were considered to be period costs and charged directly to an expense account.

9. The company gave recognition to interest and rent costs for the month (see events 2 and 3 and determine the appropriate charge for one month). Seventy-five percent of the rent costs were allocated to the factory and added to work in process. The remaining portion of the rent costs, as well as the entire amount of the interest costs, were considered period costs.

10. The company completed, and transferred from work in process to

finished goods inventory, goods that had cost $14,000 to manufacture.

11. The company sold for $20,000 (on account) goods that had cost $13,000 to manufacture.

12. Selling and other administrative costs paid in cash were $1,000.

    a. Prepare journal entries to reflect the events that took place in January.

    b. Post the journal entries to T accounts.

    c. Prepare a month-end income statement and a balance sheet.

22. *This problem is designed to illustrate a year-end* work sheet, *a device useful for the preparation of reports from an unadjusted trial balance.*

The end-of-year *unadjusted* trial balance of the Columbia Flying Service is indicated below. The following additional information has come to your attention:

1. Instructor salaries for the last week of the month have not yet been recorded. They will be payable the first week of the new year. Salaries for the one week are $1,350.

2. In the course of the previous two weeks, lessons were given that had been paid for in advance. The retail value of such lessons was $650.

3. No depreciation has been recorded in 1981. The useful life of the planes is estimated at 10 years (no salvage value) and that of the equipment at 7 years (also no salvage value).

4. Rent for December, $100, has not yet been paid.

5. The company purchases a one-year insurance policy each year which takes effect on July 1. The entire cost of the current year's policy has been charged to "insurance expense." The 12/31/81 balance in "prepaid insurance" is also that on 1/1/81. No entries to the account have been made during the year.

6. Interest on the $6,000 note outstanding is payable twice each year, April 1 and October 1. The annual rate of interest is 8 percent. The note was issued on April 1, 1981; the amount of interest expense represents the first interest payment, which was made on October 1.

7. A physical count of parts on hand indicated an unexplained shortage of parts that had cost $200. No adjustment to inventory has yet been made.

8. All purchases of supplies are charged (debited) to "supplies expense." The balance in "supplies inventory" represents supplies on hand at the beginning of the year. A physical count on December 31, 1981, indicated supplies currently on hand of $400.

9. On December 30, the company flew a charter for which it has not yet billed the customer and which it has not yet recorded in the accounts. The customer will be charged $680.

10. Based on preliminary computations, the firm estimates that income taxes for the year will be $2,200.

    a. Prepare all journal entries that would be necessary to adjust and bring the accounts up to date. (Add any additional account titles that you believe to be necessary.)

    b. On a 10-column sheet of accounting paper, copy the trial balance that follows: Leave an additional six or seven lines between the last account balance and the totals to accommodate accounts to be added by the adjusting entries. Use two columns for the account titles and two for the unadjusted account balances. Label the next two columns "Adjustments" (debits and credits), the next two "Income statement" (debits and credits), and the last two "Balance sheet" (debits and credits).

**Columbia Flying Service**
**Unadjusted Trial Balance**
**December 31, 1981**

| | | |
|---|---:|---:|
| Cash | $ 3,750 | |
| Accounts receivable | 4,500 | |
| Supplies inventory | 200 | |
| Parts inventory | 2,400 | |
| Equipment | 4,200 | |
| Equipment, accumulated depreciation | | $ 600 |
| Planes | 21,600 | |
| Planes, accumulated depreciation | | 7,100 |
| Prepaid insurance | 1,500 | |
| Accounts payable | | 800 |
| Lessons paid for but not yet given | | 2,800 |
| Notes payable | | 6,000 |
| Common stock | | 1,000 |
| Retained earnings | | 7,810 |
| Revenues from lessons | | 89,500 |
| Revenues from charters | | 15,600 |
| Salaries | 62,300 | |
| Fuel expense | 18,900 | |
| Maintenance expense | 5,100 | |
| Supplies expense | 600 | |
| Insurance expense | 3,400 | |
| Advertising expense | 1,300 | |
| Rent expense | 1,100 | |
| Interest expense | 240 | |
| Licenses and fees | 120 | |
| | $131,210 | $131,210 |

c. Instead of posting the journal entries to T accounts, post them to the appropriate accounts in the column "Adjustments." When you have finished posting the entries, sum the two columns and make certain that the totals of debits and credits are equal.

d. Add (or subtract, as required) across the columns, and indicate the total of each account in the appropriate column under the income statement or balance sheet. Take care. Remember that credits have to be subtracted from debits. Make certain that amounts are transferred to the proper column; it is easy to make an error.

e. Add each of the four income statement and balance sheet columns. The difference between the debit and credit columns of the income statement should be the net income for the year. The difference between the debit and credit columns of the balance sheet should also be the income for the year. If the two differences are not equal, then an error has been made. Why shouldn't the balance sheet balance; i.e., why shouldn't the the debits of the balance sheet equal the credits? Look carefully at the balance indicated for retained earnings. Is such balance the before or after "closing balance"? Does it include income of the current year?

f. From the work sheet, prepare in good form both an income statement and a balance sheet. Remember that retained earnings have to be adjusted to take into account income for the current year.

*solutions to exercise for review and self-testing*

a. $3,600,000 (12 months X $300 per month), regardless of how much cash was actually collected.

b.

| | | |
|---|---|---|
| Unearned rent | $300,000 | |
| Rent revenue | | $300,000 |

**To recognize rent revenue in January.**

c. (1) $3,000,000 (12 months X $300,000 per month) should have been recognized in rent revenue. Rent revenue is understated by $1,200,000 ($3,600,000 minus the $2,400,000 of revenue actually recognized).

(2) The balance in "Unearned rent" should be zero: the tenant is no longer "ahead" in rent payments.

(3) The balance in "Rent receivable" should be $600,000. The firm began the year "owing" the tenant $600,000 in services; it earned $3,600,000 and was entitled to $3,000,000 from the tenant. It collected, however, only $2,400,000; it is owed the remaining $600,000.

(4)

| | | |
|---|---|---|
| Unearned rent | $600,000 | |
| Rent receivable | 600,000 | |
| Rent revenue | | $1,200,000 |

**To adjust the year-end rent accounts.**

d. $120,000 should be reported as "Cleaning expense" regardless of the amount of cash paid.

1. $40,000 should be reported as a liability, "Cleaning costs" payable.

2. $20,000 should be reported as an asset, "Prepaid cleaning costs."

e. The reported revenue or expense depends upon the value of the services provided or received, regardless of the amount of cash received or paid. The difference between the value of the services provided or received and the amount of cash received would be added to or subtracted from a related asset or liability account.

# 5

# Revenues
# and Expenses

## Statement of the Problem

In the previous chapter it was emphasized that revenues should be *realized* (accorded accounting recognition and considered to result in an increase in net assets) when *earned,* not necessarily when the related cash is received. Omitted, however, was a discussion of when revenues should be considered to be "earned."

Recall the definition of revenues:

> *The inflow of assets into the firm as a result of production or delivery of goods or the rendering of services.*

In the illustration up to this point in the text, revenue has been recognized either with the passage of time (when earned as rent or interest) or when goods or services have been delivered to the customer (when earned in connection with sales transactions). Relatively few types of revenues can appropriately be considered to be earned with the passage of time, since relatively few types of goods or services are provided uniformly over time. Moreover, recognition of revenue at the time that goods or services are delivered to the customer may, for many types of business transactions, result in financial statements that are misleading to both management and investors. Consider, for example, two situations.

> Company A produces aircraft carriers under contract to the U.S. government. On January 2, 1979, the company signed a contract to produce one carrier at a sales price of $800 million. During 1979 and 1980 the company constructed the carrier. In 1981 it delivered the vessel to the government. Cost of producing the carrier was $600 million.

If company A were to report revenue at the time of sale (when the carrier was delivered to the government), then it would report zero revenue in both 1979 and 1980, the years of construction prior to delivery. In 1981, when the carrier was delivered, it would report $800 million in revenue. Costs of production would be *capitalized* and remain in asset accounts until charged as an expense in the period in which the revenue was recognized. Hence, ignoring certain *period* costs, the company would report expenses of zero in 1979 and 1980 and of $600 million in 1981. Income would be zero in 1979 and 1980, and $200 million in 1981. An investor who relies upon earnings of the past as a guide to those of the future could easily be misled, after two successive years bereft of profits, into prematurely abandoning his interest in what is apparently a lackluster company. But, if at the end of 1980, he sold his shares in the company, he might well, in hindsight, be accused of acting precipitously, for in 1981 the company seemed to experience a remarkable upturn.

But was the company really $200 million better off in 1981 than in either 1979 or 1980? If revenue is recognized only at time of sale, then do the financial statements really give a meaningful picture of the results of the company's economic activity in each of the three years? Would not a stockholder have received more relevant and useful information if income of the company had been matched more closely to its productive effort?

Company B sells furniture on the *installment* plan. Customers make a small down payment and have up to three years to pay the balance of the purchase price. The company sells to poor credit risks. As a consequence, it is unable to make meaningful estimates of the amount it will be able to collect and exerts far more effort (in both time and cost) in collecting its accounts than in making the initial sales. In 1981 the company had "sales" of $100,000 but collected only $20,000 in cash. The cost of the merchandise sold was $40,000. Other operating costs were $15,000.

If company B were to report revenues at the time of sale, then in 1981 it would report revenue of $100,000, cost of goods sold of $40,000, and other operating expenses of $15,000—income of $45,000.

But how much confidence could a stockholder place in the reported income? Of the $100,000 of reported revenues, only $20,000 has been collected in cash. How much of the remaining $80,000 will be collected is uncertain and cannot readily be estimated. Moreover, although the company has sold and delivered the merchandise to its customers, a major part of its economic effort— the collection of its accounts—has yet to be exerted. Can it really be said, therefore, that the company is $45,000 better off at the end of 1981 than it was at the beginning? Might not the interests of investors be better served if recognition of the sales revenue were deferred until ultimate collection became more certain and a greater portion of economic activity had been exerted?

**need for periodic reports**   The problem of determining when and how much revenue has, in fact, been earned exists only because investors and other users of financial information insist on receiving *periodic* reports of income. If they were content to receive a single report of profit or loss *after* the enterprise had completed its operations and was ready to return to stockholders their original investment plus any accumulated earnings, then determination of income would be a simple matter: Subtract from the total amount either available or already distributed to stockholders the amount of their total contributions to the firm. The difference would be income over the life of the enterprise. Indeed, in the sixteenth and seventeenth centuries, companies were frequently formed with an expected useful life of only a few years—perhaps to carry out a specific mission, such as the charter of a ship for a single voyage. Investors in such companies were satisfied to wait until the companies were liquidated to get reports of their earnings.

Most companies today have indeterminate lives, and both owners and managers demand periodic reports of economic progress. Since many transactions are not completed in the same accounting period in which they are started, accountants are forced to make determinations of when and how much revenue should be assigned to specific periods.

## Impact Upon Related Accounts

**expenses**   The issue of revenue realization does not, of course, impact solely upon revenue accounts. Directly affected also are both expense accounts and, equally significantly, balance sheet accounts. As pointed out previously, the question of when to recognize *expenses* is inherently tied to that of when to recognize revenues. To the extent that specific costs can be associated with the revenues that they generate, they are *matched* to and charged as expenses in the *same accounting period* in which recognition is given to the revenues. Costs that cannot be directly associated with specific revenues are considered *period* costs and are charged as incurred. Insofar as costs *can* be matched to specific revenues, they may be charged as expenses in an accounting period either before or after they have actually been incurred. In the previous chapter, for example, it was emphasized that costs of production may be incurred in one period but not be reported as expenses (cost of goods sold) until a later period, when the goods are actually sold. Many situations occur, however, in which costs should properly be reported as expenses in a period earlier than that in which they are incurred. Suppose a company sells and delivers manufacturing equipment to a customer in year 1. The company guarantees to provide maintenance service on the machines for one year after sale. The cost of providing the maintenance service is a cost that can be directly associated with the revenue generated by the sale of the equipment. It follows, therefore, that it should be *matched* with the sales revenue and charged as an expense (even if an estimate of the actual cost has to be made) in the same accounting period as that in which the related revenue is recognized. The journal entries required to implement this matching approach will be illustrated later in this chapter.

**balance sheet**   The valuation of assets, liabilities, and owners' equity is also related to the
**accounts**   recognition of revenue. Revenue has been defined as an inflow of cash or other assets attributable to the goods or services provided by the firm. When recog-

nition is given to revenue, so also it must be given to the resultant increase in assets or decrease in liabilities. Indeed, recognition of revenue is equivalent to the recognition of an increase of owners' equity (i.e., in retained earnings). An increase of owners' equity must be accompanied by an increase in assets or a decrease in liabilities.

*EXHIBIT 5-1*

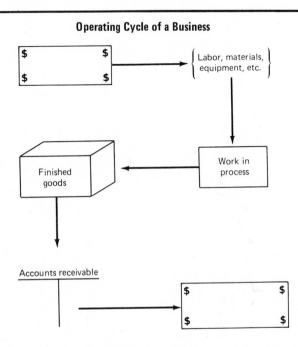

**Operating Cycle of a Business**

Exhibit 5-1 illustrates operating cycle of a typical business. The enterprise starts with an asset, generally cash, and continuously transforms it into other assets—first to materials, equipment, and labor and then to work in process, to finished goods, to accounts receivable, and eventually back to cash. If the company earns a profit, then ending cash is greater than beginning cash. The critical question facing the firm is at which point in the production cycle should the increase in the "size" of the asset package be recognized; at what point in time is the enterprise "better off" than it was before.

Most commonly, especially in a manufacturing or retail operation, the firm recognizes the increase in the value of the assets at time of sale—when goods or services are delivered to customers. By selecting that point, however, it is implicitly ignoring the value of the entire production cycle up to that point. It is asserting that all previous transactions involved nothing more than exchanges of assets and liabilities of equal magnitude—that the level of net assets remained unchanged. It is also stating that all subsequent transactions (e.g., collection of cash, fulfillment of warranty obligations, etc.) will also involve nothing more than exchanges of assets and liabilities of equal magnitude and that such exchanges will have no effect on the new level of net assets.

Point of sale is a *convenient* point to recognize revenue for *most* businesses; it is clearly unsuitable for *all* businesses. It is inappropriate in situations in which delivery of goods provides little assurance that the amount owed by the customer will be collectible. Recognition of revenue upon sale may be equally inappropriate where the enterprise has completed a significant portion of its economic activity and eventual collection of cash from a known customer is certain long before the goods are actually delivered to him.

## Guidelines for Revenue Recognition

There are, unfortunately, no pervasive principles as to when revenue should be recognized. At least four criteria, however, are cited in the accounting literature and have been generally adhered to in practice. Revenue should be recognized as soon as

1. The firm has exerted a substantial portion of its production and sales effort;
2. The revenue can be objectively measured;
3. The major portion of costs have been incurred, and the remaining costs can be estimated with reasonable reliability and precision; and
4. Eventual collection of cash can reasonably be assured.

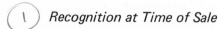

### Recognition at Time of Sale

For most manufacturing and retail concerns, the four criteria of revenue recognition are first satisfied at the point of sale. At that time the firm has exerted a major portion of its economic activity, including its sales efforts. A firm price has been established. Most of the costs have been incurred, even though there might be additional costs, such as those pertaining to product warranties, guaranteed maintenance, and collection of receivables, that might have to be incurred in the future. Collection of cash usually can reasonably be assured, although the firm may have to estimate and make allowances for merchandise that will be returned and customers who will default on their accounts.

### Recognition During Production

For some firms, especially those which provide goods or services under long-term contracts, the dual accounting objectives of providing information that is both relevant and objective can best be served by recognizing revenue as production takes place rather than waiting until point of delivery. Recognition of revenue during the entire production process enables firms to avoid the erratic —and often misleading—pattern of income that may result from point of delivery revenue recognition (as was illustrated earlier in connection with the aircraft carrier example).

A widely used means of recognizing revenue throughout the entire production process is known as the *percentage of completion method.* On any given contract, the proportion of total contract price to be recognized as revenue in each accounting period is the percentage of the total project completed during that period. If 20 percent of the project is completed in a particular year, then 20 percent of the expected total revenue from the project would be recognized during the year.

The percentage of completion or any other production-oriented means of revenue recognition is appropriate only when total costs of completing the project can be estimated with reasonable reliability and precision, the contract price is fixed and certain to be collected (as is often the case when the contract is with a government agency or major corporation), and there can be no question about the ability of the firm to complete the project and to have it accepted by the other party to the contract.

Another example of a situation in which revenue could be recognized in the course of production would be that in which a management consulting firm undertakes to advise a client on the installation of a new accounting system. Assuming that the consulting firm bills its client on the basis of number of hours of service rendered, then each of the four criteria would be reasonably satisfied as the consulting engagement progresses.

 ### Recognition at Completion of Production

For those companies that face ready markets and stable prices for their products, the four basic criteria can often be satisfied at the completion of the production process. Prior to 1972, the U.S. government guaranteed to purchase all gold offered to it at a price of $35 per ounce. From the standpoint of a gold mining company, as soon as its production process was complete, its revenue could be objectively determined; it would have few remaining expenses (storage and transportation), all of which could be readily estimated; and sale of product and collectibility of cash would be assured. Not only would the accounting interests of objectivity and relevance be best served by recognizing revenue as soon as the mining process was complete, but delay of recognition until actual sale would, by valuing gold at its cost to acquire rather than at the amount at which it was certain to be sold, understate the assets of the company.

Few situations today are as well defined as that of the pre-1972 gold mining company inasmuch as the U.S. government presently purchases gold only as needed and at fluctuating prices. Nevertheless, recognition of revenue at completion of the productive process is appropriate for those concerns which have negligible marketing costs, face stable prices, and can readily sell all goods that they produce, since they can reasonably satisfy the four criteria of revenue recognition at such time.

 *Recognition Upon Collection of Cash*

In some situations, the four criteria will not be satisfied until the production and sale processes are complete *and* cash has been collected. In those cases it is necessary to delay recognition of revenue until cash is actually in hand. In the previous installment-sales illustration, for example, the company sold to customers whose credit ratings were poor and from whom the company had no assurance that it would be able to collect its accounts receivable. Prudence dictates that no revenue be recognized until the company is certain that its customer receivables can be transformed into cash.

Obviously every company takes a risk when it sells on credit. In most situations, however, the extent of bad-debt losses can reasonably be estimated at time of sale. Only when such losses cannot be estimated would the interests of the users of financial statements be best served by delaying the recognition of revenue. If recognition were delayed, the related assets would be valued at their cost to produce or acquire rather than at the amount that the firm will eventually realize when it actually collects the cash.

The cash collection or *installment* basis of revenue recognition is not widely used today to account for routine merchandise sales—not even those in which the customer pays "on time" or on the "installment plan"—since it is generally possible to make reasonable estimates of credit losses. It is, however, widely used to account for certain types of real estate or other property transactions in which the collectibility of the receivable held by the seller is questionable. A builder, for example, might sell a recently constructed shopping center to a group of investors. The builder accepts from the investors a note for a portion of the selling price with the understanding that the investors will be able to make payments on the note only insofar as they are able to rent the stores in the shopping center. If there is uncertainty as to whether sufficient space in the shopping center can be rented to enable the investors to make payments on their note, the builder would delay recognition of revenue on the sale of the property until cash is actually in hand.

In evaluating the alternative means of revenue recognition to account for specific types of transactions, it is helpful to keep in mind the standards of reporting set forth in Chapter 1. Accounting information must be both *relevant* and *objective.* The cash basis of revenue recognition generally provides the most objective or verifiable information. By the time revenue is recognized, eventual realization is virtually certain as cash is already in hand. The methods which recognize revenue at an earlier stage in the earning process are less objective since doubts may remain as to whether cash will in fact be collected, but insofar as they provide a better indication of a company's economic effort and the rewards that will *most probably* accrue from the effort, they may result in reports that more readily facilitate financial decisions.

## Analysis of Transactions

The impact of the alternative bases of revenue recognition on revenues and expenses as well as on assets and liabilities can readily be seen when transactions are analyzed in journal entry form. The journal entry is an expression of the principles previously set forth. The journal entry process may sometimes appear a bit tricky, but it can be simplified if a few guidelines are kept in mind.

1. In those periods in which revenue is to be recognized (and *only* in such periods) a revenue account must be credited. Since recognition of revenue implies an inflow or increase of net assets, a corresponding debit must be made to an asset or liability account.

2. In the periods in which revenue is recognized (and *only* in such periods) an expense account must be debited to give recognition to the related costs. The proportion of total expected costs that is charged as an expense in any particular period would be equal to the proportion of total anticipated revenues that is recognized in that period. Since recognition of expenses implies an outflow of net assets, a corresponding credit must be made to either an asset or a liability account. (This guideline gives effect to the *matching* principle, which holds that expenses must be matched with the revenues with which they can be associated.)

3. In all periods in which revenue is *not* recognized, transactions involve *only* exchanges of assets and liabilities; hence, only asset and liability accounts should be debited or credited. Some examples will serve to illustrate these guidelines.

*example 1*

### Recognition of Revenue at Time of Sale— Warranty Obligation Outstanding

The Orange Equipment Co., in 1979, purchases equipment (intended for resale) for $50,000 cash. In 1980 it sells the equipment for $80,000 on account, giving the buyer a one-year warranty against defects. The company estimates that its cost of making repairs under the warranty will be $5,000. In 1981 the company collects the full sales price from the purchaser and incurs $5,000 in repair costs prior to the expiration of the warranty.

*1979*

**(a)**

| | | |
|---|---|---|
| Merchandise inventory (asset +) | $50,000 | |
| Cash (asset –) | | $50,000 |

**To record the purchase of the equipment.**

One asset has been exchanged for another.

*1980*

**(b)**

| | | |
|---|---|---|
| Accounts receivable (asset +) | $80,000 | |
| Sales revenue (revenue +) | | $80,000 |

**To record the sale of the equipment.**

Revenue is recognized at point of sale.

**(c)**

| | | |
|---|---|---|
| Cost of goods sold (expense +) | $50,000 | |
| Warranty expense (expense +) | 5,000 | |
| Merchandise inventory (asset –) | | $50,000 |
| Warranty liability (liability +) | | 5,000 |

**To record the expenses associated with the revenue recognized.**

Every expense associated with the revenue must be recognized. The warranty expense charged and the warranty liability credited represent an *estimate* of costs to be incurred in the future. Since such costs can be directly related to the sales revenue, they must be recorded in the same accounting period in which the revenue is recorded.

*1981*

**(d)**

| | | |
|---|---|---|
| Cash (asset +) | $80,000 | |
| Accounts receivable (asset –) | | $80,000 |

**To record customer payment.**

**(e)**

| | | |
|---|---|---|
| Warranty liability (liability –) | $ 5,000 | |
| Cash (asset –) | | $ 5,000 |

**To record costs incurred to fulfill the warranty obligations.**

The costs incurred to make repairs required under the warranty are *charged* (debited) against the liability that was established at the time the costs were charged as expenses. No additional revenues or expenses are recognized. The level of net assets remains the same. In the event that the original estimate of warranty costs proves to be incorrect, then an adjustment can be made as soon as the error becomes known. Thus, if costs were greater than $5,000, the additional amount would be charged as an expense when incurred. If less, then at the expiration of the warranty, the warranty liability account would be debited (decreased) and the warranty expense account credited (decreased) for the difference. (The credit to the warranty expense account will have the effect of reducing warranty expenses in a year subsequent to that in which the initial sale was made.)

*example 2*

### *Recognition of Revenue During Production*

The construction of the aircraft carrier described earlier can be used to illustrate the approach to recognizing revenue in which the amount of revenue recognized in any given period depends on the percentage of the entire project completed in that period. Company A contracts to build a carrier at a price of $800 million. It estimates that total construction costs will be $600 million. In 1979 it begins construction and incurs $120 million in costs; in 1980 it incurs $300 million, and in 1981 it incurs $180 million and completes the project. In 1981 the company collects the full contract price from the government.*

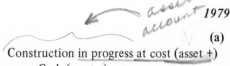

*1979*

**(a)**

| | | |
|---|---|---|
| Construction in progress at cost (asset +) | $120,000,000 | |
| Cash (asset –) | | $120,000,000 |

**To record costs incurred in construction of the carrier.**

This entry summarizes the effect of a number of entries, which would be made as construction progresses, involving various labor, materials, and overhead accounts.

**(b)**

| | | |
|---|---|---|
| Construction in progress at contract value (asset +) | $160,000,000 | |
| Revenue from construction (revenue +) | | $160,000,000 |

**To record revenue based on percentage of completion.**

---

*The example is oversimplified for purposes of illustration. In practice, the government would probably make periodic cash payments to the contractor during construction of the vessel. The timing of the cash collections, however, would have no impact upon the timing of the revenue recognition.

**(c)**

*debit inventory* →

| | | |
|---|---|---|
| Expenses relating to revenue from construction (expense +) | $120,000,000 | |
| Construction in progress at cost (asset -) | | $120,000,000 |

**To record expenses pertaining to construction.**

The company has completed 20 percent of the project (percentage of completion in this example is assumed to be equal to the proportion of estimated total costs already incurred). It is therefore appropriate to recognize 20 percent of *both* estimated revenues and expenses. It will report revenues of $160 million, expenses of $120 million, and income of $40 million. The combined effect of entries (b) and (c) is to increase the value of the construction in progress (an asset) by the amount of the income recognized. An asset ("Construction in progress at contract value") is increased by the amount of revenue recognized. Another asset ("Construction in progress at cost") is reduced by the amount of expense charged. As a consequence, construction in progress is now recorded at sales value, whereas, until entries **b** and **c** were made, it was recorded at cost.

### 1980

The entries for 1980 are similar to those for 1979.

**(d)**

| | | |
|---|---|---|
| Construction in progress at cost (asset +) | $300,000,000 | |
| Cash (asset -) | | $300,000,000 |

**To record costs incurred in construction of the carrier.**

**(e)**

| | | |
|---|---|---|
| Construction in progress at contract value (asset +) | $400,000,000 | |
| Revenue from construction (revenue +) | | $400,000,000 |

**To record revenue based on percentage of completion.**

**(f)**

| | | |
|---|---|---|
| Expenses relating to revenue from construction (expense +) | $300,000,000 | |
| Construction in progress at cost (asset -) | | $300,000,000 |

**To record expenses pertaining to construction.**

In 1980 an additional 50 percent of construction is completed; hence it is necessary to recognize 50 percent of *both* total revenues and total estimated expenses. The company will report revenues of $400 million, expenses of $300 million, and income of $100 million. By the conclusion of 1980 the firm will have reported income, for the two-year period combined, of $140 million: 70

percent of total expected income of $200 million. The work in progress will be valued at $560 million, which is $140 million more than its actual cost of $420 million.

## *1981*

The entries for 1981 correspond to those of the preceding years; additional entries are required, however, to record the completion and delivery of the ship and the subsequent collection of cash.

### (g)

| | | |
|---|---|---|
| Construction in progress at cost (asset +) | $180,000,000 | |
| Cash (asset -) | | $180,000,000 |

**To record the cost incurred in the construction of the carrier.**

### (h)

| | | |
|---|---|---|
| Construction in progress at contract value (asset +) | $240,000,000 | |
| Revenue from construction (revenue +) | | $240,000,000 |

**To record revenue based on percentage of completion.**

### (i)

| | | |
|---|---|---|
| Expenses relating to revenue from construction (expense +) | $180,000,000 | |
| Construction in progress at cost (asset -) | | $180,000,000 |

**To record expenses pertaining to construction.**

These entries are identical in form to those made in 1979 and 1980.

### (j)

| | | |
|---|---|---|
| Completed ship at contract value (asset +) | $800,000,000 | |
| Construction in progress at contract value (asset -) | | $800,000,000 |

**To record completion of the carrier.**

This entry simply reclassifies the asset.

### (k)

| | | |
|---|---|---|
| Accounts receivable (asset +) | $800,000,000 | |
| Completed ship at contract value (asset -) | | $800,000,000 |

**To record delivery of the ship.**

The completed ship is delivered. The purchaser is now indebted to the company for the contract price of the ship.

**(l)**

| | | |
|---|---|---|
| Cash (asset +) | $800,000,000 | |
|     Accounts receivable (asset –) | | $800,000,000 |

**To record the collection of cash.**

The cash has now been collected; the manufacturing cycle is now complete.

In 1981, the company will report revenues of $240 million, expenses of $180 million, and income of $60 million. The entries are summarized in Exhibit 5-2. Upon completion of the ship the company will have expended $600 million in cash to construct a ship which will be valued on its books at $800 million. Over the three-year period it will have recognized revenues of $800 million, expenses of $600 million, and income of $200 million.

*example 3*            *Recognition of Revenue at Completion of Production*

In 1980 New York Instruments Co. receives an order from an electronics manufacturer to produce 10,000 units of a part used in the production of television sets. The purchaser agrees to pay $10 a unit for the part, but under the terms of the contract the seller is to store and retain title to the goods until they are needed by the purchaser. Payment is to be made upon delivery of the goods. Cost of producing the part is $6 per unit. New York Instruments elects to recognize revenue upon completion of production. At that time the four criteria are satisfied; revenue can be objectively measured, all major costs have been incurred (storage costs are considered to be negligible), the major part of productive effort has been exerted, and collection of cash is virtually certain.

Assume that the firm begins production of the parts in 1980 and completes and delivers the parts in 1981. Each of the following entries summarizes several individual entries that would be made as costs are incurred and the groups of units are completed and delivered.

*During Production—1980, 1981*

**(a)**

| | | |
|---|---|---|
| Work in process (asset +) | $ 60,000 | |
|     Cash (asset –) | | $ 60,000 |

**To record costs of production.**

One asset is exchanged for another.

*At Completion of Production—1981*

**(b)**

| | | |
|---|---|---|
| Finished goods at cost (asset +) | $ 60,000 | |
|     Work in process (asset –) | | $ 60,000 |

**To record completion of goods produced.**

Costs are transferred from one asset account to another.

EXHIBIT 5-2

**Recognition of Revenue During Production**

Cash

| | | | | |
|---|---|---|---|---|
| Bal. 1/1/79 | | xxx | **(a)** 120,000,000 | 1979 |
| **(1)** 1981 | | 800,000,000 | **(d)** 300,000,000 | 1980 |
| | | | **(g)** 180,000,000 | 1981 |

(200,000,000)

Construction in progress at cost

| | | | | |
|---|---|---|---|---|
| **(a)** 1979 | 120,000,000 | | **(c)** 120,000,000 | 1970 |
| **(d)** 1980 | 300,000,000 | | **(f)** 300,000,000 | 1980 |
| **(g)** 1981 | 180,000,000 | | **(i)** 180,000,000 | 1981 |

( 0 )

Construction in progress at contract value

| | | | | |
|---|---|---|---|---|
| **(b)** 1979 | 160,000,000 | | **(j)** 800,000,000 | 1981 |
| **(e)** 1980 | 400,000,000 | | | |
| **(h)** 1981 | 240,000,000 | | | |

( 0 )

Completed ship at contract value

| | | | |
|---|---|---|---|
| **(j)** 1981 | 800,000,000 | **(k)** 800,000,000 | 1981 |

( 0 )

Accounts receivable

| | | | |
|---|---|---|---|
| **(k)** 1981 | 800,000,000 | **(l)** 800,000,000 | 1981 |

( 0 )

Revenue from construction[a]

| | | | |
|---|---|---|---|
| | | **(b)** 160,000,000 | 1979 |
| | | **(e)** 400,000,000 | 1980 |
| | | **(h)** 240,000,000 | 1981 |

(800,000,000)

Expenses relating to revenue from construction[a]

| | | |
|---|---|---|
| **(c)** 1979 | 120,000,000 | |
| **(f)** 1980 | 300,000,000 | |
| **(i)** 1981 | 180,000,000 | |

(600,000,000)

[a]To be *closed* to retained earnings at the end of each year.

(c)

Finished goods at market value (asset +)     $100,000

      Manufacturing revenue (revenue +)                     $100,000

**To recognize revenue upon completion of goods manufactured.**

(d)

Cost of goods manufactured (expense +)     $ 60,000

      Finished goods at cost (asset –)                         $ 60,000

**To record the expense pertaining to the manufacture of the goods.**

Revenues and expenses are given accounting recognition.

The pattern of entries is similar to that in Example 2. At the time revenue is recognized, related expenses are also recognized. The realization of revenue is accompanied by an increase in the carrying value of the goods produced–i.e., the recorded value of the finished goods increases from cost to market value, the amount of the increase being the income earned on the transaction.

### At Time of Delivery–1981

(e)

Accounts receivable (asset +)                    $100,000

      Finished goods at market value (asset –)             $100,000

**To record the delivery of goods.**

The finished products, an asset, are exchanged for a receivable, also an asset.

As in the previous examples, events in periods other than those in which revenues and expenses are recognized involve only exchanges among assets and liabilities.

*Example 4*              *Recognition of Revenue upon Collection of Cash*
                                 *(the Installment Basis)*

In 1980 a company sells a parcel of land to a developer for $200,000. The original cost of the land to the company was $150,000. Under the terms of the sales contract, the seller is to receive 5 percent of the selling price at time of closing and transfer of title, 60 percent at the end of 1981, and the remaining 35 percent at the end of 1982. Because the company views ultimate collectibility as being highly uncertain, it has decided to recognize revenue only upon actual receipt of cash.*

*In this example, recognition of revenue upon receipt of cash would be consistent with AICPA pronouncements contained in an industry audit guide, *Accounting for Profit Recognition on Sales of Real Estate.*

The pattern of entries to be followed in this example is consistent with that established in the previous illustrations. A distinguishing feature of this example, however, is that the company physically surrenders the property sold prior to the time that it recognizes revenues and expenses. Inasmuch as expenses are associated with reductions in assets, the firm must retain an *accounting* interest in the property sold equal to the portion of the original cost of the land not yet charged as an expense (cost of land sold).

*Installment Contract Receivable or use*

### At Time of Sale and Collection of First Payment—1980

**(a)**

| | | |
|---|---|---|
| Company interest in land sold (asset +) | $150,000 | |
| Land (asset –) | | $150,000 |

**To record the sale of the land.**

The purpose of this entry is simply to reclassify the property sold—to distinguish between land to which the company actually holds title and that in which it has merely an accounting interest.

**(b)**

$\times 5\%$

| | | |
|---|---|---|
| Cash (asset +) | $10,000 | |
| Revenue from sale of land (revenue +) | | $10,000 |

**To record collection of 5 percent of the selling price and to recognize 5 percent of the anticipated revenue.**

**(c)**

| | | |
|---|---|---|
| Cost of land sold (expense +) | $7,500 | |
| Company interest in land sold (asset –) | | $7,500 |

**To record 5 percent of expenses applicable to the sale of land.** (The original cost of the land to the company was $150,000; 5 percent of $150,000 = $7,500.)

The latter two entries recognize a portion of the total revenue to be realized on the sale and an identical portion of the related expense.

### At Time of Collection of Second Payment—1981

**(d)**

| | | |
|---|---|---|
| Cash (asset +) | $120,000 | |
| Revenue from sale of land (revenue +) | | $120,000 |

**To record collection of 60 percent of the selling price and to recognize 60 percent of the anticipated revenue.**

**(e)**

| | | |
|---|---|---|
| Cost of land sold (expense +) | $90,000 | |
| Company interest in land sold (asset -) | | $90,000 |

**To record 60 percent of the expense applicable to the sale of the land.**

*At Time of Collection of Third Payment–1982*

**(f)**

| | | |
|---|---|---|
| Cash (asset +) | $70,000 | |
| Revenue from sale of land (revenue +) | | $70,000 |

**To record collection of 35 percent of the selling price and to recognize the remaining 35 percent of the revenue.**

**(g)**

| | | |
|---|---|---|
| Cost of Land sold (expense +) | $52,500 | |
| Company interest in land sold (asset -) | | $52,500 |

**To record 35 percent of the expense applicable to the sale of the land.**

By the time the final payment has been made, the company will have recorded revenues of $200,000, expenses of $150,000, and income of $50,000. It will report on the balance sheet an increase in cash of $200,000 and a decrease in land of $150,000.

Although the journal entries illustrated lead to a "correct" statement of both income and assets, they are deficient in that the amount due from the customer—i.e., an account receivable—is never incorporated into the accounts. This deficiency results from the nature of the revenue recognition process. Sales revenue is recorded only upon the receipt of cash; hence the increase in assets associated with recognition of revenue can be reflected only upon the receipt of cash. The deficiency can readily be remedied, however, by establishing two related accounts, "accounts receivable" and "accounts receivable—contra." When a contract is first signed, the following entry could be made:

| | | |
|---|---|---|
| Accounts receivable (asset) | $200,000 | |
| Accounts receivable—contra (asset, contra) | | $200,000 |

Then as each payment of cash is received, the entry would be "reversed":

| | | |
|---|---|---|
| Accounts receivable—contra | $10,000 | |
| Accounts receivable | | $10,000 |

The balance in the two accounts, both of which are balance sheet accounts, will always *net* to zero. The accounts will, however, provide a measure of control over amounts due from customers and indicate the anticipated cash collections.

The criteria for revenue recognition are far easier to apply in an academic as opposed to an industrial setting. The illustrations that follow are designed to demonstrate the difficulty of implementing the guidelines. To a large extent, decisions as to the timing of revenue recognition are left to the good judgment of corporate managers and their accountants. As a consequence, companies in similar industries or even in the same industry have frequently drawn different conclusions as to the most appropriate basis of revenue recognition.

The rule-making bodies of the accounting profession, the Financial Accounting Standards Board and its predecessor, the Accounting Principles Board, have issued a number of pronouncements and industry audit guides which have done much to narrow the alternatives available to companies in similar industries. Nonetheless, differences in practice are still widespread and are likely to remain so in the foreseeable future.

**shipping industry**

In the shipping industry a period of several weeks or months may elapse between the period that cargo is first loaded on board a ship and that when the ship reaches its final destination and the cargo is unloaded. Because both selling effort and collection of cash often take place prior to the voyage, but a large portion of expenses are incurred and effort is exerted in the course, and at the conclusion, of the voyage, it is by no means clear whether revenue should be recognized at the beginning of, during, or at the end of the voyage. Practice varies considerably within the industry. Compare the following footnotes from the annual reports of three publicly owned shipping companies:

Revenue from vessel operations is recognized *upon unloading* inbound cargoes (terminated voyage basis).

—Lykes Corp., 12/31/77

Revenue from vessels time-chartered to others is recorded on a pro rata basis *over the period of the charter.* Revenues and income on voyages of other vessels are recorded on the *percent of completion method.*

—Trans Union Corporation, 12/31/77

Transportation revenues and related voyage expenses are generally recognized at *commencement of voyage.*

—R. J. Reynolds Industries, Inc., 12/31/77

Which practice is "correct"? There are neither persuasive answers nor authoritative guidelines.

**trading stamp industry**  In the trading stamp industry, a company such as Sperry and Hutchinson (S&H Green Stamps), sells stamps to retailers. The retailers distribute the stamps to their customers. The customers save the stamps and after a period of time, perhaps several months, redeem them for merchandise at outlets operated by the trading stamp company. The trading stamp company bills the retailer for the stamps at the time they are delivered.

Should the trading stamp company recognize revenue upon delivery of the stamps to the retailer or should it delay recognition until the stamps are actually redeemed? On the one hand, it is clear that the earning process is not complete until the customers exchange their stamps for merchandise. Only at that time can the company be certain of the number of stamps to be redeemed and the ultimate cost of the merchandise distributed. On the other hand, by the time the company delivers the stamps to the retailer it has completed what it views as the most significant part of its operations—it has convinced the retailer to purchase the stamps. And because of its large volume of business, it can make highly reliable estimates of the percentage of stamps to be redeemed and the cost of the merchandise to be distributed.

The following footnote to the financial statements of Sperry and Hutchinson indicates how, in fact, the company accounts for its trading stamps:

> The company records stamp service revenue and provides for cost of redemptions at the time stamps are furnished to licensees. The liability for stamp redemptions is adjusted each year based upon current operating experience and includes the cost of merchandise and related redemption expenses required to redeem 95% of the stamps issued.

**motion picture industry**  In recent years, a significant portion of the revenues of motion picture producers has been derived from the sale of television exhibition rights. Conventionally, a motion picture producer will sign a contract with a television exhibitor which, for a fixed fee, allows the exhibitor to telecast a film for a specific number of times within an established time period. The film may be one made especially for television or one to be first shown in theatres. In a typical agreement there are four significant dates or time periods:

1. The date at which the contract is signed.
2. The date or dates on which cash is collected. Bills are commonly rendered periodically over the course of the license period.
3. The date the prints are delivered to the station or network.
4. The period of the license, i.e., that during which the licensee has the right to display the film.

Compelling arguments can be made for recognizing revenue at any one of the four significant dates or time periods. Indeed, much depends on how one evaluates the economic substance of the contract between producer and exhibitor. If one views the agreement as a simple sales agreement—the sale of a print or the sale of a right to exhibit—then revenue should be recognized, as in most other sales transactions, when either the right of exhibition (i.e., the contract) or the print itself is delivered to the customer. If, however, the contract is seen as a license to display the film over a period of time, then a convincing argument can be made for recognizing revenue throughout the license period—as bills are rendered, as cash is collected, or as the films are shown.

Major film producers have recognized revenue at each of the significant dates or time periods: Columbia, upon entering into the licensing agreement; MCA, upon delivery of prints to the networks (for films produced especially for television); Disney, upon the receipt of remittances; and Metro-Goldwyn-Mayer, over the life of the contract.

The Accounting Principles Board, however, narrowed the alternatives available to motion picture producers. It established that a licensing agreement should be considered as a sale of a right and that revenue should generally be recognized at the commencement of the license period.

### Timing of Expenses

In the course of this chapter it has been emphasized that costs should be charged as expenses in the same period in which the revenues to which they are related are recognized. Net income should be determined by subtracting from revenues the expenses which were incurred to generate the revenues. Indeed, insofar as possible, expenses and revenues should be reported as if a cause and effect relationship exists between them. Regrettably, a cause and effect relationship is not always readily apparent.

As pointed out in the previous chapter, factory costs that can be directly associated with the manufacture of specific products are *capitalized* as assets and charged as expenses in the period in which the goods manufactured are sold. But other costs, such as sales and administrative costs, cannot easily be associated with specific sales and, therefore, out of practical necessity, are charged off in the period in which they are incurred.

There are many additional types of costs for which cause and effect relationships with specific revenues are also unclear. For these costs, accountants may do their best to match them with appropriate revenues, but in the absence of specific rules set forth by authoritative professional or governmental bodies, the determination as to when the costs should be charged as expenses must, in large measure, rest with the judgment of the individual accountant. As a result, similar types of costs are often accorded dissimilar treatment by firms even within a single industry.

**insurance industry** Consider, for example, costs incurred by life insurance firms. When a firm writes a policy, it will receive premiums—and therefore recognize revenue from premiums—over the life of the policy. In the period in which it first issues the policy, however, it incurs certain one-time "acquisition" costs, involving commissions, underwriting, and marketing. Should these costs be charged as expenses entirely in the year incurred, or should they be spread out over a number of years? Compare the practices of two leading companies:

> Premiums are recognized as income over the premium paying period of the policy whereas expenses, including acquisition costs such as commissions in connection with acquiring new business, *are charged to operations as incurred.*
>
> —Prudential Insurance Company of America, 12/31/76

> Costs of acquiring new life insurance business . . . *have been deferred and are being amortized over the premium paying periods in proportion to premium revenue recognized.*
>
> —Transamerica Corporation, 12/31/76

**retailing industry** Similarly, consider costs, such as those of site selection, rent, stocking the shelves, and advertising, incurred by a retailer prior to the opening of a new store. With the revenues of which accounting periods should such costs be associated? Should they be charged off as incurred (in a period in which the store might generate zero revenues), in the period in which the store opens, or in several periods subsequent to the opening of the store? Compare the manner in which costs are accounted for by three firms in the retail industry:

> Store preopening costs are charged to expense *in the year incurred.*
>
> —F. W. Woolworth & Co., 1/31/77

> Expenses associated with the opening of new stores are written off *in the year of store opening.*
>
> —J. C. Penney Company, Inc., 1/29/77

> Preopening expenses of . . . department stores are deferred and charged to operations over a three-year period.
>
> —Food Fair Stores, Inc., 7/31/77

### *Revenue and Expense Recognition—An Overview*

The issue of when to recognize revenues and expenses is pervasive in accounting. It is intrinsically related to virtually all other accounting questions.

In the remaining chapters a great deal of attention will be directed to questions of asset and liability valuation. But answers to questions of valuation must always be viewed with an eye toward their effects on revenues and expenses. After all, income can be defined as the change in net assets between two points in time. To take but a few examples: The question of whether a firm should report marketable securities, such as shares of General Motors stock, at the price the firm paid for them, or the price at which they are currently being sold is also an issue of revenue recognition—that is, should the company recognize gains or losses from market price changes as the value of the stock increases or decreases over time, or should it delay recognition until it actually sells the shares?

The question of whether inventories should be reported at cost to produce them or the price at which they will eventually be sold can also be expressed in terms of whether revenue should be recognized at point of sale or at various points throughout the production process. Disputes over whether or not a firm should assign values to seemingly worthless assets such as "organizational costs," "deferred store opening costs," or "deferred research and development costs" are also conflicts over when such costs should properly be charged off as expenses. It is vital, therefore, that every accounting question be analyzed in terms of its effect on *both* the income statement *and* the balance sheet.

## Key Accounting Concepts

In the remainder of this chapter we shall consider some key accounting concepts which have been implied in the text but which, up to this point, have not been specifically discussed.

**exchange prices** There is widespread agreement among accountants that, when first recorded, assets or liabilities should be measured by the *exchange* prices at which the transactions take place. That is, assets and liabilities should be valued with respect to the goods, the services, or the monetary consideration received or surrendered by the two parties to the transaction.

Unfortunately, even the relatively simple guidelines pertaining to the initial recording of assets and liabilities present problems of implementation. Many transactions involve more than a simple exchange of cash for goods or services. Many business transactions involve an element of barter. Goods or services are exchanged for other goods or services rather than for cash alone. In such transactions, accountants must look to the *fair value* of the consideration surrendered—that is, to the amount of money that would have been received had the goods or services been exchanged for cash alone.

The fair values of assets exchanged, however, are not always readily determinable. At what amount, for example, should a new car be recorded when purchased in exchange for cash plus an old car? The automobile salesman may well offer the purchaser a *trade-in allowance* on his old car.

But in the retail automobile industry, trade-in allowances are often significantly higher than true fair market value. Moreover, the *sticker* price on the new car may be an equally unreliable indicator of the true fair market value of the new car. The exchange price at which the new car should be recorded must, therefore, be *estimated;* either the fair market value of the old car or the new car must be appraised by the best means available—e.g., by reference to books of used car prices or by comparison of prices at which similar new cars were sold.

On a larger scale, corporations often purchase entire companies or segments of businesses in exchange for nonmonetary assets. Frequently the consideration is the common stock of the purchaser or of another company owned by the purchaser. Since the value of the stock may not be readily apparent, especially if it is not traded on a major stock exchange, the amounts at which the acquired assets are initially recorded may have to be based on the best estimates of corporate managers, accountants, or independent appraisers.

**arm's-length transactions**   The exchange prices at which assets and liabilities are first recorded are generally assumed to be the results of *arm's-length* transactions—those between independent parties. Initial measurement of assets and liabilities is especially difficult when an exchange transaction is at less than arm's length—that is, where the two parties are related to one another. It is not unusual for owners of a corporation to sell assets to the corporation itself. For example, a *closely held* corporation (one in which all outstanding shares of common stock are held by a small number of stockholders) might purchase land, buildings, equipment, or other assets from one of its shareholders. There is certainly nothing illegal or unethical about such transactions. But because the prices at which the exchanges take place do not result from negotiations among *independent* parties, they cannot be relied upon to provide fair market values at which the assets should be recorded.

Corporations may also engage in transactions with their subsidiaries—those other corporations in which they own controlling interests. Indeed, a subsidiary may have been acquired for the very purpose of being either a supplier of raw materials or a sales outlet for its finished goods. Since the prices at which goods are transferred between parent and subsidiary may be established arbitrarily by parent corporation management, they are inappropriate measures of true economic value. To the extent that the dollar amounts involved in such exchanges are material, the financial statements of both parent and subsidiary should be suspect. Indeed, revenues and expenses, as well as assets and liabilities, would be based on internally determined prices. It is, in large measure, for this reason that corporations combine the individual financial reports of related companies into single *consolidated* reports. In effect, the accountant defines the accounting entity as the sum of the two or more legal entities (the individual corporations). For reporting purposes, transfers among the related corporations are treated no differently from those among different departments of a single corporation. The values of assets and liabilities are based on the exchange transactions involving the *accounting entity* (the consolidated group of companies) and unrelated outsiders.

Accounting values are ordinarily based on monetary transactions with independent parties. Those assets and liabilities which are the result of non-monetary exchanges, in which the value of the consideration surrendered cannot objectively be determined or in which the exchange price is not arrived at as a consequence of arm's-length bargaining, should be the subject of careful scrutiny on the part of a financial analyst or other users of financial reports.

**monetary unit**

Financial statements report the results of economic activity in terms of money. In the United States, the dollar is the conventional unit of measurement. But there is no agreement among accountants that the dollar, or, more specifically, the "unadjusted" dollar, *should* be the unit of measurement.

Financial statements combine and report the results of economic measurements taken over a number of years. For example, on the balance sheet assets purchased in previous years are combined with assets purchased in the current year. An asset of $2 million—land, for example—might be composed of one parcel of land purchased 10 years ago for $1 million and another purchased in the current year, also for $1 million. But, in fact, the measuring unit, i.e., the dollar, of 10 years ago is in no way comparable to that of today. As a consequence of continuous economic inflation, the dollar of today is "worth" considerably less than that of 10 years ago. The $1 million parcel of land purchased 10 years ago cost far more in terms of economic sacrifice than did that purchased today. Adding together current dollars with dollars of 10 years ago would be similar to adding together yards of 36 inches and those of 40 inches.

The accountant's basic unit of measure, the dollar, is, unfortunately, like the elastic yard—it is constantly changing in size.

Conventional accounting reports fail to recognize the continual changes in the value of the dollar. Accounting statements are implicitly based on the assumption—a patently invalid assumption—that the dollar retains a constant value over time. Current dollars are readily combined with or compared to those of previous years with no adjustments made to take into account the impact of inflation.

Recall, for example, the question raised in Chapter 1. The net assets, as conventionally measured, of Home Heating Oil, Inc. increased during a year from $1 million to $1.06 million. Its reported income was, therefore, $60,000. As a consequence of inflation, however, it required $1.1 million in assets at year end to acquire goods and services that would have cost only $1 million at the beginning of the year. Was the company really $60,000 better off at the end of the year than it was at the beginning? Is $60,000 a fair measure of its income for the year?

The failure to take into account increases in the general level of prices and in the resultant changes in the basic measuring unit necessarily limits the usefulness of financial reports. Accountants are, of course, cognizant of the limitations but have been unable to agree either upon the most appropriate means of remedying the deficiencies or even whether proposed measures would avoid introducing additional, and perhaps more serious, distortions into the financial reports. The issue of "price level adjustments" is discussed in greater depth in Chapter 16.

**the going concern**

There is also widespread agreement among accountants that once assets have been initially recorded they should thereafter be valued on the assumption that the firm is a *going concern*—one that will continue in operation indefinitely. The concept of the going concern relates directly to an earlier discussion of the nature of assets. It was pointed out that assets are conventionally measured with respect to the particular firm reporting them—not with respect to the general marketplace. Thus, certain assets, "organizational costs," for example, can be expected to have value to the firm on whose books they are recorded, even though they are not readily marketable. The going-concern concept implies that the firm will survive at least long enough to realize the benefits of its recorded assets.

The corollary to the going-concern concept is that when there is evidence that a firm will be unable to survive, its assets should be reported at their *liquidation* values—the amounts that could be realized if the firm were to be dissolved and its assets put up for sale. Thus, if a firm is expected to be dissolved, perhaps as the result of bankruptcy proceedings, the conventional balance sheet would be inappropriate; instead, a balance sheet that indicates net realizable values should be prepared.

In recent years accountants' interest in the going-concern concept has focused largely on the issue of the point at which the public needs to be warned that the survival of a firm is in serious question.

In practice, the going-concern concept is seldom abandoned in financial statements until a firm is actually involved in legal proceedings leading to liquidation. Independent auditors do, however, have a means by which to warn readers that the assumption of indefinite existence on which the financial statements of a firm are based *may not be* valid. Instead of issuing its usual "clean" opinion, which states that the financial statements "present fairly" the firm's financial position and results of operations, the auditors will set forth the reasons for their doubts about the ability of the company to survive. They will assert only that the statements present fairly *subject to* successful resolution of the matters impinging upon its continued existence. Auditors' reservations normally stem from uncertainties as to whether a firm will be able to obtain adequate financing or essential orders for its goods or services. A "qualified" opinion, however, can only enhance the firm's financial difficulties and may even be something of a "self-fulfilling prophecy." After all, few companies are willing to lend funds to, or contract with, a firm whose survival is in doubt. If auditors issue a going-concern warning before one is really necessary, they run the risk of intensifying the financial problems of their client. If they delay beyond the point at which liquidation is likely, then they will have been a party to the issuance of misleading financial statements—those based on an invalid assumption of continued existence.

**conservatism**  Conservatism is widely regarded as one of the pervasive attitudes which underlie financial reports. Conservatism, as it relates to accounting, means that it is generally preferable that any possible errors in measurement be in the direction of understatement rather than overstatement of net income and net assets. In matters of doubt the recognition of favorable events should be delayed and that of unfavorable occurrences should be hastened. The concept of conservatism has been accorded formal recognition by the Accounting Principles Board, not as a full-fledged accounting principle, but rather as a "modifying convention."

Conservatism has its roots in the uncertainty which pervades all accounting measurements. It has been widely held that the interests of investors and creditors would be more adversely affected by overstatements of assets and profits than by understatements. More harm would accrue to them from an unforeseen or unreported loss than from an unanticipated gain. Moreover, it sometimes has been asserted that corporate managers are inherently optimistic. It is the role of the accountant to contain their optimism and to make certain that it does not spill over onto the company's financial statements.

The convention of conservatism must be applied judiciously. Insofar as accounting measurements are taken from a perspective of pessimism, they may easily be distorted. And to the extent that similar transactions (those which happen to result in gains rather than losses) are accounted for differently, the resultant financial statements may be internally inconsistent.

Moreover, understatement of earnings in one period may lead to overstatement in a subsequent period. It is not unheard of for newly appointed management teams to practice conservatism to an extreme. The new managers attempt to delay recognition of revenues to future periods and to charge costs of the future as current expenses. Such actions, of course, reduce earnings in the year that the new management group takes over—a poor showing that can be blamed on the previous managers. But they also serve to increase earnings of the future over what they might normally be by adding revenues that should properly have been recognized in the past and eliminating expenses that should not have been previously charged. This type of manipulation—sometimes referred to as taking a "big bath"—does as much to destroy the credibility of corporations and their accountants as the use of excessively liberal accounting methods.

## Summary

Revenues should be realized when earned; costs should be charged as expenses at the time the revenues to which they are related are realized. This chapter has addressed the questions of when revenues should be considered to be earned and how costs can most meaningfully be related to specific revenues. In this chapter we have not attempted to provide answers; indeed there are no definitive answers. Instead we have explored the nature of the problems and set forth general guidelines for their resolution.

Revenues are commonly recognized (considered to result in an increase in net assets) at time of sale. They may also be recognized, however, during the process of production, at the completion of the process, or after both the completion of the process and the point of sale—that is, upon collection of the cash owing to the sale. As a rule, revenue should be recognized as soon as

1. The firm has exerted a substantial portion of its production and sales effort;
2. The revenue can be objectively measured;
3. The major portion of costs have been incurred, and the remaining costs can be estimated with reasonable realiability and precision; and
4. Eventual collection of cash can reasonably be assured.

Expenses should be matched with and charged against the revenues that they serve to generate. Often, however, a clearly defined cause and effect relationship is not apparent. In the absence of such a relationship the determination of which expenses should be matched to which revenues must be based, in large measure, on the good judgment of business meanagers and their accountants.

In general, if an enterprise is neither expanding nor contracting, then total reported revenues as well as expenses would be the same regardless of to which specific policies of revenue and expense recognition the firm adhered. If, however, as is most commonly the situation, the firm is either increasing or decreasing the volume of its operations, then the impact of alternative practices on reported earnings may be substantial.

Issues of revenue and expense recognition must never be viewed in isolation from those of asset and liability valuation. They are intrinsically related. Any determination that affects reported income must necessarily affect a related balance sheet account. Questions of asset valuation will be addressed directly, however, in Chapter 6.

This chapter has also served to describe and identify the implications of several key concepts that underlie financial statements. Among the concepts discussed were those of exchange prices, arm's-length transactions, monetary units, the going concern, and conservatism.

Surfside Construction Co. contracts with the city of Portland to construct five municipal swimming pools. Contract price is $1 million ($200,000 per pool); estimated total cost of construction is $800,000 ($160,000 per pool). The contract requires that the pools be turned over to the city when all five have been completed and that payment be made at that time.

Surfside elects to recognize revenue on a percentage of completion basis, with percentage of completion being measured in terms of number of units completed.

1. In 1980 Surfside incurs $500,000 in construction costs and completes two pools. The cost of each of the completed pools was as estimated, $160,000.
   a. Prepare a journal entry to record the costs incurred.
   b. Inasmuch as Surfside completes two pools, determine the percentage of total revenues that should be recognized. Determine the dollar amount of revenue that should be recognized.
   c. Based on the percentage of revenue recognized, determine the percentage and dollar amount of estimated costs that should be recognized as expenses.
   d. If revenues on the two completed pools have been recognized, then at what value (cost or contract) must the pools be carried on the books?
   e. If the costs of constructing the two pools are to be recognized as expenses, then what asset (in an amount equal to the expenses) must be reduced?
   f. Prepare two journal entries to recognize the revenues and the related expenses.

2. In 1981 Surfside incurs the $300,000 in estimated additional costs and completes the remaining three pools.
   a. Following the pattern established in the previous section, prepare journal entries to record the costs incurred and to give recognition to revenues and expenses. Do total revenues recognized over the two-year period equal the contract price? Do total expenses equal the estimated costs?
   b. In 1981 Surfside delivered the completed pools to the city and gave accounting recognition to the amount owed by the city. Prepare the appropriate journal entry.

## Questions

1. It is sometimes pointed out that over the life of an enterprise it matters little on what basis revenues and expenses are recognized; it is only because investors and others demand periodic reports of performance that problems of revenue and expense recognition arise. Do you agree? Explain.

2. As soon as it is determined when revenues should be recognized, it should be a simple matter to determine when expenses should be recognized; match the expenses to the revenues which they generated. If this is true,

how do you account for the fact that similar companies accord different accounting treatment to expenses even though they may employ identical methods of revenue recognition?

3. "If financial statements are to be truly objective, then it is inappropriate to recognize revenue on a transaction until the seller has cash in hand; recognition of revenue at any point prior to collection of cash necessarily involves estimates of the amount of cash that will actually be collected." Do you agree?

4. The Evergreen Forest Co. raises trees intended for sale as Christmas trees. Trees are sold approximately five years after they have been planted. What special problems of income determination does the company face if it is to prepare annual financial statements?

5. What criteria as to when revenue should be recognized are widely followed in practice?

6. The Retail Furniture Co. is 100 percent owned by Furniture Manufacturers, Inc. Retail purchases its entire stock of merchandise from its parent company. Retail recently sought a loan from a local bank; the bank requested that Retail submit financial statements that were audited by an independent CPA. Retail has asked you to perform the audit. You would *not* be permitted to audit also the books and records of Furniture Manufacturers, Inc. Assuming that you were fully qualified to perform the audit, what reservations might you have about accepting the engagement? What special problems of income determination are you likely to face?

7. The Jamison Co. has suffered substantial losses in each of the past three years. The company is heavily in debt, and it appears unlikely that the company will be able to meet its obligations as they come due. After auditing the financial statements you are convinced that they "have been prepared in accordance with generally accepted accounting principles consistently applied." The statements clearly disclose the losses of the current and prior years and indicate all outstanding obligations. What additional warnings pertaining to the basis on which the financial statements were prepared would you consider giving the stockholders or potential investors or creditors? What special problems of reporting face companies whose survival is in question?

8. The Crescent Co. engaged in only one transaction in the current year. It sold for $150,000 land which it had purchased eight years earlier for $100,000. The increase in fair market price of the land could be attributed entirely to the impact of inflation—i.e., goods and services which cost $1.00 eight years ago would cost $1.50 today. How much income should the company report for the current year? How much "better off" was the company at the end of the year than it was at the beginning?

9. Accounting statements are said to be conservative. What is meant by conservatism as the concept is applied to financial reports? How does the accountant justify his conservatism? What problems might such conservatism create?

10. The question of revenue and expense recognition is inherently intertwined with that of asset and liability valuation. Explain.

## Problems

1. *This exercise compares the effects of alternative bases of revenue recognition on earnings of a particular period as well as on earnings over the life of a project.*

The Anderson Construction Company agreed to construct six playgrounds for the City of Webster. Total contract price was $1.2 million. Total estimated costs were $960,000.

The following schedule indicates for the three-year period during which construction took place the number of units completed, the actual costs incurred, and the amount of cash received from the City of Webster.

|  | Year | | |
| --- | --- | --- | --- |
|  | *1* | *2* | *3* |
| Units completed | 1 | 2 | 3 |
| Costs incurred | $480,000 | $288,000 | $192,000 |
| Cash collected | 240,000 | 360,000 | 600,000 |

a. Determine revenues, expenses, and income for each of the three years under each of the following alternatives:
  1. Revenue recognized on the basis of the <u>percentage of the project</u> completed. (Incurrence of costs indicates degree of completion.)
  2. Revenue recognized <u>as soon as each playground is completed.</u>
  3. Revenue recognized upon the <u>collection of cash.</u>
b. Are total earnings the same over the life of the project?

2. *Under the percentage of completion method, the percentage of total estimated costs recognized as expenses must equal the percentage of total contract value recognized as revenues in any particular year.*

On January 3, 1980, Eastern Electric Co. contracted with United Power Company to produce generating equipment. Estimated cost of the equipment was $2,400,000; contract price was $2,800,000. Eastern Electric recognizes revenue on such contracts on a percentage of completion basis.

In 1980, Eastern Electric incurred $1,800,000 in costs on the project; in 1981, it incurred the remaining $600,000. In 1980 it received from United Power $800,000 in cash (which may be accounted for as an advance payment), and in 1981 it received the additional $2,000,000.

a. Prepare a journal entry to recognize the costs incurred (added to work in process) in 1980. Assume that they were paid in cash.
b. Determine the percentage of revenues and expenses that should be recognized in 1980.
c. Prepare journal entries to recognize the revenues and expenses in 1980.
d. Prepare a journal entry to recognize the cash collected in 1980.
e. Prepare similar journal entries, plus any additional journal entries required in 1981 to recognize completion of the equipment and delivery to customer.

**3.** *Accounting practice does not always conform to accounting theory.*

The following statement of accounting policy was included in the annual report of Santa Fe Industries (December 31, 1976).

Revenues from rail operations are recognized in income upon completion of service. Expenses relating to shipments for which service has not been completed are charged to income and not deferred.

    a. Why might such policy be considered objectionable? What "principle" does it violate?

    b. How do you suspect the controller of Santa Fe Industries would defend the policy?

**4.** *It is sometimes necessary to recognize costs as expenses before they have actually been incurred.*

On December 31, 1979, the Valentine Roofing Co. reported among its liabilities the following balance:

Liability for roof guarantees          $4,000

During 1980 Valentine constructed roofs for which it billed customers $300,000. It estimates that, on average, it incurs repair costs, under its two-year guarantee, of 2 percent of the initial contract price of its roofs. In 1980 the company actually incurred repair costs of $7,500, which were applicable to roofs constructed both in 1980 and in prior years.

    a. Analyze both the liability and expense accounts pertaining to roof repairs in journal entry and T account forms for the year 1980.

    b. How can a company justify charging repair expenses *before* they are actually incurred, based only on an *estimate* of what actual costs will be?

**5.** *Costs of fulfilling warranty obligations must be matched to the revenues with which they are associated.*

In 1980 the Gerard Company sold for cash 20 printing presses at a price of $100,000 each. The presses cost $80,000 to manufacture. The company guaranteed each press for a period of two years starting from the date of sale. The company estimated that the costs of making repairs as required by the guarantee would be approximately 2 percent of sales.

Actual expenditures for repairs of presses sold in 1980 were as follows: 1980, $14,000; 1981, $19,000; 1982, $12,000.

Prepare journal entries to record the sale of the presses and the subsequent repair costs.

**6.** *If revenue from the sale of an asset is to be associated with the collection of cash, so too must the cost of the asset sold.*

The Walton Company sells a parcel of land for $150,000. Terms of the contract require that the seller make a down payment of $30,000 at the time the agreement is signed and pay the remaining balance in two installments at the end of each of the next two years. In addition, the contract requires the seller to pay interest at a rate of 8 percent on the balance outstanding at the time of each of the two installment payments.

Walton Company had purchased the land for $90,000.

Determine the revenues and expenses that the company should report upon each of the cash collections assuming that it elects to recognize revenues on an installment (cash collection) basis.

7. *Changing conditions require changes in accounting practices.*

The following statement appeared in the footnotes to the financial statements of Macmillan Publishing Company, Inc.

> In 1975, the Company changed its definition of the unit of sale for the domestic home study business from the entire contract amount to each individual cash payment, which is generally made when the lesson is delivered. Changing industry regulations affecting refund and cancellation policies and changing patterns of payment were proving to have such unpredictable effects on ultimate contract collectibility that the continued use of prior historical patterns to establish allowances for cancellations and doubtful accounts could have caused serious distortions in the matching of revenues and costs.

a. Which of the two definitions of unit of sale would result in the more "conservative" practice of revenue recognition.

b. Assume that in a particular month a customer contracts to take a home study course consisting of 20 lessons. Total contract price for the entire course is $500. The customer remits $25 for the first lesson.

(1) If the unit of sale is considered to be the entire contract (and the entire amount of revenue is to be recognized at time of sale), prepare one entry to recognize the signing of the contract and another to recognize the delivery of the first lesson and the collection of cash. Ignore the costs applicable to the revenues.

(2) If the unit of sale is considered to be each individual cash payment, prepare an entry to recognize the delivery of the first lesson and the collection of cash. Is it necessary to record the signing of the contract?

8. *Under the completion of production method expenses are matched with revenues upon their recognition.*

Lawncare, Inc. sells to Jaymart Stores lawnmowers that are specially manufactured for sale under a Jaymart brand name. A recent contract requires Lawncare to produce and deliver to Jaymart 1,000 mowers at a price of $150 per unit. Lawncare estimates that its manufacturing costs will be $100 per unit.

a. Lawncare recognizes revenues and expenses on a completion of production basis inasmuch as sale and collection are assured when production is completed. Prepare journal entries to reflect the following events.

1. In a particular month Lawncare incurs $90,000 in production costs, all of which are added to work in process. All expenses are paid in cash.

2. It completes 400 units and transfers them to finished goods inventory. The costs of the finished mowers were as estimated, $100 each. Lawncare gives accounting recognition to the associated revenues, expenses, and increase in the carrying value of the inventory.

3. It delivers to Jaymart 300 mowers and bills Jaymart for the items delivered.

   b. Lawncare also manufactures lawnmowers under its own brand name for sale to department stores and lawn specialty shops. Sales to these stores are not made under any special contractual arrangements. Goods are shipped as ordered. Do you think that Lawncare should use the completion of production method to recognize revenue on these sales? Would the firm not be inconsistent if it used another method?

9. *On what basis should a manufacturer of custom products recognize revenue?*

The Harrison Co. manufactures television sets for sale to Save-More Discount Stores. Save-More sells the sets under its own brand name. In 1980 Harrison Co. signed a contract to deliver to Save-More 30,000 sets at a price of $100 per set over the next three years. By the end of 1980 Harrison had not yet delivered any sets to Save-More but had 10,000 sets 90 percent complete. In 1981 Harrison completed and delivered to Save-More 23,000 sets—the 10,000 sets started in the previous year plus 13,000 sets started in 1981. In 1982 Harrison completed and delivered the remaining 7,000 sets.

Each set cost Harrison $75 to manufacture. As agreed upon in the contract, Save-More made cash payments of $1 million to Harrison in each of the three years.

   a. Determine revenues, expenses, and income for each of the three years if revenue were to be recognized (1) in the course of production, (2) at time of delivery, (3) at time of cash collection. Are total revenues, expenses, and income the same under each of the three methods?

   b. Which basis of revenue recognition do you think results in the most objective and relevant determination of corporate performance?

10. *Consider the problems of matching revenues and expenses in a mining company.*

The Fordham Mining Co. has a contract with the American Lead Co. The terms of the agreement provide that American Lead Co. will purchase at a price of $500 per ton all lead which Fordham Mining Co. is willing to sell.

Fordham Mining has determined that costs of mining lead average $400 per ton. Transportation costs to the plant of American Lead add an additional $50 per ton to the cost. In 1980 Fordham Mining Co. mined 10,000 tons of lead, shipped 9,000 tons to American, and collected payment for 6,000 tons. In 1981 it mined 12,000 tons, shipped 11,000 tons, and collected payment for 13,000 tons.

Fordham Mining Co. recognizes revenue as soon as it removes the lead from the ground.

   a. Prepare journal entries to reflect operations of Fordham Mining for 1980 and 1981. Assume all costs were paid in cash as incurred.

   b. Prepare income statements and balance sheets for 1980 and 1981. Assume that the company's only asset at the start of 1980 was $5 million cash.

   c. There is some question as to whether the transportation costs should be charged as an expense in the year in which the lead is mined and the revenue is recognized or in the year in which the lead is shipped and the costs actually incurred. Indicate the impact of the alternative that you did not select on both the income statement and the balance sheet.

**11.** *On what basis should revenues from membership fees be recognized?*

The Beautiful Person Health Club charges members an annual $240 membership fee. The fee, which is payable in advance, entitles the member to visit the club as many times as he wishes.

Selected membership data for the three-month period January to March 1980 are indicated in the table following:

|  | *Jan.* | *Feb.* | *March* |
|---|---|---|---|
| No. of new memberships sold | 20 | 30 | 10 |
| No. of renewals | 50 | 20 | 10 |
| No. of expirations (including members who renewed) | 50 | 40 | 10 |
| Total no. of active members at end of month | 600 | 610 | 620 |

Members who renew their contracts must also pay the $240 annual fee in advance of their membership year.

Monthly costs of operating the health facilities are approximately as follows:

| | |
|---|---|
| Rent | $ 1,000 |
| Salaries | 5,000 |
| Advertising and promotion | 3,000 |
| Depreciation and other operating costs | 1,500 |
| | $10,500 |

The company controller and an independent CPA disagree over the basis on which revenue should be recognized. The CPA argues that since members can use the facilities over a 12-month period, revenue from each member should be spread over a 12-month period (i.e., $20 per month per member). The controller, on the other hand, asserts that the entire membership fee should be recognized in the month the member either joins or renews. A major portion of corporate effort, he argues, is exerted *before* and at the time a new member actually joins the club. He points out that the company spends over $3,000 per month in direct advertising and promotion costs, and, in addition, a significant portion of the time of several club employees (whose salaries are included in the $5,000 of salary costs) is directed to promoting new memberships and processing both new applications and renewals.

a. Determine for the three-month period, for which data are provided, the monthly income that would result from adopting each of the two positions.

b. Which position do you favor? Why?

c. Is a compromise between the two positions possible? Would such a compromise be consistent with what you believe to be sound principles of financial reporting?

12. *The impact of alternative accounting practices on income as well as retained earnings (and thus on assets and liabilities) must be evaluated.*

Waterloo Construction Co. begins operations in 1979. The company constructs bridges. Each bridge takes three years to complete, and construction is spread evenly over the three-year period. The contract price of each bridge is $3 million. In the period between 1979 and 1983 the firm begins construction of one bridge at the start of each year. Each bridge is completed after three years; for example, that started in 1979 is completed in 1981.

a. Assume that the firm recognizes revenue only upon the completion of a bridge. Determine annual revenues for the period 1981 to 1983.

b. Assume that the firm recognizes revenue on a percentage of completion basis (one-third of the revenue on each bridge is recognized each year). Determine annual revenues for the period 1981 to 1983.

c. Is there a difference in reported revenues?

d. Determine the balance in retained earnings that the firm would report at the end of 1983 under each of the two methods. Be sure to take into account any revenues that would have been recognized in 1979 and 1980. Assume that no dividends have been declared; ignore expenses related to the revenues.

e. Suppose that starting in 1984 the firm begins construction on two bridges each year. Determine annual revenues for the years 1984 to 1986.

f. Under what circumstances does choice of accounting method have an impact upon reported revenues?

13. *Under what circumstances does choice of basis for recognizing expenditures make a difference?*

It was pointed out in this chapter that there are at least three methods by which retail chain stores charge off costs, such as those of site selection, rent, payroll, etc., incurred *prior* to the opening of a new store. Preopening costs may be

1. Charged as expense in the year incurred.

2. Charged as expense in the year a new store is opened.

3. Charged as expense over a 36-month period from the date the new store is opened.

Assume that the preopening costs of a large chain average $60,000 per store. Stores are opened on January 1, and all preopening costs are incurred during the prior year.

Prepare a table indicating the amount of preopening costs to be charged as expenses in each year of the period from 1980 through 1982 using each of the three alternative methods.

a. Assume that the company opened three stores each year from 1978 through 1981.

b. Assume alternatively that the company opened one store in 1978, two in 1979, three in 1980, four in 1981, five in 1982, and six in 1983.

14. *The effect on income of using a convenient, but theoretically unacceptable, method of accounting may be immaterial; the effect on assets and retained earnings may be substantially greater.*

Midstate Utility Company does not recognize revenue at the time it delivers electricity to customers. Instead, it recognizes revenue at the time it bills its customers for the electricity used. The company ordinarily bills customers on the 15th of each month for electricity that they had used in the previous month.

As of December 31, 1980, the company had delivered electricity for which it would bill customers, on January 15, 1981, for $86,000. As of December 31, 1981, the company had delivered electricity for which it would bill customers, on January 15, 1982, for $90,000.

In response to a suggestion by its CPA firm that the company adjust its books at the end of each year to take into account the unbilled revenues, the company controller argued that the adjustments would have but an "immaterial" impact on the financial statements. In 1981 the company had revenues of $1.1 million and income before taxes of $140,000. The company reported current assets of $170,000 and retained earnings of $830,000.

Suppose that the company consistently followed the practice of recognizing revenue in the year in which electricity was delivered rather than that in which it was billed.

a. Compute the impact of the alternative procedure, in both absolute and percentage amounts, on revenues and profits of 1981 (ignore income taxes).

b. Compute the impact on current assets and retained earnings at the end of 1981.

c. Prepare any journal entries necessary to adjust the accounts on December 31, 1981, so that revenue is recognized at the time electricity is delivered rather than when it is billed.

15. *The journal entries associated with the percentage of completion method serve to highlight the relationships among revenue recognition, expense recognition, and asset valuation.*

The Moshulu Construction Co. contracts with the Pelham Corporation to construct an office building. The contract price is $50 million. The Moshulu Co. estimates that the building will cost $40 million and will take three years to complete. The contract calls for the Pelham Corporation to make cash advances of $10 million during each of the first two years of construction and to make a final payment of $30 million upon completion of the building; these cash advances are to be accounted for on the books of Moshulu Co. as a liability until the project is completed.

The company elects to recognize revenue on the project on the percentage of completion basis. Actual expenditures over the three-year period are as follows:

| | |
|---|---|
| 1979 | $10,000,000 |
| 1980 | 25,000,000 |
| 1981 | 5,000,000 |

a. Prepare journal entries to account for the project over the three-year period. Assume that all costs are paid in cash as incurred.

b. Prepare an income statement and a balance sheet for each of the three years. Assume that at the start of the project the only asset of the company is cash of $20 million.

16. *How should revenues and expenses in the shipping industry be recognized?*

The Cromwell Co. was organized on June 1, 1980, for the specific purpose of chartering a ship to undertake a three-month, 10,000-mile voyage. On June 1, the founders of the company contributed $600,000 to the company in exchange for common stock. On the same day, the company paid the entire $600,000 to the owners of a ship for the right to use it for a period of three months.

During the three-month period the chartered ship made several stops.

Indicated in the table following are the number of miles traveled and the amount of cargo, in terms of dollar billings to customers, that the firm loaded and unloaded. (For example, in June the company loaded cargo for which it billed customers $500,000. During that same month it unloaded $300,000 of that same cargo.)

|  | Loaded | Unloaded | No. of Miles Traveled |
|---|---|---|---|
| June | $ 500,000 | $ 300,000 | 4,000 |
| July | 300,000 | 100,000 | 2,500 |
| August | 200,000 | 600,000 | 3,500 |
|  | $1,000,000 | $1,000,000 | 10,000 |

Operating and administrative expenses, in addition to the charter fee, were $100,000 per month (to be accounted for as a period cost).

The Cromwell Co. was liquidated on August 31, 1980. At that time all expenses had been paid and all bills collected.

a. Determine the income of the company over its three-month life.

b. Determine the income of the company during *each* of the three months. Make alternative decisions as to the methods used to recognize revenues and charge expenses. Assume that revenues are recognized (1) when cargo is loaded and (2) when cargo is unloaded. Assume that the $600,000 is charged as an expense (1) evenly over the three-month period and (2) in proportion to the number of miles traveled.

c. Which methods are preferable? Why?

d. The Cromwell Co. was unable to estimate, in advance, the total revenues to be earned during the voyage. If it could, is there another basis, preferable to the other two, by which the $600,000 in charter costs might be allocated?

17. *The film industry faces unique problems of income determination and asset valuation, but, as in other industries, revenues must be matched with expenses.*

Starlight, Inc. and Paramour, Inc. both produce films intended for television exhibition. The cost to produce a typical film is $150,000. The film can be licensed to a television network for $200,000. The license agreement gives exclusive exhibition rights to the network for a period of five years. At the end of the five-year period the films seldom have any commercial value.

Starlight, Inc. recognizes revenue from film productions as soon as it completes a film and signs an agreement with a network. Paramour, Inc. on the other hand, recognizes revenue only upon actual collection of license fees. Fees are contractually collectible only upon delivery of a print. Delivery is usually made several months after an agreement has been signed.

In 1979 both companies completed and signed agreements on six films; they collected the license fees on four films.

In 1980 they completed, signed agreements on, and collected the license fees, on eight films.

In 1981 they completed zero films but collected the license fees on two films.

a. Prepare income statements for each of the three years for both Starlight, Inc., and Paramour, Inc.

b. Indicate the assets related to production and licensing of the films (cash, films, license fees receivable, etc.) that would be reported on each of the corresponding balance sheets. Assume all costs of production were paid in cash in the year in which the films were completed and that each of the companies started 1979 with $100,000 cash.

Make certain that total income for the three year period as well as December 31, 1981 assets are the same for the two companies.

18. *In the advertising industry different firms use different methods to account for costs of developing advertising campaigns for clients.*

The Edward Grant Advertising Agency began operations in January 1980. In 1980 as well as in 1981 the agency billed clients for $800,000. The cost of placing its clients' ads in the media was $720,000 each year. Other operating costs were $40,000. In addition, in 1980 the agency undertook special marketing studies for one of its clients. The studies pertain to advertisements which were actually run in 1981. The cost of such studies was $30,000.

a. Assuming that the company had no assets or liabilities at the time it began operations, that all charges to clients were collected in the year billed, and that all costs were paid in the year incurred, prepare income statements and balance sheets for both 1980 and 1981 under each of two additional assumptions:

1. The cost of the special studies was charged as an expense in the year in which they were undertaken.

2. The cost of the special studies was charged as an expense in the year in which the ads with which they were associated were run.

b. Which of the assumptions results in the better matching of costs with revenues?

c. Suppose that the special studies were undertaken in an effort to *obtain* a client. As of the end of 1980, the client had still not agreed to shift its account to Edward Grant. Do you think it would be appropriate to reflect the cost of the special studies as an asset?

**19.** *Income, as determined for one purpose, may not be appropriate for another.*

Tom Ogden celebrated Christmas 1980 by purchasing a new car. In his first year as sales manager of the newly formed industrial equipment division of the Shakespeare Manufacturing Co., Ogden and his sales force had generated $750,000 in noncancelable orders for equipment.

Ogden's employment contract provided that he receive an annual bonus equal to 3 percent of his division's profits. He was aware that costs of manufacturing the equipment were approximately 60 percent of sales prices and that the company had budgeted $200,000 for administrative and all other operating costs. He could afford to splurge on a new car since, according to his rough calculations, his bonus would total at least $3,000.

In mid-January, Ogden received a bonus check for $1,200. Stunned, but confident that a clerical error had been made, he placed an urgent call to the company controller. The controller informed him that no error had been made. Although costs were in line with those budgeted, reported sales were only $600,000.

The equipment produced by Shakespeare is special-purpose polishing equipment. Since it must be custom-made, customers must normally wait for delivery at least two months from date of order.

a. Demonstrate how the amount of the bonus was calculated by *both* Ogden and the company controller. What is the most likely explanation of the difference in their sales figures?

b. The company president has asked for your recommendations with respect to the bonus plan. Assuming that the objective of the company is to give reasonably prompt recognition to the accomplishments of its sales manager, on what basis do you think revenue should be recognized for the purpose of computing sales manager's bonus? Do you think the company should use the same basis for reporting to shareholders? Explain.

**20.** *How should a computer software company, in the face of uncertainty as to whether its productive efforts will provide returns, recognize revenues and expenses?*

The University Systems Co. developed a series of computer programs designed to simplify the "back office" operations of stock brokerage firms. All costs of developing the programs have been charged to expense accounts as incurred. Although the programs can readily be applied to the operations of all firms in the industry, certain features of the programs must be custom-designed to meet the specific requirements of each customer. It is generally possible to estimate with reasonable reliability the costs of developing the custom features.

In January 1980 analysts of University Systems made a preliminary study of the "back office" operations of Conrad, Roy, Atwood, Smith, and Harris (CRASH), a leading brokerage firm. University Systems hoped that as a result of the study it could demonstrate the savings in costs and increases in efficiency that its programs could bring about and that it could thereby sell its programs to CRASH. It was agreed that the entire costs of the preliminary study would be borne by University Systems; CRASH was under no obligation to either purchase the programs or pay for the preliminary study. Cost of the preliminary study was $10,000.

The preliminary study was successful; on February 2, 1980, CRASH placed an order with University Systems for its series of programs; the contract price was $150,000.

During February and March, University Systems developed the custom features of the program for CRASH. Costs incurred in February were $8,000, and in March, $12,000. These costs were equal to amounts previously estimated.

On March 15, 1980, University Systems delivered the completed series of programs to CRASH, and they were reviewed and accepted by CRASH management.

On April 4, 1980, University Systems received a check for $50,000 plus a two-year, 8 percent note for the balance.

a. Prepare journal entries to record the events described above.

b. Prepare comparative income statements for the months ending January 31, February 28, March 31, and April 30.

c. In a short paragraph, justify your choice of basis of revenue and expense recognition. Indicate any assumptions that you may have made.

*solutions to exercise for review and self-testing*

1. a. Construction in process        $500,000

     Cash (or accounts payable)            $500,000

**To record construction costs incurred.**

b. The percentage of total revenues to be recognized equals 40 percent (two-fifths); 40 percent of $1 million is $400,000.

c. The percentage of total expenses to be recognized must also equal 40 percent; 40 percent of $800,000 is $320,000

d. Completed pools must be carried at contract value—$400,000

e. Construction in process must be reduced by $320,000.

f. Completed pools at contract value        $400,000

     Revenue from construction            $400,000

**To record revenue from construction.**

    Expenses relating to revenue from

     construction        $320,000

       Construction in process            $320,000

**To record expenses relating to revenues.**

2. a. Construction in process        $300,000

     Cash (or accounts payable)            $300,000

**To record construction costs incurred.**

    Completed pools at contract value        $600,000

     Revenue from construction            $600,000

**To record revenue from construction.**

Expenses relating to revenue from
construction                             $480,000

      Construction in process                        $480,000

**To record expenses relating to revenues.**

b. Accounts receivable                           $1,000,000

      Completed pools at contract
value                                      $1,000,000

**To record delivery of pools to the city.**

# 6

# Valuation of Assets;
# Cash and
# Marketable Securities

# Part I: Valuation of Assets

The next several chapters will be directed primarily to questions of asset and liability valuation—that is, to the problems of determining the most meaningful amounts to be assigned to the various balance sheet accounts. This chapter will be given over to both an overview of the valuation process and to consideration of two specific assets, cash and marketable securities.

Although accountants have been unable to derive a definition of an asset that has been universally accepted, almost all proposed definitions stress the notion that assets represent rights to future services or economic benefits. The question facing the accountant is what value—what quantitative measure—should be assigned to the potential services or benefits. (Such question is, of course, directly related to that discussed in the previous chapter: When should increases or decreases in the value of net assets—those associated with revenues and expenses—be accorded accounting recognition?)

The accounting profession has yet to reach a consensus on criteria of valuation. The reason is suggested, in part, by a comparison of alternative definitions of the term value. Value, as it relates to financial statements, can have at least three distinctive meanings: (1) an assigned or calculated numerical quantity; as in mathematics, the quantity or amount for which a symbol stands; (2) the worth of something sold or exchanged; the worth of a thing in money or goods at a certain time; its fair market price; (3) worth in usefulness or importance to the possessor; utility or merit. Each of the three definitions suggests differing principles of valuation.

### Historical Cost

The first definition, that value is nothing more than an assigned or calculated numerical quantity, implies that value need have nothing to do with inherent worth; it is simply a numerical quantity assigned on a basis that is, presumably, logical and orderly. It is, in fact, this first meaning that is most consistent with current accounting practice.

Financial statements are cost based. Assets are initially recorded at the amounts paid for them. Subsequent to date of purchase, assets are, in general (some exceptions will be pointed out later in this chapter), reported at either initial cost or depreciated cost. Depreciated cost is initial cost less that portion of initial cost (often indicated in a contra account) representing the services of the asset already utilized. Land is an example of an asset that is reported at initial cost; plant and equipment are examples of assets that are reported at depreciated cost.

Except at the date assets are purchased, the cost-based amounts reported on a firm's balance sheet do not represent (unless by coincidence) the prices at which they can be either purchased or sold. The reported amounts can be viewed as approximations of neither the fair market value nor the worth of the services which the assets will provide. They designate nothing more than initial cost less that portion of initial cost already absorbed as an expense.

Why do accountants "value" assets at amounts that have nothing to do with either market value or inherent worth? The justification for this practice is two-fold. First, amounts reported on the balance sheet are relatively objective. The amount at which an asset is initially recorded is established by an exchange transaction among independent parties; it is an amount that can be readily verified. Thereafter, the initial recorded amount is reduced in a systematic and orderly manner. Once useful life has been determined (and some additional assumptions, to be discussed in later chapters, are made pertaining to the method of depreciation to be used), the computation of book value is straightforward. It is unaffected by fluctuations of the market price of either the asset itself or the goods to the production of which the asset contributes.

Second, and perhaps more significant, historical cost valuations are consistent with the concepts of income determination discussed in the previous chapter. The cost of an asset is generally charged as an expense as the services associated with the asset are actually provided. That portion of cost that has not yet been charged off as an expense represents the remaining services to be provided and as such must be accorded accounting recognition. The balance sheet is the means of accounting for the unexpired costs of assets. It may be viewed as a statement of *residuals*—costs which have not yet been charged off as expenses and must, resultantly, be carried forward to future accounting periods. The balance sheet (in conjunction with the income statement) provides a measure of accountability over the *initial costs* of assets purchased. It is not purported to indicate the market value of a firm's assets; its limitations should be clearly understood.

### B Market Values

If, instead, accountants were to accept the second definition of value—the worth of a thing in money or goods at a certain time—then they would most logically look to the market place to determine the amount at which an asset should be reported. They would value assets at their market prices on the date of the balance sheet.

Numerous arguments have been advanced for a market price approach to asset valuation. Proponents assert that a balance sheet in which all assets were reported at current value would provide investors and managers with information that would be far more relevant to the decisions that they must make. Current value not only provides an indication of either the price at which an asset might be sold or that which would have to be paid to replace it but may also be used to determine the asset's *opportunity cost*—the amount that might be earned if the asset were sold and the proceeds used in the best alternative capacity.

**input value vs. output value**

The market value of an asset can be interpreted as either a current *output price* or a current *input cost*. The two are not necessarily the same, and strong support for using one or the other can be found in the accounting literature. The current output price of an asset ordinarily represents its *net realizable value* —the amount at which it can be sold less any costs that must be incurred to bring it to a salable condition. The current input cost represents the price that would have to be paid to obtain the same asset or its equivalent. From the standpoint of a manufacturing concern the current output price of goods which it had produced and were ready for sale would be the price at which the goods could be sold. The current input cost would be that of manufacturing the goods. The difference between the two would normally be the manufacturer's margin of profit.

Despite its obvious appeal, there are significant disadvantages to the current value approach to reporting assets. The reported value of an asset would be determined apart from its utility to its particular owner. An asset would be valued at its current market price regardless of whether the firm intends to sell it immediately or to continue using it for several additional years. Technological advances may cause the replacement cost of a piece of equipment to decline substantially. But such advances may not necessarily reduce the utility of that equipment to its owner. Moreover, if output values were used, assets such as nonsalable specialized equipment or intangible assets such as organizational costs or deferred start-up and preoperating costs would not be considered to be assets at all; they would be assigned values corresponding to the prices at which they could be sold—zero.

**market values in practice**

Even though conventional accounting is primarily cost based, in selected situations accountants do employ market prices in determining the appropriate asset values to report. In general, whenever revenue is recognized prior to the point of sale, the related asset is reported at either the amount that is expected to be realized or some fraction thereof. For example, when revenue is recognized upon completion of production (e.g., upon the removal of a precious mineral from the ground) the completed products are valued at their anticipated selling price—a current output price. To avoid the distortions in income that would result from delaying recognition of revenue until point of sale, accountants are forced to make estimates of the amount of revenue that will actually be realized. The best indication of the amount to be actually realized is a fixed contract price, or in the absence of such a price, the current market price of the commodity intended for sale.

The concern of accountants with conservatism also leads them to report current values whenever the market price of an asset intended for sale falls below its acquisition cost. Following the rule of *lower of cost or market,* the accountant compares the historical cost of an asset—that which the company paid to either purchase or produce it—with what it would cost to *replace* it (a current *input* cost). If the market—the replacement—price is less than the historical cost, then the asset is *written down* to the market price and the corresponding loss recognized on the income statement. The lower of cost or market rule is applied only to assets, primarily inventories and marketable securities, that the firm actually expects to sell in the normal course of business. It is grounded on the assumption that financial statements would be misleading if assets were valued at prices higher than those for which the company expects to sell them. The rule is not ordinarily applied to assets, such as plant and equipment, that are not intended for resale. The lower of cost or market rule will be examined in greater detail in Chapter 8 in connection with a discussion of inventories.

## Value to User

The third definition expresses value in terms of worth in usefulness or importance to the individual possessor. It suggests that the value of an asset be determined with respect to the particular firm that owns it. This third concept of value has considerable attraction to accounting theoreticians, but inasmuch as it requires that the future benefits of an asset be specifically identified and measured, it has received relatively little acceptance in practice. Nevertheless, it is of interest for two reasons. First, understanding the worth of an asset to a particular firm or individual offers insight into the nature of assets and into the determination of market prices. Second, in the absence of both a clearly defined exchange transaction and a current market price accountants are sometimes forced to resort to analysis of the "true" nature of an asset in order to determine an appropriate book value.

The economic benefits associated with an asset ordinarily take the form of cash receipts. An individual invests the common stock of a corporation in anticipation of cash receipts greater than the cash disbursement required by the initial purchase. The cash receipts will be derived from either periodic cash dividends paid by the company or from the proceeds resulting from the sale of the stock or both. Similarly, a manufacturer purchases a machine with the expectation that it will contribute to the production of goods which when sold will generate cash receipts. The value of an asset to its owner is, therefore, the value of the net cash receipts that the asset is expected to produce. The task of the accountant is, first, to identify and measure the cash receipts—an obviously difficult task considering that most assets result in cash receipts only when used in conjunction with other assets and that in a world of uncertainty future sales and future costs cannot be readily estimated. And, second, it is to determine the present value of those cash receipts.

Although it might appear as if the value of expected cash receipts is simply the sum of all anticipated receipts, an analysis of some fundamental concepts of compound interest will demonstrate that this is not so. Since cash may be placed in interest-bearing bank accounts or used to acquire securities that will provide a periodic return, it has a value in time. Funds to be received in years hence may be of less value than those to be received at present.

### Compound Interest and Value of Cash Receipts

**future value**  Suppose that an individual deposited $1 in a savings bank. The bank pays interest at the rate of 6 percent per year. Interest is *compounded* (computed) annually at the end of each year. To how much would the deposit have grown at the end of one year?

The accumulated value of the deposit at the end of one year would be $1 \times 1.06 = \$1.06$.

In more general terms,

$$F_n = P(1 + r)^n$$

where

$F_n$ represents the final accumulation of the initial investment after $n$ interest periods,
$P$ represents the initial investment or deposit, and
$r$ indicates the rate of interest

As indicated in Exhibit 6–1, after two years the initial deposit would have accumulated to $1.12—the $1.06 on deposit at the beginning of the second year times 1.06. After three years it would have accumulated to $1.19—the $1.12 on deposit at the beginning of the third year again times 1.06.

Employing the general formula (and rounding to the nearest cent),

At the end of two years: $F = P(1 + r)^n$; $F = \$1(1 + .06)^2 = \$1.12$
At the end of three years: $F = P(1 + r)^n$; $F = \$1(1 + .06)^3 = \$1.19$
At the end of six years: $F = P(1 + r)^n$; $F = \$1(1 + .06)^6 = \$1.42$

EXHIBIT 6-1

**Future Value of $1 Invested Today—6% Return**
**(rounded to nearest cent)**

*Years*

| 0 | 1 | 2 | 3 | 4 | 5 | 6 |
|---|---|---|---|---|---|---|

$1.00 → $1.06 → $1.12 → $1.19 → $1.26 → $1.34 → $1.42

If an amount other than $1 were deposited, then the accumulated amount could be computed simply by substituting that amount for $P$ in the basic formula. Thus $200 deposited in a bank at a rate of 6 percent would grow to $200 times $(1.06)^6$ —$283.70 at the end of six years.

To facilitate computations of compound interest, series of tables have been developed and are readily available in almost all accounting textbooks as well as numerous books of financial tables. Table 1 in the Appendix of this volume indicates the amounts to which $1 will accumulate at various interest rates and at the end of different accounting periods. The number at the intersection of the 6 percent column and the 6 periods row indicates that $1 would accumulate to $1.4185. $200 would accumulate to $200 times that amount— $200 × 1.4185 = $283.70.

Several examples may serve to illustrate the concept of future value.

*example 1*     A company sells a parcel of land for $50,000. The purchaser requests to be allowed to delay payment for a period of three years. The company agrees to accept a note from the purchaser for $50,000 plus interest at an annual rate of 8 percent. What amount would the purchaser be required to pay at the end of three years?

As indicated in Table 1 (8 percent column, 3 periods row), $1 will grow to $1.2597. Hence, $50,000 will grow to $50,000 times $1.2597—$62,985. The purchaser would be required to pay $62,985.

*example 2*     An individual deposits $300 in a savings bank. The bank pays interest at an annual rate of 4 percent *compounded semiannually.* To what amount will the deposit accumulate at the end of 10 years?

If interest is compounded semiannually and the *annual* rate of interest is 4 percent, then interest is computed *twice* each year at 2 percent—*one-half* the annual rate. (Interest is almost always stated at an *annual* rate even when compounded semiannually or quarterly.) Each interest period would be 6 months, rather than a year, so that over a 10-year span there would be 20 interest periods. Table 1 indicates that at an interest rate of 2 percent $1 will accumulate to

$1.4859 after 20 periods. Hence, $300 will accumulate to $300 times 1.4859— $445.77. As a general rule, whenever interest is compounded semiannually, the interest rate must be halved and the number of years doubled.

*example 3*
A corporation invests $10,000 and expects to earn a return of 8 percent compounded annually for the next 60 years. To how much will the $10,000 accumulate over the 60-year period?

Table 1 does not indicate accumulations for 60 years. However, the table does indicate that $1 invested at 8 percent for 50 years would accumulate to $46.9016. Over 50 years $10,000 would accumulate to $469,016. The table also indicates that $1 invested at 8 percent for 10 years would accumulate to $2.1589. If at the end of 50 years $469,016 were invested for an additional 10 years, it would increase in value to $2.1589 times $469,016—$1,012,558.

*example 4*
A corporation reached an agreement to sell a warehouse. The purchaser agreed to pay $80,000 for the warehouse but wanted to delay payment for four years. The corporation, however, was in immediate need of cash and agreed to accept a lesser amount if payment were made at time of sale. The corporation estimated that it would otherwise have to borrow the needed funds at a rate of 5 percent. What amount should the corporation be willing to accept if cash payment were made at the time of sale rather than delayed for four years?

The question can be stated in an alternative form. What amount if invested today at an interest rate of 5 percent would accumulate to $80,000 in four years? From Table 1, it may be seen that $1 invested today would increase to $1.2155. Hence, some amount ($x$) times 1.2155 would increase to $80,000:

$$1.2155x = \$80,000$$

Solving for $x$ (i.e., dividing $80,000 by 1.2155) indicates that amount to be $65,817. Thus, the company would be equally well off if it accepted payment of $65,817 today as it would be if it waited four years to receive the full $80,000. In other words, $65,817 deposited in a bank today at a 5 percent annual interest rate would increase in value to $80,000 after four years.

**present value**
As implied in Example 4, it is frequently necessary to compute the *present value* of a sum of money to be received in the future. That is, one may want to know the amount which if invested today at a certain rate of return would be the equivalent of a fixed amount to be received in a specific number of years hence.

In simplist terms, an example can be formulated as follows. If a bank pays interest at the rate of 6 percent annually, how much cash would an individual have to deposit today in order to have that amount accumulate *to* $1 one year from now? Example 4 illustrated one means of computation. In more general terms, the present value of a future sum can be calculated by rearranging the basic equation for future value—$F_n = P(1 + r)^n$. Thus,

$$P = F_n \frac{1}{(1 + r)^n}$$

where, as previously,

$F_n$ represents the final accumulation of the initial investment after $n$ years,
$r$ indicates the rate of interest (which when used in connection with present value situations is often referred to as a *discount* rate, since a future payment will be *discounted* to a present value), and
$P$ indicates the required initial deposit or investment.

$$P = \$1 \frac{1}{(1 + .06)^1} = \$.94$$

The present value of $1 to be received two years in the future would be

$$P = F_n \frac{1}{(1 + r)^n}; \quad P = \$1 \frac{1}{(1 + .06)^2} = \$.89$$

The present value of $1 to be received six years in the future would be

$$P = F_n \frac{1}{(1 + r)^n}; \quad P = \$1 \frac{1}{(1 + .06)^6} = \$.71$$

In other words, as illustrated in Exhibit 6-2, $.71 invested today at 6 percent interest compounded annually would increase to $1 at the end of six years.

## EXHIBIT 6-2

**Present Values of $1 to Be Received in the Future—6% Return**
**(rounded to nearest cent)**

*Years*

| 0 | 1 | 2 | 3 | 4 | 5 | 6 |
|---|---|---|---|---|---|---|
| $.94 ◄——— $1 | | | | | | |
| .89 ◄——————— $1 | | | | | | |
| .84 ◄————————————— $1 | | | | | | |
| .79 ◄——————————————————— $1 | | | | | |
| .75 ◄————————————————————————— $1 | | | |
| .71 ◄——————————————————————————————— $1 |

As with future value, if an amount other than $1 were to be received, then the present value of such amount could be determined by substituting that amount for $F$. Thus, if an individual wanted to receive $200 six years from the present, then the amount he would have to invest today at 6 percent interest would be

$$P = \$200 \frac{1}{(1.06)^6} = \$141$$

Table 2 in the Appendix indicates the present value of $1 for various discount rates and time periods. The present value of $1 to be received six years from today discounted at the rate of 6 percent would be $.7050. The present value of $200 would be $200 times .7050–$141.

Concepts of present value are demonstrated in the examples that follow.

*example 1*   Assume the same fact situation as in Example 4 of the previous section. A corporation agreed to sell a warehouse. The purchaser was willing to pay $80,000 four years hence or some lesser amount at time of sale. Assuming that the corporation would have to borrow the needed funds at a rate of 5 percent, what equivalent amount should it be willing to accept if payment were made at time of sale?

Per Table 2, the present value of $1 to be received in four years, at an annual rate of 5 percent, is $.8227. The present value of $80,000 is $80,000 X .8277–$65,816. Save for a $1 rounding difference, the result is identical to that computed in the earlier illustration.

*example 2*   A rich uncle wishes to give his nephew a gift of the cost of a college education. The nephew will enter college in six years. It is estimated that when he enters college, tuition and other charges will be approximately $20,000 for a degree program. The gift will be placed in a bank, which pays interest at an annual rate of 8 percent, compounded *quarterly*. What size gift is required if the full $20,000 is to be available to the nephew at the start of his college career?

Since interest is compounded *quarterly,* the question to be answered is as follows: What is the present value of $20,000 to be received *24* (4 times six years) periods away if discounted at a rate of *2* percent per period? Per Table 2, the present value of $1 to be received 24 periods in the future, discounted at a rate of 2 percent, is $.6217. The present value of $20,000 is, therefore, $20,000 times .6217–$12,434. (*Check:* Per Table 1, the future value of $1 to be received in 24 periods if invested at a rate of 2 percent is $1.6084. $12,434 times $1.6084 is $20,000.)

**future value of an annuity**

Commercial transactions frequently involve not just a single deposit or future payment but rather a series of equal payments spaced evenly apart. For example, a company interested in saving for a particular long-range goal would be concerned with the amount that it would be required to deposit during each of a certain number of years to attain that goal. A series of *equal* payments at fixed intervals is known as *an annuity.* An annuity in which the payments are made or received at the *end* of each period is known as an *ordinary annuity* or an *annuity in arrears*. One in which the payments are made or received at the *beginning* of each period is known as an *annuity due* or an *annuity in advance*. Unless otherwise indicated, the examples in this chapter will be based on the assumption that payments are made or received at the *end* of each period. (Annuity tables in the Appendix contain interest factors for ordinary annuity.)

Suppose that at the *end* of each of four years a person deposits $1 in a savings account. The account pays interest at the rate of 6 percent per year, compounded annually. How much will be available for withdrawal at the end of the fourth year?

*EXHIBIT 6-3*

**Future Value of $1 Invested at the End of Each of Four Periods–6% Return (rounded to nearest cent)**

| | *Years* | | | |
|---|---|---|---|---|
| | *1* | *2* | *3* | *4* |
| | $1.00 → | $1.06 → | $1.12 → | $1.19 |
| | | $1.00 → | 1.06 → | 1.12 |
| | | | 1.00 → | 1.06 |
| | | | | 1.00 |
| Amount available for withdrawal | $1.00 | $2.06 | $3.18 | $4.37 |

As shown in Exhibit 6–3, the $1 deposited at the end of the first period will accumulate interest for a total of three years. As indicated in Table 1, it will increase in value to $1.19. The deposit at the end of the second year will grow to $1.12, and that at the end of the third year will grow to $1.06. The payment made at the end of the fourth year will not yet have earned any interest. As revealed in the diagram, the series of four $1 payments will be worth $4.37 at the end of the fourth year.

The mathematical expression for the future value $(F)$ of a series of payments of a fixed amount ($A$) compounded at an interest rate ($r$) over a given number of years ($n$) is

$$F = A \left[ \frac{(1 + r)^n - 1}{r} \right]$$

The value at the end of four years of $1 deposited at the end of each of four years compounded at an annual rate of 6 percent is

$$F = \$1 \left[ \frac{(1 + .06)^4 - 1}{.06} \right] = \$4.37$$

Table 3 in the Appendix indicates the future values of annuities of $1 for various rates of return. Notice the relationship between Table 3 and Table 1. With a slight adjustment, the amounts in the annuity table (Table 3) represent the sum of the amounts in the simple future value table (Table 1). The adjustment is that, to get the future value of an annuity of $1 for $n$ periods, to the sum of the amounts of $n - 1$ periods in the simple annuity table (Table 1) 1.0 must be added. Thus, the sum of the amounts for *three* ($n - 1$) periods in the 6 percent column of the future value table is 3.3746. This amount plus 1.00 (i.e., 4.3746) is the same as that in the 6 percent column, *4th* period row of the annuity table. The adjustment takes into account the fact that the annuity table has been compiled on the assumption that each payment is made at the end of a period rather than at the beginning, as assumed in the single-payment table. The next three examples illustrate the concept of an annuity.

*example 1*  A corporation has agreed to deposit 10 percent of an employee's salary into a retirement fund. The fund will be invested in stocks and bonds that will provide a return of 8 percent annually. How much will be available to the employee upon his retirement in 20 years assuming that the employee earns $30,000 per year?

The future value of an annuity of $1 per year compounded at a rate of 8 percent per year for 20 years is $45.7620. Hence, the future value of an annuity of $3,000 (10 percent of $30,000) is $3,000 times 45.7620–$137,286.

*example 2*  An individual invests $1,000 per year in securities that yield 5 percent per year compounded annually. To how much will his investments accumulate at the end of 60 years?

Table 3 does not specifically indicate values for 60 periods. However, per Table 3, $1,000 deposited at the end of each of 50 periods and compounded at a rate of 5 percent will accumulate to $1,000 times 209.3480–$209,348. At the end of 50 years, therefore, the individual will have $209,348 invested in securities. Per Table 1, that sum will increase to $209,348 times 1.6289–$341,007–by the end of the 10 additional years. The $1,000 deposited at the end of years 51 through 60–an ordinary annuity for 10 years–will accumulate, per Table 3, to $1,000 times 12.5779—$12,578. The total amount that will have accumulated over the 60-year period is the sum of the two amounts, $341,007 and $12,578—$353,585.

*example 3*        A corporation has an obligation to repay $200,000 in bonds upon their maturity in 20 years. The company wishes to make annual cash payments to a fund to assure that when the bonds are due it will have the necessary cash on hand. The company intends to invest the fund in securities that will yield a return of 8 percent, compounded annually.

$200,000 represents the future value of an annuity. That is, some amount ($x$) deposited annually to return 8 percent will accumulate at the end of 20 years to $200,000. From Table 3, it can be seen that $1 invested annually would accumulate in 20 years to $45.7620. Therefore, some amount ($x$) times 45.7620 would accumulate to $200,000:

$$45.7620x = \$200,000$$

$$x = \frac{\$200,000}{45.7620}$$

$$= \$4,370$$

If deposited annually into a fund which earns a return of 8 percent, $4,370 would accumulate to $200,000 in 20 years.

**present value of an annuity**        Just as it is sometimes necessary to know the present value of a single payment to be received sometime in the future, so also there is sometimes concern for the present value of a stream of payments. An investor or creditor may wish to know the amount to be received today that would be the equivalent of a stream of payments to be received in the future.

The present value, discounted at 6 percent, of $1 to be received at the end of each of the future four periods is depicted diagramatically in Exhibit 6–4.

*EXHIBIT 6–4*

**Present Value of $1 to Be Received at the End of Each of Four Periods—6% Return (rounded to the nearest cent)**

| | | Years | | |
|---|---|---|---|---|
| *0* | *1* | *2* | *3* | *4* |
| $ .94 ◄——— $1 | | | | |
| .89 ◄——————— $1 | | | | |
| .84 ◄————————————— $1 | | | | |
| .79 ◄——————————————————— $1 | | | | |
| $3.46 | | | | |

The present value of the stream of receipts, $3.46, is nothing more than the sum of the present values of the individual receipts. The present values of the individual receipts, which are indicated in the left-hand column, could be taken directly from Table 2.

The mathematical formula for the present value ($P_A$) of an annuity of $A$ dollars per period compounded at a rate of $r$ for $n$ periods is

$$P_A = A \left[ \frac{1 - (1 + r)^{-n}}{r} \right]$$

The present value of an annuity of $1 per period for four periods compounded at a rate of 6 percent is

$$P_A = \$1 \left[ \frac{1 - (1 + .06)^{-4}}{.06} \right] = \$3.46$$

Table 4 in the Appendix indicates the present values of annuities in arrears (i.e., payments received at the *end* of each period) at various rates of return. Each amount in Table 4 is simply the sum, up to that period, of the amounts in Table 2.

The application of the concept of the present value of an annuity is demonstrated in the examples that follow.

*example 1*    An individual wishes to give his daughter a gift of a sum of money such that if she deposits the sum in a bank she would be able to withdraw $8,000 at the end of each of the four years in order to meet her college expenses. The bank pays interest at the rate of 5 percent per year compounded annually. What is the single amount that the individual should give his daughter that would be the equivalent of four annual payments of $8,000 each.

The present value of an annuity of $1 per year for four years compounded at a rate of 5 percent is, per Table 4, $3.5460. The present value of an annuity of $8,000 is $8,000 times 3.5460–$28,368.

The result can be verified as follows:

| | |
|---|---:|
| Initial deposit | $28,368 |
| First-year earnings (5%) | 1,418 |
| Balance at end of first year before withdrawal | $29,786 |
| First-year withdrawal | ( 8,000) |
| Balance at end of first year | $21,786 |
| Second-year earnings (5%) | 1,089 |
| Balance at end of second year before withdrawal | $22,875 |
| Second-year withdrawal | ( 8,000) |
| Balance at end of second year | $14,875 |
| Third-year earnings (5%) | 744 |

| | |
|---|---:|
| Balance at end of third year before withdrawal | 15,619 |
| Third-year withdrawal | ( 8,000) |
| Balance at end of third year | $ 7,619 |
| Fourth-year earnings (5%) | 381 |
| Balance at end of fourth year before withdrawal | $ 8,000 |
| Fourth-year withdrawal | ( 8,000) |
| Balance at end of fourth year | $   0 |

*example 2*   A corporation has a choice; it can either lease its new plant at an annual rental fee of $30,000 for 20 years or it can purchase it. Assuming that the company estimates that it could earn 7 percent annually on any funds not invested in the plant, what would be the equivalent cost of purchasing the plant? Assume also that the plant would have no value at the end of 20 years.

The present value of a stream of payments of $1 per year, compounded at a rate of 7 percent, for 20 years, is, per Table 4, $10.5940. The present value of a stream of payments of $30,000 is $30,000 times 10.5940–$317,820. The company would be equally well off renting the plant for $30,000 per year or purchasing it for $317,820 (ignoring, of course, both tax and risk factors).

*example 3*   A corporation issues a security (e.g., a bond) that contains the following provision: The corporation agrees to pay the purchaser $20,000 every 6 months for 20 years and make an additional single lump-sum payment of $500,000 at the end of the 20-year period. How much would an investor be willing to pay for such a security assuming that if he did not purchase the security he could, alternatively, invest the funds in other securities which would provide an annual return of 10 percent compounded semiannually?

The company promises to pay an annuity of $20,000 per period for *40* six-month periods. The present value of such an annuity when discounted at a rate of 5 *percent* (the *semiannual* alternative rate of return) is, with reference to Table 4,

$$\$20,000 \times 17.1591 = \$343,182$$

The present value of a single payment of $500,000, 40 periods hence, discounted at a semiannual rate of 5 percent is, with reference to Table 2,

$$\$500,000 \times .1420 = \$71,000$$

The present value of the stream of payments *and* the single lump-sum payment is, therefore, $343,182 plus $71,000–$414,182. Similar examples will be alluded to again in Chapter 10; they help explain why a bond with a certain face value (e.g., $500,000) might sell in the open market at a greater or lesser amount (e.g., $414,182).

*example 4*    A company wishes to contribute an amount to a pension fund such that each employee will have an annual income of $12,000 upon retirement. The firm's consulting actuary estimates that an average employee will survive 15 years after his retirement and will be employed 20 years prior to his retirement. The company anticipates that it will be able to obtain a return of 6 percent per year on contributions to the fund. How much should the company contribute each year, per employee, to the pension fund?

Upon the retirement of an employee, the company must have in its pension fund an amount equivalent to a stream of payments of $12,000 for 15 years. Per Table 4, the present value of a stream of payments of $1 per year, for 15 years, discounted at a rate of 6 percent is $9.7122. The present value of the stream of $12,000 is $12,000 times 9.7122–$116,546.

The company must, therefore, make equal annual payments of such amount that the accumulated value of the payments after 20 years (the expected number of years an employee will work prior to his retirement) will be $116,546. According to Table 3, a stream of payments of $1, invested to yield a return of 6 percent, will accumulate to $36.7856 after 20 years. Hence, some amount ($x$) times 36.7856 will accumulate to $116,546:

$$36.7856x = \$116,546$$
$$x = \$3,168$$

The firm would have to make 20 annual payments of $3,168 in order to be able to withdraw $12,000 per year for 15 years.

### Discounted Cash Flow as a Means of Determining the Value of Assets

The procedures described in the preceding section in which a stream of future cash flows is *discounted* back to the present can be employed to determine the value to a particular firm of either individual assets or groups of assets.

*example*    A firm is contemplating the purchase of new equipment. The company has determined that a new machine will enable it to reduce out-of-pocket production costs, after taxes, by $8,000 per year. If the machine will have a useful life of five years and the firm demands that it obtain a return of at least 10 percent per year on all invested funds, what is the maximum amount it would be willing to pay for the machine?

The present value of the stream of equal cash savings is (per Table 4) 3.7908 times $8,000–$30,326. The company would be willing to pay no more than that amount for the new machine.

5 yr

10 %

226

## Summary of Part 1

In accord with conventional financial reporting, the value assigned to an asset is ordinarily based on its historical cost—the amount paid to acquire it, less that portion of initial cost representing the services of the asset already consumed (i.e., allowance for depreciation or amortization). Such amount is relatively objective and is consistent with the concept of income determination by which the cost of an asset is charged as an expense as the services associated with it are actually used. The portion of the cost that represents the services that have not yet been consumed is carried forward to future accounting periods and is reported on the balance sheet.

Alternatively, even though not generally done, an asset could be stated on the balance sheet at its market value. Market value could either be an output price (that at which the asset could be sold) or an input price (that which would have to be paid to replace the asset). The market value of an asset is usually more relevant than its historical cost for most decisions that readers of financial statements have to make, since it is reasonably indicative of the economic sacrifice being made by the enterprise by holding and using the asset rather than selling it. But market value fails to take into account the utility of an asset to its particular user (e.g., the value of prior year models of equipment may be greater to a company than the market price would indicate). Moreover, the general use of market values (particularly output values) may be inconsistent with the concept that costs should be charged as expenses in the periods associated with the benefits that they provide. Start-up or organizational costs, for example, may not be considered to be assets at all, since they can not readily be sold in the open market. The entire amounts of the costs would be charged as expenses in the periods in which they were incurred.

The value of an asset could also be stated in terms of its utility to a specific user. The worth of an asset to a particular user may be defined as the present value of the anticipated cash receipts with which it is associated. The present value of the cash receipts must take into account the "time value of money"—the fact that a dollar received today is worth considerably more than one to be received in the distant future. Determination of the present value of cash flows requires an understanding of the fundamental concepts of compound interest—hence the extended discussion of that topic in this chapter. It is often impractical, however, to determine the present value of a particular asset, since individual assets are not generally associated with specific cash receipts. Thus, conventional financial statements seldom express asset values in terms of worth to the individual possessor. Nevertheless, an understanding of the concepts of present values of cash flows provides an appreciation of the underlying forces that determine the market values of assets.

In Part II of this chapter, as well as in the next several chapters, we shall deal with problems of valuing specific assets, such as cash, marketable securities, accounts receivable, inventories, and plant and equipment.

# Part II: Cash and Marketable Securities

### Cash

Of all assets and liabilities, cash would appear to present the fewest problems of valuation. Cash is ordinarily measured at its face value. Nonetheless, in recent years controversy has arisen over the most appropriate means of classifying and reporting cash balances.

Cash includes currency on hand and funds on deposit in banks that are subject to immediate and unconditional withdrawal (i.e., amounts in checking accounts). It does not in a strict sense include amounts that may be subject to withdrawal restrictions, such as funds in the form of savings accounts, which may technically require advance notification for withdrawal, or certificates of deposit, although in practice the distinction between the two is not often made. Most companies maintain several general ledger accounts for cash; in statements made available to the public, however, most cash balances are summarized into a single figure.

There are several characteristics of cash that make it of distinctive concern to the accountant and financial analyst. Cash is the most liquid of all assets and is the common medium of exchange in our society. As such, it must be the subject of especially tight safeguards and controls. As a general rule, for example, the number of persons handling currency should be kept to a minimum, all currency should be deposited in a bank as soon as feasible, and accounting recognition should be given immediately to all cash receipts via a cash register tape or a manual listing. The responsibility for particular cash funds should be assigned to particular individuals, and whenever possible, in order to better assure that the payments are made to the parties for whom they are intended, disbursements should be made by check rather than with currency.

Cash is the accepted medium of paying bills and satisfying obligations. As such it is essential that a firm have an adequate amount of cash available to meet its debts as they come due and to make the day-to-day payments required of any operating enterprise. A financial analyst or potential creditor must, therefore, be continually alert to whether the firm's available cash—or assets that can readily be turned into cash—is sufficient to meet foreseeable needs.

Cash, however, is basically an unproductive asset. Cash on hand or on deposit in a checking account earns no interest. Insofar as there is any degree of inflation in the economy, cash continually loses its purchasing power. Unlike many other assets, it produces no services or return to its owner. As a consequence, it is to the advantage of a firm to keep as little cash as possible either on hand or in checking accounts. Cash that is needed for a *safety reserve* or is being held for future purchase of other assets, distribution to share-holders, or payment of outstanding obligations should be invested temporar-ily in common stocks, short-term government notes, certificates of deposit, or other interest-bearing securities.

**cash on hand**    Cash on hand includes customer receipts that have not yet been deposited, currency necessary to conduct routine business, and *petty cash.* Petty cash represents small amounts of cash maintained to meet disbursements of insuffi-cient size that do not justify the time and inconvenience of writing a check. Petty cash funds are frequently accounted for on an *imprest* basis. That is, the general ledger balance of petty cash will always reflect a fixed amount, $100, for example. At any given time the fund itself should contain either cash or pay-ment receipts for that amount. Periodically the fund is restored to its original amount by a transfer from general cash, and at that time accounting recogni-tion is given to the particular expenses that had been incurred. The following journal entry might be made to restore $70 to the petty cash fund:

| | | |
|---|---|---|
| Postage expense | $30 | |
| Entertainment expense | 40 | |
| Cash in bank | | $70 |
| **To replenish petty cash fund.** | | |

**cash in bank**    The balance of cash indicated by a firm's general ledger is unlikely to be that actually available for withdrawal at a particular point in time. Conventional practice dictates that a firm reduce the general ledger cash balance at the time that it writes a check. However, a period of several days or even weeks may elapse before such check reaches and clears the firm's bank. During that period, the balance per the records of the bank will be greater than the balance in the books of the firm by the amount of the check. Similarly, a firm may record deposits at the time it mails them to its bank or places them in a night-deposit box. The bank will credit the firm's account only when it actually re-ceives the cash. As a consequence, the amount of cash that a firm reports may be either greater or less than that actually available for withdrawal per the records of the bank. Periodically, upon receiving a statement of its account from the bank, the firm must *reconcile* its balance with that of the bank—that is, it must add to the balance per its own books the sum of any checks that are still outstanding and subtract from such balance any deposits *in transit*. The ad-justed balance (plus or minus any other *reconciling items* such as customer checks returned by the bank for insufficient funds but not yet recorded by the firm) should be in agreement with the balance reported by the bank. An example of a bank reconciliation is provided in Exhibit 6-5.

*EXHIBIT 6-5*

**Bank Reconciliation**
**ABC Company**

| | | |
|---|---:|---:|
| Balance per bank statement, 12/31/81 | | $16,160.30 |
| Add: | | |
| Deposits in transit | $12,176.25 | |
| December bank service charge not yet recorded on books | 10.00 | |
| N.S.F. check[a] | 236.17 | 12,422.42 |
| | | $28,582.72 |
| Subtract: | | |
| Outstanding checks | | |
| # 367 | $ 126.69 | |
| 392 | 24.00 | |
| 393 | 6,200.00 | |
| 394 | 125.00 | |
| 395 | 81.50 | |
| 396 | 5.00 | $ 6,562.19 |
| Note collected by bank but not yet recorded on books | 2,000.00 | 8,562.19 |
| Balance per company books, 12/31/81 | | $20,020.53 |

[a]An N.S.F. check is one returned by the bank marked "not sufficient funds." Ordinarily, a bank gives a company credit on its books for all checks deposited. Subsequently, when it learns that it is unable to collect the full amount of a particular check because the person who drew the check has insufficient funds in his account, the bank would return the check to the depositor (the company) and debit its account. The N.S.F. check will be a reconciling item until the company records the return of the check.

Although a student could readily memorize those items that are conventionally added and those which are subtracted in the reconciliation, a more sensible approach is to pose three simple questions with respect to each item in question: That is,

1. Who "knows" about the item? On whose books—the bank's or the depositor's —has it been recorded?
2. What impact has the item had on the books in which it has been recorded? Has it increased or decreased the balance relative to that on the books on which it has not been recorded?
3. Does such amount have to be added to or subtracted from the balance of the bank so that the balance per the bank will be in agreement with the balance per the books?

In this example the books of the bank reflect a balance of $16,160.30, and those of the company, $20,020.53.

1. The company made a deposit of $12,176.00 that has been recorded on the books of the company but not yet on those of the bank. The company knows

of the deposit; the bank does not. The balance of the bank by virtue of the deposit, is $12,176.00 less than that of the company. To reconcile the two balances, $12,176.00 must be *added* to the balance of the bank.

2. The bank has deducted and recorded a $10.00 service charge. The bank knows of the service charge; the company does not. The balance of the bank is thereby $10.00 less than that of the company. To effect the reconciliation, $10.00 must be *added* to the balance of the bank.

3. The bank subtracted $236.17 from the balance of the company when it found that it could not collect a customer check for that amount. The bank knows of the deduction; the company does not. The balance of the bank is $236.17 less than that of the company. To reconcile the two balances, $236.17 must be *added* to the balance of the bank.

4. The company has written a number of checks which have not yet *cleared* the bank. The company knows of the checks and has reduced its balance at the time it wrote the checks. The bank does not know of the checks and will not learn about them until after they are deposited by the recipient. The balance of the bank is thus greater than that of the company in the amount of the outstanding checks, $6,562.19. That amount must be *subtracted* from the balance of the bank in order to bring the two balances into agreement.

5. The bank collected the proceeds of a customer note for the company and has given the company credit for it. The bank knows of the collection, but the company does not; it has not yet recorded the receipt of the cash on its own books. The balance of the bank is thereby $2,000.00 greater than that of the company. The $2,000.00 must be *subtracted* from the balance of the bank.

The reconciliation to this point has served to account for and to explain the differences between the cash balance as reported by the bank and that indicated on the books of the company. But it has also indicated that as of the date of reconciliation, December 31, 1981, the books of the company were in error. They were in error not because of any avoidable mistakes or carelessness on the part of the company accountants or bookkeepers, but only because they were not up to date. They had not taken into account those transactions which the bank knew about and recorded but which, as of the date of reconciliation, the company did not know about and had not recorded. If financial statements are to be prepared as of the date of reconciliation, then it is necessary to adjust the books and records of the company to take into account those items which should have been recorded as of the reconciliation date but which were not. Such items would involve those transactions which the bank knew about but which the company did not. In the illustration, they would include the service charge of $10.00, the N.S.F. check of $236.17, and the $2,000.00 note collected by the bank. The following entry would give effect to the adjustment:

| | | |
|---|---|---|
| Cash | $1,753.83 | |
| Bank service charge | | |
|   (expense) | 10.00 | |
| Accounts receivable | 236.17 | |
|   Notes receivable | | $2,000.00 |

To give effect to adjustments indicated by bank reconciliation. (Accounts receivable has been debited by the amount of the N.S.F. check since the person who wrote the check is now indebted to the company for the amount of such check.)

**classification of cash**   Cash is ordinarily classified as a current asset. In a sense cash is the ultimate current asset in that current assets are defined as those that will be converted into cash within the operating cycle of a business. Nevertheless there are exceptions. Cash should properly be considered a current asset only when there are no restrictions—either those imposed by contract or by management intent —upon its use as a medium of exchange with a single operating cycle. Suppose, for example, that a company is required by terms of a bond agreement to maintain a *sinking fund* for the retirement of debt that will mature in 10 years. A sinking fund consists of cash or other assets segregated in the accounts in order to repay an outstanding debt when it comes due. All such assets, although normally considered current, when set aside in sinking fund should be classified on the balance sheet as *noncurrent* assets since management has earmarked them for a specific, noncurrent purpose. The intent of management should be the key criterion for classification.

### Marketable Securities

In an effort to obtain a return on what would otherwise be temporarily idle cash, many corporations use such cash to purchase stocks, bonds, or commercial paper (short-term certificates of debt). Temporary investments are ordinarily grouped together in the current asset section of the statement of position under the heading "marketable securities." Marketable securities are distinguished from other corporate investments by corporate intent. The firm ordinarily expects to hold such securities for a relatively short period of time, until a need for cash arises, and does not anticipate exercising any significant degree of control over the company whose shares it may own. If the company has other intentions with respect to the securities, they should ordinarily be classified as "long-term investments," a noncurrent asset.

As with most other assets, marketable securities are reported on the balance sheet at their original cost. However, because the company is likely to sell them in the near future, the current market value is disclosed parenthetically on the face of the statement. Thus,

| | |
|---|---|
| Cash | $ 80,000 |
| Marketable securities (current market value, $350,000) | 335,000 |

Gains and losses on the sale of individual securities are ordinarily recognized at the time of sale. No recognition is given to fluctuations in market value. Assume, for example, that a company had purchased 100 shares of IBM at $220 per share. The stock would be reported on the statement of position at $22,000. Should the company sell the stock for $250 per share, it would record the sale as follows:

| | | |
|---|---|---|
| Cash | $25,000 | |
| Marketable securities | | $22,000 |
| Gain on sale of marketable securities | | 3,000 |
| **To record sale of marketable securities.** | | |

Revenue from dividends or interest on marketable securities is ordinarily recognized upon receipt. Thus, had IBM declared and paid a dividend of $4 per share before the company had sold it, the following entry would have been appropriate:

| | | |
|---|---|---|
| Cash | $400 | |
| Revenue from marketable securities | | $400 |

**To record receipt of dividend.**

The one critical exception to the general rule that marketable securities be reported at historical cost is that where the market price of the entire portfolio is less than cost, the carrying value of the securities should be reduced to the market value, and a corresponding loss should be recognized. The exception represents an application of the guidelines of conservatism. Unfavorable events should be accorded accounting recognition at the earliest possible time.

This "lower of cost or market" according to a pronouncement of the FASB rule need not be applied to individual securities; it may be applied to all currently marketable securities taken as a group. Assume, for example, a firm has a portfolio consisting of 100 shares of each of two stocks. Both had been purchased at a cost of $100 per share. The original cost of the portfolio is therefore $20,000. As of year end, the market price of stock A had increased to $110 per share; that of stock B had declined to $80:

| | Original Cost | Market Value | Lower of Cost or Market |
|---|---|---|---|
| Stock A | $10,000 | $11,000 | $10,000 |
| Stock B | 10,000 | 8,000 | 8,000 |
| | $20,000 | $19,000 | $18,000 |

If the lower of cost or market rule were applied on an item-by-item basis, then the portfolio would be written down to $18,000. If applied on a portfolio basis, as recommended by the FASB, then it need be written down to only $19,000. The following entry (or one similar) would be in order:

| | | |
|---|---|---|
| Decline in market value of marketable securities (expense +) | $1,000 | |
| Marketable securities (asset –) | | $1,000 |

**To record decline in market value of marketable securities.**

The portfolio basis tends to be less conservative than the item-by-item basis inasmuch as it allows increases in the market value of some securities to offset decreases in the market value of others.

## Valuation of Marketable Securities—
## An Alternative Approach

The current practice of generally reporting marketable securities at original cost is consistent with that followed in reporting other assets. Some critics, however, maintain that two important characteristics of marketable securities justify an alternative approach. First, the current market value of marketable securities (at any particular point in time) can ordinarily be objectively determined. This is especially true of securities that are widely traded since current prices are readily available either in newspapers or special brokerage service reports. Second, there is always an available market in which to sell the securities. Unlike fixed assets or inventories, marketable securities can be disposed of at the market price by a single telephone call to a stockbroker. As a consequence of these two characteristics, critics of current practice assert that the dual accounting goals of providing information that is both relevant and objective can most effectively be served by valuing securities on the balance sheet at market value rather than at historical costs.

The critics also focus attention on the impact of historical costs on the income statement. Gains or losses from holding a security are given accounting recognition only when the security is actually sold. In an accounting sense, at least, management is neither credited nor censured for holding a security as it increases or decreases in market value until the period of sale. The period of sale may be one subsequent to the one in which the increase or decrease in value actually took place.

To the extent that it has in its portfolio one or more securities that have increased in value since they were purchased, management can readily manipulate reported earnings. If management wishes to improve earnings of the current period, it simply sells those securities that have appreciated in value. If, on the other hand, it wishes to give the earnings of the following year a boost, it delays the sale until then. It is questionable, given the ease by which it can be done, that the sale of a security is of greater economic significance than the changes in its market value while it is being held.

The problem of reporting marketable securities is of special concern to industries, such as mutual funds and insurance, in which all or a sizable portion of assets consist of marketable securities. In those industries it is vital that an investor be concerned with any *unrealized* gains or losses (those representing changes in the market price of securities not yet sold). As a consequence, firms in such industries either already give effect to unrealized gains or losses on both the balance sheet and the income statement or otherwise make prominent disclosure in footnotes.

Although the issue of cost versus market value can readily be highlighted in a discussion of marketable securities, it is one that bears upon all assets and liabilities. It will be alluded to again in several subsequent chapters.

## Summary of Part II

In Part II of this chapter we have dealt with problems of accounting for and reporting cash and marketable securities, both of which are ordinarily classified as current assets.

Cash includes currency on hand as well as demand deposits in banks. It is the most liquid of all assets and is the common medium of exchange in our society. As such it must be the subject of especially tight safeguards and controls.

Cash, although generally classified as a current asset, should properly be grouped with the noncurrent assets in those situations in which it is subject to restrictions upon its withdrawal, regardless of whether the restrictions are imposed by contract or set by management itself.

Marketable securities include those securities which a firm holds as temporary investments. The key issue with respect to marketable securities pertains to the value at which they should be reported on the balance sheet and the point at which increases or decreases in value should be recognized on the income statement. Conventionally, marketable securities are reported at cost. Increases or decreases in market value are recognized only upon the sale of a security. An exception is made, however, when the market value of an entire portfolio is less than its cost. In accord with the "lower of cost or market" rule, the portfolio is written down to its overall market value. Alternatively, however, many accountants argue that all changes in the market values of securities should be given accounting recognition and all gains or losses, both *realized* and *unrealized*, should be reflected immediately in enterprise earnings.

*exercise for review and self-testing*

Try to complete this exercise without using the interest tables in the Appendix.

Assume that today is January 1, 1980. Further assume that the prevailing rate of interest paid by banks on deposits is 8 percent, compounded annually.

1. A corporation deposits $100,000 in a bank today.
   a. How much will it have in its account on December 31, 1980?
   b. How much will it have in its account on December 31, 1981?
   c. How much will it have in its account on December 31, 1982?

2. A corporation deposits $100,000 in a bank on December 31, 1980.
   a. How much will it have in its account on December 31, 1980 immediately after making the deposit?
   b. It makes another deposit of $100,000 on December 31, 1981. How much will it have in its account after making the deposit?
   c. It makes yet another deposit of $100,000 on December 31, 1982. How much will it have in its account after making the third deposit?

3. A corporation wants to be able to withdraw from its account $100,000 on December 31, 1980.

a. How much should it deposit today?

b. Assume instead that it wants to be able to withdraw $100,000 on December 31, 1981. How much should it deposit today?

c. Assume alternatively that it wants to be able to withdraw $100,000 on December 31, 1982. How much should it deposit today?

4. A corporation wants to be able to withdraw from its account $100,000 on December 31, 1980, $100,000 on December 31, 1981, *and* $100,000 on December 31, 1982.

a. How much should it deposit today?

## Questions

1. What is meant by *value* as the term is used in connection with assets reported on the conventional balance sheet?

2. The balance sheet, it is often asserted, provides little indication of a company's inherent worth. Instead, it is nothing more than a compilation of *residuals.* Do you agree?

3. Historical cost values of assets are of little relevance to most decisions faced by management, creditors, or investors. Why, then, do accountants resist efforts to convert to a market-value-oriented balance sheet?

4. Market values can be interpreted as either *input* or *output* prices. What is the distinction between the two? Give an example of each.

5. What are the economic benefits associated with an asset? How can they be quantified?

6. Current assets are defined as those which are reasonably expected to be *realized in cash,* sold, or consumed during the normal operating cycle of the business. Yet cash itself is not always classified as a current asset. Why is this so?

7. The owner of a small corporation was recently advised by his CPA that he "has too much cash sitting in his checking account." The company had a checking account balance of $100,000, and the CPA told the owner that the account was costing the company "about $5,000 per year." The owner of the corporation insisted that this could not be so; the money was deposited in a "no-charge" checking account. What do you think the CPA had in mind when he made his comment?

8. The general managers of two of a large firm's subsidiaries each reported that his company in 1980 had operating earnings, excluding income from the sale of marketable securities, of $100,000. The manager of company A also indicated that on January 5, 1980, he had purchased but had not yet sold 1,000 shares of United Mining Co. common stock at $15 per share. On December 31, 1980, United Mining was traded at $45 per share. By contrast, the manager of company B revealed that he had purchased 1,000 shares of United Mining Co. common stock on April 18, at $35 per share and had sold them on November 25 at $38 per share.

   If conventional accounting principles are adhered to, which company would report the higher income? Excluding all other factors than those discussed above, which company do you think had the superior performance in 1980?

## Problems

1. *The next several problems are intended to facilitate understanding of the four basic concepts of compound interest.*

   Assuming an interest rate of 8 percent compounded annually, $300,000 is
   a. the present value of what amount to be received in five years?
   b. the value in five years of what amount deposited in a bank today?
   c. the present value of an annuity of what amount to be received over the next five years.
   d. the value in five years of an annuity of what amount deposited in a bank at the end of each of the next five years?

2. The board of directors of a printing company decided that the company should take advantage of an unusually successful year to place in a reserve fund an amount of cash sufficient to enable it to purchase a new printing press in six years. The company determines that the new press would cost $200,000 and that funds could be invested in securities that would provide a return of 8 percent, compounded annually.
   a. How much should the company place in the fund?
   b. Suppose that the return would be compounded quarterly. How much should the company place in the fund?

3. In anticipation of the need to purchase a new equipment, a corporation decided to set aside in a special fund $40,000 each year.
   a. If the amount in the fund could be invested in securities that provide a return of 5 percent per year, how much would the company have available in eight years?
   b. Assume instead that the company knew that it would require $500,000 to replace the equipment at the end of eight years. How much should it contribute to the fund each year, assuming an annual return of 5 percent?

4. A corporation wishes to provide a research grant to a university such that the university can withdraw $10,000 at the end of each of the next three years. The university will deposit the amount received in an account that earns interest at the rate of 5 percent per year. How much should the corporation give the university? Prepare a schedule in which you indicate the balance in the account at the end of each of the three years.

5. On the day of a child's birth, the parents deposit $1,000 in a savings bank. The bank pays interest at the rate of 6 percent per year, compounded annually.
   a. How much will be on deposit by the time the child enters college on his or her eighteenth birthday?
   b. Assume instead that the interest at an annual rate of 6 percent is compounded semiannually. To how much will the original deposit increase in 18 years?

6. A corporation borrows $5,000 from a bank. Principal and interest are payable at the end of five years.

   a. What will be the amount of the corporation's payment assuming that the bank charges interest at a rate of 10 percent and compounds the interest annually?

   b. What will be the amount of the corporation's payment if interest at an annual rate of 10 percent is compounded semiannually?

7. You deposit a fixed amount in a bank. How long will it take for your funds to double if the bank pays interest at a rate of

   a. 4 percent compounded annually?

   b. 8 percent compounded annually?

   c. 8 percent compounded semiannually?

   d. 8 percent compounded quarterly?

8. A company wishes to establish a pension plan for its president. The company wants to assure the president or his survivors an income of $40,000 per year for 20 years after his retirement. The president has 15 years to work before he retires. If the company can earn 7 percent per year on the pension fund, how much should it contribute during each working year of the president?

9. *Effective interest rates can be adjusted in a number of different ways.*

   *Series EE* U.S. savings bonds differ from conventional government or corporate *coupon* bonds in that they do not have attached to them coupons that can periodically be redeemed for interest payments. Instead, they carry a face value of a fixed amount, e.g., $25, $50, or $100. The purchaser buys the bonds at a discount. For example, he might pay $75 for a $100 bond that will mature in 10 years. The difference between what he pays for the bond and its face value represents the interest for the entire period during which the bond is outstanding. Upon maturity the purchaser will present the bond to the government and receive its full face value. The government can readily adjust the effective interest rate that it pays by varying either the initial selling price of the bond or the number of years the purchaser must hold the bond before he can redeem it.

   a. Suppose the government sells a $100 face value bond for $75 and establishes a holding period of 10 years. Approximately, what is the effective rate of interest (assume that interest is compounded annually)?

   b. Suppose instead that the government wishes to establish an effective rate of 8 percent and a holding period of 10 years. At what price should it sell the bond?

   c. If the government wishes to establish an effective rate of 8 percent and a price of $75, how long a holding period should it require?

10. *Truth-in-lending laws are designed to eliminate the type of deception suggested by this problem.*

    The Helping Hand Loan Co. placed an advertisement in a local newspaper that read in part, "Borrow up to $10,000 for 5 years at our low, low, rate of interest of 6 percent per year." When a customer went to the loan company to borrow the $10,000 he was told that total interest on the five-year loan would be $3,000. That is, $600 per year (6 percent of $10,000) for five years. Company practice, he was told, required that interest be paid in full at the time a loan is made and be deducted from the amount given to the customer. Thus, the customer was given only $7,000. The loan was to be repaid in five annual installments of $2,000.

Do you think that the ad was misleading? What was the actual amount loaned to the customer? Determine what you consider to be the "true" rate of interest.

11. *Rates of discount determine firms' preferences as to alternative financing arrangements.*

Company A is presently negotiating with company B to purchase a parcel of land. Three alternative sets of terms are under consideration:
1. Company A will pay $400,000 at time of sale.
2. Company A will pay $50,000 at time of sale and give company B a five-year note for $500,000.
3. Company A will make five annual payments of $100,000 each commencing one year from the date of sale.

Company A can obtain a return of 7 percent per year on any funds that it has available for investment; company B can obtain a return of 9 percent. Both firms use discount rates to evaluate potential investments that are equal to the rates of return that they can obtain.

Rank the three sets of terms as you would expect them to be preferred by each of the two companies.

12. *Rental charges can be established so that lease arrangements are, in economic substance, equivalent to sales.*

At the request of several of its customers, a heavy equipment manufacturer has decided to give them the option of leasing or buying its products. The company expects a rate of return of 12 percent on all investments. The useful life of its equipment is eight years. Each lessee (i.e., customer) will pay all operating costs including taxes, insurance, and maintenance.

a. The company establishes an annual rental charge of $12,000. What would be the sale price that would leave the company equally well off as if it had leased the equipment for the entire useful life of the equipment? *P.V. Ans.*

b. The company previously sold the equipment for $75,000. What annual rental charge would leave the company as well off as if it had sold the equipment? *P.V. Ans.*

13. *Businesses, as well as individuals, should at least once a month compare the cash balance per a bank statement with that per their own records, account for all differences, and adjust their books as required. The next two problems are exercises in preparing bank reconciliations.*

On December 31, 1980, the general ledger of the Lincoln Company indicated that the cash balance in the firm's checking account at the First National Bank was $108,753. A statement received from the bank, however, indicated that the balance in the account was $145,974. Investigation revealed the following:
1. The company had drawn checks totaling $53,186, which had not been paid by the bank.

2. The company made a deposit on the evening of December 31 of $26,102. This deposit was included by the bank in its business of January 2, 1981.

3. On December 27, the company had deposited a check given to it by a customer for $103. On December 31, the bank returned the check to the company marked N.S.F. (not sufficient funds in customer's account). The company had given no accounting recognition to the return of the check.

4. The bank debited the account of the company for a monthly service charge of $10. The company had not yet recorded the charge.

5. On December 31, the bank collected a customer note of $10,250 for the company. The company did not receive notification of the collection until January 4.

Prepare a schedule that reconciles the balance per the general ledger with that per the bank statement.

14. The general ledger of the McGuire Corp. indicated cash in bank of $3,822.81 as of December 31, 1981. A statement from the bank, as of the same date, indicated cash in bank to be $5,666.00.

As of December 31, the company had outstanding checks of $1,800.00.

On December 29, it mailed a deposit of $465.81 to the bank. As of year end it had not been received yet.

On December 31, the bank collected for the company a note from a customer. As of year end the bank had not yet notified the company. The amount of the note was $500.

On December 18, the company made a deposit in the amount of $423.50. The bank recorded it as $432.50.

a. Prepare a schedule in which you account for the difference between the balance per the company books and that in the bank statement.

b. Determine the amount of cash in bank that should be reported on the firm's end-of-year financial statements. Prepare a journal entry to adjust the present balance.

15. *Not all economic events associated with marketable securities are given accounting recognition.*

Prepare journal entries (as necessary) to record the following transactions and events on the books of the APO Company, a firm whose fiscal year ends on December 31:

| | |
|---|---|
| 8/20/80 | The APO Company purchases 100 shares of Schaeffer Chemical Co. common stock at the price of $12 per share. |
| 8/31/80 | *The Wall Street Journal* reports that Schaeffer Chemical Co. common stock *closed* the previous day at 13½. |
| 9/30/80 | The board of directors of Schaeffer Chemical declares a quarterly dividend of $.15 per share. |
| 10/20/80 | APO Company receives a dividend check in the amount of $15. |
| 12/31/80 | A telephone call to a stockholder reveals that Schaeffer Chemical Co. common stock *closed* at 4½. |
| 1/11/81 | APO company sells 50 shares of Schaeffer Chemical at 5¼. |

During 1980 the company owned no other marketable securities.

16. *Alternative bases of asset valuation affect both earnings and assets.*

In 1980, 47th Street Diamond Mart acquired a gem for resale. The cost of the jewel to the firm was $1,000. At the end of 1980, the firm would have to pay $1,200 to acquire a stone of comparable size and quality. If the firm elects to sell the stone at year end, it could do so at a price of $1,500. However, if it would wait an additional year to sell the jewel, it could do so at a price of $1,800.

a. Indicate the amount at which the firm should report the gem on its balance sheet of December 31, 1980 if it elects to wait one year, assuming each of the following bases of valuation:
   (1) historical cost
   (2) market value (input price)
   (3) market value (output price)
   (4) value to user (the firm determines the present value of expected cash receipts using a discount rate of 7 percent)

b. Indicate the amount of any gain associated with the stone that the firm would report in 1980, assuming each of the bases indicated.

17. *The lower of cost or market rule can be applied on two different bases, each having a different effect on both assets and earnings.*

The table following gives the marketable securities (all common stocks) owned by the Colorado Co. on December 31, 1980. All securities were purchased within the previous 12 months. Also shown are the original purchase prices and the current market prices.

| Securities | No. of Shares | Purchase Price | Current Market Price |
|---|---|---|---|
| Amer. Can | 100 | 35¼ | 40 |
| Cerro | 200 | 14½ | 10 |
| Fuqua | 100 | 6 | 16 |
| GAC Corp. | 50 | 5½ | 2 |
| IBM | 20 | 250 | 240 |

a. Prepare a schedule indicating the lower of cost or market value of each security.

b. Prepare a journal entry to apply the lower of cost or market rule.
   (1) Assume the rule is to be applied on an individual security basis.
   (2) Assume the rule is to be applied on a portfolio basis (according to FASB recommendation).

c. Which basis is likely to be more conservative in that it results in lower asset values? Which minimizes the inconsistency of recognizing decreases in market values but not increases?

18. *Do earnings as computed in accord with established conventions always provide the best measure of economic performance?*

At the start of 1980 a corporation had in its portfolio of marketable securities 100 shares of each of stocks A, B, and C. Acquisition cost per share and unit market prices as of the end of 1980 and 1981 were as follows:

|  | Acquisition Cost | Market Price 12/31/80 | Market Price 12/31/81 |
|---|---|---|---|
| Security A | $100 | $150 | $80 |
| Security B | 50 | 80 | 70 |
| Security C | 60 | 90 | 63 |

During 1980 the company engaged in no securities transactions. During 1981 it sold 100 shares of security C for $65 per share.

a. Determine reported earnings related to securities for 1980 and 1981. Be sure to take into account the lower of cost or market rule applied on a portfolio basis.

b. Do you think that reported earnings is an appropriate measure of economic performance? Why?

19. *Measures of performance based on amounts reported in the income statement may be misleading.*

On January 1, 1980 the Black Corporation acquired 100 shares of common stock of company A and 100 shares of company B. Price per share of both securities was $200.

During 1980 companies A and B declared dividends of $16 and $12 per share, respectively. As of December 31, 1980, the market price of the stock of company A was $210 per share; that of company B was $230 per share.

a. Determine return on investment of each security based on the dollar amounts that would be reported on the firm's balance sheet and income statement.

b. Determine return on investment taking into account any "unrealized" gains or losses. Use *average* market value as the denominator.

c. Which security do you think was the better investment? Which basis for calculating return on investment do you think provides the better measure of economic performance? Why do you suppose that the market values of marketable securities must be disclosed in financial reports?

20. *The basis of asset valuation determines the basis for revenue recognition.*

During 1980, in its first year of operations, the Mann Company purchased, for $60 per unit, 1,000 units of a product. Of these it sold 800 units at a price of $100 per unit. On December 31, 1980, the company was notified by its supplier that in the following year the wholesale cost per unit would be increased to $70 per unit. As a consequence of the increase, Mann Company determined that the retail price would increase to $120 per unit.

Ignoring other revenues and expenses, determine the ending inventory balance, and compute income assuming that ending inventories are to be valued at

1. Historical cost (generally accepted basis).
2. A current market *input* price (a proposed alternative).
3. A current market *output* price (another proposed alternative).

In computing income, distinguish between revenue from the actual sale of product and yet to be realized gains from *holding* the product in inventory. Remember that any recorded increases in the value of the inventory must also be reflected in the determination of income (and, more specifically, of revenue).

21. *This problem describes a common banking arrangement, whereby a borrower is required to maintain a* compensating balance *with a lending institution. It suggests an accounting issue associated with the arrangement.*

    Indicated as follows are year-end balances from selected general ledger accounts of the Jefferson Co.:

    | | |
    |---|---:|
    | Cash, First State Bank | $ 50,000 |
    | Note payable, First State Bank | 500,000 |
    | Interest (expense) | 35,000 |

    The interest represents borrowing charges for one year on the note payable to First State Bank. Per terms of the loan agreement, the company will maintain in a special interest-free account an amount equal to 10 percent of any loans outstanding to the First State Bank.

    The controller of the Jefferson Co. has proposed to include the following comment among the footnotes to its published financial statements. "As of December 31, 1980, the company was indebted to the First State Bank for $500,000. The note to the bank matures in 1984. The company pays interest at the rate of 7 percent per year."

    The controller indicated that he intends to classify the cash in the special interest-free account with First State Bank as a current asset.

    a. Inasmuch as the note payable with which the special interest-free account is associated will be classified as a noncurrent liability, do you think that the compensating cash balance should be classified as a current asset?

    b. How much money did the company really borrow from the bank; how much did it have available for use?

    c. How much interest did it pay each year? What was the effective interest rate paid?

22. *Present value techniques can be used to determine the value of a business.*

    The general ledger of the Odessa Co. reflected, in summary form, the following balances (there were no material liabilities):

    | | |
    |---|---:|
    | Current assets (accounts receivable, inventory, etc.) | $ 40,000 |
    | Equipment | 80,000 |
    | Building | 120,000 |
    | Land | 60,000 |

    The Geneva Company purchased the company for a total of $400,000 (cash). Immediately after purchase an independent appraiser estimated the value of the individual assets as follows:

|                |           |
|----------------|-----------|
| Current assets | $ 40,000  |
| Equipment      | 100,000   |
| Building       | 160,000   |
| Land           | 100,000   |

a. Prepare a journal entry to record the acquisition on the books of the Geneva Company.

b. Assume instead that the Geneva Company is willing to pay for the Odessa Company an amount such that its return on investment will be 10 percent per year. Geneva estimates that the earnings (net cash inflow) of Odessa will be $50,000 for the first five years following the acquisition and $40,000 for an indefinite period thereafter.

(1) How much would the Geneva Company be willing to invest in order to receive a net cash inflow of $40,000 per year for an infinite number of years?

(2) How much would it be willing to invest in order to receive a net cash inflow of $10,000 (the "bonus" earnings) for a period of five years?

(3) How much would it be willing to pay for the Odessa Company?

*solutions to*
*exercise for*
*review and*
*self-testing*

1. a. $100,000 × 1.08 = $108,000.
   b. $108,000 × 1.08 = $116,640.
   c. $116,640 × 1.08 = $125,971.
   Verify your answers by referring to Table 1, future value of $1.

2. a. $100,000.
   b. $100,000 + ($100,000 × 1.08) = $208,000.
   c. $100,000 + ($208,000 × 1.08) = $324,640.
   Verify your answers by referring to Table 3, future value of an annuity of $1 in arrears.

3. a. $100,000 ÷ 1.08 = $92,593.
   b. $ 92,593 ÷ 1.08 = $85,734.
   c. $ 85,734 ÷ 1.08 = $79,383.
   Verify your answers by referring to Table 2, present value of $1.

4. a. It should deposit the sum of the amounts determined in part c:

$92,593 + $85,734 + $79,383 = $257,710.

Verify your answer by referring to Table 4, present value of an annuity of $1 in arrears.

# 7

# Receivables
# and Payables

This chapter will focus upon accounts and notes receivable and payable. It will also include a brief section on accounting for payroll transactions.

Receivables represent claims, usually stated in terms of a fixed number of dollars, arising from sale of goods, performance of services, lending of funds, or from some other type of transaction which establishes a relationship whereby one party is indebted to another. Claims which result from the sale of goods or services and which are neither supported by a written note nor secured by specific collateral (i.e., the creditor has no rights to specific assets in case the debtor fails to pay) are categorized as *accounts receivable.* They are distinguished from amounts backed by written notes (which may or may not arise out of a sales transaction) called *notes receivable* and those arising out of a myriad of other day-to-day business activities, such as *deposits receivable* (e.g., amounts to be received upon return of containers), *amounts due from officers* (perhaps as a consequence of loans), *dividends receivable, rent receivable,* and *interest receivable.* Accounts receivable do not ordinarily require payment of interest; notes receivable usually do.

Payables represent the corresponding obligations on the part of the recipient of the goods or services. Many of the questions pertaining to the valuation of payables are mirror images of those relating to receivables. The discussion in this chapter will center largely around receivables, with the expectation that, as appropriate, the reader can generalize to payables.

Receivables and payables that mature within one year (or one operating cycle of the business if it is greater than one year) are classified as current assets or liabilities. Those that mature in a longer period are classified as noncurrent.

### Receivables—An Overview

The amount at which a receivable should be reported in the financial statements of an enterprise is by no means obvious. Although the dollar amount of a receivable may be clearly evident from the terms of the sale or other agreement which establishes the receivable, not all receivables will prove to be collectible. One of the major causes of corporate bankruptcy is the failure to transform outstanding receivables into cash, and, not surprisingly, a considerable number of legal actions against CPA firms have resulted from alleged overstatements of the amount of recorded receivables that eventually would be collected. Moreover, the face amount of a receivable is not necessarily indicative of its economic value. Occasionally, the face amount of a receivable may include an element of *interest,* which, as will be demonstrated later in this chapter, serves to overstate the value of the receivable.

Issues relating to receivables are fundamental to those of income determination. As emphasized in Chapter 5, recognition of revenue is commonly associated with increases in receivables. Similarly, recognition of expenses— those pertaining to bad debts, for example—may correspond to decreases in receivables. The question of when to recognize increases or decreases in receivables may be viewed alternatively as when to recognize revenues or expenses.

The basic journal entries to establish and to relieve a receivable account are straightforward. Upon the sale of goods and services for $100, for example, the appropriate journal entry would be

| | | |
|---|---|---|
| Accounts receivable | $100 | |
| Sales revenue | | $100 |
| **To record the sale of goods and services.** | | |

And upon subsequent receipt of customer payment,

| | | |
|---|---|---|
| Cash | $100 | |
| Accounts receivable | | $100 |
| **To record the collection of cash.** | | |

Variations in the terms of sales and the nature of the transactions resulting in the creation of the receivable necessitate considerable modification in the basic entries in order to accommodate specific circumstances.

## Uncollectible Accounts Receivable

**direct write-off method**   There are two ways of accounting for uncollectible accounts receivable. The first, and *less preferable,* is the *direct write-off* method. As soon as it becomes obvious that an account receivable is uncollectible, it is *written off,* and a *bad-debt expense* is charged. Upon learning, for example, that a customer from whom it held a receivable of $100 is likely to default on his obligation, a company might give accounting recognition to its loss with the following journal entry:

| | | |
|---|---|---|
| Bad-debt expense | $100 | |
| Accounts receivable | | $100 |
| **To write off an uncollectible account.** | | |

Concurrently, the firm would also credit the account of the individual customer in the accounts receivable subsidiary ledger. The accounts receivable subsidiary ledger is nothing more than a book or card file of the amount owed by each customer. Each page or card is maintained as a mini general ledger account for a specific customer, with debits indicating additional debts incurred by the customer and credits signifying payments made by him. The sum of the balances due from all customers should, at all times, be equal to the balance in the accounts receivable ledger account (often called the accounts receivable *control* account). Otherwise an error has been made. In other words, the accounts receivable subsidiary ledger provides the support—or the detail—for the general ledger account.

**allowance method**

The direct write-off method, however, is inconsistent with the matching concepts discussed in Chapter 5; it may lead to an overstatement of *both* income of the period of sale and accounts receivable in the period of sale as well as in the subsequent periods. The *allowance* method overcomes these deficiencies.

Consider, for example, a company in the retail furniture industry. To attract business, the company grants credit to relatively poor credit risks. The policy results in extensive losses on uncollectible accounts, but management is nevertheless satisfied with the policy since it generates increased sales volume which more than offsets the losses. Based on several years' experience, management estimates that for every dollar of credit sales 10 cents will be uncollectible. The company vigorously pursues its delinquent debtors and writes off accounts only after it has made every reasonable attempt at recovery. Few accounts are written off before at least a year has elapsed since a customer has made a payment.

Under the circumstances, it would hardly be appropriate for the company to include among its assets the entire balance of accounts receivable. After all, only a portion of such a balance is likely to prove collectible. Similarly, and equally significantly, if in 1980 the company had $500,000 in credit sales, it would not be justified in reporting revenues of $500,000 without making allowance for the fact that only $450,000 (90 percent of $500,000) would, in all probability, be fully realized. The individual accounts related to the sales in 1980 would not be written off for at least one or two years subsequent to 1980. But such losses would be the result of decisions—the decisions to sell to customers who prove to be unworthy of credit—made in 1980. Such losses would relate directly to sales made in 1980; they should be matched, therefore, with revenues of 1980.

There are, however, two obstacles to assigning credit losses to the year in which the sales take place. First, the amount of the loss cannot be known with certainty until several years subsequent to the sales. Normally, however, such amount can be estimated with reasonable accuracy. Based on the past collection experience of the company—or on that of other firms in similar industries—it is possible to predict the approximate amount of receivables that will prove to be uncollectible. The inability to make precise estimates of the anticipated losses can hardly be a justification for making no estimate at all. For even the roughest of estimates is likely to be more accurate than no estimate at all—the equivalent of a prediction of zero credit losses.

Second, even though a firm may be able to predict with reasonable precision the overall percentage of bad debts, it certainly is unable to forecast the *specific* accounts that will be uncollectible. After all, if it knew in advance that a particular individual would be unable to pay his debts, it would never have sold to him in the first place. If a company were to recognize bad debts as expenses and correspondingly reduce its accounts receivable balance, then which subsidiary ledger accounts would it credit? Since the sum of the balances of the subsidiary ledger accounts must equal the balance in the accounts receivable control account—i.e., the general ledger balance—the firm cannot reduce the balance in the control account without, at the same time, reducing the balances in the accounts of specific customers.

The accountant circumvents this second obstacle by establishing a *contra account,* "accounts receivable—allowance for uncollectibles." The contra account will normally have a credit balance (the opposite of the accounts receivable balance) and will always be associated with and reported directly beneath its *parent* account, accounts or notes receivable. To give accounting recognition to the fact that the full amount of the balance of accounts receivable is unlikely to be collected, the accountant, instead of reducing or crediting accounts receivable directly, will credit "accounts receivable—allowance for uncollectibles."

To illustrate the procedure, continue the assumption that a firm in 1980 made $500,000 in credit sales. At year end the firm estimates that $50,000 of the outstanding balance will prove to be uncollectible. The following adjusting entry would be appropriate to give accounting recognition to its estimate:

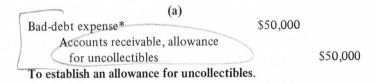

(a)

| | |
|---|---|
| Bad-debt expense* | $50,000 |
|    Accounts receivable, allowance | |
|      for uncollectibles | $50,000 |

**To establish an allowance for uncollectibles.**

*Some accountants believe that the debit should be made not to "bad-debt expense" but rather to an account "sales—uncollectibles" and that such account should be reported as a deduction from revenues. They point out that anticipated revenue has been lost; the firm will realize less than originally hoped. The approach in which "bad-debt expense" is debited for the estimated losses is illustrated in this text not because it is theoretically preferable but only because it is more commonly adhered to in practice.

The relevant T accounts would appears as follows

Accounts receivable

| 500,000 | |
|---|---|

Accounts receivable,
allowance for uncollectibles

Bad-debt expense

| | **(a)** 50,000 | **(a)** 50,000 | |
|---|---|---|---|

On the balance sheet accounts receivable (assuming none of the $500,000 has yet been collected) and its related contra account would be reported as

| | | |
|---|---|---|
| Accounts receivable | $500,000 | |
| Less: Allowance for uncollectibles | 50,000 | $450,000 |

As soon as the company is aware that a specific account cannot be collected it is then able to credit the accounts receivable control account as well as the specific accounts receivable subsidiary ledger account. Since the allowance for uncollectibles had been established for the very purpose of accommodating future bad debts, the offsetting debit would be made to the allowance for uncollectibles contra account.

Assume that in 1981 accounts totaling $7,000 are determined to be uncollectible. The appropriate entry would be

**(b)**

| | | |
|---|---|---|
| Accounts receivable, allowance for | | |
| uncollectibles | $7,000 | |
| Accounts receivable | | $7,000 |
| **To write off specific accounts.** | | |

At the same time, the specific accounts to be written off would be credited in the accounts receivable subsidiary ledger. It is important to note that at the time specific accounts are written off *no entry is made to "bad-debt expense." The effect of the uncollectible accounts on income would already have been recognized in the year the sales were made.* Hence, no further entries to revenue or expense accounts are justified. Moreover, the entry to write off the specific accounts has no effect on current assets or working capital. The *net* accounts receivable (accounts receivable less allowance for uncollectibles) remains unchanged by the entry since both the parent account and the related contra account have been reduced by identical amounts.

## Methods of Estimating Uncollectibles

There are two widely used methods of determining the charge (debit) to be made each accounting period to "bad-debt expense" and the corresponding amount to be added to the allowance for uncollectibles. The first is that illustrated above. Based on the collection experience of the company, an estimate is made of the percentage of *sales* (preferably taking into account only those made on credit) that will prove uncollectible. Each year, as long as the percentage remains stable, the same percentage is applied to the credit sales of the period, and the resultant amount is added to the allowance.

Alternatively, some firms compute the amount to be added to the allowance with specific reference to the accounts receivable outstanding at the end of the period. Such firms prepare what is known as the *aging schedule.* An aging schedule indicates what its name implies—the "age" of each account receivable. That is, it reveals the status of the various accounts—are they current, up to 30 days past due, up to 60 days past due, etc.? An aging schedule is illustrated in Exhibit 7–1.

**EXHIBIT 7-1**

**Aging Schedule as of 12/31/80**

| Customer Name | Total Balance | Current | Number Days Past Due | | | |
|---|---|---|---|---|---|---|
| | | | *0-30* | *31-60* | *61-90* | *Over 90* |
| J. Faulkner | $ 93,478 | $ 93,478 | | | | |
| F. Fitzgerald | 60,250 | 26,139 | $ 29,000 | $ 5,111 | | |
| M. Higgins | 100,000 | 75,000 | 25,000 | | | |
| A. Hawthorne | 8,222 | | | | | $8,222 |
| G. Brown | 11,650 | | | | $11,650 | |
| C. Ryder | 92,811 | 29,206 | 33,930 | 26,000 | 3,675 | |
| D. Deming | 37,220 | | 37,220 | | | |
| G. Hawkins | 110,100 | 110,100 | | | | |
| F. Cohen | 116,277 | 116,277 | | | | |
| | $630,008 | $450,200 | $125,150 | $31,111 | $15,325 | $8,222 |

Based on the aging schedule, the firm estimates the dollar amount of accounts that will be uncollectible. Such amount is indicative of the *total* balance required in the allowance for uncollectibles account.

As a rule, the longer an account is outstanding—the longer a debtor goes without paying—the less likely it is that the account will be collectible. Thus, a considerably greater proportion of accounts that are 120 days past due than those that are current will in all probability be uncollectible. A larger percentage of the balance of accounts 120 days past due must be added to the allowance for uncollectibles than for accounts that are current. The following summary based on the aging schedule in Exhibit 7-1 reveals the total balance required in the allowance for bad debts:

**Summary of Accounts Receivable as of 12/31/80**

| Number of Days Past Due | Amount | Percent Likely to be Uncollectible | Required Provision |
|---|---|---|---|
| 0 (current) | $450,200 | 2% | $ 9,004 |
| 1–30 | 125,150 | 8 | 10,012 |
| 31–60 | 31,111 | 12 | 3,733 |
| 61–90 | 15,325 | 20 | 3,065 |
| Over 90 | 8,222 | 50 | 4,111 |
|  | $630,008 |  | $29,925 |

The total required provision less the balance that is currently in the account is the amount that must be added to the account. Suppose, for example, that the balance in the allowance for bad debts as of December 31 is $7,000. The amount that must be added is $22,925 ($29,925 less $7,000):

| Bad-debt expense | $22,925 | |
| Allowance for uncollectibles | | $22,925 |

**To increase the balance in the allowance account to the required level.**

The key distinction between the two methods is that under the percentage of sales method the annual addition is determined by multiplying credit sales by a preestablished percentage. The amount of the addition is thereby computed independently of the existing balance in the allowance for uncollectibles account. Under the aging schedule method the annual addition is determined by first estimating the *required* balance in the allowance for uncollectibles account (as revealed by the aging schedule) and then subtracting from such required balance the actual balance in the account.

Which of the methods of determining the amount to be added to the allowance for uncollectibles—the percentage of sales or the aging schedule—is preferable? Insofar as the firm's estimates of either the percentage of sales to be uncollected or the percentages of the various groups of past due accounts are accurate, and uncollectible accounts are written off on a regular basis each year, then both methods will result in approximately equal credits to the allowance and charges to earnings over time. If, however, write-offs tend to follow an irregular pattern with few accounts being written off in good years and many accounts being written off in bad years, then the two methods may have differing impacts on earnings. The percentage of sales method will result in a constant percent of sales being charged to bad-debt expense regardless of the number of accounts written off in a particular year. The amount of the charge will be a function of sales volume, not of the number of accounts written off. The aging schedule approach, on the other hand, will usually result in a more erratic charge to bad-debt expense. The amount of the charge will be highly responsive to the number and size of the accounts written off. To the extent that it is desirable to match the "cost" of the bad debts to the sales to which they are applicable, then the percentage of sales methods is preferable. However, oftentimes a firm may misestimate the percentage of sales and as a result the balance in the allowance for bad debts becomes either inadequately low or unnecessarily high. Neither method, therefore, is necessarily preferable. The optimum approach may be to use both methods in conjunction with one another—to make an initial estimate of the charge to bad-debt expense by taking a percentage of credit sales and then to test the adequacy of the allowance for bad debts by preparing an aging schedule.

The industry example that follows demonstrates the importance—and the difficulty—of evaluating the collectibility of notes receivable. It is presented to highlight the fact that meaningful financial reporting is as much dependent on the sound judgment of the accountant as it is on mere mechanical accuracy.

### Industry Example: Real Estate Investment Trusts

A March 1974 story in *Forbes*, under the headline, "When Is a Lemon a Lemon," began with the exclamation "These accountants burn me up." The story related how the stock prices of real estate investment trusts had suffered major declines in recent weeks, attributable, in the words of a disgruntled investor, to the way in which accountants "let a few (firms) run wild with these paper pyramids."*

Real estate investment trusts are generally publicly owned firms which take funds received from shareholders as well as those borrowed from banks and other lending institutions and either purchase real estate directly or lend funds to other purchasers. In 1974, with the real estate industry in a tailspin as the result of inflation, high interest rates, shortages of building materials, and an excessive availability of office space, the real estate investment trusts had difficulty collecting many of their outstanding loans.

The key accounting question raised by the situation in which the real estate investment trusts found themselves was posed by *Forbes* as follows: "At what point does a 'problem loan' become a 'bad loan' on which interest should no longer be accrued?" The implication of the question is clear. Firms had not only been failing to write off or provide substantial allowances for bad

*"When Is a Lemon a Lemon," *Forbes,* Vol. 113, March 15, 1974, p. 63.

debts on loans of dubious collectibility but they had also been continuing to accrue interest revenue on such loans even though there was considerable uncertainty as to whether such interest would ever be collected.

The article went on to explain that the question of when a problem loan becomes a bad loan is not susceptible to simple answers:

> Is a loan bad just because it is 30, 60, or 90 days past due? Maybe, maybe not. At times a trust might not mind at all wanting an extra 30 or 60 days for payment. And even a lousy loan can be up to date on its payments. Florida based builder Walter J. Kassuba, who had borrowed $130 million from REITs (Real Estate Investment Trusts), was up to date on most of his debt service when he filed under Chapter 11 (i.e., declared bankruptcy) a few months ago. Everything hinges on how good a handle management has on what's going on in its profession.

Nevertheless, the article strongly implied that accountants, despite their generally "conservative" outlook, were not giving the real estate loans the careful scrutiny that they deserved:

> But, we asked (the accountants), doesn't management always think, rightly or wrongly, it can "work out" the loan—that is, get it back on schedule without a loss in revenue? Who wants "non-earnings assets," as loans on a nonaccrual basis are called? They only spoil the earnings growth and call unwanted attention to the rest of the loan portfolio. Well, the accountants replied, auditors *should* take a closer look at those portfolios in a poor real estate year.

Indeed, the article pointed out that one real estate investment trust continued to accrue interest income on three bankrupt or foreclosed properties because management felt that the loans could be worked out. Such a practice not only overstated the assets of the firm (accounts or notes receivable and accrued interest receivable) but income as well.

As of 1980, guidelines for writing off "nonearning" real estate loans still have not been developed. *Barron's* reports that "outside analysts seeking a better handle on things often run afoul of inconsistent accounting systems which make comparisons of financial statements difficult, both from bank to bank and within a bank over a period of time."* Citibank, the nation's second largest bank, in 1976 classified loans as nonearning when they had been in arrears for 180 days. In 1977, it reduced this period to 90 days. Morgan Guaranty Trust Co. waited only 30 days. The SEC recommends a period of 60 days. "In sum," according to *Barron's*, "whether a loan is nonperforming depends on whom you ask and when."

As with so many other accounting issues, the proper accounting for bad

---

*"When Loans Go Bad," *Barron's,* July 17, 1978, p. 11.

debts cannot be seen as merely the arcane concern of bookkeepers. In 1977, as *Barron's* pointed out, Citicorp had nonperforming loans of $1.6 billion, a figure greater than the total loan portfolios of all but 54 banks in the United States. Chase Manhattan, the nation's third largest bank reported nonperforming loans of $1.3 billion. Approximately 80 percent of the bad loans of both banks were in real estate. Clearly, the manner in which such loans are accounted for and disclosed is likely to have profound effects on the ability to raise capital for banks as well as real estate firms.

## Sales Returns

Sales returns involve considerations similar to those of bad debts. Insofar as goods that have been sold are expected to be returned in a subsequent accounting period, accounting recognition must be given in the period in which they are sold. Financial statements which fail to take into account goods to be subsequently returned and refunds to be given to customers would clearly overstate revenues and, hence, earnings. But as with allowances for bad debts, the necessary accounting entries must reflect the fact that until returns are actually made, the accountant has no way of knowing either the exact amount of such returns or the specific customers who will make such returns.

The accountant must follow an approach similar to that taken in recording bad debts. He must first make an estimate of anticipated returns (based, perhaps, on previous experience) and then establish an allowance for such returns.

Assume that at year end a firm estimates that merchandise that was sold for $10,000 will be returned in the following year. An appropriate journal entry would be

**(a)**

| | | |
|---|---|---|
| Sales—returns | $10,000 | |
| Accounts receivable—<br>allowance for returns | | $10,000 |
| **To record the estimate of sales returns.** | | |

Both of the accounts involved in the entry are *contra accounts.* "Sales—returns" would be reported on the income statement as a reduction of sales. "Accounts receivable—allowance for returns" would be reported on the balance sheet as an additional reduction of accounts receivable along with the allowance for uncollectibles.

If the merchandise to be returned can be resold, then it is necessary also to give effect to the fact that expense, i.e., cost of goods sold, in addition to revenues and sales, have been overstated in the year of sale. Assume that the merchandise to be returned had an original cost of $8,000. The required entry to record the anticipated return would be

**(b)**

| | | |
|---|---|---|
| Merchandise to be returned (asset) | $8,000 | |
| Cost of goods sold (expense) | | $8,000 |

**To record the cost of goods to be returned.**

When the merchandise is actually returned, only balance sheet accounts need to be adjusted; the impact on revenues and expenses would have been accounted for in the year of sale:

**(c)**

| | | |
|---|---|---|
| Accounts receivable—Allowance | | |
| for returns (asset; contra) | $10,000 | |
| Accounts receivable (asset) | | $10,000 |

**To give the customer credit for merchandise returned.**

**(d)**

| | | |
|---|---|---|
| Merchandise inventory (asset) | $8,000 | |
| Merchandise to be returned (asset) | | $8,000 |

**To record the receipt of returned merchandise.**

If the merchandise returned cannot be resold and has no value, then entries **b** and **d** need not be made.

The journal entries pertaining to sales returns are illustrated in this section not because they are especially difficult or unusual, but because they provide another example of the importance of assigning expenses to the accounting period in which their related revenues were recognized. In many industries sales returns, no matter how accounted for, would have but an immaterial impact on earnings. But in some, their effect may be substantial. In the book publishing industry, for instance, it is a common practice to guarantee retailers the right to return unsold merchandise. If a publisher were to recognize revenue at the time that books were shipped to retailers (perhaps a premature point in light of the return policy) without giving effect to the books that it will have to accept back, then both income and assets (accounts receivable) would be significantly overstated.

### Cash Discounts

Frequently, a seller will offer a customer a discount for prompt payment. A company may, for example, sell under terms 2/10/, n/30. The total amount is due within 30 days; however, if payment is made within 10 days, the customer is entitled to a discount of 2 percent. In economic substance it is difficult to view such terms as representing a true discount; a more acceptable interpretation is that the customer is subject to a penalty if he fails to make prompt payment. Suppose that a customer buys merchandise with a *stated* price of $100. If he pays on the thirtieth day following purchase rather than on the tenth day, then he has the use of his funds for an additional 20 days. The use of such funds will have cost him $2 for each $98 of merchandise purchased. His effective interest cost will be at an annual rate of approximately 37 percent—360 days/20 days × $2/$98. Only a company with a severely impaired credit rating would be willing to pay such an extraordinarily high rate. An unbiased observer might suspect, therefore, that the merchandise sold had a fair market value not of the stated sales price of $100 but rather of the stated sales price less the discount, $98.

The proper accounting for cash discounts is *not* one of the critical issues facing the business community. It is of interest to accounting students primarily because it provides another example of the importance of accounting for substance over form.

Both purchasers and sellers account for cash discounts in either of two basic ways: the net method or the gross method. The *net* method requires that both purchases and sales be recorded at the fair market value of the goods traded—that is, sales price *less* the discount—and that payments in excess of the discounted price be recorded separately as a penalty for late payment or as a financing cost. The *gross* method permits purchases and sales to be recorded at the stated price, subject to later adjustment. A simple example can be used to compare the two approaches—first from the standpoint of the purchaser and then from that of the seller.

*example*　　A company purchases on terms 2/10/, n/30 merchandise that has a sales price of $100,000:

| Net Method | | Gross Method | |
|---|---|---|---|
| Inventory　$98,000 | | Inventory　$100,000 | |
| Accounts | | Accounts | |
| payable | $98,000 | payable | $100,000 |
| To record the purchase of merchandise. | | | |

It pays within the discount period:

| Net Method | | Gross Method | |
|---|---|---|---|
| Accounts | | Accounts | |
| payable　$98,000 | | payable　$100,000 | |
| Cash | $98,000 | Cash | $98,000 |
| | | Purchase | |
| | | discounts | 2,000 |
| To record the purchase of merchandise. | | | |

Or, alternatively, it fails to pay within the discount period:

| | Net Method | | | Gross Method | |
|---|---|---|---|---|---|
| Accounts | | | Accounts | | |
| Payable | $98,000 | | payable | $100,000 | |
| Purchase | | | Cash | | $100,000 |
| discount lost | | | | | |
| (expense) | 2,000 | | | | |
| Cash | | $100,000 | | | |

**To record payment after the discount period.**

The essential difference between the two methods is that under the gross method inventory is overstated inasmuch as it is recorded at gross amount payable, which exceeds the fair market value by the amount of discount. As a consequence, upon sale of the goods, cost of goods sold is also overstated. Moreover, in the event that the firm fails to make timely payment, then the penalty charge is "buried" in cost of goods sold rather than shown in a separate account, purchase discounts lost. The distortions in the gross method can, of course, be eliminated by an appropriate year-end adjustment, which in effect, serves to convert the gross method to the net method.*

The entries recording the sales and subsequent collection from the standpoint of the seller would correspond to those of the purchaser. The gross method would result in the overstatement of both sales and accounts receivable.

### Promissory Notes

When a firm extends credit beyond a short period of time (two or three months) or makes a loan, it usually requests formal written documentation of the borrower's obligation to make timely payment. The legal instrument which provides such documentation is known as a *promissory note.* A typical promissory note is illustrated in Exhibit 7-2.

A promissory note, unlike an account receivable, generally provides that the maker (the borrower) of the note agrees to pay a fee, known as interest, for the right to use the funds provided. The promissory note is a legally binding contract. It would specify the following:

The parties involved in the contract—the payor, who is the person or organization that agrees to make the payment, and the payee, who is

---

*The adjustment would be a credit in the amount of the discount to "Merchandise inventory" (or "Cost of goods sold" to the extent that the merchandise has been resold) and a debit to either "Purchase discounts" (if the discount were taken) or to "Purchase discounts lost" (if the discount were lost).

*EXHIBIT 7-2*

**Typical Promissory Note**

Acct. No.               NAME

Austin, Texas, _____ 19____

ON DEMAND, or if no demand is made, then _____ after date, without grace, for value received, I, we, and each of us, as principals, promise to pay to the order of **THE AMERICAN NATIONAL BANK OF AUSTIN** at its banking house in the City of Austin, Travis County, Texas, the sum of

_____ DOLLARS,

with interest theron at the rate of _____ percent per annum from _____ until maturity, and if not then paid, at the rate of 10% per annum until paid.

In the event of default in the payment of this note, when due, or in performance of any agreement contained in the security agreement securing payment hereof, or in the event the holder deems itself insecure, then the holder of this note shall have the option, without demand or notice, to declare the principal and interest at once due and payable and to exercise any and all other rights or remedies provided in this note and in the security agreement, if any, including the right to set off against this note and all other liabilities of the undersigned to the holder, all money or other property in its possession held for or owed to the undersigned.

Each maker, surety, endorser, and guarantor of this note hereby waives presentment for payment or acceptance, notice of non-payment or dishonor, protest, notice of protest, and diligence in the collection hereof or in filing suit hereon and agrees that liability for the payment hereof shall not be affected or impaired by any release of or change in the security, if any, or by any extension in the time for payment; and further agrees to pay all costs and expenses of collection incurred by the holder, and if this note is placed in the hands of an attorney for collection after maturity, or is collected by legal proceedings of any kind, to pay a reasonable attorney's fee, which shall not in any event be less than 10% of the unpaid principal and interest, or the sum of $50.00, whichever is the greater, and shall bear interest at the rate of 10% per annum from the date of its accrual.

Payment of this note is secured by all money or other property of the undersigned now or at any time hereafter in the possession of the holder in any capacity and also by

NO. _____     $ _____

| Date | Int. | Principal | Balance |
|------|------|-----------|---------|
|      |      |           |         |
|      |      |           |         |
|      |      |           |         |
|      |      |           |         |

Address: _____     Name: _____

Due: _____ Phone No. _____

AB50-607-01 (1/72)

---

the person or organization to whom the money is owed (sometimes a note may be drawn to *bearer*—that is, payment is to be made to whomever presents the note to the maker);

The date the note was issued and the date payment is due (some notes state that payment is due in a specific number of days from the date it was issued);

The *principal* of the note (the amount of credit being extended), often referred to as the *face value* of the note;

The rate of interest;

Any collateral or property that the borrower either pledges or surrenders as security for the note;

Interest on a note is expressed in terms of an annual percentage rate. The formula for translating the percentage rate into the actual dollar amount is

$$\text{Interest} = \text{Principal} \times \text{Rate} \times \frac{\text{Days of loan}}{\text{Total days in one year}} \,*$$

If, for example, a company issues a note for $100,000 that bears interest at a

*To facilitate computations, it is common practice in financial circles to assume that a year has 360 days.

rate of 8 percent and is payable in 90 days, the actual interest that it will be required to pay can be computed as

$$\$100,000 \times .08 \times \frac{90}{360} = \$2,000$$

*Notes are reported on the balance sheet at their principal or face amount.* This convention is a source of confusion to many students since the total obligation of the maker is not only the principal but the interest as well. In the above illustration, for example, the total amount to be paid after 90 days is $100,000 plus $2,000 interest. Yet the note would be recorded on the balance sheet at only $100,000. The logic beyond the convention becomes apparent, however, when the impact of notes and interest on the balance sheet is viewed in conjunction with that on the income statement. Interest is a charge imposed on a borrower for the use of funds over a period of time. From the standpoint of the borrower, therefore, the interest cannot be considered an expense—and hence not a liability—until he has actually used the borrowed funds over a period of time. Over the passage of time, the borrower will recognize the expense associated with the use of funds—interest expense—and at the same time the liability—accrued interest payable. Similarly, the lender will periodically recognize the earnings attributable to the funds that he has provided the debtor and concurrently acknowledge the creation of an asset, interest receivable.

A brief example may make the relationship between income and balance sheet accounts somewhat more clear.

*example*    On June 1, Echo Co. informs Foxtrot Corp. that it will be unable to make payment on its open account, which on that date has a balance of $20,000. Echo requests that Foxtrot accept instead a 60-day note that will bear interest at the rate of 6 percent. Foxtrot agrees.

Upon accepting the note on June 1, Foxtrot Corp. would make the following entry to record the exchange of an account receivable (which does not bear interest and is unsupported by a formal legal instrument) for an interest bearing note receivable:

| | | |
|---|---|---|
| Notes receivable | $20,000 | |
| Accounts receivable | | $20,000 |
| **To record acceptance of the note.** | | |

Thereafter, with the passage of time Foxtrot Corp. must account for the revenue that it is earning on the note which it holds. Most companies, considering the clerical costs of making frequent journal entries, update their accounts quarterly or at best monthly. Assuming that Foxtrot Corp. updates its accounts monthly, the following entry would be appropriate on June 30:

| Accrued interest receivable | $100 | |
|---|---|---|
| Interest revenue | | $100 |

**To record monthly interest revenue from the note.**

The $100 represents interest for a period of 30 days computed as

$$\$20{,}000 \times .06 \times \frac{30}{360} = \$100$$

Both 6 percent and 12 percent interest rates are especially easy to work with— 6 percent represents monthly interest charges of ½ percent, and 12 percent represents monthly charges of 1 percent.

On July 30, the note would fall due. Assuming that both the note and the interest are paid in full, two entries are required to record collection. The first is identical to that made on June 30; it recognizes the interest earned during the one month period since interest revenue was previously recorded:

| Accrued interest receivable | $100 | |
|---|---|---|
| Interest revenue | | $100 |

**To record monthly interest revenue from the note.**

The balance in the accrued interest receivable account now stands at $200 and that in the notes receivable account at the original $20,000. Upon collection of both interest and principal, the appropriate entry would be

| Cash | $20,200 | |
|---|---|---|
| Accrued interest receivable | | $  200 |
| Notes receivable | | 20,000 |

**To record the collection of the note and interest.** (Note that this entry has no effect on revenues or expenses.)

From the standpoint of the payor—the maker of the note—the journal entries would be a mirror image of those of the payee.

## Notes with Interest Included in Face Value

Frequently a note will not specifically indicate a rate of interest. Instead, the face value of the note will include not only the amount originally borrowed but also the applicable interest charges as well. A borrower, for example, may give to a bank or other creditor a note for $1,000 in exchange for a 90-day loan.

The bank, however, would not give the borrower the full $1,000. Instead, if the going interest rate for that type of loan were 12 percent, it would give the borrower only $970.87. If the annual rate of interest is 12 percent, then the interest on a loan of $970.87 for 90 days would be

$$\$970.87 \times .12 \times \frac{90}{360} = \$29.13$$

The interest of $29.13, plus the principal of $970.87, exactly equals the face value of the note, $1,000.

Regardless of the manner in which the terms of the loan are stated, the difference between the amount actually received by the borrower and the amount that he must eventually repay at the maturity of the note represents the cost of borrowing—i.e., interest. In the present example, the actual amount of the loan as well as the interest could have been readily calculated as follows:

Let $x$ = The actual amount of the loan.

If interest is to be at an annual rate of 12 percent, then interest for the 90-day period, approximately ¼ year, would be a total of 3 percent of the actual amount of the loan. The total amount to be repaid is the actual amount of the loan, $x$, plus the interest, $.03x$. The total amount to be repaid has been established (the face amount of the note) at $1,000. Hence,

$$\$1,000 = x + .03x \quad \text{or}$$
$$\$1,000 = 1.03x \quad \text{or}$$
$$x = \frac{\$1,000}{1.03} = \$970.87$$

The interest must be the difference between the face amount of the note and the amount actually borrowed: $1,000 minus $970.87, or $29.13. Interest for each 30-day period is therefore $9.71.

When the amount actually loaned is less than the face amount of the note—that is, when the face amount includes both principal and interest— the note is known as a *discount* note and the interest rate as a *discount rate*. The journal entries required to record *discount* notes and the associated interest charges are similar to those for conventional interest-earning instruments.

Assume, for example, that on July 1 a lending institution accepted a three-month note of $1,000 discounted in exchange for an actual cash loan of $970.87. The entry to record the loan would be

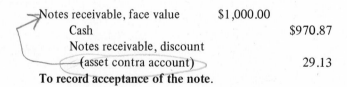

| | | |
|---|---|---|
| Notes receivable, face value | $1,000.00 | |
| Cash | | $970.87 |
| Notes receivable, discount | | |
| (asset contra account) | | 29.13 |

**To record acceptance of the note.**

The overall effect of the entry is to record the asset, notes receivable, at the amount actually loaned. "Notes receivable, discount" is a contra account associated with the account, "Notes receivable, face value." If a balance sheet were to be drawn up immediately after the loan was made, the relevant accounts would be reported on the balance sheet (among current assets) as

| | | |
|---|---|---|
| Notes receivable, face value | $1,000.00 | |
| Less: Discount on notes | 29.13 | $970.87 |

As with conventional interest-bearing notes, interest must periodically be taken into account. On July 31, the appropriate entry would be (making the simplifying assumptions that one-third of the overall interest charges will be recorded during each of the three months regardless of the actual number of days in the month)

| | | |
|---|---|---|
| Notes receivable, discount | $9.71 | |
| Interest revenue | | $9.71 |

**To record interest on the note for one month.**

The effect of such entry is to recognize the interest revenue and also to increase the value of the note (by decreasing the value of the contra account) by the amount of revenue recognized. The entry is similar to that which would have been made had the note been one with a stated interest rate. The main difference is that with the discount note the recognition of the interest results in the net increase of an asset, notes receivable, whereas with the interest-bearing note it results in the increase of a different asset, interest receivable.

The entry made for the month of July would also be made on August 31 and on September 30 to give recognition to the interest revenue earned during each month.

On September 30, when the note is paid, the balance in the "notes receivable, discount" account would have been reduced to zero. Collection of the note could be recorded as follows:

| | | |
|---|---|---|
| Cash | $1,000.00 | |
| Notes receivable, face value | | $1,000.00 |

**To record collection of the note.**

If the period of the loan were greater than one year, present value tables, the use of which was described in Chapter 6, could be conveniently used to determine the amount to be advanced to the borrower.

*example*      A finance company makes a loan to a customer on a discount basis. The company accepts from the customer a two-year note for $5,000. The actual cash advanced is determined on the basis of a 12 percent annual rate of interest.

Per Table 2 in the appendix, the present value of $5,000 discounted at a rate of 12 percent for two years is

$$\$5,000 \times .7972 = \$3,986$$

The finance company would advance the customer $3,986 and record the loan as follows:

| | | |
|---|---|---|
| Notes receivable | $5,000 | |
| Notes receivable, discount | | $1,014 |
| Cash | | 3,986 |

**To record the loan to the customer.**

Interest revenue for the first year would be 12 percent of the *net* balance of the outstanding customer obligation, that is, 12 percent of $3,986–$479. An appropriate journal entry after the note has been outstanding for one year would be

| | | |
|---|---|---|
| Notes receivable, discount | $479 | |
| Interest revenue | | $479 |

**To record interest for the first year.**

Since the customer did not actually remit an interest payment, the effective balance of his obligation would increase after the first year by $479. The increase in the effective balance is accounted for by a decrease in the discount. After the first year, the note would be reported as follows:

| | | |
|---|---|---|
| Notes receivable | $5,000 | |
| Less: Discount on notes | 535 | $4,465 |

Interest for the second year would be based on the effective customer obligation at the end of the first year. Thus, it would be 12 percent of $4,465 –$535. The entry at the end of the second year to record both interest revenue and collection of the full $5,000 would be

| | | |
|---|---|---|
| Cash | $5,000 | |
| Notes receivable, discount | 535 | |
| Notes receivable | | $5,000 |
| Interest revenue | | 535 |

**To record second-year interest and collection of the note.**

The interest revenue on a discount note would increase from year to year, corresponding to an increase in the effective obligation of the customer. Interest must be paid not only on the original amount borrowed but on any un-satisfied obligations for interest as well. (If the loan is for a relatively short period of time—less than one year—the "interest on the interest" is usually ignored because it would be immaterial.)

## Noninterest-bearing Notes

Occasionally, a firm will sell on especially generous terms of credit. In fact, sometimes the terms are so generous that they raise serious doubts as to whether the goods are really worth the price at which they were sold.

Assume, for example, that a company sells a building for $100,000. The company accepts from its customer a five-year "interest-free" note for the full sales price. As emphasized in Chapter 6, $100,000 to be received in five years is worth considerably less than the same amount to be received today. Indeed, per Table 2, the present value of a single payment of $100,000 five years hence, discounted at a rate of 8 percent, is

$$\$100,000 \times .6806 = \$68,060$$

It is hardly reasonable to expect a company to provide an interest-free loan to a customer for five years. A more credible interpretation of the trans-action is that interest charges are included in the $100,000 selling price. If the prevailing rate for similar types of loans is 8 percent, the facts suggest that the "true" selling price of the building is $68,060. The difference ($31,940) between such amount and the stated selling price of $100,000 represents interest on a five-year loan of $68,060.

If accountants are to be concerned with the substance rather than the form of transactions, they must divide the $100,000 into its component parts. They must account separately for the sales price and the interest. They must *impute* interest of $31,940. If the building had been recorded on the books of the seller at $50,000, then the following entry would be appropriate:

| | | |
|---|---|---|
| Notes receivable | $100,000 | |
| Building | | $50,000 |
| Notes receivable, discount | | 31,940 |
| Gain on sale of building | | 18,060 |
| **To record the sale of the building.** | | |

During each year that the note was outstanding, the company would ac-crue interest on the effective balance of the "loan"—the note receivable less the unamortized portion of the discount. Thus, to record interest after one year,

Notes receivable, discount      $5,445
     Interest revenue              $5,445
**To record interest for one year on a note of $68,060 at a rate of 8 percent.**

And after the second year,

Notes receivable, discount      $5,880
     Interest revenue              $5,880
**To record interest for one year on a note of $73,505 at a rate of 8 percent** ($73,505 represents the face value of the note less un-amortized discount of $26,495).

Over the life of the note, the firm will recognize earnings on the trans-action of $50,000—$100,000 received in cash less the recorded value of the building of $50,000—regardless of how the $100,000 is divided between "true" sales price and interest. If the transaction were accounted for in accordance with its form (selling price of $100,000), then a gain of $50,000 would be realized at time of sale. If accounted for in accordance with substance (sell-ing price of $68,060), then a gain of only $18,060 would be recognized in the year of sale. The remaining $31,940 would be recognized as interest and taken into income over the five-year period of the note.

From the standpoint of the purchaser of the building, if the entire $100,000 is assigned to the cost of the building, then that amount would be subject to depreciation and recognized as an expense over the useful life of the building—perhaps 40 years. If, however, the interest of $31,940 were taken into account, then only $68,060 would be assigned to the cost of the building and expensed as depreciation over its useful life. The interest, $31,940, would be charged as an expense over the five-year period of the note. The manner in which the transaction is accounted for has no effect on *total* earnings of either the purchaser or the seller; it does, however, have a significant impact on the timing and classification of such earnings.

### Industry Example: Retail Land Sales Companies

The issue of imputed interest is especially important with respect to *retail land sales* companies. Retail land sales companies purchase large tracts of land and subdivide them into small parcels for sale to consumers. They *master-plan* communities; install streets, sewers, and utilities; and sometimes construct *amenities* such as golf courses, club houses, motels, and restaurants. Often, they engage in extensive promotional efforts (e.g., free dinners or trips to the site) and frequently they direct their sales efforts at those who are interested in either retirement or vacation homes. Retail land sales companies seldom accept interest-free notes. Sometimes, however, they charge relatively low rates of interest. For example, they might charge a purchaser 6 percent interest annually at a time when the *prime rate* (that charged by banks to their most select customers) is 9 percent and the firms' own cost of borrowing is 12 percent.

Until recently, it was standard procedure in the industry to record sales at the face value of the note received. Such pratice, however, was criticized on the ground that it overstated sales revenue and understated interest revenue. Since sales revenue is recognized at the time a sales contract is signed and interest revenue is recognized over the term of the note, the effect was to speed up recognition of revenue and, according to critics, to overstate earnings in the year of the sale. Considering that the notes were often for 10 years and that the difference between the rate actually charged and that normally charged for "loans" of similar types may have been as much as 10 percent, the difference in first-year revenues on a sale of $10,000 could be almost $3,500. To eliminate the possibility of such overstatements in earnings, the Accounting Principles Board prescribed that the required payments on notes receivable that bear unreasonably low rates of interest must be *discounted* by the *prevailing* rate for similar types of credit instruments and that a portion of the stated sales price of the land be accounted for as interest rather than sales revenue.*

*example*     New Mexico Land Co. sells parcels of land for $10,000. Purchasers must pay $1,000 down and can give a 10-year note, which bears interest at a rate of 4 percent for the $9,000 balance. The note must be paid in 10 annual installments of $1,110. ($1,110 is the annual payment required to repay a loan of $9,000 in equal installments if interest is charged at a rate of 4 percent per year.)

If the company's customers had attempted to borrow the funds from a traditional lending institution, they would have had to pay the prevailing interest rate of 12 percent.

The present value of the consideration—that is, the "true" selling price of the land—can be determined by discounting *all* required payments (both principal and interest) by the *effective* rate of interest, in this example 12 percent:

| | |
|---|---:|
| Present value of $1,000 down payment | $1,000 |
| Present value of 10 annual payments of $1,110 discounted at a rate of 12 percent: Per Table 4, $1,110 × 5.6502 | 6,272 |
| Present value of all payments | $7,272 |

As a consequence, the firm would recognize sales revenue of only $7,272. $7,272 represents the worth at time of sale of all the payments to be received by

*Accounting for Retail Land Sales*. American Institute of Certified Public Accountants, 1972.

the company. The difference between that amount and $10,000 represents interest revenue and must be reported as such over the 10-year period that the note is outstanding.

## Receivables and Revenue in Practice: The Franchise Industry

The relationship between receivables and revenues cannot be overemphasized. The accounting practices of the franchise industry highlight some of the key issues pertaining to the realization of revenue and the valuation of receivables.

Franchisors sell to individual businessmen (franchisees) the right to operate a specific kind of business, to use the name of the franchisor and to provide goods or services associated with the franchisor. Companies such as McDonald's and Holiday Inn are among the best known franchisors, and their establishments appear to have become permanent additions to the American landscape. But hundreds of other franchise operations, often imitators of the well-known firms, make brief appearances on the American scene before fading into oblivion and often bankruptcy.

The revenue of a franchisor ordinarily comes from several sources. First, the franchisor sells franchises to the parties who will operate them. The franchisor receives a small downpayment and accepts from the franchisee long-term notes. Second, it generally receives royalties based on the sales volume of the franchisee. Third, it sometimes sells to the franchisee all or a portion of the product that will be sold to the public (e.g., the seasonings for fried chicken).

The source of revenue that presents the most difficult accounting problems is the first—that from the sale of the franchise. Commonly, the franchisor and franchisee will enter into a contractual arrangement many months prior to the time that the franchisee is ready to begin operations. During the intervening period and sometimes for a period subsequent to opening, the franchisor is required to provide services (advertising and management training, for example) to the franchisee. The question arises as to the point at which the revenue from the sale should be recognized and the related receivable should be recorded as an asset. Consistent with the principle that revenue should be related to productive effort, it could be recognized at the time the contract is signed, when the outlet first commences operations, or in the one or more periods in which various services are performed.

The issue of revenue recognition is compounded, however, by the fact that firms in the industry tend to face a high rate of default on notes received from the franchisees. The collectibility of the notes is directly dependent on the success of the individual franchisees. The franchisor can expect payment only insofar as the operations of a franchisee generate sufficient cash to meet its obligations as they come due.

Because eventual collection of cash cannot always be reasonably assured, it has sometimes been suggested that revenue be recognized only as the notes are actually collected; that is, on the cash collection or installment basis. Such approach would eliminate the possibility that the assets of the franchisor are overstated by the amounts that will prove uncollectible; it would make certain that revenue is not prematurely realized. But it would also be inconsistent with the general accounting practice of recognizing revenue when a transaction is substantially completed (and, as necessary, making appropriate provisions for uncollectible accounts). The installment method of accounting is ordinarily reserved for those exceptional cases where there is no reasonable basis for estimating the degree of collectibility of outstanding receivables.

Since the mid-1960s there has been an appreciable growth in the franchise industry. Firms have followed a variety of different accounting practices, and there have been allegations that some firms adopted policies which overstated both earnings and assets. In 1973, to assure greater uniformity of practice, a committee of the American Institute of Certified Public Accountants set forth guidelines for the recognition of revenue.* The committee recommended that revenue from the sale of a franchise should be delayed until the franchisor has substantially performed all of the initial services set forth in the sales agreement. It pointed out that because of a variety of practices in the industry there can be no one specific condition or event that can serve as the sole criterion for recognition of revenue. Substantial performance may occur at different times for different franchisors. Nevertheless, the committee indicated that "conservatism justifies the presumption that *commencement of operations by the franchisee* is the earliest point at which substantial performance has occurred." As a rule, the committee urged, revenue should therefore be recognized at the time that the franchisee starts its operations.

The committee took cognizance of the unusual risks of collection faced by some franchisors. But it recommended that the cash collection basis of revenue recognition be reserved for those exceptional cases where no reasonable basis of estimating the degree of collectibility exists. It urged that companies establish adequate allowances for uncollectible accounts and periodically review such allowances to make certain that they are sufficient in the light of changed conditions.

## Payroll Transactions

Although payroll transactions present few conceptual considerations that have not already been dealt with, they are worthy of discussion because they are of concern to virtually all profit and nonprofit organizations and are sometimes of major magnitude.

*\*Accounting for Franchise Fee Revenue.* American Institute of Certified Public Accountants, 1973.

The accounting for payroll transactions is characterized by the fact that the wage or salary expense pertaining to an individual employee may be considerably *greater* than the amount indicated by his wage or salary rate but that the amount actually paid to the employee may be considerably *less* than that indicated by his wage rate. The business firm must pay payroll taxes that are specifically levied on the employer and, commonly, must provide for *fringe benefits* in addition to regular wage and salary payments. Moreover, the employer must withhold from each employee's wages and salary the employee's share of payroll taxes as well as amounts for other designated purposes. Amounts withheld from the employee ordinarily represent a liability of the employer; they must be remitted either to the government or to a specific fund.

*example*   An employee is paid at the rate of $2,000 per month. From his salary must be withheld (either by law or by employee election) the following: federal income taxes (according to a schedule published by the Internal Revenue Service)—$355; Federal Insurance Contribution Act deductions (abbreviated FICA and commonly referred to as *Social Security* payments)—6 percent of gross salary—$120; Blue Cross/Blue Shield contribution—$64 per month; savings bond plan—$18 per month. As a consequence of the deductions *take-home* pay of the employee would be $1,493.

In addition, the employer incurs the following voluntary or statutory charges: employer share of FICA contributions—6 percent of gross salary—$120; contribution to company pension fund—8 percent of gross salary—$160; state and federal unemployment insurance taxes—3 percent of gross salary—$60.

The following entry would be appropriate on the payroll date:

| | | |
|---|---|---|
| Salaries (expense) | $2,000 | |
| FICA expense, employer's share | 120 | |
| Unemployment insurance (expense) | 60 | |
| Pension expense | 160 | |
|     Salaries payable | | $1,443 |
|     Liability for income taxes withheld FED'L | | 355 |
|     Liability for FICA (both employee and | | |
|       employer share) | | 240 |
|     Liability for Blue Cross/Blue Shield | | 64 |
|     Liability for savings bonds | | 18 |
|     Liability for pensions | | 160 |
|   Liability for unemployment insurance | | 60 |

**To record payroll.**

When cash payments are made to the employee or to the appropriate funds or government agencies, the various liability accounts would be debited; cash would be credited.

If employees are granted periodic vacations, then the expense of their salaries during the vacations should be allocated to those accounting periods in which they are actually performing their services. If, in the above example, the employee were granted a one-month annual vacation, then the $2,000 that he would be paid while on vacation should be charged as an expense during the 11 months in which he worked. The accrual of vacation pay could be effected by the following additional entry each month:

| | | |
|---|---|---|
| Vacation pay (expense) | $182 | |
|     Provision for vacation pay (liability) | | $182 |
| **To accrue vacation pay—one-eleventh of monthly salary.** | | |

When the employee takes his vacation—by which time the balance in the provision for vacation pay account should be approximately $2,000—the following entry (which, for simplicity, omits consideration of payroll withholdings and other deductions) would be in order:

| | | |
|---|---|---|
| Provision for vacation pay | $2,000 | |
|     Salaries payable | | $2,000 |
| **To record the amount due the employee for vacation pay.** | | |

It is particularly important for business or nonprofit organizations to spread the costs of vacation pay over the productive periods of their employees if they prepare quarterly or semiannual financial reports in addition to annual reports. If they neglect to *accrue* vacation pay, then cost of operations in the summer months may appear to be considerably higher than in other months. Such increase in operations cost is attributable to the fact that most employees take their vacations in the summer when substitute workers must be hired or production reduced.

## Summary

Three main ideas pervaded the discussion of receivables and payables:

1. Questions of the amounts at which receivables and payables should be stated are directly related to those of when revenues and expenses should be recognized.

If an enterprise grants credit to its customers, it is doubtful that all of its receivables will be transformed into cash. "Losses" on bad debts are an expected deduction from revenues. They should be charged as an expense (or a reduction of sales) in the same accounting period in which the related sales are made. Correspondingly, accounts receivable should be reduced by the amount likely to prove uncollectible.

Similarly, both sales and receivables should be reduced by the amount of expected returns, allowances and discounts of which customers may avail themselves. They should be reduced also by interest included in the face of the receivable but not yet earned. Notes receivable, for example, often include in the stated value an element of interest to be earned during the period over which the notes will be held.

2. The substance of a transaction must take precedence over its form. Accountants must look to the economic rather than the stated values of goods or services exchanged. It is not unusual, for example, for firms to allow customers to delay payments for months or even years and make no explicit charges for interest. Money, however, has a time value, and the right to use funds for an extended period of time is not granted casually. Whenever the sales price of an item is *inflated* by unspecified interest charges, the accountant must impute a fair rate of interest and account for the revenue from the sale of the item apart from the revenue from the interest.

3. Proper accounting for receivables and payables is dependent on the good judgment of both managers and accountants. The "correct" value of receivables can never be known with certainty. It is dependent on the number of customers that fail to fulfill their payment obligations, the amount of goods returned, and the amount of cash discounts taken. In determining the amount to report as a receivable as well as the amount of revenue to be considered realized, such amounts must necessarily be estimated. Accounts receivable and the related revenues can never be viewed as being "accurately" presented— only "fairly" presented.

*exercise for review and self-testing*

The LJG Company sells a unit of equipment to a customer for $1,000. The customer is permitted to defer payment for one year, but is to be charged interest at a rate of 4 percent. The company accepts a note from the customer for principal of $1,000 plus interest of $40—a total of $1,040.

In fact, the prevailing rate of interest—the rate normally charged similar customers in similar circumstances—is 12 percent, and the company often sells its equipment for less than $1,000.

a. Determine the fair market value of the equipment, taking into account the prevailing rate of interest. What is the present value of the note (both principal and interest) to the company?

b. Prepare a journal entry to record the sale of the equipment. Be sure that the amount of revenue recognized reflects the value of the consideration received. Any difference between the face amount of the note and the amount of revenue recognized should be classified as "Notes receivable, discount."

c. After one year the company collects the entire $1,040 from the customer. Prepare a journal entry to record the collection of the note and to recognize interest revenue for the year. Be sure that the amount of interest revenue recognized reflects the "true" (prevailing) rate of interest.

d. The firm estimates that of the total sales for the year for which notes were accepted, $7,000 will prove to be uncollectible. Prepare a journal entry to add that amount to "Notes receivable, allowance for uncollectibles."

e. A review of notes on hand indicates that $2,500 are presently uncollectible. Prepare a journal entry to write off the notes against the allowance provided.

## Questions

1. Why is it preferable for a firm to maintain an allowance for uncollectible accounts rather than to simply write off bad accounts as soon as it is known which specific accounts will be uncollectible?

2. On December 29 a company purchases for $100,000 merchandise intended for resale. The company is granted a 5 percent discount for paying cash within 10 days of purchase. The company records the purchase using the gross method. As of year end the company has not yet paid for the goods purchased but has resold half of them. The company intends to pay within the specified discount period. Assuming that no adjustment to the accounts has been made, in what way is it likely that the financial statements as of year end are misstated?

3. A company borrows $1,000 for one year at the prevailing interest rate of 6 percent. The note issued to the lender promises payment of $1,000 plus interest of $60 after one year. Upon borrowing the funds the company recorded a liability for $1,060. Do you agree with such accounting treatment? Explain.

4. A finance company loaned an individual $1,000 on a discount basis. The actual cash given to the borrower was only $940; interest was taken out in advance. At the time of the loan the company recorded its receivable at $1,000, reduced its cash by $940, and recognized revenue of $60. Do you agree with such practice? How would you record the loan? Explain.

5. A retail store places the following ad in the paper: "Complete Room of Furniture; $1,000; no money down; take up to 2 years to pay; no interest or finance charges." During a particular month the firm sold 10 sets of the advertised furniture. The company recorded sales of $10,000. If you were the firm's independent CPA, what reservations would you have about the reported sales?

6. A firm acquires a building at a cost of $200,000 but gives the seller a five-year interest-free note for the entire amount. Assuming that the firm would otherwise have had to borrow the funds at a rate of interest of 10 percent compounded annually, at what amount should the building be recorded? What would be the impact of failing to take into account *imputed* interest on reported earnings of the years during which the note is outstanding as well as on those of the remaining years of the useful life of the building?

7. After operating successfully in a single city, the owners of Big Top Ice Cream Parlors decide to sell franchises to individual businessmen in other cities. Within one year they sign contracts and receive down payments for 20 franchises. The total sales price of each franchise is $50,000. The required down payment is a small fraction of total sales price. During the first year only 5 outlets are actually opened. The company reported revenues from sale of franchises of $1 million. What warnings would you give an investor with respect to first-year earnings?

8. The supervisor of a large clerical department in a government agency has determined that efficiency in his department always seems to drop during the summer months. He determines efficiency by dividing total payroll costs

by the number of documents processed. Total payroll costs include amounts paid to employees on vacation. The department charges all salaries—both those of workers actually on the job and those on vacation—as an expense in the month paid. Why do you suspect efficiency appears to be low during the summer months? What improvements to the accounting system might you recommend?

9. A finance company charges customers 12 percent interest on all balances outstanding. The company continues to accrue interest revenue on outstanding loans (that is, it debits interest receivable and credits interest revenue) even though loan payments might be past due. Only when it writes off a loan does it cease to accrue interest. What dangers are suggested by such practice?

## Problems

1. *Compute simple and compound interest.*

   In each of the following situations, determine the interest revenue that a firm should recognize.
   1. It holds for 180 days a $3,000 note that earns interest at an annual rate of 8 percent.
   2. It holds for 30 days a $10,000 note that earns interest at an annual rate of 6 percent.
   3. It holds for 400 days a $1,000 note that earns interest at an annual rate of 12 percent (interest is not to be charged on interest accrued at the end of the first year).
   4. It holds for five years a $5,000 note that earns interest at a rate of 7 percent compounded annually.

2. *This is a simple exercise in accounting for uncollectibles.*

   The trial balance of the Elton Co. indicated the following:

   | | |
   |---|---|
   | Sales | $486,000 |
   | Accounts receivable | 63,000 |
   | Allowance for uncollectibles | 11,000 |

   In the current year, bad-debt expense had not yet been recorded.
   The firm estimates that approximately 5 percent of sales will prove to be uncollectible. A review of accounts receivable reveals that $21,500 of accounts presently on the books are unlikely to be collected and should therefore be written off.
   Prepare any entries that you believe are necessary in light of the facts as presented.

3. *The stated price of merchandise is not always the "true" price.*

   A firm sells merchandise for a supposed price of $1,000, but sometimes grants unusually generous terms of credit. Prevailing rates of interest are 10 percent. Determine the amount most indicative of "true" selling price of the merchandise if the buyer

a. pays $1,000 cash today.

b. pays $1,000 cash one year from today.

c. pays $1,000 cash plus interest at 6 percent (that is, $1,060) one year from today.

d. pays $500 six months from today and $500 one year from today.

4. *Compute the amount of discount notes.*

A bank makes a loan to a customer on a discount basis. Determine the amount that should be advanced to the customer in each of the following situations, assuming that the face amount of the note is $10,000 and the rate of discount is 12 percent per year.

1. The period of the loan is 1 year.

2. The period of the loan is 60 days.

3. The period of the loan is 4 years.

5. *Neither the entries to write off accounts receivable nor to restore accounts that were previously written off have a direct impact upon earnings.*

Transactions involving accounts receivable and related accounts of Warner's Department Store for 1980 and 1981 can be summarized as follows:

|  | 1980 | 1981 |
| --- | --- | --- |
| Credit sales | $3,000,000 | $3,000,000 |
| Cash collections on accounts receivable | 2,800,000 | 3,100,000 |
| Accounts deemed uncollectible and written off | 30,000 | 65,000 |

The firm estimates that 2 percent of annual credit sales will prove uncollectible.

Included in the $3.1 million of cash collections in 1981 are $3,000 from customers whose accounts had been written off in 1980. The balances in the accounts when they were written off totaled $8,000. It is the policy of the company to restore in their entirety accounts previously written off upon collection of a partial payment from a customer since a partial payment is often an indication that payment of the remaining balance will be forthcoming. (To restore an account it is necessary only to "reverse" the entry made to write it off.)

a. Prepare journal entries to record the activity reported above.

b. Compare the impact of credit losses on reported earnings of 1980 with those of 1981.

c. Comment briefly on how your answer to part b would differ if the amount to be added to the allowance for doubtful accounts were based on an aging schedule instead of a flat percentage of sales.

6. *The means of accounting for cash discounts may not be the critical issue of our time, but they point up the importance of recognizing substance rather than form.*

Indiana Industrial Supplies reported accounts receivable of $1 million as of December 31, 1980. Of that amount $800,000 represents sales of the final 20 days of the year. The company allows its customers to take a cash discount of 4 percent of sales price on all merchandise paid for within 20 days.

The company has consistently accounted for cash discounts by the *gross* method. Annual sales and year-end balances in accounts receivable have remained generally constant over the last several years. Approximately 90 percent of customers take advantage of the cash discount. Comment on whether the firm's sales and accounts receivable are likely to be fairly presented at year end. Indicate the amount of any possible over- or understatement.

7. *The gross method of accounting for cash discounts may not reflect the fair market value of goods traded.*

The Grimm Co. purchases all of its merchandise from the Anderson Co. Terms of sale are 1/15, n/30. In the month of December the following transactions took place:

| | |
|---|---|
| 12/2 | Grimm purchased $80,000 of merchandise on account. |
| 12/10 | Grimm remitted payment for the goods purchased. |
| 12/12 | Grimm purchased $50,000 of merchandise on account. |
| 12/31 | Grimm remitted payment for the goods purchased. |

a. Record the transactions on the books of the Grimm Co. using first the net method and then the gross method.
b. Record the transactions on the books of the Anderson Co. using first the net method and then the gross method. The entries from the standpoint of the seller were not illustrated in the text. They correspond closely to those of the purchaser, however.
c. Assuming that no additional adjustments were made to the accounts and that none of the merchandise acquired by Grimm has yet been sold, comment on any distortions of the accounts that might result from use of the gross method. Suppose that Grimm had sold all or part of the merchandise that it had acquired. What accounts might be misstated?

8. *Reported wage expense is generally greater than the amounts actually disbursed to employees.*

Wellman Manufacturing Co. has 100 hourly employees, each of whom worked 40 hours in a given week and was paid $6.50 per hour.

Total federal income taxes which the company was required to withhold for the week were $3,900.

The current Social Security (FICA) rate applicable to both employer and employee is 6 percent.

The company is required to pay 3 percent of gross wages into the State Unemployment Insurance Fund.

The company has a matching pension plan. Employees contribute 5 percent of their wages; the company contributes an equal amount.

The firm is required by union contract to withhold from each employee union dues of $2.50 per week.

Twenty employees have elected to join the savings bond program. The cost of a savings bond, $18, is withdrawn from wages each week and used to purchase a government savings bond.

The company pays medical insurance for each employee. The cost is $8 per week per employee.

a. Prepare a journal entry to record the weekly payroll.

b. Prepare a journal entry to record disbursement of all required payments to the various government agencies, insurance companies, pension funds, etc.

9. *The impact of an accounting change on the balance sheet may be substantially greater than on the income statement. An event may have a significant impact on the interim statements but no effect on the annual statements.*

The Sonora Co. has an annual payroll of approximately $2,000,000. Such amount does *not* include $120,000 paid to employees on vacation. The company does not *accrue* vacation pay; it charges it to expense as employees take their vacations. The controller has rejected the suggestions of the company's independent CPA that vacation pay be recognized on a week-by-week basis; he claims that such recognition would have no effect on the financial statements; it would only increase clerical costs.

The payroll of the company has remained constant for a number of years. Employees are entitled to three weeks vacation each year based on work performed in the previous fiscal year, and such vacations must be taken during July and August. Employees receive their regular wages while on vacation, and all employees must be replaced by temporary employees at the same wage rate. The company's fiscal year ends June 30.

a. Is the controller correct in his assertion that accrual of vacation pay would have no impact on the financial statements? Estimate the impact of a change in policy on both the income statement and the balance sheet.

b. Suppose the firm were to issue *interim* financial statements on December 31 for the six months ending on that date. What would be the impact of accruing vacation pay on the income statement and the balance sheet?

10. *Vacations are not to be accounted for casually—as one company found out.*

The following is an excerpt from the annual report of Eastern Airlines, Inc.

Subsequent to the issuance of the financial statements included in the 1976 Annual Report to Stockholders, the Staff of the Securities and Exchange Commission ("SEC" or "Commission"), reviewed a Registration Statement on Form S-1 filed by the company in March 1977. As a result of this review, the Staff of the SEC requested the company to change its accounting practice with respect to vacation liability, the effect of which was that the company recorded, effective January 1, 1975, a liability of approximately $35 million for earned vacation benefits, notwithstanding the CAB's deferral of implementation of such change and the company's disclosure of this matter in filings with the SEC and annual reports to stockholders. Although the company and its independent accountants continue to believe the accounting practice followed by the company was appropriate in the circumstances, the company agreed, after conferences with the Staff and consideration by the full Commission, to restate its financial statements to give effect to the accounting treatment requested by the SEC.

The cumulative effect of the accounting change, as of January 1, 1975, is shown as a one-time noncash charge against 1975 income in the amount of $35 million. The change also increased the loss before the cumulative effect of the change in 1975 by $4 million ($0.21 per share) and reduced net income in 1976 by $1 million ($0.05 per share).

    a. Indicate the entry that the firm most likely made in 1975 to record the $35 million liability for earned vacation benefits.

    b. Indicate the entry (omitting numbers) that the company will now make each time an employee takes a vacation. How does this entry differ from that which would have been made prior to 1975?

11. *In some industries it is critical that allowances be made for anticipated returns of merchandise sold.*

Division Products had gross sales in 1980 (its first year of operations) of $4 million and in 1981 of $6 million. As of December 31, 1980, the company had accounts receivable of $2 million and as of December 31, 1981, $3 million. The business of the company is highly seasonal; most of its sales are made in the last three months of the year.

The company follows standard practice in its industry. It permits the retailers with whom it deals to return for full credit any merchandise that they are unable to sell within a reasonable period of time. In January 1981, the company accepted for return merchandise which it had sold for $400,000. A return rate of 10 percent of sales is typical for the industry. None of the merchandise had yet been paid for by the retailers.

The firm's cost of goods sold is approximately 60 percent of selling price. In financial statements prepared for internal use only (and not in accord with generally accepted accounting principles of reporting to general public), the firm gives accounting recognition to merchandise returned only when it is actually received; it establishes no year-end allowances.

    a. Determine for both 1980 and 1981 the difference in income and assets that would result if the company were to adhere to generally accepted accounting principles and establish an allowance for returned merchandise. Assume that all goods returned could be resold at standard prices.

    b. Suppose that the company were in a business, such as toys, in which it is extremely difficult to predict the rate of return from pre-Christmas sales. What warnings would you give to a potential investor or creditor who is likely to rely upon the company's financial statements?

    c. How can companies in highly seasonal industries, such as toys, minimize the risk of misestimating sales returns? Why do you suppose that many department stores report on the basis of a fiscal year ending July 31?

12. *In the long run, though not in any particular year, bad debts based on an aging schedule should be equal to those based on dollar volume of credit sales.*

The Melrose Co. began operations in January 1978. The schedule below indicates credit sales and end-of-year balances in accounts receivable for 1978 through 1981. The end-of-year balances are broken down by the "age" of the receivables.

*(000 Omitted)*
*End-of-Year Balance in Accounts Receivable*

| | | | | No. of Days Past Due | | |
|---|---|---|---|---|---|---|
| *Year* | *Credit Sales* | *Total* | *Current* | *1–30* | *31–60* | *Over 60* |
| 1978 | $12,000 | $1,080 | $ 800 | $100 | $150 | $ 30 |
| 1979 | 14,000 | 1,500 | 1,100 | 300 | 50 | 50 |
| 1980 | 16,000 | 1,600 | 900 | 400 | 200 | 100 |
| 1981 | 18,000 | 1,820 | 1,280 | 220 | 200 | 120 |

The company estimates that approximately 5 percent of all credit sales will prove to be uncollectible. It has also determined that of its accounts receivable balance at any date the following percentages will likely be uncollectible:

| | |
|---|---|
| Current | 15% |
| 1–30 days past due | 40 |
| 31–60 days past due | 50 |
| Over 60 days past due | 60 |

The balance in the "allowance for uncollectibles" account was zero prior to the adjustment at the end of 1978. Actual write-offs of accounts receivable were as follows:

| | |
|---|---|
| 1978 | 260 |
| 1979 | 580 |
| 1980 | 815 |
| 1981 | 893 |

a. Determine bad-debt expense for each of the four years assuming first that the company bases its addition to the allowance for uncollectibles on credit sales and alternatively on a schedule of *aged* accounts receivables. Bear in mind that when the sales method is used the bad-debt expense is determined directly. When the aged accounts receivable method is used it is necessary to first determine the required balance in the allowance for uncollectibles account.

b. Compare total bad-debt expense over the combined four-year period under each of the two methods. (They should be the same in this example.) Which method results in the more erratic pattern of bad-debt expense in this particular example? Why?

13. *Interest on troublesome loans should not be accrued.*

The following comment was included in the notes to the financial statements of the Equitable Life Mortgage and Realty Investors:

*Non-Accrual of Interest.* When it is not reasonable to expect that interest income will be received, its recognition is discontinued. At that point, interest accrued but not received is reversed and no further interest is accrued until it is evident that principal and interest will be collected.

a. Why should the company "reverse" interest accrued but not yet received?
b. What is the most likely journal entry made to effect the reversal?

14. *The effective rate of interest on discount loans may be substantially higher than the stated rate.*

The Confidential Loan Co. placed an advertisement in a local newspaper. It read, in part, "Borrow up to $15,000. Take up to 3 Years to Repay. Low, Low, 6% Interest Rate."

Upon visiting the loan company you learn that on a three-year, 6 percent loan of $15,000, interest of $2,700 ($900 per year) is taken out in advance; you would receive only $12,300 cash. You would be required to repay the loan in three annual installments of $5,000.

Indicate the main points that you might make in a letter to the local consumer protection commission. Be sure to specify the approximate effective rate of interest charged by the company.

15. *This problem illustrates a borrowing arrangement that, although not specifically discussed in the text, represents an application of the principles which were described.*

Sometimes a firm will "discount" with a bank an interest-bearing note that it has received from a customer. The bank will advance the firm the amount to be received from the customer, less interest charges for the number of days until the note matures. When the note matures, the customer will make payment to the firm and the firm will transfer the amount received to the bank.

Suppose a firm receives a one-year note from a customer in the amount of $1,000. The note bears interest at the rate of 8 percent. Immediately upon receipt of the note, the firm discounts it with a bank. The bank, however, accepts notes only at a discount rate of 10 percent.

a. Upon the maturity of the note, how much will the customer be required to remit to the firm?
b. What is the amount that the bank will be willing to advance to the firm based on its discount rate of 10 percent?

16. *This problem provides an illustration of a real firm whose allowance for uncollectibles was inadequate to cover loan losses.*

The annual report of First Chicago Corporation contained the following comment and table regarding its provision for loan losses:

One of the most significant factors adversely affecting 1976 results was the $126.5 million provision for loan losses, up from $118.5 million in

1975. Net loan charge-offs were $145.8 million, exceeding the provision for loan losses by $19.3 million.

|                                        | 1976        | 1975        |
| -------------------------------------- | ----------- | ----------- |
| Balance, beginning of period           | $121,352    | $ 95,766    |
| Additions (deductions)                 |             |             |
|    Loans charged-off     | (153,688)   | (95,583)    |
|    Recoveries            | 7,874       | 2,669       |
| Net charge-offs                        | $(145,814)  | $ (92,914)  |
| Provisions charged to operating expense | 126,500     | 118,500     |
| Balance, end of period                 | $102,038    | $121,352    |

   a. Prepare journal entries to reflect the activity in the account, "Provision for loan losses" in 1976. (Recoveries are accounted for by reversing the entry that was made to write off the loans.)

   b. Based only on the limited information provided, do you think that the balance in the account as of the end of 1976 will be adequate to cover losses on loans to be incurred in the future? Explain.

17. *Even banks and finance companies face difficult questions of revenue recognition.*

Sunrise Finance Co. loaned a customer $10,000 for two years on a discount basis. The customer was to repay $5,000 at the end of each year. The rate of discount (the *effective* rate of interest) was 12 percent.

   a. How much cash would the company actually advance the customer? Prepare a journal entry to record the loan and the receipt by the company of a note for $10,000.

   b. How much revenue should the company recognize during the first year of the loan? Prepare a journal entry to record receipt of the first payment of $5,000. At what value will the note be reported (net of discount) after the first year? How much revenue should the company recognize during the second year?

   c. Many accountants would argue that a portion—perhaps 15 percent— of the total revenue to be earned over the two-year period should be recognized at the time the loan is made, without waiting for interest to accrue with the passage of time. Given the costs of obtaining customers (advertising) and processing loan applications, why do you suspect they feel as they do?

18. *In the real estate industry it is not uncommon for the selling price of property to include an element of interest.*

The Lincoln Co. purchased a building from the Polk Co. The stated selling price of the building was $100,000. Polk Co. agreed to accept from the Lincoln Co. an *interest-free* note, which was payable in full five years from the date the transaction was *closed.*

The building has an estimated useful life of 20 years and zero salvage value after that period. At time of sale it had been recorded on the books of the Polk Co. at $40,000. Had Lincoln Co. been required to pay cash for the building, it would have had to borrow the funds from a bank at an annual rate of interest of 10 percent.

a. Prepare a journal entry to record the purchase of the building on the books of the Lincoln Co. Be certain that the entry recognizes "substance over form."

b. Prepare any journal entries that would be required after the first year of ownership to recognize both interest expense and depreciation.

c. Determine the difference on Lincoln Co. earnings of the first year that would result from taking into account, as opposed to ignoring, the *imputed* interest.

d. Determine the difference in Polk Co. earnings of both the first year and second year that would result from taking into account the *imputed* interest. What would be the total difference in earnings in years 1 through 5? (You should not have to compute earnings in each of the five years to answer this question.)

19. *Determination of the real value of a business acquired by another may be complex.*

The following note appeared in the 1973 financial report of United Brands Company:

> On December 31, 1973, the Company sold its 83% interest in Baskin-Robbins Ice Cream Company to J. Lyons & Company Limited, a British food company, for a total of $37,600,000 including $30,300,000 in notes. The notes bear interest at 4% per annum and mature in 3 equal annual installments of $10,100,000 commencing on December 31, 1974. The notes have been recorded in the financial statements at an imputed interest rate of 12%.

a. Determine the present value, discounted at 12 percent, of *all* payments (both principal and interest) that United Brands will receive over the three-year period. Be sure to determine the interest payments as 4 percent of the outstanding balance of the notes at the time of each payment.

b. Prepare a journal entry to record the sale of the 83 percent interest in Baskin-Robbins. Assume that the 83 percent interest had been valued on the books of United Brands at $20 million. To simplify the journal entry and subsequent computation of interest, record the present value of the expected principal and interest payments to be received in a single account, "notes receivable."

c. Prepare an entry to record the first receipt of principal and interest. Be sure to base the computation of interest earned on the effective rate of 12 percent and the effective balance in the notes receivable account.

d. How much greater or less would the reported income of United Brands have been in both the year of sale and year of collection of the first principal and interest payment had the company not imputed the additional 8 percent interest?

20. *Just as it is commonly asserted that there is no such thing as a "free lunch," there is also no such a thing as "free money."*

The Davis County Land Development Co. sells real estate on terms of 10 percent down, the balance to be paid in annual installments over a three-year period. Customers are not specifically charged interest on their outstanding balances.

During 1980 the company sold several lots at a stated price of $8,000 each. The original cost to the company of each of the lots was $400. The interest rate on similar "loans" would be at a rate of 10 percent per year.

a. How much *income* do you think the company should recognize at time of sale (upon collection of the 10 percent down payment) assuming recognition of all *sales* (but not *interest*) revenue at time of down payment? Prepare a journal entry to record the transaction.

b. How much income should be recognized at the time of each of the three installment payments? What would be the balances in notes receivable and the related discount account immediately following each payment?

21. *Should a franchisor recognize revenue at the time it signs a sales contract or should it wait until it has performed substantially all of the terms of the contract?*

The Peter Pan Cheese Co., after successfully operating a single retail cheese store for several years, decided in 1980 to expand its operations. It offered to sell Peter Pan franchises, in several cities, for $40,000. For that amount an individual businessman acquired the right to sell under the name "Peter Pan" and to purchase from the franchisor several products bearing the company name.

The franchisee was required to pay $10,000 upon the opening of its outlet and could pay the balance over the next 10 years. It was to be charged interest at a rate of 8 percent per year on the balance outstanding.

The company estimated that the cost of initial services it would be required to provide the franchisee prior to the opening of his outlet would be $30,000. The company, in accord with recommendations of the franchise industry audit guide, elected to recognize revenue from the sale of the franchise at the *commencement of an outlet's operations.*

In 1980 the company signed sales contracts with 10 franchisees. Of these, 6 began operations during the year. The company incurred $180,000 in costs in connection with the outlets actually opened and $100,000 in connection with those expected to open in the following year.

In addition, the company had cash sales of merchandise to the outlets of $120,000; the cost of merchandise sold was $80,000.

The company collected $10,000 from each franchisee at the time its outlet began operations. In addition, it collected $6,000 in interest. The company estimated that 6 percent of the original balance of the notes would prove to be uncollectible.

a. Prepare an income statement for 1980 to reflect franchise operations. (Be sure to match expenses with revenues.)

b. Prepare a balance sheet as of year end. To simplify your presentation, do not include in notes receivable that portion of the notes associated with revenue that has not yet been realized. Assume that the company began the year with $200,000 in cash and owners' equity. All costs were paid in cash.

a. The fair market value of the equipment may be obtained by evaluating the value *today* of the note. Per table 2, the present value of $1 to be received one year hence, discounted at a rate of 12 percent is $0.8929. The present value of the note, therefore, is $1,040 × 0.8929–$928.62. The fair market value of the equipment, therefore would also be $928.62.

b. Notes receivable                                  $1,040.00

    Notes receivable, discount                       $111.38

    Sales revenue                                      928.62

**To record sale of equipment.**

c. Cash                                           $1,040.00

   Notes receivable, discount                     111.38

    Notes receivable                                  $1,040.00

    Interest revenue                                     111.38

**To record collection of the note and to recognize interest revenue for one year.**

d. Bad-debt expense                                $7,000

    Notes receivable, allowance

        for uncollectibles                              $7,000

**To record estimate of bad debts.**

e. Notes receivable, allowance for

   uncollectibles                                    $2,500

    Notes receivable                                   $2,500

**To write off specific notes that are uncollectible.**

# 8

# Inventories and Cost of Goods Sold

The term *inventory* refers both to goods that are awaiting sale and to those that are in the various stages of production. It includes the merchandise of a trading concern as well as the finished goods, the work in process, and the raw materials of a manufacturer. In addition, the term embraces goods that will be consumed indirectly as the enterprise manufactures its product or provides its service. Thus, stores of stationery, cleaning supplies, and lubricants would also be categorized as inventories. Proper accounting for inventories is critical not only because they often comprise a substantial portion of a firm's assets but also because they relate directly to what is frequently the firm's major expense—the cost of goods sold. The beginning inventory balance plus purchases minus the ending inventory balance equals the cost of goods sold. This chapter will be directed to several key accounting issues pertaining to inventory, some of which are currently at the center of active controversy. Among the questions to be raised are

What are the objectives of inventory measurement and valuation?
What costs should be included in inventory?
How should inventory quantities be determined?
What assumptions regarding the flow of costs are most appropriate in
    particular circumstances?
What accounting recognition should be given to changes in the market
    prices of inventories?

The discussion of inventories will be in the context of generally accepted accounting principles—how inventories are accounted for in practice. But consideration will also be given, in a concluding section, to alternatives that have been proposed but which are not presently viewed as acceptable.

## Objectives

The overriding objective of conventional inventory accounting is to match the costs of acquiring or producing goods with the revenues that they generate. In a typical operating cycle of a firm, the costs of goods which are either manufactured or purchased are included in inventory and reported as an asset. Even though the goods may have been paid for, their costs are not considered to be expenses; rather they are *stored* on the balance sheet until the goods are sold

286

and the costs can be associated with specific revenues. In the course of a year, a portion of the goods remains on hand; a portion is sold to outsiders. A portion of the costs, therefore, must be assigned to the goods that remain on hand and the rest to the goods that have been sold. That portion of the costs that is assigned to the goods on hand will continue to be carried on the balance sheet, while that assigned to the goods that have been sold will be charged to an expense account, cost of goods sold, and reported on the income statement. The question facing the accountant is, How much of the total costs should be assigned to the goods on hand and how much to the goods that have been sold? Diagramatically the issue can be depicted as shown in Exhibit 8-1.

*EXHIBIT 8-1*

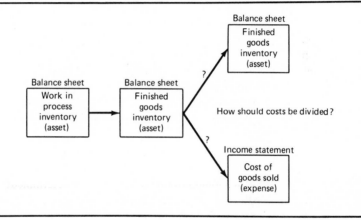

Insofar as a greater value is placed on the goods in inventory, a lesser amount will be charged as an expense. Insofar as a greater amount is charged as a current expense, then smaller amounts will remain on the balance sheet to be charged as expenses in future years.

It is sometimes asserted that another objective of inventory accounting should be to provide investors with information that will enable them to predict the future flows of cash with which inventories are likely to be associated. The arguments in favor of this objective take two forms. First, it is pointed out that inventories on hand will ordinarily be sold within a single operating cycle of the business. The inventories should be valued, it is asserted, in such a way as to provide the best indication of the amount of cash to be obtained by their sale. Logically, proponents of this position contend, inventories should be reported at the amounts for which they will eventually be sold (less, of course, any costs that will be incurred to prepare them for sale). Their position that the objective of inventory accounting is to indicate expected cash inflows, however, is in conflict with the historical cost basis of accounting. The balance sheet, as accounting is currently practiced, is not purported to indicate market values.

Rather, it is representative of nothing more than those portions of incurred (i.e., historical) costs that have not yet been matched to revenues and thereby not yet charged off as expenses.

Second, it has been observed that inventories on hand will enable the firm to reduce its outlays in future periods to acquire goods that will be sold in such future periods. The amount of the saving will be equal to the amount that would have to be spent to replace the goods that are on hand. It is averred, therefore, that an objective of inventory accounting should be to indicate to investors the cash outflow that would otherwise be required. The direct implication of this objective is that inventories should be valued at their current market values—the amounts for which they could be replaced. This form of the argument, that inventories should be a predictor of future cash flows, is similarly in conflict with the historical cost basis of accounting. It suggests that accounting recognition be given to transactions that are likely to take place in the future as well as to those that have already taken place in the past.

The preceding comments are not intended to suggest that arguments in favor of the alternative objectives of inventory accounting lack merit. But in evaluating the several choices that are currently available to business enterprises, it is important that they be appraised in the context of the historical cost framework of accounting—that which is "generally accepted" today.

## Costs Included in Inventory

Inventories are conventionally stated at historical cost—that of acquisition or production. Cost, as applied to inventories, "means in principle the sum of the applicable expenditures and charges directly or indirectly incurred in bringing an article to its existing condition and location."* If goods are purchased from outsiders, then cost would include not only the invoice price but also costs of packaging and transportation. Trade, cash, or other special discounts or allowances would ordinarily be deducted from the stated price.

As a general rule, all costs that can reasonably be associated with the manufacture or acquisition, with the storage, or with the preparation for sale of goods should be included as part of the cost of such goods. In determining whether a particular item of cost should be added to the reported value of inventory, the impact of the decision on both the income statement and the balance sheet should be taken into account. Insofar as costs are added to the reported value of goods on hand, they will be charged as expenses (as part of cost of goods sold) in the period in which the merchandise is actually sold. By contrast, if the costs are not assigned to particular items of inventory, then they will be charged as expenses in the periods in which they are incurred, regardless of when the merchandise is sold.

*Accounting Research Bulletin No. 43.* Committee on Accounting Procedure, American Institute of Certified Public Accountants, 1961.

A company purchased 100 units of product at $20 per unit. It was permitted a trade discount (one granted to all customers in a particular category) of 5 percent but had to pay shipping costs of $300. Cost per unit would be computed as follows:

| | | |
|---|---:|---:|
| Base price (100 units @ $20) | $2,000 | |
| Less trade discount (5%) | 100 | $1,900 |
| Plus shipping costs | | 300 |
| Total cost of 100 units | | $2,200 |
| Number of units | | ÷ 100 units |
| Cost per unit | | $   22 |

If goods are produced by the company itself, the problem of cost determination is considerably more complex. Cost would include charges for labor and materials that can be directly associated with the product as well as those for *overhead* such as rent, maintenance, and utilities that may be common to several products produced in the same plant. To determine the cost of a particular product, a company will have to allocate such common charges among the various products. In addition, however, the firm has to decide whether certain costs should be considered *product* costs and thereby added to the carrying value of the goods produced, or *period* costs and thereby charged off as an expense as incurred. The implications of classifying an outlay as a product rather than a period cost were discussed earlier in Chapter 4 in connection with the discussion of the manufacturing cycle. The entire question of determining the cost of goods manufactured is the focus of a branch of accounting referred to as *cost accounting.*

### Accounting for Quantities on Hand

In Chapter 4 it was pointed out that inventories may be maintained on a perpetual or a periodic basis. A perpetual basis implies that accounting recognition is given to the diminution of inventories each time a sale is made, supplies are consumed, or raw materials are added to production. When goods are removed from inventory upon a sale, for example, the following journal entry would be made:

| | | |
|---|---|---|
| Cost of goods sold | xxxx | |
| Inventory | | xxxx |

The periodic method, on the other hand, requires that recognition be given to the reduction in inventory resulting from the sale or use of goods only periodically, perhaps once a year. As goods are added to inventory, the inventory account is debited with their cost.* As goods are removed however, no entry is made. Throughout the year, therefore, the inventory *account* misstates the cost of the goods actually on hand. At the end of the period, a *physical* count of goods is taken, the goods are valued on the basis of acquisition cost, and the inventory account is adjusted to reflect the resultant dollar amount. If, for example, at year end an inventory account reflects a balance of $10,000 but a physical count reveals inventory on hand of only $500, the following entry would be appropriate (assuming that the difference between the two amounts reflects merchandise sold and not damaged or pilfered):

| | | |
|---|---|---|
| Cost of goods sold | $9,500 | |
| Inventory | | $9,500 |

**To adjust the year-end inventory account to reflect goods actually on hand.**

Although this text is not primarily directed toward the record-keeping procedures of enterprises, the two alternative methods of accounting for inventories are explained here because they *may* have an impact on the reported value of inventories at year end. The circumstances in which a difference may occur will be identified in the following discussion of the flows of costs.

### Flows of Costs

The critical issue of inventory accounting, that of flows of costs, arises because the acquisition or production costs of goods do not remain constant. As a consequence, it is sometimes necessary to make assumptions as to which goods have been sold and which remain on hand—those with the higher costs or those with the lower. (Recall the example in the first chapter of the text pertaining to the cost of heating oil sold.) In some situations, identification of specific costs with specific goods presents no problem. The goods have sufficiently different characteristics so that they can readily be tagged with specific costs. The costs to retailers of automobiles, appliances, or rare pieces of jewelry, for example, can easily be associated with specific units. Not so, however, with *fungible* (interchangeable) goods such as grains or liquids, purchases of which made at different times are mixed together, or with most small items, such as canned goods or items of clothing for which it is inconvenient to account for each unit independently. Moreover, for reasons to be indicated shortly, accountants sometimes find it desirable to make assumptions regarding the flow of *costs* which are in obvious conflict with available information regarding the flow of *goods*.

---

*Many firms, as they acquire inventory, debit an account entitled "purchases" rather than the inventory account itself. At year end, they transfer the balance in the purchases account to the inventory account by debiting "inventory" and crediting "purchases."

## ( | ) Specific Identification

The specific identification inventory method requires the enterprise to keep track of the cost of each individual item bought and sold. Ordinarily a firm would either code the cost directly on the item itself or otherwise tag each item with a control number and maintain a separate record of costs.

EXHIBIT 8-2

**Purchases and Sales of a Particular Item**

| | Purchases | | | | |
|---|---|---|---|---|---|
| Date | No. of Units | Unit Cost | Total Cost | No. of Units Sold | No. of Units on Hand |
| 1/1 (Bal. on hand) | 300 | $5 | $1,500 | | 300 |
| 3/2 | 100 | 6 | 600 | | 400 |
| 4/20 | | | | 200 | 200 |
| 5/25 | 400 | 8 | 3,200 | | 600 |
| 9/18 | 200 | 7 | 1,400 | | 800 |
| 11/8 | | | | 300 | 500 |
| Total | 1,000 | | $6,700 | 500 | |

Refer, for example, to the data provided in Exhibit 8-2, which indicates quantities of an item purchased and sold on various dates. Also indicated are the opening balance, the prices at which the various acquisitions were made, and the total cost of each acquisition. Assume that of the 200 items that were sold on 4/20, 100 units were taken from the lot that was on hand on 1/1 and 100 were taken from that purchased on 3/2. Of the 300 items sold on 11/8, 100 were taken from the lot on hand on 1/1 and 200 from that purchased on 5/25. The cost of goods sold would be computed as follows:

| | | |
|---|---|---|
| *Sale of 4/20* | | |
| From lot of 1/1 | 100 @ $5 | $ 500 |
| From lot of 3/2 | 100 @ $6 | 600 |
| | 200 | $1,100 |
| *Sale of 11/8* | | |
| From lot of 1/1 | 100 @ $5 | $ 500 |
| From lot of 5/25 | 200 @ $8 | 1,600 |
| | 300 | $2,100 |
| Cost of goods sold | 500 | $3,200 |

291

Total merchandise costs to be accounted for during the year (initial balance plus purchases) are $6,700. If the cost of goods sold is $3,200, then the balance of the total costs must pertain to the goods still on hand at year end —$6,700 minus $3,200 = $3,500. This amount can be verified by the following tabulation of ending inventory:

| | | |
|---|---|---|
| From lot of 1/1 | 100 @ $5 | $ 500 |
| From lot of 5/25 | 200 @ $8 | 1,600 |
| From lot of 9/18 | 200 @ $7 | 1,400 |
| Ending inventory | 500 | $3,500 |

The specific identification method is most appropriate for enterprises, such as automobile and appliance dealers, that sell relatively few items of large unit cost. It becomes burdensome to firms that sell large quantities of low-cost items. The specific identification method is rational in that it assures that the amounts charged as expenses are the actual costs of the specific goods sold. But at the same time, especially if the goods sold are similar to one another, it permits management the opportunity to manipulate income. If, in the above example, management wanted to report a higher income, it could simply have made certain that the units sold were taken from a lot of lower cost (e.g., the goods sold on 11/8 were taken from the $7 lot of 1/18 rather than from the $8 lot of 5/25).

### (2) First In, First Out    FIFO

In most well-managed businesses, an attempt is made to sell goods in the order in which they have been acquired. This practice minimizes losses from spoilage and obsolescence. In the absence of the ability or the willingness to expend the required time and effort to identify the cost of specific units sold, the assumption that goods acquired first are sold first is likely to provide a reasonable approximation of the actual flow of goods. Under the first-in, first-out approach, commonly abbreviated FIFO, the flow of *costs* (that which is of primary concern to the accountant) is presumed to be the same as the usual flow of goods. The FIFO method can readily be demonstrated using the data presented in Exhibit 8-2.

To compute the cost of goods sold, the items sold on 4/20 would be assumed to have come from the lot that was purchased first—that on hand on 1/1. The items sold on 11/8 would be assumed to have come from the balance of the 1/1 lot and the lots of 3/2 and 5/25. Cost of goods sold, therefore, would be $2,900:

*Sale of 4/20*

| | | |
|---|---|---|
| From lot of 1/1 | 200 @ $5 | $1,000 |

*Sale of 11/8*

| | | |
|---|---|---|
| From lot of 1/1 | 100 @ $5 | $   500 |
| From lot of 3/2 | 100 @ $6 | 600 |
| From lot of 5/25 | 100 @ $8 | 800 |
| | 300 | $1,900 |
| Cost of goods sold | 500 | $2,900 |

If 500 units were sold at a cost of $2,900, then still to be accounted for are the remaining 500 units, at a cost of $6,700 minus $2,900–$3,800. These items—the ones still on hand—would be assumed to be those that were purchased most recently:

| | | |
|---|---|---|
| From lot of 5/25 | 300 @ $8 | $2,400 |
| From lot of 9/18 | 200 @ $7 | 1,400 |
| Ending inventory | 500 | $3,800 |

Proponents of the FIFO method point out that not only is the underlying assumption that goods purchased first are sold first in accord with conventional management practice but that the method eliminates the opportunities for income manipulation that are possible if costs are identified with specific units. Regardless of which items are actually sold, for accounting purposes it will be assumed that those purchased first have been sold first. Moreover, FIFO provides a balance sheet value that is comprised of those items purchased last. In most instances the most recent acquisitions are more indicative of current replacement costs than are those purchased earlier. Insofar as current values are of interest to investors and other readers of financial statements, then FIFO provides a more useful balance sheet valuation than do any of the other methods to be discussed. [But as emphasized previously, the balance sheet, in the context of currently accepted accounting principles, should be viewed as a compendium of *residuals* (unexpired costs) as opposed to current market values.]

### (3)   Weighted Average

The weighted average inventory method is based on the assumption that all costs can be aggregated and that the cost to be assigned to any particular unit should be the weighted average of the costs of the units held during the accounting period. The weighted average method assumes no particular flow of goods. The cost of any unit sold is simply the average of those available for sale—an average that is weighted by the number of units acquired at each particular price.

In the discussion of both the specific identification and FIFO methods no distinction was made between the methods as they would be applied by firms that maintain perpetual inventory records and those which update their records only periodically after taking a physical count of goods on hand. It would make no difference in either cost of goods sold or ending inventory whether the firm followed perpetual or periodic procedures. In applying the weighted average method, however, the results would not be the same. The weighted average cost of goods on hand at the end of the year may differ from those calculated at various times throughout the year. Hence the costs assigned to the various quantities sold would also differ.

To apply the weighted average method on a *periodic* basis, the firm would assign a cost to all goods—both those that were sold and those in inventory at year end—that represents the weighted average of the cost of *all* goods available for sale during the period. The cost of the goods on hand at the beginning of the year as well as those purchased during the year would be considered in the calculation of the average. The weighted average, based on the information in Exhibit 8–2, would be calculated as follows:

| | | |
|---|---|---|
| Balance 1/1 | 300 @ $5 | $1,500 |
| Lot of 3/2 | 100 @ $6 | 600 |
| Lot of 5/25 | 400 @ $8 | 3,200 |
| Lot of 9/18 | 200 @ $7 | 1,400 |
| | 1,000 | $6,700 |

The average cost of goods available for sale would be $6,700/1,000 = $6.70.

Inasmuch as 500 units were sold during the period, the cost of goods sold would be 500 times $6.70–$3,350. Since, by coincidence, 500 units remain unsold at year end, the closing inventory would also be 500 times $6.70 –$3,350.

The weighted average method can be set forth as representing the physical flow of goods when all goods available for sale are mixed together with one another—as would be the case with liquids or other fungible goods. When applied on a periodic basis, however, such justification becomes tenuous. If goods are purchased subsequent to the last sale of the year, then the cost of those goods will enter into the average cost of the goods sold during the year, even though such goods could not possibly have been sold during the year. Suppose that in the example presented, the firm on 12/1, well after the last sale of the year, acquired 1,000 units at $20 per unit. The 1,000 units at $20 per unit would be included in the computation of the average cost of the units sold, even though it is obvious that none of them were actually sold. The weighted average method, as applied on a periodic basis, owes its popularity to its convenience; insofar as it may result in the inclusion in the cost of goods sold the costs applicable to merchandise purchased after the final sale of the year has been made, it is decidedly lacking in theoretical support.

If the weighted average method were to be applied on a perpetual basis (see Exhibit 8-3), then a new weighted (or *moving*) average of the cost of goods available for sale would have to be computed after each purchase at a different price. Such average cost would be assigned to both the goods sold and those that remain in inventory. For example, the average cost of goods available for sale, after the purchase of 3/2, would be calculated as follows:

Cost of goods available for sale on 4/20

| | | |
|---|---|---|
| Balance 1/1 | 300 @ $5 | $1,500 |
| Lot of 3/2 | 100 @ $6 | 600 |
| | 400 | $2,100 |

Average cost of goods available for sale would be $2,100/400 = $5.25.

The cost assigned to the 200 units sold on 4/20 would be 200 times $5.25–$1,050. That assigned to the 200 units that remain in inventory after the sale of 4/20 would also be $1,050.

The average cost of goods available for the next sale, that of 11/8, would be based on the average cost of goods on hand immediately following the last sale (i.e., 200 units at $5.25 per unit) plus that of the subsequent acquisitions. Thus:

Cost of goods available for sale on 11/8

| | | |
|---|---|---|
| Balance 4/20 | 200 @ $5.25 | $1,050 |
| Lot of 5/25 | 400 @ $8.00 | 3,200 |
| Lot of 9/18 | 200 @ $7.00 | 1,400 |
| | 800 | $5,650 |

Average cost of goods available for sale would be $5,650/800 = $7.0625.

## EXHIBIT 8-3

**Perpetual Inventory Record**
**Weighted (Moving) Average Method**

| | Purchases | | | Sales | | | Balance | | |
|---|---|---|---|---|---|---|---|---|---|
| Date | Units | Unit Cost | Total Cost | Units | Unit Cost | Total Cost | Units | Unit Cost | Total Cost |
| 1/1 | | | | | | | 300 | $5.00 | $1,500.00 |
| 3/2 | 100 | $6.00 | $ 600 | | | | 400 | 5.25 | 2,100.00 |
| 4/20 | | | | 200 | $5.25 | $1,050.00 | 200 | 5.25 | 1,050.00 |
| 5/25 | 400 | 8.00 | 3,200 | | | | 600 | 7.0833 | 4,250.00 |
| 9/18 | 200 | 7.00 | 1,400 | | | | 800 | 7.0625 | 5,650.00 |
| 11/8 | | | | 300 | 7.0625 | 2,118.75 | 500 | 7.0625 | 3,531.25 |

The cost assigned to the 300 units sold on 11/8 would be 300 times $7.0625—$2,118.75—and that to the 500 units remaining on hand at year end would be 500 times $7.0625—$3,531.25 (or $5,650 minus the $2,118.75 assigned to the goods sold). The total cost of goods sold for the year would be the sum of the costs assigned to each of the two lots sold:

| Total cost of goods sold during the year | |
|---|---|
| Goods sold on 4/20 | $1,050.00 |
| Goods sold on 11/8 | 2,118.75 |
| Total | $3,168.75 |

This compares to $3,350 calculated using the periodic procedures.

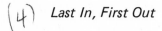

### Last In, First Out

In recent years the last-in, first-out method has been the focus of accounting controversy pertaining to inventory valuation. As its name implies, the last-in, first-out method (LIFO) assigns to goods sold the costs of those goods that have been purchased last. It is based on the assumption that, irrespective of the actual physical flow of goods, the goods sold are those that have been acquired last and the goods that remain on hand are those that have been acquired first. No pretense is made that the flow of costs even approximates the usual flow of goods.

As with the weighted average method, there will be significant differences in the cost of goods sold, as well as in the ending inventory, if a firm follows periodic as opposed to perpetual inventory procedures. If the firm determines ending inventory and cost of goods sold based on a *periodic* (i.e., annual) inventory count, then the cost of goods sold will be the cost of products that were purchased *closest to the year end.* If the firm maintains *perpetual* records, then the cost of the goods sold will be considered to be the cost of units that were purchased closest to each individual sale. Only LIFO assuming periodic procedures will be illustrated here inasmuch as firms seldom use LIFO in association with perpetual systems.*

As indicated in Exhibit 8–2, the firm sold 500 units during the year. The cost to be assigned to those 500 units will be that of the 500 units purchased most recently, i.e., those purchased on 9/18 and 5/25:

| Cost of goods sold | | |
|---|---|---|
| From lot of 9/18 | 200 @ $7 | $1,400 |
| From lot of 5/25 | 300 @ $8 | 2,400 |
| Cost of goods sold | 500 | $3,800 |

*For specific guidance on applying LIFO on a perpetual basis, see problem 3 at the conclusion of this chapter.

Since there was a total of 1,000 items available for sale at a total cost of $6,700, the costs that would be assigned to the ending inventory would be $6,700 minus the $3,800 assigned to the goods sold—$2,900. Ending inventory would be composed of the 500 items, including those that were on hand at the beginning of the year, that were purchased first:

| Ending inventory | | |
|---|---|---|
| From lot of 1/1 | 300 @ $5 | $1,500 |
| From lot of 3/2 | 100 @ $6 | 600 |
| From lot of 5/25 | 100 @ $8 | 800 |
| Ending inventory | 500 | $2,900 |

Exhibit 8–4 summarizes the costs of goods sold and the ending inventories under the FIFO, weighted average, and LIFO methods.

**EXHIBIT 8-4**

### Summary of Cost of Goods Sold and Ending Inventory

| | Cost of Goods Sold | Ending Inventory | Total Costs Accounted For |
|---|---|---|---|
| First in, first out (FIFO)[a] | $2,900.00 | $3,800.00 | $6,700 |
| Weighted average | | | |
| Periodic | 3,350.00 | 3,350.00 | 6,700 |
| Perpetual | 3,168.75 | 3,531.25 | 6,700 |
| Last in, first out (LIFO) | | | |
| Periodic | 3,800.00 | 2,900.00 | 6,700 |

[a]Cost of goods sold and inventory would be the same regardless of whether inventory records were maintained on a periodic or a perpetual basis.

### The Rationale for LIFO

Very few firms sell or use first the goods that they have acquired last. In some situations, a company might indeed store certain commodities in a pile and remove goods as needed from the top of the heap—that portion of total goods which presumably has been added last. Such would be the case in firms maintaining stores of coal or sand. But the use of LIFO is not confined to situations where the physical flow of goods follows a last-in, first-out pattern. It is applied even when there is no question but that the goods acquired first are sold first. The justification for the use of LIFO must be found in reasons other than that it is representative of the physical flow of goods.

The objective of inventory accounting, it was previously indicated, is to *match* the costs of acquiring or producing goods with the revenues that they

*current
costs*

generate. The more specific objective of the LIFO method is to match the *current costs* of acquiring or producing the goods with the current revenues from sales. Under LIFO the cost of goods sold is considered to be that of the goods most recently acquired.

Proponents of LIFO point out that a business must maintain a minimum supply of goods on hand. This basic stock of goods is as essential to the firm's continued operations as are its fixed assets, such as machinery and equipment. Under generally accepted accounting principles, accounting recognition is seldom given to increases in the market value of fixed assets. Why, then, should accounting recognition be accorded increases in the market price of inventories? Suppose, for example, that upon forming a business an entrepreneur determines that he must have 100 units of product on hand. He purchases the 100 units at a price of $1,000 each. In the course of his first year in business, he sells the units for $1,200 each. At the end of the year he replenishes his stock by purchasing another 100 units—this time, however, at a cost of $1,200 each. If inventory and cost of goods sold were to be determined on a FIFO basis, then ending inventory would be valued at $1,200 per unit; the cost of goods sold would be $1,000 per unit. The firm would report a profit of $200 per unit—a total of $20,000. Is the firm really $20,000 better off than it was at the beginning of the period?

Since the entrepreneur deemed it necessary to maintain an inventory of 100 units, he would be unable to withdraw any funds from his business without contracting operations. He would be required to use the entire $20,000 gain to replace the goods that he had sold. The $20,000, according to proponents of LIFO, is not a "true" profit; rather it represents an *inventory* profit. The inventory profit is indicative of nothing more than the difference between the initial cost of acquiring a minimum stock of goods on hand and the current cost of doing so.

Under LIFO, ending inventory would be reported at $1,000 per unit and cost of goods sold at $1,200. Since the items were sold at a price of $1,200 per unit, the firm would report zero profit for the year. Inventory would be valued on the balance sheet at the amount initially invested in the 100 units. The firm would not appear to be $20,000 "better off" when, according to the advocates of LIFO, it is in the identical position at the end of the year that it was at the beginning.

LIFO represents an attempt to reduce distortions in the income statement attributable to inflation. In a period of stable prices, both inventory and cost of goods sold would be identical under FIFO and LIFO. In a period of rising prices, compared with FIFO, LIFO would ordinarily result in a lower reported value for inventory (since goods are being valued at the earliest prices paid) and correspondingly a lower reported income (since the cost of goods sold is being determined on the basis of the most recent purchases—those at the higher prices).

Exhibit 8-5 compares reported cost of goods sold and year-end inventory for a five-year period. It is based on the assumption that at the start of

EXHIBIT 8-5

---

**Five-Year Comparison Between FIFO and LIFO**

### Table 1: FIFO

| | Cost of Goods Purchased | FIFO Cost of Goods Sold | | FIFO Ending Inventory | |
|---|---|---|---|---|---|
| | Per Unit | Per Unit | Total (1,000 units) | Per Unit | Total (1,000 units) |
| 1975 | | | | $100.00 | $100,000 |
| 1976 | $110.00 | $100.00 | $100,000 | 110.00 | 110,000 |
| 1977 | 121.00 | 110.00 | 110,000 | 121.00 | 121,000 |
| 1978 | 133.10 | 121.00 | 121,000 | 133.10 | 133,100 |
| 1979 | 146.41 | 133.10 | 133,100 | 146.41 | 146,410 |
| 1980 | 161.05 | 146.41 | 146,410 | 161.05 | 161,050 |
| Total | | | $610,510 | | |

### Table 2: LIFO

| | Cost of Goods Purchased | LIFO Cost of Goods Sold | | LIFO Ending Inventory | |
|---|---|---|---|---|---|
| | Per Unit | Per Unit | Total (1,000 units) | Per Unit | Total (1,000 units) |
| 1975 | | | | $100.00 | $100,000 |
| 1976 | $110.00 | $110.00 | $110,000 | 100.00 | 100,000 |
| 1977 | 121.00 | 121.00 | 121,000 | 100.00 | 100,000 |
| 1978 | 133.10 | 133.10 | 133,100 | 100.00 | 100,000 |
| 1979 | 146.41 | 146.41 | 146,410 | 100.00 | 100,000 |
| 1980 | 161.05 | 161.05 | 161,050 | 100.00 | 100,000 |
| Total | | | $671,560 | | |

### Table 3: Differences Between FIFO and LIFO
### (Table 1 minus Table 2)

| | Cost of Goods Sold | | Ending Inventory | |
|---|---|---|---|---|
| | Per Unit | Total (1,000 units) | Per Unit | Total (1,000 units) |
| 1976 | $10.00 | $10,000 | $10.00 | $10,000 |
| 1977 | 11.00 | 11,000 | 21.00 | 21,000 |
| 1978 | 12.10 | 12,100 | 33.10 | 33,100 |
| 1979 | 13.31 | 13,310 | 46.41 | 46,410 |
| 1980 | 14.64 | 14,640 | 61.05 | 61,050 |
| Total | $61.05 | $61,050 | | |

1976 a firm had on hand 1,000 units at $100 each. During each of the next five years the firm sold 1,000 units and purchased 1,000 units. The cost of the units purchased increased at a compounded rate of 10 percent per year.

As indicated in Exhibit 8-5, the difference each year in cost of goods sold is equal to the difference between the cost of goods purchased in the previous year and the cost of those purchased in the current year. Under FIFO goods sold in 1976 are assumed to be purchased in 1975; under LIFO goods sold in 1976 are assumed to be purchased in 1976. Proponents of LIFO argue that because FIFO matches current revenues with the cost of goods acquired in a previous period, it consistently understates the "true" cost of goods sold and as a result overstates income.

The difference in ending inventory is considerably more striking. Under FIFO goods on hand at the end of 1980 are assumed to have been purchased in 1980; under LIFO they are assumed to be purchased in 1975 (each year's sales were assumed to have been taken from the current year's purchases; the stock on hand at the start of 1976 is assumed to have never been depleted). The difference in ending inventory at the end of 1980 ($61,050) is the equivalent of the cumulative difference in cost of goods sold for the five-year period ($671,560 versus $610,510).

## LIFO—Some Reservations

The effects of LIFO on both the balance sheet and the income statement are, according to some accountants, unacceptable. LIFO results in a reported inventory that is continually out of date. If the firm never dips into its base stock (for example, in Exhibit 8-5, the inventory was never reduced below 1,000 units), then the reported inventory would be reflective of prices that existed at the time LIFO was first adopted, decades earlier perhaps. The balance sheet, as continually emphasized in this text, is not purported to be representative of current values. Nevertheless, many accountants feel uncomfortable when values that are hopelessly out of date are assigned.

More serious, however, is the impact of LIFO on reported income when the firm is required to dip into its base stock. If the firm is required to sell goods that are valued on the balance sheet at decades-old prices, then the cost of goods sold will be based on the same ancient prices. Refer back to Exhibit 8-5. Suppose that in 1980 the firm was unable to purchase its required 1,000 units. Instead, it sold its goods on hand and thereby reduced its end-of-year inventory to zero. The cost of goods sold would be $100 per unit—the price of the goods on hand when the company first adopted LIFO in 1976. This at a time when the current replacement cost of the goods is $146.41 per unit. If the cost of goods sold is misleadingly low, then reported income would, of course, be correspondingly high. Whatever its advantages when the firm is able to meet current sales out of current purchases, LIFO produces results that are absurd when it becomes necessary to reduce inventory below a level that is historically normal. Many accountants, who are opposed to LIFO, recognize the need to account for rapid increases in the replacement cost of inventories. They believe, however, that there are ways of doing so that eliminate some of the distortions of LIFO. The issue of direct price level adjustments of all accounts, not just inventories, will be addressed in Chapter 16.

## LIFO—Its Recent Popularity

In the mid-1970s several hundred major U.S. firms shifted from either a FIFO or a moving average to a LIFO inventory valuation method. Unquestionably the shifts were motivated primarily by the opportunities to reduce the federal income tax burden.

Since 1938, the Internal Revenue Code has recognized the acceptability of LIFO. In periods of rapid inflation, such as those experienced in many industrial nations in the 1970s, LIFO, by basing the cost of goods sold on the most recent purchases, reduces taxable income. The difference in taxable income between that determined on a FIFO or average cost as opposed to a LIFO basis may not be trivial. Du Pont, for example, estimated that its 1974 shift from average cost to LIFO reduced income by over $250 million and reduced its earnings per share by $3.02 (from $11.22 to $8.20). Other major corporations effected similar reductions in earnings and hence in taxes. Estimates of the overall loss in tax revenues to the federal government range up to $18 billion per year.

As a rule, when there are alternative accounting methods that are generally accepted, businesses are not required to use the same method in reporting to the Internal Revenue Service as they do in reporting to their stockholders. With respect to the method of determining inventories, however, the IRS makes an exception. If a company adheres to one method in reporting to the general public, it *must* use the same method in reporting to the IRS. As a consequence of this ruling, firms that wish to take advantage of the tax-savings opportunities provided by LIFO are required to switch to LIFO for general reporting purposes.

Quite apart from the tax advantages of LIFO, some financial analysts consider earnings of LIFO-based companies to be of higher "quality" than those of FIFO or average cost firms. What they mean is that were it not for the "inflated" value of their inventories, the earnings of the non-LIFO firms may have been considerably lower and growth trends somewhat more flat.

Not all firms, or even a majority, have shifted to LIFO. There are several reasons for their reluctance. LIFO will not result in a significant improvement of the earnings of all firms. To the extent that a firm maintains a relatively small stock of goods on hand relative to sales (that is, inventory *turnover* is rapid), the difference between LIFO and FIFO or average cost earnings is likely to be small. In the grocery industry, for example, goods are sold within days of their arrival in a store. As a consequence, inventory, as a percentage of total cost of goods sold, is sufficiently small so that a change in method of valuing inventory will have only a minor impact on overall income. Moreover, although the United States has experienced an increase in the general level of prices, the prices of some items have remained stable. For firms which deal in such items, a change would be of little significance. Perhaps most importantly, however, many firms are concerned about the consequences of having to reduce their stock below normal levels. Such a reduction might result in a major increase in earnings and a corresponding increase in taxes. The tax "savings" of several previous years might be offset entirely by an inordinately large tax expense in a single year. Since a firm would then have to replace the goods sold at the prices prevailing at the time, it may not have sufficient cash on hand both to replenish its inventory and to meet its tax obligations.

## Retail Inventory Method

Many large department stores find it inconvenient to maintain records of the cost of all merchandise on hand. Instead, as each unit is received it is tagged with the price at which it will be sold. Periodically, store clerks take a physical count of goods on hand. They record the quantity of each item on hand as well as its selling price. As a consequence, the physical count and subsequent summary results in a determination of the inventory on hand valued at expected retail prices. Since ending inventory is conventionally reported and the cost of goods sold is determined on the basis of acquisition cost, not expected selling prices, it is necessary to *estimate* the costs of the goods which are on hand and those which have been sold.

Insofar as a store has kept accurate records of all purchases, it can use the relationship between purchase prices and selling prices as its means of estimation. Assume that the firm's records provide information as to the merchandise on hand at the beginning of the period, overall quantities purchased and the amounts at which they will be sold, ending inventory at retail prices, and sales for the year (which, of course, are based on retail prices). Ending inventory, at cost, can be estimated as follows:

**Estimate of Ending Inventory (at cost)**

|  | Cost | Retail Price | Cost as a Percentage of Retail Price |
|---|---|---|---|
| Merchandise on hand 1/1 | $100,000 | $150,000 | |
| Purchases during year | 500,000 | 800,000 | |
| Goods available for sale | $600,000 | $950,000 | 63.15% |
| Sales during year | | 700,000 | |
| Merchandise on hand 12/31 | | $250,000 | |

If merchandise on hand at year end is $250,000 and the cost of the goods is approximately 63.15 percent of their retail price, then ending inventory at cost can readily be determined:

| | |
|---|---:|
| Merchandise on hand, 12/31 at retail prices | $250,000 |
| Cost as a percentage of retail price | X .6315 |
| Merchandise on hand, 12/31 at cost | $157,875 |

If $600,000 of goods (at cost) were available for sale during the year, of which $157,875 are still on hand, then the cost of goods sold for the period must be

| | |
|---|---:|
| Goods available for sale | $600,000 |
| Merchandise on hand, 12/31 (at cost) | 157,875 |
| Cost of goods sold | $442,125 |

The retail inventory method provides an approximation of the weighted average method. Goods on hand at the beginning of the period and those purchased during the period are, for cost purposes, mixed together in a common pool. In determining which goods have been sold and which remain on hand at year end, no distinction is made between goods acquired first and those acquired last. Because the retail method assumes that the ratio between cost and selling price of all goods in the pool is identical, unusually large markups and markdowns on a few selected items may not be properly reflected. As with many accounting procedures based on averages, it sacrifices a measure of accuracy for convenience.

## Lower of Cost or Market Rule

Regardless of which of the previously described inventory methods a firm adopts, the application of generally accepted accounting principles requires a departure from cost whenever the utility of the goods on hand has diminished since the date of acquisition.* Loss of utility might be the result of physical damage or deterioration, obsolescence, or a general decline in the level of prices. Loss of utility should be given accounting recognition by stating the inventories at *cost or market, whichever is lower*. As used in the expression cost or market, *market* refers to the amount that would have to be paid to *replace* the goods by purchase or reproduction. This lower of cost or market rule is grounded in the concept of *conservatism,* which holds that firms should give recognition to losses (but not to gains) as soon as they are reasonably foreseeable.

*With the exception that under federal income tax regulations application of the lower of cost or market rule is severely restricted if a firm employs the LIFO inventory method.

Suppose that a jewelry merchant purchases a lot of 100 digital watches for $100 each, with the intention of selling them at a price of $125. Prior to sale, however, as a result of manufacturing efficiencies, the wholesale price of the watches drops to $80 and the corresponding retail price to $105. Application of the lower of cost or market rule would require that the stated value of the watches on hand be reduced from original cost of $100 to the current market (replacement) price of $80. The following journal entry would be appropriate to record the decline in price:

| | | |
|---|---|---|
| Loss on inventory (expense) | $2,000 | |
| Inventory (asset) | | $2,000 |

**To record the loss attributable to the decline in the replacement cost of 100 digital watches from $100 to $80.**

The lower of cost or market rule may be applied to inventories on an individual (item-by-item) or a group basis. If applied on an individual basis, then the cost of each item in stock is compared with its current replacement cost. If the replacement cost of an item is lower than its original cost, then the item is written down to its replacement cost. If applied on a group basis, then the original cost of the inventory pool (which may be either the entire inventory or a collection of similar items) is compared with its market value, and a reduction in book value is required only if total market value is less than total initial cost. The group basis is likely to result in a considerably higher inventory valuation than the individual basis since it permits the increases in the market prices of some items to offset the decreases in others. The two bases were illustrated in Chapter 6 as part of a discussion regarding the values to be assigned to portfolios of marketable securities.

The lower of cost or market rule has been adopted by the rule-making bodies of the profession, but it has been the subject of widespread attack by accounting theoreticians. Critics assert that the rule sacrifices consistency for conservatism. The rule introduces a measure of inconsistency into financial reports, since it gives recognition to decreases in market values but not to increases. Moreover, they contend that the rule requires the recognition of losses where none have really occurred. In the previous example, the merchant purchased watches for $100 and will sell them for $105. Although he will not earn the full $25 profit for which he had hoped, he will nevertheless realize a gain (excluding all other operating costs) of $5 per unit. If the lower of cost or market rule is adhered to, his accounts will reflect a loss of $20 per unit in the period of the write-down and a gain of $25 in the period of sale.* Critics contend

---

*Authoritative pronouncements provide that inventory should never be reduced to a level that will lead to recognition of an unusually high profit in a subsequent period. Thus, if in the example the firm estimated that it would be able to sell the watches at retail for $115 rather than $105, it should reduce inventory to no less than $90. If it reduced inventory below $90, then when it sells a watch, its profit in the period of sale would be greater than its "normal" profit of $25 per unit.

that, as a consequence, earnings of both periods are distorted. In fact, they assert, the merchant earned a profit of $5 at the time of sale, not a loss of $20 in one period and a gain of $25 in the next. Although the lower of cost or market rule may be conservative with respect to both balance sheet valuations and the income reported in the period of write-down, it is most definitely not conservative with respect to the income of the period of sale.

### Proposed Alternative: Use of Current Values

Many accounting theoreticians have proposed that inventories be stated at their *current* values. In this way, they suggest, many of the deficiencies of each of the alternative assumptions regarding flow of costs, as well as the inconsistencies of the lower of cost or market rule, can be overcome. Their suggestions are worth attention, not so much because they are likely to be accepted in the foreseeable future—although there is unquestionably a trend in the direction of current value accounting—but rather because they provide an insight into the components of gains or losses attributable to the sale of goods included in inventory.

Assume that on September 1, 1980, a merchant purchases 30 cans of tennis balls at $2.00 per can. In the remainder of 1980 he sells 20 cans at $3.00 per can. On December 31, 1980, the wholesale price of tennis balls is increased to $2.50 per can. As a consequence, the merchant raises the retail price to $3.50 per can.

In 1981 he sells the 10 cans that remain from 1980. Then according to the rules of conventional practice, he will record a gain of $1.50 per can (Sales price of $3.50 minus cost of $2.00.) The $1.50 is composed of two types of gains—a *holding* gain of $.50 and a *trading* gain of $1.00.

The trading gain arises out of the normal business activities of the firm. It represents a return to the merchant for providing the usual services of a retailer—providing customers with the desired quantity of goods at a convenient time and place. The holding gain, on the other hand, can be attributed to the increase in price between the times the merchant purchased and sold the goods. The magnitude of the holding gain depends on the quantity of goods held in inventory and the size of the price increase. Most merchants are required to maintain a stock of goods adequate to service the needs of their customers— that is, to make certain that they have a sufficient number of goods on hand to minimize the risk of outages and to provide customers with an ample choice of styles, sizes, and colors. Some merchants, however, intentionally maintain an inventory greater than that necessary to meet their operating needs. Hoping to take advantage of increases in price, they employ inventory as a means of speculation. Speculative holding gains (and of course losses) are especially common in those industries which deal in commodities—e.g., grains, cocoa, and metals—that are subject to frequent and substantial fluctuations in prices.

Were inventories to be stated at their current values, it would be relatively easy to distinguish—and report separately—the holding gains from the trading gains. And more significantly, the holding gains could be identified with the accounting period in which the increase in prices actually took place, rather than delayed until the period of sale. In the example at hand, the holding gain actually occurred in 1980, the year in which the price increase was announced.

The following journal entry would be appropriate to recognize the holding gain of $.50 per can of tennis balls that took place during the year 1980:

| | | |
|---|---|---|
| Inventory | $5.00 | |
|     Holding gains on inventory (revenue) | | $5.00 |

**To record holding gain on 10 cans of tennis balls that remained on hand at year-end.**

When the 10 cans were sold in the following year, the cost of goods sold would be charged, and inventories credited, for their adjusted carrying value of $2.50 per can:

| | | |
|---|---|---|
| Cost of goods sold | $25.00 | |
|     Inventory | | $25.00 |

**To record the cost of goods sold.**

Comparative income statements which give recognition to the sale in 1980 of 20 cans of tennis balls at $3.00 per can and the sale in 1981 of 10 cans at $3.50 per can would appear as follows:

| | *1980* | *1981* |
|---|---|---|
| Sales | $60.00 | $35.00 |
| Holding gains | 5.00 | — |
|     Total revenues | $65.00 | $35.00 |
| Cost of goods sold: | | |
|     20 cans @ $2.00 | 40.00 | |
|     10 cans @ $2.50 | | 25.00 |
|     Income | $25.00 | $10.00 |

Regardless of whether inventory was adjusted to reflect the holding gains or whether conventional procedures were followed, the total gain on the sale of the 30 cans of tennis balls would be $35. Conventional income statements, in which the holding gains were not recognized, would appear as follows:

|  | 1980 | 1981 |
|---|---|---|
| Sales | $60.00 | $35.00 |
| Cost of goods sold | | |
| 20 cans @ $2.00 | 40.00 | |
| 10 cans @ $2.00 | | 20.00 |
| Income | $20.00 | $15.00 |

The effect of increasing the carrying value of the 10 cans in inventory and of concurrently recognizing a holding gain of $.50 per can would be to shift $5 of income from 1981, the year in which the cans were sold, to 1980, the year in which the price increase took place.

In the discussion to this point *current value* has been used to mean replacement cost. As indicated in an earlier chapter, however, current value can be viewed as an *output* value as well as an *input* value, such as replacement cost. Thus, some theoreticians suggest that inventories be stated at a current *output* value, such as the amount for which they could currently be sold or at net realizable value (the amount for which they are *likely* to be sold in the future, less any costs of bringing the goods to a salable condition, such as costs of completion).

Regardless of which particular current value is employed, the suggestion that inventories be valued at some current value should not be viewed as particularly radical. Recall the discussion in Chapter 5 pertaining to recognition of revenue. It was pointed out then that when, in unusual circumstances, revenue is recognized in the course of production (as in long-term construction contracts) or upon completion of production (as in the mining of precious metals), inventory is in effect stated at a curent value. Moreover, the Securities and Exchange Commission requires companies to provide in their annual reports submitted to the commission supplementary data on the replacement value of inventories. The commission does not prescribe that complete replacement cost statements be prepared, but it does insist that firms reveal what the cost of goods sold would have been had it been calculated on the basis of current, as opposed to historical, values.

## Summary

In this chapter we have dealt primarily with accounting issues pertaining to inventory within the traditional historical cost framework. Because of the overriding importance of inventories to most manufacturing and retail companies, selection of accounting alternatives may have a critical impact on both reported assets and earnings.

The primary objective of conventional accounting is to match the costs of acquiring or producing goods with the revenues that they generate. To realize such objective it is necessary to make assumptions as to the flow of costs—whether the cost of goods acquired first, or last, for example, should be associated with the revenues of a particular period. Strong arguments can be advanced in favor of or against each of the assumptions, and choice of assumption may have a significant effect on reported cost of goods sold as well as ending inventories.

Regardless of any assumption, however, inventories should be restated at the lower of cost or market to reflect declines in their replacement cost. Although some accountants have suggested that accounting recognition be given to increases in market prices as well as to decreases, current practice favors conservatism over consistency, and gains from holding inventories are considered to be realized only at the time they are sold.

*exercise for review and self-study*

The inventory records of the Simon Corp. indicate the following with respect to a particular item:

| Date | No. of Units (Purchases) | Unit Cost (Purchases) | Total Cost (Purchases) | No. of Units Sold | No. of Units on Hand |
|---|---|---|---|---|---|
| 1/01/80[a] | 400 | $20 | $8,000 | | 400 |
| 2/24/80 | 200 | 21 | 4,200 | | 600 |
| 6/16/80 | | | | 300 | 300 |
| 9/23/80 | 100 | 22 | 2,200 | | 400 |
| 11/15/80 | | | | 300 | 100 |
| 12/28/80 | 100 | 23 | 2,300 | | 200 |

[a]Beginning balance.

a. Determine the total number of units as well as the total costs to be accounted for during the year.

b. The firm maintains its records on a *periodic* basis. Determine year-end inventory and cost of goods sold assuming each of the following cost flows:
   (1) first in, first out.
   (2) weighted average.
   (3) last in, first out.

c. Suppose that the firm values its inventory on the FIFO basis. On December 31, the price per unit of the item falls to $21 and the anticipated selling price falls by $2. At what amount, in accord with the lower of cost or market rule, should year-end inventory be stated? What would be the effect of the write-down on earnings of 1980? What would be the effect on earnings of 1981 when the goods are sold?

d. Assume alternatively that the firm were to report inventory at current replacement cost (a practice *not* in accord with "generally accepted accounting principles") and that the price at year end remained at $23 per unit. At what amount should year-end inventory be stated? How much "holding gain" should be recognized? What would be the effect on cost of goods sold in 1981 of recognizing the holding gain in 1980, assuming that the goods are sold in 1981?

## *Questions*

**review and discussion**

1. "Since it is the objective of asset accounting to assign fair values to goods owned by a firm, LIFO is an inappropriate means of accounting for inventories. LIFO may result in values that are far out of date." Do you agree? Comment.

2. "Accountants make assumptions regarding the flows of goods only because it is costly and inconvenient to keep records of specific items actually sold. The specific identification method is theoretically superior to any of the other methods and eliminates the possibilities of income manipulation associated with those methods." Do you agree? Comment.

3. Very few businesses sell or use first the goods that have been received most recently. How, then, can the widespread use of LIFO be explained? Provide an example of a situation in which a company does in fact sell or use first the goods acquired last.

4. National Steel Corp. and Great Supermarkets, Inc. each has annual sales of approximately $10 million and earnings of $300,000. National Steel maintains an inventory equal in value to about 5 percent of cost of goods sold, and Great Supermarkets, about .5 percent. In other words, the inventory of National Steel *turns over* approximately 20 times per year and that of Great Supermarkets about 200 times a year. For which of the two firms would a shift from FIFO to LIFO have the greater impact on earnings? Explain.

5. It is sometimes asserted that LIFO povides a more meaningful income statement, albeit not necessarily a more meaningful balance sheet. Why does LIFO provide a more meaningful income statement? Does it always? Provide an example of a situation in which it may seriously distort income.

6. What is meant by the term market, as it is used in the expression "cost or market, whichever is lower." The lower of cost or market rule is often cited as an example of the possible conflict between conservatism and consistency. Why? Over a period of several years, is the lower of cost or market rule likely to decrease the overall income of a firm? Explain.

7. Suppose that inventories were to be stated on the balance sheet at current replacement values (which may exceed costs). What would be the impact on earnings of the year in which an increase in replacement cost was first recognized? What would be the impact on earnings of the year in which the goods were sold?

8. Conventional accounting practices require that inventories be stated at historical cost. How could a financial analyst obtain information on the replacement value of a firm's inventory?

9. What is the advantage of using the *retail* method of accounting for inventory? What is one disadvantage?

10. A firm acquires a substantial quantity of inventory on December 31, subsequent to the last sale of the year. The price paid is considerably greater than that of previous purchases. Why might use of the weighted average method, applied on a periodic basis, produce a cost of goods sold that many accountants would claim is overstated?

## Problems

1. *Choice of bookkeeping procedure may affect earnings.*

   As of January 1, 1980, a firm had 700 units of product on hand. The stated value was $1,400. During the year the firm had two sales—the first on January 17 of 600 units, and the second on November 11 of 700 units. On March 8 the firm received a shipment of 1,600 units at a cost of $4,800. Assume that the purchases were for cash.

   Prepare those journal entries which would affect inventory assuming that the firm uses
   a. Periodic inventory procedures:
      (1) FIFO.
      (2) weighted average.
   b. Perpetual inventory procedures:
      (1) FIFO.
      (2) weighted average.
   c. Compare the total cost of goods sold and the ending inventory under each of the alternatives.

2. *Cost of inventory includes all charges necessary to bring the goods to a salable condition.*

   The ABC Co. ordered 1,000 units of product at $6 per unit. It received an invoice from its supplier for $5,343 determined as follows:

   | 1000 units @ $6 | $6,000 | |
   | Less: Trade discount, 20% | 1,200 | $4,800 |
   | Plus: Taxes and import duty | | 543 |
   | Amount to be paid | | $5,343 |

   In addition, the company received a separate invoice from a freight company for shipping charges of $357.

   Prepare a journal entry to record the *costs* applicable to a sale of 200 units.

**3.** *This exercise serves to illustrate the three fundamental inventory valuation methods, each applied on both periodic and perpetual bases.*

During 1980 the Whitman Co. engaged in the following purchases and sales of an item:

|  | Purchases | | Sales |
| --- | --- | --- | --- |
|  | No. Units | Cost Per Unit | No. Units |
| Jan. 1 (Beginning bal.) | 400 | $5.00 | |
| Feb. 11 | | | 150 |
| May 6 | 200 | 5.10 | |
| Sept. 8 | | | 220 |
| Sept. 30 | 300 | 5.20 | |
| Oct. 17 | | | 310 |
| Nov. 26 | 100 | 5.25 | |
| Dec. 16 | | | 50 |
| | 1,000 | | 730 |

Determine December 31 inventory and cost of goods sold for 1980 assuming first that the company maintains inventory on a periodic basis and then on a perpetual basis. Assume also each of the following flows of costs: FIFO; weighted average; LIFO.

LIFO, applied on a perpetual basis, is not specifically illustrated in the text. The procedures are not difficult, however. Compute the cost of goods sold upon each sale. The goods sold would be assumed to be those which were acquired most recently up to the date of sale. For example, the 220 units sold on September 8 would be considered to be the 200 units acquired on May 6 plus 20 from the balance on hand as of January 1.

**4.** *The specific identification method, even if clerically feasible, may not be theoretically preferable.*

As of December 1, 1980, Big Sam Appliance Co. has 300 refrigerators in stock. All are identical; all are priced to sell at $900. Each is tagged with a card indicating in code its cost to Big Sam. Of the 300 refrigerators on hand, 100 were acquired on June 15, at a cost of $800 each, 100 on November 1 at a cost of $650, and 100 on December 1, at a cost of $700 per unit. Big Sam estimates that, in the month of December, 200 refrigerators will be sold.

a. Determine cost of goods sold on a FIFO basis, assuming that 200 refrigerators were in fact sold.

b. Suppose that Big Sam uses the specific identification method and wishes to maximize reported earnings for the year. How can he accomplish his objective by discrete selection of the units to be sold?

c. Suppose that Big Sam uses the specific identification method and, to minimize taxes, wishes to minimize reported earnings. How can he accomplish his objective?

5. *LIFO can be applied on a perpetual as well as a periodic basis.*

   If LIFO is to be applied on a perpetual basis, then it is necessary to determine the cost of goods sold immediately upon their sale rather than at the end of the accounting period.

   On January 5, 1980 a firm purchased 100 units of a product at $60 per unit. On June 11, it sold 50 units. On December 15, it purchased 60 units at $70 per unit.
   a. Determine cost of goods sold and ending inventory, applying LIFO on a periodic basis. That is, in computing the cost of goods sold on June 11, take into account all purchases and sales made through December 31.
   b. Determine cost of goods sold and ending inventory, applying LIFO on a perpetual basis. Calculate the cost of goods sold on June 11 immediately after they have been sold, without giving consideration to purchases made after that date.
   c. Comment on why LIFO applied on a periodic basis may result in cost of goods sold and ending inventory different from those that result when LIFO is applied on a perpetual basis.

6. *Is the impact of LIFO upon earnings the same in periods of falling prices as in periods of rising prices?*

   The Simons Co. began operations on January 1, 1976. In 1976 the company produced 85,000 units at a cost of $12 per unit and sold 80,000 units. In each of the next three years the company produced 80,000 units and sold 80,000 units. Costs of production were $14, $16, and $18, respectively, in each of the years.
   a. Compute both cost of goods sold and year-end inventory for each of the four years using first FIFO and then LIFO.
   b. Do the same as in part a, assuming this time that production costs were $12, $10, $8, and $6 in each of the four years. (Omit consideration of the lower of cost or market rule.)
   c. What generalizations can be made regarding the impact of LIFO as compared to FIFO on cost of goods sold and inventories in periods of rising prices versus periods of falling prices?

7. *In the "long run," choice among accounting principles seldom makes a difference.*

   The Pittsfield Co. existed in business for a period of four years. During that period, purchases and sales were as follows:

|  | Purchases | | Sales | |
|---|---|---|---|---|
|  | *Units* | *Unit Cost* | *Units* | *Sales Price* |
| 1976 | 12,000 | $10 | 8,000 | $15 |
| 1977 | 14,000 | 11 | 15,000 | 16 |
| 1978 | 9,000 | 12 | 9,000 | 17 |
| 1979 | 10,000 | 11 | 13,000 | 17 |

a. Determine income for each of the four years assuming first that the company uses FIFO and then that it uses LIFO.

b. Determine total income for the four-year period. Over the life of the business, does it matter which method of inventory is used?

8. *Earnings based on LIFO are said to be of higher quality than those based on FIFO.*

In December 1980, L. Minton established a door-to-door sales company. He invested $10,000 and purchased 2,000 units of inventory at $5 per unit— the minimum number of units required to sustain his business. He made his purchase at a propitious time, for the next day, before he had a chance to make a single sale, the price per unit of his inventory increased to $6.

During 1981 Minton purchased an additional 10,000 units at $6 per unit and sold 10,000 units at $7 per unit. He withdrew from the business for his personal use *all* cash except that necessary to assure that his inventory was maintained at its minimum level of 2,000 units.

a. Prepare journal entries to reflect the above transactions. Assume first that Minton maintained his inventories on a FIFO basis; then assume that he maintained his inventories on a LIFO basis, and indicate any entries that would be different. Prepare income statements and balance sheets comparing results under the two methods.

b. How much cash was Minton able to withdraw during 1981? Compare his cash withdrawals with income as determined by both the FIFO and the LIFO methods. What do you suppose that some financial observers mean when they say that in periods of inflation LIFO results in earnings that are of "higher quality?"

9. *An invasion of the LIFO base may seriously distort earnings.*

As of January 1, 1976, the Byron Co. had 50,000 units of product on hand. Each unit had cost $.80 to produce. During each of the next three years the company produced 100,000 units and sold the same number. In the fourth year, as the result of a strike, the company was able to produce only 50,000 units, though it was able to maintain sales at 100,000. In the fifth year the company, in order to replenish its inventory, produced 150,000 units and continued to sell 100,000 units. Unit production costs and sales prices are indicated in the table following. The company maintains its inventory on a periodic LIFO basis.

| | Units Produced | | Units Sold | |
|---|---|---|---|---|
| | No. Units | Unit Cost | No. Units | Unit Price |
| 1976 | 100,000 | $1.00 | 100,000 | $1.40 |
| 1977 | 100,000 | 1.20 | 100,000 | 1.60 |
| 1978 | 100,000 | 1.40 | 100,000 | 1.80 |
| 1979 | 50,000 | 1.60 | 100,000 | 2.00 |
| 1980 | 150,000 | 1.80 | 100,000 | 2.20 |

a. Determine the net income *after taxes* for each of the five years. Assume a tax rate of 40 percent of income.

b. Determine the *cash flow* for each of the five years. That is, determine total cash receipts and cash disbursements. Assume that all sales were for cash and that all production costs and taxes were paid in cash.

c. In a financial analyst's view, of what significance is the income of the firm for 1979?

d. Compare the total cash flow for 1979 and 1980 with that of the prior two-year period. Why is it lower?

10. *The retail method of accounting for inventories, which is widely used by department stores and other retail establishments, relates average costs to selling prices.*

On August 31, 1980, Silver's Department Store had on hand merchandise that cost $770,000 and was priced to sell at $1 million. During the fiscal year 1981, Silver's made purchases of $4.75 million which it marked up to sell at $6 million retail. Sales for 1981 (at retail) were $6.6 million. A physical count at August 31, 1981, indicated goods on hand tagged to sell at $400,000.

Determine cost of goods sold for 1981 and inventory (at cost) at August 31, 1981, using the *retail* inventory method.

11. *The retail inventory method can be used to estimate the value of goods on hand as of a particular date even if the firm maintains its records on a periodic basis.*

A fire on June 16, 1980, destroyed all merchandise of the Pearl Discount Store. Salvaged records reveal that as of July 31, 1979, the store had merchandise on hand that had cost $1.5 million and that was marked to sell at $1.76 million. In the period since that date the store had purchased merchandise that cost $7.5 million and was intended to be sold for $9,375,000. Actual sales for the period were $9.2 million.

For how much should the store submit a claim to its insurance company, assuming that the insurance company will reimburse the company for the cost of merchandise destroyed in the fire?

12. *The lower of cost or market rule does not reduce the total profits to be realized on the sale of inventories; it only transfers them from one year to the next.*

The Roscoe Corp. started in business on January 1, 1980. Its purchases and sales, as well as the replacement cost of goods on hand at year end for its first three years of operations, are indicated in the table following. The company stated its inventory on a FIFO basis and applied the lower of cost or market rule.

|  | Purchases | | Sales | | Unit Replacement Cost at Year |
|---|---|---|---|---|---|
|  | Units | Unit Cost | Units | Unit Price | End |
| 1980 | 12,000 | $20 | 10,000 | $30 | $15 |
| 1981 | 12,000 | 15 | 10,000 | 25 | 10 |
| 1982 | 6,000 | 10 | 10,000 | 20 | 5 |

a. Determine income for each of the three years.

b. Comment on the "conservative" nature of the lower of cost or market rule as it affects earnings.

13. *The lower of cost or market rule provides that declines in the value of inventory be given prompt recognition.*

Indicated in the table following is the December 31, 1980, inventory of the Albany Company, along with current replacement costs and expected selling prices:

| Items | Units | Unit Cost | Replacement Cost | Expected Selling Price |
|-------|-------|-----------|------------------|------------------------|
| A | 6,000 | $10 | $12 | $18 |
| B | 4,000 | 8 | 6 | 9 |
| C | 12,000 | 6 | 4 | 6 |
| D | 2,000 | 4 | 2 | 6 |

It is the policy of the company to sell at 50 percent above cost, but sometimes market conditions force (or enable) the company to sell at a lower (or higher) price.

Apply the lower of cost or market rule to determine the value at which December 31, 1980, inventory should be stated. Apply the rule first on an item-by-item basis and then on a group basis. (In assigning a value to item D, be sure to refer to the footnote in the text that indicates that inventories should never be reduced to a level that will lead to recognition of an unusually high profit in a subsequent period.)

14. *Problems 14 and 15 illustrate the advantages—and disadvantages—of a shift from FIFO to LIFO.*

The 1976 annual report of E. I. du Pont de Nemours & Company contained the following footnote (figures are stated in millions):

If inventory values were shown at estimated replacement or current cost rather than at LIFO values, inventories would have been $489.9 and $410.6 higher than reported at December 31, 1976 and December 31, 1975, respectively.

a. In periods of rising prices, which valuation method, FIFO or LIFO, results in inventory values which most closely approximate current market prices?

b. Assume that replacement costs are approximately equal to inventory as computed on a FIFO basis. Ignoring the impact of income taxes, by how much more, or less, as of December 31, 1975 and 1976, would retained earnings have been had the company remained on FIFO?

c. Considering the effect of the change in valuation method on retained earnings of 1975 and 1976, by how much more or less would earnings before taxes have been in 1976 if no change had taken place?

d. Based on your response to part c and assuming a tax rate of 40 percent, by how much more or less would the tax obligation of the firm have been in 1976?

e. Comment on why, in a period of rising prices, a firm would deliberately select a method of accounting that would adversely affect reported earnings.

15. The same annual report of E. I. du Pont de Nemours & Company contained the following footnote pertaining to inventories (figures are stated in millions):

> During 1975, inventory quantities were reduced from the abnormally high year-end 1974 level. This reduction resulted in a liquidation of LIFO inventory quantities carried at lower costs prevailing in prior years as compared with 1975 costs, the effect of which increased 1975 net income by approximately $38.9 or $.81 per share.

a. Explain in your own words why a liquidation of inventory served to increase net income.

b. If the liquidation served to increase the reported after-tax income by $38.9 million, by how much greater or less was the value of the goods sold based on current (1975) costs than on the historical costs at which they were actually carried on the books. Assume a tax rate of 40 percent.

c. It is clear that in 1975 the use of LIFO seriously distorted the firm's reported income. In fact, management felt compelled to include in its financial statements the previously cited footnote to warn readers of the aberrant earnings. Why did not the company shift to FIFO for 1975 and then shift back to LIFO in subsequent years when earnings would not be distorted by inventory liquidations?

16. *A CPA firm points out that there are no generally accepted standards of "preferability."*

In 1977, the Susquehanna Corporation, a firm whose securities are traded on the American Stock Exchange, changed from the FIFO to the LIFO method of accounting for inventories. The change, according to a footnote to the financial statements, was made "to better match the most recent inventory acquisition costs against current sales, thereby minimizing the effects of inflation on earnings."

In a letter to the firm's board of directors, the company's auditors, Price Waterhouse & Co. wrote the following:

> Note 2 to the consolidated financial statements of The Susquehanna Corporation, included in the Company's Annual Report to its stockholders for the year ended December 31, 1977 and incorporated by reference in the Company's Annual Report on Form 10-K for the year then ended, describes a change from the first-in, first-out method of accounting for inventories to the last-in, first-out method. We concurred with this change in our report dated February 10, 1978 on the consolidated financial statements referred to above. *It should be understood*

*that preferability of one acceptable method of inventory accounting over another has not been addressed in any authoritative accounting literature and in arriving at our opinion expressed below, we have relied on management's business planning and judgment.* Based upon our discussions with management and the stated reasons for the change, we believe that such change represents, in your circumstances, adoption of a preferable accounting principle in conformity with Accounting Principles Board Opinion No. 20.

a. What makes one accounting method preferable to another?

b. If a method of accounting, such as LIFO, is considered preferable to another method, such as FIFO, by both a company and its auditors, how can the use of the alternative method by a company in the same industry, whose financial statements might be examined by the same firm of auditors, be justified?

17) *By shifting to FIFO from LIFO, a company may increase reported earnings but incur a substantial economic cost.*

In November 1970, the president of an automobile manufacturer became concerned that actual earnings for 1970 would fall short of predicted earnings. In discussions with the corporate controller, he suggested that one way to boost earnings would be to shift from the last-in, first-out method of reporting inventories, which the company was presently using, to the first-in, first-out method.

Upon investigation, the controller found that anticipated inventories at year end would be approximately $100 million if stated on a LIFO basis. If valued on the basis of the cost of the most recent purchases (FIFO), they would be approximately $180 million.

a. What would be the effect on cost of goods sold if inventories for the year 1970 were stated on a FIFO rather than a LIFO basis? Explain.

b. What would be the impact on income tax obligations? Assume a combined federal and state tax rate of 50 percent. (In practice the Internal Revenue Service is likely to allow the company to pay the additional taxes attributable to the shift over a 20-year period.)

c. Comment on any advantages and disadvantages to the company of making the shift.

18. *The LIFO method affords an opportunity for income manipulation.*

As of January 1, 1980, the Elliot Corp. had 10,000 units of product on hand. Each had a carrying value of $20. In November of that year the president estimated that sales for the year would total 80,000 units. To date, the company had produced 70,000 units, at a cost of $25 per unit. If additional units were to be produced in the remainder of the year, they would cost $26 per unit. The company determines inventory on a periodic LIFO basis.

Determine cost of goods sold if

(1) The president ordered that no additional units be produced during the year.

(2) The president ordered that 10,000 additional units be produced.

(3) The president ordered that 40,000 additional units be produced.

19. *Inventory methods based on averages are convenient, but they allow for a measure of distortion.*

Detroit Retailers, Inc. sells only three products. Information about purchases and sales during 1980 is provided in the table following:

| | Products | | |
|---|---|---|---|
| | *A* | *B* | *C* |
| Balance on hand, 1/1 | | | |
|   No. units | 2,000 | 10,000 | 2,000 |
|   Cost per unit | $12 | $8 | $40 |
| Purchases during year excluding one shipment received on December 31 | | | |
|   No. units | 116,000 | 30,000 | 7,000 |
|   Cost per unit | $12 | $8 | $40 |
| Purchase of December 31 | | | |
|   No. units | 2,000 | 10,000 | 1,000 |
|   Cost per unit | $12 | $16 | $40 |
| Sales during year | | | |
|   No. units | 119,000 | 40,000 | 8,000 |
|   Sales price | $15 | $10 | $80 |
| Balance on hand, 12/31 | | | |
|   No. units | 1,000 | 10,000 | 2,000 |
|   Expected sales price | $15 | $20 | $80 |

a. Determine ending inventory and cost of goods sold using each of the three following inventory methods:
   (1) first-in, first-out (periodic).
   (2) weighted average (periodic).
   (3) retail method. (Remember that in using the retail method it is not necessary to make separate computations for each of the three products. Instead, the selling prices, balances on hand, purchases, ending balances, etc., of all three products are combined in determining the relationship between costs and selling prices.

b. Compare totals under each of the three methods. Comment on the hazards of using inventory methods based on averages. Why are the results under the weighted average and the retail methods distorted?

20. *Historical cost accounting may not properly reflect propitious acquisitions of inventory.*

The president of Carolina Textiles, Inc. was disappointed to learn from his controller that preliminary data indicated that his firm had suffered a loss of $25,000 in 1980. The president was surprised by the report of the controller since the price of print cloth, the product in which the company trades, had increased substantially during the year.

As of January 1, 1980, the company had on hand 400,000 yards of print cloth, for which it had paid $.25 per yard. The replacement cost of the cloth as of that date was $.27 per yeard. As of December 31, 1980, the company had in inventory 600,000 yards of cloth for which it had paid $.30 per yard. If it were to replace the cloth on December 31, it would have to pay $.45 per yard.

The president believed that creditors would be misled by financial reports on which inventories were valued, and income determined, strictly on the basis of historical cost. He requested that the controller prepare supplementary reports in which inventories were valued at net realizable value and *holding gains* were specifically recognized in the computation of income.

Determine income for 1980 assuming that inventories were stated at replacement cost in *both* 1979 and 1980.

21. *The conventional income statement can readily be modified to give effect to changes in inventory replacement costs.*

The F. C. Miller Co. trades in scrap metal. The company purchases the scrap from small dealers and sells it in bulk to the major steel manufacturers. As a matter of policy, the company sells the scrap to the manufacturers for $5 per ton more than the current price it pays the individual dealers. The price of scrap steel is volatile. The following table indicates several price changes that occurred in 1980 and the transactions engaged in by the F. C. Miller Co. in the periods between the price changes:

| Period | Price Paid to Dealers | No. of Tons Purchased | No. of Tons Sold | Price Per Ton |
|---|---|---|---|---|
| 1/1 | $ 82 | 5,000[a] | | |
| 1/2–3/11 | 85 | 16,000 | 18,000 | $ 90 |
| 3/12–6/4 | 87 | 25,000 | 22,000 | 92 |
| 6/5–9/26 | 93 | 5,000 | 9,000 | 98 |
| 9/27–12/30 | 104 | 17,000 | 13,000 | 109 |
| 12/31 | 106 | –0– | –0– | |
| | | 68,000 | 62,000 | |

[a]Opening inventory.

During the year F. C. Miller incurred operating costs of $325,000.

a. Prepare a conventional income statement in which gains or losses are recognized only upon actual sale of goods. Use the FIFO method of inventory valuation.

b. Prepare an income statement in which gains or losses are recognized upon increases in wholesale prices. Cost of goods sold should be based on replacement costs applicable at the time the goods are sold. Be sure to indicate holding gains actually realized as well as those applicable to goods still in inventory at year end.

a. The total number of units to be accounted for is the sum of beginning balance and the purchases throughout the year—800 units. Similarly, the total cost to be accounted for is $16,700.

b. 1. *FIFO*

*Ending inventory*

| | | | |
|---|---|---|---|
| From purchase of 12/28 | 100 @ $23 | $2,300 | |
| From purchase of 11/15 | 100 @ 22 | 2,200 | $ 4,500 |

*Cost of goods sold*

| | | | |
|---|---|---|---|
| From balance of 1/1 | 400 @ $20 | $8,000 | |
| From purchase of 2/24 | 200 @ 21 | 4,200 | 12,200 |
| Total | 800 | | $16,700 |

2. *Weighted Average:* Average cost = $16,700/800 units = $20.875

| | | |
|---|---|---|
| *Ending inventory* | 200 @ $20.875 | $ 4,175 |
| *Cost of goods sold* | 600 @ $20.875 | 12,525 |
| Total | 800 | $16,700 |

3. *LIFO*

| | | | |
|---|---|---|---|
| *Ending inventory* | | | |
| From balance of 1/1 | 200 @ $20 | | $ 4,000 |
| *Cost of goods sold* | | | |
| From purchase of 12/28 | 100 @ $23 | $2,300 | |
| From purchase of 9/23 | 100 @ 22 | 2,200 | |
| From purchase of 2/24 | 200 @ 21 | 4,200 | |
| From balance of 1/1 | 200 @ 20 | 4,000 | 12,700 |
| Total | 800 | | $16,700 |

c. The 200 units on hand would have to be written down to $21 per unit—$4,200. The write-down from $4,500 would cause earnings to decrease by $300. Inasmuch as the carrying value of the inventory would be reduced, then cost of goods sold, when the goods are actually sold, would be reduced by $300 and earnings thereby increased by that amount.

d. The entire inventory must be stated at $23 per unit. The 100 units that would otherwise be reported at $22 per unit would have to be increased in value by $1 per unit—a total of $100. Thus, a holding gain of $100 would be recognized. The effect of writing up the inventory by $100 in 1980 would be to increase reported cost of goods sold and reduce reported income in 1981 by the same amount.

# 9

# Long-Lived Assets and the Allocation of their Costs

This chapter will be directed to long-lived (often referred to as *fixed*) assets of the firm—assets that cannot be expected to be consumed within a single operating cycle of the business. Long-lived assets include plant assets (such as land, buildings, and equipment) as well as natural resources (such as minerals) and intangible assets (such as copyrights). Long-lived assets can be thought of as "bundles of services" which the firm will consume over time. Although they may be purchased and paid for in a single year, they will be used to generate revenues over a number of years.

Since a long-lived asset provides services for a span of time longer than one year, its cost must be charged off as an expense over more than one accounting period. The cost of the asset must be matched with the benefits to be provided—with the revenues to be generated. The process of allocating the cost of an asset over several accounting periods is referred to as *depreciation* if the asset is plant and equipment; *depletion,* if natural resources; and *amortization,* if intangible.

The basic journal entry to record the acquisition of a long-lived asset, equipment, is (assume the asset to be equipment which cost $10,000)

| | | |
|---|---|---|
| Equipment | $10,000 | |
| Cash (or notes payable) | | $10,000 |
| **To record the purchase of equipment.** | | |

The basic entry to record the periodic allocation of the cost of the asset over its useful life (assume a life of 10 years) is

| | | |
|---|---|---|
| Depreciation (expense) | $1,000 | |
| Equipment, accumulated depreciation | | $1,000 |
| **To record periodic depreciation expense.** | | |

Fixed assets are reported on the balance sheet at original cost less accumulated depreciation.

The account for accumulated depreciation or amortization (often referred to as *allowance* for depreciation or amortization) is a contra account and is always reported directly beneath the particular group of assets to which it pertains. Use of the contra account enables the firm to provide information that is more complete than if the balance in the asset account were reduced directly. Thus, after one year, the equipment might be shown on the balance sheet as

| | | |
|---|---|---|
| Equipment | $10,000 | |
| Less: Accumulated depreciation | 1,000 | $9,000 |

## Issues of Valuation

The limitations of the historical cost approach to asset valuation—that which is taken in practice today—are particularly pronounced with respect to fixed assets. Fixed assets commonly constitute a major portion of total assets of a firm, and because they are replaced relatively infrequently, differences between the value based on initial cost and that based on current measures may be substantial. Financial statements in which long-lived assets are reported at historical costs are deficient in that they provide no information as to either the market value of the assets—the price at which they could be sold or which would have to be paid to replace them—or the value of the services to be provided to the particular user.

**market values**
Insofar as the financial reports fail to account for changes in market values, *both* the balance sheet and the income statement are of limited utility to investors. The balance sheet fails to provide information on the total amount of resources available to management and for which it should be held accountable. It serves inadequately, therefore, as a basis on which to determine the return generated by the assets. Corporate performance can be meaningfully measured only in terms of current values—not historical values. Current values provide an indication of the alternative uses to which the assets could be put—the amount for which they could be sold and the proceeds invested in other ventures.

The income statement fails to provide information on the periodic increases in the value of assets (and thus of corporate net worth) over time. If income is to be a measure of how much "better off" a firm is from one period to the next, then changes in the amount for which assets could be bought or sold may be as important in determining income as actual exchange transactions. Decisions as to whether to hold or to sell fixed assets may be critical to the long-run welfare of the company. Since historical cost-based income statements omit consideration of *holding* gains or losses until such time as the assets are sold or retired, they fail to account for an important dimension of corporate performance.

At the same time, the historical cost-based income statement provides no information with respect to the market value of the services consumed as an asset is used. Depreciation expense represents the cost of a portion of an asset's service potential. If the annual depreciation charge is determined on the basis of outdated historical costs, then, in a period in which market values exceed historical costs, the charge will understate the market value of the services consumed and may thereby permit a reader of the financial report to infer that the firm is being operated with greater efficiency (less cost) than is in fact the case.

**value to users**

Measures of value based on historical costs fail to take into account not only the amounts for which assets could be bought or sold but the benefits to be provided to the particular users as well.

The value of an asset to its user is that of the services that it will provide—the revenues that it will generate or the cost savings that it will effect. It is a future-oriented measure of earnings potential.

The revenues to be generated or savings to be effected by a long-lived asset will be realized over a period greater than one year. Revenues or savings realized in the future, however, are of considerably less value than those to be realized at the present. The dollar values of services to be provided in the future must be discounted to take into account the time value of money.

Assume, for example, that a firm owns a building which it rents to outsiders. All operating expenses are paid by the tenants. The building has a remaining useful life of five years. The firm receives annual rental payments of $20,000. If the firm requires a rate of return of 8 percent on all assets, then (ignoring taxes) the value of the asset to the firm is the present value of a cash flow of $20,000 for five years. Per Table 4 in the Appendix, which indicates the present value of an annuity, present value of the rent payments (five periods, 8 percent) would be

$$\$20,000 \times 3.9927 = \$79,854$$

Such amount, in that it takes into account expected future returns, is likely to be of far greater utility to users of financial statements than a value based on historical cost.

Moreover, historical cost-based income statements fail to take into account the economic cost to the firm of the services consumed in the course of an accounting period. The economic sacrifice sustained by the firm is the loss of earnings potential. Such loss can readily be measured by comparing the value of services to be provided by the asset at the beginning of a period with that at the end. In the example of the building, the present value of the services of a building with a five-year useful life was determined to be $79,854. After another year, however, the asset could be expected to generate only four rental payments of $20,000. The present value of four payments of $20,000 discounted at 8 percent is, per Table 4,

$$\$20,000 \times 3.3121 = \$66,242$$

The economic loss, with respect to the building, sustained by the firm between the end of the fourth and the fifth years was therefore

$$\$79,854 - \$66,242 = \$13,612$$

Depreciation as conventionally determined is based on the cost to acquire an asset; it is past-oriented. It gives no explicit consideration to the loss of earnings potential sustained during the year.

**replacement cost as an alternative**    One frequently proposed alternative to reporting assets on a historical basis is to state them at *current replacement cost.* Current replacement cost is the cost of purchasing a similar asset (adjusted for age as well as technological factors) at the prevailing market price.

The use of current replacement costs would assure that the financial statements reflect at least an approximation of the costs that would have to be incurred if the asset were to be purchased in the current market. It would provide, in most instances, a reasonable estimate of the amount for which the asset could be sold. It would furnish the means to give recognition in the income statement to *holding gains* attributable to increases in market prices.

Current replacement costs do *not,* however, necessarily provide an indication of the value of the asset to the particular user. The value of an asset to a company that might use it with unusual efficiency might far exceed the price at which it is being traded in currently established markets. Nevertheless, the price that independent purchasers are willing to pay would, in general, be a reasonable approximation of the present value of the services to be provided by the asset. For most companies, replacement cost is likely to be a better indicator of value-in-use than historical cost. In fact, it is seldom feasible to measure directly the service potential of an asset. Most assets, unlike the building used in the previous example, cannot be identified with specific cash flows. They provide services only when used in conjunction with other assets. A piece of equipment used in a manufacturing process, for instance, has value only when used along with other equipment, the plant building, the land on which the plant sits, etc. Replacement cost is, therefore, as good an approximation of value-in-use as a firm could ordinarily expect to obtain.

As indicated in the following example, recognition of increases in replacement cost could readily be effected in the accounts.

The Jay Co. owns a building which originally cost $180,000 when purchased 10 years ago. It has an estimated useful life of 40 years and no salvage value. It is currently reflected on the balance sheet as follows:

| | |
|---|---|
| Building | $180,000 |
| Less: Accumulated depreciation | |
| ($\frac{10}{40}$ of $180,000) | 45,000 |
| | $135,000 |

During each of the 10 years depreciation was recorded with the conventional journal entry

| | | |
|---|---|---|
| Depreciation | $4,500 | |
| Accumulated depreciation | | $4,500 |

**To record annual depreciation expense.**

Replacement cost had remained constant for the first 10 years of asset life.

At the end of the tenth year, however, it was noted that, owing to increases in construction costs, the replacement cost of the building had increased by $20,000.

The following entry would effect recognition of the increase in replacement cost:

| | | |
|---|---|---|
| Building | $20,000 | |
| Accumulated depreciation | | $ 5,000 |
| Gain from appreciation | | 15,000 |

**To record the increase in replacement cost.**

The necessity for crediting accumulated depreciation for $5,000 may be unclear. It makes sense, however, considering that the useful life of the building has not changed. Thus, 25 percent of the building must still be considered as having been depreciated, regardless of the value placed on the building. The new value of the building is $200,000; hence 25 percent (10 years worth—$50,000) of replacement cost must be reflected in the accumulated depreciation account.

In each of the following 30 years depreciation would be recorded in the standard manner, except that the charge each year would be $\frac{1}{40}$ of $200,000:

| | | |
|---|---|---|
| Depreciation | $5,000 | |
| Accumulated depreciation | | $5,000 |

**To record depreciation expense.**

A primary objection to the use of replacement costs is the difficulty of obtaining a reasonable measure of such cost. Many assets are unique so that there do not exist readily available market prices.

How, for example, would you determine the current replacement cost of a tract of land? In some cases it may be possible to derive a value based on a recent offer to purchase the tract. In others, a reasonable value could be obtained by determining the amount for which similar tracts in the same neighborhood have recently been sold or by using price indices that reflect a general increase in commercial real estate value. Consider the problem, however, of estimating the value of land on which Ford Motor Company's River Rouge plant is located. The tract of land comprises several square miles, and the industrial influence of the plant is felt for many miles around the plant. Whatever value (or lack of it) the surrounding land has is attributable to the activities of Ford. It would be impossible to determine the value of the land either by looking at other recent offers (the plant is of such enormous value that it is reasonably certain that there have been few serious offers) or by looking at the sales prices of surrounding land (the Ford land determines the value of the surrounding land, not the other way around). Current replacement costs may be relevant for many decisions; they may not, however, be objectively determinable.

## Advantages of Historical Costs

The disadvantages of historical costs are obvious. The advantages, however, should not be understated. Historical costs are objective; the amount paid for an asset can readily be verified. Moreover, financial statements in which assets are stated at acquisition costs (less accumulated depreciation, as appropriate) are transaction based. Assets are initially recorded at the amounts for which they were acquired. The cost of an asset is allocated among the periods in which the service of the asset is provided. The total amount charged as an expense (depreciation) is exactly equal to the actual net cost (cost less salvage value, if any) incurred by the firm. Subjective judgments are held to a minimum; the financial statements present a historical record based on actual arm's-length exchanges.

It is undeniably true that financial statements based on historical costs do not provide *all* information necessary to make adequate investment or management decisions. It is questionable whether financial statements prepared on any single basis could do that. The use of historical costs, however, by no means precludes disclosure of current market values of assets or any other types of data, both of an accounting and nonaccounting nature, that financial statement users would find relevant to the decisions that they must make.

The Securities and Exchange Commission has taken a position with respect to the value of long-term assets similar to that adopted with regard to inventories. It has recognized the importance of information on current values and the limitations of historical costs. It has prescribed, therefore, that publicly

*publicly* held corporations make available to their shareholders (on Form 10-K) data on the *replacement* costs of their long-lived assets. The firms must indicate not only their best estimates of what it would cost to replace major categories of assets but, in addition, must report what the depreciation expense would have been had it been based on replacement, rather than historical, costs. With this information, as well as that relating to the current values of inventories, the knowledgeable financial analyst can reconstruct the historical cost statements issued by tne company so that they approximate reports that the company might have prepared, had it been required to do so, on the basis of replacement costs.

## Issues of Ownership

Generally, of course, a firm owns the fixed assets that it uses. But it is not always essential that a firm have formal legal title to the assets in order to record them in its own accounts. Assets are defined by accountants in economic rather than legal terms. Assets, as viewed by the accountant, are the economic resources of the firm; the contractual right to use property may be as much of an economic resource as a certificate of title. The distinction between economic and legal resources is especially important in light of current financial practice. With increasing frequency the rights and obligations of ownership are being contractually assigned to parties other than those which hold legal title.

In a common installment purchase, for example, the seller often retains formal title to the property until the buyer has made final payment of his outstanding obligations. The asset should be accounted for on the books of the purchaser as soon as he first acquires rights to its use. In a more complex financial arrangement, a financial institution might hold title to assets for a major portion of their useful lives. The financial institution leases the property to the party that will use it. The terms of the lease arrangement may be such that the annual rental payments approximate what they would have been had the user bought the property outright and borrowed the purchase price from the financial institution. Moreover, the lease contract may specify that the lessee (the user of the property) has to bear all risks and obligations of ownership; that is, he must pay all maintenance and insurance costs and make all required tax payments. Under such an arrangement the user of the property is in substance its owner; the property should, therefore, be accounted for as an asset on the books of the user.

Leasing is common in many industries; the railroad industry is an example of but one. Many freight cars bear notations indicating that they are the property of well-known banks. The banks, obviously, are not in the railroad business. Rather, they have loaned the railroad the cost of the cars and are retaining legal ownership until the railroad has repaid its loan. The loan may, however, take the form of a lease arrangement whereby the railroad rents the car from the bank. After such time as the railroad has made payments equal to the cost of the car (plus interest) the railroad would have the right to purchase the car for a nominal sum, perhaps $1. The railroad is, of course, the constructive owner of the car. The car should be recorded on the books of the railroad, not the bank.*

Lease arrangements will be discussed in greater detail in Chapter 10 in connection with long-term liabilities. The point to be emphasized at this time is that the question of whether or not property should be accounted for as an asset must be answered independently of strict legal interpretations or the peculiarities of financing arrangements.

### Cost of Plant Assets

As a general rule, plant assets are shown on the balance sheet at original cost, with the accumulated depreciation to date shown in a contra account. Normally, plant assets are said to be valued at "cost less accumulated depreciation." The cost of an asset may not simply be its stated purchase price. It would include all costs that are necessary to bring it to a usable condition. Cost would include, in addition to actual purchase price, costs of freight, installation, taxes, and title fees, among others. The costs that are included as a part of the fixed asset are said to be *capitalized*. They were incurred to benefit several periods, not just one; they should be charged as expenses over the useful life of the asset rather than in the year in which they are incurred.

The catalog or advertised price of an asset may not always be the relevant purchase price. Oftentimes the stated price of an asset is nothing more than the starting point of the bargaining process. Frequently, dealers give trade discounts (not to be confused with trade-in allowances) to customers of a certain category and cash discounts for prompt payment. Such discounts must be deducted from the originally stated price, since the purchase price must be determined on the basis of value actually surrendered by the buyer and received by the seller—that is, the *current cash equivalent.*

*example*        Assume that a firm purchases a machine for $10,000 under terms 2/10, n/30 (the company will receive a 2 percent discount if it pays within 10 days, but, in any event, must pay within 30 days). Transportation costs are $300, and the wages of the two workers who install the machine amount to $150. In addition, while the machine is being installed, three employees who worked in the vicinity of the new machine are idled for several hours, since power

---

*Until recently, because of inconsistencies in authoritative pronouncements it was possible for an asset to be recorded on the books of neither the borrower nor the lender. Some accountants have jocularly expressed profound fears of flying in airplanes that were seemingly without owners.

to other machines has to be disconnected. The wages paid to the workers while they are idle are $90. The cost of the new machine would be computed as follows:

| Purchase price: | $10,000 | |
| Less 2% discount | 200 | $ 9,800 |
| Freight-in | | 300 |
| Installation costs | | 150 |
| Payment for idle time | | 90 |
| | | $10,340 |

It may appear illogical to add the wages of the idle employees to the cost of the machine. But could the machine have been installed without such loss of time? Was the cost necessary to bring the asset to a performing state? If the answer is yes, then such costs have been incurred to benefit future periods, rather than the current period, and should rightfully be capitalized as part of the asset and should be allocated (i.e., depreciated) over the useful life of the new machine. If the answer is no, then the wages of the employees should be charged in full as an expense in the period of installation.

**purchases of land**   The same general principle applies to purchases of land. If a company purchases a parcel of land on which it intends to erect a new building, then all costs necessary to make the land ready for its intended use should be capitalized as part of the land. Thus, should a firm purchase a plot of land on which stands an old building that must first be torn down before a new building can be constructed, then the demolition costs should be added to the purchase price of land; they will serve to benefit future accounting periods.

*example*   A company purchases a plot of land for $100,000, with the intention of constructing a plant. Before construction can begin, however, an old building on the land must be removed. Demolition costs amount to $10,000, but the firm is able to sell scrap from the old building for $3,000. Title and legal fees incurred in connection with the purchase total $1,000. At what value should the land be recorded?

| Purchase price | | $100,000 |
| Add: Demolition costs | $10,000 | |
| Less: Sale of scrap | 3,000 | 7,000 |
| Title and legal fees | | 1,000 |
| Net cost of land | | $108,000 |

Land is somewhat different from other fixed assets in that it does not ordinarily lose either service potential or value with the passage of time. Indeed, most often it *appreciates* in value. Thus the cost of the land should not be depreciated or allocated over time as long as there is no evidence of a decline in its service potential or value. If the land does not decline in value and the firm can, at any time, sell the land for the amount that it originally paid, then there is no real cost to the firm and, thus, no expense need be charged. Land, therefore, is not ordinarily considered a *depreciable* asset.

**construction of assets**

When a firm constructs its own assets the *theoretical* guidelines to determine cost are quite clear. The firm should include in the cost of the asset all costs necessary to bring it to a serviceable state. Thus, the materials used, as well as the wages of all employees who work on the construction project, should quite clearly be capitalized as part of the asset. It is the *operational* questions that are the most difficult for many firms and their accountants to answer. How should a company account for those costs that are common to a number of activities that are carried out within the firm and cannot be traced directly to the construction of the asset? How, for example, should it treat the salary of a general manager who devotes only a portion of his time to supervising the construction project? Or the wages of administrative personnel who maintain records pertaining to both the construction project and other activities of the company? Should such costs be included as part of the asset constructed by the firm or should they be charged to expense as incurred?

The general answer is that the firm should *allocate* such costs between the fixed asset and the other activities. It should make estimates of the proportion of time that the general manager and the administrative personnel performed services relating to the construction project as opposed to the other activities. Only that proportion of overall costs should be added to the cost of the fixed asset.

*example*

The cost of constructing a minor addition to a plant might be computed (in oversimplified fashion) as follows:

| | |
|---|---:|
| Wages of employees directly associated with construction | $25,000 |
| Materials and supplies used in project | 40,000 |
| Salary of plant supervisor (80% of salary for 4 months) | 10,000 |
| Wages of administrative personnel (10% of wages for 4 months) | 600 |
| | $75,600 |

Decisions as to what proportions of such *joint* (common) costs should be added to the cost of fixed assets are by no means either trivial or academic. Costs that are included as part of a fixed asset will be charged as expenses, through the process of depreciation, over the life of the asset. The remaining costs that are allocated to other activities are likely to be charged as expenses in the year in which they are actually incurred. Thus, in the above example, if the decision were made that no portion of the salary of the plant supervisor should be included as part of the asset, then overall company expenses for the year would have been considerably greater, since the entire $10,000 would have been deducted from revenues. As it is, only a small portion of the $10,000 (one year's depreciation) would be charged against this year's revenues; the remainder would be spread out over the useful life of the asset.

The decision as to what proportion of joint costs to allocate to constructed fixed asset and what proportion to allocate to other company activities must to a large extent be based on the good judgment of corporate managers and their accountants. Some companies, especially if they have otherwise had a "bad" year, may attempt to artificially reduce reported expenses by allocating an excessively large portion of joint costs to the fixed asset. Others, which wish to minimize their tax liability, may do the reverse—allocate an illegitimately large portion of such costs to the other company activities—with the intent of reducing current taxable income. Such practices are not only inconsistent with accepted accounting principles; they are also unethical and, in some cases, illegal.

**capitalization of interest**

The question of which costs related to the construction of fixed assets should be capitalized is reflected in a long-standing dispute among accountants. When a company has under construction a major fixed asset, such as a new plant, it often has to borrow funds to finance the construction. On the amounts borrowed, it must pay interest. Should the interest be charged as an expense during all the years in which the loan is outstanding or should the interest, like all other costs of construction, be capitalized as part of the fixed asset and charged off, in the form of depreciation, over the life of the asset? Some accountants argue that interest costs are no different from labor costs or material costs. They are a necessary cost of construction and should, therefore, be added to the cost of the asset. Moreover, they assert, the company earns no revenues from the plant while it is under construction; hence the matching principle dictates that it should charge no expenses. The interest costs, they say, will benefit future periods; they should, therefore, be expensed in future periods. Other accountants, however, maintain that interest is a special kind of expense. The firm borrows money, they say, for all sorts of purposes. Just as it is impossible to trace capital contributed by stockholders to specific assets; so also is it impossible to trace the proceeds from the issue of bonds or other instruments of debt to particular assets. Thus, they argue, it would be improper to associate the related interest charges to specific construction projects. Interest, they say, should be expensed in the periods during which the loans are outstanding, regardless of the reason for the borrowing.

Until recently, relatively few firms capitalized interest costs. Those that did were mostly public utilities, such as gas and electric companies. In recent years, the number of firms in other industries that capitalize interest costs has increased substantially. Interest charges may be substantial in relation to overall income. In an effort to achieve greater uniformity of practice, the FASB has proposed limiting the situations in which interest may be capitalized to those where a significant period of time (one year or longer) elapses between the initial expenditure related to development of the asset and its readiness for its intended use.* Examples of the kinds of assets that would qualify for interest capitalization are assets under construction for an enterprise's own use (such as plant facilities), assets intended for sale that require a long production period (such as ships), and inventory items that require a long maturation period (such as aging whiskeys).

*capitalize interest expense*

## The Distinction Between Maintenance or Repairs and Betterments

A frequent question that faces accountants is whether to treat certain costs associated with fixed assets, especially buildings and equipment, as repair (or maintenance) costs or as betterments. The distinction between the two is often unclear, but the accounting implications are significant. In general, repair or maintenance costs are incurred to keep assets in good operating condition. They are recurring costs and do not add to the productivity of the asset or extend its originally estimated useful life. Betterments, on the other hand, enhance an asset's service potential (e.g., extend its useful life or increase its productivity) from what was anticipated when it was first purchased.

Maintenance and repair costs are usually charged off as expenses as they are incurred. Betterments, on the other hand, are added to the original cost of the fixed asset and depreciated over its remaining useful life.

*example*     In January 1979, the Z Company expended $500 to air-condition the cab of one of its trucks. At the same time, it spent $75 to replace a worn-out clutch. The journal entry to record the repair/betterment combination would be

| | | |
|---|---|---|
| Trucks (fixed asset) | $500 | |
| Truck, repairs (expense) | 75 | |
| Cash | | $575 |

**To record repairs and betterments**.

If the remaining useful life of the truck were five years, then during each of the five years, depreciation expense on the truck would be $100 (one-fifth of the air-conditioning costs) greater than what it was previously.

The "gray" area of maintenance costs involves those costs that recur every

*Capitalization of Interest Cost* (Proposed Statement of Financial Accounting Standards), Financial Accounting Standards Board, December 1978.

few years. Many firms have a policy of repainting their plants every, say, five years. Most of these firms, for the sake of clerical convenience, would record the cost of the paint job (assuming it was done by outside contractors) with the following journal entry:

| | | |
|---|---|---|
| Maintenance expense | xxxx | |
| Cash | | xxxx |

In effect, such firms are obtaining the benefit of the expenditure over a period of five years but charging the cost to one year. It would be considerably more sound to capitalize the cost of the paint job—to record it as a separate asset—and allocate the cost to each of the five years to be benefited by the expenditure.*

### Depreciation

Depreciation is the process of allocating (in a systematic and rational manner) the cost of a tangible asset, less *salvage* (also called *residual*) value, if any, over the estimated useful life of the asset. Allocation of cost is necessary if costs are to be matched with the revenues that they help to generate. By salvage value is meant the amount that can be recovered when the asset is either sold, traded in for a new asset, or scrapped. If an asset that originally cost $5,000 could be sold after 10 years (the longest the company expects to use the asset) for $500, then the total amount that must be depreciated, or allocated over useful life of the asset, is $5,000 less $500—$4,500.

Depreciation is a process of *allocation*, not *valuation*. The original cost of an asset less the accumulated depreciation (the amount of depreciation taken on an asset up to a given time) is often referred to as the *book* value of an asset. Accountants do not purport that the book value of an asset represents the value of the asset in the open market. The potential for conflict between the two values can be demonstrated in a simple example involving an automobile.

A company purchases an automobile for $13,000 with the intention of using it for five years. It estimates that the trade-in value of the auto after that time will be $1,000. The amount of depreciation to be charged each year can be calculated to be $2,400:

$$\frac{\text{Original cost} - \text{Salvage value}}{\text{Useful life}} = \frac{\$13,000 - \$1,000}{5} = \$2,400$$

Indicated on the next page is a comparison of book values and market values at the end of each of the five years of estimated useful life. The market value represents a "typical" pattern of the decline in value of an automobile.

*Refer to problem 8 for illustrations of nonconventional practices in this area.

| End of Year | Original Cost | Depreciation Taken to Date | Cost Less Accumulated Depreciation ("book" value) | Estimated Market Value |
|---|---|---|---|---|
| 1 | $13,000 | $ 2,400 | $10,600 | $9,200 |
| 2 | 13,000 | 4,800 | 8,200 | 6,200 |
| 3 | 13,000 | 7,200 | 5,800 | 3,800 |
| 4 | 13,000 | 9,600 | 3,400 | 2,200 |
| 5 | 13,000 | 12,000 | 1,000 | 1,000 |

Merely because the amounts in the last two columns are not the same it cannot be said that the decision to depreciate the asset at the rate of $2,400 per year was in error. It is *not* the objective of depreciation accounting to indicate what the asset could be sold for at the end of any given year.

It is often said that another objective of the depreciation process is to provide funds with which to replace assets when they must be sold or retired. Nothing can be further from correct. The absurdity of such a proposition is evident by examining the basic journal entry for depreciation:

| | | |
|---|---|---|
| Depreciation | xxxx | |
| Accumulated depreciation | | xxxx |

Cash is neither debited nor credited; it is neither received from outsiders nor removed from one bank account into another. It is not possible for an accountant to assure that a firm will have sufficient cash on hand to purchase a new asset when an old one is retired merely by making an end-of-month or end-of-year adjusting entry.

Only in the most indirect sense can it be said that depreciation accounting provides funds for the future replacement of assets. Depreciation, like other expenses, is deducted from revenues in order to calculate annual income. To the extent that it reduces income, it also reduces income taxes. Insofar as it reduces income taxes, it enables the firm to save for asset replacement more cash than it would if it had not recorded depreciation. In the same vein, the reduction in income attributable to depreciation expense may discourage some firms from declaring cash dividends of the same amount they might have if income were greater. In both cases, the relationship between depreciation and an asset replacement fund is far too removed to permit one to say that depreciation *provides* funds to replace assets.

## Accelerated Depreciation Methods

Up until this point, whenever depreciation has been discussed, the annual depreciation charge has been calculated by dividing the total amount to be depreciated (cost less salvage value, if any) by the number of years that the asset was expected to be in use. The depreciation charges were thereby equal during each year of the asset's life. Such procedure of calculating depreciation is known as the straight-line method. There are, however, other means of allocating the cost of an asset to the various periods during which it will be used that result in unequal annual charges. Two of the most popular of these methods are known as the sum-of-the-years' digits method and the double-declining balance method. Both of these methods result in depreciation charges which decline over the life of the asset. That is, depreciation expenses are greater in the beginning years of the asset's life than they are at the end. Both are referred to as *accelerated* methods of depreciation.

**sum-of-the-years' digits method**

Under the *sum-of-the-years' digits* method a fraction of the asset's net depreciable cost is charged off each year. The denominator of the fraction remains constant over the life of the asset. It is determined by taking a sum of numbers starting with 1 and continuing to the estimated life of the asset. Thus, if the life of the asset is three years, the denominator would be $1 + 2 + 3 = 6$. If it were five years, it would be $1 + 2 + 3 + 4 + 5 = 15$. A shortcut technique eliminates the need to count on fingers. The life of the asset $(n)$ may be multiplied by the life of the asset plus 1 $(n + 1)$ and the product divided by 2, e.g., the denominator to be used for an asset with five years of useful life would be

$$\frac{n(n + 1)}{2} = \frac{5(6)}{2} = 15$$

The numerator of the fraction would vary over the life of the asset. Each year it would be equal to the number of years remaining in the asset's life. Thus, in the first year of the life of a five-year asset, $\frac{5}{15}$ of the asset's cost (less salvage value) would be depreciated. In the second year, when the asset has a remaining life of only four years, $\frac{4}{15}$ would be depreciated. In subsequent years $\frac{3}{15}$, $\frac{2}{15}$, and $\frac{1}{15}$ respectively would be charged to depreciation expense.

*example*

A firm purchases an auto for $13,000. It estimates that the auto has a useful life of five years, after which it can be sold for $1,000. The net amount to be depreciated is $12,000 (original cost less estimated salvage value). Depreciation charges using the sum-of-the-years' digits method would be as follows:

| Year | Net Depreciable Amount | Depreciation Fraction | Depreciation Charge |
|------|------------------------|-----------------------|---------------------|
| 1 | $12,000 | $\frac{5}{15}$ | $ 4,000 |
| 2 | 12,000 | $\frac{4}{15}$ | 3,200 |
| 3 | 12,000 | $\frac{3}{15}$ | 2,400 |
| 4 | 12,000 | $\frac{2}{15}$ | 1,600 |
| 5 | 12,000 | $\frac{1}{15}$ | 800 |
| | | $\frac{15}{15}$ | $12,000 |

**double-declining balance method**

The *double-declining balance* method consists of applying to the current book value of the asset (cost less accumulated depreciation to date) a percentage rate equal to twice the straight-line depreciation rate. In the earlier example of straight-line depreciation in which the asset had a useful life of five years, one-fifth or 20 percent of the net depreciable cost was charged off each year. Hence, the depreciation rate could be said to have been 20 percent. The appropriate rate for the double-declining balance method would therefore be twice that, or 40 % percent. Unlike the straight-line or sum-of-the-years' digits methods, *the declining balance procedure requires that the rate be applied initially to the original cost of the asset—not original cost less salvage value.*

*example*

Again, the asset to be considered cost $13,000, has a useful life of five years and an estimated salvage value of $1,000. Depreciation charges using the double-declining balance method would be based on a rate of 40 percent (twice the straight-line rate of 20 percent):

| Year | Cost Less Accumulated Depreciation (book value) | Depreciation Rate | Depreciation Charge | Remaining Book Value |
|------|------------------------------------------------|-------------------|---------------------|----------------------|
| 1 | $13,000 | 40% | $5,200 | $7,800 |
| 2 | 7,800 | 40 | 3,120 | 4,680 |
| 3 | 4,680 | 40 | 1,872 | 2,808 |
| 4 | 2,808 | 40 | 1,123 | 1,685 |
| 5 | 1,685 | 40 | 674 | 1,011 — *need 1000 salv value* |

The double-declining balance method does not automatically assure that an asset will be depreciated exactly down to its salvage value. At the end of the fifth year, the book value of the asset would be $1,011—$11 more than the estimated salvage value of $1,000. To the extent that the firm continues to hold on to the asset beyond its originally estimated five-year life, then the additional $11 depreciation would be taken in the sixth year. An asset, however, should never be depreciated below its estimated salvage value. In the example, if the estimated salvage value were $1,200 instead of $1,000, the maximum amount of depreciation that could be charged in the fifth (and final) year of asset life would be $485 ($1,685 minus $1,200).

*Remember, in applying the double-declining balance method the first-year depreciation charge must be based on the original cost of the asset—not original cost less estimated salvage value. Salvage value should be disregarded in computing first-year depreciation.*

An additional observation pertaining to the two accelerated depreciation methods may be appropriate. Such methods, particularly the double-declining balance method, have grown increasingly popular in recent years. Some accountants aver that accelerated depreciation methods are preferable to the straight-line method since they tend to result in book values that more closely approximate market values. The values of many assets—autos, for example—decline by greater amounts in the early years of their lives than in later years. Such an assertion is specious, however, in that under conventional accounting there is no pretext that the book value of an asset should approximate its market value. Assets are not, by contrast, restated to reflect *increases* in market value. Others maintain that assets often provide greater services to the firm in their early years than they do in their later years. The productivity of many assets decreases with time as they operate less efficiently, require more maintenance, and are out of service for greater periods of time. Such a position is somewhat more convincing; in practice, however, accelerated depreciation methods are generally applied without consideration of the probable service patterns of particular assets. Moreover, the specific procedures were not developed on the basis of studies of asset productivity. They have received wide acceptance primarily because they provide an expedient and easily applied means for attaining a decreasing annual charge.

The popularity of the declining charge methods is most directly traceable to current tax laws. The Internal Revenue Service permits taxpayers to use such procedures in calculating taxable income. Since the methods result in greater deductible expenses in the early years of an asset's life, they result in more immediate tax savings. Although the total that the IRS allows a taxpayer to deduct over time is the same (cost less a salvage value) regardless of the depreciation method used, a dollar saved today is worth considerably more than one to be saved in the future.

## Depreciation Based on Productivity

The *unit charge* or, as it is often called, the *units of output* depreciation method directly takes into account the amount of service that an asset can provide in a given time period. The unit charge method requires that an estimate be made at the time an asset is acquired, not of useful life in terms of years as was required by the other methods, but rather of useful life in terms of units of service. Useful life might be stated in terms of machine-hours, units produced, or some other base. The useful life of an auto, for example, might be expressed as 100,000 miles. The cost of the asset is then allocated to each time period in proportion to the amount of service actually consumed.

*example*    Return again to the auto example. Assume again that the auto cost $13,000, but this time suppose that the company (as is common among auto leasing companies as well as other firms with large fleets of cars) has a policy of using the autos for a fixed number of miles—assume 100,000 miles—and then selling them, regardless of how many years an auto has actually been in service. The company estimates that after that many miles the resale value is approximately $1,000. The following schedule indicates the *actual* number of miles driven in each year and the applicable depreciation charge:

| Year | Miles Driven | Miles Driven as a % of 100,000 | Net Cost to be Depreciated ($13,000 less $1,000) | Depreciation Charge |
|------|--------------|--------------------------------|--------------------------------------------------|---------------------|
| 1 | 25,000 | 25% | $12,000 | $ 3,000 |
| 2 | 17,000 | 17 | 12,000 | 2,040 |
| 3 | 18,000 | 18 | 12,000 | 2,160 |
| 4 | 26,000 | 26 | 12,000 | 3,120 |
| 5 | 14,000 | 14 | 12,000 | 1,680 |
|   | 100,000 | 100% |   | $12,000 |

Insofar as units of service provided by an asset can be related to the revenue produced by the asset, the unit charge method provides a much better match of costs with revenues than do the other depreciation methods. As asset productivity increases, so also does the percentage of asset cost charged off as an expense. Unit charge methods of depreciation, however, are not widely used. Their lack of acceptance can be attributed to difficulties of application. For most assets it is very difficult to estimate the number of service units provided. In fact, the useful life of many assets is more a function of time than of physical wear and tear. This is especially true in periods of rapid technological advance when assets tend to become technologically obsolete long before they become physically so.

## Retirement of Fixed Assets

Upon the retirement of an asset, either by sale or by abandonment, the asset as well as the related accumulated depreciation must be removed from the books. If the asset is sold for the amount and at the time originally estimated, then the retirement entry is especially simple.

*example*     Return once again to the auto which originally cost $13,000 and had an estimated salvage value after five years of $1,000. At the end of five years the fixed asset account would have a debit balance of $13,000 (regardless of the choice of depreciation method), and the accumulated depreciation account a credit balance of $12,000 (slightly less if the double-declining balance method were used). If the asset is, in fact, sold for $1,000 then the appropriate journal entry would be

| | | |
|---|---|---|
| Cash | $ 1,000 | |
| Accumulated depreciation, | | |
| autos | $12,000 | |
| Fixed assets, autos | | $13,000 |
| **To record the sale of the asset.** | | |

If at any time during the life of the asset it is either sold or abandoned for an amount greater or less than its book value at that time, then a gain or loss on retirement would have to be recognized.

*example*

The firm has charged depreciation on the auto using straight-line depreciation. At the end of three years, after $7,200 of depreciation had been charged, the firm sold the auto for $4,000. The book value of the asset at time of sale would have been $5,800—$13,000 less $7,200. Hence, the firm has suffered a loss of $1,800.

| | | |
|---|---|---|
| Cash | $4,000 | |
| Accumulated depreciation, | | |
| autos | 7,200 | |
| Loss on disposal | 1,800 | |
| Fixed assets, autos | | $13,000 |

**To record the sale of the asset.**

Bear in mind that if an asset is sold anytime before the close of the year, depreciation for the portion of the year which the asset was actually held must first be recorded before any gain or loss can be computed.

The nature of gains or losses on retirement merits comment. Such gains or losses arise only because a company was unable to have perfect foresight when it acquired the asset as to the time of retirement and the selling price. If it had such foresight, it would have determined its depreciation schedule accordingly and hence there would be no gain or loss upon retirement.

In the previous example, the $1,800 loss on retirement indicates that insufficient depreciation in the amount of $600 per year for the three years that the asset was held had been charged. If the firm had known that it would sell the asset (which cost $13,000) for $4,000 after using it for three years, then it would have allocated $3,000 of asset cost ($13,000 cost less $4,000 salvage value, divided by 3) to each of the three years—instead of the $2,400 per year actually allocated.

Meticulous accounting might therefore dictate that, rather than recognizing a loss on retirement in the year of sale, the company should correct the earnings of the prior years for the insufficient depreciation charges. Such a correction would have the effect of reducing retained earnings without burdening reported income in the year of retirement. In practice, such an approach is virtually never taken inasmuch as it would require an excessive number of prior period adjustments and thereby complicate the process of financial reporting.

### Trade-ins

A special problem is presented when a firm *trades in* an old asset for a new one. A firm surrenders an old car, plus cash, for a later model. The most logical way of handling a trade-in is to view it as two separate transactions. In the first, the old asset is sold—not for cash but instead for a *trade-in allowance.* In the second, the new asset is purchased—for cash plus the trade-in allowance. The critical step in implementing such a procedure lies in determining the price for which the old asset was sold. In many instances, the amount that the dealer says he is offering as a trade-in allowance bears no relationship to the actual fair market value of the old asset. In the auto industry, for example, it is common practice for new car dealers to offer unusually high trade-in allowances on the used vehicles of prospective new car purchasers. If the purchaser accepts the high trade-in allowance, he may be unable to avail himself of discounts that are generally granted to purchasers who come without used cars. He may, in effect, have to pay full, or nearly full, *sticker* price for the new car, something he would not ordinarily have to do if he came to the dealer without an old car to trade.

If a meaningful gain or loss on retirement is to be computed it is essential, therefore, that the company determine as accurately as possible the actual fair market value of the asset given up. This can usually be done by consulting industry publications, such as the car dealers' "blue" book of used car prices, or by obtaining data on transactions involving similar assets.

*example*    The auto, which originally cost $13,000 (estimated life of five years, $1,000 salvage) is traded in for a new car after three years. The dealer grants a trade-in allowance of $7,000, but, according to a book of used car prices, the car is worth no more than $5,200. The sticker price of the new car is $17,000, but, in fact, an astute buyer would not normally pay more than $15,000. In addition to giving up its old car, the company pays cash of $9,800.

The book value of the old car, assuming straight-line depreciation, would at time of trade-in be

| | |
|---|---:|
| Original cost | $13,000 |
| Accumulated depreciation | |
| (three years' times $2,400) | 7,200 |
| | $ 5,800 |

Loss on the sale of the old car would therefore be $5,800 less $5,200 (fair market value of the old car)—$600.

The "sale" of the old car could properly be recorded as follows:

**(a)**

| | | |
|---|---:|---:|
| Loss on retirement | $ 600 | |
| Accumulated depreciation, autos | 7,200 | |
| Trade-in allowance (a temporary | | |
| account) | 5,200 | |
| Fixed assets, autos | | $13,000 |
| **To record the "sale" of the asset.** | | |

The entry to record the purchase of the new auto would be

**(b)**

| | | |
|---|---|---|
| Fixed assets, autos | $15,000 | |
| Cash | | $9,800 |
| Trade-in allowance | | 5,200 |

**To record the purchase of the new asset.**

Clearly, the two entries could be combined (and the trade-in allowance account eliminated).

This method of accounting for trade-ins allows the new asset to be recorded at its fair market value, which is equal to the cash price that an independent buyer would have to pay. At the same time, it permits the gain or loss on retirement of the old asset to be based upon its fair market value. It thereby gives recognition to the economic substance of the transaction, regardless of what amounts are arbitrarily assigned to the trade-in allowance and the price of the new asset.

The Accounting Principles Board (in Opinion No. 29 regarding exchanges of similar assets) prescribes a slightly different method of accounting for trade-in transactions that would result, under the procedure described, in a *gain* rather than a loss on retirement. Under the APB method, the new asset would be recorded not at its fair market value but, instead, at the book value of the old asset.*

As a consequence, no gain on retirement would be recognized. The APB method serves to prevent a firm from recognizing a gain—and increasing reported earnings—merely by exchanging one asset for another of similar type and value. The APB method is based on the underlying assumption that such an exchange is not of sufficient economic substance to justify an increase in the reported value of a firm's assets.

The contrast between the two methods serves to highlight the fact that many current accounting issues can be attributable to the practice of reporting assets on the basis of historical cost rather than market value. If the reported

---

*To the extent that the trade is not merely one asset for another, but the firm is required to pay cash as well, then the amount of cash paid would be added to the amount at which the new asset is recorded. For example, if a firm were to exchange one auto, having a book value of $8,000 (cost $10,000, accumulated depreciation $2,000), plus cash of $1,000, for a new auto that has a fair market value of $12,000, the following entry would be in order:

| | | |
|---|---|---|
| Accumulated Depreciation (old auto) | $2,000 | |
| Automobile (new) | 9,000 | |
| Automobile (old) | | $10,000 |
| Cash | | 1,000 |

**To record trade-in of automobiles.**

The amount at which the new asset is recorded represents the net book value of the old (cost of $10,000 less accumulated depreciation of $2,000) plus the cash of $1,000. The entry gives no recognition to either the fair market value of the new asset or the obvious gain in the value of the old. The new balance in the automobile account would be depreciated over the useful life of the new auto.

value of an asset were periodically increased to reflect changes in market condtions, then at the time of retirement or trade there would be little need to recognize a gain or a loss. The reported value of the asset would be nearly identical to the amount for which it could be sold or traded.

## *Determination of Useful Life*

To this point in the text, no attention has been directed toward problems of determining useful lives. Assumptions regarding length of service potential have been glibly asserted. In practice, regrettably, whereas considerable attention is directed to selection of depreciation methods, estimates of useful life are often made haphazardly. In many cases, however, overall income of the company may be as sensitive to variations in estimates of useful life as to method of depreciation.

The number of years that a firm will keep an asset is not a matter of determining only when the asset will deteriorate beyond the point at which repairs are economically feasible. Physical obsolescence is but one determinant of useful life. The service potential of an asset is to a large extent a function of technological factors. A technological breakthrough may enable a company to produce its product at considerably less cost than previously; hence the firm may decide to replace an old machine with a new. Or, a technological development in either the same or a related industry may reduce or eliminate the demand for the firm's product—and thereby make many of its production facilities obsolete. The difficulties of making meaningful estimates of useful life cannot be overestimated, and, unfortunately, there are no easy-to-follow techniques available to either accountants or managers.

The importance of correct estimates cannot be overstated, especially in companies in which depreciable assets constitute a major portion of total assets. To the extent that the estimate of useful life is greater than what is proper, annual depreciation charges will be lower and, as a consequence, income greater. Because estimates of useful life must necessarily be based on "subjective judgment," a competent financial analyst should carefully scrutinize the number of years over which a firm depreciates its major assets.

Recently, for example, the depreciation practices of several companies in the computer leasing industry came under question. One company, for example, had been depreciating IBM 360 computers, its major asset, over a 10-year period. When a new series of computers was introduced, it became unlikely that the company could continue to profitably rent out to its customers its old-model data processing machines. Its auditors qualified their opinion that the annual report of the firm presented fairly its financial position because of reservations as to the company's ability to recover the remaining undepreciated costs on its computer leasing equipment.

The depreciation practices of major airlines further highlight the subjective nature of estimates of useful life. Whereas one airline may depreciate its 727 jets over a 10-year period, another may allocate the cost over a 12-year period. The estimates are not necessarily inconsistent with one another. One may *plan* to use its planes for a shorter period of time than does the other. But since the airline industry is competitive, the seemingly conflicting policies at the very least raise questions as to the reliability of the estimates and the credibility of the financial statements.

## Natural Resources and Depletion

Natural resources, or *wasting assets*, as they are often referred to, are accounted for in a manner similar to plant and equipment. They are recorded initially at acquisition cost, and the value at which they are reported subsequently is reduced as their service potential declines.

The process of allocating the cost of natural resources over the periods in which they provide benefits is known as *depletion.* The service potential of natural resources can ordinarily be measured more meaningfully in terms of quantity of production (e.g., tons or barrels) than number of years. Hence, depletion is generaly charged on a *units of output* basis. As with other types of long-lived assets, the initial cost of a natural resource may be reported on the balance sheet for as long as it is in service. The accumulated depletion may be indicated in a contra account. In practice, however, a contra account is not always used; often the balance in the natural resource account itself is reduced directly by the amount of the accumulated depletion.

*example*    A firm purchases mining properties for $2 million cash. It estimates that the properties will yield 400,000 usable tons of ore. During the first year of production, the firm mines 5,000 tons.

The following entry would be appropriate to record the purchase of the properties:

| | | |
|---|---|---|
| Mineral deposits | $2,000,000 | |
| Cash | | $2,000,000 |

**To record the purchase of the ore deposit.**

Since the deposit will yield an estimated 400,000 tons of usable ore, cost assignable to each ton is

$$\frac{\$2,000,000}{400,000 \text{ tons}} = \$5 \text{ per ton}$$

Depletion cost of the first year would be

$$5,000 \text{ (tons mined)} \times \$5 \text{ per ton} = \$25,000$$

The entry to record the depletion would be

| | | |
|---|---|---|
| Depletion (expense) | $25,000 | |
| Mineral deposits, accu- | | |
| mulated depletion | | $25,000 |

**To record first-year depletion.**

After the first year, the mineral deposits would be reported on the balance sheet as

| | |
|---|---|
| Mineral deposits | $2,000,000 |
| Less: Accumulated depletion | 25,000 |
| | $1,975,000 |

Depletion is a cost of production, to be added along with other production costs (labor, depreciation of equipment, supplies) to the carrying value of the minerals inventory. It will be charged as an expense (cost of minerals sold) in the accounting period in which the inventory is sold and the revenue from the sale is recognized.

Often, a mining or drilling company will have to purchase or build equipment or structures that can be used only in connection with the recovery of a specific deposit. If such structures or equipment will be used for as long as the property continues to be exploited (and only so long), then depreciation charges should logically be determined using the same units of output basis as used to compute depletion. Depreciation, if based on output, is more likely in such circumstances to assure that the cost of equipment or structures is matched with the revenues realized from the sale of the minerals than if based on useful life in terms of time.

**percentage depletion**

The Federal Tax Code provides that for tax purposes depletion may be determined using a method known as *percentage depletion.* Under the percentage of depletion method, depletion is based on a percentage of gross revenues attributable to a property. The specific percentages vary from 5 percent to 22 percent depending on the specific mineral. If, for example, revenue from the sale of minerals were $1 million and the applicable percentage rate were 22 percent, then the firm would be allowed a deduction for depletion of $220,000. The depletion deduction is determined without regard to the initial cost of the property, and the deduction may continue to be taken even after the full cost of the property has been recovered. Thus, even though the mineral deposits may have cost only $2 million, the deduction of 22 percent of gross revenues is permitted to be taken indefinitely—long after accumulated depletion exceeds $2 million. Although there are some limitations on the amount of depletion that may be taken in any one year, percentage depletion has generally been viewed as an economic incentive or subsidy to firms in extractive industries. Percentage depletion is *not* a logical or legitimate means of allocating costs; it is not a generally accepted accounting method, and it may not be used for purposes of general financial reporting.

*tax code allows this*

## Intangible Assets

Intangible assets are those assets characterized by the rights, privileges, and benefits of possession rather than by physical existence. Often, the service potential of intangible assets is uncertain and exceedingly difficult to measure. As a consequence, intangible assets frequently are the subject of controversy. Examples of intangible assets are patents, copyrights, research and development costs, organizational costs, and goodwill. In this section we shall deal specifically with only a few selected intangible assets with the aim of highlighting some key accounting issues. A discussion of goodwill, one of the more controversial intangible assets, will be deferred until the chapter pertaining to ownership interests among corporations, since goodwill conventionally arises only out of the acquisition of one company by another.

Intangibles are considered to be assets either because they represent rights to future benefits or because the expenditures that were made to acquire or develop them will serve to benefit a number of accounting periods in the future. Hence, the costs must be allocated to the periods in which the benefits will be realized.

Intangible assets are recorded initially at their acquisition or development cost. The cost is then amortized over (allocated to) the periods in which the benefits will accrue. The general accounting approach to intangibles may be illustrated with respect to copyrights.

**copyrights** A copyright is an exclusive right, granted by law, to publish, sell, reproduce, or otherwise control a literary, musical, or artistic work. As of January 1, 1978, in the United States, copyrights on most new works are granted for the life of the creator plus 50 years. The cost to secure a copyright from the federal government is minimal; however, the cost to purchase one from its holder on a work that has proven successful—on a best-selling novel or musical recording, for instance—may be substantial.

If a firm were to purchase a copyright, it would record it initially as it would any other asset. Assuming a cost of $20,000, for example, an appropriate journal entry might be

| | | |
|---|---|---|
| Copyright | $20,000 | |
| Cash | | $20,000 |

**To record the purchase of the copyright.**

If the remaining useful life were determined to be 10 years, then the following entry would be appropriate each year to record amortization:

| | | |
|---|---|---|
| Amortization of copyrights | $2,000 | |
| Copyrights, accumulated | | |
| amortization | | $2,000 |

**To record amortization of copyright.**

Accounting practices with respect to copyrights focus attention on a question that is raised with respect to many types of intangibles—that of the number of years over which cost should be amortized. Although the legal life of a copyright may be firmly established, the copyright may be of significant economic value for a considerably shorter period of time. Actual useful life may depend on a multitude of factors such as public taste, critical acclaim, or future success of the author, none of which can readily be assessed. As with other long-lived assets, carrying value of the asset as well as amortization charges (the periodic decline in value) must be based, in large measure, on subjective judgments of corporate management and accountants.

**costs of drilling unsuccessful oil wells**

Accounting practices in the oil and gas industry raise another important issue with respect to intangible assets: What is the nature of the costs to be included as part of the asset; how directly must a cost be associated with a future benefit before it should properly be capitalized? Despite highly sophisticated geological survey techniques, it is usually necessary for oil and gas companies, in their search for new reserves, to drill unsuccessfully in several locations before actually striking oil or gas. Obviously the cost of drilling the productive wells should be capitalized and amortized over the years during which oil or gas will be withdrawn from the ground. But what about the costs of drilling the *dry holes*? Should they be written off as incurred, or should they also be capitalized and amortized over the period in which oil is withdrawn from the successful wells? Should they be considered losses (corporate errors, in a sense) or expenditures that are statistically necessary to discover the productive locations? Directly, the dry holes will produce no benefits to the company; indirectly they represent an inevitable cost of finding the productive wells.

In past years, some companies capitalized costs associated with unsuccessful prospects (dry hole costs), while others did not. Those that did were known as *full-cost* companies, inasmuch as the costs of the proven mineral reserves included the costs of drilling the unsuccessful as well as the successful wells. Those that did not were referred to as *successful efforts* firms, because only the costs of drilling successful wells were added to the costs of the oil and gas properties; outlays associated with unsuccessful drilling efforts were charged to expenses as soon as it was concluded that the efforts at a particular location were a failure.

In 1977, the Financial Accounting Standards Board, in Statement No. 19, prescribed that all firms must use *only* the *successful efforts* method. The

FASB

decision of the FASB was a source of consternation on the part of not only those firms that had been using the full cost method but also the federal agencies concerned with administering the antitrust statutes. The full-cost method had been used by many small exploration firms. The switch to the successful efforts method resulted, at least in the short run, in reductions in their reported earnings, as the costs of unsuccessful wells were written off in the year of failure rather than over a number of succeeding years. It was thought that the reduction in reported earnings would make the firms less attractive to investors and lenders and, thereby, less able to acquire the capital necessary to compete with the giants of the industry, many of which were already using the successful efforts method. The FASB and its defenders, however, assert that fears of reduced competition are groundless because the change affects only *reported* earnings. In terms of economic wealth—the present value of actual oil and gas reserves—the firms are neither better nor worse off merely because they make use of one accounting method as opposed to another.

The Securities and Exchange Commission failed to support the directive of the FASB that mandated the use of the successful efforts method. It took the position that both the successful efforts and the full cost methods were deficient because they failed to provide adequate information on the economic worth of the oil and gas reserves that had been discovered. The SEC proposed that a third method, referred to as *reserve recognition accounting* be developed. The new method, as outlined by the SEC, would require that proved reserves be reported at an amount indicative of the present value of the cash flows that they are likely to generate. It would require firms to estimate not only the quantities of oil and gas in their fields, but also to make assumption as to the prices at which they will be sold and the costs of lifting them from the ground. The accuracy of any assumption of prices and costs would, of course, be subject to the usual vagaries of the economy. But in the oil and gas industry even estimates of quantities available for sale may be capricious. Estimates of the quantities of oil and gas in a particular field that are made at the time of discovery are considered by industry experts to be unreliable because the eventual yield of a field is likely to be dependent upon the risks a firm is willing to take to go after the less-readily available deposits. The degree of risk will, in turn, be a function of drilling costs, probable size of deposit, selling prices, and transportation costs. Nevertheless, the SEC apparently believes that the utility of the information to be provided by the new method will outweigh its subjectivity.

In light of the SEC position, the FASB suspended the key provisions of Statement 19. As of 1980 firms can use either the full cost or the successful efforts method and attempts are underway to develop the method proposed by the SEC.

**research and development costs**

Accounting procedures with respect to research and development costs are illustrative of a third issue common to intangible assets—to what extent must theoretical concepts of intangible assets be tempered by "practical" considerations? Research and development costs are, by nature, incurred in order to benefit future accounting periods. Expenditures for research and development are made in the expectation that they will lead to new or improved products or processes that will in turn increase revenues or decrease expenses. The matching concept suggests that research and development costs be capitalized as intangible assets and amortized over the periods in which the additional revenues are generated or cost savings effected.

In practice, however, it has proven exceedingly difficult to match specific expenditures for research and development with specific products or processes. Some expenditures are for *basic* research; they are not intended to produce direct benefits. Others produce no benefits at all or result in benefits which could not have been foreseen at the time they were incurred.

The FASB in Statement No. 2 (1974) prescribed that expenditures for most types of research and development costs must be charged to expense in the year incurred rather than capitalized as intangible assets. The board was motivated by the great variety of practice among corporations as to the nature of costs that were capitalized and the number of periods over which they were amortized. Given almost unlimited flexibility in accounting for research and development, some firms capitalized costs that were unlikely to provide future benefits; others *wrote off* large amounts of previously capitalized costs in carefully selected periods so as to avoid burdening other accounting periods with amortization charges.

As a consequence of the board's actions, comparability of financial reports among companies has been facilitated. But research and development costs must now be charged as an expense as if they were to benefit but a single accounting period. And the period in which they are to be charged off— that in which they are incurred—is that which is, in fact, least likely to benefit from the expenditures, since research and development costs are almost always future-, rather than present-oriented.

The approach of the board is inconsistent with the notion that costs should be matched to the revenues with which they are associated. It substitutes a precise accounting rule for the professional judgment of managers and accountants. It can hardly be viewed as an ideal solution to the accounting problems related to intangibles. But the board's approach does represent an attempt to ensure greater comparability of financial statements and to eliminate malfeasance of reporting on the part of at least a few corporations.

## Summary

Long-lived assets provide services over a number of accounting periods. Their cost, therefore, must be allocated over all of the periods benefited.

Long-lived assets are conventionally reported on the balance sheet at their original cost, less the amount assumed to have expired to date. The amount at which they are reported may, however, bear little relationship either to what it would cost to replace them or to their value to their specific users (the present value of the revenues that they will generate or the cost savings that they will effect).

The process of allocating the cost of a long-lived asset to the accounting periods which will benefit from its services is referred to as depreciation, depletion, or amortization. There are several basic methods of cost allocation. Among them are the straight-line method, various *accelerated* methods, and the units of output method.

Regardless of how a long-lived asset is accounted for—the method of allocation selected, the useful life estimated, or the means of recognizing changes in market value chosen—its impact on reported income over its useful life will be the same. The total cost of an asset—the amount to be charged as an expense—will be the price paid for the asset less the amount for which it can be sold at time of retirement. The manner in which an asset is accounted for may, however, have a significant effect on the earnings of each individual period in which it is used. As a consequence, the issues associated with long-lived assets are of critical concern both to the accounting profession and the financial community at large.

*exercise for review and self-testing*

Airline Freight acquires a new cargo plane. The company pays $3,000,000 cash and gives to the seller an old plane with a fair market value of $500,000. The company incurs additional costs of $6,000 to have the plane delivered to its home airfield and $94,000 to have it fitted with special equipment. The firm plans to keep the plane for 10 years; it estimates that it will be able to sell the cargo plane at the end of 10 years for $900,000.

a. At what amount should the plane be initially recorded?

b. What is the total dollar amount to be allocated as depreciation expense over the period during which the plane will be in service?

c. What should be the charge for depreciation for each of the 10 years of useful life if the firm were to use the straight-line method?

d. What should be the charge for depreciation for each of the first three years of useful life if the firm were to use the double-declining balance method?

e. Suppose that the firm used the double-declining balance method and that at the end of the sixth year of useful life the book value of the plane were $943,718—that is, depreciation of $2,656,282 had been charged to date. How much depreciation should the firm charge in the seventh year of service? How much in the eighth? Be sure your answers are consistent with your response to part b.

f. Suppose that after the third year of using the plane the company elected to trade in the old plane for a new one. The company paid $7,000,000 cash for the new plane and surrendered the old cargo plane. Immediately prior to the trade, the firm had received offers from parties who were willing to buy the plane outright. All were willing to pay approximately $1,500,000 cash. At the time of the trade, the old plane had a book value of $1,843,200 (initial cost less accumulated depreciation of $1,756,800) based on use of the double-declining balance method. How much gain or loss should the firm report on the transaction? At what amount should it record the new plane?

## Questions

**review and discussion**

1. "Because fixed assets are stated on the *balance sheet* at values that are based on historical costs, the *income statement* is of limited value in evaluating corporate performance." Do you agree? Explain.

2. What is the value of an asset to a particular user? Why is it seldom feasible to measure the value of a fixed asset to a particular user?

3. It is generally agreed that market values of fixed assets are more relevant for most decisions that must be made by both investors and managers. Why, then, do accountants persist in reporting historical values?

4. A stockholder recently charged that the financial statements of a corporation in which he owned shares were false and misleading in that included among fixed assets was computer equipment which the company leased from a financial institution but did not actually own. Assuming the assertion to be correct—that leased equipment was included among assets—how might the company respond to charges that the statements were false and misleading?

5. A company recently purchased for $350,000 a parcel of land and a building with the intention of razing the building and using the land as a parking lot for employees. The land had an appraised value of $300,000, and the building, $50,000. The company incurred costs of $10,000 to remove the building. The firm recorded the parking lot on its books at $360,000. Can such value be justified?

6. "The issue of whether or not interest costs incurred while fixed assets are under construction should be capitalized and added to the stated value of the asset is a trivial one. In the long run (over the life of the asset), the decision as to whether or not to capitalize interest will have no effect on the earnings of the firm." Do you agree?

7. The term *reserve* for depreciation is sometimes used instead of *accumulated* depreciation. Some businessmen point out that it is essential that firms, through the process of depreciation, make periodic additions to such reserve in order to make certain that they have the wherewithal to replace assets when they must be retired. Explain why (or why not) depreciation assures that a firm will have sufficient resources to acquire new assets as old ones wear out.

8. "Accelerated methods of depreciation are generally preferable to the straight-line method because most assets decline in market value more rapidly in the early years of their useful life than in later years." Do you agree?

9. A company incurred $1 million in advertising costs in 1980 for radio and television ads broadcast during the year. It elected to *capitalize* such costs

as an intangible asset and charge them off as expenses over a five-year period. Such practice is *not* in accord with generally accepted accounting principles. What arguments might the firm make, however, in defense of its practice? Why do you suppose that such practice is not generally accepted?

10. What is meant by *percentage depletion*? Why is it not a generally accepted accounting method, even though it is a means of accounting for natural resources that is recognized by the Internal Revenue Service?

## Problems

1. *Depreciation, regardless of the method used, is a means of allocating the cost of an asset over its productive life.*

   The Valentine Construction Corp. purchased a crane for $150,000. The company planned to keep it for approximately five years, after which time it believed it could sell the crane for $30,000.
   a. Determine depreciation under each of the following methods for the first four years that the crane is in service:
      1. straight-line.
      2. sum-of-the-years' digits.
      3. double-declining balance.
   b. At the start of the fifth year the company sold the crane for $60,000. Determine the gain under each of the three depreciation methods.
   c. Determine for each of the methods the net impact on earnings (total depreciation charges less gain) of using the crane for the four-year period.

2. *The useful life of one asset may depend upon that of another.*

   The James Co. purchases a small plant for $250,000. The plant has an estimated useful life of 25 years with no salvage value. Included in the plant is a boiler to provide heat and hot water. At the time of purchase the company is aware that the remaining useful life of the boiler is 15 years. The firm estimates the value of the boiler to be $25,000.
   a. Record the purchase of the plant.
   b. Record depreciation during the first year.
   c. At the end of 15 years the boiler requires replacement, and the firm purchases a new boiler for $40,000. The useful life of the new boiler is also estimated to be 15 years.
      (1) Record the replacement of the old boiler with the new.
      (2) Record depreciation during the sixteenth year.
      (3) Over how many years did you decide to depreciate the new boiler? What assumptions did you make?

3. *The method of depreciation selected should provide the best possible match of costs to revenues.*

   The Strip Mining Co. decides to remove coal from a deposit on property it already owns. The company purchases for cash mining equipment at a cost of $850,000 and constructs a building on the site at a cost of $90,000.

The equipment has a useful life of 10 years, an estimated salvage value of $50,000 and can readily be moved to other mining locations. The building has a potential useful life of 12 years but would have to be abandoned when the company ceases operations at the site.

The mine contains approximately 1 million tons of coal, and the company plans to remove it over a four-year period according to the following schedule:

| Year 1 | 400,000 tons |
| 2 | 250,000 tons |
| 3 | 250,000 tons |
| 4 | 100,000 tons |

The property will be abandoned at the end of the fourth year.

a. Record the purchase of the equipment and the construction of the building.

b. Compute depreciation charges for the first year on both the building and equipment. Justify in one or two sentences your choice of depreciation method(s) and lives.

4. *Trade-in transactions must be accounted for in a manner that reflects economic substance rather than form.*

In January 1978 the Jarvis Co. purchased a copy machine for $6,000. The machine had an estimated useful life of eight years and an estimated salvage value of $500. The firm used the double-declining balance method to record depreciation.

In December 1980 the company decided to trade in the machine for a newer model. The new model had a *list* price of $12,000, but it is common in the industry for purchasers to be given a 15 to 20 percent trade discount off of list price. The manufacturer offered the company a trade-in allowance of $4,000 on its old machine. The company accepted the offer since it was considerably above the several offers of approximately $2,000 that the firm had received from other parties interested in purchasing the machine. The company paid $8,000 in addition to giving up the old machine.

Record the trade-in of the old machine and the purchase of the new. Assume that depreciation had already been recorded for 1980.

5. *Costs incurred at the end of an asset's useful life may be associated with revenues of previous accounting periods.*

National Auto Company has agreed to participate as a major exhibitor at the North American Trade Fair. The company constructs and furnishes its exhibit hall at a cost of $8 million. The fair will last for three years, after which National Auto will be required to remove its building from the fair grounds. National estimates that removal costs will be approximately $100,000 but that the building materials and the exhibits can be sold for $300,000.

a. Record the exhibit hall on the books of National Auto. Assume all payments were made in cash.

b. Calculate first-year depreciation using the straight-line method.

c. Record the removal of the exhibit hall at the completion of the fair. Assume that removal costs were as estimated.

d. Suppose instead that removal costs would be approximately $700,000 and that the building materials and exhibits could be sold for $300,000. Prepare journal entries to record the exhibit hall, to account for the hall during the three-year period, and to remove it from the books after the three-year period. Over how many periods should the removal costs (net of the amount to be salvaged) be charged as an expense?

6. *Changes in estimated useful life and residual value can have a profound impact upon reported earnings.*

The 1976 financial report of American Airlines, Inc. contains the following note:

> During 1975, American, in addition to expanding its Boeing 727 fleet, commenced various life improvement programs on its existing Boeing 727 aircraft. In recognition of the continued use and improvement of these aircraft, effective January 1, 1975 American extended the estimated useful lives of these aircraft from 12 to 16 years and reduced estimated residual values from 15% to 10% of cost.

Suppose that within the next several years American Airlines expects to acquire new Boeing 727 aircraft at a cost of $1 billion. The firm uses the straight-line method of depreciation. By how much would the change described cause annual depreciation charges on the new aircraft to decrease?

7. *Periodic maintenance costs that benefit more than one accounting period may be accounted for in at least two different ways.*

Treetop Airlines conducts maintenance overhauls on all aircraft engines every three years. The cost of each overhaul is approximately $12,000. The company owns 24 engines. In 1978 the company overhauled 10 engines, in 1979, 8 engines, and, in 1980, 6 engines.

a. How much expense should the company report in 1980 in connection with engine overhauls?

b. The financial report of Braniff Airlines indicates that "expenditures for maintenance overhauls of aircraft engines and airframes are charged to expense as incurred." Is the policy of Braniff consistent with your response in (a)? If it is, can you think of and justify an alternative policy that might as well be acceptable or even preferable? If it is not, then defend your response.

c. Suppose instead that it was the company practice to overhaul 8 engines each year. Would it matter, as far as reported expense is concerned, which accounting procedure the company used?

8. *Firms in some industries must adapt generally accepted accounting principles to their special needs.*

The statements that follow were drawn from footnotes to the financial reports of U.S. corporations. Each indicates that the company records a particular financial event in a nonconventional manner. For each statement compare the described practice with the conventional practice and indicate whether (and under what circumstances) the described practice would result in higher or lower reported earnings and balance sheet values than the conventional practice.

1. *Eastern Air Lines, Inc., December 31, 1976.* "The company capitalizes interest on advances for new flight equipment. Capitalization of interest ceases when the equipment is delivered and is depreciated over the life of the related equipment."

2. *Chessie System, Inc., December 31, 1976.* "As prescribed by the Interstate Commerce Commission, certain items of road property (principally rails and ties) are not depreciated but are accounted for under an alternative generally accepted accounting method whereby replacements are charged to expense and only additions and betterments are capitalized."

3. *Yellow Freight System, Inc., December 31, 1976.* "The cost of tires, including those purchased with new equipment, is amortized over the estimated tire lives. The unamortized balance of the cost is included in prepayments."

9. *Depreciation and depletion costs, like those of labor and materials, may be considered production, rather than period, costs if they can be associated directly with the minerals recovered.*

Wildcat Minerals, Inc. was incorporated in 1980 for the specific purpose of mining a tract of land. The company acquired the tract at a cost of $6.2 million. It estimated that the tract contained 700,000 tons of ore and that after the property was completely mined (in approximately four years) it could be sold as farm land for $600,000.

The company built various buildings and structures at a cost of $1.4 million. Such improvements have a useful life of 15 years but have utility only when used at the specific mining site; they cannot be economically moved to other locations. In addition, the company purchased other equipment at a cost of $400,000. Such equipment has a useful life of five years and an estimated salvage value of $50,000.

In 1980 the company incurred labor and other production costs of $357,000 and selling and administrative costs of $224,000. It paid taxes of $105,000.

The company mined 100,000 tons and sold 80,000 tons of ore. The selling price per ton was $19.

The company elected to charge depreciation on a unit of output basis.

a. Determine total depreciation and depletion costs for 1980.
b. Determine the cost per ton of ore sold.
c. Determine net income.
d. Determine the ending inventory.

10. *Alternative accounting practices in the oil industry may result in substantial differences in reported earnings.*

Panhandle, Inc. in 1979 drilled three exploratory oil wells at a cost of $300,000 each. Of the three, only one proved successful. The company estimates that the property on which the successful well is located will provide a cash inflow of $600,000 per year, after taking into account recovery costs, royalties, and other cash outlays for each of the next 10 years, including 1979.

  a. Determine earnings for 1979 assuming that the firm uses

    1. the "full-cost" method.

    2. the "successful efforts" method (that favored by the FASB).

  b. Assume that the firm uses the successful efforts method. It does not own the property on which it discovered oil; instead it pays a per barrel royalty to its owner.

    (1) At what value should the oil reserves (including the capitalized drilling costs) be reported on the balance sheet as of the end of 1979?

    (2) Do you think that such value fully and fairly reflects the value of the asset? What supplementary disclosures would you recommend?

11. *It is often unclear as to whether certain types of costs are necessary to bring an asset to a serviceable condition.*

On January 2, National General Corporation purchased for $10,000 an *option* on a tract of land on which it hoped to construct a plant. The option gave the company the right to purchase the land itself within a given time period and for a fixed price—in this case within 10 months and for $2 million. If the company decided to exercise its option, it would pay the seller an additional $2 million and receive title to the land. If it decided not to purchase the land, then it would allow the option to lapse and would be unable to recover the $10,000. The option arrangement allows the company additional time to decide whether to make the purchase and at the same time compensates the seller for giving the company the exclusive right to purchase the property.

  a. On July 2, National General decided to purchase the tract of land for $2 million. Prepare journal entries to record both the purchase of the option and the subsequent purchase of the land. Should the cost of the option be added to the cost of the land?

  b. Suppose instead that on January 2 National General purchased three options—each for $10,000—on three tracts of land. The company expected to purchase and build on only one of the three tracts; however, it wanted to locate its new plant by the side of a proposed highway, and the exact route of the highway had not yet been announced. The company purchased the three options in order to assure itself that the plant could be built adjacent to the road, regardless of which of three routes under consideration was selected for the highway. On July 2, the company exercised its option on one of the three tracts and purchased the land for $2 million. It allowed the other two options to lapse. Prepare journal entries to record the purchase of the three options, the purchase of the land, and the expiration of two of the options. Consider carefully whether the cost of all three options should be included as part of the cost of the land. Present arguments both for and against including the expired options as part of the cost of the land.

12. *Tax laws, as they affect depreciation, may encourage firms to sell assets long before the expiration of their useful lives.*

Commuter Airlines, Inc. was established in 1979. The firm issued common stock for $12 million and used the funds to purchase six small passenger jets at a total cost of $12 million. The firm plans to use the planes for 10 years, after which it believes they can be sold for a total of $2 million.

a. Compute depreciation for the first three years under each of the following methods:
   1. straight-line.
   2. sum-of-the-years' digits.
   3. double-declining balance.

b. Assume that income before depreciation and taxes during each of the first three years is $3 million. Compute income taxes for those years if the tax rate is 40 percent. Which method results in the least tax burden in the early years of asset life?

c. Suppose that at the end of the second year the planes are sold for $10 million. The remaining useful life of the assets is eight years. If the new owner elected to charge depreciation for tax purposes using the double-declining balance method, what would be the first-year deduction for depreciation? Compare such deduction to that which would be permitted Commuter Airlines if it used the double-declining method. Why might it be said that the asset is "worth" more to the new owner than to the previous one?

13. *Seemingly arcane issues of accounting have a direct relationship to consumer utility bills.*

In 1980, Northern Electric and Gas signed a contract to construct a new plant. The total contract price was $50 million. The plant took two years to construct. Since the company had to make periodic payments to the contractor, it was forced to borrow a considerable amount of funds. Total interest costs incurred during the period of construction were $2 million. The useful life of the plant is estimated to be 40 years with no salvage value.

The rates that Northern Electric and Gas is permitted to charge customers are fixed by a state utility commission. The commission in the state in which Northern Electric and Gas is located has a policy of establishing rates so that the company will be allowed to realize a return on assets, before taxes, of 12 percent per year. That is, the rates will be established so as to permit the company to generate annual revenues in an amount such that revenues less expenses will be equal to 12 percent of the cost of the plant.

The company estimates that once it begins operations, operating expenses, in addition to depreciation, will be $8 million per year.

A major issue among accountants is whether interest costs related to the construction of assets should be *capitalized* (added to the cost of the assets constructed).

a. Determine annual depreciation charges, on a straight-line basis, that the company would incur if it capitalized interest costs and those that it would incur if it did not. If the company did not capitalize interest, then it would charge the interest as an expense incurred during the period of construction.

b. Determine the income that the utility commission would permit the company to earn if interest were capitalized as opposed to that if it were not.

c. Determine total revenues that the firm must be permitted to generate if it were to earn the income calculated in part b.

d. Comment on what you would expect to be the attitude of public utility executives toward capitalization of interest.

14. *The impact on earnings of both alternative depreciation practices and errors may depend upon a firm's trend of growth.*

Collins Manufacturing Corporation, established in 1960, uses 18 lathes, each of which costs $10,000 and has a useful life of three years (with no salvage value). Each year the company retires 6 machines and replaces them with 6 others.

a. Compute total depreciation charges on the 18 lathes for the three-year period 1974, 1975, and 1976 using
1. the straight-line method.
2. the sum-of-the-years' digits method.

b. Suppose the company used an incorrect useful life in calculating depreciation charges. Even though it replaced the machines after a three-year period, it charged depreciation over a two-year period. It made no adjustment in the accounts for the "error"; it simply charged zero depreciation in the machines' third year. Compute depreciation using the straight-line method for the same three-year period.

c. In 1977 the company undertook an expansion program. In each of the next three years (1977, 1978, and 1979) the company purchased 7 machines and retired 6. Thus, in 1977, 1978, and 1979 the firm had in operation 19, 20, and 21 machines, respectively. Compute depreciation charges for the three-year period using
1. the straight-line method.
2. the sum-of-the-years' digits method.

d. Assume again that the firm used an incorrect useful life and depreciated the machines over a two-year period instead of three. Compute depreciation charges for the three-year period using the straight-line method.

e. What conclusions can you draw regarding the impact of choice of depreciation method and estimate of useful life on the income of a firm that is expanding its asset base as opposed to one that is maintaining it at a constant level?

15. *Complete journal entries can be reconstructed from limited amounts of data; annual reports sometimes contain misleading assertions.*

The following information relating to plant, warehouse, and terminal elevator equipment was taken from the 10-K report of General Mills, Inc. for the fiscal year ended May 29, 1977 (in thousands):

Equipment:

| | |
|---|---|
| Balance at beginning of period | $346,838 |
| Additions and miscellaneous adjustments | 70,305 |
| Balance at end of period | 384,406 |

| | |
|---|---|
| Equipment, accumulated depreciation: | |
| Balance at beginning of period | 173,964 |
| Depreciation expense and miscellaneous | |
| adjustments | 32,267 |
| Balance at end of period | 186,668 |

a. Based on the data provided, plus any other amounts that it may be necessary to derive from the data provided, prepare a journal entry that summarizes the retirement of equipment during the period. Assume that the equipment was sold for $10,000.

b. In a discussion of replacement cost information the report contains the following comment: "While inflation's annual impact on replacement of existing productive capacity is minimal because of the long time span over which replacements occur, its long-run result is that accumulated depreciation is insufficient to replace fully depreciated productive capacity."

(1) Prepare a journal entry that summarizes depreciation expense for the period.

(2) Is it the purpose of depreciation accounting to provide for the replacement of equipment? In what way, if any, does the entry you proposed enable the company to accumulate funds for replacement?

16. *Revaluation of assets to reflect changes in market values would affect not only their recorded values, but also the allocation of earnings among the years that the assets were in service.*

The Rhinegold Chemical Co. constructed a new plant at a cost of $20 million. The plant had an estimated useful life of 20 years, with no salvage value. After it had used the plant for 4 years, the replacement cost of the plant had increased to $24 million. The company decided to recognize in its accounts the increase in the fair market value of the asset. (Such practice is not, of course, in accord with currently acceptable accounting principles.)

a. Prepare the journal entry to record depreciation for each of the first four years.

b. Prepare an entry to record the revaluation of the plant.

c. Prepare an entry to record depreciation in the fifth year, the first year subsequent to the revaluation.

d. At the *start* of the eighth year the company accepted an offer to sell the plant for $19 million. Prepare an entry to record the sale.

e. Suppose the company had not readjusted its accounts after the fourth year to recognize the increase in market value. How much gain would it have recognized upon sale of the plant? Compare total depreciation expense and total gains recognized if the company recognized the increase in market value with those that would have resulted if it adhered to conventional practice and did not recognize the increase.

17. *Replacement cost data must be accepted with caution.*

The 1977 annual report of the Koppers Company (which is used as an illustration in Chapter 2) indicates that the replacement cost of its productive capacity (machinery, buildings, and equipment) is (in thousands) $1,241,000. The same capacity had cost the company $601,944 to acquire. Depreciation of $289,067 had been accumulated to date; this amount includes 1977 depreciation expense of $40,136.

1. Assume that the useful lives of the productive capacity remain unchanged and that the estimated salvage value of the productive assets increased by the same ratio that the replacement cost of the equipment bears to the historical cost.

   a. How much depreciation expense would the company have recorded for 1977 had it based the charge on current replacement costs?

   b. What would be the net replacement book value (replacement cost less accumulated depreciation) of its productive capacity?

2. The company warns in its report that the replacement cost information "is not precise and does not give a complete or balanced presentation of the impact of inflation. It does not necessarily reflect management's intent to replace existing inventory or productive facilities." The company further cautions "that the above replacement cost data are not the value of existing property, plant and equipment. Rather, they represent the Company's estimates of the costs of replacement that would have been incurred at December 31, 1977 under the hypothetical assumption that such asset had been replaced in total at that time."

   Would you characterize the replacement cost data presented as representing an "input" or "output" market value? What is the difference between the two (see Chapter 6)?

18. *Conventional practices of depreciation do not adequately satisfy the information requirements of municipalities.*

    In January 1979 the village of Rahavia acquired a new sanitation truck at a cost of $50,000. The useful life of the truck is estimated to be five years, with no salvage value anticipated. Officials of the village have budgeted $350,000 in additional expenditures for 1979. All such expenditures require the direct outlay of cash.

    State law requires that the village operate on a "balanced budget"; taxes and other revenues must be sufficiently large to cover expenses.

    1. Assume that the village elects to record depreciation on the new truck on a straight-line basis.

       a. What would be total reported expenses for 1979? What would be total required revenues?

       b. What would be total required *cash* outlays for 1979? Would the revenues as determined in part a be sufficient to cover required cash outlays?

       c. Comment on why traditional depreciation practices may be inappropriate for the types of decisions made by municipal budget officers.

    2. In fact, generally accepted accounting principles as they apply to municipalities do not require that depreciation be charged on certain types of assets. Instead, the full cost of such assets is charged as expense at the time that they are paid for and the full amount of any sums received when an asset is retired or sold is recognized as revenue. Suppose that

at the end of 1980 the village of Rahavia sold its truck for $30,000. Other expenditures were again $350,000.

a. Determine total reported expenses and the required amount of revenues, in addition to that from the sale of the truck, for both 1979 and 1980.

b. A new mayor assumed office in 1980. He asserted that, inasmuch as both reported expenditures and required additional revenues were lower in 1980 than in 1979, the village had been operated more efficiently in 1980 than in 1979. Do you agree? Comment on the usefulness in evaluating managerial performance of financial statements based on the special accounting principles applicable to municipalities.

3. Comment on the limitations of a single set of accounting practices in achieving a multiplicity of accounting objectives.

19. *Ownership arrangements that are very different in form may be very similar in economic substance.*

Deception, Inc. currently has a loan outstanding from the Gibraltar Insurance Co. that requires that Deception, Inc. maintain a *debt/equity ratio* no greater than 1:1. That is, the balance in all liability accounts can be no greater than that in the capital stock and retained earnings accounts. As of December 31, 1980, Deception, Inc. had total liabilities of $3 million and total capital stock and retained earnings of $3,150,000.

The vice-president of production of Deception, Inc. has proposed that the company purchase new equipment that would cost $257,710. The equipment would have a three-year useful life and no salvage value and during its life would result in substantial cost savings to the company. Aware that the company is short of cash, the vice-president arranged with the manufacturer of the equipment to give a three-year note for the purchase price. Interest would be at the rate of 8 percent on the unpaid balance. Payments would be made at the end of each of the three years as follows:

| | *Remaining Balance* | *Payment of Interest at 8%* | *Payment of Principal* | *Total Payment* |
|---|---|---|---|---|
| 1 | $257,710 | $20,617 | $ 79,383 | $100,000 |
| 2 | 178,327 | 14,266 | 85,734 | 100,000 |
| 3 | 92,593 | 7,407 | 92,593 | 100,000 |
| | | | $257,710 | |

The controller of Deception, Inc. rejected the proposal on the grounds that if the company incurred a liability of $257,710, it would be in violation of its loan agreement with Gibraltar.

After considerable thought and discussions with the manufacturer of the equipment, the vice-president of production returned to the controller with an alternative proposition. The manufacturer agreed to lease the equipment to Deception, Inc. for a three-year period. Annual rent would be $100,000, but Deception, Inc. would have to pay all maintenance and insurance costs. At the expiration of the lease, Deception, Inc. would have an option to purchase the machine for $1.

a. Prepare all journal entries that would be required on the books of Deception, Inc. if it agreed to *purchase* the machine and issued the note for $257,710. The company records depreciation on a straight-line basis.

b. Prepare all journal entries that would be required if the firm agreed to lease the machine.

c. What are the total charges associated with the acquisition of the machine under each of the two alternatives?

d. Comment on the difference, if any, in the *substance* of the two transactions. Viewing the transactions from the point of view of Gibraltar Insurance Co., how would you propose that the firm record the transaction if it decided to *lease* the equipment?

20. *Although not discussed in the text, increasing charge (as opposed to decreasing or accelerated charge) methods may also be used to calculate periodic depreciation charges.*

Machine Rentals, Inc. is considering purchasing a new computer that it will be able to rent to a customer for $10,000 per year starting January 1, 1980. The machine has a useful life of four years and no salvage value. The company expects a rate of return of 6 percent on all its assets.

a. What is the maximum amount the firm would be willing to pay for the machine? That is, what is the present value, discounted at a rate of 6 percent, of anticipated future cash receipts?

b. What is the present value of anticipated cash receipts at the end of each of the four years?

c. Suppose that the firm were able to purchase the machine for the amount computed in a. It elects to charge depreciation on the basis of what the machine is worth to the company (the present value of anticipated cash receipts) at the end of a year as compared to what it was worth at the beginning. How much depreciation should it charge during each of the four years? Determine total depreciation charges for the four year period.

d. Comment on the trend of charges by this method of depreciation as compared to other methods. This method is not widely used in practice, but is regarded with favor by many theoreticians. How can it be justified?

*solutions to exercise for review and self-testing*

a. The amount at which the plane should be recorded must include the fair market value of all consideration (cash and property) paid to bring the asset to a usable condition. In this case, all amounts indicated ($3,000,000 cash payment plus $500,000 old plane plus $6,000 delivery charges plus $94,000 furnishing costs) must be "capitalized" as part of the asset—a total of $3,600,000.

b. The total cost of using the plane for 10 years—the amount to be allocated— is the initial amount recorded ($3,600,000) less the anticipated residual value ($900,000)—$2,700,000.

c. If the straight-line method were used, annual depreciation charges would be $2,700,000 divided by 10, or $270,000 per year.

d. The straight-line rate of depreciation is 10 percent; twice that is 20 percent. This rate would be applied each year to the then book value (cost less accumulated depreciation) *without* regard to residual value (except as suggested in e of this exercise). Thus,

| Year | Book Value, Start of Year | Depreciation Rate | Depreciation Charge | Book Value, End of Year |
|------|---------------------------|-------------------|---------------------|-------------------------|
| 1 | $3,600,000 | 20% | $720,000 | $2,880,000 |
| 2 | 2,880,000 | 20 | 576,000 | 2,304,000 |
| 3 | 2,304,000 | 20 | 460,800 | 1,843,200 |

e. Depreciation must never be charged so as to reduce the remaining book value below expected salvage value—in this case $900,000. In the seventh year of service, therefore, the firm would charge only $43,718 of depreciation ($943,718 less $900,000); in the eighth year, zero.

f. In economic substance the firm sold an asset with a book value of $1,843,200 for $1,500,000—the apparent fair market value of the old plane. Hence, it should report a loss of $343,200. The new plane should be recorded at an amount representative of the fair market value of the consideration paid— $7,000,000 cash plus $1,500,000 the fair market value of the plane surrendered, a total of $8,500,000.

# 10

# Liabilities
# and Related Expenses

In the preceding four chapters we addressed primarily questions of valuing assets and of reporting the related revenues and expenses. This chapter will be directed to the equally important and controversial issues of valuing liabilities and of measuring their impact upon earnings of the firm.

## Bonds

Corporations, we well as governmental units and nonprofit organizations, borrow funds to finance *long-term* projects, such as plant and equipment and major public works projects. Conventionally, borrowers provide the lender evidence of their obligations to repay the funds as well as to make periodic interest payments by issuing notes or bonds. A bond is a more formal certificate of indebtedness than a note. Characteristically bonds are almost always evidence of long-term indebtedness (five years or more), while notes may be issued in connection with short- or long-term borrowings.

Corporate bonds are most commonly issued in denominations of $1,000. The *par* or *face* value of a bond indicates the *principal* amount due at the *maturity* or due date of the bond. Bonds ordinarily carry a stated annual rate of interest, expressed as a percentage of the principal. Most bond *indentures* (agreements which set forth the legal provisions of the bonds) require that interest be paid semiannually. Thus, a corporation which has issued $1,000-denomination bonds that specify an annual rate of interest of 6 percent would pay the holder of a single bond $30 on each of two interest dates six months apart.

Most corporate bonds are *coupon* bonds. Each bond contains a series of coupons which may be clipped and redeemed at six-month intervals for the interest due. Coupon bonds are distinguished from *registered* bonds in that on the latter interest is paid not to the bearer of the coupon but only to a specific party whose name is registered with the borrower.

Corporate bonds may be secured (collateralized) by property, such as a plant, or land. Or they may be unsecured, with the lender relying primarily upon the good faith and financial integrity of the borrower for repayment. Secured bonds may be categorized by the type of legal instrument used to provide the lien on the property that is pledged—e.g., mortgage bonds and equipment trust bonds. Unsecured bonds are commonly called *debentures*.

Virtually all corporate bonds indicate a specific maturity date. However, many corporate issues provide for the early retirement of the debt at the option of the *borrower* (the corporation). Such a *call provision* ordinarily requires the company to pay the lender (the bond holder) a *call premium,* an amount in addition to the par value of the bond, as a penalty for depriving the lender of his "right" to interest payments for the original term of the loan.

Bonds are generally freely negotiable—they can be bought and sold in the open market subsequent to original issue. An active market for corporate bonds is maintained by both the New York and American Stock Exchanges. A lender who no longer wishes to have his funds tied up in a loan to the issuer of a bond can sell his bond to an investor who is seeking the type of return provided by that type of bond. The price at which the bond is sold need not be that for which the bond was initially issued. Rather, it would be determined in large measure by interest rates prevalent at time of sale.

### The Nature of Bonds

Bonds provide for interest payments of a fixed amount. Ordinarily the more financially sound the lender, the lower will be the rate of interest. Yet interest rates for securities *within* the same category of risk are determined by the forces of supply and demand—the amount of funds being sought by borrowers, the amount being made available by lenders. Rates of interest that prevail throughout the country fluctuate from day to day and even from hour to hour. Although corporations conventionally set the coupon rate of interest —the amount that will be paid to the lender each interest period—and print it in the bond indentures several weeks prior to the date on which they are to be issued, the actual interest rate is determined at time of sale. The actual interest rate, often referred to as the *yield rate,* is established, not by changing the coupon rate, but rather by adjusting the price at which the bond is sold. Suppose, for example, that a $1,000 bond has a coupon rate of 8 percent—that is, the holder of the bond will be entitled to two payments of $40 each year. At the time of sale, however, the prevailing interest rate for that type of bond is 8¼ percent. Would a purchaser be willing to pay $1,000 for such a bond? Obviously not. He could lend his money to another similar company and receive $82.50 per year rather than $80. Therefore, he would be willing to pay something less than $1,000 for the bond. How much less will be considered in the next section. Similarly if the prevailing interest rate were lower than 8 percent—7½ percent, for example—a rational buyer would be willing to pay more than $1,000 for the bond. If he were to purchase the bonds of similar companies, he would receive only $75 per year in interest. He would be willing to pay something above $1,000 in order to receive a return of $80 per year. If a purchaser pays less than the face amount for a bond, then the difference between the face amount and what he actually pays is referred to as a bond *discount.* If he pays more than the face amount, then the additional payment is referred to as a *premium.*

A rational purchaser would undertake a similar analysis in deciding how much to pay for a bond that had been issued several years earlier, one to be purchased not from the issuing company directly but rather from the current holder of the bond. To the extent that prevailing interest rates are greater than the coupon rate of the bond, he would be willing to pay *less* than the face value of the bond, for he could receive the prevailing rate by purchasing a different bond on which the coupon rate is equal to the prevailing rate. To the extent that prevailing rates are less than the coupon rate, he would be willing to pay more, since the semiannual interest payments would be greater than what he could obtain elsewhere.

### Determination of Discount or Premium *

Determination of the amount that a rational purchaser would pay for a bond requires an understanding of the promises inherent in the bond agreement. A somewhat simplified and exaggerated example can be used to illustrate a logical approach to calculating the amount to be paid for a particular bond.

Suppose that on a particular day a corporation seeks bids on two bond issues. Bond A bears a coupon rate of 6 percent and bond B a coupon rate of 4 percent. Both bonds will mature in two years. Both pay interest semiannually. The prevailing annual rate of interest is 6 percent.

Both bonds contain a promise to pay the purchaser $1,000 upon maturity after two years—four semiannual periods hence. The present value of a single cash payment four semiannual periods away given an interest rate of 3 percent is, per Table 2 in the Appendix, $1,000 × .8885–$888.50. The 3 percent rate is one-half the annual rate of 6 percent; it reflects the semi-annual rather than the annual payment of interest. The 6 percent rate is the *prevailing* rate for bonds of that type, not necessarily the coupon rate on either of the two bonds in question. It is the rate that is relevant to the prospective purchaser since it is that which he could receive if he were to turn to alternative investment possibilities of comparable risk.

Bond A also promises four semiannual payments of $30. The present value of four semiannual payments, discounted at 3 percent per period (one-half the *prevailing* annual rate), is, per Table 4, $30 × 3.7171–$111.50. The total present value of the two promises—the promise to pay principal of $1,000 plus the promise to make semiannual interest payments—discounted at the prevailing rate of 3 percent per semiannual period is $1,000 ($888.50 plus $111.50). The rational buyer would be willing to pay $1,000—in this instance, the face value—for the bond.

*The reader is strongly urged to review the material on compound interest and present value contained in Chapter 6.

Bond B, on the other hand, promises four semiannual payments of only $20, since the coupon rate is 4 percent per year. The present value of four semiannual payments of $20, discounted at 3 percent is, again per Table 4, $20 × 3.7171—$74.34. The rate of 3 percent is one-half the *prevailing* rate of 6 percent. The *prevailing rate is the one that must be used to evaluate an investment opportunity*, since it (rather than the coupon rate) is indicative of the return that the investor can expect to receive. The present value of the two promises combined is, therefore, $888.50 plus $74.34—$962.84. A rational purchaser would be willing to pay only $962.84 for the bond with a face value of $1,000 and a coupon rate of 4 percent. The discount of $37.16 would assure him a *yield* of 6 percent per year, even though the coupon rate is only 4 percent per year. The analysis can be summarized as follows:

|  | Bond A<br>(6% coupon) | Bond B<br>(4% coupon) |
|---|---|---|
| Present value of $1,000 to be received at the end of 4 periods, discounted at prevailing rate of 3% ($1,000 × .8885 per Table 2) | $ 888.50 | $888.50 |
| Present value of $30 to be received at the end of each of 4 periods, discounted at prevailing rate of 3% ($30 × 3.7171 per Table 4) | 111.50 | |
| Present value of $20 to be received at the end of each of 4 periods, discounted at prevailing rate of 3% ($20 × 3.7171 per Table 4) | | 74.34 |
| Present value of bond | $1,000.00 | $962.84 |

Diagrammatically, the two bonds can be depicted as in Exhibit 10-1. Both bonds are evaluated at a rate of 3 percent per period—the prevailing yield on comparable securities. It is assumed that the bonds were sold on January 1, 1980. All discount factors are per Table 2. Bond A would sell at face value because its coupon rate is identical to the yield rate. Anytime there is a difference between the coupon and the yield rates, the bonds would be sold at an amount other than face value.

The discount of $37.16 on bond B can be viewed from a slightly different perspective. If a purchaser can obtain a yield of 6 percent per year elsewhere, then from a $1,000 bond he expects interest payments of $30 every six months. In fact, bond B will pay him only $20 per six months. He is "losing" $10 per period. The present value of $10 lost for four periods, discounted at a rate of 3 percent per period (one-half the prevailing yield of 6 percent), is, per Table 4, $10 × $3.7171—$37.16.

EXHIBIT 10-1

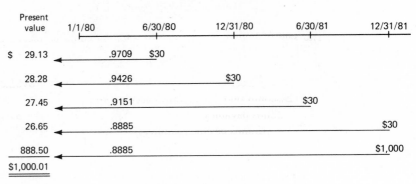

**Bond A**
**6% Coupon; 6% Yield**

| Present value | 1/1/80 | 6/30/80 | 12/31/80 | 6/30/81 | 12/31/81 |
|---|---|---|---|---|---|
| $ 29.13 | | .9709 $30 | | | |
| 28.28 | | .9426 | $30 | | |
| 27.45 | | .9151 | | $30 | |
| 26.65 | | .8885 | | | $30 |
| 888.50 | | .8885 | | | $1,000 |
| $1,000.01 | | | | | |

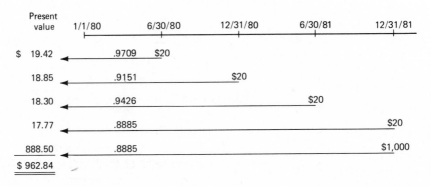

**Bond B**
**4% Coupon; 6% Yield**

| Present value | 1/1/80 | 6/30/80 | 12/31/80 | 6/30/81 | 12/31/81 |
|---|---|---|---|---|---|
| $ 19.42 | | .9709 $20 | | | |
| 18.85 | | .9151 | $20 | | |
| 18.30 | | .9426 | | $20 | |
| 17.77 | | .8885 | | | $20 |
| 888.50 | | .8885 | | | $1,000 |
| $ 962.84 | | | | | |

Computation of the bond premium or discount can be facilitated by asking four simple questions:

1. How much interest per period (based on the *coupon rate*) is a purchaser of the bond actually going to receive?
2. How much interest (based on the prevailing *yield* of comparable securities) would he expect to receive?
3. What is the difference between the two amounts?
4. What is the present value, discounted at the prevailing *yield rate*, of such difference?

The present value of the difference between the amounts a purchaser would expect to receive and what he will actually receive represents either premium or discount.

## Recording the Sale of Bonds

The sale of bond B for a price of $962.84 could be recorded by the following journal entry:

| | | |
|---|---:|---:|
| Cash (asset) | $962.84 | |
| Discount on bonds (contra account to | | |
|   bonds payable) | 37.16 | |
|     Bonds payable (liability) | | $1,000 |
| **To record issuance of the bond.** | | |

If financial statements were to be prepared immediately after the sale, the liability would be reported as follows:

| | | |
|---|---:|---:|
| Bonds payable | $1,000.00 | |
| Less: Discount | 37.16 | $962.84 |

As a consequence the *net* liability to be reported would be only $962.84, not the $1,000 face value of the bond.

## Nature of Premium or Discount

The net liability of the company at the time of sale is only $962.84. That is the amount of cash actually received. It may be argued that the company will have to repay $1,000, the face value of the bond, and that that amount, therefore, is the liability to be reported. The company will, of course, have to pay $1,000 at time of maturity. But if it only borrowed $962.84, then the "extra" $37.16 must represent interest, in addition to the semiannual coupon payments, to be paid to the lender. The additional $37.16 has the effect of increasing the rate of interest paid by the company from 4 percent to 6 percent. Interest is not ordinarily reported as a liability and recorded as an expense until the borrower has had use of the funds for an appropriate period of time. Just as the liability for each of the periodic coupon payments of $20 will not be recorded until the interest has been earned, neither should the liability for the additional interest of $37.16 to be paid upon maturity of the bond. Instead, it should be added to the liability account over the remaining life of the bond issue—as the firm has use of the funds borrowed.* Similarly, if the bonds were

---

*It could, of course, be argued that the company has a legal liability for the full $1,000. Should the company go bankrupt, however, soon after the sale of the bonds, it would be highly unusual for a bankruptcy court to award the full $1,000 to a bondholder who recently had loaned the company only $962.84.

sold at a premium, at a price of $1,020, for example, then the amount borrowed by the company is the amount actually received, $1,020. The company will, of course, have to repay only $1,000. The $20 represents a reduction, over the life of the issue, of the firm's borrowing costs and should be accounted for as such.

## Recording the Payment of Interest

As a consequence of the price adjustments attributable to the premium or discount at which the bonds were sold, the effective rate of interest to be paid by the company is that established not by the coupon rate but rather by the *yield rate (the effective rate at time of issue).* The reported interest expense should be based on such yield rate.

In the previous example, the company borrowed $962.84 at an effective interest rate of 6 percent (3 percent per interest period). Each interest date, however, it must pay the bondholder only $20. On the first interest date, its effective interest expense is 3 percent of $962.84—$28.88, an amount that is $8.88 greater than the actual payment of $20 to be made to the bondholder. The $8.88 represents the first interest period's share of the $37.16 in additional interest to be paid upon the maturity of the loan. It is, therefore, the amount of the discount that must be amortized and charged as additional interest expense in the first period. The following journal entry would reflect this interpretation of the bond discount:

| | | |
|---|---|---|
| Interest expense | $28.88 | |
| Cash | | $20.00 |
| Discount on bonds | | 8.88 |
| **To record payment of interest.** | | |

As a result of this entry, the unamortized portion of the bond discount has been reduced from $37.16 to $28.28. The bond would be reported in the liability section of the balance sheet as follows:

| | | |
|---|---|---|
| Bonds payable | $1,000.00 | |
| Less: Discount | 28.28 | $971.72 |

The effective liability of the company has increased from $962.84 to $971.72 because the company now owes not only the original amount borrowed ($962.84) but also a portion of the interest which the bondholder has earned during the first interest period. The additional interest now owed is equal to the effective interest for the period ($28.88) less the amount actually paid ($20.00).

At the end of the second interest period, the interest expense would again be based on the effective interest or yield rate that prevailed at the time the bond was issued. But now the effective liability is not $962.84 as at the end of the first period but rather $971.72, an amount reflective of the amortization of a portion of the original discount. Hence, the effective interest expense is 3 percent of $971.72—$29.15. As in the first period, the actual payment to the bondholder would be only $20.00. The difference between the two represents the portion of interest earned by the bondholder but not yet paid to him—the amount that must be subtracted from the bond discount and thereby added to the effective liability. The following journal entry would be required on the second interest date:

| | | |
|---|---|---|
| Interest expense | $29.15 | |
| Cash | | $20.00 |
| Discount on bonds | | 9.15 |
| **To record payment of interest.** | | |

As a result of this entry, the unamortized portion of the bond discount has been reduced from $28.28 to $19.13. After the second payment of interest the bond would be reported as follows:

| | | |
|---|---|---|
| Bonds payable | $1,000.00 | |
| Less: Discount | 19.13 | $980.87 |

A history of the bond is summarized in Exhibit 10-2.

## EXHIBIT 10-2

**$1,000 Bond Issued on January 1, 1980; Matures on December 31, 1981;**
**4 Percent Coupon; Sold to Yield 6 Percent**
**(3 percent per semiannual period)**

| Date | Interest (3% of effective liability) | Coupon Payment | Discount | Effective Liability |
|---|---|---|---|---|
| 1/1/80 | — | — | $37.16 | $ 962.84 |
| 6/30/80 | $28.88 | $(20.00) | (8.88) | 8.88 |
| | | | 28.28 | 971.72 |
| 12/31/80 | 29.15 | (20.00) | (9.15) | 9.15 |
| | | | 19.13 | 980.87 |
| 6/30/81 | 29.43 | (20.00) | (9.43) | 9.43 |
| | | | 9.70 | 990.30 |
| 12/31/81 | 29.70 | (20.00) | (9.70) | 9.70 |
| | | | $ 0.00 | $1,000.00 |

The effective liability, as of any date, can be determined by following the same procedures used to calculate the initial selling price of the bond. For example, as of 12/31/80 there are two interest payments of $20 remaining. The present value of such payments discounted at the effective interest or yield rate of 3 percent per period is, per Table 4, $20 × 1.9135–$38.27. The present value of the $1,000 to be received at maturity is, per Table 2, $1,000 × .9426–$942.60. The present value of the two sets of payments combined is $38.27 plus $942.60 –$980.87.

The following example deals with a bond to be sold at a premium rather than a discount.

*example*

A company wishes to sell 10-year debentures that bear a coupon rate of 10 percent. At the time of sale, bonds of comparable risk are being sold to yield 8 percent.

1. For how much will the company be able to sell each $1,000 bond?

The present value at the effective yield rate of 4 percent per half-year period (8 percent per year) of a single payment of $1,000, 20 periods hence, is, per Table 2, $1,000 × .4564–$456.40.

The present value of a stream of 20 payments of $50 each (based on the coupon rate discounted at 4 percent per period) is, per Table 4, $50 × 13.5903 –$679.52. The sum of the two present values is $1,135.92, the amount for which the company will be able to sell the bond.

| | |
|---|---:|
| Present value of $1,000 to be received after 20 periods discounted at prevailing rate of 4% per period ($1,000 × .4564 per Table 2) | $ 456.40 |
| Present value of $50 to be received at the end of each of 20 periods, discounted at prevailing rate of 4% per period ($50 × 13.5903 per Table 4) | 679.52 |
| Present value of bond | $1,135.92 |

Alternatively the same result could have been obtained by focusing on the premium. The company is offering the purchaser 20 payments of $50 each. The purchaser, based on the prevailing interest rate of 8 percent, would be willing to accept 20 payments of $40 each. The present value of the series of the $10 "bonuses" is, per Table 4, $10 × 13.5903–$135.90. The latter figure represents the bond premium; hence the sale price would be the face value of $1,000 plus a premium of $135.90–the same (with allowance for rounding discrepancies) $1,135.92 as computed earlier.

2. Prepare a journal entry to record the sale of one bond.

| | | |
|---|---|---|
| Cash | $1,135.92 | |
|     Bonds payable | | $1,000.00 |
|     Premium on bonds payable | | 135.92 |
|     **To record sale of the bond.** | | |

3. How would the bonds be reported on the balance sheet immediately after sale?

| | | |
|---|---|---|
| Bonds payable | $1,000.00 | |
| Premium | 135.92 | $1,135.92 |

4. Prepare a journal entry to record the first interest payment. The total amount borrowed by the company was $1,135.92. The effective rate of interest, the yield rate, was 8 percent. The effective semiannual interest would therefore be 4 percent times the outstanding balance of $1,135.92—$45.43. The amount of interest actually to be paid at the time of the first payment is, based on the coupon rate, $50.

| | | |
|---|---|---|
| Interest expense | $45.43 | |
| Premium on bonds payable | 4.57 | |
| Cash | | $50.00 |

**To record payment of interest.**

5. How would the bonds be reported immediately after the first payment of interest?

| | | |
|---|---|---|
| Bonds payable | $1,000.00 | |
| Premium | 131.35 | $1,131.35 |

6. Prepare a journal entry to record the second interest payment. The effective liability just prior to the second payment of interest is $1,131.35. Effective interest charges, based on the yield rate at the time of sale, are $1,131.35 × .04—$45.25.

| | | |
|---|---|---|
| Interest expense | $45.25 | |
| Premium on bonds payable | 4.75 | |
| Cash | | $50.00 |

**To record payment of interest.**

The net liability will now be $1,131.35 less that portion ($4.75) of the premium just amortized—$1,126.60.

7. For how much could the bondholder sell the bond immediately after the second payment of interest, assuming that the prevailing interest rate is still 8 percent?

| | |
|---|---|
| Present value of $1,000, 18 periods away, discounted at 4%, per period (per Table 2), $1,000 × .4936 | $ 493.60 |
| Present value of 18 coupon payments of $50 each (per Table 4), $50 × 12.6593 | 632.97 |
| Price at which the bond could be sold | $1,126.57 |

$$60 - .04(1000 + x) = x$$
$$60 - 40 - .04x = x$$
$$20 = .96x$$

$$.04(1000 + x) = x$$
$$40 + .04x = x$$
$$40 = .96x$$

This amount is the same amount that would be reported on the books of the issuing company as calculated for part 6 of this example (save for a minor rounding discrepancy). It is the same only because the prevailing interest rate is the same as it was at the time when the bond was first issued—8 percent.

## End-of-Year Accruals

If a bond interest date does not occur exactly at year end, it is necessary to accrue interest for the expense incurred from the time of either the issue date or the last payment date to the year end. Suppose, for example, that a 6 percent, 20-year coupon bond was sold on December 1, 1980, for $893.20—a price that would result in a yield of 7 percent. Interest is payable each year on May 31 and November 30. Interest expense for the first full six-month period would be 3.5 percent of $893.20—$31.26. That portion of the discount amortized would be the difference between the interest expense of $31.26 and the actual coupon payment of $30.00—$1.26. The accrual entry on December 31, 1980, would reflect one-sixth of these amounts:

| | | |
|---|---|---|
| Interest expense ($\frac{1}{6}$ of $31.26) | $5.21 | |
| Discount on bonds payable | | $ .21 |
| Accrued interest payable | | 5.00 |
| **To record accrual of interest.** | | |

The entry on May 31, 1981, when the first payment was made would be reflective of the remaining five-sixths (note that consistent with conventional practice the interest expense on May 31 is *not* based on the effective liability at December 31—after the *partial* amortization of the discount—but rather on the liability as of December 1):

| | | |
|---|---|---|
| Interest expense ($\frac{5}{6}$ of $31.26) | $26.05 | |
| Accrued interest payable | 5.00 | |
| Discount on bonds payable | | |
| ($\frac{5}{6}$ of $1.26) | | $ 1.05 |
| Cash | | 30.00 |
| **To record payment of interest.** | | |

## Straight-Line Amortization

Some firms, instead of determining interest charges and amortization of discount or premium as described in the preceding paragraphs, have in the past amortized the premium or discount on a straight-line basis. Total interest charges for the month are calculated by adding to the cash coupon payment (or subtracting from, in the case of a premium) the portion of the discount (premium) amortized. The amount of the discount or premium amortized each period is determined simply by dividing the initial discount or premium by the total number of periods for which the bond will be outstanding. As a consequence, effective interest charges remain constant over the life of the issue. In the illustration used earlier, a 4 percent coupon bond was issued at a price of $962.84 —a discount of $37.16. Since the bond would be outstanding for four periods, one-fourth of $37.16—$9.29—would be amortized each period. Total interest costs each period would be $29.29—the portion of the discount amortized plus the $20 coupon payment. The straight-line method is convenient; it eliminates the need to recompute interest each period. But it is deficient in that it results in a constantly changing *rate* of interest when interest expense is compared to effective liability (face value plus or minus discount or premium). Since, in the example, the effective liability would increase by $9.29 each period, the effective interest rates over the life of the bond (interest expense ÷ effective liability) would be as follows:

$$\frac{29.29}{962.84} = 3.04\%; \quad \frac{29.29}{972.13} = 3.01\%; \quad \frac{29.29}{981.42} = 2.98\%; \quad \frac{29.29}{990.71} = 2.95\%$$

The effective rate of interest tends to increase over time when a bond is sold at a premium. Because of such distortions, the Accounting Principles Board, in Opinion No. 21, "Interest on Receivables and Payables," specifically prohibited firms from using the straight-line method for their reports to the public.

## Redemption of Bonds

When a firm redeems its bonds outstanding upon their maturity, no special accounting problems are presented. Once the interest expense of the final period is recorded, the discount or premium should have been amortized to zero. Thus, for a single bond, the following entry would be appropriate:

| | | |
|---|---|---|
| Bonds payable | $1,000.00 | |
| Cash | | $1,000.00 |

**To record redemption of the bond.**

If, however, the firm decides to redeem the bonds before they mature, then the accounting questions are more complex.

Assume that a company 20 years ago had issued 30-year, 7 percent coupon bonds at a price of $1,025.50 to yield 6.8 percent. With 10 years remaining until maturity, the firm decides to redeem the bonds since it no longer needs the funds that it borrowed. According to the bond indenture agreement, the company has the right to call the issue any time after 15 years of issuing date at a price of $102. (Bond prices are frequently quoted in terms of $100 even though they are conventionally sold in denominations of $1,000. Thus the company would have to pay $1,020 to redeem a single bond.) The bond was originally issued at a price of $1,025.50; if the company had amortized the premium correctly, the net value of the bond after 20 (10 years remaining) years per the corporate books would be $1,014.34. If the company exercised its option to redeem the bond for $1,020.00, the following entry would be appropriate:

| | | |
|---|---:|---:|
| Bonds payable | $1,000.00 | |
| Premium on bonds payable | 14.34 | |
| Redemption costs (call premium) | 5.66 | |
|     Cash | | $1,020.00 |
| **To record redemption of the bond.** | | |

The redemption costs represent a penalty payment that management has elected to make to the bondholders in return for depriving them of the return which their investment in the bonds was providing them.

A corporation may also realize a gain by redeeming its bonds prior to maturity. This is especially true if the company does not officially *call* its outstanding issue but instead purchases its bonds in the open market. The company would pay the current bondholders the prevailing price for the security. By purchasing the bonds outstanding the company would eliminate its liability to outsiders, and it would recognize as a gain the difference between the book value of the bonds and the purchase price.

Bond prices, as pointed out earlier, are determined by the relationship between the coupon rate and the prevailing return that an investor is able to obtain elsewhere. It is commonly believed that bonds are a relatively riskless investment—that bond prices remain reasonably stable. Nothing could be further from the truth. If, for example, prevailing interest rates increase from 6 percent to 7 percent, then the market price on a bond which bears a coupon rate of 6 percent and has 30 years remaining until maturity could be expected to decline from $100.00 to $87.53—almost a 12½ percent change. If a company had initially issued such a 6 percent coupon bond at a price to yield 6.1 percent, then the bond would be recorded on its books at a net value of $98.63 (a discount of $1.37 per hundred dollars). The purchase (i.e., the redemption) of a single $1,000 bond at a price of $87.53 would be recorded as follows:

| | | |
|---|---:|---:|
| Bonds payable | $1,000.00 | |
|     Cash | | $875.30 |
|     Discount on bonds payable | | 13.70 |
|     Gain on redemption | | 111.00 |
| **To record redemption of the bond.** | | |

## Interpreting Gains and Losses on Redemptions

Gains or losses on the redemption of bonds must necessarily be viewed by a financial analyst with a critical eye. Such gains or losses are recognized and reported on the income statement in the year in which the redemption takes place. As a result corporate management could readily time its redemptions in such a manner as to provide a source of discretionary income whenever it is believed that a boost in reported earnings would be helpful. Assume, for example, that in 1965 a firm issued (at par) $10 million in 5 percent coupon bonds payable in 45 years. In 1980, 15 years later, the prevailing rate of interest for similar securities was 7 percent. A 5 percent bond with 30 years remaining until maturity would be traded in the open market for approximately $75. The company could purchase the entire issue for $7.5 million and thereby realize a $2.5 million gain. Insofar as management believes that interest rates in the 1980s will continue to remain substantially above the level of the earlier period, then management is free to select the year in which it redeems the bonds and thereby reports the gain.

Viewed from another perspective, a gain or loss on redemption of bonds may be seen as being very similar to a gain or loss on the sale of long-term assets. If a company is blessed with perfect foresight and is able to predict exactly when and for how much it will redeem its bonds, it would calculate its periodic charges or credits for the amortization of the bond discount or premium in a manner that would assure that the net book value of the bonds at time of redemption is exactly equal to the redemption price. Thus, there would be no gain or loss on redemption. If a company does not have perfect foresight, then, upon redeeming its bonds, it must make adjustment for its failure to amortize correctly the discount or premium in the years that the bond was outstanding. Just as the gain or loss on the retirement of long-lived assets may be interpreted as a correction of depreciation expense, the gain or loss on redemption of bonds may be considered to be a correction of the amortization of the bond discount or premium and, thus, as an adjustment to the interest charges of previous periods.

### Leases

In recent years several new methods of financing business growth have been developed and popularized. One financial arrangement that has been of special concern to accountants is that of *leasing.* In a strict sense a lease involves the right to use land, buildings, equipment, or other property for a specified period of time in return for rent or other compensation. In practice, however, many lease arrangements are the equivalent of installment purchases or other forms of borrowing arrangements.

Suppose that a construction firm is in need of earth-moving equipment. The cost of the equipment is $100,000; the estimated useful life is 10 years. Since the company does not have sufficient cash on hand to purchase the equipment, it secures a loan for its full cost. The terms of the loan specify that principal and interest are to be paid in 10 annual installments of equal amount. The amount of each payment is to be determined on the basis of an annual interest rate of 8 percent. If $100,000 is viewed as the present value of an annuity for 10 periods, discounted at a rate of 8 percent, then the annual payment required to amortize the loan can be determined (per Table 4 of the Appendix) as follows:

$$\$100,000 = 6.7101x$$
$$x = \$14,903$$

Upon purchasing the equipment and borrowing the necessary funds, the company would make the following journal entries:

| | | |
|---|---|---|
| Cash | $100,000 | |
| Note payable | | $100,000 |
| **To record the loan of $100,000.** | | |

| | | |
|---|---|---|
| Equipment | $100,000 | |
| Cash | | $100,000 |
| **To record the purchase of earth-moving equipment.** | | |

Each year the company would make the required payment on the note and would record depreciation on the equipment. The division of the payment between principal and interest would, of course, vary from year to year. As the balance of the loan declines, a smaller portion of the payment would be for interest and a larger portion for reduction of the principal. The entry for the payment of the first year would be

| | | |
|---|---|---|
| Interest expense | $8,000 | |
| Note payable | 6,903 | |
| Cash | | $14,903 |
| **To record the first payment on the note.** | | |

The entry for depreciation (assuming the straight-line method is being used) would be

| | | |
|---|---|---|
| Depreciation expense | $10,000 | |
| Allowance for depreciation | | $10,000 |
| **To record depreciation for one year.** | | |

Suppose instead, however, that the transaction took a slightly different form. The manufacturer of the earth-moving equipment, upon arrangement with the construction company, sold the equipment to a financial institution, such as a bank or an insurance company. The financial institution thereupon leased the equipment to the construction company. The agreement specified that the term of the lease was to be for 10 years, after which time the construction company would have the option to purchase the equipment for $1. Annual rental charges would be $14,903, and the construction company (the lessee) would have to pay all insurance, maintenance costs, and license fees on the equipment. In economic substance all parties are in the identical position in which they would have been had the company purchased the equipment outright and borrowed the required funds from the financial institution. Annual cash payments by the construction company are the same $14,903. Compare, however, the manner in which the lease, as opposed to the borrow/purchase, transaction might be accounted for. At the time the lease agreement was signed no entry would be required. Each year upon payment of the "rent" the following journal entry would be made:

| | | |
|---|---|---|
| Rent expense | $14,903 | |
| Cash | | $14,903 |

**To record payment of rent for one year.**

Depreciation, of course, would not be taken on the equipment, since the equipment itself would never be recorded on the books of the lessee (the construction company).

The fundamental accounting distinction between the transaction as a purchase/borrow arrangement and as a lease is that when considered as a lease the company records on its books neither the asset nor the accompanying liability. From the standpoint of the company, the omission of the liability may represent an important advantage of the lease transaction. Potential creditors and investors view with disfavor excessive amounts of debt appearing on a balance sheet. Moreover, some loan agreements specify the maximum amount of debt that a company is permitted to incur. The leasing arrangement would be a convenient means of circumventing such restrictions. In effect it would permit the company to arrange for "off the balance sheet" financing of its equipment acquisitions.

**accounting for financing leases**

There would be little justification for permitting two transactions, the purchase/borrow arrangement and the lease, which are in economic substance identical, to be accounted for differently. The construction company, as a lessee, has the same rights and obligations as it would if it were the legal owner of the equipment. The company bears all risks and has acquired all rights of ownership. Should the equipment last for longer than the estimated 10 years, the company has the option to purchase it for a negligible amount. Should it suffer a major breakdown, the construction company has the obligation to repair it. Moreover, the company has both a legal and a moral obligation to make the specified payments over the life of the lease. The firm that holds title to the equipment, the financial institution, is the owner in name only.

The Accounting Principles Board determined, and the Financial Accounting Standards Board affirmed, that leases which are clearly in substance purchases of property (*financing leases*) should be recorded as such. The acquisition of the construction equipment would be recorded as a purchase. The transaction would be accounted for as the purchase illustrated previously except that appropriately descriptive account titles would be used for both the asset and the liability:

| | | |
|---|---|---|
| Equipment held under lease (asset) | $100,000 | |
| Present value of lease obligations | | |
| (liability) | | $100,000 |

**To record acquisition of earth-moving equipment under a lease arrangement.**

The asset, "equipment held under lease," would be amortized over the useful life of the equipment;* the liability, "present value of lease obligations," would be accounted for as if it were an ordinary interest-bearing note:

| | | |
|---|---|---|
| Amortization of Equipment held | | |
| under lease (expense) | $10,000 | |
| Equipment held under lease, | | |
| allowance for amortization | | $10,000 |

**To record first-year amortization** (straight-line method, useful life of 10 years).

| | | |
|---|---|---|
| Interest expense (8% of $100,000) | $8,000 | |
| Present value of lease obligations | 6,903 | |
| Cash | | $14,903 |

**To record the first lease payment.**

Many lease agreements indicate only the amount of annual payments; they do not reveal either the actual purchase price (i.e., the fair market value) of the property transferred or the interest rate used to determine the required amounts of the annual payments. Insofar as the lease agreement is silent on these points, the accountant must look to other borrowing arrangements into which the firm

---

*This asset could be amortized over the life of the lease if ownership of the property is not likely to be transferred to the lessee.

has entered to identify an appropriate rate at which to discount the periodic payments required by the lease.

**accounting for operating leases**

Not all lease arrangements are the equivalent of purchases. Businesses enter into rental agreements for a variety of reasons: They need property for only a short period of time; they do not wish to accept the risks of ownership; they do not have the cash necessary to make a purchase and are unable or unwilling to incur additional debt; they want the service and maintenance that might be provided by the lessor.

Traditionally, *operating* leases, those which cover merely the right to use property for a limited time in exchange for periodic rental payments, have been accorded no balance sheet recognition. No entry is made at the time the lease is executed; entries to record the rent expense are made periodically. Many accountants argue, however, that *all* lease agreements (assuming that they are not cancellable) create property rights as well as obligations that deserve to be reported on the balance sheet. A lessee ordinarily has the right to hold and use the property in a manner consistent with the applicable laws, the rights of others, and the provisions of the lease agreement. It often has most of the rights of an owner, with the exception of the right to dispose of the property at its discretion. At the same time, it has the obligation to make rental payments as they come due. The present value of the rights obtained in a lease agreement, according to many accountants, should be *capitalized* and recorded as an asset; the corresponding present value of the obligation should be recorded as a liability. The asset should be amortized (depreciated) over the life of the lease. The stated value of the obligation should be reduced as the periodic rental payments are made. Each rental payment would be considered in part a payment of *principal,* the initial liability being equal to the present value of the property rights, and in part a payment of interest on the unpaid balance of the original obligation.

There are, however, serious obstacles to *capitalizing* (recording as an asset) the value of the property rights inherent in *all* noncancellable lease commitments. It is exceedingly difficult to measure the value of such property rights. Many leases, for example, provide not only for the right to *use* the property but also for services on the part of the lessor. The lessor of an office building, for example, may provide heat, electricity, and janitorial and security services. Consistent with other accounting principles, the rights to receive those types of services are not capitalized as assets—no more than accounting recognition is given to an employment contract at the time it is signed. The task of allocating the lease payments between the right to use the property and the other services provided is likely to be inordinately difficult. Moreover, determination of an appropriate rate at which to discount the lease payments to arrive at their present value is also likely to present difficulties. Whereas in

*Capitalize = record as asset*

transactions involving purchase-type leases the effective interest rate is often a subject for negotiation, in those pertaining to *operating* (nonpurchase) leases the question of interest may not even be specifically considered.

In 1977, in Statement No. 13, the FASB set forth criteria for distinguishing between financing leases and operating leases. According to the board, leases should be considered financing leases and thus capitalized, if the present value of required lease payments is approximatley equal to the fair market value of the lease property, if the term of the lease is 75 percent or more of the leased property's estimated useful life, if the lessee has the right either during or at the expiration of the lease agreement to purchase the property from the lessor at an amount less than what the property is actually worth, or if ownership is transferred to the lessee by the end of the lease term. If the agreement does not satisfy any one of these criteria, it should be considered an operating lease and not capitalized. Nevertheless, disclosure of the terms of the lease should be made in a footnote to the financial statements.

## Accounting for Income Taxes

**nature of problem**    For many companies, taxes based on income represent their single largest recurring expenditure. The combined federal, state, and local income tax rate is sometimes over 50 percent of earnings. Income taxes must obviously be a major factor to be accounted for in any business decision. The proper determination of tax liability is also a critical element of financial reporting.

As a general rule, corporate earnings on which income taxes are based are determined in the same manner as for general financial reporting. There are, however, a number of exceptions. The exceptions fall into two broad categories: permanent differences and timing differences. A permanent difference is one in which, because of special legislative consideration, particular revenues or expenses are omitted from computation of taxable income. Interest on municipal bonds, for example, is not taxable by the federal government and hence, in calculating the income on which the federal income tax is based, it would be omitted from the revenues. Similarly, under certain circumstances charitable contributions, officers' salaries, and life insurance premiums may be corporate expenses which are not deductible in the determination of taxable income and would therefore be excluded from expenses.

A timing difference, on the other hand, is one in which an item is includable or deductible in income for tax purposes in one period but in income for general reporting purposes in another. For example, a dance studio may sell to a customer a series of dance lessons. The customer pays for the lessons in advance. As illustrated previously in the text, for purposes of general reporting the company would properly record the revenue in the periods in which the lessons were actually taken. In the computation of taxable income, however, the revenue would be taken into account in the period in which the cash was collected. An oil company, in searching for new oil, incurs costs of drilling dry holes. Such costs for general reporting purposes may be considered unavoidable costs of discovering the actual location of the oil and thereby capitalized and written off over the period during which the oil is removed from the producing wells. For tax purposes, however, the costs may be considered expenses in the year in which actually incurred.

Because of the magnitude of the tax rate, financial statements can easily be distorted if the tax associated with a particular revenue or expense is reported in a period other than that in which the revenue or expense is recorded. Consider the following (somewhat exaggerated) example.

The income of a company before consideration of depreciation and income taxes is $1,000 in both year 1 and year 2. Equipment had been purchased at the beginning of year 1 for $1,000 and has an estimated useful life of only two years and no salvage value. For purposes of financial reporting the company computes depreciation using the straight-line method. Hence, depreciation is $500 per year. The federal government, however, permits the use of accelerated depreciation for computation of taxable income. The company elects to compute depreciation for tax purposes using the double-declining balance method, because it would result in the postponement (though by no means a reduction) of taxes. Since, in the absence of a salvage value, the double-declining balance method results in a depreciation charge in the first year of twice that determined by the straight-line method, depreciation in year 1 would be $1,000. In year 2, the asset would have been fully depreciated; hence zero depreciation would be charged. (Note that in this particular case depreciation in year 2 is zero. As a general rule, however, the number of years over which an asset is depreciated is the same regardless of depreciation method used.) Assume that the tax rate is 40 percent.

As illustrated in Exhibit 10-3, reported income of the company, before income taxes, is $500 in both year 1 and year 2. *Taxable* income, however, is zero in year 1 and $1,000 in year 2. Therefore, required tax payments are zero in year 1 and $400 in year 2.

If the company were to report a tax expense of $0 in year 1 and $400 in year 2, then income after taxes in year 1 and year 2 would be $500 and $100, respectively:

|  | Year 1 | Year 2 |
|---|---|---|
| Income before taxes (from Exhibit 10–3) | $500 | $500 |
| Tax expense (from Exhibit 10–3) | –0– | 400 |
| Income after taxes | $500 | $100 |

EXHIBIT 10-3

**Reported Income as Compared to Taxable Income**

| | |
|---|---|
| Asset cost: | $1,000 |
| Useful life: | 2 years |
| Tax rate: | 40% |
| Methods of depreciation: | Straight-line for general reporting purposes, double-declining balance for tax purposes. |

**Income Before Taxes—General Reporting Purposes**

| | Year 1 | Year 2 |
|---|---|---|
| Income before depreciation and taxes | $1,000 | $1,000 |
| Depreciation | 500 | 500 |
| Income before taxes | $ 500 | $ 500 |

**Required Tax Payment**

| | Year 1 | Year 2 |
|---|---|---|
| Income before depreciation and taxes | $1,000 | $1,000 |
| Depreciation | 1,000 | -0- |
| Taxable income | $ -0- | $1,000 |
| Tax rate | 40% | 40% |
| Required tax payment | $ -0- | $ 400 |

Many accountants would argue, however, that such computation of income after taxes is misleading. They would question whether the company really earned $400 more in year 1 than in year 2. They would assert that to the extent that an investor relies upon earnings of the past as a guide to earnings of the future, he would be seriously misled by the year 1 report of income. They would contend that income before taxes was the same in both year 1 and year 2 and that since income taxes are based on income, the reported tax expense should be the same in each of the two years. At the end of the first year the company had an effective liability (though certainly not a legal one) for taxes of $200 (40 percent of $500). The federal government, through special provisions of tax laws, allowed the company to *postpone* the payment of the taxes until the following year. The following journal entries, they contend, would give effect to the economic substance of the taxes on income:

Year 1

| | |
|---|---|
| Tax expense (40% of $500) | $200 |
|     Taxes deferred until future years | |
|     (liability) | $200 |
| **To record tax expense.** | |

*Year 2*

| | | |
|---|---|---|
| Tax expense (40% of $500) | $200 | |
| Taxes deferred until future years | 200 | |
| Taxes payable in current year | | $400 |

**To record tax expense.**

As the taxes are actually paid, the usual recognition would be given to the payment:

| | | |
|---|---|---|
| Taxes payable in current year | $400 | |
| Cash | | $400 |

**To record tax payment.**

The procedure by which the reported tax expense is based on reported *income,* as opposed to the actual legal liability (the taxes indicated as due per the tax return), is often referred to as *interperiod tax allocation.* The Accounting Principles Board in Opinion No. 11, "Accounting for Income Taxes," specifically prescribed that interperiod tax allocation be an integral part of the determination of the income tax expense.

   *In essence, tax allocation requires that the reported income tax expense be based on pretax accounting income.* The reported tax liability is divided into two parts: (1) the portion that is currently payable and (2) that which can be deferred until future periods.

   The portion that is currently payable is based on the liability per the tax return (that is, based on *taxable* income). The deferred portion is ordinarily the difference between the reported tax expense and the portion of the liability that is currently payable. In years in which the firm is able to postpone taxes, the deferred portion of the liability is ordinarily credited (that is, the deferred liability is increased); in years in which the firm must "repay" the taxes that had been postponed, the deferred liability is debited (and thereby decreased). The following example illustrates a timing difference in which revenue is included in years subsequent to those in which it is included in accounting (reported) income.

*example*     The Ann Arbor Bridge Co. received in 1980 a $40 million contract to construct a bridge across the Huron River. The company estimates that construction costs will total $36 million and that the bridge will be built over a two-year period.

   The company estimates that construction and collection of cash will adhere to the following timetable:

| | Percent Completed in Year | Percent Cash Collected in Year |
|---|---|---|
| 1980 | 20% | — |
| 1981 | 80 | 25% |
| 1982 | — | 75 |

The company decides to report in its financial statements earnings from the contract on a percentage of completion basis but elects to report the earnings on its income tax return on an installment basis (i.e., as cash is collected). The tax rate is 40 percent.

### Required Tax Payments (installment basis)

|  | 1980 | 1981 | 1982 |
|---|---|---|---|
| Revenue | $ –0– | $10,000,000 (25%) | $30,000,000 (75%) |
| Expenses applicable to revenues (36/40ths of revenues) | –0– | 9,000,000 (25%) | 27,000,000 (75%) |
| Taxable income | $ –0– | $ 1,000,000 | $ 3,000,000 |
| Tax rate | 40% | 40% | 40% |
| Tax | $ –0– | $ 400,000 | $ 1,200,000 |

### Income Statement for Purposes of Financial Reporting (percentage-of-completion basis)

|  | 1980 | 1981 | 1982 |
|---|---|---|---|
| Revenue | $8,000,000 (20%) | $32,000,000 (80%) | $ –0– |
| Expenses applicable to revenues (36/40ths of revenues) | 7,200,000 (20%) | 28,800,000 (80%) | –0– |
| Income before taxes | $ 800,000 | $ 3,200,000 | $ –0– |
| Tax expense (40%) | 320,000 | 1,280,000 | –0– |
| Net income | $ 480,000 | $ 1,920,000 | $ –0– |

In the income statement, the tax expense is based on the reported income before taxes, irrespective of the required tax payment. *The tax expense follows the income.*

The following journal entries would effect the appropriate *allocation* of taxes. It is assumed for convenience that the required tax payment (the current portion of the liability) is made entirely in the year to which it is applicable, although in practice a part of the payment is likely to be delayed until the following year.

*Year 1980*

| Tax expense | $320,000 | |
|     Taxes deferred until future years | | $320,000 |

**To record tax expense.** (No tax payment need be made in 1980; tax expense represents 40 percent of reported income before taxes of $800,000.)

*Year 1981*

| | | |
|---|---|---|
| Tax expense | $1,280,000 | |
| Taxes payable in current year | | $400,000 |
| Taxes deferred until future years | | 880,000 |

**To record tax expense.** (Required tax payment is $400,000; tax expense represents 40 percent of reported income before taxes of $3,200,000.)

| | | |
|---|---|---|
| Taxes payable in current year | $400,000 | |
| Cash | | $400,000 |

**To record payment of taxes.**

*Year 1982*

| | | |
|---|---|---|
| Taxes deferred until future years | $1,200,000 | |
| Cash | | $1,200,000 |

**To record payment of taxes.** (Required tax payment is $1,200,000; reported income is zero so no tax expense need be charged.)

The liability, "taxes deferred until future years" would be reported on the balance sheet among the current or noncurrent liabilities, depending on when it is likely to be liquidated. The balance in the account will increase in those years in which the tax expense exceeds the required tax payments and decrease in those years in which required tax payments exceed the tax expense.

Taxes deferred until future years

| | | | |
|---|---|---|---|
| | | (1980) | 320,000 |
| | | (1981) | 880,000 |
| (1982) | 1,200,000 | | |

**controversy continues**   The issue of whether or not taxes should, in fact, be allocated among accounting periods, as presently required, has been the subject of considerable debate among accountants. Tax allocation is rooted in the matching concept; it is designed to give effect to a cause and effect relationship between income and tax expense. It is intended to prevent businesses from reporting a relatively high income in one period only to have to report a correspondingly low income in a future period, when taxes that have been postponed from the earlier years must be paid.

Many accountants contend, however, that income taxes are sufficiently different from other types of costs that application of the matching principle may be inappropriate. Income taxes, they assert, are not functionally related to revenues or even to pretax reported income but rather to *taxable* income. They believe, therefore, that requirements that the taxes be matched to reported income are of questionable validity.

They also point out that tax allocation can result in financial statements in which liabilities are materially overstated in that deferred tax obligations may never, in fact, have to be paid. For most companies, the deferred tax liability is attributable primarily to the use of accelerated depreciation methods for tax purposes but straight-line depreciation for general financial reporting. Insofar as a company continually replaces its assets, each year it would be able to postpone a portion of its taxes. As the taxes associated with assets purchased earlier must be paid, taxes associated with the more recent acquisitions may be postponed. The deferred tax liability will continuously *roll over,* and in a sense be postponed indefinitely. If, on the other hand, the firm is expanding, then the deferred tax liability will increase year by year. The continuous buildup of such liabilities has been of concern to many financial analysts. They contend that, in reality, it is sometimes unlikely that the reported deferred tax obligation will have to be liquidated in the foreseeable future. Therefore, they assert, the tax allocation process results in financial reports in which liabilities are substantially overstated.*

## Investment Tax Credit

In the early 1960s, in an effort to stimulate corporate investment in plant and equipment, Congress provided for a tax credit of up to 7 percent of the cost of new facilities. Since then the credit has periodically been revoked and reinstituted; in 1975, the maximum credit was increased to 10 percent. From the time it was introduced, however, the proper means of accounting for the credit has been a major source of controversy.

A tax credit must be distinguished from a tax deduction. A tax deduction reduces the income on which tax is computed. A tax credit, by contrast, directly reduces the tax itself. The investment tax credit provides that up to 10 percent (1979 rates) of the cost of eligible plant and equipment can be used to offset a firm's required tax payment. If, for example, a firm purchased $500,000 of eligible plant and equipment, then it could reduce its current tax liability by $50,000. In addition, it could take *deductions* for depreciation on the full $500,000 (less any salvage value) over the useful life of the equipment.

The accounting question evoked by the investment tax credit is whether such credit should reduce the *reported* tax expense only in the year the equipment is purchased (and the year in which the credit is granted) or whether it should be spread over the useful life of the equipment. On the one hand, it has been argued that the credit represents a permanent reduction of tax (as opposed to the temporary reductions discussed in the preceding section) and that the

*The antidote to the argument that the deferred tax liability will continuously roll over and thus be postponed indefinitely is that accounts payable also continuously roll over. As long as a firm continues to function at its present level or to expand, then its liability for accounts payable, like that for deferred taxes, is unlikely to ever be liquidated. Few, if any, accountants would argue that accounts payable should not be reported on the balance sheet.

benefits from such reduction should be reported to investors in the year in which they are granted. On the other hand, it has been asserted that the tax credit has the effect of reducing the net cost of the asset. The cost of an asset is charged to expense (through the process of depreciation) over its useful life. The tax credit should be accounted for in a way that would reduce the costs that would otherwise have to be charged as expenses over the useful life of the equipment.

The accounting method by which the credit reduces *reported* tax expense in the year in which it is granted is known as the *flow-through* method (because the credit "flows" directly into income) and the method by which it reduces expenses over the life of the property is referred to as the *deferral,* or *amortization,* method.

Suppose that a firm has a tax obligation of $1,000,000 prior to consideration of an investment tax credit of $50,000. Useful life of the property acquired is ten years. If it were to use the deferral method in the year it acquired the property, the firm could make the following two entries relating to income taxes:

**(a)**

| | | |
|---|---|---|
| Tax expense | $1,000,000 | |
| Investment tax credit | | $ 50,000 |
| Cash (or taxes currently payable) | | 950,000 |
| **To record tax expense.** | | |

**(b)**

| | | |
|---|---|---|
| Investment tax credit | $5,000 | |
| Tax expense | | $5,000 |

**To record the amortization of the investment tax credit** (based on an estimated useful life of the property of 10 years).

The net effect of the two entries is to reflect a reported tax expense of only $995,000. During each of the remaining nine years of the asset's useful life, the reported tax expense would be reduced by $5,000 [by way of an amortization entry like (b)], and the remaining balance in the "investment tax credit" account would also be reduced by the same amount.* The "investment tax credit" account would of course always have a credit balance. It could be reported on the balance sheet either as a deferred revenue (similar to revenues received but not yet earned) or as an account contra to the property with which it is associated.

If the firm were to use the flow-through method then reported tax expense would be equal to the required tax payment—$950,000. As a consequence of the deferral method, *reported* expenses would be $45,000 greater in

*Alternatively, the credit could be reflected each year as a reduction of depreciation expense rather than tax expense.

the year the property is acquired than if the flow-through method were used. In each of the subsequent nine years, however, they would be $5,000 less under the deferral method. The actual tax payments that the firm is required to make would, however, be unaffected by choice of method.

At one time, the Accounting Principles Board specified that the allowable investment credit should be reflected in income over the productive life of the acquired property (the deferral method) and not only in the year in which it is placed in service. Subsequently, however, while reaffirming its preference for the deferral method, it permitted firms to use either of the two methods.

In 1972 Congress passed into law a provision that prohibited any professional accounting body (it was aimed at the Accounting Principles Board and the Securities and Exchange Commission) from requiring that firms use the deferral method exclusively. The provision was intended to ensure that the credit had maximum impact on earnings in the year a firm purchased the eligible property.

The Congressional action was significant for at least two reasons. First, it demonstrated that Congress has, and may sometimes be willing to exercise, the authority to establish accounting principles. Second, it emphasized the importance that some groups place on *reported* earnings of corporations. The legislation was apparently passed in response to pressure from both industry groups and the U.S. Treasury Department. They believed that the credit would provide a stimulus to the economy that was both more pronounced and more immediate if it could be reflected in full in corporate earnings in the year in which it was granted. Whether or not they are correct is questionable. Financial statements do not establish the financial health of an enterprise; they only report upon it. The tax credit serves to reduce taxes (and thereby reduce cash outflow) in the year in which the eligible property is purchased—regardless of the manner in which it is accounted for. The economic well-being of the corporation is, in substance, unchanged by the manner in which accountants elect —or are required—to describe it.

## Pensions

Pensions represent periodic payments to retired or disabled employees owing to their years of employment. Although there is a great variety of pension plans, most require that a company make fixed monthly payments to an employee from the time of his retirement to the date of either his death or that of his surviving spouse.

At one time pensions were viewed as discretionary payments made by a company to its loyal and dedicated employees. Today they are contractual obligations of a company and are incorporated into almost all collective bargaining agreements.

The accounting issues pertaining to pension plans arise from the fact that payments to an employee do not have to be made until he retires, yet the cost to the company clearly arises from the service that he provides during his period of employment. Most companies make periodic payments into a pension fund in order to assure the availability of cash as required. The amount that a company must provide in current periods, in order to meet the future pensions of employees who are presently active, is *actuarially* determined. (An actuary is a statistician who computes insurance risks and premiums.) It is dependent on estimates of life expectancy, employee turnover (since only a portion of present employees is likely to remain with a company sufficiently long to be eligible for pension benefits), and the rate of return that the company will earn on investments purchased with the cash that has been contributed to the pension fund. The specific method that a firm uses to determine the amount of its required payments to the pension fund is referred to as its *actuarial cost method.*

The importance of proper accounting for pensions was vividly demonstrated in the mid-1970s when it became widely known that the financial status of several major U.S. cities was substantially worse than indicated by their financial reports. These cities did not adhere to generally accepted accounting principles and failed to disclose pension obligations of hundreds of millions of dollars to both current and previous employees.

Pension costs must be accounted for on an accrual basis. Regardless of when a company actually *funds* (makes the required payment to the pension fund) its pension plan, the company receives the benefit of an employee's services in the years in which he has actually worked. Pension costs, like direct wage payments, must be charged as expenses in the periods in which the employees provide their services.

The *pension fund* itself is ordinarily a separate legal and accounting entity. Its assets consist entirely of cash, securities, and other income-earning investments. Its liabilities are composed primarily of the *estimated* claims of the employees—the actuarial value of their vested (contractually required) benefits. Neither the assets nor the liabilities of the pension fund are reported on the balance sheet of the corporation.

The amount that the corporation reports as its pension expense represents its *required* payments to the pension fund as determined by the actuarial cost method that it elects to use. The difference between the required payment and the amount that it actually pays into the fund is recorded as a liability, accrued pension expense, if the required payment exceeds the actual payment. The difference is recorded as an asset, prepaid pension expense, if the actual payment exceeds the required payment. Assume, for example, that the required payment to the pension fund, as determined by an appropriate actuarial cost method, is $500,000. In fact, however, the company contributes only $400,000. The following journal entries would be required.

**(a)**

| | | |
|---|---|---|
| Pension expense | $500,000 | |
| Accrued pension costs (liability) | | $500,000 |
| **To record pension expense.** | | |

**(b)**

| | | |
|---|---|---|
| Accrued pension cost (liability) | $400,000 | |
| Cash | | $400,000 |

**To record contributions to the pension fund.**

The pension liability, as reported on the balance sheet, is increased each year by the recorded pension expense; it is decreased by payments to the pension fund.

The problem of accounting for pension costs is further complicated by the fact that when a firm first adopts a pension plan, or makes significant improvements to its plan, it is likely to incur an immediate obligation to make payments to the pension funds, because additional benefits must be made available to all employees presently on the payroll—including those who are near retirement age. The new benefits may be attributed to their *prior service* to the company, but the company will not yet have funded such benefits.

It would generally cause a company serious economic hardship if it had to fund all *prior service costs* (those based on service in past years) in the year in which the plan or changes to the plan are adopted. Similarly, it would seriously distort income if the costs of such prior services were charged to income in a single year. As a consequence, firms are permitted to amortize (spread) such costs over a 40-year period. Since the expense may not be fully accounted for until 40 years after the plan or change is adopted, then neither will be the corresponding liability for the required contributions to the pension fund. The amount of the liability for such past service costs must, however, be reported in footnotes to the financial statements.

Because there are several actuarial cost methods by which a firm can elect to determine its required payments to the pension fund, reported pension expenses of firms with similar pension obligations may not be readily comparable. The essential point to bear in mind, however, in reviewing financial reports is that the reported pension expense represents actuarially *required* payments to a pension fund (*not actual* payments to pensioners or even to the pension fund) and that the reported balance sheet liability represents the cumulative difference between such required payments and the actual payments (not the actual liability to the pensioners).

## Summary

In this chapter we have reviewed the means by which several types of liabilities —bonds, as well as those relating to leases, taxes, and pensions—are accounted for. Each of the liabilities is directly related to an expense—interest expense, income tax expense, and pension expense. A central theme of the chapter has been that the amount at which the liability is stated on the balance sheet has a direct impact upon the amount of expense reported on the income statement.

As emphasized in each of the chapters pertaining to assets, all questions of balance sheet valuations must necessarily be considered within a context of income determination.

*exercise for review and self-testing*

On January 1, 1980 a company issued bonds. The bonds had an established coupon rate of 14 percent, but they were issued at a price that provided bondholders a return of only 12 percent. The bonds were to mature in 20 years.

a. For each $1,000 bond, how much interest will the company be required to pay each six months?

b. For each $1,000 bond held, how much interest would a bondholder expect to receive semiannually based on the prevailing yields of comparable securities?

c. What is the difference between the two amounts?

d. What is the present value of such a difference based on the effective yield rate (compounded semiannually) and the number of periods until maturity?

e. What is the amount of premium or discount at which the bond will be issued? What is the selling price of each $1,000 bond?

f. What is the amount of interest, based on the effective yield rate, that the company should record as an expense when, on June 30, 1980, it is required to make the first interest payment?

g. What is the actual amount of required payment?

h. What is the difference between the two amounts? By how much should the recorded value of the bond premium be reduced?

i. What is the effective liability of the company, per bond, on July 1, 1980?

j. What is the amount of interest expense that the company should record on December 31, 1980, when it is required to make its second payment of interest?

## Questions

**review and discussion**

1. A friend recently purchased $10,000 of American Telephone & Telegraph Company bonds. The company is considered as financially sound as any major U.S. corporation. The bonds are scheduled to mature in 30 years, but your friend intends to sell them within 2 or 3 years in order to provide funds for his child's education. He wants a "safe" investment. He decided not to purchase the common stock of the same company because he viewed it as too risky. Do you think he made a wise decision? Would he have been better off buying AT&T bonds that matured in only 3 years? Explain.

2. The account "discount on bonds payable" ordinarily has a debit balance. It has sometimes been argued that bond discount, like most other accounts which have debit balances, should be reported as an asset rather than as *contra* (as an adjustment) to a long-term liability. Considering the nature of bond discounts, do you agree?

3. For many years there has been controversy over the accounting for gains and losses which may arise when a company repurchases or redeems its own bonds at a price different from the value at which they are recorded on its books. Why have some financial observers charged that major corporations have engaged in repurchases or redemptions in order to give an artificial boost to earnings? How is this possible?

4. Why are some lease arrangements accounted for as if they were installment purchases? Why do some accountants believe that almost all long-term noncancellable lease agreements should be *capitalized* (i.e., assets and corresponding liabilities recorded) on the balance sheet? Why might a company believe that it is able to present a more favorable balance sheet by leasing, rather than purchasing, plant or equipment?

5. Why might a company report a tax expense on its income statement that is greater or less than the required tax payment as indicated on its income tax return?

6. Why do some accountants contend that interperiod tax allocation results in an overstatement of liabilities, in that amounts which may never have to be paid are included among reported obligations?

7. Distinguish between a tax *deduction* and a tax *credit*.

8. What is the impact on both income and assets of accounting for the investment tax credit by the flow-through as opposed to the amortization method?

9. What does reported pension expense represent? What does the liability for accrued pension costs represent?

10. On the books of which accounting entity would a firm's actual liability to its employees for pension benefits be reported?

11. What is meant by "prior service costs?" How are they accounted for?

## Problems

1. *The amount for which a bond is issued, as well as subsequent charges to income, are dependent upon the prevailing yield rate at the time of issue.*

   On January 2, 1980, the Black Company issued 12 percent coupon bonds at a price which provided purchasers a yield of 10 percent. The bonds paid interest on June 30 and December 31 and were scheduled to mature at December 31, 1981.
   a. Record the sale of a single $1,000 bond.
   b. Determine interest expense for each of the four periods and record the first payment of interest.
   c. Record the redemption of the bond (including final interest payment).

2. *The prices at which outstanding bonds can be resold fluctuate with changes in the prevailing rates of interest.*

   On May 1, 1980, the Baltimore Co. issued at par (i.e., at a price of $100) $10 million in 8 percent, 20-year coupon bonds. Interest is payable semi-annually.

    a. Within two years, prevailing interest rates had increased to 10 percent. At what price could a bondholder sell a single $1,000 bond in the open market?

    b. By the fourth year, prevailing interest rates had increased to 12 percent. At what price could a bondholder now sell a single $1,000 bond?

    c. What impact would the increase in prevailing interest rates have upon the reported interest expense of the Baltimore Co.?

    d. "In comparison to common stocks, bonds provide a relatively risk-free investment." Do you agree?

3. *Call provisions may establish a ceiling on the prices at which outstanding bonds are traded.*

The Universal Drilling Co. issued, in 1965, $100,000 of 6 percent 30-year bonds. The bond indenture agreement provided that the company could redeem the bonds any time after 1975 at a price of $102.

    In 1980, with 15 years remaining until maturity, the company decided to retire the bonds. Since the prevailing interest rate was 8 percent, the company elected to repurchase the bonds in the open market at the prevailing price.

    a. Determine the price that the company would have to pay for the bonds.

    b. Assume instead that the prevailing annual interest rate in 1980 was 4 percent. Determine the price that the company would have to pay for the bonds. Be sure to consider the maximum price at which the bonds are likely to trade in light of the call provision.

4. *Bonds may also be issued between interest dates, and, although not specifically discussed in the text, the accounting problems associated with such issues are not overly complex.*

The United Tire Company on January 31, 1980 issues 6 percent coupon bonds to mature in 20 years. The bonds are sold, at par, to yield 6 percent. The bonds require the payment of interest on June 30 and December 31.

    a. What will be the required interest payment on June 30, 1980, on a single $1,000-denomination bond? (All coupons, including the first, require the payment of the same amount of interest.)

    b. Since the bondholder on June 30 would have held the bond for only five months, how much interest would he have earned (i.e., would he actually "deserve" to receive)?

    c. Suppose the bondholder agreed to *advance* the company the amount of that portion of the first interest payment that he did not actually earn. How much would he advance the company?

    d. Prepare a journal entry to record the issue of one bond, assuming that the company received the principal plus the unearned portion of the first interest payment.

    e. Prepare a journal entry to record the first interest payment. The interest expense should represent the cost of borrowing funds only for the period during which the company had the use of such funds.

5. *Principles of accounting for financial reporting may not be appropriate for managerial decision making.*

In January 1955, the Bowman Co. issued $100,000 of 6 percent, 30-year coupon bonds. The indenture agreement stipulates that the company has the right to *call* (redeem) the bonds at a price of $103 any time after the bonds have been outstanding for 10 years. In 1980 the bonds were stated on the company's books at a value of $98,300; there was a reported discount of $1,700.

In January 1980, when 5 years remained until maturity, the company controller debated whether or not he should refund the entire bond issue— that is, whether he should redeem the bonds and reborrow the entire cost of redemption. The prevailing rate of interest at the time he was making his decision was 5 percent. The controller determined that he could borrow the entire $103,000 necessary to call the outstanding issue at that rate.

In 1980 the company earned a return of 8 percent on all invested capital.

a. Prepare a journal entry that would be required to record the redemption of the bonds.

b. In view of the fact that the company would have to report a loss on the redemption of the bonds the controller decided against redeeming the bonds. Do you agree with his decision? [*Hint:* Identify all cash flows that would result in the next 5 years (10 semiannual periods) under both of the alternatives. Determine the present value *to the company* of such cash flows. In discounting the cash flows, use the rate that is most appropriate to the company—the rate (8 percent per year or 4 percent per period) that indicates what it could earn on the borrowed funds.]

6. *The straight-line method of bond amortization distorts the cost of borrowing.*

In the past, companies, wishing to avoid the complexities of the *effective interest* means of accounting for bond premium or discount, used the *straight-line* amortization method.

Suppose a company issues 12 percent coupon bonds at a price which would provide a return to the bondholders of 10 percent. The bonds will mature in 20 years.

a. Prepare a journal entry to record the issue of a single $1,000 bond.

b. Prepare journal entries to record both the *first* and the *last* payments of interest. Assume first that the company uses the effective interest method and second the straight-line method. Be sure to determine the *effective* liability outstanding at the *start* of each of the periods.

c. Determine the effective rate of interest recorded as an expense under each of the two methods for both the first and the last payments. That is, express the recorded interest expense as a percentage of the reported effective liability (bond payable plus unamortized premium).

7. *By redeeming its debt at a "bargain" price, a firm is able to realize a substantial gain.*

The 1976 financial statements of Chessie System, Inc. contained the following note:

During 1975 [the company] purchased $11.6 million principal amount of its 4½% convertible debentures due 2010 at a price of $550 each under a tender offer. The resulting net gain was $2.6 million after related deferred Federal income taxes of $2.4 million.

a. Chessie System, Inc. is a financially sound company. Why do you suspect that it was able to redeem its outstanding debt at a "bargain" price?

b. The note makes reference to *deferred* federal income taxes. What does the use of the term *deferred* suggest about the provisions of the tax laws pertaining to gains on the redemption of bonds?

c. Suppose that the company were unable to pay off its debt without reducing the scale of its operations. It therefore had to reborrow the amount that it paid to the holders of the 4½ percent debentures. How do you think the rate of interest on the new debt would compare with that on the old (much higher, much lower, etc.)? Will the company really be better off as a consequence of having "refunded" (paid off and reborrowed) its debt? What is the real nature of the gain of $5 million (before taxes)? When did the gain really occur—at the time of refunding or in the several previous accounting periods?

8. *An important issue facing banks and other financial institutions is whether they should give immediate accounting recognition to unfavorable modifications in the terms of debt arrangements.*

In January 1980 a bank acquired $1 million of the bonds of Gotham City. The bonds paid interest at a rate of 10 percent and were sold to yield 10 percent (that is, they were sold "at par"). The bonds were to mature in five years.

Shortly after the bank made its investment in the bonds, Gotham City faced a fiscal crisis. After a series of complex legal maneuvers, it was able to "restructure" its debt. The city was permitted to extend the maturity of the debt from five years to ten years and to reduce the rate of interest paid from 10 percent to 6 percent. The amount of principal owed (the face value of the bonds) was to remain unchanged.

a. What is the value to the bank of its Gotham City bonds immediately following the restructure? That is, what is the present value, discounted at the prevailing yield rate of 10 percent per year (5 percent per period), of the anticipated payment of $1 million in principal and the anticipated 20 semiannual payments of $30,000 in interest?

b. Do you think that the bank should "write down" the carrying value of the bonds from $1 million to the amount determined in a and thereby recognize an immediate loss? If it did, what would be the impact on earnings of the current year and future years as compared to that if it did not? Would total earnings, over the remaining life of the issue, be affected by a decision to recognize an immediate loss?

(*Note:* The question of how to account for "restructured debt," although not specifically dealt with in the text, was an important issue in the mid-1970s as a consequence of fiscal crises that faced New York City as well as a large number of firms in the real estate industry. The FASB, in Statement No. 15, ruled that in situations similar to the one described in this problem no write-down would be required. However, in cases where total anticipated receipts of both principal and interest, without regard to their *present* value, are less than the carrying value of the debt, an immediate loss would have to be recognized.)

**9.** *The distinction, in economic substance, between an installment purchase and a financial lease may be trivial.*

The indenture agreement associated with the outstanding bonds of the Eastern Machine Co. stipulates the maximum amount of debt that the company can incur. The company wishes to expand its plant and purchase new equipment, but the company has insufficient funds to purchase the equipment outright. Since the company is prohibited by the existing bond indentures from borrowing the needed funds, the controller of the company has suggested that the firm arrange for the manufacturer of the equipment to sell the equipment to a lending institution. The lending institution would, in turn, lease the machine to the company. The lending institution would provide no maintenance or related services, and the company would have responsibility for insuring the equipment. Upon the expiration of the lease, the company would have the option of purchasing the equipment. If the company were to acquire the equipment outright, its cost would be $500,000. If it were to borrow the funds, it would be required to pay interest at the rate of 8 percent per year. The financial institution has agreed to a noncancellable lease with a term of 15 years, a term corresponding to the useful life of the equipment.

a. If the company decides to lease the equipment, what would be the most probable annual rental payments?

b. How do you suspect the controller intends to account for the acquisition of the equipment? What journal entries do you think he would propose at the time the equipment is acquired? At the time the first payment of rent is made?

c. Do the proposals of the controller in your opinion reflect the substance of the transaction? Are they in accord with provisions of the Financial Accounting Standards Board? What alternative journal entries would you propose?

**10.** *Recent pronouncements of the FASB are intended to prevent firms from avoiding balance sheet disclosure of financial obligations by leasing rather than purchasing long-lived assets.*

The managers of Business Services, Inc. are debating whether to buy or to rent a computer. A computer manufacturer has offered the company the opportunity to lease, for a period of 15 years, a machine for $100,000 per year. Alternatively, the company could purchase the machine outright and could borrow the purchase price from an insurance company at an annual rate of 10 percent. The note to the insurance company would be repaid in 15 equal installments, each installment representing both a repayment of principal and a payment of interest on the unpaid balance.

Costs of operating the equipment would be the same under either alternative; the salvage value after 15 years would be negligible.

Currently the company has total assets of $5 million and total liabilities of $2 million.

a. What is the maximum that the company should be willing to pay to purchase the machine?

b. Suppose that the company paid such maximum amount. Compare total expenses that would be reported during the first year if the company purchased the machine as opposed to leasing it assuming that it accounts for the transaction as an operating lease (although under current FASB pronouncements the lease would satisfy the criteria of a financial lease). The company uses the straight-line method of depreciation.

c. Determine the ratio of total debt to total owners' equity under each of the alternatives.

11. *The perceptive financial analyst would adjust for differences between companies relating to the means of financing and accounting for long-term assets and obligations.*

As a financial analyst you are reviewing annual reports for the year 1980 of two chains of discount department stores. The reports indicate that one of the two companies owns all of its stores; the other leases them. A footnote to the financial statements of the firm that leases contained the following information:

The company operates principally in leased premises. The basic terms of the leases generally range from 10 to 20 years. Many of the leases meet the criteria of noncapitalized financing leases (operating leases) as defined by the Financial Accounting Standards Board and accordingly have not been included among long-term liabilities. Total minimum rental commitments are as follows (in thousands):

| | |
|---|---|
| 1981–1985 | $30,000 per year |
| 1986–1995 | $25,000 per year |
| 1996–2000 | $10,000 per year |

An additional note in the financial statements indicates that the companies' cost of borrowing is 8 percent.

What adjustments to the assets and liabilities of the firm that leases its stores would make its financial reports comparable with those of the firm that owns the stores?

(Remember that the present value of an annuity of $1 per year to be received in years 6 to 10 can be determined by subtracting the factor for year 5 from that for year 10.)

12. *Under deferred tax accounting, reported tax expense may differ from the required tax payment.*

A company acquires an asset at a cost of $30,000. The asset has an estimated useful life of three years and an estimated residual value of $6,000. The company computes depreciation on the straight-line basis for purposes of financial reporting but uses the sum-of-the-years' digits method in reporting to taxing authorities. In each of the three years that the company uses the asset, it expects to have earnings, before taking into account depreciation and taxes, of $20,000. The applicable tax rate is 40 percent.

Complete the following table:

|  | *Year 1* | *Year 2* | *Year 3* |
|---|---|---|---|
| *Depreciation* | | | |
| Reporting purposes | | | |
| Tax purposes | | | |
| *Income before taxes* | | | |
| Reporting purposes | | | |
| Tax purposes | | | |
| *Taxes* | | | |
| Reported expense | | | |
| Required payment | | | |
| *Deferred tax account* | | | |
| Amount to be added or | | | |
| subtracted during year | | | |
| Balance at end of year | | | |

13. *Reported tax expense may be substantially greater than the required tax payment.*

    In 1980 the ELS Company had income, before depreciation on assets purchased in that year and before taxes, of $20 million. During the year it purchased equipment for $4 million. The equipment has a useful life of eight years and no salvage value. All of the equipment purchased is eligible for the 10 percent investment tax credit.

    The company charges depreciation on a straight-line basis for financial reporting purposes but uses the double-declining balance method for tax purposes. It accounts for the investment credit by the amortization or deferral method. The tax rate is 40 percent.

    a. Compute the actual amount of taxes for 1980 that the company will be required to pay.

    b. Determine reported tax expense and net income (i.e., income after taxes).

14. *By the time an asset is fully depreciated, the balance in the deferred tax account related to that asset should be reduced to zero.*

    The Frost Co. purchased equipment in 1980 at a cost of $100,000. The equipment had an estimated useful life of four years with zero salvage value. The company elected to use straight-line depreciation for general reporting purposes but decided to take advantage of the provisions of the tax code which permit the use of accelerated (double-declining balance) depreciation to determine taxable income.

    In each of the four years from 1980 through 1983 the company had earnings, before taking into account both depreciation on the equipment and taxes, of $50,000. The tax rate is 40 percent.

    a. Determine taxable income and taxes for each of the four years. Assume that the asset is depreciated to zero in the fourth year.

b. Determine reported tax expense and net income for each of the four years, assuming that tax expense is based on reported, rather than taxable, income.

c. Prepare journal entries necessary to give effect to the allocation of taxes for each of the four years. Assume that all taxes are paid in the year in which they are incurred. Determine, and keep track of, the year-end balances in the deferred taxes account.

15. *As long as a company continues to expand, the balance in its deferred tax liability account will continue to increase.*

A company made purchases of fixed assets as follows:

| 1975 | $ 60,000 |
|------|----------|
| 1976 | 90,000 |
| 1977 | 120,000 |
| 1978 | 120,000 |
| 1979 | 0 |
| 1980 | 0 |

The company uses straight-line depreciation for accounting purposes but sum-of-the-years' digits depreciation for tax purposes. The useful life of all fixed assets purchased is three years; the assets have a zero salvage value. The income tax rate is 40 percent.

a. Determine, for each of the six years, total depreciation that would be reported on the financial statements and that which would be deductible for tax purposes. Indicate the difference each year.

b. Determine the taxes that would be *saved* (postponed) or would have to be *repaid* during each of the six years.

c. Determine the amount that would be reported as a deferred tax liability each year.

d. Suppose that the firm continued to increase its purchases of fixed assets after the third year. What would be the effect on the deferred tax liability? Why do you suppose some accountants are opposed to *interperiod tax allocation?*

16. *A liability for taxes that will have to be paid in the future should be established whenever a company is permitted to recognize revenue for financial reporting purposes in one period and for tax purposes in a later period.*

The Arizona Land Co. was organized on January 1, 1980. The corporation issued 1,000 shares of common stock for $100,000 cash. The company elected to recognize revenue on the installment basis (i.e., upon collection of cash) for income tax purposes but at time of sale for general accounting and reporting purposes.

In 1980 the company purchased for cash a parcel of land for $60,000. In the same year it sold the land for $100,000; the buyer made a down payment of $50,000 and paid the balance in 1981.

In 1981 the company purchased for cash another parcel of land for $180,000 and sold it for $200,000. The buyer paid the entire amount in cash at time of sale.

The effective tax rate is 40 percent. The company pays all taxes in the year to which they are applicable. The company allocates taxes as appropriate.

Prepare a statement of income and a balance sheet for the years 1980 and 1981.

17. *The deferral method of accounting for the investment tax credit requires that the credit be taken into income over the life of the related asset.*

    A firm acquires an asset at a cost of $32,000. The asset has an estimated useful life of eight years and qualifies for an investment tax credit of 10 percent. The firm estimates that in each of the next eight years it will have a tax obligation, prior to giving consideration to the investment tax credit, of $20,000.

    Complete the following table assuming that the firm uses the deferral method to account for the tax credit:

|  | Year 1 | Years 2 through 8 (per year) |
|---|---|---|
| Required tax payment |  |  |
| Tax expense to be reported on income statement |  |  |
| Net amount to be added to (subtracted from) deferred investment tax credit account on balance sheet |  |  |

18. *In comparing firms, differences in the methods used to report the invest-ment tax credit must be taken into account.*

    In analyzing the financial statements of two firms in the same industry, an investor noticed that one firm accounted for the investment tax credit by the flow-through method and the other by the amortization method.

    The firm that accounted for the credit by the flow-through method had taxable earnings in 1980 of $100,000. In 1980 it acquired assets, which were eligible for the tax credit of 10 percent, of $300,000. The useful life of the equipment is 15 years. If has no salvage value. The applicable tax rate is 40 percent.

    a. To make the two firms comparable, what adjustments to both the income statement and balance sheet of the flow-through firm would you suggest for 1980?

    b. What adjustment would you suggest for the remaining 14 years over which the assets will be depreciated?

19. *The full cost of increasing employee pension benefits attributable to prior service with the firm does not necessarily have to be reflected in the in-come statement or balance sheet in the year of the change.*

    The 1976 financial statements of the Colgate-Palmolive Company reported:

    Effective January 1, 1977, the Board of Directors, subject to stockholders' approval, amended the Colgate plan to increase the benefits. These amendments will create an additional unfunded prior service cost of $57,000,000. The effect on pension expense of the increased benefits, amortization of the increased prior service cost, and revision of the actuarial assumptions will be an increase of approximately $1,400,000 per year.

   a. What is the effect of the change, as of January 1, 1977, (to the extent revealed or implied by the note) on
      1. recorded expenses?
      2. recorded liabilities?
      3. cash disbursements?
   b. Over how many years would you estimate Colgate is amortizing the prior service costs? (Assume the entire $1,400,000 relates to prior service costs.)
   c. What would be the long-term effect of the change, during 1977 and subsequent years, on
      1. reported expenses?
      2. required cash payments?

20. *Pension costs should be charged as expenses when the firm receives the benefits of employee services, not when the firm makes cash payments to either the employees themselves or to a pension fund.*

   A corporation reported on its income statement pension expense of $17 million. Its balance sheet indicated accrued pension costs (liability) of $6 million. A footnote to its financial statements revealed that the company's actual contribution to the pension fund was $14.5 million and that the actuarially computed liability for *unfunded* prior service costs was $36 million.
   a. Prepare a journal entry to summarize the pension expense and the cash contribution to the pension fund for the year.
   b. Distinguish between the liability for accrued pension cost as reported in the balance sheet and that for the unfunded prior service costs as reported in the footnotes.
   c. From the information provided, is it possible to determine the present actuarial value of the firm's overall pension liability to its past and current employees? On the books of which accounting entity would such liability be recorded?

*solutions to*   a. 7% (½ of 14%) of $1,000—$70 interest payable each six months.
*exercise for*   b. 6% (½ of 12%) of $1,000—$60 interest expected each six months.
*review and*    c. $10 difference.
*self-testing*  d. The present value of an annuity of $10 for 40 semiannual periods at a discount rate of 6% is, based on Table 4.

$$\$10 \times 15.0463 = \$150.46$$

   e. Each bond will sell at a premium of $150.46 and at a total price of $1,150.46.

f. 6% of $1,150.46—$69.03.

g. $70 (see part a).

h. $70.00 – $69.03 = $.97 amortization of bond premium.

i. $1,150.46 – $.97 = $1,149.49 effective bond liability on July 1, 1980.

j. 6% of 1,149.49—$68.97 interest expense.

# 11

# Transactions
# Between a Firm
# and its Owners

This chapter is the first of two chapters that will be directed primarily to transactions between a firm and its owners. In this chapter we shall compare partnerships with corporations, consider the problems associated with the formation of a new enterprise, and identify the characteristics of preferred stock and common stock. In addition, we shall digress from our main concern with the accounting issues associated with commercial enterprises to explore some of the unique reporting problems of municipalities and other nonprofit organizations.

## Proprietorships and Partnerships

There are three major types of business enterprises: the individual proprietorship, the partnership, and the corporation. The proprietorship is a business firm owned by a single party. The partnership is one owned by two or more parties. The corporation is a separate, legal entity which operates under a grant of authority from a state or other governmental body and is owned by one or more stockholders.

The proprietorship is far and away the most common type of business enterprise in the United States. Indeed, proprietorships comprise almost 70 percent of all business concerns, whereas partnerships account for about 17 percent of enterprises and corporations only 13 percent. Corporations, however, generate approximately 75 percent of the national income.

Corporations are often thought of as large enterprises whereas proprietorships and partnerships as small. While it is true that most proprietorships and partnerships are small businesses, *most* corporations are also relatively small, often family-owned firms. The corporation is associated with bigness because most large businesses—those that account for the major part of industrial output —are corporations. Nevertheless, many large enterprises are organized as partnerships. Service organizations such as brokerage firms or CPA firms are commonly organized as partnerships even though they generate hundreds of millions of dollars in annual revenues.

Proprietorships and partnerships are, in a legal sense, extensions of their owners. One or more parties simply establish a business. They purchase or rent whatever equipment or space is needed, acquire supplies or inventory, and obtain any local operating licenses that might be required. No formal charter or state certificates are required. If the business is to be operated as a partnership, it is generally wise to have an attorney draw up a partnership agreement which specifies the rights and obligations of each partner—how profits will be distributed, who will perform what services, how much each partner must contribute initially, what rights of survivorship will accrue to each partner's estate, what limitations there will be upon sale of a partner's interest in the business—but such a document is for the protection of the individual partners; it is not ordinarily required by law. Significantly, a proprietor, as well as each partner of a partnership, is usually personally responsible for all obligations of his business. If the enterprise suffers losses, the owners are jointly and severally responsible for all debts incurred. A partner will generally be held liable not only for his share of the debts but, should his partners be unable to meet their share of the claims against the business, for those of his partners as well. As a consequence, few investors are willing to purchase an equity interest in a partnership as they might purchase one in a corporation. In the event the partnership is liquidated and fellow partners are unable to meet their share of obligations, the personal assets of the investors might be subject to the claims of creditors. Their risk of loss is unlimited, extending beyond their original investment.

There are no limits on the number of partners who might compose a partnership. Because of the extended liability to which each partner is subject, most partnerships are small—two or three members. However, many partnerships are considerably larger. Some large CPA firms which are organized as partnerships have well over 1,000 partners.

Neither the proprietorship nor the partnership form of organization provides for the ready transfer of interest from one owner to another. Partners do not individually own or have a share in the ownership of *specific* partnership assets. As with a corporation, property is held in the name of the firm itself. Each partner, like each stockholder, owns a share in *all* partnership property. Nevertheless, most partnership agreements prohibit a partner from freely transferring his interest to a person outside of the partnership. Generally, the agreements stipulate that a partner may sell his interest to an outsider only if all the partners agree to accept the new member. Similarly, the death or the withdrawal of a partner may automatically dissolve the partnership; a partner is not ordinarily free to bequeath his interest to his heirs. In many partnerships, especially those with a large number of partners, special provisions are made to assure the continuity of the business despite the loss of an individual partner. Nevertheless, because of the difficulty of transferring shares, the partnership form of organization is not well suited to induce casual investors—those who are either unable or unwilling to take an active role in management—to purchase a small interest in a business.

Neither proprietorships nor partnerships are subject to federal or state taxes on income. Instead, the tax is assessed on the individual owners. If the organization is a partnership, then each partner is taxed on his share of partnership earnings. The rate of tax is determined by the tax bracket in which the individual partner falls after taking into account his earnings from nonpartnership sources. Each partner is taxed on his share of the entire earnings of the partnership, not just on his withdrawals from the business. Thus, especially if the partnership requires capital for expansion, a partner may be taxed on earnings that are retained in the business, and are not readily available for his discretionary use, as well as on funds actually taken from the business.

## Corporations

A corporation, by contrast, is a legal entity separate and distinct from its managers. It is a legal "person" created by the state. A corporation is owned by its stockholders, but its stockholders are not compelled to take an active role in its management. In many corporations there is a distinct separation of ownership and operating control, with managers typically holding only a small fraction of total shares outstanding. A corporation has an indefinite life. It continues in existence regardless of the personal fortunes of its owners. Its owners are commonly free to transfer or sell their share of stock to anyone they wish.

Corporations, unlike proprietorships or partnerships, are creatures of the state. A corporation has the right to own property in its own name, and it can sue or be sued. Upon its formation, it must be chartered by the state. Although at one time charters were granted only upon special acts of the legislature, today they are routinely issued upon submission of certificates of incorporation and supplementary application forms, and payment of necessary fees. The certificate of incorporation specifies the name of the proposed corporation, its purposes (most certificates of incorporation are drawn so as to allow the company to engage in an unlimited range of business activities), the number of shares authorized to be issued, and the number of directors.

Once the charter has been issued the corporation has to adopt formal bylaws, which would govern a number of critical areas of operation. They would cover such matters as the issuance and transfer of stock and the conduct of meetings of directors and stockholders.

The single most significant distinction between corporations and proprietorships or partnerships is that the liability of stockholders of a corporation is limited to the amount of their initial investment in the company, whereas that of the owners of proprietorships or partnerships is unlimited. With few exceptions, the maximum loss that a stockholder can sustain on purchase of an interest in a corporation is the amount of his initial investment. Should the corporation fail, creditors can avail themselves of only the assets of the corporation; they cannot seek redress against the personal assets of the individual stockholders. Only in rare circumstances—the involvement of corporate stockholders in fraud, for example—is it possible for creditors or others who may have judgments against the corporation to "pierce the corporate veil" and bring a successful legal action against the individual stockholders. Because it is able to protect investors against unlimited loss, the corporation is a vehicle that is well suited to raise large amounts of capital. Large numbers of persons may be willing to purchase an ownership interest in a company knowing that they can share in the gains of the company to an unlimited extent but that their losses will be limited by the amount of their direct contributions. They need not be overly concerned with the day-to-day operations of their business, since neither the managers nor their fellow owners can so mismanage the business as to put any of their personal assets in jeopardy.

Corporations, like other legal persons, are subject to both federal and state income taxes. Earnings of a corporation are taxed, albeit at rates different from those of individuals, regardless of whether or not they are distributed to its owners. The individual owners of the corporation, unlike those of a partnership, are not taxed on their share of the earnings that are retained in the business; they are, however, taxed on the earnings as they are distributed to them in the form of dividends. Earnings of a corporation are taxed twice—once when earned by the corporation and again when they are distributed to the stockholders.

### Corporations vs. Partnerships: Distinctions in Perspective

It is easy to place too much emphasis on the distinctions between partnerships and corporations. For some businesses, especially smaller enterprises, the differences may be more of form than of substance. For a small business the corporate form of organization is unlikely to facilitate acquisition of required capital any more than would the partnership form. Most small enterprises have difficulty obtaining equity capital not so much because potential investors are concerned about subjecting all of their personal assets to possible loss but rather because they are unwilling to risk any funds on the venture. Small businesses are inherently hazardous, and the corporate form of organization does not measurably enhance prospects for success.

Equally significant, the limited liability feature of the corporate form of organization may actually deter potential suppliers of capital. To a bank or other lending institution, the limitation on owner's liability is an obstacle rather than an inducement to making a loan. The bank, after all, wants assurance that in the event of default it can have access to all the assets of owners, not merely those devoted to the business. As a consequence, many lenders circumvent the limitations on stockholder liability by requiring that the stockholders personally cosign any notes issued by the corporation.

Moreover, the distinction between the corporate and partnership form of organization has been diminished in recent years by legislation in some states which, in fact, provides for the limitation on the liability of certain partners in certain circumstances. As long as there exists one *general* partner whose liability is unlimited, the liability of other partners, particularly those who take no part in the day-to-day management of the enterprise, may be limited.

③ The advantage of a corporation over a partnership in that shares of ownership are readily transferable may also be more illusory than real. Although the shares of major corporations can be sold without difficulty, those of companies that are *closely held* by a small number of stockholders could probably not be sold any more easily than could a similar interest in a partnership. Indeed, agreements among stockholders of smaller companies sometimes provide that all sales of shares to outsiders must meet with the approval of existing owners.

The tax distinctions between partnerships and corporations have also been diminished greatly by statute. The current federal tax code provides that if certain criteria are met small corporations may elect to be taxed as partnerships. As a consequence, small corporations can avoid the burden of "double" taxation; only stockholders and not the corporation will be taxed on corporate earnings.

## Distinctive Features of Partnership Accounting

There are relatively few differences between accounting for a proprietorship or partnership and a corporation. What differences there are relate primarily to the owners' equity accounts and are more of form than of substance. Although in this section we shall deal exclusively with partnerships rather than proprietorships, the points made will generally be applicable to proprietorships as well. For accounting purposes the proprietorship may be viewed as a special case of a partnership—a "partnership" with only a single partner.

The owners' equity section of a partnership general ledger usually consists of one capital account for each partner. Each capital account is credited (increased) by the amount of a partner's contributions to the firm and by his share of partnership profits. It is debited (decreased) by a partner's withdrawals from the firm and by his share of partnership losses.

*example*  Lee and Grant decide to form a partnership. Lee contributes $200,000 cash, and Grant contributes a building, which has been appraised at $150,000 but on which there is a mortgage of $50,000. The building had been carried on Grant's personal books at a value of $75,000. The partnership agrees to assume the liability for the mortgage. The following entry would be required to establish the partnership:

(a)

| | | |
|---|---|---|
| Cash | $200,000 | |
| Building | 150,000 | |
| Mortgage note payable | | $ 50,000 |
| Capital, Lee | | 200,000 |
| Capital, Grant | | 100,000 |

**To record formation of the partnership.**

Property contributed is valued at its fair market value, regardless of the value at which it might have been carried on the books of the individual partners prior to being assigned to the partnership.

The partners agree to share profits and losses in the same ratio as their initial capital contributions, 2 to 1. During the first year of operations the partnership had revenues of $240,000 and expenses of $180,000—income of $60,000. The following *closing entry* would be required, assuming that revenues and expenses were properly recorded throughout the year.

**(b)**

| | | |
|---|---|---|
| Revenues (various accounts) | $240,000 | |
| Expenses (various accounts) | | $180,000 |
| Capital, Lee | | 40,000 |
| Capital, Grant | | 20,000 |

**To close the revenue and expense accounts.**

During the course of the year Lee withdrew $20,000 in cash, and Grant, $40,000. In addition, each partner was paid $25,000 in salaries, included in expenses above. At the time of withdrawal the appropriate entry would be

**(c)**

| | | |
|---|---|---|
| Withdrawals, Lee | $20,000 | |
| Withdrawals, Grant | 40,000 | |
| Cash | | $60,000 |

**To record withdrawals.**

The "withdrawals" account is the equivalent of the "dividends" account maintained by corporations. At year end it would be *closed* to partners' capital:

**(d)**

| | | |
|---|---|---|
| Capital, Lee | $20,000 | |
| Capital, Grant | 40,000 | |
| Withdrawals, Lee | | $20,000 |
| Withdrawals, Grant | | 40,000 |

**To close withdrawals accounts.**

It is critical that a partnership agreement set forth any amounts that the individual partners are to receive in salaries apart from the shares of earnings to which they are entitled. Payments of salaries to partners may be accounted for just as they would be if they were ordinary expenses. They have no direct impact on the withdrawals account or the individual capital accounts.

| Lee, capital | | | | Grant, capital | | | |
|---|---|---|---|---|---|---|---|
| (d) | 20,000 | (a) | 200,000 | (d) | 40,000 | (a) | 100,000 |
| | | (b) | 40,000 | | | (b) | 20,000 |
| | | | 220,000 | | | | 80,000 |

At the conclusion of the year, Lee would have a capital balance of $220,000, and Grant, $80,000. The capital balances would no longer be in the original ratio of 2 to 1. Whether or not a partner should be permitted to draw his capital account below a specified level is a question that must be addressed in the partnership agreement. Some partnership agreements provide for the payment of interest to any partner who maintains an *excess* capital balance in relation to those of his partners.

### Admission of New Partners

The difficult conceptual issues pertaining to partnership accounting relate to the sale of partnership interests and the admission of new partners. The critical question—one to which there is no widespread agreement on an answer—is whether such events demand an overall revaluation of partnership assets. Suppose, for example, that at the conclusion of its first year of operations the Lee-Grant partnership decides to admit a third partner, Sherman. Sherman agrees to pay $200,000 for a one-third interest in the partnership. Just prior to his admission, the combined balance in the capital accounts of the two partners is $300,000. Hence, reported net assets must also be $300,000. After admission of Sherman and acceptance of his contribution of $200,000, net assets of the partnership will be $500,000.

Sherman is willing to pay $200,000 for a one-third interest in the partnership. In his eyes—and probably those of the marketplace, assuming an arm's-length transaction—the total value of the partnership must be three times $200,000—$600,000. Yet the reported net assets of the company after his admission will be only $500,000. Should the additional $100,000 in value be accorded accounting recognition; if so, how?

**revaluation approach**    There are two probable explanations for the apparent $100,000 excess of *market* value over reported value. First, the market value of one or more specific assets is worth more than its reported value. For example, plant and equipment recorded at a value net of depreciation of $200,000 may, in fact, have a market value of $300,000. Or, second, the company possesses assets that have not been accorded accounting recognition. More than likely, such assets are intangible—the good name of the firm, special skills of management, an advantageous location or economic environment. Such intangible assets could be grouped together in the broad category of *goodwill.*

Recognition of the market value of the "new" asset, goodwill, or the increase in the existing assets, plant and equipment, as well as the corresponding increase of the equity of the two original partners can readily be effected by a simple journal entry:

Goodwill (or plant and
equipment)                    $100,000
Capital, Lee                                        $66,667
Capital, Grant                                       33,333
**To record goodwill.**

The increase in owners' equity is divided among the two partners *in proportion to the agreed upon profit/loss sharing ratio,* 2 to 1, even though their capital balances are not in such ratio.

The admission of the new partner can now be recorded as follows:

Cash                                    $200,000
Capital, Sherman                                   $200,000
**To record admission of a new partner.**

After his admission, the balance sheet of the partnership would reveal net assets of $600,000 and owners' equity as follows:

Capital, Lee        $286,667
Capital, Grant       113,333
Capital, Sherman     200,000

The revaluation approach is based on the contention that the transfer of the partnership interest in an arm's-length transaction provides an objective means of determining the fair market value of partnership assets. Proponents of the approach assert that the transfer is of sufficient economic significance to justify a restatement of assets. Indeed, they argue, the admission of a new partner is the equivalent of the dissolution of one business entity and the formation of another.

The objection to the revaluation approach is that it is inconsistent with the historical basis of accounting. Assets of an enterprise are generally reported at original cost, less any allowances for depreciation or amortization. No recognition is given to goodwill developed by the enterprise. The balance sheet provides an indication of unexpired costs, not current market values. Moreover, the approach is inconsistent with accounting principles as applied by corporations. In corporate accounting, neither the sale of existing shares nor the issue of new shares at a price reflective of a market value in excess of *book* values is considered to be proper cause for an overall revaluation of corporate assets.

**bonus
approach**   As an alternative to recognizing the increase in fair market value, the partnership can account for the additional payment by the new partner as a *bonus* paid to the existing partners. After the admission of the new partner, the net worth of the partnership will be $500,000 (the $300,000 in assets prior

to his admission plus the new partner's contribution of $200,000). For his contribution of $200,000 the new partner will receive a one-third equity in a partnership that has a net worth of $500,000. He will be credited, therefore, with a capital interest of one-third of $500,000—$166,667. The difference of $33,333 between his contribution of $200,000 and the capital interest with which he will be credited ($166,667) may be interpreted as a bonus to be divided among the existing partners *in proportion to the profit/loss sharing ratio* of 2:1. Thus, the admission of Sherman could be recorded as follows:

| | | |
|---|---|---|
| Cash | $200,000 | |
|     Capital, Sherman | | $166,667 |
|     Capital, Lee | | 22,222 |
|     Capital, Grant | | 11,111 |
| **To record admission of a new partner.** | | |

After his admission, the balance sheet of the partnership would reveal net assets of $500,000 (as compared to $600,000 under the *goodwill* approach), and partners' capital accounts would be reported as follows:

| | |
|---|---|
| Capital, Lee | $242,222 |
| Capital, Grant | 91,111 |
| Capital, Sherman | 166,667 |

The issue of accounting for the admission of a new partner is not one that is currently under consideration by the rule-making authorities. It is of interest to students of accounting primarily because it provides so vivid an example of the type of problem that arises when book values are inconsistent with market values.

## Corporate Capital Accounts

In contrast to the owners' equity section of a partnership balance sheet, in which the capital balances of the partners are reported, that of a corporation would indicate the par values of different classes of stock, the amount received by the corporation in excess of such par values, and the earnings retained in the business. Exhibit 11-1 illustrates the stockholders' equity section of the Bausch & Lomb Corporation.

There are two major categories of capital stock: common stock and preferred stock. Common stock is the "usual" type of stock; when only one class of stock is issued, it is almost certain to be common stock. Preferred stock, when issued, ordinarily has certain preferences as to dividend payments and rights in liquidation.

EXHIBIT 11-1

**Bausch & Lomb Corporation**
**Stockholders' Equity**

| | Shares | December 31, 1978 | December 31, 1977 |
|---|---|---|---|
| 4% cumulative preferred stock, par value $100 per share— | | | |
| Authorized | 60,000 | | |
| Issued and outstanding | 50,000 | $ 5,000,000 | $ 5,000,000 |
| Class A preferred stock, par value $1 per share— | | | |
| Authorized | 600,000 | | |
| Issued and outstanding | None | | |
| Common stock, par value $2.50 per share— | | | |
| Authorized | 8,000,000 | | |
| Issued and outstanding | 5,700,436 | 14,251,000 | 14,166,000 |
| Class B stock, par value $.50 per share— | | | |
| Authorized | 550,000 | | |
| Issued and outstanding | 108,550 | 54,000 | 57,000 |
| Capital in excess of par value | | 26,507,000 | 25,821,000 |
| Earnings retained | | 128,831,000 | 107,767,000 |
| | | $174,643,000 | $152,811,000 |

As indicated in Exhibit 11–1, the balance sheet includes, often parenthetically, information on the numbers of shares of each class of stock authorized, issued, and outstanding. The number of shares *authorized* is the maximum number of shares, per its corporate charter, that the company is permitted to issue; the number of shares *issued* is the amount that has actually been put into circulation; the number of shares *outstanding* indicates those currently in circulation. It represents the number of shares issued less those that have been repurchased by the company. Shares held by the company, often referred to as *treasury* shares, are considered to be issued but not outstanding.

## Common Stock: Characteristics and Rights of Shareholders

Common stock is characterized by rights to income and of control. Common stockholders receive distributions of the assets of the corporation if and when dividends are declared by its board of directors. Common stockholders, however, have a *residual* interest in their company. Upon dissolution of the corporation, they have the right to share in the remaining assets of the company after all claimants, including preferred stockholders, have been satisfied.

Common stockholders ordinarily possess rights to vote. They can elect members of the board of directors and can vote on such matters of corporate policy as are specifically reserved in corporate bylaws for decision by the stockholders-at-large. Corporate voting is conducted on the basis of one *share* (not one shareholder), one vote.

Sometimes a company may issue more than one class of common stock. The alternative classes are typically restricted in certain rights made available to, or granted certain privileges denied, the others. A footnote to the annual report of the Bausch & Lomb annual report, for example, indicates that Class B stock has the same voting, dividend and liquidation rights as ordinary common stock, but is reserved for issuance to employees in connection with stock option plans.

### Preferred Stock: Characteristics and Rights of Shareholders

Preferred stock is a hybrid between common stock and bonds: It combines some of the benefits—and limitations—of both. Preferred stock ordinarily stipulates that a fixed or minimum dividend will accrue to the holder each year. The dividend may be stated as a dollar amount (e.g., $3 per share) or as percentage of the par value (e.g., 5 percent). In this regard, preferred stock is similar to bonds. However, the obligation to pay such dividends is not quite so binding on the corporation as it would be if the company had issued bonds. Most commonly, the company would not be in immediate default if it failed to make a single dividend payment. Instead, the company would be prohibited from making any dividend payments to common stockholders until it satisfied its current and, in most instances, accumulated obligations to the preferred stockholders. Similarly, in the event of liquidation, the preferred stockholders would have preference over the common stockholders. Before any distributions could be made to the common stockholders, the preferred stockholders would have to have been returned both their initial investment as well as any accumulated dividends.

The specific features of preferred stock vary from issue to issue. Generally, preferred stockholders do not have voting rights, except when the company has failed to pay preferred stock dividends for a specified number of periods. Some issues, called *participating* issues, entitle the preferred stockholders to share in income in excess of the stipulated dividend. For example, an issue may carry a minimum dividend of $3 per share. It may provide that once the preferred stockholders have received their minimum dividend—and usually once the common shareholders have received a dividend of a stated amount—any additional funds available for distribution will be divided, in a specified proportion, between the two groups of stockholders.

Unlike bonds, preferred stock does not mature on a particular date. Usually, however, the corporation has the option to *call* (redeem) the stock at a stipulated price after a number of years have elapsed. Many issues (approximately 40 percent in recent years) provide that preferred shares can be *converted*, at the option of the holder, into shares of common stock. The specific conversion ratio—how many shares of common stock may be exchanged for each share of preferred stock—is ordinarily established at the time the preferred stock is issued.

From the standpoint of the issuing corporation, preferred stock has one critical disadvantage over bonds or other pure debt securities. The dividends on preferred stock (like those on common stock) are not deductible from corporate income for tax purposes, whereas interest payments are. The effective cost of the capital acquired through the issue of preferred stock is therefore magnified substantially. Suppose, for example, that a company wishes to raise $1 million in capital. It could issue bonds which could be sold to yield 6 percent or preferred stock which would bear a dividend rate of 8 percent. Preferred stock, especially if it is not convertible into common stock, often provides the holder with a higher return since interest payments take precedence over dividend payments. The interest payments would require an outlay of $60,000 per year, and the dividend payments, $80,000. If, however, the income tax rate were 48 percent, then the *effective* outlay would be $80,000/ (1 - .48)—$153,846. That is, the company would have to earn $153,846 in order to meet its preferred stock dividend payments of $80,000:

| | |
|---|---:|
| Income before taxes | $153,846 |
| Tax at 48% | 73,846 |
| Income available for payment of dividends | $ 80,000 |

By contrast, the company would have to earn only $60,000 to meet its required interest payments of $60,000. Since the interest payments are fully deductible, if the corporation earned $60,000 and paid interest of $60,000, it would have no taxable income and hence no tax liability. The full $60,000 of earnings could be used to meet the interest payments:

| | |
|---|---:|
| Income before taxes | $60,000 |
| Taxes | 0 |
| Income available for payment of interest | $60,000 |

Whereas when taxes are ignored, the cost of capital, if the preferred stock rather than the bonds were issued, would be in the ratio of 8:6, when taxes are taken into account the ratio increases to 15:6.

The mechanics of forming a corporation are straightforward; the central accounting problems relate to the values to be placed upon the assets or services contributed by its organizers.

A corporation is ordinarily formed by one or more individuals known as promoters. The *promoters* organize the corporation, apply for a charter, and establish the bylaws under which the corporation will initially operate. Commonly, the promoters contribute cash, other assets, or services to the company in exchange for all or a portion of the capital stock to be issued. If additional equity (ownership) financing is required, then the promoters arrange for shares of the stock to be sold either to the general public or to specific parties known to the promoters. The promoters are in a fiduciary relationship —one of highest trust—to the corporation. They are under obligation to make certain that they themselves do not benefit at the expense of those who will subsequently purchase shares of corporate stock—that they receive an interest proportionate to the value of the assets or services which they have contributed.

Corporate stock traditionally bears an indication of *par value* per share. Par value is the nominal value of the stock, a value that has been arbitrarily assigned. Common stock can be sold for an amount above or below par value. If sold above, it is said to have been sold at a *premium,* and if below, at a *discount.* Originally par value was intended to protect creditors. It was to provide them assurance that stockholders had contributed assets worth at least as much as the par value of the shares. If they had not—that is, if they had purchased the stock at a discount—then in the event of corporate dissolution they could be held responsible for the difference between what they paid for the stock and its par value, despite the usual limitations on stockholder liability.

Par value did not prove to be an effective means of protecting creditors inasmuch as a new corporation could assign to its shares a par value far below the price at which it expected the shares to be sold. Many states have substituted a concept of *stated* or *legal* capital for par value. Commonly, stated or legal capital is either an amount established by the company (similar to par value) or that for which the stock was actually issued. Typically, stated or legal capital establishes a floor on the payment of dividends; the corporation is prohibited from paying dividends that will reduce its owners' equity below its stated or legal capital.

When a corporation issues common stock for cash or other assets, either to the original promoters or anytime subsequent to its formation, a simple journal entry is in order. Asset accounts are debited and owners' equity accounts are credited for the *fair market* value of the property received by the corporation. The credit to the capital account is divided into two parts—the par (or stated) value of the stock issued and the amount in excess of par (or stated) value. Suppose, for example, a corporation issues 10,000 shares of $2.50 par value stock at $80 per share. The appropriate entry would be

| | | |
|---|---|---|
| Cash | $800,000 | |
| Common stock, par value | | $ 25,000 |
| Contributed capital in excess | | |
| of par value, common stock | | 775,000 |

**To record the issue of common stock.**

The two credited accounts combined indicate the capital contributed by common stockholders. Some accountants believe that the significance of par value is sufficiently small so that the interests of clear and concise financial reporting would be better served if the two accounts were consolidated on the balance sheet into a single account, "capital contributed by common stockholders."

Corporations are often organized from a nucleus of assets previously employed by proprietorships, partnerships, or other corporations. The assets must be recorded on the books of the new corporation at their fair market value, regardless of the value at which they were accounted by the previous entity.

*example*    Moore decides to incorporate his existing business. The fair market value of all assets to be contributed to the corporation is $400,000. The corporation will also assume liabilities of the business, which amount to $50,000. As part of his incorporation plan, Moore will sell shares to outside investors, who have agreed to contribute $336,000 cash. Moreover, an attorney has agreed to accept shares of stock in exchange for legal and other services connected with the organization of the company. The services have a fair market value of $14,000. The charter of the new company authorizes the issue of 20,000 shares of common stock, $10 par value. The promoter (in this case, Moore) decides, however, to issue only 10,000 shares.

The net amount contributed to the corporation will be $700,000— $350,000 contributed by Moore, $336,000 contributed by the other investors, and $14,000 contributed by the attorney. The new company will issue 1 share of common for each $70 contributed. The following entry would record its initial capitalization:

| | | |
|---|---|---|
| Various assets | $400,000 | |
| Cash | 336,000 | |
| Organizational costs | 14,000 | |
| Various liabilities | | $ 50,000 |
| Common stock, par value ($10) | | 100,000 |
| Contributed capital in excess | | |
| of par value | | 600,000 |

**To record formation of the corporation.**

The various assets and liabilities, including any intangible assets, would be classified and recorded in separate accounts as appropriate. Each stockholder would receive a number of shares indicative of his percentage contribution. Thus,

|  | Contribution | Percentage | No. of Shares |
|---|---|---|---|
| Moore | $350,000 | 50% | 5,000 |
| Other investors | 336,000 | 48 | 4,800 |
| Attorney | 14,000 | 2 | 200 |

The important consideration is that each stockholder receives an ownership interest reflective of the fair market value of his contribution. Prior to the enactment of protective state legislation, it was not unusual for the promoters to overvalue their own contribution and thereby take for themselves a disproportionate share of stock to be issued. But even today, because of the subjective nature of the valuation process, an investor who purchases stock of a newly formed corporation should carefully review the contributions of the promoters to make certain that they have not been overstated. Of particular concern should be the value of intangible assets, such as patents, lists of customers, and organizational services provided by the promoter.

## Issuance of Additional Shares

Should a firm issue additional shares of stock subsequent to its formation, similar entries would be in order. The resultant increase in owners' equity would be reflected first in the "common stock, par value" account, and then, to the extent of amounts received above par, in the account, "contributed capital in excess of par value."

The price at which additional shares of stock may be issued would be dependent on the market value as opposed to the book value of the company's existing shares outstanding.

*example*    A firm has reported assets of $100,000, liabilities of $50,000, and owners' equity of $50,000. Owners' equity is composed of the following accounts:

| | |
|---|---|
| Common stock, $1 par value, 10,000 shares issued and outstanding | $10,000 |
| Contributed capital in excess of par value | 25,000 |
| Retained earnings | 15,000 |
| Total owners' equity | $50,000 |

The book value per share is $50,000 divided by 10,000 shares—$5 per share.

*Book Value = 5*

The company wishes to raise $100,000 in capital. The market price of the company's stock is $20 per share. (Large discrepancies between book value and market value are not uncommon. Book value is based on historical costs; market value is based on investor expectations as to future earnings.) Assuming that the market price is unaffected by the impending issue of the new stock (a major financial event which may itself affect investor expectations of future earnings), the company could acquire the $100,000 in needed capital by issuing an additional 5,000 shares at $20 per share. *(market)*

The journal entry to record the issue would be

| | | |
|---|---|---|
| Cash | $100,000 | |
|     Common stock, par value | | $ 5,000 |
|     Contributed capital in excess | | |
|       of par value | | 95,000 |
| **To record the issue of additional stocks.** | | |

$\frac{100,000}{5,000} = 20$

Owner's equity would now be made up as follows:

| | |
|---|---|
| Common stock, $1 par value, 15,000 shares issued and outstanding | $ 15,000 |
| Contributed capital in excess of par value | 120,000 |
| Retained earnings | 15,000 |
| | $150,000 |

*Net assets*

$A = L + OE$

$OE = A - L$
↑
*net assets*

Book value per share would now be $10 ($150,000 divided by 15,000 shares), compared to $5 prior to the sale of the additional shares.

The increase in book value can be attributed to the willingness of the new investors to pay $20 per share for stock that had a book value of only $5 per share. The new investors contributed $100,000 in return for a one-third interest (5,000 shares out of 15,000 shares) in a company that will have *reported* net assets of $150,000. In effect, existing shareholders received a "bonus" in the same manner as did the partners in the example earlier in this chapter.

### Issuance of Preferred Stock

The mechanics of recording the issuance of preferred stock are almost identical to those of recording common stock. However, the characteristics of any amounts received in excess of or below par value are, in essence, more similar to the premium or discount associated with bonds than with common stock.

The amount that an investor will pay for a corporation's common stock is dependent on his expectation of the firm's earnings in the future. He will share in the *residual* income of the company—that which remains after the claims against earnings of bondholders and preferred stockholders are satisfied. The price that he is willing to pay for a share of common stock will rise and fall with his assessment of the company's earning potential.

The owner of preferred stock, however, is less concerned with anticipated profits of the company. His dollar share in the income of the company is contractually fixed. He will receive only the dollar amount of the dividend specified on his shares. As long as the company has sufficient earnings to meet its required dividend payments, he will be unaffected by swings in income.

The primary concern of the purchaser of preferred stock is the yield that he will obtain from one company as opposed to another with similar risk characteristics. Suppose, for example, the preferred stock of a company has a par value of $100 per share and a dividend rate of $6 per year. If similar securities are being sold to yield 7 percent per year, then a rational purchaser would be willing to invest in the shares only if he could purchase them at a discount sufficiently great to assure a return equivalent to the rate prevailing in the market. If similar securities are being sold to yield only 5 percent, then he would be willing to pay a premium of such magnitude as to reduce his return to that which he could obtain elsewhere. Preferred stock has many of the characteristics of bonds. The price at which a share of preferred stock is traded is determined in a manner similar to that of bonds.

*example*

The ABC Co. wishes to issue 10,000 shares of $100 par value preferred stock which will pay dividends of $10 per year. On the day of issue the prevailing yield on similar types of securities is 9 percent.

For how much is each share likely to be sold?

If a share of stock which pays dividends of $10 per year is to be sold to yield 9 percent, then it would be sold at a price equal to $10/.09—$111.11. Since, unlike bonds, there is no maturity date, the return can be assumed to be a perpetuity (one for an infinitely long duration); hence, there is no need to refer to present value tables to determine the selling price. Similarly, there is no need to amortize the premium ($11.11 per share in this case), which is commonly classified on the balance sheet as "Contributed capital in excess of par."

## Transactions in a Corporation's Own Shares

Companies may purchase their own outstanding shares of stock for a number of reasons. They may wish to reissue the shares to executives or other employees in connection with stock option or related compensation plans. They may desire to *invest* temporarily in their own shares, just as they might invest in shares of other corporations. Or they may want to reduce the scale of their operations—to return to stockholders a share of the capital they had contributed. Stock which is acquired and retained by the issuing corporation is known

_Contra accnt to O.E._

as _treasury stock._ Treasury shares may not be voted, do not receive dividends, and carry none of the usual rights of ownership.

The manner in which treasury stock is accounted for has a direct impact on a firm's reported capital structure. There are two primary methods of accounting for treasury stock. One method is referred to as the _cost_ method and the other as the _par value_ method. Under the cost method treasury shares are accounted for in a separate account. Under the par value method treasury shares are treated as stock to be permanently retired.

**cost method**   Assume that prior to acquisition of treasury stock, the owners' equity section of a firm's balance sheet is as follows:

| | |
|---|---:|
| Common stock, $1 par value, 10,000 shares issued and outstanding | $ 10,000 |
| Contributed capital in excess of par value | 20,000 |
| Retained earnings | 70,000 |
| Total owners' equity | $100,000 |

The firm purchases 100 shares of its own common stock at a price of $15 per share. Under the _cost_ method, the acquisition could be recorded with a simple journal entry:

| | | |
|---|---:|---:|
| Treasury stock | $1,500 | |
| Cash | | $1,500 |

**To record the purchase of treasury stock.**

Treasury stock would be reported in an account which is _contra_ to the other equity accounts. Thus,

| | |
|---|---:|
| Common stock, $1 par value, 10,000 shares issued, 100 shares held in treasury | $ 10,000 |
| Contributed capital in excess of par value | 20,000 |
| Retained earnings | 70,000 |
| | $100,000 |
| Less: Shares held in treasury (at cost) | 1,500 |
| Total owners' equity | $ 98,500 |

Some accountants assert that treasury stock should be reported among the current assets—just like other marketable securities. They argue that the stock could be converted to cash at any time, even more readily, perhaps, than most other current assets. Those who reject this assertion point out that it is illogical for a corporation to own itself; retention of treasury shares represents a reduction in the outstanding equity of the remaining stockholders. Moreover, they assert, the firm has the potential to sell for cash an unlimited number of *unissued* shares. Yet few would argue that unissued shares should be reported as assets. The position of those who maintain that treasury stock should be accounted for as a reduction in stockholders' equity, rather than as an asset, prevails (though by no means universally) in practice.

Should the company sell the shares, the treasury stock amount is reduced by the amount of their original reacquisition cost. If the selling price exceeds (or is less than) the original cost, then any difference is added to (or subtracted from) contributed capital in excess of par.* Assume, for example, the 100 shares, originally purchased at $15 per share, were resold for $17 each. The following entry would be in order:

| | | |
|---|---|---|
| Cash | $1,700 | |
|     Treasury stock | | $1,500 |
|     Contributed capital in excess of | | |
|       par value | | 200 |
| **To record the sale of treasury stock.** | | |

The entry is reflective of the widely held view among accountants that a company cannot recognize gains or losses in transactions in its own securities. Such transactions involve nothing more than increases or decreases in the amount of contributed capital. *Thus, the sale of treasury stock, unlike the sale of marketable securities, would not result in revenues or expenses to be included in the computation of net income.*

**par value method**
Under the *par value* method, the acquisition of the treasury shares is accounted for as a retirement of the stock purchased. First, both the common stock, par value, and the contributed capital in excess of par accounts are reduced (debited) by amounts reflective of the percentage of shares being retired. Then, retained earnings are reduced (debited) by any amounts in excess of the reduction in both common stock and contributed capital in excess of par.†

---

*There is an exception with respect to sales of treasury stock where selling price is less than original cost. *Losses,* according to APB Opinion 6, should be subtracted from capital contributed in excess of par only to the extent that previous net *gains* from sales or retirements of the same class of stock are included therein; otherwise they should be subtracted from retained earnings. The rationale behind this approach lies in the belief among accountants that the original contributed capital (an amount that often has legal significance) should not be dissipated by purchases and sales of treasury stock.

†If the price paid is less than the original issue price, then, for each share, common stock would be debited with par value and contributed capital in excess of par would be debited by the difference between par and purchase price.

Using the data previously presented, for example, the purchase of 100 shares at a price of $15 per share represents the retirement of 1 percent (100/10,000) of the outstanding shares. Common stock ($1 per share par value) would be reduced by 1 percent of $10,000–$100. Contributed capital in excess of par, previously $20,000, would be reduced by 1 percent of $20,000–$200. Retained earnings would be reduced by the difference between the total amount paid for the shares ($1,500) and the sum of the reductions to the other two accounts ($300)–$1,200. Thus,

| | | |
|---|---|---|
| Common stock | $ 100 | |
| Contributed capital in excess of par | 200 | |
| Retained earnings | 1,200 | |
| Cash | | $1,500 |

**To record the purchase of treasury stock.**

Subsequent to the retirement, the capital accounts would appear as follows:

| | |
|---|---|
| Common stock, $1 par value, 9,900 shares issued and outstanding | $ 9,900 |
| Contributed capital in excess of par value | 19,800 |
| Retained earnings | 68,800 |
| Total owners' equity | $98,500 |

Were the *treasury* shares to be reissued in the future, the sale would be accounted for as any other issue of new shares of stock.

The choice between the cost method and the par value method should ordinarily be governed by the *intent* of the corporation. If the corporation expects to resell the shares or to use them in connection with employee compensation plans or for some other business purposes other than retirement, the cost method has practical advantages. It avoids disruption of the retained earnings account as a consequence of transfer of shares, by the corporation, from one stockholder to another. If, however, the company does not plan to reissue the shares, then the par value or retirement method better recognizes the substance of the acquisition. Unfortunately, because of the subjective nature of corporate intent, similar situations are not in practice always accounted for uniformly.

## Is Interest an Expense or a Distribution of Earnings?

Throughout the text interest has been accorded the same accounting recognition as other costs to the company. It has been referred to as an *expense* and grouped on the income statement along with other expenses—cost of goods sold, rent, administrative salaries, etc.

From a procedural standpoint it is convenient to account for interest in the same manner as other costs. But whether or not interest is, in fact, an expense is by no means a settled matter among accountants.

A corporation or any other business enterprise requires an initial, and sometimes continuing, infusion of capital. At least a portion of such capital is provided by stockholders. The corporation grants the stockholders the right to share in the profits of the enterprise and periodically distributes such profits in the form of dividends. Dividends, of course, are not considered an expense of the corporation; they are a distribution of earnings.

In addition, capital may also be provided by individuals or institutions who lend the company funds. This is especially true of bondholders who commit substantial amounts of capital for long periods of time. Indeed, many companies view the amounts obtained through the issuance of long-term bonds as *permanent* capital.

Often it is to the advantage of the company to raise capital by issuing bonds rather than common stock. Interest on bonds, for example, is tax deductible; dividend payments are not. Whereas an issue of common stock increases the number of shares outstanding, and hence increases the number of shares among which profits have to be divided, an issue of bonds allows the earnings to remain undiluted (although, of course, substantially diminished by virtue of the interest payments). The specific advantages and disadvantages of issuing bonds as opposed to stock are beyond the scope of this text. The point to be emphasized at present, however, is that a company can obtain long-term financing by issuing either debt (bonds) or equity (stock) securities. The choice between the two is often dependent on somewhat technical characteristics of the firm's own capital structure as well as existing relationships between prevailing stock and bond prices. As of December 31, 1978, for example, a major corporation such as American Telephone & Telegraph was financed by substantial amounts of both long- and intermediate-term debt ($34.5 billion) and equity ($44.1 billion), including retained earnings.

If in economic substance (though obviously not in legal form) common stock and bonds are equivalent forms of long-term capital, then it follows, according to some accountants, that the return to bondholders (i.e., interest payments) should be accorded accounting recognition similar to that of the return to stockholders (dividends). Since dividends are accounted for as a distribution of earnings—not an expense—so, also, should be interest payments.

Whether interest is accounted for as an expense or as a distribution of earnings, the impact on retained earnings will, of course, be the same. If accounted for as an expense, then interest will be reported on the income statement among other operating costs; if accounted for as a distribution of earnings, then it would be reported, along with common and preferred stock dividends, either in a section of the income statement in which changes in retained earnings are indicated or in a separate statement of changes in owners' equity.

### Financial Statements: Proprietary vs. Entity View of a Company

The issue relating to the classification of interest may be viewed by some as being of little consequence. It is of importance, however, in that it relates to a more important question: Should financial statements be prepared from the standpoint of the proprietors (the owners) of the entity or from that of the entity as a separate and distinct organization apart from the proprietors? If the financial statements are prepared from the perspective of the proprietors, then the emphasis would be placed upon the residual interests of stockholders—what would remain for them after the liabilities have been liquidated. Since proprietors are concerned primarily with earnings available for distribution to stockholders, interest would be considered a cost of operations and thereby accounted for as would any other charge against revenues.

If, on the other hand, the statements are prepared from the perspective of the business entity apart from that of the owners, then the claims of the owners would be viewed as being little different from those of other creditors who have made funds available to the business. Stockholders would be considered as but one group among several which have claims against the assets of the firm. Interest would be viewed, and accounted for, as being similar in basic characteristics to dividends. Both would be considered as returns to the individuals or institutions which have financed the enterprise by their contributions of capital.

### Accounting for Nonprofit Organizations

Reference to the accounting entity provides an opportunity to identify the unique features of accounting for municipalities and other nonprofit organizations. One of the key differences between the accounting practices of commercial enterprises and those of nonprofit organizations relates to the definition of the accounting entity.

The accounting problems of municipalities and other nonprofit organizations have, until recently, received relatively little attention from independent CPAs. The fiscal crisis of New York City, which resulted in part because the financial reports of the city failed to warn of impending insolvency, represented a turning point with respect to active interest in, and concern for, nonprofit accounting on the part of the accounting establishment. Today, government accounting is one of the most controversial and rapidly expanding areas of the profession. Nonprofit organizations contribute a sizable proportion of the gross national product and are major recipients of private investment capital. In terms of dollar volume of new offerings, the market for municipal securities is only slightly smaller than that for corporate securities, and in recent years the number of individual offerings by municipalities has been over five times the number of primary corporate issues that have been registered with the SEC.

Accounting practices of nonprofit organizations are basically the same as those of commercial enterprises, but there are several noteworthy differences. In the discussion to follow attention will be directed to the accounting practices of municipalities; those of other nonprofit organizations are similar but not always the same in all respects.

## the accounting entity

In commercial accounting, a single set of accounts is maintained for each corporation. In municipal accounting, by contrast, several sets of accounts are usually employed for a single government entity. Each set of accounts is known as a *fund*. The term *fund* as used here bears little relationship to the term as defined earlier with reference to commercial accounting (i.e., cash or working capital). A fund is used to account for certain related activities of a government enterprise. Conventionally, one fund is maintained for general operations of government, another for revenues that are restricted for special purposes, a third for capital projects under construction, a fourth for assets accumulated to repay outstanding loans, and a fifth for business-like enterprises, such as hospitals or utilities, that the municipality may control.

The accounts of each fund, like those of a commercial enterprise, are self-balancing and may be summarized by the fundamental accounting equation:

$$\text{Assets} - \text{Liabilities} = \text{Owners' equity}$$

The individual asset and liability accounts are comparable in nature and terminology to those described throughout this text. The owners' equity account like that of commercial organization represents a residual interest in the enterprise—what would remain if all assets were to be sold at amounts equal to their book values and all liabilities were to be liquidated. In nonprofit accounting, the residual interest is referred to *not* as owners' capital or capital stock, but rather as *fund balance*. Except for the name, however, it has most of the accounting characteristics of owners' equity.

The various funds are seldom combined. The financial statements of municipalities consist of several independent balance sheets and statements of revenues and expenditures.

The use of several accounting entities to account for a single economic entity can be explained by the need to maintain strict separation and control over assets that are *legally* earmarked for specific purposes. Should, for example, a municipality use funds that were acquired by issuing long-term utility bonds to finance day to day operations, then the responsible government officials may be in violation of applicable city or state statutes and bond covenants and subject to legal sanctions.

**the modified
accrual basis**

Municipalities and other nonprofit organizations generally recognize revenues and expenditures on the accrual basis, just as do commercial enterprises. There are, however, several important exceptions. The most prominent of these regards expenditures. In the commercial sector, accounting recognition is first given to goods and services acquired when they are received. Municipalities, however, commonly give recognition to them when they are first ordered. At that time the cost of the goods or services is recorded as an *encumbrance* and a reserve for the required payment is established. The encumbrance account, while not exactly like an expense, has many of the same accounting characteristics, and when financial reports are prepared it is commonly linked closely with actual expenses. Later, when goods or services are received, the encumbrance is eliminated and an expenditure account charged. Concurrently, the reserve (*reserve for encumbrances*) is also eliminated and an actual liability is set up. The practice of giving accounting recognition to goods and services ordered can be attributed to the importance placed upon the municipal budget and the consequences of exceeding allowable expenditures. Municipalities want to be certain that, once they have committed themselves to acquiring goods and services, the accounts reflect immediately the reduction in resources available for other purposes.

Most of the other modifications to the accrual basis require that certain types of revenues and expenditures be recognized upon the receipt or disbursement of cash. Municipal decision makers tend to focus, to a greater extent than their commercial counterparts, on flows of cash. The accounting principles applicable to municipalities and other nonprofit organizations reflect their preference for information on cash receipts and disbursements rather than on inflows and outflows of resources.

**fixed assets
and long-
term debt**

Municipalities and other nonprofit organizations do not generally—there are several notable exceptions—give formal accounting recognition in the individual funds to fixed assets or to the debt used to acquire them. If an asset is acquired for cash, then an expenditure account is charged at the time of purchase. If it is financed by long-term bonds, then the expenditure account is charged as payments are made to liquidate the debt. Neither the asset nor the debt is recorded on the balance sheets of the various funds. Instead, they are listed separately in special "groups of accounts" that are, in effect, nothing more than supplementary "memo" ledgers. Inasmuch as the expenses associated with the acquisition of assets are recorded when the cash payments are made, there is no need to reflect the cost a second time by way of charges to depreciation.

The accounting practices with respect to fixed assets can be traced directly to the relationship between tax revenues and expenditures. Tax rates are established so that a municipality can meet its expenditures. The municipality must gear its tax collections to cash payments, not to expenses as they might be determined using an accrual basis of accounting. The financial statements, therefore, report expenditures for fixed assets when cash disbursements are made, rather than, as in commercial accounting, as the services provided by the assets are consumed.

**financial statements**  The financial statements of nonprofit organizations are comparable to those of commercial establishments. For each fund, a balance sheet, which indicates the assets, liabilities, and fund balance as of a particular point in time, is prepared. Inasmuch as nonprofit organizations do not attempt to "earn" income, no income statement is prepared. Instead, a statement that indicates revenues and expenditures is presented. Commonly, the statement would compare actual amounts with budgeted amounts. Such comparison reflects the greater importance attached to budgets in nonprofit organizations. In nonprofit organizations, the budget is not merely a set of managerial guidelines; it is a document that is formally adopted by the governing authorities, it sets forth the manner in which the resources of the organization are to be allocated, and it specifies the contributions that will be required from its members (e.g., citizens). In addition, the financial report of a nonprofit organization will generally include for each fund a statement of cash receipts and disbursements and a statement of changes in fund balance. The latter is comparable in many respects to the statement of changes in retained earnings that is required of commercial entities.

Each of these distinctive features of nonprofit accounting has come under attack. Within the next several years there are likely to be substantial changes in the manner in which nonprofit organizations are accounted for; many of these changes are likely to diminish the differences between nonprofit and commercial accounting procedures.

## Summary

In this chapter we have focused on the equity accounts of proprietorships, partnerships, and corporations. Although there are important legal and organizational differences among proprietorships, partnerships, and corporations, form of organization is often of less significance in the operations of the enterprise than is at first apparent. Many of the distinctions have been diminished by both statute and business practice.

We have considered in this chapter alternative means of accounting for the admission of new partners and of accounting for treasury stock. We have also touched on the question of whether interest is really an expense and the related issue of whether financial statements should be prepared from the standpoint of the entity itself or its proprietors. In addition, we have looked at some unique features of the accounting systems and financial reports of non-profit organizations. A corporation's purchases and sales of its own capital stock are seldom, if ever, reported on its income statement. Yet transactions between a corporation and its shareholders can have a profound impact on its earnings per share as well as on the value of outstanding shares.

In the mid-1960s, for example, many companies took advantage of relatively high stock market prices to issue additional shares. Since the price that the new investors were willing to pay was substantially above the *book* value of the new shares, the added premium served to increase the book value of the existing shares. Inasmuch as the cost of the capital acquired was low in relation to the return that could be generated by the additional capital, sale of the new shares served to increase overall earnings per share. Numerous firms that were previously privately owned *went public* in order to benefit from the ease of obtaining capital through the sale of common stock.

In the mid-1970s, when stock market prices were depressed, a number of companies engaged in the reverse process; they reacquired shares that they had issued previously. If the market price of the shares acquired was less than their intrinsic value, then the proportionate value of the remaining shares increased. Since relatively little capital had to be surrendered to reacquire the shares, the overall earnings capacity of the firms may have declined only slightly. But since earnings now had to be divided among a significantly smaller number of shares, earnings per share may have increased substantially.

The perceptive investor and financial analyst examines carefully the transactions between a company and its owners and the manner in which they are accounted for. They can have a critical effect on a stockholder's interest in past and future corporate earnings.

*exercise for review and self-testing*

Scopus, Inc. decides to reorganize its corporate structure. To facilitate additional financing, it is going to incorporate one of its divisions. The company will transfer to the new corporation plant and equipment that is presently recorded on its books at a cost of $8,900,000 less accumulated depreciation of $4,500,000 and patents that were developed by the company itself and have not been accorded formal accounting recognition. The fair market value of the plant and equipment is $8,200,000; that of the patents, $2,000,000.

1. The new company issues 100,000 shares of common stock, par value $50. Initially, all the shares will be held by the parent company.
    a. What value should the new company assign to the plant and equipment? To the patents?
    b. What value should the new company assign to "Common stock, par value"? To "Common stock, capital in excess of par"?
    c. Prepare a journal entry to record the issuance of the common stock.

2. The new company also issues 10,000 shares of preferred stock. The preferred stock is assigned a par value of $100 and pays dividends at a rate of 9 percent per year. At the time the stock is issued comparable securities are being sold to yield 8.5 percent.
   a. What is the dollar amount per share that the firm will pay in dividends?
   b. How much is an investor likely to pay for a share of stock that pays a dividend of such amount if he expects a return of 8.5 percent?
   c. Prepare a journal entry to record the issuance of the preferred stock, assuming that the stock is issued for cash at the price determined in part b.

3. After a year, the new company acquires 1,000 of its outstanding shares of common stock for the purpose of reissuing them to employees as part of a stock option plan. The company acquires the shares for cash at a price of $180 per share.
   a. Do you think that the acquisition of the treasury stock should be accounted for by the cost or the par value method?
   b. Based on your answer to part a, prepare a journal entry to record the acquisition of the stock.

4. Shortly after reissuing the shares described in part 3 the company reacquires an additional 20,000 shares of common stock with the intention of retiring them. The company purchases the shares for $160 each. At the time of purchase the company has a balance in its retained earnings account of $2,000,000.
   a. Do you think that the acquisition should be accounted for by the cost or par value method?
   b. By what percentage would the number of shares outstanding be reduced?
   c. By what percentage and by what amount should the balance in the account "Common stock, par value" be reduced?
   d. By what percentage and by what amount should the balance in the account "Common stock, capital in excess of par" be reduced?
   e. By what amount—the difference between total amount paid and the sum of the reductions in the other capital accounts—should the balance in "Retained earnings" be reduced?
   f. Prepare a journal entry to record the retirement of the shares.

## Questions

**review and discussion**

1. The risks of being a *silent* (one who takes no active role in management) partner of a business organized as a partnership are far greater than that of being a silent stockholder of a firm organized as a corporation. Do you agree? Explain.

2. It is often pointed out that the limitations on liability afforded stockholders of a corporation make it easier for a corporation as opposed to a partnership to raise capital. Cite an example of a situation where the limitations on liability may, in fact, make it more difficult for a corporation to acquire needed funds.

3. A corporation, it is said, is a legal "person." Why is a corporation, but not a partnership or a proprietorship, so described?

4. An incoming partner is willing to pay $400,000 for a one-third interest in a partnership that after his admission will have, if no revaluation of assets is made, recorded owners' capital of $900,000. Why would he be willing to pay such a *premium* price? What accounting issues are raised by his willingness to pay such a price?

5. Why is *preferred* stock preferred? What preferences are attached to it?

6. A friend wants to purchase "safe" securities for a period of two to three years. He wants assurance that the original amount of his investment will remain intact. Assume that you are satisfied that the company in which he is considering investing is sound—that it is highly unlikely that it will be unable to pay required preferred stock dividends or interest. Would you necessarily suggest to him that the preferred stock of the company is a safer investment than the common stock? What factors are most likely to influence the market price of the preferred stock, assuming that it is not convertible into common stock?

7. What are the critical accounting problems involved in the formation of a corporation? What warnings would you give to someone who is about to purchase the common stock of a newly organized corporation?

8. The financial statements of RCA Corporation contained the following footnote:

> At December 31, 1976, 78,331 shares of treasury stock, included in Investments and Other Assets [a noncurrent asset] at cost to RCA of $1.9 million, were available to cover undistributed awards payable in RCA common stock.

What objections might many accountants have to classifying treasury stock as a noncurrent *asset?*

9. Why do some accountants contend that interest "expense" is a misnomer—that interest is not really an expense at all? What do they believe interest to be? What are the reporting implications of their position?

10. How does use of the term "funds" in nonprofit accounting differ from that in commercial accounting?

11. By accounting for long-lived assets on a cash basis, governmental units are able to readily match tax collections to required cash outlays. What is an important disadvantage of accounting for long-lived assets on a cash basis?

## *Problems*

1. *The method of financing used by a "closely held" corporation must take into account the distinctions in the tax code between dividends and interest.* William Elton is the sole stockholder of the Elton Co. Mr. Elton intends to contribute $1 million of his personal funds to the corporation in order to fi-

nance expansion of a plant. He expects that the added capacity of the plant will enable the company to earn $300,000 per year additional income, before taxes. Mr. Elton has asked your advice as to whether he should have the corporation issue common stock or bonds in return for the $1 million. Mr. Elton intends to withdraw $100,000 of the additional earnings each year, either in the form of interest on bonds or dividends on the common stock. The corporation pays taxes at a rate of 48 percent. Mr. Elton personally is in the 60 percent tax bracket. Mr. Elton would be required to pay taxes on all returns from the corporation, regardless of whether in the form of interest or dividends.

What advice would you give to Mr. Elton?

2. *The tax consequences of incorporating a closely held business depend to a great extent upon the owner's plans to withdraw funds.*

John Albert operated his business as a sole proprietorship for several years. His attorney had advised him that in order to limit his liability he ought to incorporate his firm. He has asked you for an evaluation of the tax consequences.

The firm has annual earnings, before taxes, of $250,000. The effective corporate income tax rate would be approximately 40 percent. Since he has several additional sources of income, Mr. Albert is in the 70 percent personal income tax bracket.

Were Mr. Albert to incorporate his business, he would be the sole stockholder.

a. Determine the total tax obligation on income attributable to the business assuming first that the business remains a sole proprietorship and alternatively that it is incorporated. Consider the total tax impact on both Mr. Albert and his firm—both corporate and personal taxes. Assume that Mr. Albert intends to withdraw $50,000 per year from the business (either in the form of proprietor withdrawals or corporate dividends) and retain the remainder of earnings in the business.

b. Again determine total tax obligations. Assume this time, however, that Mr. Albert intends to withdraw $150,000 per year from the business.

c. Can you generalize from your analysis?

3. *Accounting principles applicable to partnerships are essentially the same as those applicable to corporations.*

Simmons and Ross decided to form a partnership to engage in the sale of real estate. Simmons contributed land that had an appraised value of $400,000; Ross contributed cash of $100,000. The land was subject to a liability of $100,000, which the partnership agreed to assume. The land had been recorded on the personal books of Simmons at a value of $200,000. The partners agreed that profits and losses would be shared in proportion to the initial contributions of the owners. In addition, however, Ross would be paid a management fee of $10,000 per year.

During its first year of operations the partnership purchased additional land for $800,000, paying $150,000 cash and giving a note for the balance. It sold for $300,000 land that it had acquired for $200,000. The buyers paid cash of $90,000 and agreed to assume liabilities of $210,000 that the partnership had incurred when it had acquired the land.

During the first year the partnership borrowed $80,000 from Simmons. It agreed to pay Simmons interest at the rate of 6 percent per year. As of year end the loan had been outstanding for six months, but the partnership had neither paid nor accrued any interest.

The firm incurred additional interest expenses, paid in cash, of $40,000. At year end, Ross withdrew $30,000 cash from the partnership and, in addition, was paid his management fee; Simmons withdrew nothing. (Assume that all other operating expenses are negligible.)

a. Prepare all necessary journal entries to record the formation of the partnership and to summarize all transactions in which it engaged during its first year of operations. Prepare also any required adjusting and closing entries.

b. Prepare a balance sheet as of year end.

4. *The admission of a new partner may be accounted for by the asset revaluation method or the bonus method.*

The balance sheet of a partnership indicated the following:

| | |
|---|---|
| Total assets | $100,000 |
| | |
| Capital, Gail | 50,000 |
| Capital, Dan | 50,000 |
| | $100,000 |

The partners share profits and losses equally.

In need of additional capital, the partnership elects to admit a third partner. The new partner, Julie, has agreed to contribute $80,000 cash in return for a one-third interest in the firm.

a. If a one-third interest in the partnership has a fair market value of $80,000, then what is the most probable value of the entire partnership after admitting Julie as a partner?

b. (1) Prepare a journal entry to record the cash contributions of the new partner.

(2) Prepare a second journal entry to write up the assets of the partnership to the amount determined in part (1) and to increase the capital accounts of the original partners as appropriate.

(3) Prepare an alternative second entry in which you merely adjust the capital accounts of all three partners so that they are consistent with the terms of admission of the new partner as well as with the book value (unadjusted) of the partnership assets (including the cash contributed by the new partner).

c. Which alternative do you prefer? Why?

5. *Some accountants aver that the admission of a new partner is just cause for revaluing the assets and liabilities of a partnership; others say that it is not.*

As of the end of 1980, the KLM partnership had assets of $1 million, liabilities of $400,000, and partners' capital of $600,000 as follows:

|  |  |
|---|---|
| Partner K | $200,000 |
| Partner L | 150,000 |
| Partner M | 250,000 |

The three partners share profits and losses equally.

Partner K has decided to sell his entire one-third interest in the partnership to P. P has agreed to pay, *directly* to K, $250,000 for his interest.

a. Prepare a journal entry to record the sale of the interest on the books of the partnership. (Assume that the sale will *not* be used as an occasion to revalue *partnership* assets.)

b. Suppose instead that the offer of $250,000 will be considered indicative of the value of partnership assets and that, prior to the sale of K's interest, the increase in value of partnership assets will be given accounting recognition. Prepare the journal entries that would be required to effect the revaluation of the assets and the transfer of interest. Indicate the balances in the partners' capital accounts immediately following the sale.

c. Indicate briefly the arguments in favor of each of the two approaches. Which approach is consistent with corporate practice with respect to a sale of an ownership interest by one party to another?

6. *Distributions to partners upon liquidation of a partnership must be based upon the balances, after appropriate adjustments, in the partners' capital accounts.*

After 10 years, Freeman Brothers Men's Shop is going out of business. Freeman Brothers is operated as a partnership. Just prior to liquidation, its balance sheet reflected the following:

|  |  |
|---|---|
| Cash | $ 20,000 |
| Merchandise inventory | 80,000 |
| Total assets | $100,000 |
| Current liabilities | $ 5,000 |
| Capital, J. Freeman | 45,000 |
| Capital, L. Freeman | 50,000 |
| Total liabilities and owners' equity | $100,000 |

The two Freeman brothers share profits and losses equally.

The firm holds a "going-out-of-business" sale and sells its entire merchandise inventory for $100,000. It pays its creditors and distributes the remaining cash between the two partners.

a. Prepare the required journal entries to record the sale of the merchandise and payment of the liabilities. (Prepare any closing entries that might be required with respect to any revenues and expenses associated with the sale of the merchandise.)

b. Determine the balances in the partners' capital accounts immediately prior to the final distribution of cash between the partners. How do you explain the fact that although the partners share profits and losses equally, their capital balances are not also equal?

c. How much cash should be distributed to each of the partners? Prepare a journal entry to record the final distribution to the partners.

7. *The initial values assigned to the assets of a newly established corporation must be indicative of their fair market value.*

You have recently been offered the opportunity to purchase 1,000 shares of the common stock of Computer Service Corporation at a price of $15 per share (a price well below its book value). The company has just been formed; it has not yet commenced operations. It was organized by three computer systems analysts, who are presently the only stockholders. The company intends to lease office space and computers; it will provide auto-mated bookkeeping services to small businesses.

A balance sheet provided you by the company reveals the following:

| | |
|---|---:|
| Cash | $100,000 |
| Inventories and supplies | 20,000 |
| Goodwill | 50,000 |
| Total assets | $170,000 |
| | |
| Common stock, par value $1 (20,000 shares authorized, 10,000 shares issued and outstanding) | $ 10,000 |
| Common stock, contributed capital in excess of par | 160,000 |
| Total equities | $170,000 |

A footnote to the financial statements indicates that the $50,000 of goodwill represents the accumulated expertise of the founders of the cor-poration. All three promoters have had extensive experience with a leading computer manufacturer and have held management positions with other computer service companies. The goodwill was authorized by the firm's board of directors.

a. What reservations might you have about purchasing the stock of the company?

b. Assume instead that you were an independent certified public accoun-tant called upon to audit the company shortly after its formation. What adjusting journal entry might you propose?

8. *The amount for which shares of common stock were issued can be de-rived from information provided upon their retirement.*

The financial report of Warner Communications, Inc. contains the fol-lowing note:

During 1976, 9,000,000 Common treasury shares, $1 par value, having an aggregate cost of $157,798,000 were retired resulting in charges of

$9,000,000 to capital stock, $36,440,000 to paid in capital and $112,358,000 to retained earnings.

    a. How much did the company pay to acquire each share?

    b. What was the initial issuance price per share?

    c. Prepare a journal entry to record the retirement of the shares assuming that just prior to their retirement they were recorded at acquisition cost in a treasury stock account.

9. *The price at which preferred stock, like bonds, is issued is reflective of the relationship between prevailing yields and the promises inherent in the security.*

The Thoreau Electric Co. has decided to issue 100,000 shares of preferred stock that will pay an annual dividend of $6 per share. The preferred stock will have a stated value of $100 per share. At the date of issue, similar grades of preferred stock are being sold to provide a return to investors of 7 percent.

    a. At what price is the issue of Thoreau likely to be sold?

    b. Prepare a journal entry to record the sale of the preferred stock.

    c. Prepare an entry to record the payment of the first annual cash dividend.

    d. Suppose instead that the preferred stock will have a stated value of $1 per share. Prepare an entry to record the sale of the stock.

10. *Prices at which securities are issued and acquired can be derived from changes in the balances of owners' equity accounts.*

The stockholders' equity section of the balance sheet of the Intercontinental Corp. reveals the following:

|  | 1980 | 1979 |
|---|---|---|
| Common stock, $10 par value | $ 1,200,000 | $ 1,000,000 |
| Preferred stock, $100 par value, 8% | 500,000 | 450,000 |
| Contributed capital in excess of par |  |  |
|    Common stock | 11,500,000 | 8,900,000 |
|    Preferred stock | 8,000 | — |
| Retained earnings | 18,143,000 | 20,220,000 |
| Less: Common stock held in treasury (1,300 shares in 1980, 1,000 shares in 1979) | (173,000) | (130,000) |
|  | $31,178,000 | $30,440,000 |

No treasury stock was retired or reissued during 1980.

    a. How many shares of common stock did the company issue in 1980? What was the issue price per share?

    b. How many shares of preferred stock did the company issue in 1980? What was the issue price per share?

    c. What would you estimate to be the prevailing yield rate for comparable types of securities at the time the preferred stock was issued? That is, what was the yield rate used to determine the issue price of the preferred stock?

d. What was the price paid for the 300 shares of common stock acquired by the company in 1980?

11. *The price at which common stock of a newly formed corporation is issued should be reflective of the fair market value of the corporate assets.*

Filmore and Francis are partners in a firm that operates a chain of drugstores. They decide to incorporate their business and sell shares in the enterprise to the general public. Filmore has a 60 percent interest in the partnership and Francis a 40 percent interest.

The net assets (assets less liabilities) of the partnership are recorded on the books of the partnership at $8 million. However, after considerable study and consultation with independent appraisers, the partners decide that the fair market value of their business is $12 millon. Indeed, just prior to their decision to incorporate they received an offer to sell their entire business to an independent party for that amount.

The partners intend to issue 200,000 shares of common stock. They plan to keep 60 percent of such shares for themselves and sell the rest to the public. Each share of stock will have a par value of $20.

a. At what price should the shares be sold to the public?

b. Prepare any journal entries required to record the formation of the new corporation.

12. *The conversion of preferred stock to common stock requires an adjustment only to owners' equity accounts.*

The annual report of Chromalloy American Corporation, a firm listed on the New York Stock Exchange, contains the following note:

*Preferred Stock*—The Company's preferred stock is issuable in series and is entitled to one vote per share. The outstanding $5 Cumulative Convertible Preferred Stock is convertible at the rate of 3.888 shares of common for each share of preferred stock.

The stockholders' equity section of the balance sheet indicates the following:

| | |
|---|---:|
| Preferred stock—authorized 1,825,000 shares, par value $1 per share: | |
| $5 cumulative convertible preferred stock; outstanding 561,164 shares | $    561,164 |
| Common stock—authorized 20,000,000 shares, par value $1 per share; issued 10,748,462 shares | 10,748,462 |
| Other capital ascribed to shares | 42,930,965 |
| | $ 54,240,591 |
| Retained earnings | 122,696,044 |
| | $176,936,635 |

Suppose that all 561,164 shares of preferred stock were converted (exchanged) into common stock. The company receives no cash in the exchange; it realizes no gain or loss; the transaction has no impact upon retained earnings.

Prepare a journal entry to record the exchange. Be sure that as the result of your entry the balance in the common stock, par value account is reflective of the new number of shares outstanding.

13. *A shift from partnership to corporate status is an event of sufficient economic and legal significance to justify revaluing the assets and liabilities of an enterprise.*

Bryan and Moore are partners in a retail stereo business. After several successful years of operation as a partnership, the two decide to incorporate their business as Stereo, Inc. Bryan and Moore share profits and losses in the ratio of 3:1. Prior to the liquidation of the partnership and its subsequent incorporation, the balance sheet of the partnership indicated the following:

| *Assets* | | |
|---|---:|---:|
| Cash | | $ 12,000 |
| Accounts receivable | | 26,000 |
| Inventory | | 83,000 |
| Furniture and fixtures | $ 75,000 | |
| Less: Allowance for depreciation | 22,000 | 53,000 |
| Land | | 18,000 |
| Building | $102,000 | |
| Less: Allowance for depreciation | 60,000 | 42,000 |
| Total assets | | $234,000 |
| *Liabilities and owners' equity* | | |
| Accounts payable | | $ 29,000 |
| Notes payable | | 80,000 |
| Capital, Bryan | | 93,750 |
| Capital, Moore | | 31,250 |
| Total liabilities and owners' equity | | $234,000 |

Prior to transferring the assets to the corporation, the partners decided to adjust the books of the partnership to reflect current market values.

The building had a current market value of $85,000; the land, $26,000; and the furniture and fixtures, $30,000.

The firm had not previously provided for uncollectible accounts. However, it was estimated that $4,000 of the accounts would be uncollectible. It was also determined that $8,000 of inventory was obsolete. The new corporation was to assume the liabilities of the partnership except as noted below.

The new corporation was authorized to issue 100,000 shares of $10 par value common stock. Common stock was to be issued at par value, with the number of shares proportionate to the fair market value of one's contribution.

Shares were also issued to the following parties in addition to the partners:

To an attorney for providing services pertaining to the organization of the corporation. The fair market value of the services was $8,000.

To the party holding the note payable. He agreed to accept common stock in full payment of his $80,000 note.

To a venture capital financial institution. It agreed to invest $50,000 cash in the new corporation.

a. Prepare journal entries to revalue the partnership, to transfer the assets to the new corporation in exchange for common stock, and to distribute the shares of the common stock to the partners.

b. Prepare journal entries to organize the new corporation.

c. Indicate the number of shares each investor would receive.

14. *Transactions involving a firm's own stock are often based upon the price at which the shares are being traded in the open market.*

The Frost Co. was organized on June 1, 1979. According to the terms of its charter, the firm was authorized to issue capital stock as follows:

*Common stock:* $2 par value, 100,000 shares.
*Preferred stock:* $100 par value, 5 percent dividend rate, 10,000 shares.

During the first year of operations the following transactions, which affected capital accounts, took place:

1. The corporation issued for cash 50,000 shares of common stock at a price of $30 per share.
2. The corporation issued for cash 10,000 shares of preferred stock at $90 per share.
3. The company purchased a building, giving the seller 10,000 shares of common stock. At the time of the purchase, the common stock of the company was being traded in the open market at $25 per share.
4. The firm's advertising agency agreed to accept 3,000 shares of common stock, rather than cash, in payment for services performed. At the time of payment the market price of the stock was $28 per share.
5. The firm agreed to purchase the stock of a dissident shareholder. The firm purchased 3,000 shares at a price of $30 per share.
6. The company subsequently sold 2,000 of the shares to one stockholder at a price of $28 per share and at a later date 1,000 shares to another shareholder at a price of $31 per share.

Prepare journal entries to record the above transactions.

15. *Treasury stock may be accounted for by the cost or par value method.*

As of January 1, 1980, the owners' equity section of the Dunham Corp. contained the following balances:

| | | |
|---|---|---|
| Common stock ($3 par value, 100,000 shares issued and outstanding) | $300,000 | |
| Common stock, capital in excess of par | 800,000 | $1,100,000 |

| | | |
|---|---:|---:|
| Preferred stock ($1 par value, 10,000 shares issued and outstanding) | $ 10,000 | |
| Preferred stock, capital in excess of par | 1,000 | 11,000 |
| Retained earnings | | 2,000,000 |
| Total owners' equity | | $3,111,000 |

During January the company purchased in the open market 10,000 of its own common shares at a price of $50 per share. Later in the same month it reissued 5,000 of those shares at a price of $60 per share.

a. Prepare journal entries to record the purchase and reissue of the stock using first the *cost* method and then the *par value* method.

b. Compare the balances in the capital accounts pertaining to common stock and retained earnings subsequent to the reissue of the shares under each of the two methods.

c. Where, under the cost method, would *treasury stock* be reported on the balance sheet?

16. *The value of a business, which is about to be acquired by another firm, can be established in a number of different ways.*

Alliance Department Stores, Inc. has agreed to purchase McKay Bros. Discount Store. McKay Bros. is operated as a partnership. The owners' equity accounts on the books of the partnership indicate that each of the two partners has a recorded capital balance of $100,000. An independent appraiser has determined that the value of the individual assets of the company (there are no significant liabilities) is $250,000. The partners, however, have had several offers to sell the entire business for $300,000.

Alliance Department Stores, Inc. has offered to purchase the store for shares of its own common stock. The number of shares to be issued is currently being negotiated between the two parties. Alliance currently has 50,000 shares of common stock outstanding. The par value of each share is $2. The company has $300,000 in capital in excess of par and $600,000 in retained earnings. The current market price for shares of Alliance is $25 per share.

Six possible ways of determining the number of shares to be issued to the McKay Bros. partners are under consideration. The value of a share to be issued by Alliance can be based on either its *book* or its *market* value. The value of the interest to be purchased by Alliance can be based on the book value of McKay Bros.' assets, the appraised value of its assets, or its market value as a going concern.

a. Determine the number of shares to be issued by Alliance under each of the six combinations:
   - Value of Alliance shares based on (1) book value *or* (2) market value, *and*
   - Value of McKay Bros. based on (1) book value, (2) appraised value, *or* (3) market value.

b. How do you account for the differences among book value, appraised value, and market value?

   c. On which basis do you recommend the number of shares should be determined?

17. *Prevailing tax laws are a key factor in a corporation's decision as to whether it should issue bonds or preferred stock.*

   A firm wishes to construct a new plant. The estimated cost of the plant is $5 million. The firm is undecided as to whether to raise the required capital by issuing bonds or preferred stock. The current prevailing yield on bonds of similar grade is 7 percent, and that on preferred stock is 9 percent.

   What would be the minimum earnings, before taxes, that the firm would have to realize, under both alternatives, if it were to break even on the proposed project? The current tax rate is 40 percent.

18. *In choosing among alternative instruments of financing, a firm must take into account its expectations as to future earnings.*

   A corporation has decided to construct an addition to its plant. The cost of the addition is $5 million; it is expected to increase earnings by $900,000 per year before taking into account income taxes.

   The firm is considering three alternatives to acquire the needed $5 million capital:

   1. Sell bonds. Current yield rates are 8 percent per year.
   2. Issue preferred stock. Current yield rates are 12 percent per year.
   3. Issue common stock. The firm currently has 600,000 shares outstanding. It estimates that additional shares could be sold at a price of $10 per share. The company has not paid any dividends on common stock in recent years and does not plan to do so in the foreseeable future. The current tax rate is 48 percent.

   a. Prepare a table that has one column for each of the three alternatives and the following headings:
     1. Anticipated additional earnings (before taxes)
     2. Required interest or dividend payments
     3. Additional "earnings" less direct cost of capital (1 – 2)
     4. Income taxes
     5. Net additional earnings (3 – 4)
     6. Shares of common stock outstanding
     7. Additional earnings per share of common stock (5 ÷ 6)
     Which alternative do you think the company ought to select if impact on earnings per share of common stock is to be the most important criterion?
   b. Suppose that anticipated earnings from the new addition were $1.5 million per year. Which alternative do you think the firm ought to select? (You need not recompute earnings per share; simply use judgment.)
   c. Suppose that estimated additional earnings were $900,000 per year but that the market price of the firm's common stock was $20 per share. Which alternative should now be favored?

19. *Municipalities are accounted for on the basis of "funds," each of which is an independent accounting entity; they adhere to a "modified" accrual basis of reporting.*

The table following is the trial balance of the general fund of the town of Elat. Based on the brief discussion of nonprofit accounting in this chapter as well as on inferences that may be drawn from the various accounts listed in the trial balance provided, describe the effect, if any, on the accounts of the events reported. For convenience, put your description in the form of journal entries. Note any differences between the entries that you recommend and those that would be appropriate in a commercial enterprise.

**Town of Elat**
**General Fund**
**Trial Balance as of**
**May 15, 1980**

|  | Debits | Credits |
| --- | --- | --- |
| *Cash | $ 30,000 |  |
| *Taxes and other amounts receivable | 15,000 |  |
| *Marketable securities | 25,000 |  |
| *Due from other funds | 10,000 |  |
| *Vouchers and accounts payable |  | $ 58,000 |
| *Due to other funds |  | 6,000 |
| *Reserve for encumbrances |  | 12,000 |
| *Fund balance |  | 9,000 |
| Tax revenues |  | 79,000 |
| Revenues from fines, grants, interest and other sources |  | 13,000 |
| Expenditures for general operations | 68,000 |  |
| Expenditures for repayment of debt | 11,000 |  |
| Other expenditures | 6,000 |  |
| Encumbrances | 12,000 |  |
| Total | $177,000 | $177,000 |

*Indicates a balance sheet account; other accounts would be reported on the statement of revenues and expenditures or the statement of changes in fund balance.

1. The town receives a cash grant of $3,000 from the federal government.
2. The town constructs a new fire station at a cost of $400,000. The town borrows the full cost and issues $400,000 of long-term bonds.
3. The town pays interest of $16,000 on the bonds.
4. The town transfers $10,000 from the general fund to the debt service fund, a fund used to accumulate the resources required to repay the outstanding bonds. (Bear in mind that each fund is a separate accounting entity. Hence, even an intragovernmental transfer may result in revenue to the receiving fund and expenditure to the disbursing fund.)
5. The town orders $5,000 of supplies. (It is no coincidence that the balances in the encumbrance and reserve for encumbrance accounts are the same.)

6. The town receives, uses, and pays for $4,000 of the supplies ordered. (It would no longer be necessary to maintain an encumbrance or a reserve for encumbrance for the $4,000; it is necessary, however, to recognize an expenditure for that amount.)

20. *A corporation can increase the equity of existing (and remaining) stock-holders by judiciously issuing and retiring shares of its own common stock.*

In 1976 the Black Corporation reported earnings of $6 million. Its owners' equity at the end of that year was $30 million. The firm had 1 million shares of common stock issued and outstanding.

At the start of 1977 the company decided to expand its operations. To raise an additional $15 million in capital, it elected to issue additional common stock. It was able to issue the stock at a price of $100 per share. The additional capital enabled the firm to increase earnings by $3 million per year after taxes.

a. Determine the *book* value per share and earnings per share both before and after the issue of the additional common stock.

b. In 1980, the market price of the firm's common stock had fallen to $50 per share. The firm decided to reacquire, at market price, $7.5 million of common stock. To avoid having to reduce its scale of operations the firm decided to issue long-term bonds for $7.5 million. The bonds could be sold at a price such that the effective interest cost to the company, after taxes, would be 5 percent. Determine the book value per share and earnings per share after the reacquisition of the shares and the issue of the bonds. Assume that in the intervening years all earnings had been distributed to stockholders in the form of dividends.

*solutions to*
*exercise for*
*review and*
*self testing*

1a. The assets should be recorded at their fair market values. Hence, plant and equipment, $8,200,000; patents, $2,000,000.

b. Common stock, par value: 100,000 shares × $50 per share = $5,000,000. Common stock, capital in excess of par: $10,200,000 – $5,000,000 = $5,200,000.

c.
| | | |
|---|---|---|
| Plant and equipment | $8,200,000 | |
| Patents | 2,000,000 | |
|     Common stock, par value | | $5,000,000 |
|     Common stock, capital in excess of par | | 5,200,000 |

**To record issuance of common stock.**

2a. The firm will pay $9 per share in dividends.

b. $9 ÷ .085 = $105.88, which equals the market value per share of preferred stock.

c.
| | | |
|---|---|---|
| Cash | $1,058,800 | |
|     Preferred stock, par value | | $1,000,000 |
|     Preferred stock, capital in excess of par | | 58,800 |

**To record issuance of preferred stock.**

3a. Inasmuch as the company intends to reissue the shares in the near future they should be accounted for by the cost method.

   b.  Treasury stock $180,000

       Cash $180,000

   **To record acquisition of 1,000 shares of common stock.**

4a.  Inasmuch as the company intends to retire the shares they should be accounted for by the par value method.

   b.  20%.

   c.  20%; 20% of $5,000,000 = $1,000,000.

   d.  20%; 20% of $5,200,000 = $1,040,000.

   e.  20,000 shares $\times$ $160 per share minus $2,040,000 = $1,160,000.

   f.  Common stock, par value $1,000,000

       Common stock, capital in excess of par 1,040,000

       Retained earnings 1,160,000

         Cash $3,200,000

   **To record retirement of 20,000 shares of common stock.**

# 12

Special Problems
of Measuring and
Reporting Dividends
and Earnings

This chapter, as did the previous one, will focus on transactions between a corporation and its owners. Specifically, it will consider the means of measuring and reporting distributions of earnings—dividends in cash, "in kind," and in stock. It will also deal with the unique problem of accounting for employee salaries when the compensation is in the form of options to acquire common stock, and it will examine the question of when an impairment of asset value should be considered a loss. It will conclude with a discussion of two controversial issues with respect to reports of earnings—those relating to calculation of earnings per share and those relating to the determination of earnings for an *interim* period.

*RE = Earnings − Div.*

## Retained Earnings and Cash Dividends

Retained earnings represent the total accumulated earnings of a corporation less amounts distributed to stockholders as dividends and any amounts transferred to other capital accounts.

Dividends are distributions of assets (or shares of common stock) which serve to reduce retained earnings. They are *declared* by a formal resolution of a firm's board of directors. The announcement of a dividend would indicate the amount per share to be distributed, the *date of record* (that on which the stock records will be closed and ownership of the outstanding shares determined), and the *date of payment*. A typical announcement might read as follows: "The board of directors of the XYZ Corporation, at its regular meeting of December 9, 1979, declared a quarterly dividend of $2 per share payable on January 24, 1980, to stockholders of record on January 3, 1980."

The entry to record the declaration of a dividend is straightforward. On the date of declaration, when the liability for payment is first established, the entry (in this case to record a dividend of $2 per share on 100,000 shares outstanding) would be

| | | |
|---|---|---|
| Common stock dividends | $200,000 | |
| Dividends payable | | $200,000 |
| **To record declaration of the cash dividend on common stock.** | | |

At year end "common stock dividends" would be *closed* to retained earnings.

When payment is subsequently made it would be recorded as follows:

| | | |
|---|---|---|
| Dividends payable | $200,000 | |
| Cash | | $200,000 |

**To record payment of the dividend.**

Although conventional (nonstock) dividends are charged to retained earnings, they are paid in cash or other tangible assets. It does not follow that merely because a company has a balance in retained earnings it has the wherewithal to make dividend payments. Retained earnings are a part of owners' equity. Owners' equity corresponds to the excess of assets over liabilities. It cannot be associated with specific assets to which stockholders have claim.

The nature of retained earnings is a common source of misunderstanding —a misunderstanding that can be attributed in large measure to the widespread use, until recently, of the term *earned surplus* in place of retained earnings. *Surplus* implies something extra—an amount over and above what is needed. Retained earnings may not, in fact, represent *surplus*. Rather, a balance in retained earnings may be indicative of earnings that have been reinvested in the corporation. By not distributing its earned assets to stockholders, the corporation may have internally financed expansion. The retained earnings, therefore, may not denote the availability of cash or other assets that can readily be distributed to stockholders; instead the company may have used its available resources to acquire land, buildings, and equipment. The owners' equity section of the Ford Motor Co. balance sheet (1978), for example, comprises the following accounts (in millions):

| | |
|---|---:|
| Common stock | $ 239.9 |
| Capital in excess of par | 492.7 |
| Retained earnings | 8,953.7 |
| | $9,686.3 |

Retained earnings account for 92 percent of owners' capital. It is obvious that distribution of assets represented by the entire $8.95 billion in retained earnings would force the company to retrench its operations back to the scale of its Model T days.

Decisions as to when and how much of a dividend to declare are ordinarily made with primary reference to the corporation's current cash position and anticipated cash flow. The company must determine whether the available and projected cash is sufficient to meet its other operating requirements—the need to meet payrolls, maintain inventories, replace worn-out equipment, etc. In addition, however, the corporation must consider also the interests of shareholders. To the extent that assets are not distributed to stockholders, the stockholders are being forced to increase their investment in the corporation.

Whether they wish to increase their investment will ordinarily depend in large measure on the return they could obtain from competing investment opportunities. If the funds to be retained in the corporation are likely to provide a return greater than stockholders could obtain elsewhere, then stockholders are often willing to permit the company to retain all or a portion of its assets. In fact, many corporations, particularly *growth* companies, omit payment of dividends for years at a time. Stockholders of such companies are willing to forgo immediate cash returns for long-term corporate expansion and enhancement of their investment.

The payment of dividends is sometimes constrained by statutory restrictions. The corporation laws of some states prescribe that dividends cannot be paid "out of capital"; they can be paid only "out of earnings." That is, the payment of dividends cannot serve to reduce the stockholders' equity of the company beneath the amount contributed by the stockholders. The motivating force behind such restrictions is protection of creditors. The state laws are designed to make certain that assets that should properly be used to liquidate outstanding debt are not, by way of dividends, returned to stockholders, who, because of their limited liability, are not otherwise responsible for the obligations of the corporation.

## Dividends in Kind

Although dividends are conventionally paid in cash, it is not uncommon for a company to distribute other types of assets. A company, for example, may own a substantial number of shares in another corporation and wish to distribute those shares in lieu of a cash dividend. Suppose, for example, the Gamma Co. owns 100,000 shares of XYZ Corporation stock. It declares and pays a *dividend in kind* (as such dividends in property are known) of 4 shares of XYZ stock for each of its own 25,000 shares outstanding. If the stock of the XYZ Corporation had been recorded on the books of the Gamma Co. at $5 per share but had a fair market value of $8 per share, then the following two entries would be in order:

| | | |
|---|---|---|
| XYZ Corp stock | $300,000 | |
| Gain on investment | | $300,000 |

**To write up XYZ Corp. stock to reflect market value.**

| | | |
|---|---|---|
| Common stock dividends | $800,000 | |
| XYZ Corp. stock | | $800,000 |

**To record declaration and payment of dividend in kind.**

As a consequence of the dividend, the corporation is able to realize a holding gain in the amount of the difference between book value and market value of the property distributed.

Many accountants assert, however, that a corporation should *not* be permitted to realize gains or losses as the result of discretionary, non-arm's-length transactions with stockholders. If it were, they contend, it could readily manipulate earnings by distributing to shareholders assets that it could not otherwise sell to outsiders at the value assigned to them. Other accountants point out, however, that the recipients of the assets would unquestionably record, and would be taxed upon, the property at fair market value. Moreover, they observe, a corporation should not have to incur the transaction costs of selling its assets to outsiders to realize a gain, when it could readily transfer them directly to its shareholders, who could sell them for as much cash as they would otherwise receive. By definition of the term "market value," they aver, assets distributed to the stockholders could alternatively have been sold to outsiders at the market values assigned to them. The Accounting Principles Board, in Opinion No. 29, held that dividends in kind should generally be accounted for at fair market values and appropriate gains or losses recognized.

Distributions of the stock of other companies (dividends in kind) should not be confused with *stock dividends,* which will be discussed in a following section.

## Stock Splits

Corporations will sometimes *split* their stock. That is, they will issue additional shares for each share outstanding. A firm might, for example, split its stock three for one, meaning that, for each one share presently held, a shareholder will receive an additional two.

Stock splits are ordinarily intended to reduce the market price per share, to obtain a wider distribution of ownership, and to improve the marketability of the outstanding shares. The common stock of a corporation might be trading at $300 per share. The board of directors determines that at such a high price the stock is less attractive to investors than it would be at a lower price. Many investors like to acquire stock in round lots of 100 shares since brokerage commissions tend to be relatively higher when fewer shares are purchased. The board might, therefore, vote a three for one stock split. Each shareholder will end up with three times as many shares as he had previously, but the market price per share could be expected to fall to nearly one-third its previous price. Neither the corporation nor the individual stockholder would be intrinsically better or worse off as a result of the split.

Commonly, the corporation would reduce the par value of the common stock to reflect the split and would so notify shareholders. If the stock previously had a par value of $1, it would subsequently have a new par value of $.33$\frac{1}{3}$. As a consequence, no accounting entries are required to effect the split. Common stock, par value, will in total remain unchanged. So, too, will capital contributed in excess of par and retained earnings.

## ③ Stock Dividends

A special form of stock split is known as a *stock dividend.* As with a stock split, a stock dividend results in the issuance of additional shares. Ordinarily the ratio of new shares to outstanding shares is decidedly lower for a stock dividend than for a stock split. Seldom would the number of new shares to be issued exceed 20 percent of previously outstanding shares; generally it is less than 5 percent. More significantly, the motivation underlying a stock dividend is considerably different from that of a stock split. A corporation would issue a stock dividend not to improve the marketability of its shares but rather to provide its shareholders with tangible evidence of an increase in their ownership interest. A company may view a stock dividend as a substitute for a dividend in cash or other property. Lacking the available cash, it will distribute to each shareholder, on a *pro rata* basis, additional shares of its own stock. Sometimes, for example, a company that has consistently paid cash dividends will be caught in a *cash squeeze.* Rather than omitting the dividend entirely, the company will distribute additional shares of stock instead of cash. A stock dividend may also provide a means for a company to *capitalize* a portion of accumulated earnings. The company will transfer a portion of accumulated earnings from the retained earnings account (which is sometimes viewed as a temporary capital account) to common stock, par value and capital received in excess of par accounts (which are considered to be of a more permanent nature). Such a transfer provides formal evidence that a portion of accumulated earnings has been invested in the business and is no longer available for the payment of dividends.

A stock dividend, like a stock split, has no effect on the intrinsic worth of the corporation. It leaves the shareholders neither better nor worse off than previously. A stock dividend has no effect on corporate assets and liabilities. As a consequence of the dividend, additional shares of common stock are outstanding. But since the net worth of the corporation remains the same, each share of common stock represents a proportionately smaller interest in the corporation.

Suppose, for example, that a corporation, prior to declaration of a stock dividend, had net assets of $100,000 and 1,000 shares of common stock outstanding. A stockholder who owned 100 shares would have held a 10 percent interest in a company with a book value of $100,000. If the corporation declared a 3 percent stock dividend, then the stockholder would receive 3 additional shares. He would now own 103 shares out of a total of 1,030 shares—still a 10 percent interest in a company with a book value of $100,000. Insofar as the market price for the stock is determined in a rational manner, then the market price per share could be expected to be reduced proportionately.

The underlying nature of a stock dividend has been well expressed by the U.S. Supreme Court. In a case in which the court was called upon to rule whether stock dividends constituted income subject to tax under the provisions of the Sixteenth Amendment, Justice Pitney reaffirmed a statement in a previous case in which it was stated

> A stock dividend really takes nothing from the property of the corporation, and adds nothing to the interest of the shareholders. Its property is not diminished, and their interests are not increased. . . . The proportional interest of each shareholder remains the same. The only change is in the evidence which represents that interest, the new shares and the original shares together representing the same proportional interest that the original shares represented before the issue of the new ones.*

Although stock dividends are, in essence, a form of stock split, the rule-making authorities of the accounting profession have determined that they should be accounted for somewhat differently. According to a pronouncement of a committee on accounting procedures, a predecessor of the Accounting Principles Board, when a corporation issues less than 20 percent additional shares as a dividend, it should transfer from retained earnings to "permanent" capital an amount equal to the *fair value* of the shares issued.† Assume, as before, a company which previously had 1,000 shares of stock outstanding declared a 3 percent stock dividend. Assume additionally that each share had a par value of $10 and that the market price at the time of the declaration was $150 per share. The fair value of the 30 shares to be issued and the accumulated earnings to be capitalized would be 30 times $150—$4,500. Conventionally, because of the relatively small number of additional shares to be issued, a company would *not* reduce the par value of its shares. Instead, it would transfer from retained earnings to "common stock, par value" an amount reflective of the par value of the new shares to be issued—in this example $300—and to "common stock, contributed capital in excess of par" the remaining amount—in this example $4,200.

The following entry would give effect to the stock dividend:

| | | |
|---|---:|---:|
| Retained earnings | $4,500 | |
|     Common stock, par value | | $ 300 |
|     Common stock, contributed capital | | |
|       in excess of par | | 4,200 |
| **To record the issue of a stock dividend.** | | |

The rationale behind the *capitalization* of retained earnings rests largely with the interpretation placed upon stock dividends by the recipients. The professional committee which issued the official pronouncement with respect

---

*Eisner *v.* Macomber (252 U.S. 189, 40 S. Ct. 189).

†*Accounting Research Bulletin No. 43.* American Institute of Certified Public Accountants, Chapter 7. (New York, 1961).

to stock dividends took note of the fact that a stock dividend does not, in fact, give rise to any change whatsoever in either the corporation's assets or its respective shareholders' proportionate interests. However, it said, "it cannot fail to be recognized that, merely as a consequence of the expressed purpose of the transaction and its characterization as a *dividend* in related notices to shareholders and the public at large, many recipients of stock dividends look upon them as distributions of corporate earnings and usually in an amount equivalent to the fair value of the additional shares received." Moreover, the committee pointed out, in many instances the number of shares issued is sufficiently small in relation to shares previously outstanding so that the market price of the stock does not perceptibly decline. Hence, the overall market value of a stockholder's interest may, in fact, increase by the amount of the market value of the new shares. Because both recipients and the investing public *think* that the dividend shares are of value, the committee implied, the corporation should account for them as if they were of value. It should transfer a portion of accumulated earnings from "temporary" to "permanent" capital accounts so as to indicate that such portion of earnings is no longer available for the payment of dividends. Whatever merit the rationale of the committee might have had when it was first set forth has unquestionably been reduced by the increased sophistication of investors. Today, only the most naive of investors see the new shares *per se* as having value—although they do, of course, recognize that the earnings that they represent have served to enhance the value of their investment.

## When Is A Loss A Loss?

Inherent in almost all issues facing the accounting profession is the question, "When is a company better off than it was previously?" Implicit in this question is its corollary, "When is a company worse off," or, to phrase it somewhat differently, "When should a loss be recognized as a loss?"

Suppose, for example, that a U.S. company that has interests abroad has been threatened with the expropriation of one of its foreign manufacturing facilities. Unquestionably, the mere threat of the expropriation leaves the firm worse off than it was previously. No doubt, the market price of the firm's outstanding common stock would fall in reaction to such a threat. But should the mere possibility of expropriation be a cause for the firm to write off its foreign assets and charge income with a "loss from expropriation"?

Consider also a company that has been accused by federal authorities of having engaged in price-fixing activities. As a consequence, its customers announce their intention to sue for recovering of damages. At what point should the firm recognize an impairment of its value: when the suits are actually filed; when an initial judgment against the firm is rendered; or when all available appeals have been exhausted?

The question of when to recognize such *contingencies* (losses that are uncertain as to both occurrence and amount) is particularly troublesome to accountants. On the one hand, the convention of conservatism dictates that prompt recognition be given to losses. But, on the other hand, financial statements must be objective. The probability of many types of losses does not suddenly go from remote to certainty. It increases gradually over a period of time. Firms cannot be permitted unlimited discretion in selecting the period in which to recognize losses. If they were, then reported income would be nothing more than an arbitrary determination of corporate management.

The difficulty of establishing guidelines as to when a loss should be recognized arises in large measure because the type of losses with which accountants must deal form a continuum from "reasonably certain and estimable" to "remotely possible and not estimable." On the one end of the continuum are losses such as those arising from warranty obligations and uncollectible accounts. As indicated previously, such losses are conventionally recognized at the time of the related sale of merchandise. They are statistically certain to occur, and the amount of the loss is subject to reasonable estimation, even though the particular account that will have to be written off or the party to whom payment might have to be made is unknown at the time of sale. On the other end of the continuum are losses from fires and natural disasters, which, although sure to occur at some time, are in fact random happenings.

The Financial Accounting Standards Board, in Statement No. 5, "Accounting for Contingencies," has prescribed that a loss may be charged to income only when

(1) information available prior to issuance of the financial statements indicates that it is probable that an asset had been impaired or a liability had been incurred at the date of the financial statements, *and*
(2) the amount of loss can be reasonably estimated.

These guidelines are, of course, vague, but the complete statement of the board provides a number of examples as to when various types of losses should be recognized. The statement directs that, even if a loss contingency does not satisfy the criteria for formal recording within the accounts, it must nevertheless be disclosed in a footnote to the financial statements. The disclosure must indicate the nature of the contingency and give, if possible, an estimate of, or range of, the possible loss.

## Appropriations of Retained Earnings

Some firms provide for the possibility of a loss within the formal accounting structure without actually charging an expense. They *appropriate* (designate) a portion of retained earnings to "cover" the loss. When a firm first believes that a loss is possible (but prior to the time that the loss satisfies the FASB criteria for a charge to earnings), it would make an entry such as the following (assuming a potential liability of $4,000,000):

Retained earnings $4,000,000
    Retained earnings appro-
        priated for contingency $4,000,000
      **To establish a reserve for a contingency (the specific nature of the contingency would be indicated in the account title).**

The retained earnings appropriated for contingencies would be reported in the equity section of the balance sheet directly above or below the unappropriated retained earnings. When the loss actually occurs, the entry would be reversed— the reserved portion of retained earnings restored to the unreserved portion— and the normal entry to record an expense would be made. Similarly, if the danger of an actual loss passes, the appropriated retained earnings would also be returned to the unappropriated portion.

Appropriations of retained earnings, although commonly referred to as *reserves,* do not, in fact, represent reserves at all. They do not assure that the firm will have the financial ability to carry out the activities for which they were intended.

Retained earnings, as has previously been stressed, cannot be associated with particular assets. The appropriation of retained earnings does *not* result in the establishment of a cash reserve or in any way increase the ability of the firm to make cash payments. It does not cause specific assets to be set aside for specific purposes. It represents nothing more than a bookkeeping entry—a reclassification of retained earnings. It is indicative of no substantive financial transaction. To the extent that investors believe that the existence of the reserve is evidence that the firm has the financial means to meet the need for which it was established, they will have been seriously deceived.

## "self-insurance"

A special question of when to recognize losses arises when a firm *self-insures* a portion of its assets. Most firms, like individuals, carry insurance to protect themselves against losses too great for them to bear at any one time. To the extent that a firm is likely to incur an estimable number of losses over a period of years, the effect of the insurance is that the cost of the losses is spread over a period of years (as the insurance premiums are paid) rather than charged in the years in which the losses actually take place.

Some firms which self-insure their assets actually set aside a cash reserve to cover potential losses. Others do not specifically segregate any assets but make certain that they do not declare dividends to an extent which would impair their ability to cover possible losses. Most firms do not self-insure against major catastrophies. Instead, they self-insure against losses that occur with reasonable regularity—damage to automobiles or trucks, for example. Insurance rates are established by independent insurance companies on the basis of the actual or anticipated loss experience of the insured. Premiums are designed to cover actual losses plus costs of administering the policy and, in addition, to provide the insurer with a profit. By maintaining its own insurance coverage a firm is able to restrict its costs to the actual losses.

The accounting issue with respect to self-insurance is whether firms that self-insure should properly charge to expense each year an amount approximately equal to what they would pay in insurance premiums had they insured their assets with outside companies. Suppose, for example, a firm estimates that, on the average, it can expect to incur $30,000 in property losses every five years. Each year it might make the following entry:

| | | |
|---|---|---|
| Self-insurance expense | $6,000 | |
| Retained earnings appropriated | | |
| for self-insurance | | $6,000 |

**To establish a reserve for anticipated property losses.**

As it actually incurs a loss and has to repair or replace damaged property it would charge the loss against the reserve. Thus, assuming that it had to pay $12,000 to repair a truck, it would record the expenditure as follows:

| | | |
|---|---|---|
| Retained earnings appropriated | | |
| for self-insurance | $12,000 | |
| Cash | | $12,000 |

**To record the expenditure to repair a damaged truck.**

There are opposing views as to whether it is appropriate to make periodic charges against income for self-insurance. On the one hand, it is argued that as long as the losses are predictable and occur with regularity, they are an ordinary cost of operations and should be charged to income uniformly—not only in the years that, by chance, they happen to occur. Moreover, it is asserted, the objective of financial statement comparability among firms is advanced by periodic charges to income. Otherwise, those firms that insure with an outside company would report an insurance expense, and those which self-insure would not.

On the other hand, it is contended that self-insurance is *no insurance*. By its very nature insurance involves a transfer of risk to an outside party. Firms that elect to self-insure elect not to insure at all. Losses, therefore, should be charged only as incurred.

The Financial Accounting Standards Board has specifically placed reserves for self-insurance in the same category as reserves for other contingencies. It has therefore precluded firms from charging periodic income with self-insurance expenses. Property losses, the board made clear, should be charged to income only when there is evidence that the value of an asset has been impaired or a liability incurred.

## Employee Stock Options

In recent years, stock options have become an increasingly popular means of compensating executives and other employees. They present intriguing accounting issues because of the uncertainty that attaches to the value of the compensation.

Stock options permit an employee to purchase shares of his company's stock at a fixed price at some date in the future. Although the employee will have to pay for his shares, the price he will have to pay remains constant regardless of fluctuations in market value. Should the market value of the shares increase above the set price (the *exercise* price), he could acquire the shares at a considerable savings over what he would otherwise have to pay. Should the market price fall below the exercise price, then he need not exercise his option and could allow it to lapse.

The difficult accounting issues with respect to employee stock options relate to the measurement of the compensation paid and the value of the shares of stock to be issued. If the employee had to exercise the option immediately upon receipt, then the problems of valuation would be reasonably straightforward. The approximate value of the option would be the number of shares that could be purchased times the difference between the current market price of the stock and the exercise price of the option. If, for example, an option permitted an employee to purchase 100 shares of stock at $40 per share at a time when the stock was being traded at $45 per share, then the employee could "save" $5 per share. The value of the option would be

$$100 (\$45 - \$40) = \$500$$

Most stock option plans stipulate that an option can be exercised only after a specified period of time has elapsed and only if the employee has remained with the company during that period. Indeed, one of the primary objectives of stock option plans is to reduce employee turnover. As a consequence, at the time the option is granted, neither the number of shares to be issued nor the total amount to be received from an employee as payment for his shares is known.

Moreover, once an option plan has been adopted, the exercise price—the price that the employees will have to pay for their shares—is adjusted only periodically. Because of fluctuations in the market price of the firm's shares, the exercise price may sometimes be *greater* than the market price. For example, the option may allow employees the right to purchase shares of stock at a price of $40 even though the current market price is only $35. If the value of the option is to be based on the excess of the exercise price over the market price, then the option would appear to have a negative value.

The option, however, clearly has a positive value regardless of the relationship between exercise and market prices. The recipient has the *right* to purchase the shares at $40 per share. If in the period during which he is eligible to exercise the option the market price increases to more then $40, he can purchase the shares at a *discount* price. If the price remains below $40 per share, he need not exercise the option; he has lost nothing.

Despite these problems of measurement, the Accounting Principles Board has ruled that stock options should be recorded as compensation expense in the periods in which an employee performed the services for which the option was granted. The injunction of the board is intended to ensure that the cost of employee services is matched with the benefits (revenues) that they serve to generate. The value of the option should be determined as of the date that the option is granted.

The board prescribed that the value of each option be measured by the difference between the exercise price and the market price so long as the market price exceeds the exercise price. But, if, as in the situation just described, the exercise price is greater than the market price, then the option and the related compensation should be assumed to have a zero value. The board recognized that there is, in fact, value in options that are granted when the exercise price is greater than the market price. However, it considered the practical difficulties of determining such value to be insurmountable.

*example*

On February 28, 1980, a firm grants an executive the option to purchase 1,000 shares of $1 par value common stock at a price of $8 per share. The option can be exercised during a five-year period beginning January 1, 1984 providing the executive is still employed by the firm. The market price of the stock on February 28, 1980 is $10 per share.

The compensation and the option would be assigned a value of 1,000 times $2 ($10 minus $8)–$2,000–and would be recorded on the date granted as follows:

| | | |
|---|---|---|
| Executive compensation (expense) | $2,000 | |
| Capital received, stock options | | $2,000 |

**To record the issue of the employee stock options.**

The account "Capital received, stock options" would be reported among the other owners' equity accounts. It would represent capital contributed by employees in the form of services rather than cash or other property. When the option is actually exercised, the issue of the 1,000 shares would be recorded as follows:

| | | |
|---|---|---|
| Capital received, stock options | $2,000 | |
| Cash | 8,000 | |
| Common stock, par value | | $1,000 |
| Common stock, contributed capital in excess of par | | 9,000 |

**To record the issue of 1,000 shares of common stock.**

If, alternatively, the employees elected not to exercise the options and they lapsed, then no entry would be required (although "Capital received, stock options" could be reclassified to an account with a title indicative of the lapsed status of the options).

On March 31, 1980 the firm grants the executive an identical option. The market price of the stock has now fallen to $7 per share, however. Since the exercise price is greater than the market price, the option, for accounting purposes, is deemed to have a zero value; no journal entry is required to record the grant of the option.

When the option is actually exercised, the issue of the 1,000 shares would be recorded with the following entry:

| | | |
|---|---|---|
| Cash | $8,000 | |
| Common stock, par value | | $1,000 |
| Common stock, contributed capital in excess of par | | 7,000 |

**To record issue of 1,000 shares of common stock.**

Note that the recorded value of the capital received is directly dependent on the market price of the common stock on the *date the options are granted* rather than the date on which the options are exercised and the shares issued.

### Income Statement: All-inclusive vs. Current Operating Performance

The income statement presents the revenues and expenses of a period. There is a diversity of opinion, however, on whether the income statement should focus upon the normal, recurring operations of the firm or upon all transactions that affect the equity of owners (excluding dividends as well as issues and retirements of capital stock).

Under one viewpoint, only those transactions which are indicative of the *current operating* performance of an enterprise should be taken into account in calculating net income. Other transactions, those of an unusual, nonrecurring nature, should be segregated from the ordinary transactions and reported separately. The income statement should be a report on the normal operations of the firm.

Proponents of the current operating performance approach assert that net income for a given period is useful primarily in that it can serve as a basis for making comparisons among firms and among accounting periods as well as for making predictions about earnings in the future. To the extent that net income is "contaminated" by transactions that are highly unusual and unlikely to recur, its utility is diminished.

Those who favor the alternative approach, the *all-inclusive* income statement, maintain that the income statement should provide a complete record of *all* transactions, excluding dividend distributions, that have an impact upon the retained earnings of a business. They argue that the aggregate of periodic net incomes should provide a complete history of the earnings of the enterprise. They point out that the all-inclusive concept avoids the necessity of making highly subjective judgments as to what constitutes a charge or credit sufficiently unusual as to warrant exclusion from net income. Although proponents of the all-inclusive concept recognize the importance of distinguishing between recurring and nonrecurring revenues and expenses, they believe that the needs of analysts can best be served by providing in footnotes to the financial statements full disclosure of the nature of any unusual items affecting income.

Over the past several decades the profession has wavered between the two concepts of the income statement. In recent years, however, there has been a decided swing toward the all-inclusive concept; the most recent opinions of authoritative bodies reflect the view that, with few exceptions, net income should include all items of profit and loss recorded during the period. Extraordinary items, however, should be distinguished from recurring items.

## Extraordinary Items

Extraordinary items are those that are *unusual in nature and infrequent in occurrence*. In Opinion Nos. 9 and 15, the Accounting Principles Board directed that extraordinary items be segregated from other revenues and expenses and reported separately on the income statement. The board recommended that they be included as part of the income statement as follows:

| | |
|---|---|
| Income before extraordinary items | $xxxx |
| Extraordinary items (less applicable taxes of $_____ ) (Explanatory note: _____ ) | xxxx |
| Net income | $xxxx |

As indicated by the suggested presentation, the taxes associated with the extraordinary items should be presented along with those items. The taxes applicable to the extraordinary items should, therefore, be excluded from the tax expense reported in the main body of the income statement.

To help assure uniformity of practice, the board established rigorous criteria as to what constitutes an extraordinary item. To qualify as extraordinary, an item (as set forth in Opinion No. 30) must be unusual in nature in that "the underlying event or transactions should possess a high degree of abnormality and be of a type clearly unrelated to or only incidentally related to the ordinary and typical activities of the entity." It should be characterized by infrequency of occurrence in that it should be "of a type not reasonably expected to recur in the foreseeable future." Examples of events or transactions that would ordinarily be categorized as extraordinary items are losses resulting from major casualties such as earthquakes, expropriations of property by foreign governments, or governmental prohibitions against the sale or use of products which the company had previously manufactured. Examples of events or transactions that would not be categorized as extraordinary items and should thereby be reported along with ordinary expenses are write-offs of receivables, losses on the sale of a plant, and losses from foreign currency revaluations.

## Earnings per Share

If there is any one single measure of corporate performance that is of primary concern to common stockholders and potential investors, it is unquestionably earnings per share (EPS). In its simplest form, calculation of earnings per share is straightforward:

$$\frac{\text{Net earnings} - \text{Preferred stock dividends}}{\text{Number of shares of common stock outstanding}}$$

Net earnings should be those after taxes. Preferred stock dividends must be deducted from earnings whenever the ratio is being computed for the benefit of common stockholders, since preferred dividends serve to reduce the equity of common stockholders.

The number of shares outstanding should be based on the average number of shares outstanding during the year. Such average would be weighted by the number of months the shares may have been outstanding. The average number of shares outstanding, rather than simply the number outstanding at year end, must be used in the denominator to take into account the fact that the corporation may have had the use of the capital associated with any additional shares issued during the year only for a part of the year. The company's opportunity to generate earnings on the additional capital would have been limited by the number of months it had the use of such capital.

*example*      A firm had earnings after taxes of $800,000. It paid preferred stock dividends of $200,000. It had 200,000 shares of common stock oustanding since January 1. On October 1, it issued an additional 100,000 shares of common stock.

Earnings available to common stockholders would be $600,000 (earnings after taxes less preferred dividends paid).

The average number of shares outstanding would be

| | |
|---|---:|
| 200,000 shares × 9 months | 1,800,000 |
| 300,000 shares × 3 months | 900,000 |
| | 2,700,000 |
| Divided by 12 months | ÷ 12 |
| | 225,000 shares |

Earnings per share of common stock would be

$$NI - DIV \equiv \frac{\$600,000}{225,000} = \$2.67$$

**accounting for potential dilution**

As a consequence of the complex capital structures of many firms, the straight-forward computation of earnings per share may be misleading. Although the average number of shares actually outstanding during a year is, by year end, a historical fact, many firms have commitments to issue additional shares in the future. If earnings per share are to have predictive value—if they are to be a useful guide toward future earnings—then the number of shares reasonably expected to be issued in the future must also be taken into account. Otherwise earnings per share may take a precipitous drop in the period in which the additional shares are issued.

The obligation to issue the additional shares of common stock stems largely from commitments contained in other securities that may be outstanding: stock rights, warrants, and options as well as bonds and preferred stock that might be converted into common stock.

*Stock rights,* often called *preemptive* rights, represent commitments on the part of a company to issue, at an established price, a specified number of shares of common stock. A company would typically grant stock rights to existing shareholders whenever it intends to issue new shares of stock. The rights give the existing stockholders first opportunity to acquire the new shares and thereby to preserve their proportionate interests in the company.

*Warrants,* like rights, are promises on the part of a company to issue a stated number of shares at a set price. Warrants, however, are usually issued by companies in connection with the sale of bonds to make the bonds more attractive to prospective purchasers.

When a firm has a complex capital structure—one that includes such securities that could potentially result in the *dilution* of earnings per share—the calculation of earnings per share becomes both subjective and complicated: subjective because it must necessarily be based on a number of estimates and assumptions, and complicated because the issue of the additional shares will affect not only the number of shares outstanding but overall corporate earnings as well. In 1968 the Accounting Principles Board, in Opinion No. 15, set forth specific guidelines on the computation of earnings per share. An overview of its provisions will serve to indicate some of the difficulties of determining earnings per share when the capital structure is complex.

Opinion No. 15 requires that a firm with a complex capital structure present two types of earnings per share data on the face of its income statement. The first would indicate *primary earnings per share* and the second *fully diluted earnings per share*. The calculation of *both* of the earnings per share figures would take into account the impact of additional shares of common stock that might be issued. They differ, however, in that in the primary earnings per share calculation the denominator (shares outstanding) of the EPS fraction is based on common stock presently outstanding as well as those other types of securities that are considered to be, in substance, *common stock equivalents*. In the computation of fully diluted earnings per share, the denominator includes all shares of common stock presently outstanding plus *all* (with a few exceptions) shares which the firm might have to issue in the future.

**common stock equivalents**    Securities that are in substance *common stock equivalents* are those which are not, in form, common stock but which contain provisions which enable their holders to convert the securities into common stock. They are securities that derive their value from that of the common stock in that they can readily be converted into common stock. The holders of such securities can expect to participate in the appreciation of the value of the common stock and share in the earnings of the corporation. An option to purchase shares of common stock, for example, would ordinarily be considered to be a common stock equivalent as long as the exercise price is less than the prevailing market price of the common stock. As the common stock appreciates in value, so also will the option, since it can be converted into common stock.

Preferred stock that is convertible to common stock may or may not be a common stock equivalent. An issue of convertible preferred stock that provides its holders with a return approximately equal to that which they could obtain by purchasing similar securities without the conversion privilege would *not* be considered a common stock equivalent. It has a value in its own right; holders receive periodic dividend payments sufficient to provide them with a return comparable to that which they could obtain elsewhere. An issue of convertible preferred stock that provides its holders with a yield significantly less than they could obtain elsewhere *would*, however, be considered a common stock equivalent. Holders can be presumed to have purchased such securities in order to be able to convert their shares into common stock. The security derives its value primarily from the common stock into which it could be converted. Suppose, for example, that the prevailing rate of return that an investor could expect to receive is 6 percent. If an issue of convertible preferred stock is sold at a price to yield 6 percent, then it would *not* be considered a common stock equivalent; it does not derive its value primarily from the common stock. The potential number of shares of common stock to which it could be converted would not be taken into account in determining primary earnings per share. If, however, the stock is sold at a price to yield only 1 percent, then it would be considered to be a common stock equivalent, and the number of shares to which it could be converted would be included in the calculation of primary earnings per share. The convertible preferred stock that is not considered to be a common stock equivalent would, however, be taken into account in the calculation of fully diluted earnings per share. Opinion No. 15 sets forth, in detail, rules to be adhered to in determining whether a particular security is a common stock equivalent and whether the number of shares of common stock into which it could be converted should thereby be included in the computation of primary earnings per share. In general, a security would be considered a common stock equivalent if its yield at the time it was issued was less than two-thirds of interest rates (the *prime* bank lending rates) prevailing at the time.

**adjustments**
**to earnings**

If, in computing earnings per share, both primary and fully diluted, it is assumed that certain securities will be converted into common stock and thereby increase the number of common shares outstanding, it is also necessary to give consideration to the impact of such conversion on the *earnings* of the company that are available to common stockholders. To the extent, for example, that it is assumed that outstanding bonds or preferred stock will be converted to common stock, the firm will no longer have to pay interest or dividends on such securities. The amounts saved will serve to increase the earnings in which the common stockholders have an equity interest. In determining the numerator (earnings) of the EPS fraction, the interest or dividends on preferred stock or bonds which are assumed to be converted into common stock must be added to the actual earnings for the year.

Outstanding stock warrants or options permit the holder to *purchase* (for cash) shares of common stock. If, in computing number of shares outstanding, it is assumed that warrants and options will be exercised and additional shares of common stock issued, it is also necessary to take into account the cash that will be received in exchange for the additional shares. Few firms will permit such cash to remain idle in a checking account. Instead, they will invest it in income-producing projects. To the extent that the shares to be issued are added to the number of shares outstanding, it is necessary also to add the potential increase in corporate earnings to actual earnings for the year.

The Accounting Principles Board recognized the practical difficulties of estimating the additional income that would be derived from the cash received from the exercise of warrants and options. To avoid the confusion and diversity of practice that might result if each firm made arbitrary assumptions regarding income to be earned, the board directed that a firm presume that, instead of investing in income-producing projects the proceeds from the exercise of the warrants and options, the firm use the proceeds *to purchase and retire* shares of its own common stock, that is, to reduce the scale of its operations. The number of shares to be purchased and retired would be based on the present market price of the stock. If, for example, a company had 10,000 warrants outstanding, each of which could be used to acquire one share of common stock at a price of $54 per share, it would be assumed that the firm would receive $540,000 in cash. If the current market price of the common stock were $60 per share, then it would be assumed also that the $540,000 would be used to purchase and retire 9,000 shares of common stock. The effect of the method required by the board would be that 1,000 shares would be added to the outstanding common shares but that no change in earnings would be assumed.

The board recognized that few firms would, in fact, use the proceeds from the exercise of warrants or options to retire common stock outstanding. It viewed the assumption as a practical means of taking into account the use of the funds received in exchange for the additional shares of common stock.

*example*

The capital structure of a firm included the following throughout all of 1980:

Common stock: 200,000 shares issued and outstanding.

Preferred stock, Class A: 50,000 shares issued and outstanding. Each share is convertible into *one* share of common stock. Each share pays a dividend of $2. The stock was initially sold to yield shareholders a return of 3 percent—a yield *substantially below* (less than two-thirds) the rate of 6 percent that prevailed at the time.

Preferred stock, Class B: 100,000 shares issued and outstanding. Each share is convertible into *one* share of common stock. Each share pays a dividend of $6. The stock was initially sold to yield shareholders a return of 7 percent—a yield approximately *equal* to the rate that prevailed at the time.

Executive stock options outstanding: Options to purchase 90,000 shares at a price of $40 per share are outstanding.

The current market price of common stock is $60 per share.

The firm had net earnings of $3 million. Out of this amount, $100,000 was paid in dividends to holders of preferred stock, Class A and $600,000 was paid in dividends to holders of preferred stock, Class B. Earnings available to common stockholders were, therefore, $2.3 million.

## Primary Earnings Per Share

*Number of shares outstanding*

| | | |
|---|---|---|
| Common stock | | 200,000 shares |
| Common stock equivalents: | | |
| Preferred stock, Class A | | 50,000 |
| Options | 90,000 shares | |
| Less: Shares of common stock assumed to be purchased and retired with proceeds of $3,600,000 ($40 × 90,000); $3,600,000 ÷ $60 (market price) | 60,000 | 30,000 |
| Shares outstanding for primary EPS calculation | | 280,000 shares |

*Earnings*

| | |
|---|---|
| Earnings available to common stockholders (per above) | $2,300,000 |
| Add: Dividends on preferred stock, Class A, considered to be a common stock equivalent | 100,000 |
| Income for primary EPS calculation | $2,400,000 |

$$\text{Primary EPS} = \frac{\$2,400,000}{280,000 \text{ shares}} = \$8.57$$

Preferred stock, Class B would *not* be considered a common stock equivalent, since it has value in its own right—its yield at time of initial issue was greater than two-thirds of prevailing yields.

Preferred stock, Class A would be considered a common stock equivalent, since it apparently would derive its value directly from the common stock.

## Fully Diluted Earnings Per Share

*Number of shares outstanding*

| | |
|---|---|
| Per primary EPS calculation | 280,000 shares |
| Preferred stock, Class B (not a common stock equivalent but nevertheless convertible into common stock) | 100,000 |
| Shares outstanding for fully diluted EPS calculation | 380,000 shares |

*Earnings*

| | |
|---|---|
| Income for primary EPS calculation | $2,400,000 |
| Add: Dividends on preferred stock, Class B assumed in calculation of number of shares outstanding to be converted into common stock | 600,000 |
| Income for fully diluted EPS calculation | $3,000,000 |

$$\text{Fully diluted EPS} = \frac{\$3,000,000}{380,000 \text{ shares}} = \$7.89$$

## Interim Financial Reports

Publicly traded corporations are required, and many other firms elect, to issue interim financial reports. Interim financial reports are those that cover less than a full year; commonly they cover a quarter- or half-year period. The interim reports of most companies are not nearly so detailed as their annual reports; usually they indicate only a few key indicators of performance such as sales or net income and earnings per share.

The accounting principles to be followed in calculating income for a period of a quarter or half year are the same as those followed for a full year. Nevertheless, meaningful determination of income for short periods presents inherent difficulties. In an earlier chapter it was pointed out that over the life of an enterprise determination of income is relatively simple. Most accounting problems arise because of the need for financial information on a periodic basis. Revenues and expenses must be assigned to specific accounting periods long before the full consequences of a transaction are known with certainty. Prepaid and deferred costs must be *stored* in asset and liability accounts pending allocation to earnings of particular years. To the extent that interim periods are shorter than annual periods, the related problems of income determination and asset valuation are correspondingly greater. It becomes considerably more difficult to associate revenues with productive effort and to match costs with revenues.

The problems of preparing interim financial reports are compounded by the fact that whereas a period of one year will often correspond to a firm's natural business cycle, periods shorter than a year may be characterized by seasonal fluctuations in both revenues and expenses. Indeed, some revenues and expenses are determined on an annual basis; they cannot readily be calculated for a period less than a year until results for the entire year are known. As a consequence, meaningful interim reports cannot be prepared for any one period without consideration of anticipated financial activities in subsequent periods.

The rate at which income is taxed, for example, is based on earnings for an entire year. In 1979 the corporate tax rate was 22 percent on the first $25,000 of income and 48 percent on amounts above $25,000. Suppose that a corporation had taxable income of $20,000 in each of four quarters of a year. If tax expense for the first quarter, when taxable earnings were only $20,000, were to be based on a rate of 22 percent, then reported earnings would be misleadingly high. Income during the remaining three quarters would be taxed at the rate of 48 percent. The actual effective rate of tax (total tax as a percentage of total taxable income) could not be known with certainty until year end.

Some firms permit customers quantity discounts based on cumulative purchases during the year. The discounts may not take effect until the customer has reached a specified level of purchases—a level not likely to be attained until the third or fourth quarter of the year. Prices—and revenues—will appear to be higher in the earlier quarters than the later ones. Unless an adjustment to revenues is made to take into account the discounts to be granted in the future, the interim reports will overstate earnings.

In the same vein, firms may traditionally incur certain major costs in a particular season. Major repairs, for example, may be undertaken during a firm's "slow" season, but they benefit the entire year. Discretionary bonuses to employees may be paid at the year end, but they represent additional compensation for work performed during the entire year. Unless these expenditures are taken into account and spread over the entire year, the interim reports for each individual period may be misleading.

An opinion of the Accounting Principles Board (Opinion No. 28) deals specifically with issues of interim reports. It emphasizes that each interim period should be viewed as an integral part of an annual period and that, as appropriate, adjustments should be made to expenses and revenues to take into account benefits received or costs incurred in other periods.

Although the opinion helped provide for greater uniformity of practice among firms, it did not (and, of course, could not) eliminate the underlying weaknesses of interim reports. Interim reports necessarily are based on an even greater number of subjective assumptions, estimates, and allocations than are annual reports. They provide financial information for a relatively short period of time; especially if a business is seasonal, they cannot be relied upon as predictors of earnings for the remaining periods of the year. If carefully prepared, they can serve as a useful means of comparing performance in one quarter with that in a corresponding quarter of a prior year, though usually not among quarters of the same year. Interim reports unquestionably provide information that is of value to investors and other users of financial reports—but only if the users are aware of their inherent limitations.

## Summary

In this chapter we have dealt with distributions of earnings, stock options, losses and contingencies, earnings per share, and interim reports. Although we discussed several diverse accounting problems, the general approach to resolving them must, in essence, be the same as that to the issues discussed in previous chapters. Accountants must discern the substance, as well as the form, of a transaction, they must measure and assign values to the goods, services, or securities exchanged and must make a judgment as to the appropriate accounting period in which to give recognition to the impairment or enhancement of company resources.

*exercise for review and self-testing*    A corporation had earnings after taxes and preferred dividends of $500,000. It had, for the entire year, 100,000 shares of common stock outstanding.

The company also had outstanding 10,000 shares of preferred stock. The shares were issued at par ($100) and provide the holders with a return of 4 percent. Each share is convertible into one share of common stock. At the time the shares were issued, the prevailing rate of interest, as measured by the prime bank lending rate, was 10 percent.

The firm's capital structure also includes 2,000 convertible bonds, each of which is convertible into 15 shares of common stock—a total of 30,000 shares of common stock. Each bond pays interest at a rate of 8 percent per year. The bonds were issued at a time when the prime bank lending rate was also 8 percent. Total annual interest costs are $160,000, but after-tax interest costs are only 52 percent (one minus the tax rate of 48 percent) of that amount —$83,200.

a. Which of the two issues of convertible securities would be considered a *common stock equivalent*? Why?

b. In determining *primary* earnings per share, how many shares of common stock should be considered outstanding? Such amount would include the actual number of shares of common stock plus the number of shares of common stock into which the common stock equivalent could be converted.

c. If the common stock equivalent were converted into common stock, by how much would interest or preferred dividends be reduced? What would be total earnings available to common stockholders?

d. Based on the calculations in b and c, what would be *primary* earnings per share?

e. How many additional shares of common stock would the company be required to issue if the convertible security that is not considered a common stock equivalent were converted? How many shares of common stock should be considered outstanding in determining *fully diluted* earnings per share?

f. If the bonds were converted into common stock, by how much more would interest (after taking into account tax costs) be reduced? What would now be total earnings available to common stockholders?

g. Based on the calculations in e and f, what would be *fully diluted* earnings per share?

## Questions

review and
discussion

1. The *Wall Street Journal* of July 17, 1975, reported, "Gulf & Western Industries, Inc. declared a 100% stock dividend, said it intends to raise its quarterly dividend by the equivalent of 2.5 cents a current share and predicted record earnings for fiscal 1975." Explain the significance of each of the three elements of the announcement. Which of the three is of most significance to the welfare of the stockholders? Which is of the least?

2. Dividends are sometimes said to be "paid out of retained earnings." Yet for

many corporations, especially those that have been in existence for, and have expanded over, a period of several years, the balance in retained earnings is of little consequence in the decision as to the amount of dividends that can be declared. Why?

3. A firm owns 10,000 shares of stock in another corporation. It wishes to distribute the stock to its shareholders as a dividend in kind. The stock was purchased by the company as a temporary investment at a price of $4 per share. It has a present market value of $10 per share. If the company were to distribute the shares to its stockholders, how much gain on the transaction should the company report? Some accountants oppose recognizing gains or losses on distributions to stockholders. Why?

4. The following excerpt of a conversation was overheard in a crowded elevator in a Wall Street office building: "I just heard that IBM is going to split its stock two for one. The announcment will be made later this week so you'd better purchase a few hundred shares before everyone else hears about it and the price skyrockets." Assuming that the tip is reliable, is there any rational reason for the price of IBM to "skyrocket?"

5. Why is it important that accounting recognition be given to executive stock options in the period that they are first issued? Why would it not be preferable to wait until the period in which the options are exercised—and the company actually receives cash and issues the additional shares—to record the option transactions?

6. In calculating earnings per share, why is it necessary to make assumptions as to what a firm will do with any cash received when options are exercised? Why not simply add the potential number of shares to be issued to the number of shares currently outstanding?

7. What is the distinction between primary earnings per share and fully diluted earnings per share? Are primary earnings per share necessarily based on the average of the actual number of shares outstanding during the year?

8. Distinguish between the *current operating* and the *all-inclusive* concepts of income. What types of events are likely to be accounted for differently if one, as opposed to the other, concept were to be accepted?

9. "The deficiencies and limitations of financial statements are magnified many times when such reports are prepared on a quarterly rather than annual basis." Do you agree? Explain.

10. *Reserves for contingencies* are an indication of prudent and sound management. Their presence on the balance sheet assures investors that the company has "saved for a rainy day." Do you agree? Explain.

## Problems

1. *Are stockholders really better off if they receive a cash, rather than a stock, dividend?*

As of January 1, 1979, the owners' equity section of Arrow Industries contained the following balances:

| Common stock, ($2 par value, 12,500,000 shares | |
| --- | --- |
| issued and outstanding) | $ 25,000,000 |
| Capital in excess of par value | 230,000,000 |
| Retained earnings | 300,000,000 |
| | $555,000,000 |

In 1979 the company had earnings of $20,000,000.

In 1978 the company had declared cash dividends of $1.50 per share. In 1979, however, the board of directors wished to use all available cash to expand facilities. It decided instead to issue a stock dividend "equivalent in value" (based on market prices) to the cash dividend.

The market price of the firm's common stock on December 31, 1979 was $60 per share.

a. How many additional shares of common stock should the company issue?

b. Prepare a journal entry to record the distribution of the additional shares.

c. Comment on whether the stockholders are equally well off having received the stock rather than the cash dividend.

2. *You be the judge. Does a stock dividend represent income to the recipient?*

The case before the court presents the question whether, by virtue of the Sixteenth Amendment, Congress has the power to tax, as income of the stockholder, a *stock dividend* made lawfully and in good faith against earnings accumulated by the corporation since March 1, 1913.

The facts, as outlined, are as follows:

On January 1, 1916, the Standard Oil Company of California declared a *stock dividend;* the company issued additional shares to its stockholders and transferred a portion of its retained earnings to permanent capital (common stock and capital received in excess of par).

Plaintiff, a shareholder of Standard Oil Company of California, received her pro rata number of additional shares. She was called on to pay, and did pay under protest, a tax imposed on the shares. The amount of the supposed income was her proportionate share of the retained earnings transferred to the other capital accounts.

Plaintiff has brought action against the Collector of Taxes to recover the tax. In her complaint she contends that the stock dividend was not income within the meaning of the Sixteenth Amendment.

Put yourself in the position of a judge hearing the case. Outline an opinion in which you decide whether the shareholder can recover the tax paid. The only issue you need to consider is whether a stock dividend constitutes income. Make certain that in your outline you summarize the arguments most likely to be made by *both* plaintiff (shareholder) and defendant (tax collector).

3. *The economic as well as the accounting impacts of three types of dividends of "equal value" may be somewhat different.*

   The balance sheet of Cannon Industries reports the following amounts:

   | | |
   |---|---:|
   | Cash | $ 1,000,000 |
   | Marketable securities | 4,000,000 |
   | Other assets | 15,000,000 |
   | Total assets | $20,000,000 |

   | | | |
   |---|---:|---:|
   | Liabilities | | $ 7,000,000 |
   | Common stock ($1 par value, 500,000 shares issued and outstanding) | $ 500,000 | |
   | Common stock, capital in excess of par | 3,500,000 | |
   | Retained earnings | 9,000,000 | 13,000,000 |
   | Total liabilities and owners' equity | | $20,000,000 |

   Marketable securities include 300,000 shares of Consolidated Industries, which were purchased at a cost of $6 per share.

   In past years the company has paid annual dividends of $4 per share. This year the company is considering two other alternatives to a cash dividend which it hopes will have "equal value" to shareholders:

   1. A dividend in kind of shares of Consolidated Industries. The market value of the shares is $8 per share. The company would distribute to stockholders one share of Consolidated for each two shares of Cannon owned—a total of 250,000 shares.
   2. A stock dividend. The market value of Cannon Industries' stock is $80 per share. The company would distribute one additional share for each 20 shares presently owned—a total of 25,000 shares.

   a. Prepare journal entries that would be required if the company were to issue (1) the dividend in kind, (2) the stock dividend, (3) the cash dividend of $4 per share.
   b. Comment on any problems the company might face in issuing the cash dividend.

4. *Although a stock dividend is comparable in economic substance to a stock split, it is not accounted for in the same manner.*

   The owners' equity section of the Cortland Co. includes the following balances as of June 30, 1980.

   | | |
   |---|---:|
   | Common stock (80,000 shares par value $20, issued and outstanding) | $ 1,600,000 |
   | Common stock, capital in excess of par | 9,200,000 |
   | Retained earnings | 30,000,000 |
   | | $40,800,000 |

As of June 30 the market price of the firm's stock was $700 per share. On that date the firm issued to its stockholders an additional 16,000 shares.

a. Record the issuance of the additional shares if the transaction were to be accounted for as (1) a six-for-five stock split, (2) a stock dividend.

b. At what price would you anticipate the common stock would be traded subsequent to the issuance of the new shares?

c. Comment on how the individual stockholders should account for the additional shares received in their own books and records. How much income should they report for federal tax purposes?

5. *The distinction between a stock split and a stock dividend may be a source of confusion.*

*Barron's* (August 28, 1978) contained the following two news items, back-to-back in the same article:

McQuay-Perfex, Inc. declared a 50% stock dividend and raised its quarterly cash dividend to 24 cents a share from 20 cents.

Stanley Works directors declared a three-for-two stock split and boosted the cash dividend on presplit shares to 40.5 cents from 36.0 cents.

a. Assume that the stockholders' equity of both firms comprised the following:

| | |
|---|---:|
| Common stock, par value $3 (100,000 shares outstanding) | $  300,000 |
| Additional paid-in capital | 800,000 |
| Retained earnings | 2,000,000 |
| | $3,100,000 |

Prepare the journal entry, if any, that each of the firms would make to record the stock "dividend" or stock split.

b. Comment on why accountants, businessmen, as well as journalists are sometimes accused of using needlessly confusing jargon.

6. *A firm accounts for dividends in kind in apparent violation of generally accepted accounting principles.*

The 1976 annual report of American Express Company explains that the company had recently declared a dividend in kind. It distributed to its shareholders approximately 1,955,000 shares of the common stock of Donaldson, Lufkin & Jenrette, Inc. (DLJ) that it had held as an investment. The shares of DLJ had been carried on the books of American Express at $26,773,000 ($13.70 per share). The market value of the shares on the date of the declaration of the dividend was only $6,352,000 ($3.25 per share).

a. Prepare any journal entries that the company should make in connection with the dividend in kind. Remember that generally accepted accounting principles require that property distributed to shareholders be valued at market value and the difference between that value and carrying value should be reflected as a gain or loss.

b. The annual report of American Express also notes: "In management's opinion, the difference between the carrying value and market value of the DLJ investment . . . did not represent a permanent impairment in value (in which case a charge to income to the extent of the impairment would have been required under generally accepted accounting principles). Accordingly, the entire carrying value of the DLJ investment . . . was charged to retained earnings."

Prepare the entry most likely made by the company.

c. What reservations might you have regarding the manner in which American Express accounted for the dividend in kind?

7. *Restrictions on the payment of dividends that are based on balances in retained earnings may be inappropriate for some companies.*

The Mineral Wells Mining Co. was organized in 1979 for the sole purpose of extracting ore from a deposit that the company intended to purchase. It is anticipated that after the property is mined, the company will be dissolved.

The company issued 10,000 shares of common stock ($1 par value) at a price of $110 per share. It purchased the properties for $1 million cash.

During its first year of operations the company extracted 25 percent of the available ore. It had sales revenue of $400,000 and operating expenses and taxes of $100,000, *excluding* depletion. All revenues were received, and all operating expenses were paid, in cash.

The company estimates that it requires an operating cash balance of $100,000.

a. Prepare an income statement and a balance sheet which would reflect the results of operations for the first year.

b. Based entirely on the cash requirements of the firm, what is the maximum cash dividend it can afford to pay?

c. Prepare a journal entry to record payment of such "dividend." (Debit owners' equity accounts directly rather than "dividends.")

d. The statutes of many states prohibit companies from paying dividends in amounts greater than the existing balance in retained earnings. The purpose of the restriction is to assure that distributions of corporate assets are not made to stockholders at the expense of creditors. Do you think that such restrictions should apply to companies organized to extract minerals from specific properties? What would be the impact, over time, of such restrictions on the assets of the companies?

8. *The protection afforded by a firm's practices with regard to casualty insurance may be illusory.*

Three firms in the same industry adopted different policies with respect to casualty insurance. Firm A purchased insurance from an outside company for $10,000 per year. Firm B *self-insured* against losses. Each year it contributed $10,000 to a special insurance fund (e.g., a bank account designated for the purpose) and charged the expense against current earnings (a method no longer in accord with generally accepted accounting principles as set forth by the Financial Accounting Standards Board). Firm C established a *reserve for insurance*. Each year it set aside $10,000 of retained earnings and added it to the reserve. The charge to retained earnings was made directly; it was not initially charged as a current expense.

Each of the three firms estimated that, over a long period of time, it would incur a major loss ($50,000) on the average of once every five years.

Assume that each of the three firms incurred a loss of $50,000 in the third year after having adopted its policy with respect to insurance.

a. Compare the impact of the policies on earnings of the three firms during the three-year period.

b. Comment on the relative abilities of the firms to sustain the loss.

9. *Employee stock options represent a cost of compensating employees. They should be recorded as an expense in the accounting period during which the employees performed the related services.*

The Warwick Co. has adopted a stock option plan which entitles selected executives to purchase shares of its common stock at $40 per share, the price at which the stock was being traded in the open market on the date the plan was adopted.

The plan provides that the options may be exercised one year after being received provided that the executive is still employed by the company. The options lapse, however, 2½ years after they have been issued.

Each option entitles the executive to purchase one share of common stock, which has a par value of $5.

The following transactions or events with respect to the option plan took place over a period of years:

12/31/80: The company issued 1,000 options to its executives. Market price of the stock on that date was $52.

12/31/81: The company issued an additional 2,000 options. Market price of the stock was $35.

7/1/82: Executives exercised 800 of the options issued in 1980. Market price of the common stock was $42.

3/6/83: Executives exercised 1,000 of the options issued in 1981. Market price of the common stock was $48.

6/30/83: The remaining 200 of the options issued in 1980 lapsed. Market price of the common stock was $47.

Prepare journal entries, as required, to record the above transactions and events.

10. *This problem provides a review of several types of transactions that affect owners' equity.*

As of January 1, 1980, the owners' equity section of the Green Mountain Co. contained the following balances:

| | |
|---|---:|
| Common stock, $4 par value (100,000 shares issued and outstanding) | $   400,000 |
| Common stock, capital received in excess of par | 600,000 |
| Retained earnings | 800,000 |
| | $1,800,000 |

During 1980 the following events took place:

1. On January 7, the company issued to executives options to purchase 2,000 shares of common stock at a price of $25 per share. The market price of the common stock on that date was $28 per share.

2. On February 1, the company purchased 2,000 shares of its own stock in the open market at a price of $20 per share. The firm intended to use the stock to satisfy obligations on outstanding options.

3. On February 10, the company declared a cash dividend of $.50 per share. The dividend was paid on February 23.

4. On March 7, executives exercised options to purchase 2,000 shares. The market price of the common stock on that day was $26 per share.

5. On May 10, in lieu of its usual quarterly cash dividend, the company declared and paid a dividend in kind. The company distributed to shareholders 5,000 shares of Pacific General Co. common stock that had been held as an investment. The prevailing market price for the shares was $10 per share; they had been purchased previously, and recorded on the books of Green Mountain Co., at a price of $2 per share.

6. On August 10, the company declared and paid a stock dividend equal in value (based on the current market price of the shares issued) to the $.50 per share of its traditional quarterly dividend. The market price of the shares on that date was $25.

7. On December 17, the company declared a stock split. For each old share owned, stockholders would be given *two* new shares.

8. On December 28, the company issued to executives the options to purchase 4,000 shares at a price of $12.50 per share. The market price of the common stock on that date was $10 per share.

Prepare journal entries to record the above events. (Debit any dividends directly to the owners' equity accounts affected rather than to "dividends.")

11. *End-of-year changes in number of shares outstanding will have but little effect upon earnings per share.*

In November 1981 the controller of a firm estimated that net earnings for the year ending December 31 would be approximately $500,000, an amount considerably less than the $600,000 for the previous year. Aware that the newspapers commonly focus on earnings per share, the controller devised a scheme to boost EPS. On December 1 the firm would acquire in the open market 20,000 shares of its own common stock. It would immediately retire those shares. The acquisition and retirement would serve to reduce the denominator of the EPS ratio and thereby boost EPS. Throughout 1980 and the first eleven months of 1981 the firm had 100,000 shares of common stock outstanding.

a. Determine EPS for 1980 and 1981, based on 100,000 shares outstanding.

b. Determine EPS for 1981 as the controller apparently expects it will be computed.

c. Will the scheme of the controller be successful? Determine EPS for 1981 in accord with generally accepted accounting principles.

12. *An understanding of the principles underlying the computation of earnings per share helps in interpreting information contained in a firm's annual report.*

The following information pertaining to earnings per share appeared in an annual report of the Monsanto Company:

### Earnings per Common Share

Income and the number of shares used in the computation of earnings per common and common equivalent share were determined as follows:

| Income (In millions) | Primary | Fully Diluted |
|---|---|---|
| Net income | $ 366.3 | $ 366.3 |
| Preferred dividends | (2.2) | |
| Interest (less tax) on: | | |
| Loan stock of Monsanto Limited | 0.3 | 0.3 |
| Debentures of Monsanto International Finance Company | | 0.5 |
| | $ 364.4 | $ 367.1 |
| *Number of Shares (In thousands)* | | |
| Weighted average shares: | | |
| Outstanding | 35,835 | 35,835 |
| Incremental shares for outstanding stock options | 161 | 167 |
| Shares issuable upon conversion: | | |
| Loan stock of Monsanto Limited | 276 | 276 |
| Debentures of Monsanto International Finance Company | | 269 |
| $2.75 Preferred Stock | | 983 |
| | $36,272 | $37,530 |

a. Is the firm's $2.75 preferred stock a common stock equivalent? How can you tell?

b. Why were preferred dividends of $2.2 million deducted from the computation of primary earnings but not fully diluted earnings?

c. Are the debentures (bonds) of Monsanto International Finance Company (a consolidated subsidiary) common stock equivalents? How can you tell?

d. Why is the term "incremental" used in describing the shares to be issued in connection with outstanding stock options?

13. *The procedure for determining earnings per share, although complex, is designed to make certain that potential dilution is taken into account.*

In 1979 the Sutton Company had earnings after taxes and before dividends of $300,000. The company has 100,000 shares of common stock issued and outstanding. The corporate income tax rate may be assumed to be 40 percent.

In addition, the company has outstanding $500,000 of bonds that are convertible into common stock. Each $1,000 of bonds may be converted into 40 shares of common stock. The bonds were sold to yield 4 percent.

When they were issued, the prime interest rate for corporate borrowers was 8 percent.

The company also has outstanding 3,000 shares of $100 par value convertible preferred stock. Each share of preferred stock may be exchanged for five shares of common stock. The preferred stock carries a dividend rate of $10 per share. The stock was issued at par (no discount or premium) at a time when the prevailing interest rates were 7 percent.

a. Determine primary earnings per share.

b. Determine fully diluted earnings per share.

**14.** *In computing earnings per share a firm must make an assumption as to what it does with cash received when outstanding stock options are exercised.*

Riggs Corporation had earnings after taxes in 1980 of $800,000. The company had 200,000 shares of common stock outstanding. The current market price of the common stock is $25 per share.

In 1979 the company adopted a stock option plan. Currently outstanding are 50,000 options which enable the holder to purchase one share each at $20 per share and 10,000 options which may be exercised for one share each at $10 per share.

The company has 10,000 shares of 8 percent convertible preferred stock outstanding. Par value of the stock is $100; each share is convertible into *three* shares of common stock. The current market price of the preferred stock is $105. The preferred stock was issued at a time when the prevailing interest rates were 6 percent.

a. Determine primary earnings per share.

b. Determine fully diluted earnings per share.

**15.** *The question of how best to report upon pending litigation and final settlement of claims resulting from such litigation has always been a troublesome one to accountants.*

Assume the following facts:

In 1975 a major manufacturer of electrical equipment is charged by a group of customers with engaging in pricing practices that are in violation of antitrust statutes. The alleged illegal activities took place in the years 1972 to 1974. The customers file suit in federal court; they seek treble damages totaling $36 million. Attorneys for the defendant confidentially advise their client to "be prepared for a final judgment between $10 million and $20 million."

In 1978, after a lengthy trial, the company is found liable to the plaintiffs for $20 million in damages. The company announces its intention to appeal.

In 1979 an appeals court reverses the decision of the lower court and orders a new trial.

In 1980 the company agrees to an out-of-court settlement with the plaintiffs. The firm will pay damages of $6 million.

In 1981 the company pays the agreed upon amounts to the plaintiffs.

How, in your judgment (irrespective of any official pronouncements on the subject), do you think the company ought to account for the litigation?

Indicate any specific journal entry that you think the company should make during or at the end of each of the years in question. Consider the possibility of making supplementary disclosures in footnotes to the financial statements. Bear in mind that the financial statements will be public documents, available to the plaintiffs and their attorneys.

16. *Seasonal businesses have special problems of interim reporting.*

Lakeview, Inc. operates a summer resort. The resort is open for guests during the summer months only. In the first quarter (January 1 through March 31) of its fiscal year the company had zero revenues but made cash disbursements as follows:

| | |
|---|---:|
| Property taxes for the period January 1 to December 31 | $ 60,000 |
| Administrative salaries for the first quarter | 30,000 |
| Advertising | 12,000 |
| Repair and maintenance (annual overhaul of boats and docks) | 7,000 |
| Total disbursements | $109,000 |

a. For each disbursement consider whether, for purposes of interim reporting, (1) it should be charged as an expense as incurred, (2) it should be allocated evenly to each of the four quarters, or (3) it should be allocated on some other basis. (Use your judgment; the answer cannot be found in the text.)

b. Comment on the special difficulties faced by seasonal businesses in preparing interim reports. (In practice, policies with regard to the allocation of costs such as those indicated in this problem vary from firm to firm. There are no specific professional guidelines that deal with seasonal industries.

17. *First period "interim" earnings must be adjusted to take into account events of subsequent periods.*

For the first three months in 1980, the Warwick Company, according to its president, had earnings before taxes of $140,000, determined as follows:

| | | |
|---|---:|---:|
| Sales | | $420,000 |
| Cost of goods sold | $200,000 | |
| Other expenses | 80,000 | 280,000 |
| Income before taxes | | $140,000 |

The following additional information has come to your attention:

1. The company gives quantity discounts to its customers based on total purchases for the year. No quantity discounts have been allowed to date. The firm estimates that total sales for the year, at *gross* sales price, will be $2 million. After taking into account quantity discounts, $200,000 of the sales will be at 95 percent of gross sales price (a discount of $10,000) and $400,000 will be at 90 percent of gross sales price (a discount of $40,000).

2. The company uses the LIFO inventory method and determines year-end inventory and the annual cost of goods sold on the basis of a periodic inventory count, which is taken on December 31 of each year. The cost of goods sold for the quarter ending March 31 was calculated as follows:

| | | |
|---|---:|---:|
| Goods on hand 1/1/80: 30,000 units @ $5 | $150,000 | |
| Production, 1st quarter: 10,000 units @ $10 | 100,000 | $250,000 |
| Estimated goods on hand 3/31/80: | | |
| 10,000 units @ $5 | | 50,000 |
| Cost of goods sold, 30,000 units | | $200,000 |

The company estimates that it will complete the year with an inventory of 30,000 units. As a consequence, the ending inventory will be stated at $5 per unit: The firm will not have to "dip" into its LIFO stock. The cost of goods sold for the entire year will be based on current production costs of $10 per unit.

3. The company overhauls its plant once a year in July at a cost of $20,000. The cost of the overhaul has not been taken into account in computing first-quarter expenses.

4. Each December the company gives its salaried employees a bonus equal to approximately 10 percent of their annual salaries. First-quarter salaries (included in other expenses), without taking into account the bonus, amounted to $75,000.

5. The current federal income tax rate is 22 percent of the first $25,000 of taxable income and 48 percent on all earnings above that amount. The company estimates that taxable income for the entire year will be $80,000.

Determine earnings after taxes for the first quarter of 1980 as you believe they should be reported to the general public.

*solutions to exercise for review and self-testing*

a. A convertible security is considered a common stock equivalent if it derives its value from that of the common stock. The pragmatic test is whether its yield at the time it was issued was less than two-thirds of the prime bank lending rate. The preferred stock was issued to yield 4 percent at a time when the prime rate was 10 percent. It would, therefore, be considered a common stock equivalent. The convertible bonds were issued to yield 8 percent at a time when the prevailing rate was also 8 percent. It would not, therefore, be considered a common stock equivalent.

b. 100,000 shares of common stock + 10,000 shares that would be issued if the preferred stock were converted = 110,000 shares.

c. Preferred dividends would be reduced by $40,000. Total earnings available to common stockholders would be $540,000.

d. Primary earnings per share = $540,000/110,000 shares = $4.91.

e. An additional 30,000 shares would be issued; 140,000 shares would now be outstanding.

f. Interest would be reduced by $83,200, after taking into account income taxes. Total earnings available to common stockholders would be $540,000 + $83,200 = $623,200.

g. Fully diluted earnings per share = $623,200/140,000 shares = $4.45.

# 13

## Intercorporate Investments and Earnings

In this chapter we shall consider issues of accounting for and reporting intercorporate investments. Because they are sometimes of major magnitude, intercorporate investments are a source of continuing controversy. The means by which an investment in another company is recorded initially and updated subsequently are likely to be of considerable consequence for the valuation of assets and the determination of income.

A corporation may acquire an equity interest (ownership of common or preferred stock) in another company for a number of reasons. A company may have cash that is temporarily idle. It may, therefore, purchase a relatively small number of the shares of another company in order to obtain a short-term return—as an alternative, perhaps, to purchasing short-term government notes or certificates of deposits. Such securities are categorized on the books of the acquiring corporation as "marketable securities"; the accounting for marketable securities was discussed in Chapter 6. On the other hand, a company may purchase the stock of another corporation as a long-term investment. It may do so because it believes that the securities will provide a long-term return equivalent to, or greater than, that which could be obtained by internal use of available funds. Or, it may seek to obtain a sufficient number of shares to exercise a measure of influence and control over the other corporation in order to gain entry into new markets or new industries, to develop sources of raw materials, or to integrate its own operations with those of the other company.

A company may acquire the stock of another company by purchasing it for cash or other assets. Or, especially if it intends to get possession of all, or almost all, of the outstanding shares, it may exchange shares of its own common stock for those of the company it seeks to acquire. Moreover, a firm may obtain shares of another company simply by itself organizing such a company and retaining all, or a portion, of the shares issued. Many companies, to satisfy various legal requirements, to obtain certain tax advantages, or to enhance organizational efficiency, divide their operations into several subsidiary corporations, in each of which the *parent* corporation will hold controlling interest. Each subsidiary corporation may represent nothing more than a manufacturing or sales division or even a branch office. To take an extreme example, a well-known commercial loan company maintains separate corporations not only for each of its numerous branch offices but for each major type of loan made within a branch office. The parent corporation owns 100 percent of the common stock of all of the individual corporations.

## Level of Influence

The critical determinant of the means by which intercorporate investments are accounted for is the degree of influence that the investor corporation exerts over the acquired company. To the extent that the investor corporation exerts relatively minor influence, the investment would generally be accounted for by the *cost* method; to the extent that it exerts substantial influence, it would be accounted for by the *equity* method. (Both of these methods will be defined and evaluated shortly.) Insofar as the investor company is able to *control* the other company (control ordinarily being defined as ownership of over 50 percent of the voting stock), the investment is commonly reported by means of *consolidated financial statements*. Consolidated financial statements report the financial position and earnings of two or more corporations as if they were a single entity. The three methods of accounting for corporate investments—the cost, the equity, and the consolidated statement methods—are not, it should be emphasized, categorically consistent. *Since each corporation is a separate legal entity, a separate set of accounting records must, by law, be maintained for it. On the books of the investor corporation the shares of the other company must be accounted for by either the cost or the equity method. If, however, the investor company has control over another corporation, then, for purposes of reporting, the individual financial statements of the two companies can be combined into a single, consolidated, set of statements.* The relationships and distinction among the methods will be brought out in the next several sections.

**criteria for presumption of significant influence**

Where an investor corporation is unable to maintain significant influence over the company in which it owns an interest because of the small proportion of its holdings, then it should account for its investment by the cost method. Evidence of an ability to influence significantly the key financial and operating policies over an investee company may be manifest by several factors: percentage of shares owned, representation on the corporate board of directors, membership on key policy-making committees, interchange of managerial personnel, material purchases or sales between the two companies, and exchanges of technological information. Even though a company may not own a majority of a corporation's outstanding shares, it may nevertheless exercise a predominant impact on that company's policies. While recognizing that degree of influence cannot be readily measured, the Accounting Principles Board, in order to achieve a greater degree of uniformity of practice, prescribed that an investment of 20 percent or more of the voting stock of an investee should lead to a presumption that the investor has the ability to exercise significant influence over the investee.*

*"The Equity Method of Accounting for Investments in Common Stock," Opinion No. 18 of the Accounting Principles Board, American Institute of Certified Public Accountants, (New York, 1971).

It directed, therefore, that investments of less than 20 percent of voting stock should be accounted for by the cost method and investments of 20 percent or more by the equity method.

## Cost Method

Under the cost method, a company records its investment in the stock of another company at cost—the amount paid to acquire the stock. It recognizes revenue from its investment only to the extent that the investee company actually declares dividends. In the absence of unusual declines in market values, the investment would be maintained on the books of the investor at original cost. The carrying value of the investment would be unaffected by changes either in the market value of shares owned or in the net worth of the company that they represent.*

*example*

On March 1, the Adams Company purchases 10,000 of 100,000 (10 percent) shares of the outstanding common stock of the Cain Company. It pays $30 per share. The following entry would be required on the books of the *investor* company, the Adams Company:

| | | |
|---|---|---|
| Investment in Cain Company | $300,000 | |
|     Cash | | $300,000 |

**To record the purchase of 10,000 shares of Cain Company common stock.**

On December 31, 1980, the Cain Company announces that earnings for the year were $500,000 ($5 per share of common stock).

No entry is required to record the announcement of the annual earnings. The Adams Company recognizes revenue from its investment only upon the actual declaration of dividends by the company whose shares it owns.

On the same date, December 31, 1980, the Cain Company declares dividends of $2 per share, payable on January 20, 1981.

| | | |
|---|---|---|
| Dividends receivable | $20,000 | |
|     Revenue from investment in | | |
|     Cain Company | | $20,000 |

**To record dividends to be received from the Cain Company.**

---

*Financial Accounting Board Statement No. 12, "Accounting for Certain Marketable Securities" (1976), provides that investments in other corporations which are accounted for by the cost method should be reported and valued in a manner similar to marketable securities in general. That is, they should be valued at cost unless the market value of the entire portfolio of securities is less than its cost. In such event, the entire portfolio should be written down to, and reported at, market value.

The cost method of maintaining investments is that illustrated in previous chapters in connection with marketable securities and recognition of dividend revenue. Dividends are recognized as revenue when they are declared, not when they are paid.

## Equity Method

Under the equity method, a company records its investment in another company at cost (same as under the cost method), but it periodically adjusts the carrying value of its investment to take into account its share of the investee's earnings subsequent to the date it acquired the stock. It recognizes its share of increases or decreases in the net worth of the investee as soon as they are known to it. If net worth increases as a result of investee corporate earnings, then the investor company recognizes promptly, on its own books, revenue in the amount of its proportionate share of such earnings; it does not wait until such earnings are distributed in the form of dividends. Since earnings of the investee company serve to increase the equity of the investor company in the investee company, the investor company will concurrently increase the carrying value of its investment by its share of total revenue recognized.

If net worth of the investee corporation decreases, then the investor will also recognize such decreases. Net worth will decrease as a consequence of operating losses. But it will also decrease whenever dividends are declared (a liability for the payment of a dividend is established; retained earnings are decreased). Hence, as the investee company declares a dividend, the investor company recognizes the dividend receivable and at the same time adjusts the carrying value of its investment to reflect the decline in the net worth of the investee. An example may help to clarify the accounting procedures.

*example*    Assume the same facts as in the previous example, except that this time, on March 1, 1980, the Adams Company purchases 20,000 of 100,000 (20 percent) shares of the common stock outstanding of the Cain Company. Again, it pays $30 per share. This time, however, since Adams has acquired 20 percent of the shares outstanding, it may be presumed that it exerts substantial influence over the Cain Company; hence, it is appropriate to account for the investment by the equity method.

**(a)**

| | | |
|---|---|---|
| Investment in Cain Company | $600,000 | |
| Cash | | $600,000 |

**To record the purchase of 20,000 shares of Cain Company common stock for $30 per share.**

This entry is identical in form to that illustrated previously in connection with the cost method.

On December 31, the Cain Company announces that earnings for the year were $500,000 ($5 per share of common stock).

**(b)**

| | | |
|---|---|---|
| Investment in Cain Company | $100,000 | |
| Revenue from investment | | |
| in Cain Company | | $100,000 |

**To record the proportionate share of the 1980 income reported by the Cain Company.**

The net worth of the Cain Company increased by $500,000 as a consequence of 1980 earnings. The Adams Company must recognize 20 percent of that amount as its own revenue. Since the Adams Company receives no cash or other assets as a direct result of the Cain Company having realized the income, its share of the earnings would be reflected by an increase in the carrying value of its investment.

When the Cain Company declares a dividend of $2 per share, the Adams Company would establish a receivable account for the dividends but would recognize a corresponding *decrease* in the carrying value of its investment.

**(c)**

| | | |
|---|---|---|
| Dividends receivable | $40,000 | |
| Investment in Cain Company | | $40,000 |

**To record dividends to be received from the Cain Company.**

Upon learning that the Cain Company had declared a dividend, the Adams Company would *not*, under the equity method, recognize revenue. Revenue representing the earnings of the Cain Company had been recognized at the time it was first reported. To recognize it again when it is distributed to shareholders in the form of dividends would be to count it twice. The carrying value of the investment in the Cain Company would be reduced by the amount of the dividend received because, as a result of cash distributions to its shareholders, the Cain Company has reduced both its assets and its retained earnings. The share of the Adams Company in such retained earnings has thereby been proportionately reduced.

As indicated in the accompanying T accounts, the net effect of the last two entries (**b** and **c**) has been to increase the assets of the Adams Company by $100,000 (investment in Cain Company, $60,000; dividends receivable, $40,000). Correspondingly, the Adams Company recognized $100,000 in revenue from its investment in the Cain Company. The $100,000 represents, of course, 20 percent of the reported earnings of the Cain Company.

| Investment in Cain Company | | | | Revenue from investment in Cain Company | |
|---|---|---|---|---|---|
| (a) | 600,000 | (c) | 40,000 | (b) | 100,000 |
| (b) | 100,000 | | | | |

*% earnings* · *660,000*

| Dividends receivable | | | *Dividends decrease asset value* | Cash | |
|---|---|---|---|---|---|
| (c) | 40,000 | | | (a) | 600,000 |

## Cost and Equity Methods Compared

The justification for the cost and the equity methods and the distinctions be-tween them can readily be appreciated when the two methods are viewed within the context of issues of revenue recognition. A company owns stock in another company. If the investee company is profitable, the investor company is ob-viously better off than if the investee company is not. Since, in the long run, earnings of a company represent revenue to its owners, earnings of the investee company signify revenue to the investor company. The question facing the ac-countant of the investor company relates to the point in time at which such revenue should be recognized.

Under the cost method the investor company recognizes as revenue its share of investee corporation earnings only as the investee corporation actually declares dividends—that is, as it announces its intention to distribute to share-holders the assets corresponding to the earnings available for distribution. The cost method is thereby more conservative than the equity method. Under this method revenue is recognized by the investor company only as cash (assuming that the dividend is to be paid in cash) is about to be received. The cost method makes sense when an investor company has but little influence on the dividend or other operating policies of the company in which it owns shares, for al-though the investee company may be profitable, it need not necessarily declare dividends, and the investor company cannot require it to do so. It may be many years, therefore, before earnings of the investee company are trans-lated into liquid assets of the investor company.

Under the equity method, the investor company recognizes as revenue its share of investee company earnings as soon as such earnings are reported, regardless of when such earnings are likely to be distributed to shareholders in the form of dividends. The equity method is appropriate when the investor company does have significant impact on the dividend policy of the investee firm. The rationale for the equity method can easily be understood if the consequences of *not* using the method are considered. If the investor had suffi-cient influence on the investee so that it could control if and when the investee could declare dividends, then it could readily control its own earnings. If the investor firm otherwise had an unprofitable year, it could direct that the investee firm increase its dividend payout. Its share of the dividends would be reflected immediately in higher reported revenues. If the investor firm otherwise had an unusually profitable year and did not "need" additional revenues in order to report satisfactory earnings, it could request that the investee firm delay payment of dividends until future periods. In Chapter 5 it was pointed out that revenue should be recognized only when it can be objectively measured and when eventual collection of cash can reasonably be assured. When a firm is able to exert substantial influence (defined by the Accounting Principles Board as ownership of 20 percent or more of voting stock) over the company in which it maintains an interest, then the two criteria are reasonably satisfied at the time the investee company reports its earnings. The equity method is thereby considered more appropriate. When the firm is unable to exert such influence, then the criteria are not reasonably satisfied until the investee company declares its intention to distribute cash or other assets. Hence, the cost method is more appropriate.

## Consolidated Reports

When a company is able to control, as opposed to merely influence, the financial and operating policies of another company, then the interests of investors as well as other users of financial statements are usually most meaningfully served by the preparation of consolidated financial statements. Consolidated financial statements report the financial position and results of operations of two or more corporations, each a separate legal entity, as if together they were a single economic entity. They are designed to give effect to the economic substance as opposed to the legal form of the corporate relationship. They combine the assets, liabilities, equities, revenues, and expenses of the two or more companies into a single balance sheet and income statement.

Consolidated statements are a means of reporting. The preparation of consolidated financial statements does not preclude the preparation of individual financial statements for specific purposes. Indeed, each member of a group of corporations whose financial statements may be combined into a single consolidated set of statements must maintain separate accounting records. An investor corporation must, therefore, account for its ownership in other companies by either the cost or the equity method—although, as will be seen shortly, choice of method becomes immaterial since both the investment accounts and the revenue from investment accounts are eliminated in the process of consolidation.

The usual condition for consolidated statements is voting control of one company by another—that is, ownership of more than 50 percent of the voting stock. There are, however, exceptions to this rule. Consolidated statements would not generally result in the most meaningful presentation and are, therefore, not required when the two or more companies are not, in fact, a single economic entity (if, for example, voting control is likely to be only temporary). Similarly, if a subsidiary company is in a specialized industry, one in which unique accounting practices are adhered to, the presentation of individual reports might be more useful to investors than a consolidated report.

As a general rule, if an investor company owns less than 20 percent of the voting stock of another company, it would *account* for its investment on the cost basis; if it owns 20 percent or more, then it would *account* for its investment on an equity basis; if it owns over 50 percent, it would *report* to stockholders on a consolidated basis, unless because of special circumstances consolidation is deemed inappropriate.

A company that has control (over 50 percent ownership) of another company is referred to as a *parent;* the controlled company is known as a *subsidiary*.

## Principles of Consolidation—
## Balance Sheet

In simplest form consolidated statements represent the sum of the balances in accounts of the individual companies which are to form the consolidated entity. However, as will be demonstrated in the discussion and examples to follow, certain eliminations and adjustments are required if double counting is to be avoided.

The objective of consolidated statements is to depict the financial position and results of operations of two or more companies as if they were a single economic entity. It is necessary, therefore, to adjust for the effect of certain intercompany transactions on both the income statement and the statement of position. Consider the following illustration: If a parent company sells for $100 merchandise to a subsidiary company, which in turn sells it to outsiders for $120, then the sum of the sales of the two companies would be $220. But if the two companies were viewed as a single entity, then the sale from the parent to the subsidiary would be accounted for as an internal transfer as opposed to a sale. Total sales—those to outsiders—would be only $120. Elimination of the sale from parent to subsidiary is thereby required. Similarly, the cost of the goods sold by the parent to the subsidiary would have to be eliminated, and if the subsidiary is still indebted to the parent for the goods which it purchased, so also would the account receivable (on the books of the parent) and the account payable (on the books of the subsidiary).

The examples to follow will center first upon the effects of consolidation on the balance sheet and then on the income statement.

Assume that Parent company purchases 100 percent of the common stock out-standing of Subsidiary company. Immediately after acquisition, the trial bal-ances of the two individual companies appear in condensed form, as follow:

|  | Parent | Subsidiary |
|---|---|---|
| Cash | $ 20,000 | $10,000 |
| Account receivable (from subsidiary) | 10,000 | |
| Investment in subsidiary | 40,000 | |
| Other assets | 80,000 | 40,000 |
| | $150,000 | $50,000 |
| | | |
| Account payable (to parent) | | $10,000 |
| Common stock | $ 30,000 | 10,000 |
| Retained earnings | 120,000 | 30,000 |
| | $150,000 | $50,000 |

Since the balances indicated are those immediately following acquisition, it is clear that the parent company must have paid $40,000 to acquire the sub-sidiary—the amount indicated in its investment in subsidiary account. If the two companies are to be combined, there is no need for an investment in subsidiary account; from a consolidated standpoint, a company cannot have an investment in itself. At the same time, if the two sets of statements are to be combined, it would be inappropriate to report $40,000 owners' equity (common stock, $10,000, plus retained earnings, $30,000) of the subsidiary, since it is the parent company which is the sole owner of the subsidiary and which has such equity in the subsidiary. To effect a consolidation, it would be necessary to eliminate *both* the investment in the subsidiary *and* the equity of the owners. For convenience, the eliminations can be expressed in journal entry form:

(a)

| | | |
|---|---|---|
| Common stock (of subsidiary) | $10,000 | |
| Retained earnings (of subsidiary) | 30,000 | |
| Investment in subsidiary (by parent) | | $40,000 |

**To eliminate the investment in subsidiary and corresponding subsidiary owners' equity accounts.**

The trial balance indicates that the subsidiary company owes the parent company $10,000. From the standpoint of the combined enterprise, both accounts receivable and payable would be overstated if assets and liabilities were simply added together; a company cannot have a payable to or a receiv-able from itself. The payable and receivable must be eliminated:

**(b)**

| | | |
|---|---|---|
| Account payable (to parent) | $10,000 | |
| Account receivable (from subsidiary) | | $10,000 |

**To eliminate intercompany payable and receivable.**

*The two entries would be posted to the books of neither the parent nor the subsidiary. They are nothing more than worksheet eliminations to effect a combination of the two individual sets of statements.* Thus, the consolidated balance sheet would appear as indicated in the far right-hand column.

| | Original Statements | | Adjustments | | Combined |
|---|---|---|---|---|---|
| | Parent | Subsidiary | Debit | Credit | Statements |
| Cash | $ 20,000 | $10,000 | | | $ 30,000 |
| Account receivable (from subsidiary) | 10,000 | | | (b) $10,000 | |
| Investment in subsidiary | 40,000 | | | (a) 40,000 | |
| Other assets | 80,000 | 40,000 | | | 120,000 |
| | $150,000 | $50,000 | | | $150,000 |
| | | | | | |
| Account payable (to parent) | | | $10,000 | (b) $10,000 | |
| Common stock | $ 30,000 | 10,000 | (a) 10,000 | | $ 30,000 |
| Retained earnings | 120,000 | 30,000 | (a) 30,000 | | 120,000 |
| | $150,000 | $50,000 | $50,000 | $50,000 | $150,000 |

**interests of minorities**

A firm does not always acquire 100 percent of the outstanding common stock of another firm. *Minority stockholders* may also own an equity interest in an investee firm. Assume facts similar to those in the previous example, but this time suppose that the parent company purchased only 80 percent of the common stock of the subsidiary. The parent company paid $32,000 for its interest, an amount exactly equal to 80 percent of the *book value* of the subsidiary, as represented by common stock of $10,000 and retained earnings of $30,000.

The parent company's investment in subsidiary of $32,000 must be eliminated against $32,000 of the $40,000 owners' equity of the subsidiary:

| | | |
|---|---|---|
| Common stock (of subsidiary) | $ 8,000 | |
| Retained earnings (of subsidiary) | 24,000 | |
| Investment in subsidiary (by parent) | | $32,000 |

**To eliminate investment in subsidiary and corresponding amounts in subsidiary's owners' equity accounts.**

But that leaves $8,000 remaining in the owners' equity accounts of the subsidiary. This amount represents the equity of the minority shareholders—those who hold the remaining 20 percent interest in the firm. Consolidated financial statements are prepared from the perspective of the *majority* stockholders, those of the parent company. From the standpoint of a majority stockholder, it would be both confusing and misleading to report on the balance sheet common stock and retained earnings in two companies—those of the parent and those of the subsidiary. Hence, the minority interest in each of the owners' equity accounts (the amounts that remain after the majority interest has been eliminated) are reclassified into a single account, "minority interest in subsidiary":

| | | |
|---|---|---|
| Common stock (of subsidiary) | $2,000 | |
| Retained earnings (of subsidiary) | 6,000 | |
| Minority interest in subsidiary | | $8,000 |

**To reclassify the equity of minority shareholders in the subsidiary.**

The minority interest in subsidiary account represents the equity of the minority shareholders in the consolidated corporation. It is, in a sense, the portion of the residual interest in the subsidiary that may be assigned to the minority rather than the majority stockholders. As a consequence, many corporations report minority interest in subsidiaries among *long-term liabilities*. The amounts reported in the owners' equity section of the consolidated balance sheet represent only the equity of the parent company stockholders.

**acquisition price in excess of investment book value**

In the discussion so far, the price paid by the parent to acquire its investment in the subsidiary was exactly equal to its proportionate share of the *book value* (which is equal to the *owners' equity*) of the subsidiary. If, as is common, the parent company acquires its interest at an amount greater than the book value of the assets acquired, then such excess must be accounted for and reported in a manner indicative of its nature.

Assume now that Parent Co. pays $37,000 to acquire an 80 percent interest in Subsidiary Co. but that the 80 percent interest has a value on the books of Subsidiary Co. of only $32,000. As in the previous examples, if the financial positions of the two individual companies are to be shown as if they were a single economic entity, then both the investment of the parent and its corresponding owners' equity as recorded on the books of the subsidiary must be eliminated. This time, however, although the investment is recorded on the books of the parent at $37,000, the corresponding equity is recorded on the books of the subsidiary at only $32,000.

The portion of the investment ($32,000) that represents its value as recorded on the books of the subsidiary can be eliminated against the corresponding owners' equity with an entry identical to that made in the previous example. The minority interest can also be reclassified with an identical entry. That leaves $5,000 (the excess of $37,000 paid over the corresponding book value of $32,000) of the investment still to be accounted for.

## TANGIBLE ASSETS

This excess of cost over book value is often a source of confusion and misunderstanding. There are at least three reasons a firm may pay for an interest in a subsidiary an amount in excess of the book value of such interest. First, the book value of individual assets (and hence the recorded owners' equity) is based on historical cost—the amount initially paid to acquire the assets, less amortization and depreciation. Book value, as frequently emphasized throughout this text, is not necessarily indicative of fair market value. Thus, the price paid by the company to acquire its shares of stock in the subsidiary may be indicative of the fair market value of the individual assets represented by such shares. If such is the case, then the excess of cost over book value should be assigned to the particular assets acquired. Consistent with the historical cost basis of accounting, assets should be valued at purchase price. The mere fact that the parent company may not have purchased the assets directly, but instead acquired the common stock of the company that has title to the assets, does not change the substance of the transaction. Nor should it change the manner in which the assets are to be accounted for. The following additional adjustment would be required insofar as the excess of cost over book value is to be allocated to specific assets:

Specific tangible assets (land, buildings,
  equipment, etc.)                          $5,000
       Investment in subsidiary                    $5,000
**To allocate the excess cost of investment over book value to specific tangible assets.**

Subsequent to the acquisition, the consolidated enterprise should base its charge for depreciation on the amounts at which the assets are recorded on the consolidated balance sheet. Depreciation charges, as a consequence, may be greater on the consolidated income statement than the sum of the separate depreciation charges on the financial statements of the two individual companies. The acquired subsidiary, on its own financial statements, will maintain its assets and continue to base depreciation at the initial values of the assets.

## INTANGIBLE ASSETS

Second, a firm may pay for an interest in a subsidiary an amount in excess of the book value of such interest because the subsidiary possesses certain intangible assets which it has not recorded on its own books. The subsidiary, for example, may have title to patents, copyrights, or trademarks which, because they have been developed internally (as opposed to purchased from outsiders), have not been given accounting recognition. When such assets are obtained in connection with the purchase of a subsidiary, they should properly be recorded at their fair market values. If the excess of cost over book value can be ascribed to specific intangibles, then it should be so reclassified:

| | | |
|---|---|---|
| Specific intangible assets (patents, copyrights, etc.) | $5,000 | |
| Investment in subsidiary | | $5,000 |

**To allocate the excess of cost over book value of investment to specific intangible assets.**

The values assigned to the specific intangibles should be amortized, and periodic charges reflected on the consolidated income statement, over their estimated useful lives. The amortization charges would not be recorded on the books of either the parent or the subsidiary—only on the statements of the two companies combined.

## GOODWILL

Third, a firm may pay to acquire another company an amount in excess of recorded book value because the company possesses certain intangible assets that cannot be specifically identified. Such assets may arise because of favorable customer attitudes toward the company, unusual talents of corporate managers, advantageous business locations, or special monopolistic or political privileges. Or they may arise because the individually identifiable assets when used together are worth considerably more than the sum of the fair market values of the assets employed independently. Whatever may be the attributes of such assets, however, they enable the firm to earn amounts in excess of "normal" returns. Such assets—that is, the amount in excess of book value that cannot be specifically allocated to other assets—may be classified as *goodwill:*

| | | |
|---|---|---|
| Goodwill | $5,000 | |
| Investment in subsidiary | | $5,000 |

**To allocate the excess of cost over book value of investment to goodwill.**

Goodwill, in a sense, is a residual. It represents that portion of the cost of acquiring a subsidiary that cannot be assigned directly to any specific assets. Goodwill is one asset that arises *only* out of business combinations. Although firms may over a number of years develop the attributes that comprise goodwill, they may not, under conventional accounting principles, give recognition to them. Goodwill may be recorded only when one firm purchases another and the excess of cost over book value cannot be specifically assigned to other assets.

The conventional practice of recording goodwill only to the extent purchased, however, has by no means been beyond criticism. In the example at hand, a company purchased for $37,000 an 80 percent interest in a company that has a total book value of $40,000. The 80 percent interest, therefore, has a book value of $32,000, and the maximum amount of goodwill that can be recognized is $5,000. Many observers contend that it is illogical to record goodwill of only $5,000. They assert that if 80 percent of the company is worth $37,000, then 100 percent would be worth $46,250—$37,000/.80. Recognition should be given to the entire $6,250 of goodwill ($46,250 less book value of $40,000 *or* $5,000/.80). To record less than the full $6,250 is to pretend that the 80 percent share of the subsidiary owned by the parent company has increased as the result of the development of the goodwill but that the share of the minority has not. Such an approach thereby leads to an undervaluation of the assets of the acquired company. The arguments of the critics, however, have not been accepted by the Financial Accounting Standards Board or its predecessor bodies. Their rejection stems, no doubt, in large measure from their desire to avoid giving accounting recognition to any assets not specifically acquired and paid for in an arm's-length exchange transaction.

The issue of whether to give recognition to the full value of goodwill as implied by the price paid for a partial interest in a corporation or merely to the fraction of goodwill actually paid for is similar to one discussed earlier in the text—whether the assets of a partnership should be revalued to reflect the price paid for an equity interest in a partnership. As was noted in the discussion pertaining to partnerships, such issues arise because increases in market values of assets are not conventionally given accounting recognition as they occur over time.

As a consequence of the very nature of goodwill—it is a residual asset—its useful life is not readily determinable. Nevertheless, the Accounting Principles Board has prescribed that firms should make their best efforts to estimate the useful lives of all intangible assets, including goodwill, and that such assets should be amortized over their useful lives.* In no event, however, should the amortization period exceed 40 years. To the extent, therefore, that a consolidated entity records goodwill, it must each year reduce the balance in the goodwill account (a credit to goodwill) and increase expenditures by a like amount (debit to amortization of goodwill) by no less than one-fortieth of the initial amount recorded. Both the goodwill itself and the charge for amortization would appear only on the consolidated statements, not on those of either the parent or the subsidiary by itself.

---

*"Intangible Assets," Opinion No. 17 of the Accounting Principles Board. American Institute of Certified Public Accountants (New York, 1970).

Characteristic of the examples to this point was the assumption that consolidated statements were being prepared immediately upon the acquisition of the
subsidiary by the parent. As a consequence, the account on the books of the
parent, "Investment in subsidiary," reflected the cost to the parent of its interest
in the subsidiary.

As pointed out earlier in this chapter, a corporation on its own books
must account for an owernship interest in another company by the equity
method if it is greater than 20 percent of the outstanding voting stock. The
equity method requires that the firm periodically recognize revenues and *increase*
the balance in its investment in subsidiary account to reflect the earnings of the
subsidiary. At any given time after the date of acquisition, the investment in
subsidiary account may not, therefore, reflect the amount initially paid for the
shares of the subsidiary.

Assume, for example, that Parent Co. paid $40,000 for a 100 percent
interest in Subsidiary Co. During its first year after being acquired, Subsidiary
Co. had earnings of $6,000 and declared no dividends. As a consequence, both
its retained earnings and its net assets would be $6,000 greater than what they
were at date of acquisition. If Parent Co. accounted for its investment by the
equity method, then its net assets (investment in Subsidiary) and retained earnings (owing to the earnings of Subsidiary that it recognizes) would also be
$6,000 greater.

The $6,000 of subsidiary earnings would have served to increase the net
worth of both the parent and the subsidiary by $6,000. If, however, the two
firms were to be viewed as a single economic entity, then net worth of the two
firms combined would have increased by a total of only $6,000. It is necessary,
if double counting is to be avoided, to reduce assets (investment in subsidiary)
and retained earnings by $6,000. Thus,

| | | |
|---|---|---|
| Retained earnings | $6,000 | |
| Investment in subsidiary | | $6,000 |

**To eliminate double counting of subsidiary earnings attributable to parent
company's use of equity method.**

This entry will restore the investment in subsidiary account to an amount indicative of the original price paid for the interest in the subsidiary. The remaining balance can be eliminated with the entries illustrated in the previous examples.

## Principles of Consolidation—
## Income Statement

In essence, the consolidated income statement, like the consolidated balance
sheet, presents the sum of the balances in the accounts of the component corporations. However, as with the balance sheet, numerous adjustments and

eliminations may be necessary to give effect to transactions among the individual companies.

The consolidated income statement provides an indication of the change in enterprise welfare between two points in time as if the various components of the enterprise were a single economic entity. Principles of revenue and expense recognition must be applied as if the individual companies whose statements are to be consolidated were, in fact, combined into a single company. As a consequence, revenues and expenses, if they are to be recognized, must be the result only of arm's-length transactions with parties *outside* of the *consolidated* entity.

Many of the eliminations and adjustments which affect the income statement directly affect the balance sheet also. It is generally convenient, therefore, to make the elimination and adjustment entries on a work sheet in which the initial positions of the individual companies are drawn from their respective trial balances and thereby include both income statement and balance sheet accounts. Such a work sheet is illustrated in Exhibit 13-1.

Intercompany transactions take many forms; the specific eliminations and adjustments that might be required must be determined in light of the particular nature of the transactions. Some typical intercompany transactions, on which the trial balances as contained in Exhibit 13-1 are based, may be used to provide an insight into the general approach to consolidations. In Exhibit 13-1 it may be assumed that the parent company owns an 80 percent interest in the subsidiary. Consolidated statements are to be prepared for the first year of combined operations.

**interest**   The individual components of a company may enter into arrangements which result in revenues to one company and expenses to another but involve no transactions with outsiders. Suppose, for example, that a parent company makes a loan to its subsidiary. Interest on the loan would be recognized as a revenue to the parent and as an expense to the subsidiary. From the standpoint of the consolidated entity, the "loan" is nothing more than an intracompany transfer of funds from one "division" to another. Just as any intercompany payable and receivable outstanding at year end would be eliminated from the consolidated balance sheet, so too must the interest revenue and expenses be eliminated from the income statement. If $7,000 of the interest revenue and expense reported on the individual statements were intercompany interest, then the following elimination would be required:

**(a)**

| | | |
|---|---|---|
| Interest revenue | $7,000 | |
| Interest expense | | $7,000 |
| **To eliminate intercompany interest.** | | |

EXHIBIT 13-1

## Consolidated Work Sheet

| | Parent Debit | Parent Credit | Subsidiary Debit | Subsidiary Credit | Adjustments Debit | Adjustments Credit | Combined Debit | Combined Credit |
|---|---|---|---|---|---|---|---|---|
| | *Preclosing Trial Balances* | | | | | | *Combined Preclosing Trial Balance* | |
| Inventory | $ 40,000 | | $ 12,000 | | | | $ 52,000 | |
| Land | 50,000 | | 45,000 | | | (e) $ 6,000 | 89,000 | |
| Investment in subsidiary | 200,000 | | | | | (e) 20,000 (f) 180,000 | | |
| Other assets | 600,000 | | 218,000 | | | | 818,000 | |
| Excess of cost over book value (goodwill) | | | | | (e) $ 20,000 | (d) 500 | 19,500 | |
| Liabilities | | $ 30,000 | | $ 20,000 | | | | $ 50,000 |
| Minority interest in subsidiary | | | | | | (g) 45,000 | | 45,000 |
| Common stock | | 80,000 | | 50,000 | (f) 40,000 (g) 10,000 | | | 80,000 |
| Retained earnings | | 687,000 | | 175,000 | (f) 140,000 (g) 35,000 | | | 687,000 |
| Sales | | 400,000 | | 300,000 | (b) 100,000 | | | 600,000 |
| Gain on sale of fixed assets | | 6,000 | | | (c) 6,000 | | | |
| Interest revenue | | 7,000 | | | (a) 7,000 | | | |
| Cost of goods sold | 240,000 | | 210,000 | | | (b) 100,000 | 350,000 | |
| Interest expense | | | 7,000 | | | (a) 7,000 | | |
| Other expenses | 80,000 | | 53,000 | | | | 133,000 | |
| Amortization of goodwill | | | | | (d) 500 | | 500 | |
| | $1,210,000 | $1,210,000 | $545,000 | $545,000 | $358,500 | $358,500 | $1,462,000 | $1,462,000 |

Handwritten annotations: "80%"; "for 80% of"; "Should be 39M — 6M from gain on..."; "Goodwill — amort of"; "minority"; "45,000 = 10 + 35 — C.S. R.E."; "80%"; "200-20-40"; "from sale of land"

In Exhibit 13-1, no intercompany payable or receivable is indicated on the trial balance. It may be assumed that all loans had been repaid by year end.

**sales and cost of goods sold**

From the standpoint of a consolidated enterprise, a sale of merchandise by one member of a consolidated group to another is not an event worthy of revenue recognition. A sale takes place only when merchandise is sold to a party outside of the consolidated enterprise. Intercompany sales should, of course, be given accounting recognition on the books of the individual companies; they must, however, be eliminated when reporting on the operations of the companies as a consolidated economic entity.

Assume, for example, that included in the revenues of the parent are $100,000 in sales to the subsidiary. The goods sold to the subsidiary were manufactured by the parent at a cost of $80,000. The subsidiary company in turn sold the goods to outsiders at a price of $120,000. The transactions would be reflected in the books of the two companies as follows:

|  | Parent | Subsidiary |
|---|---|---|
| Sales revenue | $100,000 | $120,000 |
| Cost of goods sold | 80,000 | 100,000 |

From the standpoint of the consolidated entity, sales to outsiders were $120,000 and the cost of goods sold only $80,000. It is necessary to eliminate $100,000 in both sales revenue (the sale by the parent to the subsidiary) and cost of goods sold (the cost of the goods sold by the subsidiary to outsiders):

**(b)**

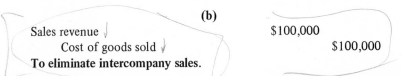

| | | |
|---|---|---|
| Sales revenue | $100,000 | |
| Cost of goods sold | | $100,000 |
| To eliminate intercompany sales. | | |

The required adjustments for intercompany sales becomes considerably more complex when, at year end, one member of the corporate group has not yet sold to outsiders its entire stock of goods purchased from another member. It then becomes necessary to reduce the value of inventory in the amount of any profit recognized on its sale from one company to another. Inventory must be stated at its cost to the consolidated entity, rather than at the intercompany selling price.

**sales of fixed assets**

Fixed assets must be reported on the consolidated statements on the basis of their initial cost to the consolidated enterprise. If a fixed asset has been sold by one member of the consolidated group to another, then the amount at which the asset is carried on the books of an individual company may be greater or less than that based on original cost.

Assume, for example, that the $6,000 in the account of the parent company, "gain on sales of fixed assets" represents in its entirety the gain on the sale of land to the subsidiary. The land was sold to the subsidiary at a price of $45,000, which also represents the entire balance in the "land" account of the subsidiary. It had been purchased for, and had previously been carried in the accounts of the parent at $39,000.

To report the consolidated results of operations and financial positions of the two companies, it is necessary to eliminate the effects of transactions that would be considered nothing more than internal transfers if the two companies were viewed as a single economic entity. Thus,

(c)

| | |
|---|---|
| Gain on sale of fixed assets (by parent) | $6,000 |
|     Land (of subsidiary) | $6,000 |

**To adjust for gain on intercompany sale of land.**

The intercompany sale of land will have to be accounted for in the preparation of consolidated statements in years subsequent to that in which the sale took place—in fact, for as long as the asset remains on the books of the subsidiary. The land will continue to be "overvalued" by the amount of the gain recognized by the parent. Since, on the books of the parent, the gain will have been *closed* at year end to retained earnings, retained earnings will be permanently overstated.

The complexities of adjusting for the sale of fixed assets are substantially compounded when the assets transferred are subject to depreciation. From the standpoint of the consolidated enterprise, depreciation charges must be determined on the basis of the original cost of the asset to the first member of the consolidated group that acquired it. On the books of the company on which the asset is presently recorded, however, it would be maintained on the basis of the price paid to the seller company, a member of the consolidated entity. If, for example, the fixed asset sold were equipment rather than land, then the subsidiary would properly depreciate, on its own books, an asset that had cost $45,000. If the useful life were 10 years and zero salvage value were assumed, annual depreciation charges would be $4,500. For purposes of consolidated reporting, however, the asset initially cost only $39,000, the original acquisition cost of the parent (seller) corporation. Hence annual depreciation charges would be only $3,900. Adjustment would be required to reduce annual depreciation charges by $600. But, in addition, adjustments would also be required in each year after the first to "correct" for the cumulative effect on "accumulated depreciation" attributable to the previous "overstatements" of depreciation charges.

**amortization of goodwill** As was indicated in the discussion relating to the interpretation of the excess of investment cost over book value, *goodwill* is an asset that arises exclusively out of the process of consolidation. Goodwill is recorded only on a consolidated balance sheet, not on those of the component companies of a consolidated group. When, in accordance with authoritative professional pronouncements, the goodwill is amortized, then the amortization expense is reported only on the consolidated income statement, not on those of the individual companies. In the data contained in Exhibit 13-1, Parent Co.. paid $200,000 for an 80 percent interest in a company with a book value (as evidenced by the balances in Subsidiary Co.'s common stock and retained earnings accounts) of $225,000. The book value of the 80 percent interest was, therefore, $180,000. The excess of cost over book value—assumed in this case to represent goodwill—was, at time of acquisition, $20,000.

If the goodwill is to be amortized over 40 years, the maximum amortization period permitted by current professional pronouncements, then the following consolidation entry would be in order:

**(d)**

| | | |
|---|---|---|
| Amortization of goodwill (expense) | $500 | |
| Goodwill (asset) | | $500 |
| **To amortize goodwill.** | | |

**completing the consolidation** To complete the process of consolidation, three additional entries, the nature of which was discussed in the section dealing with the balance sheet, are necessary.*

First, the portion of the investment in subsidiary that represents the excess of cost over book value must be reclassified. As indicated previously the excess of cost over book value was $20,000:

**(e)**

| | | |
|---|---|---|
| Goodwill | $20,000 | |
| Investment in subsidiary | | $20,000 |
| **To allocate the excess of cost over book value of investment to goodwill.** | | |

Second, the remaining balance in the investment in subsidiary account (the initial investment) must be eliminated against the equity of the parent as reflected on the books of the subsidiary:

*In this example the trial balances presented are those for the first year after acquisition of the subsidiary. The balances are preclosing balances. The revenue and expense accounts have not yet been closed to retained earnings, and it has been assumed that the parent company has not yet recognized its share of subsidiary earnings.

**(f)**

| | | |
|---|---|---|
| Common stock (of subsidiary) | $ 40,000 | |
| Retained earnings (of subsidiary) | 140,000 | |
| Investment in subsidiary (by | | |
| parent) | | $180,000 |

**To eliminate investment in subsidiary and corresponding amounts in subsidiary's owners' equity accounts.**

Third, the interests of the minority stockholders (the remaining balances in the equity accounts of subsidiary) must be reclassified:

**(g)**

| | | |
|---|---|---|
| Common stock (of subsidiary) | $10,000 | |
| Retained earnings (of subsidiary) | 35,000 | |
| Minority interest in subsidiary | | $45,000 |

**To eliminate minority interest in subsidiary and corresponding amounts in subsidiary's owners' equity accounts.**

**minority interests in earnings of subsidiary**    Consolidated statements, as already emphasized, are prepared from the perspective of the stockholders of the parent corporation. The parent corporation, however, is entitled to only a portion of the earnings of its subsidiary. The minority stockholders of the subsidiary are then entitled to remaining earnings. Conventionally, therefore, the portion of subsidiary earnings that can be ascribed to the minority stockholders is deducted from total consolidated income and reported on the consolidated income statement as an expense.

Based on the preclosing trial balance in Exhibit 13–1 the earnings of Subsidiary Co. were $30,000:

| | | |
|---|---|---|
| Sales | | $300,000 |
| Cost of goods sold | $210,000 | |
| Interest expense | 7,000 | |
| Other expenses | 53,000 | 270,000 |
| Subsidiary income | | $ 30,000 |

Inasmuch as Parent Co. owns only 80 percent of the outstanding shares of Subsidiary Co., the minority share of subsidiary earnings would be 20 percent of $30,000—$6,000.

From the data in the *combined* trial balance, and taking into account the minority interest in earnings, a consolidated statement of income can readily be prepared:

**Parent Co.**
**Consolidated Statement of Income**
**for First Year of Combined Operations**

| | | |
|---|---:|---:|
| Sales | | $600,000 |
| Cost of goods sold | $350,000 | |
| Other expenses | 133,000 | |
| Amortization of goodwill | 500 | |
| Minority interest in earnings of subsidiary | 6,000 | 489,500 |
| Consolidated income | | $110,500 |

*Treat as Expense* (handwritten annotation)

**consolidated balance sheet**

From the combined trial balance a consolidated balance sheet can also be prepared. However, insofar as the amounts reported in both the retained earnings accounts and the minority interest in subsidiary accounts represent *preclosing* balances, it is necessary to adjust both accounts to give effect to current year earnings:

| | *Retained Earnings* | *Minority Interest in Subsidiary* |
|---|---:|---:|
| Per preclosing trial balance | $687,000 | $45,000 |
| Share of current year income | 110,500 | 6,000 |
| Adjusted balance | $797,500 | $51,000 |

*O.E.* *Income* (handwritten annotations)

**Parent Co.**
**Consolidated Balance Sheet**
**at End of First Year of Combined Operations**

| | |
|---|---:|
| Assets | |
| Inventory | $ 52,000 |
| Land | 89,000 |
| Other assets | 818,000 |
| Goodwill | 19,500 |
| Total assets | $978,500 |
| | |
| Equities | |
| Liabilities | $ 50,000 |
| Minority interest in subsidiary | 51,000 |
| Common stock | 80,000 |
| Retained earnings | 797,500 |
| Total equities | $978,500 |

*45 + 6* (handwritten annotation)

## Instant Earnings

A company may, of course, purchase for cash all, or a portion, of the out-standing stock of another corporation. But quite often interests in other companies are obtained in exchange for the common stock of the acquiring corporation. If the investment is accounted for as a purchase (an alternative means will be discussed shortly), no special accounting problems are presented. Suppose, for example, Alpha Company acquired 500,000 shares of Beta Company at a price of $10 per share. In exchange for the shares, Alpha Company issued to Beta Company stockholders 50,000 shares of its own common stock, each share having a market value of $100. The common stock has a par value of $1 per share. The following journal entry would be in order:

| | | |
|---|---|---|
| Investment in Beta Co. *(asset +)* | $5,000,000 | |
|     Common stock, par value | | $ 50,000 |
|     Common stock, capital | | |
|        in excess of par | | 4,950,000 |

**To record purchase of Beta Co. by Alpha Co.**

An acquisition for stock, rather than cash, may have a striking impact on the reported earnings of the parent company. Indeed, acquisitions may result in instant increases in reported profits even in the absence of any substantive improvements in the operations of either the parent or the subsidiary company. Consider the following additional information pertaining to the acquisition of Beta by Alpha:

### Selected Financial Data Immediately Prior to Acquisition

| | Alpha | Beta |
|---|---|---|
| Number of shares outstanding | 100,000 shares | 500,000 shares |
| Net assets | $1,000,000 | $5,000,000 |
| Capital stock ($1 par value) | 100,000 | 500,000 |
| Retained earnings | 900,000 | 4,500,000 |
| Book value per share | 10 | 10 |
| Latest annual income | 200,000 | 500,000 |
| Latest earnings per share | 2 | 1 |
| Market price of common stock | 100 per share | 10 per share |

Alpha Company is the smaller of the two companies in terms of assets and total earnings. Yet investors obviously consider its prospects for future earnings to be more promising than those of Beta. The price/earnings ratio (market price of common stock to earnings per share) of Alpha is 50 to 1 and that of Beta is only 10 to 1. Suppose that the exchange of stock were to be based on the market prices of the shares of the two companies. The 500,000 shares of Beta Company have a total market value of $5 million (500,000 shares at $10 per share). Since each share of Alpha has a market value of $100, the number of shares that Alpha would be required to issue would be $5 million divided by $100—50,000.

If Alpha Company were to issue 50,000 additional shares to the owners of Beta Company, then it would have outstanding a total of 150,000 shares. Consolidated earnings, assuming no substantive improvement in the operations of either firm, would be the sum of the earnings of the two individual companies—$700,000 ($200,000 plus $500,000). No amortization of excess of cost over book value is required since the total market price of Beta Company stock is exactly equal to its book value. Earnings per share of Alpha Company, reported on a consolidated basis, would now be $4.66 ($700,000 divided by 150,000 shares)—an increase of 133 percent over previously reported earnings of $2 per share.

The ramifications of this simplified example are critical to an understanding of the merger movement of the 1960s and 1970s. In that period numerous firms acquired subsidiaries. Frequently, the acquired companies were in industries totally unrelated to those of the parents. Commonly the acquisitions were made for common stock rather than cash, and often, as in the example, a whale of a firm was swallowed up by a minnow.

The acquisition in the example, as is common in practice, was facilitated by the substantial difference in the price/earnings (P/E) ratios of the two firms. The P/E ratio of Alpha was considerably higher than that of Beta. Stock market prices tend to be based, in large measure, on reported earnings—and most particularly on the trend in earnings over a number of years. The relatively high P/E ratio of Alpha would likely be accounted for, at least in part, by a trend of rapidly increasing earnings. The acquisition of Beta will likely help sustain that trend or even accentuate it. The P/E ratio of Alpha may thereby remain high or even increase, thus making it even easier for the firm to acquire additional firms in the future. And future acquisitions may further add to reported earnings per share. To a considerable degree, the recent merger movement was supported by the circle of acquisition, increase in earnings, increase in market price of stock, additional acquisitions, etc.

It must be pointed out, however, that the increase in earnings is seldom as dramatic as in the example. To the extent that the acquiring corporation pays to stockholders of the company to be acquired a price in excess of the firm's book value, then the excess might (exceptions will be discussed below) have to be amortized over a number of years. The charge for amortization would serve to reduce earnings.

## Pooling of Interests

**rationale**   In the discussions of business combinations to this point it has been assumed that one company acquires another. The combinations have been accounted for as purchase-type transactions—one company purchases, either for cash or common stock, the outstanding common stock of another. In those instances where a business combination is effected by an exchange of common stock— where one company, be it a new or existing company, acquires substantially all of the voting stock of another in return for its own common stock—the transaction may be accounted for as an alternative type of business combination—a pooling of interests. The financial consequences of accounting for a business combination as a pooling of interests rather than a purchase may be profound; reported earnings as well as values assigned to assets may be significantly different.

Underlying the pooling of interests method of accounting for business combinations is the rationale that two firms join together to operate as a single economic enterprise. Neither of the two purchases the other, and the owners of both of the component companies are granted a proportionate interest in the combined enterprise. The combination represents a marriage of equals, or if not exactly of equals, then at least a marriage where one party does not clearly dominate the other.

The key feature of the pooling of interests method is that each of the component companies retains its former basis of accounting. That is, the assets and liabilities of neither company are revalued at the time of combination. The recorded assets and liabilities of both companies are carried forward to the consolidated enterprise at their previously recorded amounts. So also are their retained earnings. No accounting recognition is given to goodwill, nor are other assets written up to their fair market values. Retention of the former basis of accounting is justified on the grounds that there has been no sale of the assets of one firm to another; there has merely been a fusion of two companies into one.

The pooling of interests method has had great appeal to firms effecting business combinations in that it commonly allows the consolidated enterprise to report higher earnings than if the combination were accounted for as a purchase. The pooling of interests method may result in higher reported earnings because it does not require the consolidated enterprise to increase the carrying values of the assets of the acquired firm to reflect an excess of purchase price over book value. No goodwill need be recorded. Therefore, the firm does not have to charge either depreciation or amortization on the amounts by which the fair market values of either of the two firms exceed their book values.

*example*   An example can be used to illustrate the pooling of interests approach and to highlight the differences between the pooling of interests and the purchase methods of accounting for business combinations. Indicated in the table following is selected information about two firms, Delta Corp. and Echo Corp., prior to their merger:

|  | Balance sheets | |
| --- | --- | --- |
|  | Delta Corp. | Echo Corp. |
| Miscellaneous assets | $1,500,000 | $6,000,000 |
|  |  |  |
| Miscellaneous liabilities | $ 500,000 | $1,000,000 |
| Common stock, par value $1 | 100,000 | 500,000 |
| Contributed capital in excess of par | 300,000 | 700,000 |
| Retained earnings | 600,000 | 3,800,000 |
|  | $1,500,000 | $6,000,000 |
|  |  |  |
| Number of shares outstanding | 100,000 | 500,000 |
| Net income, in year prior to merger | $ 200,000 | $ 500,000 |
| Earnings per share | 2 | 1 |
| Recent market price per share | 100 | 20 |

Delta and Echo agree to combine their operations. Delta Corp. will issue to the current stockholders of Echo Corp. new shares of its own common stock in exchange for their existing shares in Echo Corp. The number of shares to be issued by Delta will be based on the relative market prices of the shares just prior to the negotiations leading to the merger. Since the shares outstanding of Echo Corp. have a current market value of $10 million (500,000 shares at $20 per share), Delta Corp. will have to issue 100,000 shares ($10 million divided by $100, the market price of Delta Corp. stock).

Although the two firms may be combined into a single economic entity for reporting purposes, they are still independent legal entities; hence each firm must keep separate sets of accounting books and records. If the merger is to be accounted for as a pooling rather than a purchase, it is conventional practice for the firm which has issued the additional shares of common stock to carry its investment in the other company at its *book value*—that is, at the net worth of its investment per the books of the other firm. This is in contrast to the value at which the investment would be assigned if the combination were to be accounted for as a purchase. If it were to be accounted for as a purchase, then the investment would be recorded at the market value of the shares of common stock issued to acquire the interest in the other firm. The reason the investment is carried at book rather than market value relates to the under-lying rationale of a pooling of interests. A pooling of interests is a merger of two existing companies, the owners of both of which will continue to retain their respective equity interests. Unlike a purchase transaction, a pooling transaction is not considered an event of the type that justifies revaluation of assets. Subsequent to the merger the individual balance sheets of the two firms would appear as follows:

|  | Balance sheets | |
|  | Delta Corp. | Echo Corp. |
| --- | --- | --- |
| Miscellaneous assets | $1,500,000 | $6,000,000 |
| Investment in Echo Corp. | 5,000,000 | — |
|  | $6,500,000 | $6,000,000 |
| Miscellaneous liabilities | $ 500,000 | $1,000,000 |
| Common stock, par value $1 | 200,000[a] | 500,000 |
| Contributed capital in excess of par | 5,200,000[a] | 700,000 |
| Retained earnings | 600,000 | 3,800,000 |
|  | $6,500,000 | $6,000,000 |

*Handwritten annotations near Investment in Echo Corp.: Echo / Com St 500 M / Cap Ex 700 M / Ret E 3800 / 5000*

*Handwritten: shares 100M / 1 + MM*

*Handwritten: 49 in → / excess*

*Handwritten: 100M × 50 = 5MM*

[a]Reflects the issue of 100,000 additional shares. The book value of the Echo Corp. is $5 million (assets less liabilities). Each share is considered to be issued at a price of $50 ($5 million divided by 100,000 shares). Of the $50, $1 represents common stock, par value, and the remaining $49, contributed capital in excess of par.

To prepare a balance sheet on a consolidated basis, it is necessary to eliminate the "Investment in Echo Corp." and the corresponding owners' equity accounts of Echo Corp. Under pooling of interests accounting the specific elimination entry is sometimes a bit tricky, but the general rule is that the balance in the investment account is offset against the entire balance in the other company's common stock, par value account plus whatever other amount in "contributed capital in excess of par" is needed to make up the difference. In other words, the debit to contributed capital in excess of par is nothing more than a "plug." Thus,

| | | |
| --- | --- | --- |
| Common stock, par value $1 | $ 500,000 | *all of Echo* |
| Contributed capital in excess of par | 4,500,000 | |
| Investment in Echo Corp. | | $5,000,000 |

**To eliminate investment in Echo Corp. and corresponding balances in owners' equity accounts.**

As a result of the elimination entry, the consolidated balance in the common stock par value account would reflect the par value of shares outstanding (those of the "parent" company). The balance in the retained earnings account would reflect the sum of the previous balances of the two individual companies. The consolidated balance sheet would appear as indicated on the following page.

The assets and liabilities are stated on the same basis as on the books of the component companies. In contrast to the purchase method no adjustment has been made to asset values—either by revaluation of specific assets or by the addition of goodwill—to reflect the difference between the market value of the

*Handwritten: no asset revaluatn or goodwill*

**Consolidated Balance Sheet**

| | |
|---|---:|
| Miscellaneous assets | $7,500,000 |
| Miscellaneous liabilities | $1,500,000 |
| Common stock, par value $1 | 200,000 |
| Contributed capital in excess of par | 1,400,000 |
| Retained earnings | 4,400,000 |
| Total liabilities and owners' equity | $7,500,000 |

common stock issued by Delta Corp. ($10 million) and the value at which the assets were recorded on the books of the Echo Corp. ($5 million).

If there were no substantive increase in the earnings of the two firms as a consequence of the merger, then earnings after the merger would be the sum of the earnings of the two individual firms—$200,000 contributed by Delta, $500,000 contributed by Echo, a total of $700,000. The earnings per share, based on 200,000 shares of Delta Corp. stock outstanding, would be $3.50. The earnings per share of Delta Corp., the firm whose stock remains outstanding, would thereby have increased as a result of the merger by $1.50 from what they were prior to the merger—an increase that can be attributed merely to the *instant earnings* effect described earlier.

By contrast, if the combination had been accounted for as a purchase, then the combined entity would have reported either goodwill of $5 million, or specific assets would have been increased in carrying value by that amount. If the $5 million in additional assets or in goodwill were depreciated or amortized over a period of, say, 20 years, then earnings would be $250,000 per year lower than under the pooling method. If earnings after the merger were the same as those prior to the merger, then consolidated earnings, if the combination were accounted for as a purchase, would be only $450,000 as opposed to $700,000 if it were accounted for as a pooling. Hence, earnings per share would be only $450,000 divided by 200,000 shares—$2.25.

**abuses and reforms**  The term *pooling of interests* was at one time used to describe a type of business combination rather than an accounting method. Two corporations of similar size joined together to carry out their operations. The owners of the two firms obtained, and retained, an interest in the new firm proportionate to their respective contributions, and the new company was managed jointly by the previous managers of the two firms. A pooling of interests was viewed as a merger of two great rivers as contrasted with a purchase which was seen as a stream feeding into a river. The ill-fated merger of the New York Central Railroad and the Pennsylvania Railroad into the Penn-Central Corp. was a classic example of a pooling of interests.

In the late 1950s and early 1960s the traditional criteria for a pooling of interests began to erode. Business combinations that were not in spirit poolings of interests were accounted for as if they were. First, the relative size test was abandoned. Combinations of giant firms, often conglomerates, with small firms were treated as poolings of interests. Then, the criteria of continuity of ownership and management were disregarded. One of the two firms involved in the combination may have paid sizable amounts of cash, rather than simply exchanged common stock, for a portion of the common stock of the other firm. Thus, the owners of one of the firms were, to the extent that they received cash payments, *bought out* by those of the other. Eventually, even those combinations in which it was clear that one company had acquired (purchased) another were accounted for as poolings. *Poolings of interests* and *purchases* came to be recognized as *accounting* alternatives from which managements could select, rather than as types of business combinations.

Today, as set forth in Opinion No. 16, "Business Combinations," issued by the Accounting Principles Board in 1970, a business combination may be accounted for as a pooling of interests only if a number of specific conditions are satisfied. Primary among the criteria for a pooling of interests is that the merger must be effected almost entirely by an exchange of common stock. Purchases of stock for cash (except in minor amounts) are prohibited and one company must acquire substantially all (at least 90 percent) of the common stock of the other firm. Moreover, stockhoders who receive the newly issued shares must either retain them or sell them to outsiders; they cannot redeem them for cash to the issuing corporation.

Opinion No. 16 does not require adherence to the spirit of the traditional pooling of interests in the sense that the two combining companies must be of similar size. One company is permitted to be dominant over another. But Opinion No. 16 does restrict the freedom of firms to choose whether a combination should be accounted for as a purchase or as a pooling of interests. If it satisfies certain criteria, it *must* be accounted for as a pooling of interests; if it does not, it *must* be accounted for as a purchase.

Despite the issuance of Opinion No. 16, the issue of business combinations remains controversial. The critical issue on which attention is focused relates to the values that should be assigned to the assets of the combining companies—and most particularly those of a company acquired by another. The values assigned to the assets have, of course, a direct bearing on depreciation and amortization charges and, hence, on reported earnings. As a pooling, the assets of each company are stated at their previous basis; as a purchase, assets are restated to reflect the consideration paid for them.

### *Summary*

Intercorporate ownership may take a variety of forms. The objective of the accountant is to give effect to the economic substance of the relationship between the parties involved.

As a general rule, the manner in which the interest of one company in another is accounted for is determined by the degree of control that it is able to exercise. If an investor company is unable to exert substantial influence over the company whose shares it owns, it would account for its interest on the *cost basis.* If it is able to exercise substantial influence, it would account for its interest on the *equity basis.*

When a corporation has control over another, then the information needs of the stockholders of the controlling company are usually best served by combining the financial positions and results of operations of the merging firms into a single set of *consolidated* financial statements. If the business combination were effected entirely by an exchange of common stock, then the consolidated statements would ordinarily be prepared on a pooling of interests basis. If, on the other hand, one company acquired for cash or other assets the outstanding stock of another, the combination would be accounted for as a purchase.

*exercise for review and self-testing*

Parent Co. acquired 90 percent of the outstanding common stock of Subsidiary Co. On January 1, 1980, immediately following the acquisition, the balance sheets of the two firms revealed the following:

|  | Parent Co. | Subsidiary Co. |
|---|---|---|
| Investment in Subsidiary Co. | $320,000 | — |
| Other assets | 500,000 | $300,000 |
| | | |
| Capital contributed by stockholders | 200,000 | 120,000 |
| Retained earnings | 620,000 | 180,000 |

Subsidiary Co. reported earnings for the year ending December 31, 1980 of $30,000 and declared dividends of $10,000. Parent Co. reported earnings, *excluding* any revenues attributable to Subsidiary Co., of $100,000.

a. Parent Co. maintains its investment in Subsidiary Co. on the equity basis. What would be the amount that it should report in 1980 as earnings from subsidiary? At what amount should it value "Investment in Subsidiary Co." on December 31, 1980?

b. If the financial statements of Parent Co. and Subsidiary Co. were to be consolidated, what amount should be reported on the balance sheet as excess of cost over book value (goodwill) prior to amortizing such excess in 1980?

c. What would be the amount of Subsidiary Co.'s 1980 earnings that could be ascribed to minority stockholders?

d. If the excess of cost over book value were to be amortized over a period of 40 years, by how much would the combined earnings of the two companies be reduced when the income statements of the two firms were consolidated?

e. What would be the consolidated income of the two companies, assuming that the earnings of the subsidiary company owing to minority stockholders was considered as an expense?

f. Suppose alternatively that Parent Co. acquired 100 percent of the stock of Subsidiary Co. in exchange for shares of its own common stock. At time of acquisition, the common stock issued by Parent Co. had a fair market value of $400,000 and the book value of Subsidiary Co. was $300,000. What would now be the consolidated income of the two companies for 1980 assuming that the merger satisfied the conditions of the pooling of interests accounting method?

## Questions

1. Under what circumstances should a firm account for an investment in another company by the cost method? By the equity method? When should it prepare consolidated financial statements?

2. Why is the cost method considered inappropriate for investments in which the investor company can exert significant influence over the operating policies of the investee?

3. Why, under the equity method, does a firm *reduce* its balance in its investment account upon declaration of a dividend by the investee?

4. When under the equity method does an investor recognize revenue attributable to the earnings of the company in which it maintains an investment? When under the cost method? When is revenue recognized if consolidated statements are prepared?

5. Why do consolidations relate only to corporate *reports* rather than to the underlying corporate books and records? On which set of books, those of the parent or the subsidiary, those of both, or those of neither, are consolidation adjustments made?

6. From the standpoint of which group of stockholders—those of the parent, those of the subsidiary, or those of both—are consolidated statements prepared?

7. Under what conditions may a company improve its earnings per share simply by acquiring controlling interest in another company?

8. What is *goodwill?* When is it recorded? From what does it arise? Suppose a firm acquires an interest in a subsidiary for an amount in excess of its book value. What difference might it make on consolidated net income if such excess were classified as goodwill rather than assigned to specific assets?

9. What is the underlying rationale of a pooling of interests? What critical differences arise in terms of asset valuation and income determination if a combination is accounted for as a pooling rather than as a purchase?

10. What four accounts—two income statement accounts and two balance sheet accounts—appear only on consolidated financial statements, never on those of individual companies?

## Problems

1. *The equity method provides for more timely recognition of subsidiary earnings and losses than does the cost method.*

On January 2, 1980, the Colorado Co. purchased for $60 per share (cash) 2,000 of the 10,000 outstanding shares of the Denver Corp.

On July 5, 1980, the Denver Corp. reported earnings of $40,000 for the first six months of the year.

On July 15, the board of directors of the Denver Corp. declared and paid a $1 per share cash dividend.

On December 31, the Denver Corp. reported a loss of $15,000 for the second six months of the year.

a. Prepare journal entries to account for the investment of the Colorado Corp. in the Denver Corp. using first the *cost* method and then the *equity* method.

b. Compare total revenues of the Colorado Co. attributable to its investment under the two alternative methods. Compare the year-end carrying values of the investment.

2. *The earnings of a subsidiary can be derived from information on the carrying value of the investment and dividends declared.*

On January 1, 1976, the Eagleton Co. purchased for $80,000 a 40 percent interest (4,000 of 10,000 shares) in the common stock of Alexander, Inc.

On December 31, 1978, the Eagleton Co. sold 1,000 of the shares at a price of $25 per share. It recorded a gain of $2,000 on the sale.

On December 31, 1980, the remaining shares were reported on the books of Eagleton at a value of $78,000.

During the five-year period from 1976 through 1980 Alexander, Inc. paid annual dividends of $1.50 per share.

a. Determine the earnings of *Alexander, Inc.* during the period January 1, 1976 to December 31, 1978.

b. Determine the earnings of Alexander, Inc. during the period January 1, 1979, to December 31, 1980.

3. *The equity method prevents an investor company from regulating its own earnings by manipulating the dividend practices of the investee firm.*

The Maine Co. owned 40 percent (10,000 shares) of the voting stock of the Bangor Corp. and controlled a majority of seats on the latter's board of directors. Toward the end of 1980, it was estimated by the controllers of the two firms that Maine Co. would have earnings for the year of approximately $10,000 (exclusive of earnings attributable to Bangor Corp.) and that Bangor Corp. would have earnings of approximately $50,000.

The president of Maine Co. was disappointed that his firm would earn only $10,000 plus its share of Bangor Corp. earnings. Prior to 1980 Maine Co. had increased its earnings by 10 percent each year; consistent with that trend Maine Co. would have to report total earnings in 1980 of $45,000.

a. In accord with APB guidelines, Maine Co. accounts for its interest in Bangor Corp. on the equity basis. If Bangor Corp. were to declare its usual dividend of $.50 per share, what would be the total reported income of Maine Co.?

b. The president of Maine Co. suggested to his controller that Bangor Corp. be directed to declare a special dividend of $3 per share. What impact would the additional dividend have on earnings of Maine Co.?

c. Suppose that Maine Co. accounted for its investment in Bangor Corp. on the cost basis. What would be the total reported earnings of Maine Co. if the latter declared its regular dividend of $.50 per share? What impact would the additional dividend specified in part b have on earnings of Maine Co.?

d. Comment on why the equity rather than the cost method is considered appropriate for firms which can exert substantial influence over companies in which they have an interest.

4. *Consolidating adjustments may have varying effects on consolidated earnings.*

The consolidated income of two companies is the sum of their individual earnings after certain adjustments have been made. For each of the transactions listed, indicate with brief explanation whether the required adjustments would increase, decrease, or have no effect upon consolidated income as determined simply by summing the earnings of the two individual companies. Assume that company A owns 100 percent of the outstanding shares of common stock of company B.

1. Company B acquired $100,000 of bonds issued by company A. Company A paid company B interest of $8,000.
2. Company B sold $100,000 of the merchandise to company A. The goods had cost company B $80,000 to produce. By year end company A had resold all of the goods to outsiders.
3. Company A sold $50,000 of merchandise to company B. The goods had cost company A $30,000 to produce. At year end all the goods remained in the inventory of company B.
4. Company B owned 5,000 shares of the preferred stock of company A. Company A paid dividends of $3 per share on the preferred stock.
5. Company A sold Company B land for $25,000. The land had cost company A $40,000.
6. Two years earlier, company A sold Company B equipment for $10,000. The equipment had cost company A $6,000. The equipment had an estimated useful life of 10 years and zero salvage value. Company B has been charging depreciation based on its cost of $10,000—$1,000 per year.

5. *Consolidated income represents the sum of the earnings of the individual firms plus or minus any revenues or expenses that would not have been recognized had the individual firms been divisions of a single entity.*

Chicago Corp. owns 100 percent of the outstanding stock of the Woodlawn Co. In 1980 Chicago Corp. had earnings of $200,000 (exclusive of its share of Woodlawn Co. earnings) and Woodlawn Co. had earnings of $80,000. Given the additional information that follows, determine consolidated earnings for the year:

1. Chicago Corp. sold merchandise to Woodlawn Co. at a price of $60,000. The cost of the merchandise was $48,000. Woodlawn Co. has not yet resold any of the merchandise.
2. Chicago made a loan of $100,000 to Woodlawn. During the year, Woodlawn Co. paid interest on the loan of $6,000.

3. Chicago Corp. purchased from Woodlawn equipment for $25,000. The equipment has a remaining useful life of 10 years and no anticipated salvage value. The equipment had a net value on the books of Woodlawn of $15,000 (cost of $30,000 less accumulated depreciation of $15,000). Woodlawn had been depreciating the equipment over a period of 20 years ($1,500 per year).

4. Woodlawn Co. leased office space from Chicago Corp. In 1978 Woodlawn made rent payments of $500 per month—a total of $6,000 during the year.

5. Chicago Corp. paid for its interest in Woodlawn an amount that was $60,000 in excess of Woodlawn Co.'s book value. The $60,000 was allocated entirely to goodwill and is being amortized over a period of 20 years.

6. *The sale of equipment by one member of a consolidated group of firms to another may result in complex adjustments to a number of accounts for as many years as the equipment is used.*

The Wayside Co. purchased manufacturing equipment from its subsidiary, The Gardner Co. The Wayside Co. paid $40,000 for the equipment five years ago. The equipment had been recorded on the books of the Gardner Co. at a cost of $50,000 less accumulated depreciation of $25,000. The Gardner Co. had been depreciating the asset over a period of 10 years. The Wayside Company will depreciate the asset over its remaining useful life of 5 years.

a. At what amount should the Wayside Co. record the asset on its own books? How much depreciation should it charge each year?

b. At what amount should Wayside Co. report the asset on its consolidated balance sheet? How much depreciation should it report?

c. Suppose that depreciation charges on the equipment enter into the computation of cost of goods sold. Explain the nature of any adjustments to cost of goods sold that might have to be made when a consolidated income statement is prepared. Suppose that not all goods manufactured in the course of a year are actually sold. Explain the nature of any adjustments to year-end inventory that might have to be made.

7. *Intercompany sales may require the adjustment of inventory as well as sales and cost of goods sold.*

Retail Co. serves as the marketing division of Manufacturing Co. It purchases all the goods that it sells to outsiders from Manufacturing Co. Manufacturing Co., which sells only to Retail Co., does so at prices that exceed costs by 66 2/3 percent.

The following data were taken from the year-end trial balances of the two firms:

|  | Manufacturing Co. | Retail Co. |
|---|---|---|
| Sales revenue | $200,000 | $216,000 |
| Cost of goods sold | 120,000 | 180,000 |
| Ending inventory | — | 20,000 |

The financial statements of the two firms are to be consolidated.

a. What is the total amount that should be reported as sales (i.e., sales to outsiders)?

b. What was the cost (to the consolidated entity) of the goods sold?

c. What is the amount at which the ending inventory should be reported (i.e., what was its cost to the consolidated entity)?

d. Prepare a journal entry to eliminate intercompany sales and cost of goods sold and to eliminate any "unearned" profit from the ending inventory. Such entry should serve to reduce the combined trial balances of the two firms to the amounts computed in parts a, b, and c.

8. *The financial statements of three or more companies can be consolidated using the same principles that are applicable to consolidation of two firms.*

Condensed balance sheets of three companies, A, B, and C, appear as follows:

|  | *A* | *B* | *C* |
|---|---|---|---|
| Miscellaneous assets | $500,000 | $134,000 | $90,000 |
| Investment in B (80 percent) | 190,000 | | |
| Investment in C (60 percent) | | 66,000 | |
|  | $690,000 | $200,000 | $90,000 |
| Common stock | $ 50,000 | $ 5,000 | $10,000 |
| Retained earnings | 640,000 | 195,000 | 80,000 |
| Total owners' equity | $690,000 | $200,000 | $90,000 |

B acquired its 60 percent interest in C for $60,000 at a time when the balance in the retained earnings account of C was $70,000. Company A just recently acquired its 80 percent interest in B.

a. Prepare any necessary journal entries to eliminate, for purposes of consolidation, the investment of B in C and to reclassify the interest of the minority stockholders. Be sure to take into account the earnings of C since the acquisition; consider the effect they have had on the carrying value (on the books of B) of "Investment in C."

b. Prepare any necessary journal entries to eliminate the investment of A in B and to reclassify the interest of the minority stockholders.

c. Combine the remaining balances into a consolidated balance sheet. Assign any excess of cost over book value to goodwill.

9. *The preparation of a consolidated balance sheet in years subsequent to acquisition, although seemingly complex, can readily be accomplished if broken down into individual steps.*

Barry industries owns 80 percent of Debs, Inc. It purchased its interest in 1976 at a price of $80,000. At the time of purchase, Debs, Inc. had assets of $110,000 and liabilities of $20,000. Since 1976 neither firm has issued additional shares of stock or redeemed outstanding shares. Statements of position of the two firms as of December 31, 1980 are as follows:

|  | Barry Industries | Debs, Inc. |
|---|---|---|
| Cash | $200,000 | $ 50,000 |
| Fixed assets | 600,000 | 100,000 |
| Other assets | 80,000 | 40,000 |
| Investment in Debs, Inc. | 112,000 | – |
| Total assets | $992,000 | $190,000 |
| Accounts payable | $ 62,000 | $ 10,000 |
| Bonds payable | 150,000 | 50,000 |
| Common stock | 20,000 | 5,000 |
| Contributed capital in excess of par | 80,000 | 35,000 |
| Retained earnings | 680,000 | 90,000 |
| Total liabilities and owners' equity | $992,000 | $190,000 |

a. On what basis, cost or equity, is it likely that Barry Industries maintains its interest in Debs, Inc.?

b. By how much did the retained earnings of Debs, Inc. increase since Barry Industries acquired its interest in 1976? How is such increase reflected in the accounts of Barry Industries?

c. Prepare a journal entry, required for consolidation, to eliminate from "Investment in Debs, Inc." the amount that has been added to such account since the date of acquisition. (*Hint:* the debit should be to "Retained earnings.")

d. How much in excess of the book value of its equity in Debs, Inc. did Barry Industries pay to acquire its interest in Debs, Inc. (*Hint:* Compare purchase price of $80,000 with 80 percent of Debs' net worth—assets less liabilities—at the time of acquisition.)

e. Prepare a journal entry to reclassify the excess of cost over book value as goodwill.

f. Prepare a journal entry to eliminate the remaining balance ($72,000) in the "Investment in Debs, Inc." account against 80 percent of any remaining balances in Debs, Inc.'s equity accounts.

g. Prepare a journal entry to reclassify the remaining balances in the equity accounts of Debs, Inc. as "Minority interest in subsidiary."

h. The goodwill is being amortized over a period of 20 years. Prepare a journal entry to reflect the fact that goodwill for 5 years has already been amortized. (*Hint:* Debit retained earnings)

i. Included in "Other assets" of Barry Industries is $50,000 in bonds issued by Debs, Inc. Prepare a journal entry to eliminate the intercompany payable and receivable.

j. Determine the remaining balances, after the journal entries just made, and prepare a consolidated balance sheet.

**10.** *This exercise, which requires the preparation of a worksheet, can serve as a review of the various types of adjustments that are generally required to effect a consolidation of financial statements.*

Indicated below are the preclosing trial balances of X Co. and its subsidiary Y Co. as of December 31, 1979.

|  | X Co. | | Y Co. | |
|---|---|---|---|---|
|  | Dr. | Cr. | Dr. | Cr. |
| Cash | $ 20,200 |  | $ 3,000 |  |
| Accounts and notes receivable | 50,000 |  | 16,000 |  |
| Interest receivable | 4,000 |  | 3,000 |  |
| Inventory | 25,000 |  | 10,000 |  |
| Fixed assets | 185,000 |  | 30,000 |  |
| Investment in Y Co. | 29,000 |  |  |  |
| Accounts and notes payable |  | $ 44,000 |  | $ 17,000 |
| Interest payable |  | 2,000 |  | 1,000 |
| Common stock |  | 10,000 |  | 10,000 |
| Capital contributed in excess of par |  | 50,000 |  | 20,000 |
| Retained earnings |  | 181,200 |  | 10,000 |
| Sales |  | 100,000 |  | 40,000 |
| Interest and other revenues |  | 12,000 |  | 2,000 |
| Cost of goods sold and related expenses | 80,000 |  | 32,000 |  |
| Interest expense | 6,000 |  | 6,000 |  |
|  | $399,200 | $399,200 | $100,000 | $100,000 |

The following information suggests adjustments to the accounts of the two firms that must be made before they can be summed:

1. X Co. owns 60 percent of the common stock of Y Co. It acquired its interest in Y Co. on January 1, 1979. The difference between what it paid for its interest ($29,000) and the book value of such interest can be attributed entirely to the fact that land owned by Y Co. was worth more than its recorded value. (Be sure to eliminate the remainder of investment in Y Co. after reclassification of excess of cost over book value against X Co.'s interest in the three owners' equity accounts of Y Co. and to reclassify the equity of Y Co.'s minority stockholders as "Minority interest in subsidiary.")

2. In 1979 X Co. made $20,000 of sales to Y Co. X Co.'s cost of goods sold was $16,000. None of the goods purchased by X Co. remain in its inventory.

3. Y Co. still owes X Co. $6,000 for the merchandise purchased.

4. In the course of the year X Co. made loans to Y Co. X Co. charged Y Co. $2,000 of interest on the loans. Although there was no out-standing balance on the principal of the loans at year end, Y Co. was

still indebted to X Co. for $1,000 of interest. Both companies have properly accrued the interest revenue or expense.

5. During the year X Co. sold to Y Co. some land. Selling price was $6,000. The land had originally cost X Co. $3,000. X Co. included the gain on the sale of land in "Interest and other revenues."

6. X Co. has not yet recognized its share of Y Co. 1979 earnings. Thus, no adjustment is required to adjust for any earnings since acquisition that might have been added to the "Investment in Y Co." account. However, in preparing a consolidated balance sheet from the trial balance, it is important to remember that the balance in X Co. "Retained earnings" does not reflect earnings for 1979 and the balance in "Minority interest in subsidiary" does not include the interests of the minority stockholders in the earnings of the subsidiary in 1979.

   a. Make all journal entries necessary to effect consolidated financial statements.

   b. Prepare a consolidated income statement and balance sheet. Be sure to include minority share of subsidiary earnings as an expense. You will probably find it useful to prepare a worksheet in which you establish columns for original balances, adjustments, and consolidated balances.

11. *The case against amortization of goodwill may be more persuasive in theory than in practice.*

Shortly after the Accounting Principles Board imposed the requirement that goodwill be amortized over a period of not longer than 40 years, International Telephone & Telegraph Corporation (ITT) indicated in a footnote to its financial statements that it disagreed with the position of the board because, it asserted, the value of goodwill does not necessarily diminish over time.

a. If an asset, such as goodwill or land, does not diminish in value over time, do you think that it should be amortized?

b. Suppose that a company, such as ITT, wishes to acquire a plant that manufactures solar energy cells. Solar Energy, Inc. offers to sell the company such a plant, its only asset, for $1 million. The remaining useful life of the plant is 40 years. Its value on the books of Solar Energy, Inc. is $100,000.

   Alternatively, the *owners* of Solar Energy, Inc. offer to sell their *stock* (not the plant) to ITT for $1 million.

   a. Assume that ITT acquires the *plant* for $1 million. How much depreciation would it charge each year?

   b. Assume instead that ITT acquires the *stock* for $1 million. Based on the "judgment" of management it allocates the entire excess of cost of its investment in Solar Energy, Inc. over its book value of $100,000 to goodwill. If the company were not required to amortize goodwill, how much depreciation would it charge each year? If, instead, it were required to amortize goodwill over a period of 40 years, what would be the combined charge for depreciation and amortization?

   c. Why do you suppose the APB decided as it did that goodwill must be amortized?

12. *A merger or acquisition, particularly if accounted for as a pooling, may provide "instant earnings" to the firm whose shares remain outstanding.*

The following information pertains to the Cambridge Co. and the Leeds Co. as of December 31, 1980.

|  | Cambridge Co. | Leeds Co. |
|---|---|---|
| Number of shares of common outstanding | 1,000,000 | 500,000 |
| Net assets | $15,000,000 | $5,000,000 |
| Latest annual income | $ 2,000,000 | $1,000,000 |
| Recent market price of common stock (per share) | $40 | $20 |
| Earnings per share | $ 2 | $ 2 |

The Cambridge Co. and the Leeds Co. have agreed to a business combination. Cambridge Co. will acquire 100 percent of the common stock of Leeds Co. at the recent market price of $20 per share.

a. Suppose that Cambridge Co. were to purchase all 500,000 shares of Leeds Co. for $20 per share in cash. Cambridge Co. would borrow the required funds at an interest rate (after taxes) of 5 percent per year. The combination would be accounted for as a purchase, and the excess of cost over book value would be amortized over a period of 20 years. Determine anticipated earnings per share of Cambridge Co. after the acquisition, assuming no substantive changes in the earnings of either company.

b. Suppose alternatively that Cambridge Co. were to acquire all 500,000 shares in an exchange of stock. The number of shares to be issued would be based on relative market values, and the combination would be accounted for as a pooling of interests. Determine the anticipated earnings per share of Cambridge Co.

13. *Alternative means of effecting a merger may have differing impacts upon reported assets and equities.*

Indicated as follows are condensed balance sheets of the MNO Co. and PQR Co.

|  | MNO Co. | PQR Co. |
|---|---|---|
| Assets | $5,000,000 | $2,000,000 |
| Common stock, par value $10 | $1,000,000 | $ 500,000 |
| Contributed capital in excess of par | 1,500,000 | 650,000 |
| Retained earnings | 2,500,000 | 850,000 |
| Total owners' equity | $5,000,000 | $2,000,000 |

Prepare balance sheets of the MNO Co. (consolidated as appropriate) to reflect the acquisition of the PQR Co. by the MNO Co. under each of the following conditions.

1. The MNO Co. purchases the *assets* of the PQR Co. at a price of $2.5 million cash. To raise the necessary cash, MNO Co. issues 50,000 shares of common stock at $50 per share.
2. The MNO Co. purchases 100 percent of the outstanding stock of the PQR Co. at a total price of $2.5 million cash. To raise the necessary cash, MNO Co. issues 50,000 shares of common at $50 per share.
3. The MNO Co. issues 50,000 shares of its own common stock in exchange for 100 percent of the outstanding shares of the PQR Co. The market price of the MNO Co. stock at the time of the exchange is $50 per share. The transaction is to be accounted for as a pooling of interests.

14. *Alternative means of accounting for excess of cost over book value can have substantially different effects on reported earnings.*

In 1978, the National Products Company acquired, for $200,000 in common stock, 100 percent control of State Industries, Inc. At the time of the acquisition the net assets (assets less liabilities) of State Industries were recorded on its books at a value of $120,000. In 1979, National Products had earnings of $90,000, exclusive of earnings of State Industries, Inc. State Industries, Inc. had earnings of $20,000. There were no material intercompany transactions during the year. Determine the consolidated earnings of National Products Company and its subsidiary under the following alternative assumptions:

1. The combination is accounted for as a purchase, and the excess of acquisition cost over book value is allocated to various fixed assets that have an average remaining useful life of 10 years.
2. The combination is accounted for as a purchase, and the excess of acquisition cost over book value is allocated entirely to "goodwill." The goodwill is to be amortized over the maximum period allowed by Accounting Principles Board guidelines—40 years.
3. The business combination is accounted for as a pooling of interests. (A firm cannot in practice choose whether to account for a merger as either a purchase or a pooling. If, and only if, an acquisition satisfies the criteria for a pooling can it be accounted for as such. Otherwise, it must be accounted for as a purchase.)

15. *Poolings and purchases have markedly different effects upon asset and equity accounts.*

Indicated as follows are the condensed balance sheets of the ABC Co. and the DEF Co. as of December 31, 1980. On that date, ABC Co. issued 25,000 new shares of common stock in exchange for 100 percent of the outstanding stock of the DEF Co. On the date of the exchange the market price of ABC Co. stock was $50 per share.

|  | *ABC Co.* | *DEF Co.* |
|---|---|---|
| Assets | $2,500,000 | $1,000,000 |
| Common stock, $1 par value | $ 100,000 | $ 50,000 |
| Contributed capital in excess of par | 400,000 | 200,000 |
| Retained earnings | 2,000,000 | 750,000 |
| Total owners' equity | $2,500,000 | $1,000,000 |

a. Prepare a journal entry to record the exchange of stock on the books of the ABC Co. Assume that the exchange will be accounted for as a pooling of interests.

b. Make any entries that would be necessary for the preparation of a consolidated balance sheet, and prepare such a consolidated balance sheet.

c. Indicate any key differences in parts a and b that would result if the transaction had been accounted for as a purchase rather than as a pooling.

16. *In the absence of intercompany transactions, the equity method of accounting for an investment will have an effect on parent company earnings comparable to that of a full-scale consolidation.*

The preclosing trial balances of the Mann Co. and the Rudolph Co. as of December 31, 1980, are as follows:

|  | *Mann Co.* | *Rudolph Co.* |
|---|---|---|
| Cash | $100,000 | $20,000 |
| Investment in Rudolph Co. | 54,000 | |
| Other assets | 76,000 | 75,000 |
| Common stock | 10,000 | 10,000 |
| Retained earnings | 190,000 | 80,000 |
| Sales | 140,000 | 60,000 |
| Cost of goods sold | 95,000 | 50,000 |
| Other expenses | 15,000 | 5,000 |

The Mann Co. owns 60 percent of the outstanding stock of the Rudolph Co. It acquired its investment in 1976 for $30,000 at a time when the net worth of Rudolph Co. was $50,000. Mann maintains its investment in Rudolph on the equity basis. Mann Co. has not yet taken into account its share of Rudolph Co.'s 1980 earnings.

a. Prepare a 1980 income statement and balance sheet for Mann Co. assuming that it is deemed inappropriate to consolidate its accounts with those of Rudolph.

b. Prepare a *consolidated* income statement and balance sheet. Be sure that the last line of the income statement excludes the minority share of Rudolph Co. earnings.

c. Compare net worth and income under the two procedures. Why is the equity basis of accounting for business combinations sometimes referred to as a *one-line consolidation?*

17. *Generally accepted accounting practices provide for recognition of only a portion of the difference between the market value and the book value of a subsidiary's assets.*

Stef Industries recently purchased a 60 percent interest in Federal Electronics. Immediately following acquisition, the individual balance sheets of the two firms appeared as follows:

|                                  | Stef Industries | Federal Electronics |
|----------------------------------|-----------------|---------------------|
| Cash                             | $ 20,000        | $ 10,000            |
| Other assets                     | 200,000         | 185,000             |
| Investment in Federal Electronics| 120,000         |                     |
| Total assets                     | $340,000        | $195,000            |
| Liabilities                      | $ 50,000        | $ 20,000            |
| Common stock                     | 20,000          | 10,000              |
| Retained earnings                | 270,000         | 165,000             |
| Total liabilities and owners' equity | $340,000    | $195,000            |

a. Stef Industries can be presumed to have paid a market price for its acquisition. If a 60 percent interest in Federal Electronics has a fair market value of $120,000, how much must the entire company be worth?

b. Assume that Stef Industries was willing to pay an amount in excess of the book value because Federal Electronics had developed patents on several electronic devices. The value of such patents is not recorded on the books of Federal. In preparing consolidated financial statements, what value should be assigned to the patents (i.e., what is the excess of cost over book value)?

c. If the book values of all other assets and liabilities of Stef Industries approximate their fair market values, then what must be the fair market value of the patents?

d. How do you account for the fact that on the consolidated statements only 60 percent of the value of the patents will be recorded, whereas 100 percent of the value of the other assets of Stef Industries will be recorded?

e. Prepare a consolidation entry—one in addition to those that would be conventionally made—to increase the value of patents to 100 percent of their presumed value. To which interest, majority or minority, did you assign the additional value? (Note that such entry would not ordinarily be made under present-day practice. It is one that many critics suggest *should* be made.)

18. *The "value" of shares received by stockholders of a firm being acquired may be less than what is readily apparent.*

Octopus Corp., a conglomerate, decided to acquire controlling interest in Meek Co.

The common stock of Octopus Corp. had been trading at $20 per share and that of Meek Co. at $60 per share. Octopus had 1 million shares outstanding, and Meek had 300,000 shares outstanding.

The management of Meek Co. was opposed to the takeover. To circumvent the opposition of management, Octopus offered to purchase all outstanding shares of Meek Co. stock at a price of $80 per share—a price that was $20 greater than the market price prior to the announcement of its offer. Octopus would not, however, pay cash for the stock. Instead it would issue to Meek stockholders common stock of Octopus Corp. with a market value of $80 for each share that it received. Hence, it would issue four shares of Octopus stock for each share of Meek Co. stock received.

In the year prior to the offer, Octopus Corp. had earnings of $500,000; Meek had earnings of $1 million. At the time of the offer, Meek Co. had a book value (net worth) of $15 million.

a. Determine the earnings per share of Octopus Corp. in the year prior to the acquisition.

b. Determine the earnings per share of Octopus in the year immediately following the acquisition. Assume that Octopus will prepare consolidated financial statements and that the operating earnings of the two individual companies will remain unchanged. Any excess of cost over book value will be assigned to goodwill and amortized over a period of 40 years. Assume also that 100 percent of the outstanding shares of Meek were tendered (sold) to Octopus.

c. Suppose an investor owned 1,000 shares of Meek. How much better off is he in terms of market value of his holdings after he sold his shares to Octopus than before?

d. How much better (or worse) off is he with respect to earnings that can be ascribed to his shares?

*solutions to exercise for review and self-testing*

a. Parent Co. would report as earnings from subsidiary in 1980 90 percent of Subsidiary Co. income of $30,000—$27,000. It would value "Investment in Subsidiary" at $338,000. Such amount is the original investment of $320,000 plus $27,000, its share of subsidiary earnings less $9,000 of dividends received (or recognized as receivable) from the subsidiary.

b. Parent Co. paid $320,000 for a 90 percent interest in a firm with a book value of $300,000. The excess of cost over 90 percent of total book value ($270,000) is $50,000.

c. Subsidiary Co. had earnings of $30,000. The minority share would be 10 percent of earnings—$3,000.

d. Inasmuch as excess of cost over book value is $50,000, consolidated earnings would be reduced by one-fortieth of that amount—$1,250.

e. Consolidated earnings would be the combined earnings of the two firms, $130,000, less the minority interest in earnings of $3,000 and less amortization of the excess of cost over book value of $1,250—$125,750.

f. If an acquisition is accounted for as a pooling, then the investment in subsidiary is recorded on the books of the parent at the book value of its equity in the subsidiary—in this case, $300,000. No goodwill is recognized; none need be amortized. Consolidated earnings would simply be, therefore, the sum of the earnings of the two individual companies—$130,000.

# 14

## Statement
## of Changes in
## Financial Position

In 1976 Pan American World Airways reported an operating loss of approximately $18 million. Nevertheless, ordinary operations served to increase working capital by $110 million. In 1977 Pan Am reported a modest operating profit of $33 million, but working capital from operations increased by $186 million. This information is revealed directly in the firm's statement of changes in financial position (Exhibit 14-1), in which sources and uses of working capital are indicated.

Change in working capital, is, by itself, a measure of financial performance that is neither superior nor inferior to income. It is an additional criterion, and the statement in which changes in working capital are reported provides another dimension to the picture of financial health painted by the income statement and the balance sheet. In the case of Pan Am, the dimension added by the statement of changes in financial position makes the firm appear significantly more robust than does the two-dimensional view presented by only the income statement and balance sheet.

The changes in working capital could, in fact, have been deduced from the income statement and balance sheet. But neither of these two statements focuses directly upon working capital and the reasons for its increase or decrease during an accounting period.

Working capital—its sources and its uses—is of critical concern to the investor. Working capital is composed of cash and other liquid assets such as marketable securities, accounts receivable, and inventories—those that could be transformed into cash within a relatively short period of time—less accounts payable and other liabilities that would be expected to consume cash within the same short period of time. As a general rule, cash is what is needed by a business to satisfy its obligations as they come due, to meet day-to-day operating expenses, and to make distributions of assets to stockholders eager for a return on their investment.

Investors are vitally concerned with flows of cash. With the purchase of securities an investor makes a sacrifice of cash in the expectation of receiving in the future a greater amount of cash than he initially surrendered. He expects his return to be derived from cash dividends declared by the firm in which he has become a part owner and/or from the eventual sale of his shares of stock for an amount greater than that which he paid to acquire them.

Over time the cash returns to an investor are directly dependent on the ability of the firm in which he has an interest to generate cash. The wherewithal

EXHIBIT 14-1

## PAN AMERICAN WORLD AIRWAYS, INC. AND CONSOLIDATED SUBSIDIARIES
### CONSOLIDATED STATEMENTS OF CHANGES IN FINANCIAL POSITION

| | Year Ended December 31, | |
| --- | --- | --- |
| | 1977 | 1976 |
| | (In thousands) | |
| Sources of Working Capital: | | |
| Income (loss) before equity in income of unconsolidated subsidiaries and associated companies and extraordinary items . . . . . . . . . . . | $ 33,489 | $ (17,928) |
| Items not involving working capital: | | |
| Depreciation and amortization . . . . . . . . . . . . . . . . . . . . . . . . . | 152,915 | 133,906 |
| Deferred federal income tax (credit) . . . . . . . . . . . . . . . . . . . . . | | (5,513) |
| Total from operations . . . . . . . . . . . . . . . . . . . . . . . . . . . . | 186,404 | 110,465 |
| Disposal of property and equipment . . . . . . . . . . . . . . . . . . . . . . | 48,282 | 25,732 |
| Termination of capital leases . . . . . . . . . . . . . . . . . . . . . . . . . . | 26,803 | |
| Increase in long-term debt . . . . . . . . . . . . . . . . . . . . . . . . . . . . | 70,460 | 75,000 |
| Increase in long-term obligations under capital leases . . . . . . . . . | 26,771 | 125,245 |
| Deposits returned upon lease or purchase of flight equipment . . . . . | 10,639 | 19,693 |
| Dividends received from unconsolidated subsidiaries . . . . . . . . . . | 2,000 | 5,014 |
| Proceeds from long-term receivables and transfers to current assets | 1,343 | 3,226 |
| Other—net . . . . . . . . . . . . . . . . . . . . . . . . . . . . . . . . . . . . . . . | 5,879 | 9,304 |
| | 378,581 | 373,679 |
| Uses of Working Capital: | | |
| Property and equipment additions . . . . . . . . . . . . . . . . . . . . . . . . | 189,680 | 58,696 |
| Capital lease additions . . . . . . . . . . . . . . . . . . . . . . . . . . . . . . . | 27,850 | 129,048 |
| Long-term debt becoming currently payable . . . . . . . . . . . . . . . . . | 25,875 | 25,875 |
| Obligations under capital leases becoming currently payable . . . . . | 24,923 | 21,501 |
| Retirement of long-term debt . . . . . . . . . . . . . . . . . . . . . . . . . . . | 16,079 | 9,383 |
| Reduction of long-term obligations under capital leases . . . . . . . . . | 27,703 | |
| Deposits pledged as security . . . . . . . . . . . . . . . . . . . . . . . . . . . | 53,000 | 10,639 |
| Advances on aircraft purchase contracts . . . . . . . . . . . . . . . . . . . | 38,487 | |
| | 403,597 | 255,142 |
| Increase (Decrease) in Working Capital . . . . . . . . . . . . . . . . . . . . | $ (25,016) | $ 118,537 |
| Summary of Changes in Working Capital: | | |
| Increases in current assets: | | |
| Cash and cash investments . . . . . . . . . . . . . . . . . . . . . . . . . . | $ 15,955 | $ 72,203 |
| Receivables, inventories and other current assets . . . . . . . . . . | 35,662 | 1,870 |
| Decreases (increases) in current liabilities: | | |
| Notes payable—bank loans . . . . . . . . . . . . . . . . . . . . . . . . . . | | 30,000 |
| Current maturities of long-term debt . . . . . . . . . . . . . . . . . . . . | (4,369) | 7,244 |
| Accounts payable and accrued liabilities . . . . . . . . . . . . . . . . . | (60,502) | (20,252) |
| Air traffic liability . . . . . . . . . . . . . . . . . . . . . . . . . . . . . . . . . | (11,762) | 27,472 |
| Increase (Decrease) in Working Capital . . . . . . . . . . . . . . . . . . . . . | $ (25,016) | $ 118,537 |

of the firm to pay dividends is contingent upon its ability to produce cash inflows that exceed outflows. And the market value of the firm's common stock is determined primarily by perceptions of investors as to how well the firm will succeed in generating the cash that can be used to pay dividends. In virtually all "models" designed to evaluate investments, expected cash inflow is a key element.

One important objective of financial statements is to provide both investors and potential investors with the information needed to make predictions about the ability of the enterprise to generate cash in the future. The balance sheet reflects the assets and liabilities of the enterprise—the resources that can be exchanged directly for cash or that can be used to generate other assets that can be exchanged for cash as well as the obligations that will have to be satisfied by the disbursement of cash. The income statement reports on historical changes between two points in time in the level of resources, net of liabilities, available to the firm. It provides a record of financial performance in the past—one that might serve as a guide to expected performance in the future.

The income statement serves to indicate how much better off a firm is at the end of an accounting period than it was at the beginning. It is based on the accrual concept. Revenues are reported in the period in which they are earned; costs are charged as expenses in the same period that recognition is given to the revenues with which they are associated. As a consequence, the income statement is deficient in that it fails to present a factual history of a firm's cash transactions. The determination of periodic income is necessarily based on a number of estimates, judgments, and allocations. These relate to such matters as the useful lives of assets owned (depreciation), the ultimate collectibility of accounts receivable (bad-debt expense), and the life expectancy of employees (pension expense). Moreover, an income statement provides an incomplete record of transactions involving cash. It may fail to report several types of important financial events. Payment and repayment of debt, issuance of common or preferred stock, and purchase or sale of fixed assets are but a few examples of the types of transactions about which no information is likely to be revealed on the income statement. A balance sheet, of course, provides information only on the financial position of an enterprise at a specific point in time. A comparison of two balance sheets, at different points in time, indicates the net change in cash during the period covered, but it provides only limited insight as to the reason for the change.

The statement of changes in financial position serves as a supplement to the income statement and balance sheet. Until 1971, relatively few firms included statements of changes in financial position in their annual reports to stockholders. The Accounting Principles Board, in Opinion No. 19, "Reporting Changes in Financial Position," required that subsequent to that year a statement of changes in financial position must be presented as a basic statement for each period for which an income statement is presented.

The statement of changes in financial position presents a summary of all significant transactions—the exchanges with outside parties—in which an enterprise engaged during an accounting period. Reported in the statement are transactions involving the financing and investing activities of the firm, such as the sale of new securities, the purchase of fixed assets, and the payment and repayment of debt—transactions of the type that are excluded from the income statement.* The statement of changes in financial position presents primarily *factual* information. The transactions summarized are *actual* transactions with independent parties. The data presented are considerably less "contaminated" by estimates, judgments, or allocations than those in the statement income.†

The statement of changes in financial position is intended to provide an additional source on which investors or other users of financial statements can rely to make predictions about cash flows of the future. It by no means can be viewed as a better or more reliable financial report than either the income statement or the balance sheet; it is only a supplementary one.

The statement of changes in financial position is often referred to as a *statement of sources and applications of funds.* "Funds" has alternative meanings, and in practice there is considerable variation in the nature of the statements. On the one hand, "funds" is sometimes interpreted to mean *cash;* as a consequence, the statement of changes in financial position is a summary of cash receipts and cash disbursements. More commonly, "funds" is interpreted to mean *working capital*—current assets less current liabilities—and the statement of changes in financial position is a summary of the means by which the enterprise accumulated working capital and the uses to which it was applied.** In this chapter we shall be concerned primarily with the statement of changes in financial position based on the working capital concept of funds; a section of the chapter will, however, be directed to the statement based on the cash concept of funds.

In light of the preceding discussion of the importance of cash, it may seem odd that it is the working capital, rather than the cash, concept of funds that is most widely accepted. But it is the statement of changes in financial position based on the broader concept of funds that is likely to serve as the more reliable basis on which to predict cash flows of the future. Current assets generally can be either readily transformed into cash or may obviate the future disbursement of cash. Current liabilities usually require the near-term payment of cash. For example, the total sales of a company during a period—sales for cash as well as on credit—are likely to be a better indicator of the ability of a firm to generate cash than merely the total cash collections from sales. Credit sales would immediately serve to increase working capital but not cash. In the normal course of business, however, the accounts receivable generated by the credit sales would shortly be converted into cash.

---

*The statement of changes in financial position may also report upon certain reclassifications of assets or liabilities between current and noncurrent categories. To avoid undue complexity, consideration of these reclassifications is omitted from this chapter.

†"Less" contaminated rather than "uncontaminated" mainly because the value of accounts receivable is affected by estimates of bad debts and that of inventory is affected by choice of valuation method (FIFO, LIFO, etc.).

**In nonprofit accounting "fund" is used to signify an independent accounting entity with a self-balancing set of accounts.

## Changes in Working Capital

Working capital represents the current assets of a firm (commonly cash, marketable securities, accounts receivable, and inventories) less the current liabilities (wages and salaries payable, accounts payable, and short-term notes payable).

By the very nature of the accounting equation and the double-entry bookkeeping process, changes in working capital must be associated with changes in nonworking capital accounts—noncurrent assets, noncurrent liabilities, and owners' equity. A change in one working capital account that is offset by a corresponding change in another working capital account will have no effect on net working capital.

The basic accounting equation indicates that current assets (CA) plus other assets (OA) are equal to current liabilities (CL) plus other liabilities (OL) plus owners' equity (OE); that is,

$$\$CA + \$OA = \$CL + \$OL + \$OE$$

By rearranging the terms in the equation, it can be seen that working capital (current assets minus current liabilities) must equal other liabilities plus owners' equity minus other assets:

$$\underbrace{\$CA - \$CL}_{\text{Working capital}} = \$OL + \$OE - \$OA$$

Changes in working capital can be identified with changes in other liabilities, owners' equity, or other assets. *Increases* in working capital can be explained by *increases* in noncurrent liabilities or owners' equity (such as those attributable to the issuance of bonds or stock) and by *decreases* in noncurrent assets (such as those attributable to the sale of long-lived assets). *Decreases* in working capital can be explained by *decreases* in noncurrent liabilities or owners' equity (such as those attributable to the repayment of debt or the declaration of dividends) or *increases* in noncurrent assets (such as those attributable to the purchase of long-lived assets). Changes in working capital are most commonly associated with profits and losses—in effect, increases and decreases in owners' equity (retained earnings). To summarize:

| Sources of Working Capital (events associated with increases in working capital) | Uses of Working Capital (events associated with decreases in working capital) |
|---|---|
| Increases in noncurrent liabilities | Decreases in noncurrent liabilities |
| Increases in owners' equity (including those attributable to periodic income) | Decreases in owners' equity (including those attributable to periodic losses and declarations of dividends) |
| Decreases in noncurrent assets | Increases in noncurrent assets |

## The Statement of Changes in Financial Position: A Report on Long-Term Financial and Investment Activity

Inasmuch as changes in working capital are necessarily associated with changes in noncurrent assets, noncurrent liabilities, and owners' equity, the statement of changes in financial position can also be seen as a report that focuses on the long-term financing and investing activities of a firm. It indicates how much the firm spent on the acquisition of plant, equipment, or other long-term assets and how it obtained the financial wherewithal to do so.

In a broad sense, there are only three types of transactions in which a firm can engage:

1. Those in which the components of working capital are affected but the net amount of working capital remains unaffected.
2. Those in which the net amount of working capital is changed but so also are one or more of nonworking capital accounts (noncurrent assets or liabilities or owners' equity).
3. Those in which no working capital account is affected; only noncurrent asset, noncurrent liability or owners' equity accounts are increased or decreased.

The statement of changes in working capital pays no heed to the transactions in which net working capital remains unchanged (type 1). Instead, it focuses primarily on the second type transactions as a result of which net working capital increases or decreases and correspondingly long-term assets, long-term liabilities, or owners' equity changes. In addition, however, it reports upon the third type of transactions—those that involve changes in only noncurrent asset, noncurrent liability, or owners' equity accounts. This type of a transaction has no effect upon working capital. But it may have an important impact upon the firm's productive capacity as well as the structure of its debt and equity.

Suppose, for example, that a firm acquires a new plant in exchange for long-term notes. No cash is paid, nor is any other component of working capital involved in the transaction. If the statement of changes in financial position were to report only those transactions which directly affect working capital, then the acquisition of the plant would be omitted from the statement. Moreover, since the acquisition would have no effect on revenues or expenses (except insofar as depreciation is charged) in the year of exchange, it could not properly be reported on the income statement.

Because of the long-term significance of such transactions, the Accounting Principles Board directed that they be specifically reported upon in the body of the financial statements. It prescribed, therefore, that they should be reported "as if" they were made for cash. That is, the issuance of the long-term notes should be reported as a source of funds and the acquisition of the plant as a use of funds. In other words, such transactions should be reported as offsetting

535

sources and uses of funds. Commonly, a note beside the reported amounts would indicate the nature of the transaction.

Other examples of transactions that do not directly affect working capital but which should be reported as if they did are those involving exchanges of one noncurrent asset for another, acquisition of assets in exchange for common or preferred stock, exchanges of one class of stock for another (e.g., common stock for preferred), or redemption of long-term debt in exchange for common or preferred stock.

## Changes in Components of Working Capital

The statement of changes in financial position comprises two related tables. One indicates the change between two points in time in the balances in the accounts that constitute working capital. The other indicates the reason for the change in working capital—that is, the changes in those other accounts (noncurrent assets and liabilities and owners' equity) that provide an explanation for the change in working capital.

Determining the change in working capital and in its various component accounts is a reasonably simple, mechanical task. The balances (per the balance sheet) at the beginning of the year are compared to those at the end of the year and the differences computed. Current assets and current liabilities at the end of the year are subtracted from those at the beginning. The net change in current liabilities is then subtracted from the net change in current assets. The table on the next page, for example, indicates the change in working capital of the Kingston Corp. during 1980.

Working capital increased during the year by $24,000—an increase that would have to be accounted for in the second table.

The importance of changes in the components of working capital should not be overlooked. In the Kingston Corp., for example, net working capital increased. The increase, however, is primarily attributable to a build-up of accounts receivable and inventories and would, in fact, have been much greater had it not been for a substantial increase in current notes payable. The build-up in receivables, payables, and inventories, if not associated with an increase in sales, could be a sign of financial deterioration rather than strength. The customers of the firm may not be paying their bills on time, the firm may be unable to sell the goods that it has produced, and it may have had to resort to short-term borrowing to meet its obligations.

Determining the reason for the change in working capital is considerably more complex. The analyst must be a detective. He must gather, from a number of sources, bits and pieces of information which together account for the entire change in working capital. His primary sources are the income statement and the balance sheet, but sometimes he must delve further into the underlying accounts.

**Kingston Corp.**
**Changes in Working Capital (000s omitted)**

|  | December 31, 1980 | December 31, 1979 | Increase (decrease) |
|---|---|---|---|
| Current assets |  |  |  |
| Cash | $ 41 | $ 28 | $ 13 |
| Accounts receivable (net of allowance for uncollectibles) | 231 | 180 | 51 |
| Note receivable | 11 | — | 11 |
| Inventories | 275 | 219 | 56 |
| Prepaid expenses | 8 | 6 | 2 |
| Total current assets | $566 | $433 | $133 |
| Current liabilities |  |  |  |
| Accounts payable | $114 | $110 | $  4 |
| Wages and salaries payable | 42 | 39 | 3 |
| Notes payable | 196 | 83 | 113 |
| Interest payable | 5 | 2 | 3 |
| Dividends payable | 5 | 5 | 0 |
| Taxes payable | 14 | 28 | (14) |
| Total current liabilities | $376 | $267 | $109 |
| Working capital | $190 | $166 | $ 24 |

In light of the fact that changes in working capital can be explained in terms of changes in other balance sheet accounts, the analyst's basic approach is to reconcile the beginning balance with the ending balance in each noncurrent asset, noncurrent liability, and owners' equity account. He attempts to reconstruct the transactions or events that resulted in an increase or a decrease in the account and to determine which of those transactions or events created a source of working capital.

## Earnings as a Source of Working Capital

Retained earnings is a logical account with which to begin a quest for sources and uses of working capital. Retained earnings are conventionally increased as a consequence of periodic income; they are decreased by the declaration of dividends. Operations, as represented by income, are a source of working capital, and dividends, a use.

Income is a primary measure of an increase in working capital in that *most* components of income—that is, most revenues and expenses—involve either cash receipts or disbursements, or short-term promises of cash receipts or disbursements. Suppose, for example, that income of a merchandising company was $20,000, determined as follows:

| | | |
|---|---:|---:|
| Sales revenue | | $100,000 |
| Less: Cost of goods sold | $40,000 | |
| Salaries | 25,000 | |
| Taxes | 8,000 | |
| Other expenses | 7,000 | 80,000 |
| Income | | $ 20,000 |

Insofar as sales revenue resulted in an increase in cash or accounts receivable and that the expenses resulted in a decrease in cash or inventories, or an increase in a short-term payable (all being components of working capital), then operations (income) were a *source of funds* in the amount of $20,000. Commonly, however, if income is to be considered a source of funds, it must be adjusted to take into account any revenues or expenses that were not associated with increases or decreases in working capital.

**depreciation**  Suppose that of the $7,000 in other expenses, $3,000 represented depreciation on store and office equipment. The likely journal entry to record the depreciation expense was:

| | | |
|---|---:|---:|
| Depreciation expense | $3,000 | |
| Store and office equipment, | | |
| accumulated depreciation | | $3,000 |
| **To record depreciation.** | | |

The depreciation did not require an outlay of cash or other current assets in the current year. Neither did it result in an increase in current liabilities. "Store and office equipment—accumulated depreciation" is a contra account to a non-current asset; no components of working capital were affected by the charge for depreciation.

Under the assumption that $3,000 of the other expenses represented depreciation charges, sales revenue resulted in an increase in working capital of $100,000, but expenses resulted in a decrease of working capital of only $77,000. Operations, therefore, served to increase working capital by $23,000. Inasmuch as $3,000 of expenses were of the type that did not require an outlay of cash or other components of working capital, $3,000 must be added to reported net income to derive the total increase in working capital attributable to operations.

It is common for firms to report depreciation as a source of funds. Thus (assuming no other sources of funds),

Sources of working capital:

| | |
|---|---|
| Net income | $20,000 |
| Depreciation | 3,000 |
| | $23,000 |

Such reporting practice has no doubt contributed to a great deal of misunderstanding with respect to depreciation. Depreciation is *not* a source of funds. Depreciation provides no cash to an enterprise. It neither increases nor decreases current assets or current liabilities. Depreciation is nothing more than an expense that does not require a current outlay of cash. It is a means of allocating to a current year a cost that had been incurred in a previous year. It is a source of funds only in the sense that if reported income is to be considered a source of funds, then reported income must be adjusted (increased) by the amount of depreciation included among reported expenditures. A statement of changes in financial position is likely to be more meaningful to investors if depreciation, when included among the sources of working capital, is specifically described as an adjustment to net income, required because it is an expense that does not result in a current year reduction of working capital.

In addition to depreciation there are other components of income that do not result in either an increase or decrease in working capital. They, too, must be either added to or subtracted from net income if operations are to be considered a source of funds.

**amortization and depletion**

Most similar to depreciation are charges for amortization or depletion of non-current assets. The amortization of patents, copyrights, franchises, or goodwill or the depletion of mineral deposits requires a charge to income that results in the reduction of a long-term asset rather than an outlay of working capital. Insofar as income is categorized as a source of funds, those expenditures that did not result in a reduction of working capital must be added back to net income.

Amortization of a bond discount is another type of expense that does not result in a reduction of working capital. When a bond discount (a contra account to a liability—hence an account that has a debit balance) is amortized the net balance of long-term liabilities is reduced. No cash or other assets or liabilities are exchanged. The amount of the amortization expense must be *added* to net income; it is a charge that does not require the use of funds.

Correspondingly, amortization of a bond premium must be *subtracted* from income. A bond premium has a credit balance and is reported as an addition to bonds payable. The amortization of a bond premium serves to *reduce* interest expense. Recall, for example, that if a $1,000 bond is sold at a premium, then the effective interest rate must be less than the coupon rate. If, for example, a 20-year, 6 percent, $1,000 bond were sold to yield 5 percent (at a price of $112.55) then the following entry might be made to record the first semi-annual interest payment:

| | | |
|---|---|---|
| Bond premium | $ 1.86 | |
| Interest expense | 28.14 | |
| Cash | | $30.00 |
| **To record payment of interest.** | | |

The enterprise would record an interest expense of $28.14, but a cash payment of $30.00 would be made to the bondholder. The amortization of the premium serves to understate reported expenses as a use of funds and thereby to overstate reported income as a source of funds. The amortization of the bond premium ($1.86) must be subtracted from reported income if reported income is to be shown as a source of funds.

**gains and losses**    Gains or losses on the sale of fixed assets are additional types of revenues and expenses for which income must be adjusted. Consider, for example, the sale of a parcel of land. The land had cost $5,000 and had been carried on the books at that value. It was sold for $7,000. The following entry would have been made to record the sale:

| | | |
|---|---|---|
| Cash | $7,000 | |
| Land | | $5,000 |
| Gain on sale of land | | 2,000 |
| **To record the sale of land.** | | |

The sale of the land would provide the firm with $7,000 in working capital. Included among the sources of funds would be a separate item, "sale of land–$7,000." But included in reported income would be the $2,000 gain on the sale of land. If income, including the gain of $2,000, were shown as a source of funds and so also was the $7,000 received in exchange for the land, then sources of funds would be overstated by $2,000; the gain would have been counted twice. It is necessary to subtract from reported income, if reported income is to be presented as a source of funds, any gains on sale of non-current assets that have been included in the determination of reported income. Similarly, any losses must be added to income. Such losses, although they served to reduce reported income, would not have reduced working capital.

**deferred income taxes**    A further adjustment to income is required to take into account the difference between reported tax expense and taxes that are actually payable. In Chapter 10, it was pointed out that the reported income tax expense is conventionally determined as a percentage of reported earnings. Yet special features of the tax laws—those which permit the use of *accelerated* methods of depreciation, for example—often provide for long-term postponement of taxes. A typical journal entry to record an annual tax liability might appear as follows:

| | | |
|---|---|---|
| Tax expense | $100,000 | |
|     Taxes payable in current year | | $80,000 |
|     Taxes deferred until future years | | 20,000 |
| **To record tax expense.** | | |

That portion of the tax which is payable in the current year increases current liabilities and hence decreases working capital; it is a use of funds. But that portion which is deferred until future years increases a long-term liability; it has no effect on working capital. Insofar as reported income has been reduced by reported tax expense ($100,000), net income as a source of funds is understated by the portion of taxes deferred until future years ($20,000), for only the portion of the tax that is payable in the current year ($80,000) resulted in a reduction of working capital. The deferred portion of income taxes must therefore be added back to net income.

In the same vein, if a portion of pension expense has not been funded or recorded as a current liability, then the entire amount of the pension expense would not have resulted in a reduction of working capital. Net income must be adjusted by that portion of pension expense which was offset by a credit to a long-term liability account (accrued pension costs, for example) as opposed to either cash or a current liability.

**other changes in retained earnings**

Retained earnings are characteristically increased by earnings and decreased both by losses and by dividends. Dividends paid in cash are a use of working capital and should be reported as such. Stock dividends, like cash dividends, result in a decrease in retained earnings. But stock dividends do not result in a reduction of working capital. Stock dividends result in an increase in common stock and contributed capital in excess of par. They should not, therefore, be classified as a use of funds.

It is incumbent upon the analyst to make certain that the entire change in retained earnings from the end of one year to the end of the next can be accounted for by earnings or losses or by the declaration of dividends. That is, the beginning balance plus income minus dividends must equal the ending balance. In extraordinary circumstances retained earnings may have been increased or decreased in the course of a year by adjustments to the earnings of prior years. Such adjustments may have resulted in either an increase or decrease in working capital and may therefore have been a source or use of funds.

Changes in capital stock accounts invariably result from either the issuance of additional shares or the redemption of existing shares. Suppose, for example, that a firm's common stock and the related contributed capital in excess of par accounts contained the following balances at the beginning and at the end of 1980:

|  | December 31, 1980 | December 31, 1979 |
|---|---|---|
| Common stock (par value $1) | $120,000 | $100,000 |
| Contributed capital in excess of par | 524,000 | 480,000 |
|  | $644,000 | $580,000 |

In the absence of offsetting redemptions, it is almost certain that the combined increase of $64,000 was attributable to the issuance of 20,000 shares of common stock. Insofar as the shares were issued in exchange for cash or other current assets, they represent a *source* of funds and should so be reported. If, however, the shares were issued to acquire noncurrent assets (to acquire a new corporation, for example) or in exchange for outstanding bonds or preferred stock, then the addition to the capital accounts would *not* represent a source of funds. Nevertheless, because the transaction would have had an important effect upon the firm's long-term financial structure, it would be reported "as if" it involved working capital. The issue of the new securities would be reported as a source of working capital; the acquisition of the assets or retirement of the debt would be reported as a use.

Changes in the balance in preferred stock and related accounts are also likely to be attributable to the issue or redemption of shares in exchange for cash. The analyst must therefore account for all changes in such balances and verify whether in fact they resulted in increases or decreases in working capital.

### Noncurrent Assets

Changes in noncurrent assets are generally associated with changes in working capital. It is important, therefore, that the increases or decreases in noncurrent asset accounts, as well as in accounts directly associated with noncurrent assets, such as accumulated depreciation, be fully explained. Increases in fixed asset accounts conventionally result from purchases; hence they represent a *use* of funds. Decreases conventionally result from either sales or retirements; hence they often represent a *source* of funds. Moreover, increases in accumulated depreciation ordinarily are associated with periodic depreciation charges —a nonfund expense requiring an adjustment to net income. Decreases are tied to the sales and retirements and may thereby be associated with the source of funds attributable to the sale of the related asset.

Assume that the reported balances in an equipment account and the related accumulated depreciation account at the end of years 1980 and 1979 appear as follows:

|  | December 31, 1980 | December 31, 1979 |
|---|---|---|
| Equipment | $310,000 | $290,000 |
| Accumulated depreciation | 75,000 | 90,000 |
|  | $235,000 | $200,000 |

The underlying accounts reveal:

| | |
|---|---|
| Amount (in cash) for which equipment was sold | $ 3,000 |
| Original cost of equipment sold | 60,000 |
| Accumulated depreciation on equipment sold | 56,000 |
| Loss on sale of equipment | 1,000 |
| Annual depreciation charge on all equipment | 41,000 |
| Purchase of new equipment | 80,000 |

It is clear that the activity in the fixed asset accounts was associated with changes in working capital:

1. Equipment was acquired at a cost of $80,000. Purchase of equipment usually requires the use of cash or other components of working capital.

2. Equipment was sold for $3,000. The cash received served to increase working capital. The sale of equipment can be considered a source of working capital.

3. The equipment that was sold for $3,000 had a book value of $4,000 (initial cost of $60,000 less accumulated depreciation of $56,000). If the price at which equipment is sold is reported as a source of working capital, then the related gain or loss cannot also be reflected in income, if income is to be considered a source of funds. The recorded loss on the sale of equipment ($1,000) must be added back to income.

4. Periodic charges for depreciation are a type of expense that does not require the use of funds. Insofar as income is considered a source of funds, then depreciation charges, in this example $41,000, must also be added back to income.

In determining the sources and uses of working capital, it is imperative that an analyst make certain that he has accounted for the complete increase or decrease in each nonworking capital balance sheet account. The activity described here does, in fact, serve to explain the changes in both the "Equipment" and "Accumulated Depreciation" accounts:

## EQUIPMENT

Beginning balance + Purchases – Retirements = Ending balance
$290,000    + $80,000 –   $60,000   =    $310,000

## ACCUMULATED DEPRECIATION

Beginning balance + Annual depreciation – Accumulated de-    = Ending
preciation on equip-   balance
ment retired
$90,000     +         $41,000      –        $56,000      = $75,000

The activity in the accounts relating to equipment would have been associated with the following changes in working capital:

## SOURCES OF WORKING CAPITAL

Adjustments to income (expenses not associated with an outflow of working capital)

| | | |
|---|---|---|
| Add: Annual depreciation charges | $41,000 | |
| Loss on sale of equipment | 1,000 | $42,000 |
| Sale of equipment | | 3,000 |
| Total sources associated with equipment | | $45,000 |

## USES OF WORKING CAPITAL

| | |
|---|---|
| Purchase of new equipment | $80,000 |
| Net *use* of working capital associated with activity in equipment accounts | $35,000 |

## Noncurrent Debt

Long-term obligations can be analyzed in a manner similar to long-term assets. The issuance of long-term bonds is ordinarily a source of funds and the retirement a use. The related discount or premium, like accumulated depreciation, must be reviewed in conjunction with the *parent* accounts to determine the exact amount of the increases or decreases in working capital.

Assume that the balances in a long-term debt account and the related discount account at the end of 1980 and 1979 appear as follows:

|  | December 31, 1980 | December 31, 1979 |
|---|---|---|
| Bonds payable | $150,000 | $200,000 |
| Discount on bonds payable | 4,000 | 10,000 |
|  | $146,000 | $190,000 |

The accounting records also reveal the following:

| | |
|---|---|
| Face value of bonds issued | $ 50,000 |
| Discount on bonds issued | 1,000 |
| Face value of bonds retired | 100,000 |
| Discount on bonds retired | 5,000 |
| Amount paid to retire bonds | 102,000 |
| Loss on retirement of bonds | 7,000 |
| Bond discount amortization expense | 2,000 |

This information suggests several transactions that must be reported on the statement of changes in financial position:

1. Bonds were issued at a total price of $49,000. This amount represents the face amount of the bonds ($50,000) less discount on sale ($1,000). The issuance of long-term debt represents a source of working capital.

2. Bonds with a book value of $95,000 (face value of $100,000 less discount of $5,000) were retired during the year. The amount paid to retire them was $102,000. This amount represents a use of working capital.

3. The bonds were retired at a loss of $7,000, the difference between amount paid ($102,000) and book value ($95,000). The loss of $7,000 is reflected in the determination of net income. If, however, the amount paid to retire the bonds ($102,000) is to be reported as a use of working capital, then the $7,000 cannot be counted again as an expenditure requiring the use of funds. To avoid double counting, the $7,000 must be added back to income.

4. In the course of the year, $2,000 of bond discount amortization expense was charged. The expense reduced income, but it did not decrease working capital. Instead, it reduced the discount on bonds payable, an account that is contra to a noncurrent liability. If income is to be considered a source of working capital, then the $2,000 of amortization expense must be added back to income.

These transactions serve to explain the entire change in "Bonds payable" and "Discount on bonds payable" during 1980:

**BONDS PAYABLE**

Beginning balance + Bonds issued – Bonds retired = Ending balance
$200,000 + $50,000 – $100,000 = $150,000

**DISCOUNT ON BONDS PAYABLE**

Beginning + Discount on – Annual amor- – Unamortized dis- = Ending
balance    new bonds    tization charge   count on bonds    balance
       issued                    retired
$10,000 + $1,000 – $2,000 – $5,000 = $4,000

The activity in the two accounts affected working capital as follows:

**SOURCES OF WORKING CAPITAL**

| | | |
|---|---:|---:|
| Adjustments to income (expenses not associated with an outflow of working capital) | | |
| Add: loss on retirement of bonds | $7,000 | |
|       annual amortization expense | 2,000 | $ 9,000 |
| Issuance of bonds | | 49,000 |
| Total sources associated with bond transactions | | $ 58,000 |

**USES OF WORKING CAPITAL**

| | |
|---|---:|
| Retirement of outstanding bonds | 102,000 |
| Net *use* of working capital associated with activity in bond accounts | $ 44,000 |

## Preparation of Funds Statement—
## an Example

An example of the derivation of a statement of changes in financial position from an income statement and a balance sheet may help to clarify the relationships between changes in working capital and changes in other accounts. The example is based on the income statement, balance sheet, and other information of the Taconic Corp., presented in Exhibit 14-2.

Although there are many approaches that may be taken in preparing a statement of changes in financial position, the one illustrated here will be that of first determining the change in working capital to be accounted for and then

EXHIBIT 14-2

**Taconic Corp.**
**Comparative Statement of Position**
**December 31, 1980 and 1979**

| | 1980 | 1979 |
|---|---|---|
| *Assets* | | |
| Current assets | | |
| Cash | $ 40,000 | $ 30,000 |
| Accounts receivable | 76,000 | 80,000 |
| Inventories | 60,000 | 62,000 |
| Other current assets | 160,000 | 50,000 |
| Total current assets | $336,000 | $222,000 |
| Other assets | | |
| Buildings and equipment | $403,000 | $328,000 |
| Less: Accumulated depreciation | 90,000 | 72,000 |
| | 313,000 | 256,000 |
| Land | 40,000 | 40,000 |
| Investment in subsidiary | 6,000 | |
| Miscellaneous assets | 27,000 | 27,000 |
| Total other assets | $386,000 | $323,000 |
| Total assets | $722,000 | $545,000 |
| *Liabilities and owners' equity* | | |
| Current liabilities | | |
| Accounts payable | $ 50,000 | $ 48,000 |
| Other current liabilities | 12,000 | 8,000 |
| Total current liabilities | $ 62,000 | $ 56,000 |
| Other liabilities | | |
| Income taxes deferred until future years | $ 69,000 | $ 62,000 |
| Bonds payable | 371,000 | 250,000 |
| Premium on bonds payable | 10,000 | 11,000 |
| Total bonds payable | 381,000 | 261,000 |
| Total other liabilities | $450,000 | $323,000 |
| Owners' equity | | |
| Common stock ($1 par value) | $ 13,000 | $ 12,000 |
| Contributed capital in excess of par | 127,000 | 122,000 |
| Retained earnings | 70,000 | 32,000 |
| Total owners' equity | $210,000 | $166,000 |
| Total liabilities and owners' equity | $722,000 | $545,000 |

EXHIBIT 14-2 (cont)

**Taconic Corp.**
**Statement of Income**
**Year Ended December 31, 1980**

| | | |
|---|---:|---:|
| Sales | $1,045,000 | |
| Other revenues | 26,000 | $1,071,000 |
| Cost of goods sold | | |
| (excluding depreciation) | $895,000 | |
| Depreciation | 51,000 | |
| Interest | 11,000 | |
| Taxes | 30,000 | |
| Other expenses | 24,000 | 1,011,000 |
| Net income | | $    60,000 |

*Other information (from journal entries or specific accounts):*

1. The company declared dividends of $22,000.
2. It acquired buildings and equipment at a cost of $112,000.
3. It sold assets for $10,000. The assets had originally cost $37,000. At time of sale depreciation of $33,000 had been accumulated. The gain on sale of $6,000 is included in "Other revenues."
4. The subsidiary was acquired in exchange for 1,000 shares of common stock.
5. The company paid $23,000 in taxes. The difference between that amount and tax expense of $30,000 was credited to "Income taxes deferred until future years."
6. The company paid $14,000 in interest. The difference between that amount and reported interest expense of $11,000 represents amortization of bond premium.
7. The company issued for $123,000 bonds having a face value of $121,000.

reconstructing, in summary form, the journal entries that most likely affected each of the *nonworking capital* accounts. The reconstructed entries will be slightly different from the original entries, however.

First, whenever one side of the original entry involved a working capital account, the debit or credit in the reconstructed entry will not be to that working capital account. Instead, it will be to either "Sources of working capital" or "Uses of working capital." A brief explanation as to why working capital was received or disbursed will be provided in parentheses.

Second, whenever one side of the original entry involved a revenue or expense that did not result in either an inflow or an outflow of working capital (depreciation expense, for example) and must thereby be added to or subtracted from income if income is to be considered a source of funds, the debit or credit in the reconstructed entry will not be to that revenue or expense. Instead, inasmuch as income represents a source of funds, it will be to "Sources of working capital." A few words indicating that the entry represents an adjustment to income and the reason for the adjustment will be placed in parentheses.

The reconstructed entries will be posted to a worksheet. The worksheet will have four columns: one for beginning balances, two for the reconstructed entries, and one for ending balances. The top portion of the worksheet will contain one line representing working capital and other lines for each of the nonworking capital balance sheet accounts. The lower portion of the worksheet will contain accounts descriptive of the reasons for the changes in working capital—the part of the reconstructed journal entries that do not involve debits or credits to the nonworking capital accounts.

The mechanics of preparing the worksheet are reflective of the relationship between working capital and nonworking capital accounts. Changes in working capital must be associated with increases or decreases in nonworking capital accounts. The worksheet is a means of assuring that all changes in nonworking capital accounts have been analyzed and that their impact upon working capital has been described.

During 1980, the working capital (current assets less current liabilities) of the Taconic Corp. increased by $108,000. The changes in the component accounts are indicated in Exhibit 14–3.

*EXHIBIT 14–3*

| | Taconic Corp.<br>Change in Working Capital | | |
|---|---|---|---|
| | *December 31,<br>1980* | *December 31,<br>1979* | *Increase<br>(decrease)* |
| Current assets | | | |
| Cash | $ 40,000 | $ 30,000 | $ 10,000 |
| Accounts receivable | 76,000 | 80,000 | (4,000) |
| Inventories | 60,000 | 62,000 | (2,000) |
| Other current assets | 160,000 | 50,000 | 110,000 |
| Total current assets | $336,000 | $222,000 | $114,000 |
| Current liabilities | | | |
| Accounts payable | $ 50,000 | $ 48,000 | $ 2,000 |
| Other current liabilities | 12,000 | 8,000 | 4,000 |
| Total current liabilities | $ 62,000 | $ 56,000 | $ 6,000 |
| Working capital | $274,000 | $166,000 | $108,000 |

The $108,000 increase in working capital may be accounted for by reconstructing the entries, in summary form, that affected each of the non-working capital balance sheet accounts.

**retained earnings** Retained earnings increased by $38,000 in 1980. This increase can be accounted for by income of $60,000 less dividends of $22,000 (per other information). Income (subject to adjustments for noncash revenues and expenses) represents a source of funds and dividends a use of funds:

(a)

| | | |
|---|---|---|
| Sources of working capital (net income) | $60,000 | |
|     Retained earnings | | $60,000 |
| **To record net income.*** | | |

(b)

| | | |
|---|---|---|
| Retained earnings | $22,000 | |
|     Uses of working capital (declara- | | |
|       tion of dividends) | | $22,000 |
| **To record declaration of dividends.** | | |

**buildings and equipment** The next nonworking capital balance sheet account for which it is relatively easy to account for the change during the year is "Buildings and equipment." "Buildings and equipment" increased by $75,000. As indicated in other information, new equipment was acquired at a cost of $112,000, and equipment that had an initial cost of $37,000 was retired during the year. These two transactions account for the entire increase of $75,000.

The entry to record the acquisition of equipment can be reconstructed as follows:

(c)

| | | |
|---|---|---|
| Buildings and equipment | $112,000 | |
|     Uses of working capital (pur- | | |
|     chase of buildings and | | |
|     equipment) | | $112,000 |
| **To record the purchase of buildings and equipment.** | | |

The equipment was sold at a price of $10,000. At the time of sale it had a book value of only $4,000 (initial cost of $37,000 less accumulated depreciation of $33,000). The company realized a gain of $6,000 on the sale. The amount for which the equipment was sold is, of course, a source of funds. In-

---

*Unfortunately, this very first entry represents a minor exception to the general policies to be followed in reconstructing the original entries. Originally, as revenue was earned, a working capital account was debited and a revenue account was credited. As expenses were incurred, a working capital account was credited and an expense account was debited. At year end, the revenues and expenses were closed to retained earnings. In the entry given the credit to retained earnings represents, therefore, the net amount closed to retained earnings—the difference between revenues and expenses.

sofar as the $10,000 is reported as a source of funds, the gain on sale must be subtracted from income if double counting is to be avoided. Thus, in the following reconstructed entry, the gain is recorded as a reduction of (credit to) sources of working capital:

**(d)**

| | | |
|---|---|---|
| Sources of working capital (selling price of the equipment) | $10,000 | |
| Accumulated depreciation | 33,000 | |
| Buildings and equipment | | $37,000 |
| Sources of working capital (adjustment to income owing to gain on sale of equipment) *reductn* | | 6,000 |

**To record the sale of equipment.**

**accumulated depreciation**

Accumulated depreciation, per the comparative balance sheets, increased by $18,000. The balance in the account was reduced by $33,000 as the result of the sale of equipment (see entry **d**). Depreciation charges for the year, per the income statement, were $51,000. The difference between the two amounts is equal to the net $18,000 change to be accounted for.

Depreciation charges are a nonfund expense; they must be added back to income if income is to be considered a source of working capital. Thus,

**(e)**

| | | |
|---|---|---|
| Sources of working capital (adjustment to income owing to depreciation charges, a nonfund expense) | $51,000 | |
| Accumulated depreciation | | $51,000 |

**To record depreciation.**

**investment in subsidiary; capital accounts**

Taconic Corp. acquired its investment in the subsidiary, $6,000, in exchange for 1,000 shares of $1 par value common stock (per the comparative balance sheets and other information). As a consequence of the transaction, the balance in the common stock account must have increased by $1,000 and that in the contributed capital in excess of par account by $5,000. In fact, the increases of $1,000 and $5,000, respectively, account for the entire changes in the two accounts during the year.

The acquisition of the interest in the subsidiary in exchange for common stock neither increased nor decreased the working capital of the company. Nevertheless, the issue of common stock in exchange for noncurrent assets is included in that category of transactions that are considered sufficiently significant that they should be reported in the statement of changes in financial position *as if* they resulted in offsetting sources and uses of funds. Thus,

**(f)**

| | | |
|---|---|---|
| Sources of working capital (issuance of common stock) | $6,000 | |
| Common stock | | $1,000 |
| Capital contributed in excess of par | | 5,000 |

**To record the issue of 1,000 shares of stock.**

**(g)**

| | | |
|---|---|---|
| Investment in subsidiary | $6,000 | |
| Uses of working capital (acquisition of subsidiary) | | $6,000 |

**To record the acquisition of the subsidiary.**

**deferred income taxes**   Income taxes deferred until future years increased by $7,000 (per the comparative balance sheets). Increases in deferred taxes can almost always be attributable to the difference between income tax expense as reported on the income statement and income taxes which are legally due and currently payable. Of the $30,000 in reported taxes, only $23,000 was actually paid. Hence only $23,000 served to reduce working capital. The remaining $7,000 did not require an outlay of funds; along with other expenses that did not require an outlay of funds, it must be added back to reported income.

**(h)**

| | | |
|---|---|---|
| Sources of working capital (adjustment to income owing to taxes that were deferred and thereby did not require an outlay of working capital) | $7,000 | |
| Income taxes deferred until future years | | $7,000 |

**To record deferred portion of tax expense.**

(There is no need to record the portion of the tax expense that is not deferred inasmuch as it was included in the determination of reported earnings and does not require adjustment.)

**bond premium**   The only nonworking capital accounts remaining to be analyzed are bonds and the related premium. The entries to both accounts can be reconstructed in a manner similar to that of buildings and equipment.

As revealed in the supplementary information, actual interest paid was

$14,000. Reported interest was only $11,000. The difference can be attributable to the amortization of the bond premium. Upon the payment of interest, the following entry must have been made:

| | | |
|---|---|---|
| Interest expense | $11,000 | |
| Premium on bonds payable | 3,000 | |
| Cash | | $14,000 |

**To record the payment of interest.**

The reported interest expense understates the actual interest payment by $3,000. The following entry reconstructs the portion of the entry pertaining to the premium. It gives recognition to the fact that operations actually provided $3,000 less in the way of working capital than would be apparent from reported net income. Included among expenses in the determination of net income was $11,000 in interest expense; in fact $14,000 was paid.

**(i)**

| | | |
|---|---|---|
| Premium on bonds payable | $3,000 | |
| Sources of working capital (adjustment to income owing to amortization of bond premium, a credit that was not associated with an inflow of working capital | | $3,000 |

**To record amortization of bond premium.**

Per the comparative balance sheets, bond premium decreased by only $1,000. Entry **i** accounted for a $3,000 decrease. A $2,000 increase remains, therefore, to be explained.

**bonds payable**    Bonds payable increased during the year by $121,000. As indicated in the supplementary information, bonds with a face value of $121,000 were issued at a premium of $2,000. The issuance of the bonds served to increase working capital, therefore, by $123,000.

**(j)**

| | | |
|---|---|---|
| Sources of working capital (issuance of bonds) | $123,000 | |
| Bonds payable | | $121,000 |
| Premium on bonds payable | | 2,000 |

**To record the issuance of bonds.**

This entry explains not only the change in the bonds payable account but also the remaining unexplained balance of $2,000 in the premium account.

EXHIBIT 14-4

**Taconic Corp.**
**Worksheet for Preparation of Statement of**
**Changes in Financial Position**
**(working capital basis)**

| | Beginning Balance (12/31/79) Debit (credit) | Reconstructed Journal Entries Debits | Reconstructed Journal Entries Credits | Ending Balance (12/31/80) Debit (credit) |
|---|---|---|---|---|
| Working Capital | $166,000 | $108,000 | | $274,000 |
| *Noncurrent assets* | | | | |
| Buildings and equipment | 328,000 | (c) 112,000 | (d) $37,000 | 403,000 |
| Accumulated depreciation | (72,000) | (d) 33,000 | (e) 51,000 | (90,000) |
| Land | 40,000 | | | 40,000 |
| Investment in subsidiary | | (g) 6,000 | | 6,000 |
| Miscellaneous assets | 27,000 | | | 27,000 |
| Total assets | $489,000 | | | $660,000 |
| *Noncurrent liabilities and owners' equity* | | | | |
| Income taxes deferred until future years | $ (62,000) | | (h) 7,000 | $ (69,000) |
| Bonds payable | (250,000) | | (j) 121,000 | (371,000) |
| Premium on bonds payable | (11,000) | (j) 3,000 | (f) 2,000 | (10,000) |
| Common stock ($1 par value) | (12,000) | | (f) 1,000 | (13,000) |
| Contributed capital in excess of par | (122,000) | | (f) 5,000 | (127,000) |
| Retained earnings | (32,000) | (b) 22,000 | (a) 60,000 | (70,000) |
| Total noncurrent liabilities and owners' equity | $(489,000) | | | $(660,000) |

*Sources of working capital*

| | | | |
|---|---|---|---|
| Income | (a) | | 60,000 |
| Adjustments to income: | | | |
| Depreciation | (e) | | 51,000 — *off by year* |
| Gain on sale of buildings and equipment | (d) | 6,000 — *decrease* | |
| Deferred income taxes | (h) | | 7,000 |
| Amortization of bond premium | (i) | 3,000 — *decrease* | |
| Sale of equipment | (d) | | 10,000 |
| Issuance of common stock | (f) | | 6,000 |
| Issuance of bonds | (j) | | 123,000 |

*Uses of working capital*

| | | | |
|---|---|---|---|
| Declaration of dividends | (b) | 22,000 | |
| Purchase of buildings and equipment | (c) | 112,000 | |
| Acquisition of subsidiary | (g) | 6,000 | |
| Net increase in working capital (per first line) | | | 108,000 |
| | | | $541,000 |

$541,000

When all the entries have been posted to the worksheet (Exhibit 14–4), the changes in all of the nonworking capital accounts will have been accounted for, and the $108,000 increase in working capital will have been explained.

Exhibit 14–5 summarizes the various sources and uses of working capital.

*EXHIBIT 14-5*

**Taconic Corp.**
**Statement of Changes in Financial Position**
**Year Ended December 31, 1980**

| | | | |
|---|---:|---:|---:|
| *Sources of working capital* | | | |
| Net earnings | | $ 60,000 | |
| Adjustments to net earnings | | | |
| Add: Depreciation | $51,000 | | |
| Income taxes deferred | | | |
| until future years | 7,000 | $ 58,000 | |
| Deduct: Gain on sale | | | |
| of equipment | $ 6,000 | | |
| Amortization of premium | | | |
| on bonds payable | 3,000 | (9,000) | $109,000 |
| Sale of buildings and equipment | | 10,000 | |
| Issue of bonds | | 123,000 | |
| Issue of common stock (see note A) | | 6,000 | 139,000 |
| Total sources of working capital | | | $248,000 |
| *Uses of working capital* | | | |
| Dividends declared | | | $ 22,000 |
| Purchase of buildings and equipment | | | 112,000 |
| Acquisition of interest in subsidiary (see note A) | | | 6,000 |
| Total uses of working capital | | | $140,000 |
| Net increase in working capital (see Exhibit 14–3) | | | $108,000 |

*Note A:* 1,000 shares of common stock (par value $1) were issued in exchange for an interest in a subsidiary. At the time of acquisition the fair market value of such interest was $6,000.

## Statement of Changes in Financial Position on a Cash Flow Basis

Accounting Principles Board Opinion No. 19, which requires that a statement of changes in financial position be included in a firm's annual report along with the income statement and the balance sheet, allows a company to prepare the statement on a cash rather than a working capital basis. A statement which indicates the sources and uses of cash may be of more utility to some investors than one dealing with working capital in that it provides direct information on the one resource, cash, that is likely to be of greatest interest. As pointed out previously, however, a statement which focuses on cash may, ironically, be of less value in predicting future flows of cash than one which focuses on working capital. Some of the elements of working capital other than cash may be interchangeable with cash and can readily either be exchanged for cash at the discretion of management or will be converted into cash in the ordinary course of business operations within a short period of time.

The statement of changes in financial position on the basis of working capital is grounded on the fact that a net change in working capital can be explained by changes in all nonworking capital accounts. Similarly, the statement of changes in financial position on the basis of cash finds its roots in a comparable relationship. Changes in cash must be associated with changes in noncash accounts. The basic accounting equation indicates

$$\text{Cash} + \text{All other Assets} = \text{Liabilities} + \text{Owners' equity}$$

Therefore,

$$\text{Cash} = \text{Liabilities} + \text{Owners' equity} - \text{All other assets}$$

An increase in cash can be associated with an increase in a liability or equity account or a decrease in any other asset account. And a decrease in cash can be associated with a corresponding decrease in a liability or equity account or an increase in any other asset account.

The statement of changes in financial position based on cash is, therefore, not very different from that based on working capital. Indeed, the statement of changes in cash will ordinarily report all financial events that would be reported in the statement of changes in working capital. The major distinction between the two results from the fact that increases or decreases in cash may be attributable to increases or decreases in the other elements of working capital as well as in noncurrent assets, noncurrent liabilities, and owners' equity.

Cash, like working capital, is derived primarily from operations. But if net income is to be reported as a source of cash, several adjustments must be made—all of the adjustments that have to be made when the statement is prepared on the basis of working capital, plus a few others. The additional adjustments arise because revenues and expenses are conventionally reported on the accrual rather than on the cash basis of accounting. Whereas a sale generally results in a corresponding increase in working capital (i.e., accounts receivable), it does not necessarily result in an increase in cash. Similarly, the cost of goods sold can usually be associated with a decrease in working capital (i.e., inventory) but not necessarily in cash.

Perhaps a simple example can highlight the distinctions between the statement of changes in financial position on a cash basis and on a working capital basis.

*example*    The following information was taken from the books and records of a firm after its first year of operations.

| | |
|---|---:|
| Sales | $100,000 |
| Cost of goods sold | 65,000 |
| Net income | 35,000 |
| Cash collections | 95,000 |
| Total goods purchased | 80,000 |
| Total goods for which payment was made | 30,000 |

At year end its balance sheet showed

| | | | |
|---|---:|---|---:|
| Cash | $65,000 | Accounts payable | $50,000 |
| Accounts receivable | 5,000 | Owners' equity (re- | |
| Inventory | 15,000 | tained earnings) | 35,000 |
| Total assets | $85,000 | Total equities | $85,000 |

Working capital increased by $35,000 (assets, all current, of $85,000 less accounts payable of $50,000). The statement of changes in financial position based on working capital would attribute the entire increase to a single source, net income.

By contrast, cash increased by $65,000. The statement of changes in financial position on a cash basis would appear as follows:

| | |
|---|---:|
| *Sources of cash* | |
| Net income | $35,000 |
| Increase in accounts payable | 50,000 |
| Total sources of cash | $85,000 |
| *Uses of cash* | |
| Increase in accounts receivable | $ 5,000 |
| Increase in inventory | 15,000 |
| Total uses of cash | $20,000 |
| Net increase in cash | $65,000 |

The statement of changes in financial position on the cash basis, unlike that on the working capital basis, makes clear that

1. not all sales resulted in collections of cash. This is indicated by the $5,000 increase in accounts receivable.
2. not all the cost of the goods sold required the disbursement of cash. As revealed by the $15,000 increase in inventory, the firm acquired more goods than it sold, but, as shown by the $50,000 increase in accounts payable, it paid for only a portion of the acquired inventory.

### Summary

Investors, managers, and other users of financial statements have a vital interest in the uses to which a firm puts its cash and in the manner in which it is derived. In the short run, cash is what is needed by an enterprise to meet its day-to-day expenses and to satisfy its obligations as they come due. In the long run, investors, who likely acquired for cash an interest in the enterprise, expect to receive cash returns that exceed the amount of their initial sacrifice.

The statements of income and position fail to reveal directly the sources of a firm's cash and the uses to which it was applied. Both statements are prepared on the accrual basis of accounting. As a consequence, they provide little information on those transactions that involve exchanges among assets, liabilities, and equities but which do not affect the overall level of resources on hand.

The statement of changes in financial position is intended to supplement the income statement and the balance sheet by focusing directly upon changes in funds. Most commonly, the statement of changes in financial position indicates sources and uses of working capital rather than cash. Changes in working capital are likely to provide a better means of assessing future cash flows since working capital can readily be converted into cash.

The statement of changes in financial position is commonly prepared by accounting for all changes in nonworking capital accounts. Income (a change in retained earnings) is a primary source of funds. But reported income may include numerous nonfund revenues and expenses. Reported earnings, if they are to be considered sources of funds, must be adjusted for the nonfund elements such as depreciation and gain on disposal of fixed assets.

The statement of changes in financial position may be prepared on a cash as well as on a working capital basis. The underlying procedures are the same, but a few additional adjustments are required to take into account increases or decreases in cash attributable to changes in the other components of working capital.

A firm's condensed balance sheets for the years ending December 31, 1982 and 1981 and statement of income for 1982 indicated the following:

|  | 1982 | 1981 |
|---|---|---|
| *Balance Sheet* | | |
| Working capital | $189,000 | $140,000 |
| Fixed assets | 245,000 | 250,000 |
| Accumulated depreciation | ( 36,000) | ( 30,000) |
| Total assets | $398,000 | $360,000 |
| Deferred income taxes | $ 11,000 | $ 4,000 |
| Bonds payable | 200,000 | 200,000 |
| Discount on bonds payable | ( 4,000) | ( 5,000) |
| Contributed capital | 15,000 | 15,000 |
| Retained earnings | 176,000 | 146,000 |
| Total equities | $398,000 | $360,000 |

*Statement of Income*

| | | |
|---|---|---|
| Sales revenue | $274,000 | |
| Gain on sale of fixed assets | 2,000 | $276,000 |
| Cost of goods sold | $200,000 | |
| Depreciation | 10,000 | |
| Interest | 17,000 | |
| Taxes | 19,000 | 246,000 |
| Net income | | $ 30,000 |

a. By how much did working capital change during 1982? What must be the net change in the combined balances of all nonworking capital accounts?

b. Suppose that net income is to be considered a source of working capital. In which nonworking capital account is income of $30,000 reflected?

c. Did net income really provide exactly $30,000 in working capital? How much working capital was required by depreciation expense? If depreciation did not affect working capital, then which nonworking capital account did it affect?

d. The accounts reveal that the firm actually paid $12,000 in taxes. Hence working capital was reduced by only $12,000, rather than by $19,000 as suggested by reported tax expense. In which balance sheet account is the difference of $7,000 reflected?

e. The accounts also indicate that the firm sold for $3,000 equipment that had originally cost $5,000. The firm had already charged $4,000 of depreciation on the equipment; its book value was only $1,000.

    (1) If the sale of equipment is to be reported as a source of $3,000 in working capital, can the $2,000 gain on sale of fixed assets be properly included

in the determination of income, inasmuch as income is also to be reported as a source of working capital?

(2) In what two nonworking capital balance sheet accounts is the sale of fixed assets reflected?

f. The firm reported interest expense on bonds payable of $17,000. How much interest did the firm actually pay? In what account is the difference reflected? What journal entry did it most likely make upon paying the interest?

g. Have all the changes in nonworking capital accounts been fully accounted for? (Note that the accumulated depreciation account is affected by both the depreciation charges and the sale of equipment.)

h. Prepare a schedule in which you summarize the adjustments that must be made to income if it is to be considered a source of working capital. Your schedule must include all other sources of working capital as well. Does the sum of all sources of working capital equal the increase in working capital as determined in question a? Has any working capital been used during the year?

## Questions

**review and
discussion**

1. A statement of changes in financial position, especially one based on the cash concept of funds, is sometimes said to be more "objective" than an income statement. Do you agree? Why?

2. Why are changes in the working capital balance of a firm, as well as reasons for such changes, of vital concern to investors, creditors, and other users of financial statements?

3. In a recent collective bargaining session, management argued that even though reported earnings were at record highs, the company was nevertheless unable to afford even a small increase in wages. In another session involving different companies and unions, the union asserted that even though the company incurred a severe loss, the company could well afford to grant a substantial wage increase. What do you think the two positions have in common? What argument with respect to reported earnings is likely to be made in both sets of negotiations?

4. A magazine article contained the following comment with respect to a major U.S. corporation: "For the first time, the company's cash flow exceeded its income. The firm was basking in riches as depreciation write-offs poured a golden stream of cash into its treasury." In what way is such a statement misleading?

5. Why do most firms elect to define funds in terms of working capital rather than cash?

6. Why must reported earnings be adjusted before they can properly be included as a source of funds?

7. Why are some types of transactions (e.g., an exchange of bonds for preferred stock) reported as sources and uses of funds even though they resulted in neither an increase nor a decrease in working capital? Provide examples of such transactions.

8. "The statement of changes in financial position is superfluous. A sophisticated analyst can derive from comparative balance sheets and the income statement all the information contained in the statement." Do you agree? Explain.

9. In what way does the statement of changes in financial position based on a cash concept of funds differ from that based on a working capital concept? In preparing the statement based on the cash concept, what additional accounts must be analyzed?

10. The president of Presidential Realty Corporation, a firm whose shares are traded on the American Stock Exchange, made the following comment in his letter to stockholders: "In our opinion, however, conventionally computed 'operating income' has never adequately measured the performance of real estate development and investment companies such as ours. We believe that the best measure of our performance is the 'Sum' of the operating income, the non-cash charges against such income (consisting of rental property depreciation, write-off of mortgage origination costs, and deferred federal income taxes), and the funds generated from net gains from capital transactions. It is this 'Sum' that is available for all corporate purposes, such as payment of mortgage debt, reinvestment in property replacements and new properties or enterprises, and distributions to shareholders."

The president of the company is, in essence, advocating a cash basis of reporting. Why, in light of his comments, has the accounting profession insisted that financial statements be prepared on the accrual basis and that noncash as well as cash charges be deducted from revenues in determining income? Do you believe that a better measure of performance is obtained if noncash expenses are added back to income? Can you think of any special characteristics of the real estate industry that may have influenced the position of the president?

## Problems

1. *Seemingly similar types of transactions may have very different effects on working capital.*

Indicate the impact each of the following transactions would have on the working capital position of a company. Specify whether it would increase (I), decrease (D), or have no effect (NE) on working capital.

1. Declaration of a $150,000 stock dividend.
2. Declaration of a $150,000 cash dividend.
3. Purchase of marketable securities for $12,000 cash.
4. Sale, for $15,000 cash, of marketable securities that had initially cost $12,000.
5. Declaration of $8,000 in dividends by a firm in which the company has a 5 percent interest.
6. Declaration of $8,000 in dividends by a firm in which the company has a 40 percent interest.
7. Write-off of an uncollectible account of $3,000 against the allowance provided.

8. Acquisition of another company in exchange for $1 million in long-term notes.
9. Acquisition, for $4,500 cash, of treasury stock.
10. Sale for $600 of merchandise that had cost $400.

2. *Transactions that affect working capital may not affect cash; those that affect cash may not affect working capital.*

The following describes several transactions in which the Ramara Corp. engaged in 1981.

1. Sold merchandise, on account, for $6,000. Cost of the goods sold was $5,000.
2. Collected $3,200 of the amount owed by customers.
3. Purchased additional inventory for $1,700 (on account).
4. Paid $1,500 of the amount owed to suppliers.
5. Purchased marketable securities for $700 cash.
6. Sold the marketable securities for $500 cash.
7. Recorded one month's interest on notes payable, $50.
8. Paid one month's interest on the notes payable, $50.
9. Recorded one month's rent due from tenant, $200.
10. Received payment of one month's rent from tenant.

    a. Indicate whether the transactions would increase (I), decrease (D), or have no effect (NE) on the working capital of the corporation.
    b. Indicate whether the transactions would increase (I), decrease (D), or have no effect (NE) on the cash balance of the corporation.

3. *"Missing" information on sources and uses of funds may be deduced by analyzing the changes in nonworking capital accounts.*

The following account balances appeared on the financial statements of the Rackham Corp.:

|  | 1981 | 1980 |
|---|---|---|
| Buildings and equipment | $475,000 | $400,000 |
| Accumulated depreciation | 125,000 | 100,000 |
| Depreciation | 40,000 | 35,000 |
| Gain on sale of equipment | 12,000 | 57,000 |

During 1981 the Rackham Corp. purchased $134,000 in new equipment.
a. Compute the increase in funds attributable to the *sale* of equipment in 1981. (*Hint:* Analyze the changes in the buildings and equipment and related accumulated depreciation accounts, giving consideration to the types of events that cause their balances to increase or decrease.)
b. Indicate any adjustments to 1981 income that would be required if income were to be considered a source of funds.

4. *Careful analysis of owners' equity accounts can provide information on sources and uses of funds.*

The owners' equity section of the Driscoe Corp. balance sheet as of December 31, 1980 and 1981 contained the following balances:

|                                        | *1981*    | *1980*    |
|----------------------------------------|-----------|-----------|
| Common stock (par value $10)           | $105,000  | $100,000  |
| Contributed capital in excess of par   | 43,000    | 40,000    |
| Retained earnings                      | 256,000   | 244,000   |

At the start of 1981 the company declared a cash dividend of $.50 per share and a stock dividend of $.20 per share. Reported earnings of the firm included a loss of $20,000 attributable to a fire at a company plant, depreciation of $10,000, and a gain of $2,000 on the retirement of outstanding bonds.

Based on the above information, determine, as best you can, the increase in working capital associated with changes in the owners' equity accounts. (*Hint:* Determine first the reduction in retained earnings owing to the declaration of the cash dividend and the stock dividend. Be sure to base your computations on the number of shares outstanding at the start of the year. Then, by analyzing the retained earnings account, determine 1981 earnings and adjust for any nonfund revenues or expendiures. Consider the possibility that new shares of stock were issued during the year.)

5. *Reported changes in flow of funds as well as reported earnings can be "manipulated" by actions of management.*

The president of the Trans-Dakota Airways is considering several means of improving financial performance in 1980.

a. Indicate the likely impact of each of the following suggestions on 1980 (1) reported earnings, (2) flow of funds (defined as working capital) and (3) flow of cash. Ignore any income tax implications.

  1. Change from the LIFO to the FIFO method of accounting for inventories. (The prices of the goods purchased by the company have been consistently increasing.)
  2. Recognize revenue from the sale of tickets at the time a ticket is sold rather than at the time a passenger completes his flight. In 1980 the number of tickets sold exceeded the number of flights taken.
  3. Delay payments to certain suppliers until 1981.
  4. Delay until 1981 required payments to the firm's pension fund.
  5. Amortize (for reporting purposes) prior period service costs relating to pensions over a period of 20 years rather than 10 years, as is done currently.

b. Another suggestion was to depreciate the company's fleet of 727 jets over a period of 15 years—the number of years over which a competitor depreciates similar planes—rather than 10 years, as is currently done. The initial cost of the planes was $30 million. What would be the impact of the change on reported earnings and flow of working capital? Assume that the company pays income taxes at a rate of 40 percent and that the change would have to be made for tax as well as reporting purposes.

c. It is sometimes asserted that the statement of changes in financial position provides a more "objective" measure of financial performance than does the statement of income. Do you agree? Does it make a difference whether the statement of changes in financial position is based on working capital as opposed to cash? Comment.

6. *In the long run patterns of earnings are likely to correspond to those of changes in working capital.*

David Wise established the Polarus Electronic Corp. in January 1976. The corporation issued $1.2 million in stock to Wise and several of his friends and relatives. During its first three years of operation the company was remarkably successful. Sales as well as earnings increased substantially each year. Condensed income statements for the first three years appear as follows:

|  | 1976 | 1977 | 1978 |
|---|---|---|---|
| Sales | $700,000 | $1,400,000 | $2,100,000 |
| Cost of goods sold and other expenses | 550,000 | 1,100,000 | 1,650,000 |
| Net income | $150,000 | $ 300,000 | $ 450,000 |

The company expanded its physical facilities during the period. According to the president, approximately $1 in fixed assets was necessary to generate $1 in sales. Comparative balance sheets in condensed form, as of December 31, for the three-year period appear as indicated:

|  | 1976 | 1977 | 1978 |
|---|---|---|---|
| Working capital | $ 650,000 | $ 250,000 | $ -0- |
| Fixed assets | 700,000 | 1,400,000 | 2,100,000 |
| Total assets | $1,350,000 | $1,650,000 | $2,100,000 |
| Common stock | $1,200,000 | $1,200,000 | $1,200,000 |
| Retained earnings | 150,000 | 450,000 | 900,000 |
| Total equities | $1,350,000 | $1,650,000 | $2,100,000 |

The financial trends of the first three years of operations continued into 1979. Yet at the end of 1979 the firm was forced to declare bankruptcy because it was unable to meet its current obligations as they came due.

a. How would you explain the bankruptcy of such an apparently successful company? Prepare a *pro forma* ("as if") income statement and balance sheet for 1979. In preparing the balance sheet, first project retained earnings, common stock, and fixed assets, then determine working capital.

b. Suppose that the company were able, at the end of 1979, to obtain a one-year loan in the amount of any working capital deficiency. Assuming that the expansionary trend were to continue, do you think that such a loan would have "saved" the company? Explain.

7. *For some decisions information on changes in working capital may be more relevant than that on income.*

The Badlands Mining Co. was organized to remove ore from a specific tract of land over a period of five years. In its second year of operations the company incurred a loss of $200,000, determined as follows:

| | | |
|---|---:|---:|
| Sales of ore | | $2,000,000 |
| Less: Depletion of ore | $1,000,000 | |
| Depreciation on equipment | 200,000 | |
| Wages and salaries | 400,000 | |
| Other operating costs | 600,000 | 2,200,000 |
| Net Loss | | $ 200,000 |

In spite of the loss the president of the company recommended to the board of directors that it declare a dividend of $300,000. One member of the board declared the recommendation to be nonsense. "How can we justify declaring a dividend in a year when we 'took a financial beating?' "

a. How, in fact, might the board justify the declaration of a dividend?

b. Why would a statement of changes in financial position provide a better indication of the ability of the company to declare dividends than would a statement of income?

c. Suppose that the company had to acquire during the year $400,000 of equipment. Prepare a schedule which would support the position of the president that the company could "afford" to declare a dividend despite the required outlay for the equipment.

8. *In some industries changes in fund balances may provide a better measure of corporate performance than income.*

In January 1980 Real Estate Investors Corp. purchased an apartment building for $100,000. The company paid $10,000 in cash and gave a 10-year note for the balance. The company was required to pay only interest on the note for the first 5 years. In year 6 through 10 it was required to make principal payments of $18,000 per year.

In 1981 (the second year after the purchase of the property) the income statement of the company appeared as follows:

| | | |
|---|---:|---:|
| Revenues from rents | | $20,000 |
| Less: Depreciation | $9,000 | |
| Interest | 5,400 | |
| Other expenses | 6,000 | 20,400 |
| Net loss | | $ 400 |

Depreciation was based on the double-declining balance method with an estimated useful life of 20 years.

a. Determine net cash inflow during 1981.

b. Compute return on investment on a cash basis (cash inflow divided by company investment in the apartment building).

c. Comment on why some real estate experts believe that the statement of changes in financial position provides a better indication of corporate performance in the real estate industry than does the statement of income. Consider the fact that many properties are sold long before the end of their useful (depreciable) lives.

9. *After only one year of a firm's operations it is relatively easy to identify the sources of working capital and the uses to which it was put.*

The Earl Company began operations in 1980. Its income statement and balance sheet for its first year of operations are as follows:

**Earl Company**
**Statement of Income**
**Year Ended December 31, 1980**

| | | |
|---|---:|---:|
| Sales | | $ 94,000 |
| Less: Cost of goods sold | $48,000 | |
| Depreciation | 3,000 | |
| Amortization of organization costs | 2,000 | |
| Taxes | 7,000 | |
| Interest | 1,000 | |
| Other expenses | 20,000 | 81,000 |
| Net income | | $ 13,000 |

**Balance Sheet**
**as of December 31, 1980**

| | | |
|---|---:|---:|
| Assets | | |
| Current assets | | $ 37,000 |
| Plant and equipment | $53,000 | |
| Less: Accumulated depreciation | 3,000 | 50,000 |
| Land | | 20,000 |
| Organization costs | | 8,000 |
| Total assets | | $115,000 |
| Equities | | |
| Current liabilities | | $ 19,000 |
| Income taxes deferred until future years | | 2,000 |
| Note payable | $40,000 | |
| Less: Discount | 6,000 | 34,000 |
| Common stock | | 50,000 |
| Retained earnings | | 10,000 |
| Total liabilities and stockholders' equity | | $115,000 |

*Note:* The reported interest expense of $1,000 represents, in its entirety, amortization of discount on note payable.

Reconstruct, as necessary, the transactions of the year and prepare a statement of changes in financial position. (*Hint:* Try to account for the change in each nonworking capital account. Make assumptions that are consistent with the information presented and with standard accounting practice. For example, inasmuch as income was $13,000, but the ending balance in

"Retained earnings" is only $10,000, it may be assumed that dividends of $3,000 were declared.)

10. *It is possible to derive a statement of changes in financial position entirely from comparative balance sheets and a statement of income.*

    Comparative income statements and balance sheets of the Hassel Corp. are as follows:

**Hassel Corp.**
**Statement of Income**
**Years Ending December 31**

|  | 1981 | 1980 |
|---|---|---|
| Sales | $160,000 | $146,000 |
| Gain on sale of land sold | 8,000 | |
|  | $168,000 | $146,000 |
| Less: Cost of goods sold | $118,000 | $ 95,000 |
| Other expenses | 20,000 | 10,000 |
| Income taxes | 8,000 | 11,000 |
|  | $146,000 | $116,000 |
| Net income | $ 22,000 | $ 30,000 |

*Note:* Included in cost of goods sold is depreciation expense of $10,000 in 1981 and $9,000 in 1980.

**Balance Sheet**
**as of December 31**

|  | 1981 | 1980 |
|---|---|---|
| Assets | | |
| Current assets | $ 60,000 | $ 47,000 |
| Equipment | $150,000 | $120,000 |
| Less: Accumulated depreciation | (40,000) | (30,000) |
|  | $110,000 | $ 90,000 |
| Land | 35,000 | 50,000 |
| Total assets | $205,000 | $187,000 |
| Equities | | |
| Current liabilities | $ 20,000 | $ 31,000 |
| Income taxes deferred until future years | 9,000 | 7,000 |
| Notes payable | 30,000 | 25,000 |
| Common stock | 100,000 | 100,000 |
| Retained earnings | 46,000 | 24,000 |
| Total liabilities and owners' equity | $205,000 | $187,000 |

a. Determine the net change in working capital.
b. Analyze each of the nonworking capital accounts. Determine the most likely reason for the change in each of the accounts and reconstruct the journal entries that affected each account. Identify the entries associated with sources or uses of working capital. Be especially cautious about the change in working capital associated with the reduction in the land account.
c. Prepare a statement of changes in financial position.

11. *Use of a worksheet facilitates preparation of the statement of changes in financial position.*

The table following gives the balance sheets of the Inman Corp. as of June 30, 1982 and 1981, and the income statement for 1982:

**Inman Corp.**
**Balance Sheet**
**as of June 30, 1982 and 1981**

|  | 1982 | 1981 |
|---|---|---|
| Assets | | |
| Current | | |
| Cash | $  46,000 | $  13,000 |
| Accounts receivable | 65,000 | 12,000 |
| Inventories | 66,000 | 54,000 |
| Total current assets | $  177,000 | $  79,000 |
| Noncurrent | | |
| Property, plant, and equipment | $  925,000 | $1,090,000 |
| Less: Accumulated depreciation | 228,000 | 298,000 |
| | $  697,000 | $  792,000 |
| Investment in subsidiary | 230,000 | 219,000 |
| Other assets | 120,000 | 140,000 |
| Total noncurrent assets | $1,047,000 | $1,151,000 |
| Total assets | $1,224,000 | $1,230,000 |
| Liabilities and shareholders' investment | | |
| Current | | |
| Accounts payable | $  40,000 | $  35,000 |
| Other payables | 145,000 | 15,000 |
| Total current liabilities | $  185,000 | $  50,000 |
| Noncurrent | | |
| Notes payable | 74,000 | 280,000 |
| Shareholders' investment | | |
| Common stock ($2 par value) | $  20,000 | $  20,000 |
| Contributed capital in excess of par | 80,000 | 80,000 |
| Retained earnings | 865,000 | 800,000 |
| Total shareholders' investment | $  965,000 | $  900,000 |
| Total liabilities and shareholders' investment | $1,224,000 | $1,230,000 |

## Statement of Income
### Year Ending June 30, 1982

| | | |
|---|---:|---:|
| Sales | $555,000 | |
| Proportionate share of subsidiary earnings | 26,000 | $581,000 |
| Less: Cost of goods sold | 326,000 | |
| Interest | 20,000 | |
| Taxes | 30,000 | |
| Other expenses | 140,000 | 516,000 |
| Net income | | $ 65,000 |

*Other information:*
1. Included in cost of goods sold and other expenses is a total of $90,000 in depreciation.
2. The company incurred an uninsured loss at its plant. Equipment that had a book value of $80,000 (original cost $240,000, accumulated depreciation $160,000) was destroyed. The loss is included among "other expenses." No other "Property, plant and equipment" was sold or retired. The remaining change in the account balance can be attributed to the purchase of new equipment.
3. Other assets include patents of $40,000 in 1982 and $60,000 in 1981. Amortization expense of $20,000 is included in other expenses.
4. The company owns a 30 percent interest in another company. It accounts for its investment by the equity method. The subsidiary paid dividends of $15,000 to Inman Corp. during 1982.
5. The entire decrease in the balance of "Notes payable" is the result of repayment of the liability.

Prepare, on a working capital basis, a statement of changes in financial position. You will probably find it useful to reconstruct the journal entries that affected the nonworking capital accounts and to post them to a worksheet.

12. *The nature of "real world" sources and uses of funds may not always be obvious; conclusions regarding the significance of net changes in working capital must be drawn with care.*

Examine the statement of changes in financial position of Pan American World Airways, Inc., which is included in Exhibit 14–1.
   a. In 1976, a year in which the firm incurred a loss, working capital increased. In 1977, a year in which the firm had a profit, working capital decreased. What are the primary reasons for this apparent contradiction? Is the "deterioration" in working capital in 1977 an indication of financial weakness?
   b. Consider three sources and uses of working capital associated with lease obligations: "Increase in long-term obligations under capital leases"; "Obligations under capital leases becoming currently payable"; "Capital lease additions."

(1) Explain why each is reported as either a source or a use of working capital.

(2) The December 31, 1976 balance in "Long-term obligations under capital leases" (a noncurrent liability) was $365,024 (000 omitted). The December 31, 1977 balance was $339,169. From the information in the statement of changes in financial position can you reconcile the two amounts?

c. Included among sources of working capital is "Termination of capital leases." This description is not very revealing as to the nature of the transaction that led to the increase in working capital. From what you know about the way in which leased property is recorded as well as the types of events that are associated with increases in working capital, explain, as best you can, why termination of capital leases is reported as a source of working capital.

d. Dividends received from *unconsolidated* subsidiaries is reported as a source of working capital. Why are not dividends received from *consolidated* subsidiaries also reported as a source of working capital?

13. *The financial report of Koppers Company, Inc. highlights some of the differences between an actual statement of changes in financial position and those used for illustration in a textbook.*

Refer to the financial statements of Koppers Company, Inc. in Chapter 2.

a. The firm reported earnings of $66,199 (000 omitted in this and subsequent questions), yet working capital decreased by $28,963. What were the primary factors contributing to this decrease? Are these factors indicative of financial strength or weakness?

b. Reported as a source of funds is "Book value of fixed assets and other noncurrent assets disposed of or sold." In this text, it was indicated that the full amount received from the sale of fixed and other noncurrent assets disposed of or sold—not just book value—should be reported as a source of working capital. If book value, rather than full amount, is to be reported as a source of working capital, in what other related way must the statement of changes in financial position as prepared by Koppers Company differ from that described in the text?

c. Why is "Equity in earnings of affiliated companies, less dividends received" subtracted from net income in determining funds provided by operations?

d. Because of the way in which the sources and uses of working capital have been combined and summarized, it is impossible to reconcile the balances in all nonworking capital accounts with the amounts reported on the income statement and the statement of changes in working capital. With some accounts, however, it is possible.

1. How can you explain the increase of $41,949 in retained earnings between 1976 and 1977?

2. How do you explain the decrease of $5,647 in noncurrent "term" debt?

e. Deferred compensation, a noncurrent liability, increased by $1,051. How is such increase most likely reflected in the statement of changes in financial position?

**14.** *Preparation of a statement of changes in financial position requires the analysis of each nonworking capital account.*

The consolidated balance sheets of the Sorrells Co. as of December 31, 1981 and 1980, are as follows. So also is the income statement for 1981.

**Sorrells Co.**
**Consolidated Balance Sheet**
**as of December 31, 1981 and 1980**

| | 1981 | 1980 |
|---|---|---|
| **Assets** | | |
| Current | | |
| Cash | $    88,000 | $    61,000 |
| Accounts receivable | 250,000 | 211,000 |
| Inventory | 269,000 | 245,000 |
| Total current assets | $  607,000 | $  517,000 |
| | | |
| Other assets | | |
| Plant and equipment | $  950,000 | $  958,000 |
| Less: Accumulated depreciation | 180,000 | 102,000 |
| | $  770,000 | $  856,000 |
| Investment in unconsolidated | | |
| subsidiary | 50,000 | –0– |
| Goodwill | 65,000 | 74,000 |
| Total other assets | $  885,000 | $  930,000 |
| Total assets | $1,492,000 | $1,447,000 |
| | | |
| **Equities** | | |
| Current liabilities | | |
| Accounts payable | $  218,000 | $  179,000 |
| Other current liabilities | 63,000 | 176,000 |
| Total current liabilities | $  281,000 | $  355,000 |
| Other liabilities | | |
| Deferred income taxes | $    24,000 | $    20,000 |
| Bonds payable | 200,000 | 200,000 |
| Less: Unamortized discount | 13,000 | 14,000 |
| | $  187,000 | $  186,000 |
| Total other liabilities | $  211,000 | $  206,000 |
| | | |
| Owners' equity | | |
| Common stock ($1 par value) | $  110,000 | $  100,000 |
| Contributed capital in excess of par | 340,000 | 300,000 |
| Retained earnings | 550,000 | 486,000 |
| Total owners' equity | $1,000,000 | $  886,000 |
| Total liabilities and owners' equity | $1,492,000 | $1,447,000 |

**Sorrells Co.**
**Statement of Income**
**Year Ended December 31, 1981**

| | | |
|---|---:|---:|
| Sales | | $883,000 |
| Less: Expenses | | |
| Cost of goods sold | $596,000 | |
| Depreciation | 87,000 | |
| Amortization of goodwill | 9,000 | |
| Interest | 13,000 | |
| Other expenses | 8,000 | |
| Income taxes | 76,000 | 789,000 |
| Net income | | $ 94,000 |

Using the statements as well as the other information provided below, prepare a statement of changes in financial position. Use the working capital concept of funds. Reconstruct journal entries as required and post them to a worksheet.

*Other information:*

1. The company declared cash dividends of $30,000.
2. "Other expenses" includes a loss of $2,000 on equipment sold. The equipment had cost $17,000 and had a book value at time of sale of $8,000. (You have sufficient information to determine the proceeds from the sale.)
3. The firm also acquired new equipment. (By analyzing the plant and equipment account you should be able to determine the cost of the equipment purchased.)
4. The bonds payable carried a 6 percent coupon rate. They had been sold at a price to yield a 7 percent return. (By examining the accounts related to the bonds payable you should be able to determine any required adjustments to net income.)
5. The company acquired a 15 percent interest in the unconsolidated subsidiary in exchange for 10,000 shares of common stock. There were no other changes in the common stock accounts during the year.
6. The company credits the difference between taxes reported on the income statement and those actually payable within one year to "deferred income taxes."

15. *Preparation of a statement of changes in financial position on a cash basis requires the analysis of* all *accounts other than cash.*

Comparative income statements and balance sheets for the Rushmore Sales Corp. for the years ended December 31, 1981 and 1980, are indicated as follows:

## Rushmore Sales Corp.
### Balance Sheet
### as of December 31, 1981 and 1980

|                                              | 1981      | 1980      |
|----------------------------------------------|-----------|-----------|
| Assets                                       |           |           |
| Cash                                         | $ 40,000  | $ 19,000  |
| Accounts receivable                          | 60,000    | 45,000    |
| Inventories                                  | 20,000    | 28,000    |
| Fixed assets (net of accumulated depreciation) | 107,000   | 112,000   |
| Total assets                                 | $227,000  | $204,000  |
| Equities                                     |           |           |
| Accounts payable                             | $ 89,000  | $ 85,000  |
| Common stock                                 | 100,000   | 100,000   |
| Retained earnings                            | 38,000    | 19,000    |
| Total equities                               | $227,000  | $204,000  |

### Income Statement
### for Years Ending December 31, 1981 and 1980

|                    | 1981      | 1980      |
|--------------------|-----------|-----------|
| Sales              | $100,000  | $ 85,000  |
| Cost of goods sold | $ 70,000  | $ 50,000  |
| Depreciation       | 5,000     | 5,000     |
| Other expenses     | 6,000     | 8,000     |
| Total expenses     | $ 81,000  | $ 63,000  |
| Net income         | $ 19,000  | $ 22,000  |

a. All sales were made on account. By analyzing "Accounts receivable," determine the amount of cash collected in 1981.

b. All "Other expenses" were paid directly in cash. Indicate the amount of cash applied to the payment of "Other expenses."

c. Determine the amount of inventory purchased during 1981. Then, by analyzing "Accounts payable," determine the amount of cash payments made during the year in connection with purchases of inventory in 1981 and in prior years.

d. Indicate any other expenses not requiring an outlay of cash.

e. Prepare two statements of changes in financial position based on the cash concept of funds. In the first, indicate directly all sources and applications of cash (e.g., collections, purchases). In the second, start with net income as a source of cash and indicate any required adjustments (e.g., for changes in inventories, accounts receivable).

a. Working capital increased by $49,000, an amount that must be equal to the net change in the nonworking capital balance sheet accounts.

b. The net income of $30,000 is reflected in an increase of the same amount in retained earnings.

c. Income did not provide $30,000 in working capital; some revenues and expenses involved neither an inflow nor an outflow of working capital. Depreciation did not require the use of working capital. It served to increase accumulated depreciation by $10,000.

d. The $7,000 difference is reflected in the deferred tax account.

e. (1) The $2,000 cannot be included in the determination of income if income is to be considered a source of funds. It must be deducted from income; otherwise it would be counted twice.

   (2) The sale of fixed assets is reflected in "Fixed assets" ($5,000) and its related contra account, "Accumulated depreciation" ($4,000).

f. The firm most likely paid only $16,000, the difference of $1,000 being reflected by the reduction in the bond discount account. It probably recorded interest as follows:

| | | |
|---|---:|---:|
| Interest expense | $17,000 | |
| Cash | | $16,000 |
| Discount on bonds payable | | 1,000 |

**To record interest expense.**

g. All the changes in nonworking capital accounts would now have been accounted for.

| | | |
|---|---:|---:|
| h. Net income | | $30,000 |
| Adjustments to net income | | |
| Depreciation | $10,000 | |
| Income taxes deferred | 7,000 | |
| Amortization of bond discount | 1,000 | |
| Gain on sale of land | ( 2,000) | 16,000 |
| Net income as a source of working capital | | $46,000 |
| Other source: Sale of fixed assets | | $ 3,000 |
| Total sources of working capital | | $49,000 |

The sum of all sources of working capital equals the change in working capital computed in question a. No working capital was used during the year.

# 15

## Financial Statements: The Perspective of the Analyst

In Chapter 1 of this text it was emphasized that if the information provided by the accountant is to be useful, then above all it must be *relevant*—it must bear upon or be associated with the decisions it is designed to facilitate. In this chapter we shall focus upon the decisions made by investors, one group that financial reports are designed to serve. This chapter is intended to shed light on some of the considerations that sophisticated investors take into account in deciding whether to purchase or sell the securities of a corporation and on some of the analytical techniques that they commonly employ. Occasional reference will be made to the special concerns of other groups that rely upon financial reports. It is hoped that the discussion will be sufficiently broad so that the reader will be able to apply, with slight modification perhaps, the analytical techniques described to a wide range of decisions for which the financial prospects of an enterprise must be evaluated.

In large measure, this chapter is designed to serve as a summary of the preceding chapters. In examining financial reports, it is essential that the analyst be cognizant of the accounting principles, estimates, and judgments on which they are based.

Another objective of this chapter is to convey two critical yet seemingly contradictory messages. The first is that financial statements provide an abundance of information about the company whose financial affairs they describe. The financial statements of a company enable an analyst to gain an insight into its economic well-being with a clarity that cannot be matched by any other documents or sources of information. A measure of expertise, however, may be required to discern the true nature of its financial situation. Financial statements may readily be compared to aerial photographs. An untrained observer may not only learn considerably less from an examination of the photographs than a skilled analyst, but the conclusions that he draws from them may be seriously misleading. A layman, for example, may see in a series of aerial photographs nothing more than a pastoral landscape of rolling hills and farms dotted with residential homes and barns. An expert, however, by carefully focusing on changes over time and relationships among the various structures, roadways, and power lines, may detect the presence of underground missile batteries. Similarly, a casual observer may see in a set of financial statements a seemingly stable, financially sound corporation. A skilled analyst, however, by studying trends over time and relationships among accounts, may discern the existence of financial factors that may lead to the company's immediate demise or to a period of unusual prosperity.

The second message is that the importance of financial statements can easily be overemphasized. For any decisions in which the financial prospects of a company must be taken into account, an analysis of the data contained in the financial statements is unquestionably necessary. But it is hardly sufficient.

Financial statements do not explicitly provide information on a number of factors that are likely to have an effect on the future success of a company. Financial statements, for example, do not generally report upon scientific or technological breakthroughs that the company might have made. And they are generally silent about changes in the economic or social environment in which the firm operates. Changes in the real income or in the tastes of the consumers served by the firm could have a major impact on its profitability, but even a detailed examination of financial reports may not provide a hint of such changes.

Expertise in accounting must be accepted with humility. It enables one to prepare and interpret financial statements. But financial statements are only one source of information among many (albeit a critical source) that must be taken into account in deciding whether to invest in a corporation. For every million-aire whose investment success can be attributed to his keen ability to interpret financial statements, there is undoubtedly another who cannot distinguish a debit from a credit.

## Corporate Personality

Corporations, because of the individuals who own and manage them, have personalities. Some are liberal; some conservative. Some are aggressive; some are passive. Some are risk takers; some are risk averters. Financial statements are a window into the nature of a firm. They provide an insight into its character. It is essential that an investor understand the personality of the company whose stocks or bonds he is considering and make certain that such personality is either consistent with or complementary to his own.

**pattern of growth**   The personality of a corporation manifests itself in many ways. Some corporations are basically conservative. Their objective may be to grow slowly over a number of years, each year reporting a consistent upward trend in earnings. Compare, for example, the trend of earnings of General Mills and Kellogg. Both firms are in the food industry, primarily in cereals and grains. Data for both companies for the last ten years are depicted in Exhibit 15-1.

During the period shown the earnings of both firms increased substantially —those of General Mills by 184 percent and those of Kellogg by 206 percent. The growth pattern of Kellogg, however, was somewhat more consistent than that of General Mills. With the exception of two unusually successful years, the earnings of Kellogg increased by moderate amounts each year. The percentage changes in the increases or decreases of the earnings of General Mills were considerably more pronounced. In terms of consistency of earnings, therefore, Kellogg is the more conservative of the two firms.

**means of expansion**    The personality of a corporation may also be evident by its method of expansion. Some firms concentrate on manufacturing and selling a limited range of products. They attempt to increase dollar sales primarily by increasing prices, expanding into new geographical markets, and by increasing penetration into those markets which they currently serve. Other firms may continually introduce new products or may acquire additional companies.

*EXHIBIT 15-1*

**Trend of Net Earnings**

| | General Mills | | Kellogg | |
|---|---|---|---|---|
| $Year^a$ | Earnings per share$^b$ | % Increase over previous year | Earnings per share | % Increase over previous year |
| 1968 | $ .83 | — | $ .59 | — |
| 1969 | .92 | 11% | .62 | 5% |
| 1970 | .63 | (32) | .68 | 10 |
| 1971 | .99 | 57 | .76 | 12 |
| 1972 | 1.02 | 3 | .83 | 9 |
| 1973 | 1.40 | 37 | .89 | 7 |
| 1974 | 1.59 | 14 | .97 | 9 |
| 1975 | 1.59 | 0 | 1.42 | 46 |
| 1976 | 2.04 | 28 | 1.71 | 20 |
| 1977 | 2.36 | 16 | 1.81 | 6 |

[a] General Mills reports on the basis of a fiscal year ending the last week in May.
[b] After extraordinary items; adjusted for two-for-one split in 1975.

Kellogg Company has increased its sales primarily by concentrating on breakfast foods, its traditional line of products. In recent years it has acquired several existing companies in areas throughout the world, but all have been manufacturers of food products. In addition, it has introduced a number of new products, but most are varieties of either cereals or snacks.

General Mills, by contrast, has ventured into industries that are, at best, only peripherally related to its traditional product line of cereals and grains. Its annual report (in descriptive and statistical sections that supplement the basic financial statements) indicates that the company operates restaurants and manufactures and sells toys, costume jewelry, fashion apparel, outdoor recreational clothing and equipment, furniture, and specialty chemicals. Between June 1973 and April 1977 the company acquired controlling interest in 14 significant additional companies.*

Another revealing indicator of corporate character is the manner in which a company finances its expansion and, more specifically, the extent to which it uses funds supplied by parties other than owners. It is generally considered more hazardous to finance operations by borrowing from outsiders as opposed to issuing additional shares of capital stock. Debt securities require fixed annual interest payments regardless of company earnings. Equity securities, by contrast, contain no promises of a fixed return. Should income decline in a particular year, the company with equity rather than debt securities outstanding can omit a dividend without suffering the dire consequences of default on interest payments. The extent to which a firm makes use of other parties' money to increase return to its shareholders is referred to as *leverage*.

General Mills is considerably more levered than is Kellogg. General Mills, as of May 29, 1977, had total debt of $722,401,000 and total equity of only $724,870,000—a debt to equity ratio of 1.0 to 1.0.

Kellogg, on the other hand, as of December 31, 1977, had a total debt of $294,400,000 as compared to stockholders' equity of $544,600,000—a debt to equity ratio of only .54 to 1. Comparative income statements and balance sheets of the two firms are presented in Exhibits 15-2 and 15-3 on pp. 583-587.

**reporting practices**   Corporate personality may be revealed not only by substantive, economic factors as described in the preceding paragraphs but by differences in reporting practices as well.† Firms, for example, that adopt "conservative" reporting practices (generally those which result in lower reported earnings, e.g., using straight-line depreciation method for both financial reporting and tax purposes as opposed to accelerated depreciation for tax purposes and straight-line depreciation for financial reporting purposes) tend to have more conservative financial ratios

---

*With respect to product line, Kellogg is unquestionably the more "conservative" firm insofar as *conservative* is defined as "tending to preserve established traditions or institutions." One could argue persuasively, however, that Kellogg, by concentrating on a single product line, is really taking a greater risk than is General Mills. By placing all of its resources in a single industry, Kellogg may be subject to financial catastrophe if there is a sudden (although in its case unlikely) consumer rejection of its products.

†For two studies of corporate personality, see John M. Shank and Ronald M. Copeland, "Corporate Personality Theory and Changes in Accounting Methods: An Empirical Test," *Accounting Review,* Vol. XLVIII, July 1973, pp. 494–501, and George H. Sorter, Selvin W. Becker, T. Ross Archibald, and William H. Beaver, "Accounting and Financial Measures as Indicators of Corporate Personality—Some Empirical Findings," in *Research in Accounting Measurement,* R. Jaedicke, Y. Ijiri, and O. Neilson, eds. Sarasota, Fla.: American Accounting Association, 1966, pp. 200–211.

(e.g., less debt relative to equity) than their more liberal counterparts. Moreover, some firms are more apt to make accounting changes than others. Firms that may be categorized as *change receptive* based on their having made certain changes in accounting principles or methods are more likely than other companies to make additional accounting changes. General Mills, in its financial statements for year-end May 1975 changed from the FIFO to the LIFO method of valuation for a substantial portion of its inventories. Kellogg continues to state its inventories, as it has in the past, on the basis of average cost.

Even a brief overview of a firm's annual report provides an insight into its character. Such an insight may be as valuable to an analyst as a detailed quantitative evaluation. The annual report of General Mills paints a picture of an aggressive, expansion-oriented company, and that of Kellogg, a successful yet more conservative firm.

## Quality of Earnings

Throughout this text it has been emphasized that companies must make many selections among accounting methods. The choice of one method over another may result in higher or lower reported earnings. To the extent that the differences in reporting earnings are material, they must obviously be taken into account in weighing the operating results of one company against those of another. In this section we shall review several key accounting alternatives and areas of management discretion. Although the emphasis will be on differences in reported *earnings,* it must be kept in mind that differences in reported revenues and expenses are necessarily associated with corresponding differences in assets or liabilities as well as in owners' equity.

Differences in reported earnings may be attributed in large measure to the basic accounting principle that revenues should be realized when earned, not necessarily when the related cash is received. Many accounting issues arise over disagreements as to *when* a productive activity can be said to have produced earnings. Similarly, costs should be charged as expenses in the same accounting periods in which the revenues to which they are associated are recognized. Such periods may be prior to or subsequent to the periods in which the disbursements of cash are made. Frequently, however, it is not clear to which revenues costs should be associated.

In recent years it has become fashionable to characterize earnings in terms of *quality.* High-quality earnings are those in which the recognition of revenue is postponed until the actual receipt of cash, and expenses are charged no later than the period in which the cash is disbursed. Low-quality earnings are those in which revenues are recognized well before collection of cash can be reasonably assured and recognition of expenses is delayed beyond the period in which the cash disbursement has been made. High-quality earnings are associated with "conservatism" and result in lower reported income.

EXHIBIT 15-2

**Kellogg Company and Subsidiaries**
**Consolidated Balance Sheet at December 31**

| (In millions) | 1977 | 1976 |
|---|---|---|
| Current assets | | |
| Cash, including certificates of deposit of $38.2 ($78.9 in 1976) | $ 48.8 | $ 87.7 |
| Marketable securities, at cost which approximates market | 32.4 | 30.0 |
| Accounts receivable, less allowances of $1.5 ($1.6 in 1976) | 108.7 | 84.1 |
| Inventories: | | |
| Raw materials and supplies | 98.6 | 87.8 |
| Finished goods and materials in process | 72.8 | 61.1 |
| Prepaid expenses | 20.7 | 14.0 |
| Total current assets | 382.0 | 364.7 |
| Plant and Equipment | | |
| Land | 17.3 | 13.3 |
| Buildings | 180.7 | 176.0 |
| Machinery and equipment | 407.6 | 329.7 |
| Construction in progress | 39.2 | 56.2 |
| | 644.8 | 575.2 |
| Less accumulated depreciation | 227.7 | 198.2 |
| | 422.1 | 377.0 |
| Intangible Assets | 29.4 | 19.1 |
| Other Assets | 5.5 | 4.7 |
| Total Assets | $ 839.0 | $ 765.5 |
| Current Liabilities | | |
| Accounts payable | $ 58.9 | $ 54.6 |
| Loans payable, including current maturities of long-term debt | 27.4 | 17.0 |
| Income taxes | 34.6 | 35.4 |
| Accrued liabilities | 44.7 | 45.1 |
| Total Current Liabilities | 165.6 | 152.1 |
| Long-term Debt | 80.3 | 85.9 |
| Other Liabilities | 8.0 | 6.5 |
| Deferred Income Taxes | 40.5 | 31.5 |
| Shareholders' Equity | | |
| 3½% Cumulative preferred stock, $100 par value: Authorized and issued 70,513 shares less 47,686 shares in treasury (74,263 less 51,169 in 1976) | 2.3 | 2.3 |
| Common stock, $.50 par value: Authorized 80,000,000 shares; issued 76,389,877 shares (76,219,064 in 1976) | 38.2 | 38.1 |
| Capital in excess of par value | 31.0 | 28.3 |
| Retained earnings | 473.1 | 420.8 |
| Total Shareholders' Equity | 544.6 | 489.5 |
| Total Liabilities and Shareholders' Equity | $ 839.0 | $ 765.5 |

EXHIBIT 15-2 (cont)

**Kellogg Company and Subsidiaries**
**Consolidated Earnings for Year Ended December 31**

| (In millions) | 1977 | 1976 |
|---|---|---|
| Net sales | $1,533.4 | $1,385.4 |
| Interest and other income, net | 7.6 | 8.3 |
| | 1,541.0 | 1,393.7 |
| Cost of goods sold | 988.0 | 890.6 |
| Selling, general and administrative expenses | 281.2 | 241.9 |
| Interest expense | 9.2 | 9.0 |
| | 1,278.4 | 1,141.5 |
| Earnings before income taxes | 262.6 | 252.2 |
| Income taxes | 124.4 | 121.8 |
| Net earnings | $ 138.2 | $ 130.4 |
| Earnings per common share | $ 1.81 | $ 1.71 |

**timing of revenue recognition**

In Chapter 5, it was pointed out that most businesses recognize revenue at time of sale—sale being the point at which title to goods passes from seller to buyer. Alternatively, however, revenue is sometimes recognized during the production process (for example, on long-term construction projects) or upon actual collection of cash (where ultimate collectibility of a customer's obligation may be questionable). Although the accounting profession is moving in the direction of uniformity of practice among industry groups, there remains, within a number of industries, substantial diversity. In Chapters 5 and 7, for example, differences in timing of revenue recognition in the shipping, motion picture, and franchise industries were illustrated. The means by which a firm recognizes revenue is likely, especially in periods of expansion or contraction, to have a profound impact on reported earnings. An analyst should not even begin to compare one company with another until he has ascertained their methods of revenue recognition and adjusted for any differences.

**gains from appreciation**

Conventionally, increases in the market prices of assets are recognized only at the time of sale. If, for example, a firm owns marketable securities or real estate which have appreciated in value, it would realize no gains as long as it holds the property. Correspondingly, if the firm wants to take into income the difference between the current market price of the asset and the amount for which it was acquired, it need only sell the asset. The full amount of the appreciation would

EXHIBIT 15-3

**General Mills**
**Consolidated Balance Sheet**

| Assets | May 29, 1977 | May 30, 1976 |
|---|---|---|
| | (in thousands) | |
| **Current Assets:** | | |
| Cash | $ 14,794 | $ 4,478 |
| Marketable securities (at cost, approximates market value) | 7,521 | 77,351 |
| Receivables: | | |
| Customers | 222,997 | 199,966 |
| Miscellaneous | 16,983 | 22,425 |
| | 239,980 | 222,391 |
| Less allowance for possible losses | (8,373) | (6,428) |
| | 231,607 | 215,963 |
| Inventories | 425,832 | 353,654 |
| Prepaid expenses | 33,640 | 21,351 |
| Total Current Assets | $ 713,394 | $ 672,797 |
| **Other Assets:** | | |
| Land, buildings and equipment | | |
| Land | 49,127 | 41,806 |
| Buildings | 291,882 | 256,570 |
| Equipment | 435,324 | 393,265 |
| Construction in progress | 52,751 | 47,621 |
| | 829,084 | 739,262 |
| Less accumulated depreciation | (289,003) | (267,770) |
| | 540,081 | 471,492 |
| Miscellaneous assets: | | |
| Investment in 20–50% owned companies | 11,081 | 11,339 |
| Other | 22,473 | 23,071 |
| | $ 33,554 | $ 34,410 |
| Intangible assets: | | |
| Excess of cost over net assets of acquired companies | 150,416 | 138,802 |
| Patents, copyrights and other intangibles | 9,826 | 10,695 |
| Total Other Assets | $ 733,877 | $ 655,399 |
| Total Assets | $1,447,271 | $1,328,196 |

EXHIBIT 15-3 (cont)

**General Mills**
**Liabilities and Stockholders' Equity**

| *Assets* | May 29, 1977 | May 30, 1976 |
|---|---|---|
| | *(in thousands)* | |
| Current Liabilities: | | |
| Notes payable | $ 27,725 | $ 24,098 |
| Current portion of long-term debt | 3,435 | 4,405 |
| Accounts payable and accrued expenses: | | |
| Accounts payable—trade | 234,147 | 194,622 |
| Accounts payable—miscellaneous | 43,779 | 46,671 |
| Accrued payroll | 36,090 | 29,933 |
| Accrued interest | 5,380 | 5,546 |
| | 319,396 | 276,772 |
| Accrued taxes | 61,380 | 69,045 |
| Thrift accounts of officers and employees | 3,269 | 3,363 |
| Total Current Liabilities | $ 415,205 | $ 377,683 |
| Other Liabilities: | | |
| Long-term debt, excluding current portion | 276,136 | 281,763 |
| Deferred Federal income taxes | 14,834 | 11,231 |
| Deferred compensation | 7,529 | 6,442 |
| Other liabilities and deferred credits | 3,400 | 5,773 |
| Total Liabilities | 301,899 | 305,209 |
| | $ 717,104 | $ 682,892 |
| Minority Interests | $ 5,297 | $ 5,059 |
| Stockholders' Equity: | | |
| Common stock | 192,475 | 172,897 |
| Retained earnings | 546,960 | 469,009 |
| Less common stock in Treasury, at cost | (14,565) | (1,661) |
| Total Stockholders' Equity | $ 724,870 | $ 640,245 |
| Total Liabilities and Stockholders' Equity | $1,447,271 | $1,328,196 |

EXHIBIT 15-3 *(cont)*

**General Mills**
**Consolidated Results of Operations**

| | Fiscal Year Ended | |
|---|---|---|
| | May 29, 1977 *(52 Weeks)* | May 30, 1976 *(53 Weeks)* |
| | *(in thousands)* | |
| Sales | $2,909,404 | $2,644,952 |
| Costs and Expenses: | | |
| Costs of sales, exclusive of items shown below | 1,786,210 | 1,654,169 |
| Depreciation expense | 46,206 | 45,006 |
| Amortization expense | 1,919 | 1,701 |
| Interest expense | 26,739 | 29,400 |
| Contributions to employees' retirement plans | 20,617 | 17,903 |
| Profit sharing distribution | 4,275 | 3,527 |
| Selling, general and administrative expenses | 794,846 | 692,985 |
| Total Costs and Expenses | $2,680,812 | $2,444,691 |
| Earnings Before Taxes on Income and Other Items shown below | $ 228,592 | $ 200,261 |
| Taxes on Income | (112,119) | (99,964) |
| Other Items: | | |
| Add share of net earnings of 20–50% owned companies | 1,481 | 1,094 |
| Deduct minority interests in net earnings of consolidated subsidiaries | (920) | (853) |
| Net Earnings | $ 117,034 | $ 100,538 |
| Earnings per Common Share and Common Share Equivalent | $ 2.36 | $ 2.04 |
| Average number of common shares and common share equivalents | 49,572 | 49,203 |

be recognized as revenue in the year of sale. The sophisticated analyst should be aware of the possibilities of both *manipulating* income and *hiding* assets that arise from the accounting practice of recognizing *holding* gains only upon sale. In comparing the earnings of two companies the analyst should recognize that one of the two may have "improved" its earnings simply by selling off appreciated assets. The other, by reporting at cost assets that have appreciated in value, may have a discretionary *reserve* of earnings that it can release in any desired period.

**losses on receivables**
Firms follow various practices with respect to actual and potential losses on accounts and notes receivable. On the one hand, some firms do not even recognize as assets accounts or notes receivable if there is serious doubt about their collectibility. That is, they recognize revenue only upon collection of cash (the installment basis) even though they may have a legal claim against the party to which they provided goods or services. Firms in the real estate and retail land sales industries will, under certain circumstances, delay recognition of revenue until cash is in hand. The common practice in most industries, however, is to establish an allowance for uncollectible accounts. The provision of an allowance (a contra account) serves to reduce the balance in the related asset account and to recognize potential losses on receivables prior to the period in which the receivables are actually written off. The questions of both the adequacy of the allowance and the conditions that must exist before an account is written off— the two of which relate to the amount reported as a bad-debt expense—are matters of management discretion. As illustrated in Chapter 7, some firms are considerably more reluctant than others both to provide for possible losses and to write off accounts that have turned sour.

It is exceedingly difficult, without access to the underlying receivable records, for an analyst to evaluate the reasonableness of a firm's policy with respect to bad debts. There are, however, a few indicators in the financial statements that might serve to raise doubts. First, the analyst can compute the ratio of the balance in the allowance for uncollectibles account to that in the related receivable account and compare it with that of other firms in the same industry. If such ratio is unusually low, it might be a sign that the company has inadequately protected itself against possible losses on bad debts. Second, the analyst can determine a ratio of sales to accounts receivable. If the ratio (called the accounts receivable turnover ratio) is unusually low in comparison to that of previous years, an analyst should be put on notice that the firm may be having collection problems and that the balance in the receivables account may be "building up" as customers delay payments on their outstanding obligations. Third, an analyst can review financial reports of previous years for any sudden and material increases in bad-debt expenses. Such extraordinary increases might be an indication that in past years the amounts added to the allowance for uncollectibles had been inadequate and occasional *catch-up* adjustments were required.

**costs of goods sold**   Corporations have the option of employing one of the three basic methods of accounting for inventories: first in, first out; weighted average; and last in, first out—along with several variations of each of the three. Choice of method, of course, has a direct bearing upon the reported cost of goods sold.

In periods of rising prices, LIFO would ordinarily result in higher reported cost of goods sold and lower reported income, because under LIFO goods acquired last, at presumably higher prices, are assumed to be sold first. The dollar difference in reported earnings that would result from using LIFO rather than FIFO generally depends on two major factors: the magnitude of the increase in prices and the length of time that each item of inventory is held before it is sold. Moreover, if LIFO is used, significant distortions in reported earnings may occur in any year in which the firm is forced to "dip into" its LIFO base—that is, to sell goods that have been carried on the books at costs of years earlier.

An analyst is seldom able to convert with accuracy FIFO earnings to LIFO earnings or vice versa. It is often possible to make estimates of the differences, and if such differences are determined to be material, then no comparisons of financial position or results of operations between two companies can properly be made without adjusting both inventory and cost of goods sold.

**depreciation**   The primary variables with respect to depreciation relate to the method of depreciation and the estimate of asset life. Fixed assets generally constitute a major portion of total assets. Differences in the manner in which they are accounted for may have a profound effect on reported earnings.

Companies may allocate the cost of an asset by either the straight-line or one of several *accelerated* methods of depreciation. The straight-line method results in smaller depreciation charges in the early years of an asset's life than do accelerated methods; accelerated methods, such as sum-of-the-year's digits or double-declining balance, result in smaller charges in the later years.

The accounting useful life of an asset is a consequence of the best estimate of corporate management. Many companies disclose the estimated useful lives of major groups of assets in footnotes to their financial statements.* As indicated in Chapter 10, it is not uncommon to find similar companies depreciating similar

---

*Publicly held corporations are required to reveal the useful lives of assets in the 10K or 12K reports that they must submit each year to the Securities and Exchange Commission. Such reports contain a great deal of financial information in addition to that contained in the annual reports to stockholders. They are in the public domain and may be found in business libraries.

assets over substantially different lengths of time. The analyst must, of course, take cognizance of such differences when making intercompany comparisons.

In the same fashion, the analyst must consider the number of years assumed to be benefited by noncurrent assets other than plant and equipment. The period of time over which intangible assets such as organization costs are amortized may vary significantly from company to company.

**other expenses**   The manner in which several other types of costs are accounted for is also a matter of management discretion. The investment tax credit, which serves to reduce a company's required tax payment by up to 10 percent of the cost of eligible property, may be accounted for by either the flow-through or the deferral method. If accounted for by the flow-through method, then tax expense in the year the eligible property is acquired is reduced by the full amount of the credit. If accounted for by the deferral method, then the benefit of the tax credit is recognized over the entire useful life of the property.

The means by which pension expense is determined may also differ from company to company. In estimating the required contribution to the pension fund in any given year, a firm may select among several *actuarial cost methods.* Choice of actuarial cost method directly affects reported pension expense. In addition, the company has wide latitude in selecting the number of periods over which it can amortize *past service* costs—those costs which are attributable to changes in a pension plan made in a current year but which are based on the service of employees in past years. In accord with pronouncements of the Accounting Principles Board, a firm may amortize such costs over a period of up to 40 years.

Gains or losses on the retirement of long-term debt are additional items of revenue or expense over which management can have direct control. Although the accounting treatment of such gains or losses is *not* subject to management determination—they must be recognized in their entirety in the year of sale or redemption—the decision as to *when* to retire the bonds is at the discretion of management. If, for example, the prevailing level of interest rates had increased substantially in the years since a firm's bonds were first issued, it is probable that they are being traded in the open market at a price considerably below face value. The company could therefore redeem them at less than the amount at which they are stated on its books and thereby realize a gain. It is up to management to determine when to redeem the bonds and how much of the outstanding issue should be redeemed. It may, therefore, be able to "control" reported earnings by redeeming bonds as necessary to reflect desired profitability.

A central theme of this book is that reported earnings (as well as reported assets and liabilities) should not be taken at face value. The analyst should be certain to consider the effect on reported earnings of alternative principles and policies and to recognize that earnings can be evaluated in terms of quality as well as quantity.

## Ratio and Percentage Analysis

Few accounting numbers are of significance by themselves. They have meaning only as they relate to other numbers. The fact, for example, that Kellogg had earnings in 1977 of $138 million is by itself of little interest. It provides no insight as to whether the company is well managed, the stockholders are receiving an adequate return on their investment, or earnings are increasing or decreasing over time. It takes on meaning only as it is associated with other financial measures, such as total invested capital, gross sales, or market value of common stock.

This section will be directed to some ratios and percentages that analysts find particularly useful in conducting financial evaluations. There may be several variations of each of the ratios illustrated, and it would be improper to infer that the form presented is superior to others. Indeed, there is no correct form for any of the ratios or percentages. Ratios or percentages should be computed in a manner that best serves to facilitate the specific decisions at hand.

Ratios must never be evaluated in a vacuum. What are important to an analyst are trends over time and comparisons with firms in the same or related industries. Should a key ratio or series of ratios increase or decrease from one year to the next, it may be a sign of either financial deterioration or improvement. Moreover, there are no fixed minimum or maximum values below which a ratio should not fall or above which it should not rise. It is, of course, possible to determine industry averages and distributions of the values of particular ratios. Obviously, whenever the ratio of a particular firm is substantially out of line with those common in the industry, the analyst should be alert to either potential financial difficulty or unusual financial strength.

Normal ranges for most ratios and percentages vary considerably from industry to industry. Some industries, electric utilities, for example, require large amounts of invested capital in order to support their operations. Other industries, supermarkets, for instance, require relatively small amounts of permanent capital. As a consequence, supermarkets can be expected to have a much higher ratio of net income to total invested capital (return on investment) than would electric utilities. Supermarkets, on the other hand, tend to earn a relatively small profit on each dollar of sales since the *markup* on grocery products is relatively small. By contrast, once the physical facilities have been acquired, the cost of generating electricity is relatively low. Thus, electric utilities would generally have a much higher ratio of net income to sales revenue (return on sales) than would supermarkets. Industry norms for a number of key indicators can be obtained from publications of industry trade associations or of financial service bureaus such as Dun and Bradstreet or Standard & Poor's.

The objectives of ratio analysis can be expressed in terms of the three major types of ratios:

*Profitability and activity ratios:* To measure the profitability and efficiency of the activities carried out by the enterprise.

*Liquidity ratios:* To indicate the ability of the firm to meet its obligations as they mature.

*Financing ratios:* To compare the claims of the creditors of the firm with the equity of its owners.

In the section to follow we shall illustrate only a small sample of widely used ratios.

**profitability and activity ratios**

*Return on Investment.* The single most significant measure of corporate profitability and efficiency is return on investment, the ratio of income to capital. Return on investment provides an indication of how effectively the enterprise is employing the resources under its command.

Return on investment may be computed in numerous ways. The differences between two of the more common ways point out the importance of adapting ratios to the particular objectives of the financial review which is being undertaken.

Return on investment may be viewed as a measure of the profitability of the enterprise without regard to the manner in which it has been financed. Income, before taking into account distributions to the parties which supplied the capital—that is, interest or dividends—is compared to total capital employed in the business. Total capital may be represented by either total assets (the left-hand side of the accounting equation) or total liabilities plus total owners' equity (the right-hand side).

Alternatively, return on investment may be seen as a measure of the return to the owners of the enterprise. Net income, after taking into account distributions to all parties other than the owners, is compared to equity of the stockholders. Interest, a distribution to creditors, is considered an expense no different from other operating costs. This measure of profitability is of primary interest to stockholders since it relates their share of income to the capital in which they have a residual equity. The other measure, the *all-capital* ratio, is of more immediate concern to managers of the firm since it reveals the success of the business in employing *all* the resources within its command.

During 1977 Kellogg (per Exhibit 15-2) employed on *average* $802,250,000 of capital. The average available capital was determined by summing the total assets at the end of 1976 ($765,500,000) and those at the end of 1977 ($839,000,000) and dividing by 2. It is preferable to base the computation on average, rather than year-end capital, in order to avoid distortions that would result if additional capital were acquired or returned to investors in the final months of the year. Since the firm did not have use of such capital during the entire year, it should not be expected to have earned a return on it for the entire year. In 1977, Kellogg had net earnings of $138,200,000. Deducted in the calculation of net income was $9,200,000 which was distributed in the form of interest to parties which supplied debt capital. The interest expense must be added back to net income if total income available to suppliers of capital is to be compared with total capital employed by the company:*

$$\text{Return on investment} = \frac{\text{Net income} + \text{Interest}}{\text{Average assets}}$$
(all capital)

$$= \frac{\$138,200,000 + \$9,200,000}{\$802,250,000} = 18.4\%$$

The average stockholders' equity during 1977 was $517,050,000 [($489,500,000 + $544,600,000)/2].

The return on stockholders' equity may thus be determined as follows:

$$\text{Return on investment} = \frac{\text{Net income}}{\text{Average stockholders' equity}}$$
(stockholders' equity)

$$= \frac{\$138,200,000}{\$517,050,000} = 26.7\%$$

Return on stockholders' equity (26.7 percent) is considerably higher than return on all capital (18.4 percent). This indicates that the company is making effective use of borrowed funds. It is earning a return on the borrowed funds in excess of their cost (i.e., interest expense).

Other variations of the same ratio may have greater utility for specific purposes or to specific users. From the standpoint of common stockholders, for example, a ratio that compares earnings applicable only to common stockholders (as opposed to both common and preferred stockholders) to their equity might be more relevant than either of the two other ratios. Earnings applicable to common stockholders represent net income less dividends declared to preferred stockholders. The consolidated statement of shareholders' equity (not illustrated) indicates that Kellogg paid preferred stock dividends of $100,000. As can be determined from the balance sheet, the average equity of common stockholders during 1977 was $514,750,000. The return on equity of common stockholders can be computed as follows:

$$\text{Return on equity of common} = \frac{\text{Net income} - \text{Preferred stock dividends}}{\text{Average equity of common stockholders}}$$
stockholders

$$= \frac{\$138,200,000 - \$100,000}{\$514,750,000} = 26.8\%$$

---

*Many analysts subtract from the interest to be added to net income the saving in income taxes associated with the interest. In computing taxable income, interest expense is deductible. If the tax rate is 48 percent, then the company would have saved 48 percent of the interest cost of $9,200,000–$4,416,000.

## PRICE/EARNINGS RATIO

The profitability of a company may also be measured by comparing net earnings to the price at which the shares of common stock are being traded. The ratio is conventionally expressed on a per share basis. Earnings per share of Kellogg in 1977 were $1.81. If, at year end, the market price per share were $22, then the price earnings ratio would be 12.2 to 1:

$$\text{Price/earnings ratio} = \frac{\text{Market price per share}}{\text{Earnings per share}}$$

$$= \frac{\$22}{\$1.81} = 12.2\%$$

Expressed in another way, the company provided stockholders with a return of 8.2 percent (earnings per share divided by market price) on the market value of their investment. The relationship between earnings and market price is of particular relevance to common stockholders. It enables them to compare the return that they are presently receiving with that which they could receive were they to sell their shares and invest the proceeds in other ventures.

## PERCENTAGE OF REVENUE

Another means of measuring corporate efficiency as well as detecting expenditures that are out of line is to express each expenditure or group of expenditures as a percentage of revenues. Exhibit 15-4 indicates each main group of Kellogg's expenses in dollars and as a percentage of total 1977 revenues.

*EXHIBIT 15-4*

**Kellogg Company**
**Revenues and Expenses as a Percentage of Total Revenue**
**1977**
**(in millions)**

|  | *$ Amount* | *Percent* |
|---|---|---|
| Net sales | $1,533.4 | 99% |
| Interest and other income | 7.6 | 1 |
| Total revenue | $1,541.0 | 100% |
| Expenses: |  |  |
| Cost of goods sold | 988.0 | 64% |
| Selling, general, and administration expenses | 281.2 | 18 |
| Interest expense | 9.2 | 1 |
| Taxes | 124.4 | 8 |
| Total expenses | $1,402.8 | 91% |
| Net income | $ 138.2 | 9% |

Significant changes in the percentage from year to year may be a natural consequence of the behavior of costs. An increase in sales, for example, would not necessarily result in a proportionate increase in interest. But unusual changes may also signal the need for tighter controls over cost.

As indicated in Exhibit 15-4, the *profit margin* of Kellogg (net income as a percent of revenues) is 9 percent. The *gross margin* (1 – cost of goods sold percentage) is 36 percent. (In determining both the profit margin and gross margin it is generally useful to base percentages on net sales, excluding interest or other revenues. In the case at hand, interest and other revenues are sufficiently immaterial as to have no significant impact on the percentages.)

## ACTIVITY RATIOS

Activity ratios measure the effectiveness of management in utilizing specific resources under its command. Activity ratios are often referred to as *turnover* ratios. They relate specific asset accounts to sales or to some other revenue or expense accounts with which they are logically associated.

The inventory turnover ratio, for example, measures corporate efficiency in employing inventory. Inventory turnover is the number of times the annual cost of sales exceeds average inventory during the year. It is computed by dividing cost of goods sold by average inventory:

$$\text{Inventory turnover} = \frac{\text{Costs of goods sold}}{\text{Average inventory}}$$

The greater the number of times per year that inventory *turns over,* the more efficiently the investment in inventory is being used. The smaller the inventory in relation to cost of goods sold, the greater the sales activity that the inventory is able to support. Ideally, average inventory should be based on a 12-month average; otherwise the average may be distorted by seasonal fluctuations. (Indeed a company may intentionally choose to end its fiscal year in a month when inventories are at a yearly low in order to facilitate its physical count.) In the absence of monthly information, however, the average of Kellogg can be determined roughly by dividing by two the sum of beginning and ending inventories. Average inventory (both raw materials and supplies) equals $160,150,000 [($171,400,000 + $148,900,000)/2].

$$\text{Inventory turnover} = \frac{\text{Cost of goods sold}}{\text{Average inventory}}$$

$$= \frac{\$988,000,000}{\$160,150,000} = 6.2 \text{ times}$$

*Accounts receivable turnover* can be determined in a similar manner. However, since accounts receivable are stated at the price at which the sales were made, the average balance in accounts receivable must be compared with sales, not cost of goods sold:

$$\text{Accounts receivable turnover} = \frac{\text{Sales}}{\text{Average accounts receivable}}$$

Average accounts receivable for Kellogg equals $96,400,000 [($84,100,000 + $108,700,000)/2].

$$\text{Accounts receivable turnover} = \frac{\$1,533,400,000}{\$96,400,000} = 15.9 \text{ times}$$

The greater the number of times that accounts receivable turn over, the smaller the amount of funds that the company has "tied up" in accounts receivable, and the greater the amount of funds that it can invest in other assets.

The same ratio can be expressed in an alternative form, *number of days' sales in accounts receivable.* Assuming that all sales were made on account, then on average the company made $4,259,444 in sales per day:

$$\text{Average sales per day} = \frac{\text{Total sales}}{360} = \frac{\$1,533,400,000}{360} = \$4,259,444$$

The number of days' sales in accounts receivable may be determined by dividing accounts receivable as of any particular day by average sales per day:

$$\begin{array}{l}\text{Number of days' sales in} \\ \text{accounts receivable} = \\ \text{(as of December 31, 1977)}\end{array} \quad \frac{\text{Accounts receivable}}{\text{Average sales per day}}$$

$$= \frac{\$108,700,000}{\$4,259,400} = 25.5 \text{ days}$$

Expressed in another way, on the average, it takes 25.5 days for the company to collect its accounts receivable. Should the collection period increase from one year to the next, or should it be greater than the number of days in the payment period specified in the company's terms of sales, then there would be reason to suspect that the company is experiencing difficulty collecting from its customers.

The efficiency of plant and equipment is often measured by the *plant and equipment turnover* ratio, determined by comparing sales to average book value of plant and equipment:

$$\text{Plant and equipment turnover} = \frac{\text{Sales}}{\text{Average plant and equipment}}$$

Average plant and equipment of the Kellogg Company in 1977 was $399,550,000 [($377,000,000 + $422,100,000)/2].

$$\text{Plant and equipment turnover} = \frac{\$1,533,400,000}{\$399,550,000} = 3.8 \text{ times}$$

The greater the turnover ratio, the more effectively plant and equipment are being employed. In years when sales are down and physical facilities are not being used to capacity, the ratio would tend to decline. In years when sales are up and the plant is being used to the fullest extent possible, the ratio would tend to increase.

**liquidity ratios**   Liquidity ratios indicate the ability of a firm to meet its obligations as they mature.

### CURRENT RATIO

As indicated in Chapter 2, the primary measure of liquidity is the *current* ratio. The current ratio compares current assets with current liabilities. The higher the ratio of current assets to current liabilities, the less likely the company will be to default on its obligations. Current assets, however, commonly provide either no direct return to the company or a return smaller than could be obtained if funds were invested in long-term securities. Insofar as the current ratio is high, therefore, the company may be incurring an *opportunity cost*—it could be losing revenue by tying up funds in current assets rather than by taking advantage of other financial opportunities.

The current ratio of the Kellogg Company as of December 31, 1977 is 2.31 to 1:

$$\text{Current ratio} = \frac{\text{Current assets}}{\text{Current liabilities}} = \frac{\$382,000,000}{\$165,600,000} = 2.31$$

The current ratio is of special concern to short-term creditors, those who are concerned about the firm's ability to meet its obligations within a period of one year. The current ratio, however, should be viewed with considerable care. It is one ratio that can readily be manipulated by management. For example, by paying off short-term loans just prior to year end (and subsequently reborrowing at the start of the next year), management may be able to increase its year-end current ratio. It is important to bear in mind that an identical change in both current assets and current liabilities will, in fact, alter the current ratio. If, for example, a firm had current assets of $400,000 and current liabilities of $200,000 and subsequently repaid an outstanding current obligation of

$100,000, its current ratio would increase from 2:1 prior to repayment to 3:1 after repayment. The practice of taking deliberate steps to inflate the current ratio is known as *window dressing*.

## QUICK RATIO

A test of liquidity more severe than the current ratio is the *quick ratio*. The quick ratio matches cash, marketable securities, and accounts receivable to current liabilities. It provides an indication of the ability of the company to satisfy its obligations without taking into account both inventories, which are less readily transformed into cash than other current assets, and prepaid expenses, which save the company from having to disburse cash in the future but which are not themselves transformed into cash. The quick ratio of the Kellogg Company as of December 31, 1977 is 1.15 to 1:

$$\text{Quick ratio} = \frac{\text{Cash} + \text{Marketable securities} + \text{Accounts receivable}}{\text{Current liabilities}}$$

$$= \frac{\$48,800,000 + \$32,400,000 + \$108,700,000}{\$165,600,000}$$

$$= \frac{\$189,900,000}{\$165,600,000} = 1.15$$

**financing ratios**    Financing ratios compare claims of creditors with the equity of stockholders.

## DEBT TO EQUITY RATIO

The debt to equity ratio compares capital provided by creditors with that supplied by owners. Debt includes all outstanding liabilities, both current and noncurrent. Equity includes balances in all owners' equity accounts—common and preferred stock, capital provided in excess of par, and retained earnings.

Total debt of the Kellogg Company, composed of current liabilities, long-term debt, other liabilities, and deferred income taxes, is $294,400,000. Total stockholders' equity is $544,600,000. The debt to equity ratio as of December 31, 1977, therefore, is .54 to 1:

$$\text{Debt to equity ratio} = \frac{\text{Total debt}}{\text{Total equity}}$$

$$= \frac{\$294,400,000}{\$544,600,000} = .54$$

The debt to equity ratio is of particular concern to creditors. The claims of creditors against the assets of a firm have priority over those of the stockholders. The higher the debt to equity ratio, the greater the amount of the *priority* claims against the assets, and in the event the firm is unable to meet all its outstanding obligations, the less likely that any individual claim will be liquidated in full. Moreover, a high debt to equity ratio suggests the obligation to make high periodic interest payments. As a consequence, there is an increased risk that corporate earnings will be insufficient to cover all required principal and interest payments.

The debt to equity ratio is also of interest to stockholders. Stockholders can expect no return on their investment, either periodically in the form of dividends or upon liquidation, until all senior claims of creditors have been satisfied. The lower the debt to equity ratio, the less the risk of loss assumed by stockholders. But in contrast to the possible preference of stockholders to be assured a return on their investment, there may be a conflicting desire to make use of leverage—to take advantage of other people's money to enhance the return on their invested capital. Insofar as the debt to equity ratio is high as a consequence of reliance upon debt, then any earnings on the borrowed capital above the required interest payments would increase the return to stockholders. Leverage, however, works both ways. If the firm should be unable to earn on its borrowed capital an amount sufficient to cover the cost of such capital, then the return on stockholders' equity would be comparably reduced.

## TIMES INTEREST EARNED

Insight into the ability of a company to satisfy its fixed obligations to creditors may be obtained by comparing earnings with interest charges. Although the times interest earned ratio may be expressed in a variety of ways, the simplest form indicates the relationship between income *before* deducting both interest and income taxes. The objective of the ratio is to indicate the margin of safety afforded bondholders and noteholders. If earnings only barely cover interest charges, then the creditors' promised interest payments are in jeopardy. If, however, earnings are several times greater than interest charges, then in the absence of a business reversal their return is reasonably assured.

Since the objective of the ratio is to indicate the earnings available for the payment of interest, it is important that the interest charges themselves be added back to net income. Moreover, since interest payments are a deductible expense in the determination of taxable income, income taxes should also be added back. In a sense, the payment of interest takes precedence over the payment of federal, state, and local income taxes. Required income tax payments are calculated after deducting payments to creditors. If the firm, after payment of interest, has zero income or a net loss, then the tax liability is also zero.

The Kellogg Company covered its required interest payments 29.5 times in 1977:

$$\text{Times interest earned} = \frac{\text{Net income} + \text{Interest} + \text{Income taxes}}{\text{Interest}}$$

$$= \frac{\$138,200,000 + \$9,200,000 + \$124,400,000}{\$9,200,000}$$

$$= \frac{\$271,800,000}{\$9,200,000} = 29.5$$

Kellogg is financed primarily by equity rather than long-term debt capital. Its earnings relative to its required interest payments are exceedingly high. Barring any extreme drop in earnings, the company is in little danger of defaulting on its obligations.

**ratio analysis— concluding comment**

Ratio analysis is a useful tool by which to evaluate current financial strength as well as past operating performance and by which to make predictions about the future. Ratio analysis, for example, has proved to be an especially effective means of forecasting corporate bankruptcy. It has been demonstrated that in a large number of instances bankruptcy has been preceded by a deterioration of a few key ratios.

Ratios, however, have virtually no significance by themselves. They are of use only when compared with similar measures of other companies in the same industry or with those of previous accounting periods.

Most significantly, it must be emphasized that ratios are no better than the underlying accounting data. To the extent that the underlying data are deficient with respect to a particular decision at hand, then so too are the ratios. Marketable securities, for example, are conventionally reported on the balance sheet at cost if such cost is less than their market value. If a firm's current ratio is calculated on the basis of reported current assets, as opposed to the fair market value of the current assets, then the current ratio may be substantially understated and thereby be inappropriate for most investment decisions. There is no "correct" formula for calculating ratios. The analyst is free to adjust the underlying accounting data in any manner that is likely to enable him to establish relationships that may facilitate the decision at hand.

Several key ratios are summarized in Exhibit 15-5.

### Footnotes

Footnotes are occasionally difficult for anyone but an expert to interpret. But they contain disclosures that are far too important for a serious analyst to ignore. They contain information which supplements that contained in the body of the

EXHIBIT 15-5

## Summary of Selected Ratios

| Name | Formula | Objective |
|---|---|---|
| **I. Profitability and activity ratios** | | |
| A. Return on investment (all capital) | $\dfrac{\text{Net income} + \text{Interest}}{\text{Average assets}}$ | To indicate effectiveness of business in employing *all* resources within its command |
| B. Return on investment (stockholders' equity) | $\dfrac{\text{Net income}}{\text{Average stockholders' equity}}$ | To indicate effectiveness of business in employing capital provided by stockholders |
| C. Return on equity of common stockholders | $\dfrac{\text{Net income} - \text{preferred stock dividends}}{\text{Average equity of common stockholders}}$ | To indicate effectiveness of business in employing capital provided by common stockholders |
| D. Price/earnings ratio | $\dfrac{\text{Market price per share}}{\text{Earnings per share}}$ | To measure return on market value of common stock |
| E. Inventory turnover | $\dfrac{\text{Cost of goods sold}}{\text{Average inventory}}$ | To measure efficiency of employment of inventory |
| F. Accounts receivable turnover | $\dfrac{\text{Sales}}{\text{Average accounts receivable}}$ | To measure efficiency of employment of accounts receivable |
| G. Number of days' sales in accounts receivable | $\dfrac{\text{Accounts receivable}}{\text{Average sales per day}}$ | To determine the average number of days in which accounts receivable are outstanding |
| H. Plant and equipment turnover | $\dfrac{\text{Sales}}{\text{Average plant and equipment}}$ | To measure efficiency in employment of plant and equipment |
| **II. Liquidity ratios** | | |
| A. Current ratio | $\dfrac{\text{Current assets}}{\text{Current liabilities}}$ | To measure firm's ability to meet current obligations as they come due |
| B. Quick ratio | $\dfrac{\text{Cash} + \text{Marketable securities} + \text{Accounts receivable}}{\text{Current liabilities}}$ | To measure, by a more severe test, the firm's ability to meet current obligations as they come due |
| **III. Financing ratios** | | |
| A. Debt to equity ratio | $\dfrac{\text{Total debt}}{\text{Total equity}}$ | To indicate proportion of capital provided by creditors rather than by owners |
| B. Times interest earned | $\dfrac{\text{Net income} + \text{Interest} + \text{Income taxes}}{\text{Interest}}$ | To measure firm's ability to meet fixed interest charges |

financial statements and without which the financial statements themselves may be misleading.

In recent years there has been a sharp increase in the amount of information contained in footnotes and, as a consequence, in their importance to the analyst. In part, the trend toward greater amounts of explanatory material stems from the frustration of accountants in selecting among alternative principles and procedures. By disclosing the nature of a transaction, the accountant minimizes the significance of his own choices among alternatives. If the user of the financial statements prefers another alternative, he is provided with sufficient information to adjust the financial statements to satisfy his own particular requirements.

Moreover, it is being increasingly recognized that regardless of the accounting principles followed, the basic financial statements provide an inadequate amount of information about a company's financial affairs. Certain critical types of information—that relating to pending legal actions against a firm, for example—cannot meaningfully be described within the framework of the three basic financial statements.

In addition, different users want different levels of information. A degree of detail that is appropriate for one user may represent *information overload* to another. Footnotes may be viewed as appendices to the financial reports. For those readers who want information in addition to that contained in the main body of the statements, it is readily available to them.

The information contained in footnotes varies from company to company. Examples of the footnotes in the annual report of the Kellogg Company (Exhibit 15-6) serve adequately, however, to illustrate the typical matters disclosed.

## ADDITIONAL DETAIL

The main body of the financial reports generally summarizes groups of accounts in a single figure. In the balance sheet of the Kellogg Company, for example, long-term debt is summarized in a single figure. Footnote 8 provides a breakdown of the debt by category.

## OUTSTANDING COMMITMENTS

The footnotes provide information with respect to commitments and contractual rights and obligations that may have been made or entered into by the firm but which are not otherwise revealed in the financial statements. Note 9 discloses the rights of redemption with respect to preferred stock and commitments relating to preferred stock.

An additional note (not shown) indicates that Kellogg Company had no material rental obligations under noncancelable leases. If, however, the firm had entered into long-term leases, it would be required to disclose both the annual required payments and the present (discounted) value of such payments. Such disclosure would enable an analyst to make comparable, by adjustment, the financial statements of the firm that leases a portion of its plant and equipment with those of a firm that purchases similar assets and borrows the required funds.

EXHIBIT 15-6

## Kellogg Company and Subsidiaries
## Selected Footnotes
## Year Ended December 31, 1977

### Note 8. Long-Term Debt

Long-term debt consists of:

|  | 1977 | 1976 |
|---|---|---|
| 8 5/8% Notes, due 1985 | $75.0 | $75.0 |
| Other | 1.8 | 8.4 |
| Foreign | 4.4 | 6.6 |
| Capitalized lease obligations | 3.5 |  |
|  | 84.7 | 90.0 |
| Less current maturities | 4.4 | 4.1 |
|  | $80.3 | $85.9 |

The company may redeem the 8 5/8% Notes after October 1, 1982 at principal amount plus accrued interest. The Indenture includes, among other things, limitations on the incurring of debt secured by mortgages on principal properties within the United States.

### Note 9. Preferred Stock

The Company may redeem its outstanding preferred shares at a price of $101 ($100 after 1985). Each year the Company must offer to purchase 3,750 shares of preferred stock at a maximum price of $100, or apply previously acquired shares (47,686 in treasury at December 31, 1977) against this requirement.

### Note 11. Legal Matters

The Company is involved in various litigations incidental to the conduct of its business. Management does not consider that any such litigation, either individually or in the aggregate, can have, except as stated below, a material adverse effect on the Company.

In 1972 the Federal Trade Commission commenced a proceeding against Kellogg Company and three other cereal manufacturers charging that these companies have maintained a "highly concentrated, non-competitive market structure in the production and sale of (ready-to-eat) cereal" in violation of the Federal Trade Commission Act. The relief requested includes divestiture of assets, licensing of trademarks, prohibition of future acquisitions of competitors, and prohibition of shelf space activities. It is the position of Kellogg Company that it has not violated the Act and the Company, therefore, is contesting the charges vigorously.

In 1974 the U.S. Justice Department filed a suit against Mrs. Smith's Pie Company alleging that the 1973 acquisition of the Lloyd J. Harriss Pie

*EXHIBIT 15-6 (cont)*

Company and affiliates was a violation of the Clayton Anti-Trust Act. On April 28, 1977 the U.S. District Court entered an order requiring Mrs. Smith's to divest the acquired companies. Mrs. Smith's is taking action to comply with the order.

*Contingent Liabilities.* The foonotes also provide information with respect to *contingent* liabilities. Contingent liabilities are potential liabilities. They would be transformed into actual liabilities—those requiring recognition on the balance sheet—only if certain unfavorable events were to occur. Contingent liabilities commonly result from pending legal proceedings. In note 11, for instance, federal antitrust actions against Kellogg and its subsidiaries are described.

The importance of contingent liabilities cannot be overemphasized. They are not given specific accounting recognition in the main body of the financial statements because the outcome of the related event cannot be predicted with even a modicum of certainty. But the consequences of an unfavorable outcome may in some instances overwhelm the information contained in the main body of the financial statements. If, for example, an antitrust action were to result in the division of the company into several smaller units, then reported asset values (based on the concept of the going concern) may be of little significance and reported income would be of little use in predicting operating results of the future.

In recent years the amount of information pertaining to pending legal actions that should be disclosed has been a source of controversy among independent auditors, the firms that they audit, and the attorneys of such firms. On the one hand, certified public accountants have been urging companies to provide the public with specific information about the probable outcome of pending litigation. On the other hand, companies, on the advice of counsel, have been increasingly reluctant to provide such information. First, they argue that in light of the uncertainty surrounding many legal actions, predictions about the outcome of a case may be misleading to the public. Second, they assert that predictions about the results of litigation may undermine a firm's own position in a case. Consider, for example, a situation in which a firm is contesting a damage suit which has been filed against it. The plaintiffs are demanding $10 million in damages; attorneys for the defendant company believe that the suit can be settled out of court for $200,000 but have publicly denied any wrongdoing or liability. Were the company to predict in its financial reports that the case would be settled for $200,000, its bargaining position would likely be severely weakened, perhaps to the extent that the prediction would be self-defeating.

The accounting and legal professions have now reached an agreement that assures that companies provide at least minimal information about pending litigation. The conscientious analyst, however, should view the corporate disclosures as nothing more than warning flags. He should attempt to learn all he can about the pending litigation through publicly available legal filing or reliable secondary sources and consider the financial consequences of alternative outcomes.

## Other Required Disclosures

The Securities and Exchange Commission requires additional disclosures in the annual reports to stockholders (although not necessarily in the financial statements per se) which do much to facilitate financial analysis. Among the information to be disclosed is:

A brief description of the company's business, which indicates the general nature and scope of its operations;

Information on the company's lines of business and its classes of products;

A five-year summary of operations;

A summary of significant accounting policies. The policies to be revealed pertain to those matters in which the firm has some degree of discretion, such as inventory, fixed assets, and investments in subsidiaries. Exhibit 15-7 provides excerpts from Kellogg Company's statement of accounting policies.

## EXHIBIT 15-7

---

**Kellogg Company and Subsidiaries**
**Excerpts from Statement of**
**Significant Accounting Policies**
**Year Ended December 31,1977**

**Consolidation**

The consolidated financial statements include the accounts of Kellogg Company and its wholly-owned subsidiaries. Significant intercompany transactions are eliminated in consolidation.

**Inventories**

Inventories are valued at the lower of cost (principally average) or market.

**Plant and Equipment**

Fixed assets are stated at cost and depreciated over estimated useful lives using straight-line methods. The cost and accumulated depreciation of properties sold or retired are eliminated from the accounts and gains or losses on disposition are reflected in earnings. Expenditures for maintenance and repairs are charged against earnings. Renewals and improvements are capitalized.

*EXHIBIT 15-7 (cont)*

### Intangible Assets

Intangible assets represent the excess of unamortized cost over the fair market value of net assets of businesses acquired by purchase. An amount of $19.0 million recorded prior to November 1, 1970 is not being amortized as it is considered to have continuing value over an indefinite period. The balance is being amortized over twenty-five to forty years.

A brief explanation as to the reason for changes in earnings from those of the previous year is given. This statement generally focuses upon material increases or decreases in selected revenues and expenses. The analysis of the management of Kellogg Company for 1977 is contained in Exhibit 15-8.

*EXHIBIT 15-8*

**Kellogg Company and Subsidiaries**
**Management's Analysis of**
**the Summary of Operations**
**Year Ended December 31, 1977**

**1977 Compared to 1976**

Net sales increased $148.0 million, with higher selling prices accounting for approximately $113.0 million of the total. The balance of the increase represents sales of products of businesses acquired during the year, the sales of new products and increases in volume on existing products. Lower currency translation rates on foreign sales had an off-setting effect of approximately $26.0 million.

An increase of $97.4 million in costs of goods sold resulted principally from higher costs for raw material, labor, energy and other manufacturing costs. Raw material costs including those of businesses acquired and new products were up $53.8 million, labor rose $17.3 million and increases in freight, energy, employee benefits and fixed charges accounted for most of the balance. Maintenance and repairs were up $6.0 million primarily because of increased costs of labor and repair parts. Depreciation increased $5.2 million reflecting the continuing expansion and modernization of our plants.

Selling, general and administrative expenses rose $39.3 million principally due to increased advertising and promotion expenses associated with new product introductions and increased costs of purchasing equivalent media advertising and promotion exposure.

In addition, the annual report must include an offer to send stockholders, free of charge, a copy of the report (Form 10-K or 12-K) that the company is required to file annually with the SEC. The report filed with the SEC contains financial information in considerably more detail and abundance than is conventionally provided in the annual report intended primarily for stockholders.

The disclosure requirement with respect to lines of business and classes of products is of particular importance to financial analysts. Many companies are *conglomerates;* they are composed of divisions in a number of unrelated industries. Their consolidated financial statements combine the financial position and results of operations of all their activities and provide no indication of the corporate resources devoted to any particular industry or to the profits derived therefrom. Yet financial analysis is meaningful only when it is possible to make comparisons among different firms in the same industry. Insofar as the financial statements fail to provide data by industry, such comparisons are impossible.

Firms traditionally have been reluctant to disclose financial information on the basis of individual lines of business because of the inherent difficulties of allocating common costs (e.g., headquarters costs) to the separate businesses and of classifying, in a meaningful way, all products into lines of business. The SEC requires the disclosure of sales and revenues as well as income only for each line of business that exceeds 15 percent (10 percent for companies with over $50 million in revenues) of total sales and revenues or income before income taxes. While the disclosure requirements by the Securities and Exchange Commission are inadequate from the standpoint of many financial analysts, they do assure the availability of a substantial amount of valuable information that was usually not previously made public.

As this text is being written, proposals for more comprehensive disclosure are under consideration. Almost certainly, annual reports of the future will contain greater amounts of "soft" information than do those of today. "Soft" information is that which cannot be readily verified or "attested" to, but which may, nevertheless, be of critical importance to an investment decision. It has been suggested, for example, that management include in the annual report to shareholders projections of future economic performance, a summary of its plans and objectives, and an explanation of its dividend and capital structure policies.

## Summary

Financial statements provide information that is critical to the evaluation of a corporation's past operating performance, its current financial position, and its prospects for the future. To use financial statements, however, one must first understand them. In this chapter we have stressed the importance of examining financial statements with a critical eye, of being aware of their inherent limitations, and of being cognizant of the potential impact of different accounting principles and policies.

Accounting numbers taken by themselves seldom provide very much insight into a corporation. Calculation of ratios, and comparison of such ratios with those of similar firms and with those of the same firm over one or more accounting periods, enable the analyst to measure the efficiency with which the firm has utilized the resources within its command, to evaluate its ability to meet its obligations as they come due, and to compare the interests of stockholders with those to whom the company is indebted.

Not all significant financial data are contained in the body of the financial reports, however. Additional notes and statements of management provide information that supplements the data contained in the basic statements. They contain disclosures pertaining to accounting policies, outstanding commitments, and contingent liabilities as well as schedules that support summary figures included in the body of the statements.

*exercise for review and self-testing*

You wish to compare the financial performance and investment characteristics of General Mills, Inc. with that of Kellogg Company. Your evaluation is to be based on the 1977 financial reports of the two firms, which are reproduced, in part, in this chapter. The relevant ratios for Kellogg Company have been computed and are indicated in the text.

a. Which of the firms had greater earnings, prior to deducting dividend and interest distributions in relation to all the resources within its command?

b. Which of the firms provided a greater return to common stockholders as measured by income available to them as a percentage of their average equity?

c. Which of the firms used its inventory more effectively, if effectiveness is measured by the number of times that average inventory "turned over"?

d. Which of the firms had less capital tied up relative to sales in accounts receivable; in which firm did accounts receivable "turn over" the greater number of times?

e. Which of the firms was more likely to be able to meet its current obligations as they came due; in which of the firms was the ratio of current assets to current liabilities the greater?

f. Which of the firms was more highly levered; in which was the ratio of capital provided by creditors (debt) to that provided by owners (equity) the greater? Include in debt the minority interests in consolidated subsidiaries.

g. Which of the firms was likely to be better able to meet its fixed interest obligations; in which firm was interest "covered" the greater number of times by earnings?

## Questions

*review and discussion*

1. "Financial analysis is nothing more than a subset of accounting. An analyst who understands a firm's accounting reports understands just about all there is to know about a company." Do you agree? Explain.

2. Provide an example of how a firm's "personality" may be revealed by its mode of financing expansion. Provide an example of how it may be indicated by its *accounting* practices.

3. What is meant by *quality* of earnings? What are the major characteristics of *high-quality* earnings?

4. In what way do the conventional means of accounting for marketable securities limit the usefulness of net earnings as a measure of corporate performance in a particular year?

5. One financial analyst recently commented to another, "As you can see, over each of the last three years, company A has had a higher rate of return on investment than company B. Since both firms are in the same industry, it seems pretty clear that company A is the better managed of the two." Cite five examples of how the difference in return on investment may be attributable entirely to choice among accounting alternatives.

6. Why do normal ranges for most ratios and percentages vary from industry to industry? Provide an example.

7. The specific manner in which a ratio is determined should depend on the specific decision at hand. Illustrate this statement by comparing return on investment as computed using total investment with that computed using stockholders' equity.

8. "From the standpoint of the stockholders, the lower the debt to equity ratio, the better, since there are smaller claims against the resources of the firm on the parts of creditors." Do you agree? Explain.

9. Why is it desirable that a corporation relegate certain types of financial data to footnotes rather than including them in the main body of the financial reports?

10. Why have accountants and attorneys sometimes been at odds with respect to disclosure of pending litigation in footnotes to the financial statements?

## Problems

1. *Ratio analysis provides useful, but by no means sufficient, information on which to base an investment decision.*

   Examine the financial statements of General Mills presented in the chapter.
   a. As compared with Kellogg, which company in the latest year for which data are presented provided the greater return on all classes of stockholders?
   b. Assume that during 1977, the common stock of General Mills traded, on average, at a price of $30 per share. If Kellogg's traded at an average price of $22 per share, which company had the greater price/earnings ratio?
   c. Which of the two companies had the greater earnings as a percentage of total revenues?
   d. Which had the greater gross margin? Why are the gross margin percentages of the two companies not readily comparable?

    e. Based solely on your calculations, which company had the superior record of performance? Would you be willing to recommend that a friend purchase the stock of one company over that of the other?

2. *Choice among generally accepted accounting practices affects the "quality" of earnings.*

A central theme of this text has been that a firm has the opportunity to select among several methods of accounting and reporting. Review the financial statements of Koppers Company in Chapter 2. For each of the following areas, indicate the nature of the choice made by the company, describe an alternative practice that the firm could have adopted, and state whether the practice selected by the firm likely resulted in greater or lesser reported earnings than the alternative:

    1. inventories.

    2. fixed assets.

    3. income taxes.

3. *A forward-looking management will consider the impact of its actions upon widely used financial ratios.*

What effect would each of the following transactions have on a firm's (1) current ratio, (2) quick ratio, (3) debt to equity ratio? Indicate whether each transaction would cause the ratio to increase (I) or decrease (D) or whether it would have no effect (NE). Assume that any transactions involving revenues or expenses have an immediate impact upon retained earnings. Assume that all ratios were initially *greater* than 1 : 1.

    1. The firm sells goods on account. Assume that the firm maintains its inventory records on a perpetual basis and that the price at which the goods are sold is greater than their initial cost.

    2. The firm collects the amount receivable from the customer to whom it made the sale.

    3. The firm issues long-term bonds.

    4. The firm issues preferred stock in exchange for cash.

    5. The firm declares, but does not pay, a dividend on common stock.

    6. The firm pays the previously declared dividend.

    7. The company purchases merchandise inventory on account.

    8. The company pays for the merchandise previously purchased.

    9. The firm purchases equipment, giving the seller a three-year note for the entire amount payable.

    10. The firm recognizes depreciation for the first year.

    11. The company writes off an uncollectible account receivable against the allowance for uncollectibles.

    12. The firm writes off inventory as obsolete.

4. *An increase in the current ratio may not necessarily be indicative of an improved financial position.*

The president of a company, in requesting a renewal of an outstanding loan, wrote to an officer of a bank: "In spite of a decline in sales and earnings, we were able to strengthen our working capital position." He went on to cite the increase in the current ratio as evidence of the improvement.

The balance sheet of the company reported the following current assets and liabilities:

|  | December 31, 1981 | December 31, 1980 |
|---|---|---|
| Cash | $ 60,000 | $120,000 |
| Accounts receivable | 270,000 | 190,000 |
| Inventories | 420,000 | 300,000 |
| Total current assets | $750,000 | $610,000 |
| Accounts payable | $370,000 | $330,000 |
| Notes payable | 140,000 | 140,000 |
| Total current liabilities | $510,000 | $470,000 |

The income statement (in summary form) revealed the following:

|  | 1981 | 1980 |
|---|---|---|
| Sales | $1,400,000 | $1,560,000 |
| Cost of goods sold | $ 840,000 | $ 936,000 |
| Other expenses | 240,000 | 260,000 |
| Total expenses | $1,080,000 | $1,196,000 |
| Net income | $ 320,000 | $ 364,000 |

a. Determine the current ratio for both years.

b. (1) Determine the quick ratio.

   (2) Calculate number of days' sales in accounts receivable.

c. Provide a possible explanation for the increase in accounts receivable and inventories that would undermine the contention of the president that the firm's working capital position has improved. Has the current position of the company really improved?

5. *Information on product lines is essential to comparisons involving "conglomerates."*

   Refer to the income statement of General Mills for the year ended May 29, 1977.

   a. Prepare a schedule in which you express each expense and net income as a percentage of sales.

   b. Compare the percentages to those of Kellogg Company. Which firm had the greater gross margin. Which had the greater profit margin?

   c. Included in the annual report of General Mills are data on sales and earnings by major product groups. It is revealed that sales of breakfast and snack items represented 25.4 percent of total sales. These same items, however, contributed 35.1 percent of total earnings.

  a. Determine the approximate profit margin on sales of breakfast and snack items.

  b. In light of the fact that Kellogg Company manufactures and sells primarily breakfast and snack foods, does the efficiency of General Mills with respect only to those products appear any greater compared than that of Kellogg?

**6.** *Comparisons of performance based on ratios may be meaningless if made between firms in different industries.*

Cohen-Hatfield Industries, a firm whose shares are traded on the American Stock Exchange, is primarily in the retail jewelry business. A substantial portion of its revenue is generated from jewelry departments that it leases in department stores.

    Its annual report of January 29, 1978 indicated the following:

| | |
|---|---:|
| Net sales | $44,966,000 |
| Cost of merchandise sold | 27,487,000 |
| Net income | 510,000 |
| Inventory | 13,815,000 |
| Property and equipment | 1,742,000 |

  a. Consider the operating characteristics of the retail jewelry industry as compared with those of the cereal industry. In which industry would firms be likely to have the greater amount of plant and equipment in relation to sales? In which would inventory be kept on hand for the longer period of time? In which would the "mark-up" on goods sold be the greater?

  b. Compute the following ratios for Cohen-Hatfield and compare them with those of Kellogg Company (which are indicated in the text):

    1. plant and equipment turnover.

    2. inventory turnover.

    3. gross margin.

Base the computations of Cohen-Hatfield ratios on year-end rather than average amounts. Are the differences in the ratios consistent with your "intuitive" analysis in part a?

**7.** *To assure interfirm and interyear comparability of ratios it may be necessary to adjust for differences in method of accounting for inventory.*

The 1977 annual report of General Mills contained the following note:

If the FIFO method of inventory accounting had been used in place of LIFO, inventories would have been $18,746,000 and $12,496,000 higher than reported at May 29, 1977 and May 30, 1976, respectively.

Suppose that you want to adjust the 1977 financial statements of General Mills in order to make them comparable with either those of competitors which maintain inventory on a FIFO basis or with years prior to 1975 when General Mills maintained its inventory on a FIFO basis.

If the company had maintained its inventory on a FIFO basis:

a. How much less would cost of goods sold have been in 1977?

b. How much greater would reported income *after taxes* have been? Assume a marginal income tax rate of 48 percent.

c. How much greater would current assets as of May 29, 1977 have been?

d. How much greater would retained earnings have been? Assume a marginal income tax rate of 48 percent.

e. Compute the following ratios taking into account the required adjustments:

   1. current ratio.

   2. inventory turnover.

   3. return on investment (stockholders' equity).

   (For convenience, base the computation of the ratios on balances as of May 29, 1977 rather than on average balances during the year.)

8. *The factors that affect return on investment may be depicted graphically.*

   Return on investment may be computed in several ways. One way, often associated with the Du Pont Company, is illustrated in the accompanying diagram. The diagram is intended to direct the attention of management to the various elements that have an impact upon return on investment.

   a. Refer to the 1977 financial statements of General Mills. Determine return on investment (all capital) as illustrated in the text. Assume average investment to be the same as year-end investment.

   b. Determine return on investment by "filling in" each of the boxes in the diagram and carrying out the required operations. Compare your results.

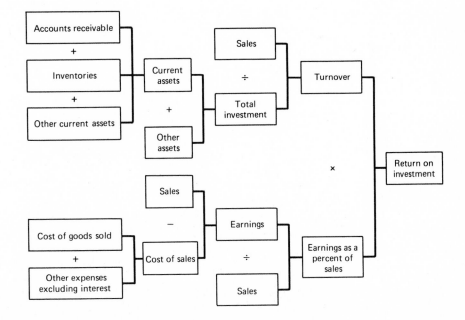

9. *Financial ratios incorporate all of the deficiencies of the underlying accounting data.*

A friend, who is president of Statistical Software, Inc., asked if you would like to invest in his company. In explaining to you the advantages of such an investment, he pointed to the firm's profitability as evidenced by a high rate of return on stockholders' equity and the security of the investment as measured by *times interest earned.*

The firm develops and sells to industrial firms customized computer programs. The programs are intended to enable a firm to generate statistical information about its operations.

The president of Statistical Software, Inc. provided you with the company's 1980 financial statements. The statements of earnings and of changes in financial position (cash basis) are as follows:

### Statement of Income
### Year Ended December 31, 1980

| | | |
|---|---:|---:|
| Sales | $540,000 | |
| Other revenues | 260,000 | $800,000 |
| Cost of programs developed | $530,000 | |
| Other expenses | 90,000 | |
| Interest | 20,000 | |
| Taxes | 40,000 | 680,000 |
| Net income | | $120,000 |

### Statement of Changes in Financial Position
### Year Ended December 31, 1980

| | | |
|---|---:|---:|
| Sources of cash | | |
| From operations | | |
| Income | $120,000 | |
| Add: Depreciation and amortization | 60,000 | |
| Subtract: Gain on sale of land | (160,000) | $ 20,000 |
| Sale of land | | 220,000 |
| Total sources of cash | | $240,000 |
| Uses of cash | | |
| Increase in accounts receivable | | $170,000 |
| Increase in advertising and promotion costs expected to benefit future periods | | 30,000 |
| Increase in program development costs applicable to software to be delivered in future | | 120,000 |
| Total uses of cash | | $320,000 |
| Decrease in cash | | $ (80,000) |
| Cash balance beginning of year | | 410,000 |
| Cash balance end of year | | $330,000 |

The balance sheet reveals that average stockholders' equity during the year was $600,000.

a. Determine the rate of return on stockholders' equity and the times interest earned measure of coverage of fixed charges.

b. Review carefully the two statements presented. Recognizing that no investment decisions can be made on the basis of statements for a single year, what questions would you raise (or what reservations would you have) pertaining to the firm's *quality* of earnings?

10. *Differences in return on investment may be more apparent than real.*

Rent-a-Truck, Inc. was founded in January 1980. The company issued 300,000 shares of common stock at $10 per share.

The company acquired trucks at a cost of $3 million. The useful lives of the trucks were estimated to be five years, with zero salvage value.

During its first year of operations the revenues of the firm, less all expenses other than depreciation and income taxes, were $1.3 million. The applicable income tax rate is 40 percent. The company *defers* its tax expense; that is, reported tax expense is based on *reported* income; it is not indicative of the required current tax payment.

a. Determine the first year's return on investment (stockholders' equity) under each of the following assumptions:

1. The firm uses straight-line depreciation for book purposes and straight-line depreciation for tax purposes.

2. The firm uses double-declining balance depreciation for book purposes and double-declining balance depreciation for tax purposes.

3. The firm uses straight-line depreciation for book purposes and double-declining balance depreciation for tax purposes.

Base your computation on year-end stockholders' equity as opposed to average stockholders' equity.

b. Comment on any substantive (i.e., "real" economic) differences in rate of return under each of the three methods.

11. *Use of return on investment (all capital) as a criterion of corporate performance may lead to dysfunctional management decisions.*

The president of Burnside, Inc. is faced with the decision as to whether to expand the corporation by acquiring a new plant. The cost of the new plant would be $500,000. The necessary capital could be acquired by issuing bonds which would provide a return to lenders of 12 percent per year. The new plant would increase corporate pretax earnings by $70,000 prior to taking into account required interest payments of $60,000.

Burnside, Inc. in recent years has had annual pretax income, after deducting $50,000 in interest payments, of $250,000. The firm, as of December 31, 1980, has outstanding debt of $500,000 and owners' equity of $1.5 million.

The financial vice-president favors acquisition of the new plant, arguing that corporate earnings would be increased by $10,000. The corporate controller opposes acquisition, maintaining that it would result in reduction of the firm's return on invested capital.

a. Determine return on investment (all capital) if (1) the plant is not acquired and (2) the plant is acquired. Assume that earnings on the old facilities will be the same in the future as they have been in the past. Disregard income taxes.

b. Determine return on investment (stockholders' equity) under the two alternatives.

c. Calculate earnings per share under the two alternatives. The company has 10,000 shares of common stock outstanding.

d. Do you think the company should acquire the plant? Explain.

e. Comment on the potential dangers of using return on investment (all capital) as a criterion for making investment decisions.

12. *Alternative practices with respect to acquisition of property would affect differently the debt to equity ratio.*

Review the financial statements of General Mills.

a. Calculate the debt to equity ratio as of May 29, 1977.

b. A footnote to the financial statements indicates that "non-cancellable lease commitments for the next five years are: $17,000,000 in 1978; $15,000,000 in 1979; $12,000,000 in 1980; $10,000,000 in 1981; and $9,000,000 in 1982."

c. Suppose that General Mills had elected to purchase the property that it presently rents. The company would have financed its purchase by borrowing the required funds at a rate of 8 percent per year. Determine the amount the company would have had to borrow. Make the simplifying assumption that the useful life of the property does not extend beyond 1982 and that the loans would be repaid by then. In other words, determine the present value of the lease obligations.

c. Recompute the debt to equity ratio assuming that the company would *capitalize* its lease obligations.

d. In comparing the financial position of General Mills with that of Kellogg, do you think it is appropriate to adjust the balance sheet of General Mills for lease obligations? Why? (Kellogg does not have any material lease obligations that are not reflected on its balance sheet.)

13. *Corporate debt, though it increases financial risk, may work to the benefit of common stockholders.*

Refer to the financial statements of Koppers Company in Chapter 2.

a. Determine the ratio of debt to equity as of December 31, 1977.

b. Calculate return on investment based on all resources within the company's command.

c. Calculate return on investment based only upon the equity of the common stockholders.

d. Calculate the rate of interest paid during 1977 on the average balance of term debt outstanding.

e. From the standpoint of the common stockholders, did the company make effective use of borrowed funds (i.e., leverage) during 1977?

14. *The advantages of debt financing as opposed to equity financing may be illusory.*

The Dement Corporation has $30 million in total assets. It has $10 million in current liabilities outstanding and $20 million in stockholders' equity. There are presently 100,000 shares of common stock outstanding. After-tax earnings over the past several years have averaged $2.1 million per year.

The company has decided to expand its operations by constructing a new plant. The new plant will cost $6 million, and it is estimated that it will increase earnings by $360,000 after taxes, not taking into account costs of financing.

The company has two options available to it to finance the plant. First it can issue additional shares of stock. The additional shares could be sold for $400 per share.

Alternatively, it can raise the required $6 million by issuing bonds. The bonds would be sold to yield purchasers 10 percent per year. The interest costs would be tax deductible to the company. The applicable tax rate is 48 percent.

a. Assume that the company will construct the new plant. For each of the alternatives determine anticipated (1) return on investment (all capital), (2) return on investment (stockholders' equity), and (3) earnings per share.

b. After reviewing the figures just computed, the president of the company stated, "It is obvious that we are better off financing expansion with debt rather than equity. In the future, let's finance all additions by issuing bonds rather than stock." Comment on the logic of the president.

15. *Insofar as financial statements fail to take into account current values, so also do the financial ratios.*

The financial statements of the Yorkville Bottling Co. revealed the following data for 1981:

| | |
|---|---|
| Current assets | $   420,000 |
| Other assets (property, plant and equipment) | 6,580,000 |
| Current liabilities | 670,000 |
| Other liabilities | 2,308,000 |
| Sales | 11,500,000 |
| Interest expense | 350,000 |
| Net income | 1,400,000 |

a. Determine the following relationships (based on year-end balances):
   1. return on investment (all capital).
   2. current ratio.
   3. debt to equity.
   4. plant and equipment turnover.

b. Investigation reveals that included in current assets are marketable securities that are recorded at a cost of $100,000. Their current market value is $350,000. Moreover, the company's plant is located on land that had originally cost $500,000. The land currently has a fair market value of $1 million. Recompute the above relationships to take into account the additional information. Which set of relationships do you think is more relevant to most decisions required of both managers and investors?

c. Comment on how the revised ratios may affect the analyst's view of both financial position and operating performance.

16. *A balance sheet and an income statement can be derived from selected financial ratios.*

The Ventnor Company had net earnings in 1980 of $50,000.

a. Its return on investment based on stockholders' equity as of year end was 10 percent. Determine year-end stockholders' equity.

b. The firm's debt to equity ratio was 0.4 : 1. Determine year-end debt.

c. Ventnor Company's return on investment (all capital) was 8 percent based on year-end capital. Determine interest expense for the year.

d. Its *times interest earned* ratio was 13 : 1. Determine income taxes.

e. The company's net earnings as a percent of sales was 5 percent. Determine sales.

f. Its gross margin was 40 percent. Determine cost of goods sold.

g. Its inventory turned over 6 times. Determine inventory.

h. The firm's accounts receivable turned over 25 times. Determine accounts receivable.

i. Its fixed assets turned over 2 times. Determine fixed assets.

j. Its only remaining asset was cash. Determine year-end cash.

k. Its current ratio was 2 : 1. Determine current liabilities.

l. All expenses not yet determined may be classified as "sales and administration." Reconstruct, as best you can, the income statement of Ventnor Company for 1980 and its balance sheet as of year end 1980.

17. *Ratio analysis may assist an investor in predicting whether a firm will "turn around" or go bankrupt.*

The financial statements as of January 31, 1974 and 1975, of the M. R. Lee Co. are presented below and on page 619. The M.R. Lee Co. operates a chain of low-priced department stores located in 42 states. Most of its merchandise is priced under $10, but the stores also carry a line of major appliances.

a. Explain as best you can the reason for the decline in earnings in 1975.

b. Compare the liquidity of the company in 1975 with that of 1974.

c. Compare the debt to equity ratio of 1975 with that of 1974.

d. Comment on the firm's ability to meet fixed interest charges.

e. Comment on the critical problems that the firm will face in the following year. Do you see any bright spots? Do you believe that the ability of the firm to survive is in question?

### Consolidated Statement of Income
### (000s omitted)

|  | Years ended | |
|---|---|---|
|  | *1/31/75* | *1/31/74* |
| Net sales | $1,761,952 | $1,845,802 |
| Other revenues | 10,700 | 15,617 |
| Total revenues | $1,772,652 | $1,861,419 |
| Cost of goods sold | $1,303,267 | $1,282,944 |
| Selling and other expenses | 726,420 | 546,202 |
| Interest | 37,771 | 18,082 |
| Income tax expense (refund) | (117,466) | 3,289 |
| Total expenses | $1,949,992 | $1,850,517 |
| Net income (loss) | $ (177,340) | $ 10,902 |

### M. R. Lee Co.
### Consolidated Balance Sheet as of January 31
### (000s omitted)

|  | 1975 | 1974 |
|---|---|---|
| **Assets** | | |
| Current | | |
| Cash and Equivalent | $ 79,642 | $ 45,952 |
| Accounts receivable (net) | 431,191 | 540,802 |
| Inventories | 407,357 | 450,636 |
| Other current assets | 6,591 | 7,299 |
| Total current assets | $ 924,781 | $1,044,689 |
| Noncurrent | | |
| Property and equipment (net) | $ 101,932 | $ 100,983 |
| Investment in subsidiaries | 49,764 | 44,251 |
| Other assets | 5,790 | 5,063 |
| Total noncurrent assets | $ 157,486 | $ 150,297 |
| Total assets | $1,082,267 | $1,194,986 |
| **Liabilities and stockholders' equity** | | |
| Current | | |
| Accounts payable | $ 50,067 | $ 58,192 |
| Notes and other payables | 600,995 | 453,096 |
| Miscellaneous accruals | 79,144 | 46,691 |
| Taxes payable | 19,700 | 103,078 |
| Total current liabilities | $ 749,906 | $ 661,057 |
| Noncurrent | | |
| Notes payable | $ 99,005 | $ 100,000 |
| Bonds payable | 117,336 | 120,336 |
| Other liabilities | 2,183 | 18,845 |
| Total noncurrent liabilities | $ 218,524 | $ 239,181 |
| Stockholders' equity | | |
| Preferred stock | $ 7,465 | $ 7,464 |
| Common stock ($1.25 par value) | 18,599 | 18,599 |
| Capital in excess of par | 83,914 | 85,909 |
| Less: Stock held in treasury | (33,815) | (36,696) |
| Retained earnings | 37,674 | 219,472 |
| Total stockholders' equity | $ 113,837 | $ 294,748 |
| Total liabilities and stockholders' equity | $1,082,267 | $1,194,986 |

a.  Note: 000 omitted in all dollar amounts.

$$\text{Return on investment} = \frac{\text{Net income + Interest}}{\text{Average assets}}$$
$$\text{(all capital)}$$

$$\text{Average assets} = \frac{\$1,447,271 + \$1,328,196}{2} = \$1,387,733.5$$

$$\text{Return on investment} = \frac{\$117,034 + \$26,739}{\$1,387,735.5} = 10.4\%$$

The comparable return on investment for Kellogg Company was considerably greater, 18.4 percent.

b.  
$$\text{Return on investment} = \frac{\text{Net income + Preferred stock dividends}}{\text{Average equity of common stockholders}}$$
$$\text{(stockholders' equity)}$$

$$\text{Average equity} = \frac{\$640,245 + \$724,870}{2} = \$682,557.5$$

$$\text{Return on investment} = \frac{\$117,034 + \$0}{\$682,557.5} = 17.1\%$$

The return to stockholders of Kellogg Company, based on their equity in the firm, was 26.8 percent.

c.  
$$\text{Inventory turnover} = \frac{\text{Cost of goods sold}}{\text{Average inventory}}$$

$$\text{Average inventory} = \frac{\$353,654 + \$425,832}{2} = \$389,743$$

$$\text{Inventory turnover} = \frac{\$1,786,210}{\$389,743} = 4.58 \text{ times}$$

Kellogg Company appears to have used its inventory more efficiently as its inventory turned over 6.2 times.

d.  
$$\text{Accounts receivable turnover} = \frac{\text{Sales}}{\text{Average accounts receivable}}$$

$$\text{Average accounts receivable} = \frac{\$215,963 + \$231,607}{2} = \$223,785$$

$$\text{Accounts receivable turnover} = \frac{\$2,909,404}{\$223,785} = 13.0 \text{ times}$$

The accounts receivable of Kellogg Company turned over more, 15.9 times.

e.
$$\text{Current ratio} = \frac{\text{Current assets}}{\text{Current liabilities}} = \frac{\$713,394}{\$415,205} = 1.72 \text{ to } 1$$

The current ratio of Kellogg Company was greater, 2.31 to 1.

f.
$$\text{Debt/equity ratio} = \frac{\text{Total debt}}{\text{Total equity}} = \frac{\$722,401}{\$724,870} = 1.0 \text{ to } 1$$

Kellogg Company was less levered as its debt to equity ratio was only .54 to 1.

g.
$$\text{Times interest earned} = \frac{\text{Net income} + \text{Interest} + \text{Income taxes}}{\text{Interest}}$$

$$= \frac{\$117,034 + \$26,739 + \$112,119}{\$26,739} = 9.6 \text{ times}$$

Kellogg Company was able to cover its fixed interest charges with considerably greater ease. The net income before interest and taxes for Kellogg was 29.5 times its interest obligations.

# 16

## Accounting for Increases in Prices and Values

In this chapter we shall deal with the need for, and means of, adjusting financial statements to take into account changes in the general level of prices as well as in the value of specific resources held by a firm. In addition, we shall consider issues relating to assets and liabilities of a firm that are stated in foreign currencies. We shall conclude the text with a brief discussion as to whether the use of one accounting practice as opposed to its alternatives really does affect the allocation of capital in our economy.

## Historical Costs: Adjusting for Changes in the Level of Prices

One of the implicit assumptions underlying traditional accounting is that the basic unit of measure (e.g., the U.S. dollar) is stable. To this point in the text, for example, it has been assumed that the U.S. dollar has remained unchanged in value over time—that a dollar was worth the same in 1979 as it was in 1972. It is for this reason that measurements (e.g., costs of assets) taken in 1972 could readily be added to those of 1979. In fact, of course, such an assumption is patently untenable. Between 1972 and 1979 the general level of prices in the United States approximately doubled. In a sense, therefore, the dollar of 1979 was worth about one-half that of 1972.

Inflation has been a major force in the United States. Inflation works to the benefit of some parties and to the detriment of others. A firm, for example, that issued bonds in 1972 with the stipulation that they be redeemed in 1979 may have benefited from the increase in the general level of prices. The dollars that it borrowed in 1972 could purchase considerably more goods and services than those which the company had to repay in 1979. By contrast, the parties which purchased the bonds in 1972 sacrificed far more purchasing power when they surrendered the cash to acquire the bonds than they received in return seven years later.

Financial statements that do not take into account the changing value of the dollar are deficient in that they fail to provide a basis for assessing the impact of inflation upon the company being reported upon. They establish no basis on which to determine whether the firm has gained or lost from the increase in prices. Effective 1980, large publicly-traded corporations will be required by FASB Statement No. 33 (1979) to provide in their annual reports two sets of supplementary financial disclosures. One will take into account changes in the general level of prices (constant dollar data); the other will give recognition to changes in the replacement costs of the specific resources held by the firm (current cost data).

**changes in prices vs. changes in values**

Prices of goods and services increase (or decrease) for at least two reasons. First, there might be a change in either the demand for or the supply of a specific product. An increase in demand would cause the price to increase; a decrease in supply would also cause the price to increase. Second, as a consequence of in-flationary forces in the economy, there might be a general increase in the pre-vailing level of prices. The dollar itself may decline in value. On average, taking into account *all* goods and services purchased by consumers as well as businesses, a dollar might buy less today than it did in a previous period. This section is directed exclusively to increases in prices resulting from a *general* increase in the level of prices. It does *not* deal with changes in the *value* of *specific* goods or services. Such changes will be discussed later in this chapter.

Suppose that in 1972, $1,000 could have served to acquire a *basket* of goods or services of a typical consumer. By the end of 1979 that same basket of goods had a cost of $2,010.* Suppose further that the increase in prices (101 percent) was typical of the rise in prices throughout the economy. In terms of goods and services—the only terms in which a dollar has meaning—it can be said that 1.00 1972 dollar was the equivalent of 2.01 1979 dollars:

$$\$^{72}1.00 = \$^{79}2.01$$

If a company had purchased a parcel of land in 1972 for $1,000, then assuming no change in the inherent value of land—that is, assuming that there was no change either in the demand for such land or in the availability of similar parcels of land—one would expect that the parcel of land would be priced at $2,010 in 1979. Indeed, in terms of 1979 dollars, the price paid for such land was $2,010. The *historical cost* of the land can be expressed as *either* $^{72}1,000 or $^{79}2,010.

Many accountants and businessmen have come to recognize that it is in-appropriate to add together, in the same financial statements, dollars of one year with dollars of another. Financial information, they point out, should be ex-pressed in terms of the dollars prevailing at the time the statements are issued (e.g., 1979 statements should be based on 1979 dollars). Stated values of goods or services which were acquired with different monetary units (e.g., 1972 dollars) should be *translated* into the monetary unit in use as of the date of the financial statements (e.g., 1979). Thus, the land referred to in the previous paragraph should be reported on the balance sheet at $^{79}2,010 as opposed to $^{72}1,000.

*Price level data for 1979 are based on an estimate of the GNP Price Deflator rather than on official government statistics.

It is essential that proposals to state all values in terms of current dollars be distinguished from those (to be discussed later in this chapter) which require that all assets be expressed in terms of current *market* values. Proposals to express all values in terms of current *dollars* are firmly rooted in the historical cost basis of accounting. They require that assets be stated at historical cost expressed in terms of current purchasing power. They differ from proposals to take into account changes in market value in that, as under conventional reporting, changes in prices resulting from increases in supply or in demand will remain unrecognized until an asset is actually sold. Under proposals to recognize changes in market values, increases in market prices, regardless of cause, will be recognized as soon as they occur.

Suppose, for example, that the market value of the land purchased in 1972 for $1,000 was $2,500 in 1979. Under proposals to adjust for price level changes the land would be reported on the balance sheet at $2,010—its historical cost expressed in 1979 dollars. Were the company to sell the land in 1979, it would report a gain of $$^{79}$490—the difference between its historical cost of $$^{79}$2,010 and its selling price of $$^{79}$2,500. Had the market value decreased in 1979 to $$^{79}$1,200, then the company would report a loss of $$^{79}$810—the difference between the price paid of $$^{79}$2,010 and the selling price of $$^{79}$1,200.

**restatement using index numbers**

The key to restating financial statements so that they are expressed in common (current) dollar terms is the translation of dollars of the past into dollars of the present. The U.S. Department of Commerce maintains an index, known as the Gross National Product Implicit Price Deflator (GNP Deflator), which expresses prices of various years as percentages of prices of a selected base year. The index is updated quarterly. As of 1979, the base year was 1972. Hence the price level of 1972 is expressed as 100. The average price level which prevailed in 1976, for example, is expressed as 142.5, indicating that prices increased by 42.5 percent between 1972 and 1976.

To translate a value into current dollars, it is necessary to multiply the value, which is expressed in dollars of the past, by the ratio of the GNP Deflator (or any other similar index) for the current year to that of the past year.

*example*

A company acquired a building in 1971 for $200,000. The building had a useful life of 20 years. At the end of 1979, it was carried on the books as follows:

| | |
|---|---|
| Building | $200,000 |
| Less: Accumulated depreciation | 90,000 |
| | $110,000 |

Assume that the GNP Deflator was 201 at the end of 1979. It was 95 at the time of acquisition in 1971. To translate the carrying value of the building to current dollars, it is necessary to multiply both the building and the accumulated depreciation by the ratio of 201 to 95.

| Asset | Cost in Unadjusted Dollars | Conversion Factor | Cost in 1974 Dollars |
|---|---|---|---|
| Building | $200,000 | 201/95 | $423,158 |
| Accumulated depreciation | 90,000 | 201/95 | 190,421 |
| | | | $232,737 |

The building would be reported on the 1979 balance sheet at the adjusted historical cost of $423,158 less accumulated depreciation of $190,421. Depreciation charges to be reported on the 1979 income statement would be one-twentieth of the adjusted historical cost of $423,158—$21,158 (or $10,000 unadjusted depreciation per year times 201/95).

Assume further that the company had prepaid insurance at year end of $5,000. The insurance was acquired at midyear, at a time when the GNP Deflator had a value of 190. The value at year end was 201. Prepaid insurance would be converted by multiplying the $5,000 by the ratio of 201 to 190.

| Asset | Cost in Unadjusted Dollars | Conversion Factor | Cost in Year-end 1974 Dollars |
|---|---|---|---|
| Prepaid insurance | $5,000 | 201/190 | $5,289 |

**monetary vs. non-monetary items**

Not all balance sheet items should properly be translated from original to current dollars. Many assets and liabilities are classified as monetary items. Monetary items are assets and liabilities which are contractually fixed or which are convertible into a fixed number of dollars regardless of changes in prices. Suppose, for example, that in 1972 a company deposited $1,000 in a non-interest-bearing bank account. The price level increased 101 percent between the date of deposit and the end of 1979. But, if at the end of 1979 the company elected to withdraw its funds, it would still receive only $1,000. Over the years, the company clearly suffered a loss in purchasing power. But the bank is unlikely to indemnify the company for such loss and return to the company $2,010. Although the company in 1972 deposited $$^{79}$2,010, it holds a promise from the bank of only $$^{79}$1,000. It would be improper, therefore, to report the cash at a value greater than that stated on its face.

Other monetary items include accounts and notes receivable as well as most forms of debt. If a firm holds a note receivable, the amount that it will receive is contractually fixed. The company will receive no more or no less than the stated amount of the debt regardless of changes in the purchasing power of the dollar. Similarly, if the firm has obligations to make contractually fixed payments, its liability will be unchanged by fluctuations in the value of the dollar. In periods of inflation, creditors incur purchasing power losses as they are repaid with dollars worth less than those promised at the date of the contract. Debtors, on the other hand, reap purchasing power gains as they are able to repay their obligations in devalued dollars.

Nonmonetary items are defined as all assets and liabilities which are not contractually fixed in terms of a specific dollar amount and include all items which are not classified as monetary items. Among nonmonetary assets are marketable securities; inventories; most prepaid costs such as insurance, advertising, and rent; property, plant, and equipment; and goodwill. Among nonmonetary liabilities and equities are *deferred revenues* (e.g., obligations to perform services), common stock, contributed capital in excess of par, and retained earnings.

**adjusting the balance sheet**

The unadjusted balance sheet of a company can readily be converted to one expressed entirely in current dollars by multiplying each of the *nonmonetary* items by the appropriate conversion factor. The conversion factor would represent the ratio of the current value of the GNP Deflator to the value at the time each nonmonetary asset was acquired or each nonmonetary liability was incurred. No adjustment need be made for monetary assets or liabilities since the amount to be paid or received is contractually fixed.

Common stock is considered to be a nonmonetary item, one that must be adjusted, since it does not carry a promise to pay a fixed amount. Retained earnings is also a nonmonetary item. Retained earnings is a residual amount; it represents undistributed earnings of several accounting periods. It can be adjusted most readily by adding to or subtracting from the unadjusted amount the sum of the adjustments made to the other accounts.

*example*

The December 31, 1978 balance sheet of the Inflation Co. appears as follows:

**Inflation Co.**
**Balance Sheet at December 31, 1978**

*Assets*

| | | |
|---|---:|---:|
| Cash | | $ 20,000 |
| Accounts receivable | | 90,000 |
| Inventory | | 80,000 |
| Land | | 40,000 |
| Plant and equipment | $180,000 | |
| Less: Accumulated depreciation | 72,000 | 108,000 |
| Total assets | | $338,000 |

*Liabilities and Owners' Equity*

| | |
|---|---:|
| Accounts payable | $ 30,000 |
| Rent received in advance | 5,000 |
| Bonds payable | 50,000 |
| Common stock | 100,000 |
| Retained earnings | 153,000 |
| Total liabilities and owners' equity | $338,000 |

The following information is also relevant:

> The inventory was acquired in the fourth quarter of 1978. For computational purposes it may be assumed to have been acquired at year end. $10,000 of land was acquired at the end of 1964 and $30, 000 at the end of 1966.
>
> Plant and equipment was acquired at the end of 1974.
>
> The rent paid in advance represents six months' rent on property owned by the company. The rent was received in the second quarter of 1978.
>
> The common stock was issued at the end of 1964.
>
> Selected values of the GNP Deflator may be assumed to have been:

| | | | |
|---|---|---|---|
| 1964 (year end) | 71 | 1978 (1st quarter) | 170 |
| 1966 (year end) | 75 | 1978 (2nd quarter) | 175 |
| 1974 (year end) | 122 | 1978 (3rd quarter) | 179 |
| 1977 (year end) | 167 | 1978 (4th quarter) | 183 |
| | | Average for 1978 = 177 | |

The balance sheet can be adjusted as follows:

### Inflation Co.
### Adjusted Balance Sheet at December 31, 1978

| | Unadjusted Amounts | Conversion Factor | Adjusted Amounts (1978 Dollars) |
|---|---|---|---|
| *Assets* | | | |
| Cash (monetary item) | $ 20,000 | — | $ 20,000 |
| Accounts receivable (monetary item) | 90,000 | — | 90,000 |
| Inventory (4th quarter 1978) | 80,000 | 183/183 | 80,000 |
| Land (1964) | 10,000 | 183/71 | 25,774 |
| Land (1966) | 30,000 | 183/75 | 73,200 |
| Plant and equipment (1974) | 180,000 | 183/122 | 270,000 |
| Accumulated depreciation (1974) | (72,000) | 183/122 | (108,000) |
| | $338,000 | | $450,974 |
| *Liabilities and Owners' Equity* | | | |
| Accounts payable (monetary item) | $ 30,000 | — | $ 30,000 |
| Rent received in advance (2nd quarter, 1978) | 5,000 | 183/175 | 5,229 |
| Bonds payable (monetary item) | 50,000 | — | 50,000 |
| Common stock (1964) | 100,000 | 183/71 | 257,746 |
| Retained earnings | 153,000 | — | 107,999 |
| | $338,000 | | $450,974 |

Special note should be taken of two accounts in the adjusted balance sheet shown on the preceding page. The land is reported and adjusted in two parts to give recognition to acquisitions that were made in two separate years. Adjusted retained earnings of $107,999 represent adjusted retained earnings of $153,000 plus the difference between unadjusted and adjusted amounts of assets less the differences between unadjusted and adjusted amounts of liabilities and common stock. More simply, it may be viewed as a "plug"—the adjusted assets less the sum of the adjusted liabilities and the adjusted common stock.

As a consequence of the adjustments, each *nonmonetary* item is expressed in terms of its *historical* exchange value. Historical exchange value, however, is expressed in dollars of December 31, 1978, rather than dollars of a time past. Each *monetary* item, by contrast, is expressed at its contractually stated amount. The difference between that amount and the value that would have been reported had the item been adjusted represents a cummulative purchasing power gain or loss, a concept to be discussed in the section that follows.

**gains and losses in purchasing power**

One of the important measures to be derived by adjusting financial reports for changes in the overall level of prices is that of the net gain or loss from holding monetary items. Insofar as a company holds monetary assets, be they cash or receivables, during a period in which the level of prices is increasing, it suffers a monetary (purchasing power) loss. The dollars or the promises of dollars are worth less—they could be used to acquire fewer goods or services—at the end of the period than at the beginning.

Assume, for example, that at the start of 1978, when the GNP Deflator was at 167, a company held cash and accounts receivable (monetary assets) of $100,000. During 1978 the level of prices increased by 9.6 percent and the GNP Deflator, by year end, increased to 183. At year-end 1978 the company held the same cash and receivables; it engaged in no transactions during the year. As a consequence of holding the monetary assets, the company incurred a purchasing power loss of 9.6 percent. Had it held assets that could have been transformed into current, year-end 1978, dollars, then it would have been able to exchange such assets (assuming no change in substantive values) for $100,000 times 183/167—$109,581—and would have retained the same purchasing power that it had at the start of the year. Instead, however, it had at the end of 1978 only $100,000 in purchasing power, at a time when $109,581 was required to acquire the same goods and services that a year earlier cost only $100,000. In terms of current, year-end 1978 dollars, the company incurred a loss in purchasing power of $9,581. Price-level-adjusted statements would reflect such losses on the statement of income.

The overall gain or loss in purchasing power associated with a monetary item can readily be determined by subtracting the face amount of the item from the amount of current dollars that would be required to achieve the same degree of purchasing power as when the asset or liability was first acquired. The gain or loss within a particular period of time may be computed by subtracting the purchasing power of the item (expressed in current dollars) at the start of the period from that at the end of the period.

If a company acquires a monetary item in the middle of a year, then the purchasing power gain or loss with respect to that item must be measured from the date acquired to the end of the year. If during the year it disposed of a monetary item that it had on hand at the beginning of the year, then the gain or loss must be determined from the start of the year to the date of disposal. As a consequence, it is necessary to determine exactly (or otherwise make reasonable assumptions) as to when monetary items were acquired and disposed of.

*example*   The illustration of the Inflation Co. will be continued. At the conclusion of 1978 (the start of 1979) the company held the following monetary items:

| | | |
|---|---:|---:|
| Assets | | |
| Cash | $20,000 | |
| Accounts receivable | 90,000 | $110,000 |
| Liabilities | | |
| Accounts payable | $30,000 | |
| Bonds payable | 50,000 | 80,000 |
| Net monetary assets | | $ 30,000 |

Evenly throughout the year, the company made sales of $500,000. At the end of the second quarter of the year it collected rent on land leased to outsiders in the amount of $10,000. Evenly throughout the year it purchased $360,000 of merchandise and incurred other expenses (excluding depreciation) of $92,000. At year end, therefore, it had net monetary assets of $88,000:

| | | |
|---|---:|---:|
| Net monetary assets, December 31, 1978 | | $ 30,000 |
| Add: Sales | $500,000 | |
| Rent received | 10,000 | 510,000 |
| | | $540,000 |
| Less: Purchases | $360,000 | |
| Other expenses (excluding depreciation) | 92,000 | 452,000 |
| Net monetary assets, December 31, 1979 | | $ 88,000 |

The GNP Deflator for year-end 1978 and for 1979 by quarter, and on average, may be assumed to have been:

| Year end, 1978 | 183 | |
|---|---|---|
| 1st quarter, 1979 | 187 | |
| 2nd quarter, 1979 | 192 | Average for 1979 = 194 |
| 3rd quarter, 1979 | 196 | |
| 4th quarter, 1979 | 201 | |

To determine the gain or loss on purchasing power, each of the monetary inflows and outflows will be translated into year-end 1979 dollars (GNP Deflator = 201) by multiplying the amount of the flow by the ratio of the deflator at year end to that existing at the time of the flow. In this illustration, all purchases and sales are assumed to have taken place evenly throughout the year. For convenience, they will be converted using the average value of the GNP Deflator. The rent, however, was received in the second quarter. Thus, it will be converted using the second-quarter value. The difference in the ending balance of net monetary assets between that computed using the adjusted and that using the unadjusted data will constitute the gain or loss in purchasing power:

| | Unadjusted Amounts | Conversion Factor | Adjusted Amounts (12/31/75 Dollars) |
|---|---|---|---|
| Net monetary assets, December 31, 1978 | $ 30,000 | 201/183 | $ 32,951 |
| Add: Sales | 500,000 | 201/194 | 518,041 |
| Rent | 10,000 | 201/192 | 10,469 |
| | $540,000 | | $561,461 |
| Less: Purchases | $360,000 | 201/194 | $372,990 |
| Other expenses | 92,000 | 201/194 | 95,320 |
| | $452,000 | | $468,310 |
| Net monetary assets, December 31, 1979 | $ 88,000 | | $ 93,151 |
| Net monetary assets, December 31, 1979— unadjusted amounts | | | 88,000 |
| Difference—Loss in purchasing power | | | $ 5,151 |

By holding monetary assets for all or a portion of a year in which the price index rose from 183 to 201 the company incurred a loss in purchasing power of $5,151.

The conventional statement of income can be translated into end-of-period dollars by adjusting each of the individual revenues and expenses and by adding or subtracting any gain or loss in purchasing power attributable to holding monetary assets (that computed in the previous example).

In adjusting the income statement, each revenue and expense must be related to the transaction from which it arose. The conversion factor must be based on the level of prices that existed at the time such transaction took place. Depreciation, for example, arises from the acquisition of fixed assets. Depreciation expense, therefore, must be adjusted by the ratio of the current value of the price index to the value of the price index at the time fixed assets were first acquired.

Similarly, cost of goods sold arises from the purchase of merchandise. Since a portion of goods sold during the current year may have been purchased in a previous year or at different times during the current year, the differences in dates of acquisition must be taken into account.

*example*    The unadjusted income statement of the Inflation Co. for 1979 appears as follows:

**Inflation Co.**
**Statement of Income**
**for the Year Ended December 31, 1979**

| | | |
|---|---|---|
| Sales | $500,000 | |
| Rent revenue | 10,000 | $510,000 |
| | | |
| Less: Cost of goods sold | $370,000 | |
| Depreciation | 18,000 | |
| Other expenses | 92,000 | 480,000 |
| Net income | | $ 30,000 |

As indicated in the discussion of purchasing power gains and losses, sales took place evenly throughout the year. Hence, the average value (194) of the GNP Deflator for 1979 may be used to restate sales in terms of December 31, 1979 dollars. Thus,

$$\$500,000 \times 201/194 = \$518,041$$

The rent revenue, however, must be adjusted in two stages. As indicated in the balance sheet of December 31, 1978, the company had recorded on its books $5,000 of rent received in advance. The $5,000 was part of a payment of $10,000 that had been received in the second quarter of 1978, at a time when the price index was at 175. The payment represented rent for both the second six months of 1978 and the first six months of 1979. In the second quarter of

1979 when the price index was at 192, the company received another rent payment of $10,000. Of this amount, $5,000 represented rent for the last six months of 1979. The remaining $5,000, to be recorded on the 1979 balance sheet as "rent received in advance," represents rent for the first six months of 1980. Rent revenue for 1979, therefore, arose out of $5,000 received in the second quarter of 1978 when the price index was at 175 and $5,000 received in the second quarter of 1979 when the price index was at 192. Rent revenue could be restated in terms of end-of-year 1979 dollars as follows:

$$\$5,000 \times 201/175 = \$5,743$$
$$\$5,000 \times 201/192 = \underline{\$5,234}$$
$$\underline{\underline{\$10,977}}$$

Cost of goods sold arises out of purchases of inventory. The balance sheet of December 31, 1978 reveals inventory on hand of $80,000. The inventory was acquired during the fourth quarter of 1978 when the price level was at 183. As indicated previously, $360,000 of merchandise was acquired evenly throughout 1979. The average price level during the year was 194. Since unadjusted cost of goods sold equals only $370,000, the ending inventory as of December 31, 1979, must be $70,000 (beginning inventory of $80,000 plus purchases of $360,000 less cost of goods sold of $370,000). The goods that remain on hand at year end, however, cannot be assumed to have been acquired at a time when the *average* level of prices was at 194. If the company maintains its inventory on a FIFO basis, it is more reasonable to assume they were acquired during the fourth quarter of the year—when the GNP Deflator was at 201. Cost of goods sold, expressed in terms of year-end 1979 dollars, can be determined as follows:

|  | Original Amounts | Conversion Factors | Adjusted Amounts (1979 Dollars) |
|---|---|---|---|
| Inventory, December 31, 1978 | $ 80,000 | 201/183 | $ 87,869 |
| Add: Purchases, 1979 | 360,000 | 201/194 | 372,990 |
| Goods available for sale, 1979 | $440,000 |  | $460,859 |
| Less: Inventory, December 31, 1979 | 70,000 | 201/201 | 70,000 |
| Cost of goods sold, 1979 | $370,000 |  | $390,859 |

Depreciation expense may be attributed to the acquisition of fixed assets. In the case at hand, plant and equipment was acquired at the end of 1974 when the GNP Deflator was at 122. Depreciation ($18,000) may be adjusted as follows:

$$\$18,000 \times 201/122 = \$29,656$$

Other expenses ($142,000), it will be assumed, arose out of transactions occurring evenly throughout 1979 and can be adjusted on the basis of the average value of the price index in 1979. Thus,

$$\$92,000 \times 201/194 = \$95,320$$

The adjusted statement of income, taking into account the loss in purchasing power of $5,151 (computed in the previous example), would appear as follows:

**Inflation Co.**
**Adjusted Statement of Income**
**for the Year Ended December 31, 1979**
**(expressed in terms of current 1979 dollars)**

| | | |
|---|---:|---:|
| Sales | $518,041 | |
| Rent revenue | 10,977 | $529,018 |
| | | |
| Less: Cost of goods sold | $390,859 | |
| Depreciation | 29,656 | |
| Other expenses | 95,320 | |
| Loss of purchasing power | 5,151 | 520,986 |
| Net income | | $   8,032 |

**price level adjustments: why bother?**

Price level adjustments unquestionably add a measure of complexity to financial reporting. Is the additional complexity worth the benefits to be obtained? The arguments in favor of price level adjustments are persuasive.

First, price level adjustments increase the internal consistency of financial statements. They assure that all revenues and expenses and all assets and liabilities that appear on the financial statements of a particular year are expressed in dollars of the same value, rather than in a mixture of dollars of varying values for a number of different periods.

And second, price-level-adjusted statements enable managers and stockholders of an enterprise to determine whether the "real" capital of the business has increased or decreased within an accounting period. The difference between adjusted and unadjusted earnings may be substantial. Studies have demonstrated that many firms which had been reporting healthy profits over a long period of time had, in fact, incurred losses when the impact of inflation was taken into account. Moreover, price-level-adjusted statements specifically set forth the gains or losses attributable to holding monetary items.

**factors that determine magnitude of price level adjustments**

The primary determinants of the magnitude of the difference between price-level-adjusted earnings and conventional earnings are:

1. the rate of inflation
2. the average age of the firm's assets
3. the composition of its balance sheet in terms of monetary and non-monetary items.

### RATE OF INFLATION

The greater the rate of inflation, the greater its impact on earnings. Indeed, interest in price level adjustments has been influenced to a large extent by the prevailing rate of inflation. The roots of price level accounting may be traced to Germany, which, in the years following World War I, experienced a period of exceedingly rapid cost of living escalation. Serious interest in price level adjustments in the United States developed in the 1970s when the price level was increasing at rates in excess of 10 percent per year.

Suppose a firm had fixed assets that cost $100,000. They had a useful life of 10 years. If the rate of inflation were 10 percent per year, then the difference between adjusted and unadjusted depreciation charges can be seen in Exhibit 16–1.

*EXHIBIT 16–1*

**Illustration of Impact of Inflation on Depreciation Expense**

|  | *Years Since Acquisition of Assets* | | |
|---|---|---|---|
|  | *3* | *6* | *9* |
| Historical cost of assets, unadjusted | $100,000 | $100,000 | $100,000 |
| Accumulated depreciation, unadjusted | 30,000 | 60,000 | 90,000 |
| Depreciation expense, unadjusted | 10,000 | 10,000 | 10,000 |
| Historical cost of assets, adjusted[a] | 133,100 | 177,156 | 235,795 |
| Accumulated depreciation, adjusted[a] | 39,930 | 106,294 | 212,215 |
| Depreciation expense, adjusted[a] | 13,310 | 17,716 | 23,580 |

[a]Unadjusted amount times $(1.10)^n$, where $n$ = number of years since acquisition.

The difference in annual depreciation charges by the ninth year of useful life is dramatic—adjusted depreciation charges are 235 percent of unadjusted charges.

## RATE OF TURNOVER

The slower the turnover of assets and liabilities, both monetary and non-monetary, the greater will be the difference between adjusted and unadjusted financial statements. Insofar as assets and liabilities turn over rapidly, they are carried on the books at dollars that are either current or nearly current.

Price level statements will have significantly different effects on firms in different industries. Compare, for example, a firm in the retail grocery business with that in the steel industry. The firm in the grocery business maintains relatively small amounts of fixed assets. Its primary asset, inventory, turns over daily or weekly. It offers no credit and hence has no accounts receivable. Insofar as its outstanding debt is also low, its assets and liabilities are all likely to be stated in current dollar terms; price level accounting would have but a small impact on its financial reports. The firm in the steel business, by contrast, must maintain substantial amounts of plant and equipment, the useful lives of which are likely to be long. As a consequence, a major portion of its assets is likely to be stated in dollars of many years past, and its depreciation expense, if no adjustments are made, will be expressed in such earlier dollars. Were its statements to be recast in price-level-adjusted format, then reported fixed assets and depreciation charges would be substantially higher.

## COMPOSITION OF BALANCE SHEET

Two general guidelines may be expressed with respect to the composition of the balance sheet and its impact on price-level-adjusted earnings. The greater the proportion of net monetary items, the greater will be the purchasing power gains or losses; the greater the proportion of fixed assets, the greater will be the difference in depreciation charges.

Companies which have high debt to equity ratios—and in particular those whose debt consists of long-term obligations—will generally report substantially *higher* earnings if price level adjustments are taken into account. Suppose, for example, that a company had issued $1 million in bonds. If the rate of inflation were 10 percent, then each year, as the inflation rate is compounded, the company would realize a purchasing power gain of over $100,000.

The greater the proportion of fixed assets, the greater will be the increase in the carrying value of assets and, hence, the greater will be the increase in depreciation charges. The earnings of firms that are *capital intense* (i.e., that require large amounts of fixed assets) will likely be reduced substantially when their financial statements are adjusted to take into account the effects of inflation.

The financial reports of some firms—public utilities, for example—are likely to be significantly altered by price level adjustments. Such companies must maintain large amounts of plant and equipment and conventionally finance such plant and equipment with large amounts of bonds. Hence, their earnings are likely to be decreased by additional charges for depreciation but increased by purchasing power gains on outstanding debt.

Public utilities have been among the most enthusiastic proponents of price level adjustments. The rates which public utilities are permitted to charge their customers are ordinarily regulated by state or federal regulatory commissions. Rates are established at levels which should enable companies to generate revenues sufficient to provide them with a fair rate of return. Rate of return is measured by income as a percentage of total assets. By adjusting their financial statements for changes in the price level, public utilities would be able to *increase* their reported assets. At the same time they would likely *decrease* their reported earnings (in general the increase in depreciation charges would be greater than the offsetting gains in purchasing power from having outstanding bonds). Hence, to allow the utilities to earn their pre-established fair rate of return (assuming no change in what is considered a fair rate of return), the regulatory authorities would have to grant them an increase in the rates charged to customers.

Obviously, a change to price level accounting has no effect on the economic value of a firm's assets or liabilities or on its substantive earnings. It affects only *reported* assets, liabilities, and equities. The utilities would benefit, therefore, only insofar as the regulatory commissions fail to "see through" the accounting changes and make no change in the established rate of return to give consideration to the changes in the underlying data on which rate of return is based.

### An Alternative Approach to Accounting— Current Values

Price level accounting is nothing more than an extension of the traditional historical cost approach to accounting. Assets and liabilities are stated at values resulting from exchange transactions. Similarly, the determination of income is firmly rooted in historical exchange transactions. The primary difference between price level accounting and traditional accounting is that all accounting measurements are expressed in terms of common (i.e., current) dollars instead of a mix of current and previous dollars.

There are, however, other *models* of accounting that are not based primarily on historical exchange prices. Some of these are distinctly future oriented. They are of primary interest to the student of accounting not only because they may be implemented in the future but also because they help to place the conventional model in its proper perspective—as one among several approaches to measurement of income and valuation of assets.

**replacement cost model**

One *model* of financial reporting in which accountants are forced to venture outside of the relatively safe harbor of historical costs is based on *current values.* Under a typical variant (there are several) of the current value model, all assets are reported on the balance sheet at their current values. Current value is defined to mean the amount that would have to be paid to replace an asset.

Under the current value approach, increases in the market price (the replacement value) of an asset would be given recognition as soon as the increases were identified. In sharp contrast to the historical cost approach, there would be no need to wait until an exchange transaction with outsiders took place (i.e., the asset is sold) before accounting for the gain. An asset would be *written up* to reflect its replacement cost regardless of whether the increase in cost could be attributed to a fundamental change in the supply or demand for the asset or merely to a general decline in the purchasing power of the dollar. No distinction as to the reason for the increase would be made.

In accord with current value conventions, monetary assets and liabilities would commonly be reported at their stated values (assuming that stated value does not include an element of unearned interest)—just as under historical cost accounting. Monetary assets and liabilities include cash as well as those receivables and payables that can be expected to be settled in specified amounts of cash regardless of changes in the purchasing power of the dollar. Other assets, however, would be reported at the best approximation of the amount that the firm would have to pay to replace them, either by purchasing them from outsiders or by manufacturing them itself.

The current value approach to accounting was discussed earlier in the text in the chapters directed toward both inventories and long-lived assets. In both those chapters it was emphasized that if recognition were to be given to increases in value on the balance sheet, then so also must it be given on the income statement.

Under most proposals for current value accounting, the income statement would report two types of gains from holding assets during a period of rising replacement costs:

*Unrealized gains,* which relate to assets that were neither sold nor used during the year.

*Realized gains,* which relate to assets that were either sold or used during the year.

Suppose, for example, that a firm was organized on January 1, 1980. Its balance sheet immediately upon formation appeared as follows:

**Balance Sheet
as of January 1, 1980**

| | |
|---|---:|
| *Assets* | |
| Marketable securities | $ 5,000 |
| Inventories | 25,000 |
| Plant and equipment | 50,000 |
| Total assets | $80,000 |
| *Equities* | |
| Owners' equity | $80,000 |

During 1980 a limited number of events occurred:

1. The firm purchased inventory at a cost of $50,000. During the year it had sales of $100,000. The actual cost of the goods sold was $60,000. However, it would cost the firm $75,000 to replace the goods sold during the period. The firm thereby *realized* a holding gain of $15,000—the difference between the historical cost and the replacement cost of the goods actually sold.

2. At year end, the firm had goods on hand that had cost $15,000. The cost to replace them would have been $19,000. The difference of $4,000 between historical cost and replacement value represents a gain to the firm of $4,000, but, inasmuch as the goods have not yet been sold, the gain, as of year end, is still *unrealized*.

3. The useful life of the plant and equipment that cost $50,000 is estimated to be 10 years; no salvage value is anticipated. During the year the replacement cost of the assets increased from $50,000 to $60,000. As a result of the increase the firm had a total gain of $10,000. On the basis of historical costs, the firm charges depreciation of $5,000 per year—one-tenth of $50,000. On the basis of replacement cost, it must charge depreciation of $6,000—one-tenth of $60,000. The $1,000 difference between the depreciation charges represents the *realized* portion of the gain. The $1,000 gain is associated to the portion of the plant and equipment used during the year. The remaining $9,000 represents the *unrealized* portion.

4. The replacement value of the marketable securities increased from $5,000 to $7,000. None of the marketable securities was sold during the year; the entire gain of $2,000 remains *unrealized*.

The 1980 income statement of the firm on the basis of replacement costs may be compared with that on the basis of historical costs, and the balance sheets for the same period may also be contrasted:

## Statement of Income
### for the Year Ending December 31, 1980

|  | Historical Costs | Replacement Costs |
|---|---|---|
| Sales | $100,000 | $100,000 |
| Cost of goods sold | 60,000 | 75,000 |
| Depreciation | 5,000 | 6,000 |
| Total expenses | $ 65,000 | $ 81,000 |
| Operating income | $ 35,000 | $ 19,000 |
| Holding gains | | |
| *Realized* | | |
| On goods sold | | $ 15,000 |
| On plant and equipment used | | 1,000 |
| Total realized holding gains | | $ 16,000 |
| *Unrealized* | | |
| On marketable securities | | $ 2,000 |
| On inventory | | 4,000 |
| On plant and equipment | | 9,000 |
| Total unrealized holding gains | | $ 15,000 |
| Total holding gains | | $ 31,000 |
| Net income | $ 35,000 | $ 50,000 |

## Balance Sheet
### as of December 31, 1980

|  | Historical Costs | Replacement Costs |
|---|---|---|
| *Assets* | | |
| Cash (note a) | $ 50,000 | $ 50,000 |
| Marketable securities | 5,000 | 7,000 |
| Inventory | 15,000 | 19,000 |
| Plant and equipment (note b) | 45,000 | 54,000 |
| Total assets | $115,000 | $130,000 |
| *Equities* | | |
| Owners' equity (note c) | $115,000 | $130,000 |

Note a: Based on the assumption that cash was received in connection with the sales of $100,000 and disbursed in connection with the purchases of $50,000.
Note b: Initial plant and equipment less depreciation.
Note c: Initial owners' equity plus net income.

The advantages and disadvantages of the replacement cost model as compared with the historical cost model have been debated extensively in the accounting literature. A few of the main points (each subject to challenge) can be summarized briefly:

## ADVANTAGES OF THE REPLACEMENT COST MODEL

1. It provides more relevant information for making predictions regarding the future economic performance (and, more specifically, future cash flows) than does the historical cost model. First, it distinguishes between earnings arising from routine operations and those resulting from changes in prices. Thus, it enables the analyst to forecast future performance in light of his own estimates as to both changing operating conditions and expected increases in prices. Second, it provides a measure of the current value of the resources within the command of the organization. Cash flows of the future are more likely to be related to the current value of such resources than to a past value.

2. It provides more relevant information on which to evaluate the past performance of corporate managers. Corporate managers should be held accountable for earning an adequate return on the current value of the assets under their control. The cost of using the assets is more meaningfully determined on the basis of their current rather than their past economic value.

3. The replacement value model, if used by all corporations, would facilitate comparisons among firms. The resources held and consumed by each firm would be expressed in terms of their value today rather than as of the dates they were acquired, which vary from firm to firm.

## DISADVANTAGES OF THE REPLACEMENT COST MODEL

1. The values assigned to assets may be highly subjective. In an era of rapid technological change, it is exceedingly difficult to determine the "replacement" value of an asset that, in fact, will not and cannot be replaced in the same form. Although there are ways to estimate the replacement costs of outdated assets (e.g., industry price indices and catalogs of used equipment prices), the range of managerial discretion may be sufficiently wide so as to detract from the credibility of the statements taken as a whole.

2. Replacement costs may not be relevant to investors and other groups of statement users if a firm has no intention of either selling or replacing its assets in the near future. The reported holding gains may never be realized, and the amounts at which the assets are reported may never be received or paid by the company.

3. The replacement cost model increases reported cost of goods sold and depreciation, but it has no effect upon sales revenue. Many firms base their selling prices upon the actual (historical) cost of producing or purchasing their products. As such costs increase, the firms compensate by raising prices. Fi-

nancial statements based upon replacement costs may give the false impression that earnings of the future may be lower than those of the present or past, when in fact they will not.

Although both the SEC and the FASB have now taken steps to assure that firms provide data which give recognition to changing prices and/or values, neither organization has been willing to reject the traditional historical cost (unadjusted) financial statements. The decade of the 1980s will undoubtedly witness continued experimentation and change in the area of inflation accounting.

## Accounting for Transactions in Foreign Currency

Akin to the issue of accounting for assets and liabilities stated in dollars of different years is that of accounting for assets and liabilities expressed in foreign currencies. In both cases accountants must take cognizance of changing units of measurement. Today, virtually all major U.S. corporations have interests in other countries, and in recent years the value of the dollar has been subject to wide fluctuations against other major currencies. The problem of accounting for transactions in foreign currencies can be explicated by way of an example.

Suppose that a U.S. firm invested $8,840 and formed a subsidiary company in Germany. At the time the new firm was organized, one U.S. dollar was equivalent in value to 1.92 German deutschemarks (DMs). Conversely, 1 DM was the equivalent of $.52. Immediately after the new company was organized, its balance sheet, expressed in deutschemarks and converted into dollars appeared as follows:

|  | DMs | Conversion Factor | $'s |
|---|---|---|---|
| *Assets* |  |  |  |
| Cash | DM 1,000 | .52 | $ 520 |
| Accounts receivable | 3,000 | .52 | 1,560 |
| Plant and equipment | 15,000 | .52 | 7,800 |
|  | DM 19,000 |  | $9,880 |
| *Equities* |  |  |  |
| Accounts payable | DM 2,000 | .52 | $1,040 |
| Owners' equity | 17,000 | .52 | 8,840 |
|  | DM 19,000 |  | $9,880 |

Shortly after the company was formed the value of the deutschemark increased against the dollar. Whereas previously one deutschemark could be acquired for $.52, it would now cost $.60.

The parent company clearly benefited from the increase in the value of deutschemarks. It holds in cash DM 1,000. In addition, it holds accounts receivable for DM 3,000. The receivables are stated in terms of deutschemarks, not dollars. The company will receive payments in deutschemarks, which can be converted into a greater number of dollars than when the receivables were first recorded. By contrast, the advantage of holding DM 4,000 in cash and accounts receivable is offset in part by the obligation to make payment of DM 2,000—deutschemarks that are more costly in terms of dollars than when the obligation was first recorded.

Thus, the company holds net assets of DM 2,000 (cash of DM 1,000 plus receivables of DM 3,000 less payables of DM 2,000) that can be said to be *denominated* in deutschemarks. Assets and liabilities that are *denominated* in a foreign currency are very much like monetary assets and liabilities as described in the section on price level adjustments. They are contractually fixed; the number of monetary units to be received or paid will remain the same regardless of whether the value of these units increases or decreases. Inasmuch as the company holds DM 2,000 in denominated assets and the value of each deutschemark increased by $.08 ($.60 less $.52), the company is $160 (DM 2,000 times $.08) better off as the result of the change in the rate of exchange.

The company also holds plant and equipment, which is recorded on its balance sheet at DM 15,000. Unlike that of cash or accounts receivable, the value of plant and equipment is not contractually fixed. The firm cannot automatically sell the plant and equipment for an established number of either deutschemarks or dollars. The plant and equipment have an intrinsinc value apart from that of any particular currency. As the value of the deutschemark, relative to the dollar, increases, the number of deutschemarks for which the plant and equipment can be sold may remain the same (thereby increasing their value in terms of dollars) or may decline in proportion to the increase (thereby causing their value in terms of dollars to remain the same). Thus, it cannot be said with assurance that the firm has benefited from the change in exchange rates on account of its ownership of plant and equipment.

The key accounting issues with respect to assets and liabilities in foreign currencies relate to the rates of exchange at which they should be translated into dollars and to the timing of gains or losses associated with the adjustments in their balance sheet values. Should balance sheet accounts be translated at the current rate of exchange or the rate of exchange that existed when an asset was first acquired or a liability first incurred? Should a distinction be made between assets and liabilities that are denominated in a foreign currency and those that are not? Should gains or losses on currency fluctuations be recognized in the periods in which the exchange rates increase or decrease, or should recognition be delayed until an asset or liability is actually liquidated?

In 1975 the FASB issued Statement No. 8 that sets forth specific rules for translating currency transactions. In essence, FASB states that all assets and liabilities that are *denominated* in foreign currencies must be translated at the rate in existence when the asset or liability was first acquired or incurred. Thus, cash, payables and receivables should generally be translated at the current exchange rate; inventory and fixed assets should be translated at the rate in effect when the assets were first acquired.* Gains or losses arising from the "revaluation" of the denominated assets should be reported in the period of the change in the rate of exchange.

Per the guidelines of the FASB, if a balance sheet of the illustrative company were prepared immediately after the rate of exchange changed from $.52 to $.60 per each deutschemark, it should be converted as follows:

|  | DMs | Conversion Factor | $'s |
|---|---|---|---|
| *Assets* | | | |
| Cash | DM 1,000 | .60 | $ 600 |
| Accounts receivable | 3,000 | .60 | 1,800 |
| Plant and equipment | 15,000 | .52 | 7,800 |
| Total assets | DM 19,000 | | $10,200 |
| *Equities* | | | |
| Accounts payable | DM 2,000 | .60 | $ 1,200 |
| Owners' equity | 17,000 | (residual) | 9,000 |
| Total equities | DM 19,000 | | $10,200 |

Cash, accounts receivable and accounts payable would be translated at the current rate of exchange. Plant and equipment would be translated at the "historical" rate of exchange—that which was applicable when the assets were acquired. Owners' equity is a residual; it reflects the original owners' equity of $8,840 plus the gain of $160 from holding the denominated assets.

Statement No. 8 has proven to be one of the most controversial statements issued by the FASB. Most objectionable to many corporations is the requirement that gains or losses from holding assets denominated in foreign currencies be recognized as the rate of exchange fluctuates, even if a firm does not actually sell those assets or convert them into dollars. It has been alleged (but certainly not proven) that the statement has had a substantial impact on the supply and demand for foreign currencies inasmuch as some firms attempt to "hedge" their foreign exchange holdings to avoid having to give recognition in their financial reports to gains and losses arising out of currency translation.

---

*Assets that would normally be reported at market values should also be translated at the current rate of exchange.

## Accounting Alternatives—Do They Make a Difference?

Financial information plays a major role in the allocation of capital in our economy. In large measure, investment capital is divided among the firms that seek it in proportion to reported earnings. The price of a firm's common stock is to a great extent a function of *anticipated* profits. Since investors wish to maximize the returns on their investments, they are willing to pay more for the stock of a firm with a brighter rather than a dimmer future. The higher the market price of a firm's common stock relative to earnings, the greater its capability to obtain equity financing.

Reported earnings of the past are often viewed as the primary predictor of earnings of the future. In this text we have emphasized that over a limited number of years a firm can increase the income figures reported to the public simply by selecting judiciously among accounting alternatives. One might hypothesize, therefore, that the market price of the stock of a firm that *reports* higher earnings than others as a consequence of adopting more liberal accounting principles and policies would also be relatively higher than those of its more conservative counterparts. If the hypothesis is correct, then the capital markets would have been "fooled" by accounting information, and a measure of inefficiency would thereby have been introduced into the free market system.

There is a substantial body of literature to suggest, however, that the capital markets as a whole are not so fooled—that, in fact, investors give consideration to differences in accounting practices and adjust accordingly. Assume, for example, that the common stocks of firms in a specific industry were being traded, on average, at a price that was equal to 10 times annual earnings. If a company reported earnings of $5 per share, its common stock could be expected to sell for $50 per share. If it reported earnings of $4 per share, its stock could be expected to sell for $40 per share. But suppose that a company reported earnings of $5 per share because, relative to other firms in the industry, it adhered to more liberal accounting principles. Otherwise it would have reported earnings of only $4 per share. Would its stock still be traded at $50 per share? According to a number of studies, it is likely that the common stock would be sold for only $40 per share.

The studies are encouraging in that they support the contention that investors, as a group, are sufficiently sophisticated to distinguish among various accounting practices and to look beyond the "bottom line" of the income statement. Moreover, they suggest that the accounting profession need not be so concerned about mandating specific practices as was once generally believed. Regardless of alternatives selected, investors will make the adjustments necessary to make earnings of one company comparable with those of others.

Obviously, however, investors can make the necessary adjustments only if they have available the requisite information—the details of the underlying transactions—to do so. If, therefore, the studies suggest that the accounting profession need not be especially concerned about specifying particular accounting practices, they also imply that the profession need be very concerned about making certain that corporations disclose enough about their operations and financial position to enable investors to evaluate the results of transactions in a manner other than the one selected by the corporation.

The studies in no way suggest that *individual* investors properly interpret financial statements. They deal exclusively with investors as a group. Individual investors, as well as creditors, labor union officials, and other users of financial statements, must still bear the burden of carefully analyzing the financial statements and evaluating the impact of alternative accounting practices.

Although greater disclosure—up to the point of "information overload"—may well facilitate investment decisions, policy makers must take cognizance of its cost. Information is not a free commodity. W. R. Grace & Co., for example, complained in its annual report that over 13,000 hours of time were expended in satisfying SEC requirements with respect to replacement costs. The cost of providing additional data must be weighed against the benefits to be realized.

## Concluding Comment

In this text we have stressed the controversial nature of accounting. We have attempted to demonstrate that even upon the most fundamental principles of accounting—those dealing with valuation of assets and recognition of revenue, for example—there are disagreements. Indeed "generally accepted" accounting principles are not nearly as generally accepted as the phrase implies.

This issue-oriented approach has been taken in an effort to convey the message that accounting is an extremely dynamic discipline. The controversies that surround so many of its principles and procedures are evidence of its vigor and vitality.

In the years to come professional and regulatory agencies, such as the Financial Accounting Standards Board and the Securities and Exchange Commission, will continue to set forth guidelines intended to improve the quality of financial reporting. The general thrust will probably be twofold: to narrow the alternatives to account for similar transactions in similar circumstances and to increase the amount of information disclosed about corporate financial activities.

It is certain that there will be disagreement over whatever accounting procedures the professional or regulatory bodies recommend. In accounting there are few "correct" answers. No single procedure can best satisfy all of the objectives of financial reporting.

One of the themes of this text has been that two primary standards of financial reporting—relevance and objectivity—are often in conflict. Information that is most relevant may not be most objective; that which is most objective may not be most relevant. Current market values, for example, may be more useful to most users of financial reports than historical transaction-based values. They may not, however, be as readily verifiable.

Another theme has been that there is an integral relationship between the income statement and the balance sheet. Some accounting procedures that are likely to provide a more useful income statement may result, however, in a less useful balance sheet. The LIFO inventory method, for example, insofar as it generally results in a cost of goods sold expense that is representative of current costs, is believed by many to produce an income statement that is more relevant in evaluating corporate performance than does the FIFO method. At the same time, however, in that it requires out-of-date inventory costs to be carried forward in an asset account, it produces a less meaningful balance sheet.

At best, therefore, the pronouncements of the professional and regulatory bodies will be compromises. They will balance the various objectives of financial reporting. If in the future the fundamental accounting *questions* do not change, then most assuredly the *answers* will.

*exercise for review and self-testing*

A firm was organized on January 1, 1980. On that date it issued common stock in exchange for $100,000 cash. The values of the price index during 1980 were as follows:

| | |
|---|---|
| January 1, 1980 | 110 |
| Average for 1980 | 120 |
| December 31, 1980 | 130 |

Provide two answers to each of the questions. Assume first that the firm will prepare price level adjusted statements and then that it will prepare its statements on the basis of replacement costs.

1. On January 1, 1980 the firm acquired equipment for $60,000 cash. The useful life of the equipment is 10 years; it has no anticipated salvage value. The firm records depreciation on a straight-line basis. By December 31, the replacement cost of the equipment had increased to $75,000.
   a. At what amount should the firm report the equipment on December 31, 1980 prior to adjusting for depreciation?
   b. How much depreciation expense should it record?
   c. What should be the reported net book value of the equipment?

2. Evenly throughout the year the firm acquired inventory for $40,000 cash. Evenly throughout the year it sold goods for which it had paid $30,000. At the time of sale, the goods sold had a replacement value of $34,000. As of December 31, the $10,000 of inventory on hand had a replacement value of $12,000.
   a. At what amount should the firm report cost of goods sold?
   b. At what amount should it report year-end inventory?

3. Sales revenue, which was received evenly throughout the year, was $50,000. At what amount should the firm report sales revenue?

4. At what amount should it report common stock?

5. What was the amount of the loss in purchasing power that the firm incurred by holding various amounts of monetary assets (in this example, only cash) during the year. (This need be computed only for price level statements.)

6. What were the amounts of gains from holding inventory and equipment during the year. For each asset, separate the holding gains to *realized* and *unrealized* portions. (This need be computed only for replacement cost statements.)

7. Prepare an income statement for 1980 and a balance sheet as of December 31, 1980 assuming that the firm uses each of *three* alternative accounting models: historical cost, no price level adjustments; historical cost, with price level adjustments; replacement cost. Be certain that the amount reported for retained earnings is equal to net income.

## Questions

**review and discussion**

1. It has been suggested that price level adjustments are required because one of the underlying assumptions of traditional accounting is untenable. What assumption is this?

2. Increases in the prices of goods and services can be attributable to at least two fundamental economic forces. What are these forces? With which of the two do price level adjustments attempt to deal?

3. "Price level adjustments in no way undermine the historical, transaction-based underpinning of financial accounting. Price-level-adjusted statements must be distinguished from those in which assets are recorded at current market values in that the former are firmly rooted in historical costs, while the latter are not." Do you agree? Explain.

4. "U.S. corporations should logically oppose price level adjustments because in a period of inflation they result in lower reported earnings." Does such a statement make sense? Do price level adjustments necessarily reduce reported earnings? Explain.

5. What is the difference between monetary and nonmonetary items? Why is it generally unnecessary to convert monetary items into current dollars?

6. What are purchasing power gains or losses? How are they computed?

7. What are the major determinants of the difference between price-level-adjusted earnings and conventional earnings?

8. A U.S. firm holds assets in a foreign country. Why might different rates of exchange be used to convert different assets (e.g., cash, plant and equipment) into dollars?

9. In December 1980 a U.S. firm receives a note for £1,000 (British pounds). On the day the note is received, £1 can be exchanged for $1.93. By Decem-

ber 31, the value of the pound has decreased to $1.89. On January 1, 1981 the U.S. firm receives payment on the note and exchanges the pounds for dollars. In which year, 1980 or 1981, should the firm recognize a loss attributable to the unfavorable change in the exchange rate? Explain.

10. Distinguish between *realized* and *unrealized* gains as they apply to replacement cost accounting.

11. What do recent studies suggest about the relationships between a firm's *reported* earnings and the market value of its common stock? Is a change to an accounting principle that increases reported earnings likely to increase the price at which a firm's securities are traded?

12. Many of the controversies in accounting can be traced to the desire of accountants to satisfy more than one standard. What are two standards of financial reporting? Provide an example of how one standard may sometimes be achieved only at the expense of another.

## Problems

1. *In adjusting for changes in price levels, monetary items must be distinguished from nonmonetary items.*

   Indicate whether each of the following items should be considered a monetary (M) or a nonmonetary (N) item:
   1. Cash on hand.
   2. Cash in bank.
   3. Marketable securities (e.g., stocks).
   4. Accounts and notes receivable.
   5. Inventories.
   6. Refundable deposits.
   7. Property, plant, and equipment.
   8. Accumulated depreciation.
   9. Goodwill.
   10. Patents, trademarks, licenses.
   11. Accounts and notes payable.
   12. Dividends payable.
   13. Bonds payable.
   14. Common stock, par value
   15. Common stock, capital contributed in excess of par.
   16. Retained earnings

2. *Increases in prices must be distinguished from increases in value.*

   In 1975, a certain grade of lumber sold for $115 per 1,000 board feet. In 1980, the same grade of lumber sold for $165 per 1,000 board feet. In 1975 the GNP Deflator was at 135; in 1980 it was at 188. By how much did the cost of lumber actually increase, after taking into account the decline in the overall value of the dollar? Express your answer in terms of 1980 dollars.

3. *Price level adjustments affect not only the carrying value of fixed assets, but also related depreciation charges and gains and losses from disposition of such assets.*

As of December 31, 1980, a company reported a balance in its truck account of $106,000 and a balance of $62,800 in the related accumulated depreciation account. Supporting documentation reveals the following:

| Year | Number of trucks acquired | Cost per truck | Balance in truck account | Balance in accumulated depreciation account |
|---|---|---|---|---|
| 1977 | 3 | $12,000 | $ 36,000 | $28,800 |
| 1978 | 2 | 15,000 | 30,000 | 18,000 |
| 1979 | 2 | 20,000 | 40,000 | 16,000 |
| 1980 | 0 | — | — | — |
| | | | $106,000 | $62,800 |

Depreciation is recorded on a straight-line basis. The useful life of a truck is assumed to be five years; salvage value is considered to be zero.

For the years 1977 to 1980 the GNP Deflator was at the following levels:

| | |
|---|---|
| 1977 | 148 |
| 1978 | 159 |
| 1979 | 178 |
| 1980 | 188 |

a. Determine depreciation charges for 1980 on both a conventional and a price-level-adjusted basis.

b. Suppose that on December 31, 1980, after 1980 depreciation had been recorded, one of the trucks acquired in 1977 was sold for $3,000. Determine the gain or loss to be recognized under both conventional and price-level-adjusted accounting.

4. *"Earnings" from marketable securities may, in fact, be more than offset by losses in purchasing power.*

As of the beginning of 1980 an investor had $200,000 in cash. On the first day of the year he purchased for $100,000 a certificate of deposit and for $50 per share, 2,000 shares of common stock (a nonmonetary asset) of a well-known company.

In the course of the year, the investor earned interest of $6,000 on the money placed in the certificate of deposit. He earned dividends of $3,000 on the common stock which he held. At year end, he sold the 2,000 shares of common stock at a price of $52 per share.

A general-purpose price index at the start of 1980 was at a level of 159. On average during the year it was at 170, and at year end it was at 178.

a. Determine income for the year on a conventional basis.

b. Determine the gain or loss in purchasing power for the year.

c. Determine the gain or loss, on a price-level-adjusted basis, on the sale of the common stock.

d. Determine price-level-adjusted earnings for the year, including the gains or losses in purchasing power and on the sale of common stock.

e. Reconcile, on a price-level-adjusted basis, the equity of the investor at the start of the year with that at the end.

5. *A price-level-adjusted balance sheet requires that each nonmonetary asset and liability be adjusted by the ratio of the current price index to the price index at the time the asset or liability was acquired or incurred.*

The balance sheet of the Daedalus Flying Service, as of Decemer 31, 1980, appears as follows:

**Daedalus Flying Service**
**Balance Sheet as of December 31, 1980**

*Assets*

| | | |
|---|---:|---:|
| Cash | | $   5,000 |
| Accounts receivable | | 6,000 |
| Inventories | | 9,000 |
| Planes and equipment | $320,000 | |
| Less: Accumulated depreciation | 80,000 | 240,000 |
| Total assets | | $260,000 |

*Liabilities and owners' equity*

| | |
|---|---:|
| Accounts payable | $   7,000 |
| Wages payable | 2,000 |
| Tickets sold for trips not yet taken | 1,000 |
| Notes payable | 150,000 |
| Common stock | 40,000 |
| Retained earnings | 60,000 |
| Total liabilities and owners' equity | $260,000 |

The inventory was acquired throughout 1980. The average GNP Deflator for 1980 was 170.

The planes and equipment were acquired in 1976 at a time when the price index was at 135.

Accounts receivable, accounts payable, wages payable, and tickets sold for trips not yet taken arose from transactions that took place during the third and fourth quarters of 1980. The average GNP Deflator for those quarters was 175.

The notes payable were issued in connection with the purchase of the planes and equipment in 1976 when the price index was 135.

The common stock was sold in 1975 when the price index was at 128.

The price index as of December 31, 1980 was at 178.

Prepare an adjusted balance sheet expressed in terms of year-end 1980 dollars.

**6.** *Price level adjustments have varying effects upon the earnings of firms in different industries.*

Two companies, firm A and firm B, are in different industries. Both, however, are of the same size and do the same volume of business. The 1980 income statements and balance sheets for the two firms are as follows:

### Income Statements
### for the Year Ending December 31, 1980

|  | *Firm A* | *Firm B* |
|---|---|---|
| Sales | $1,000,000 | $1,000,000 |
| Cost of goods sold (excluding depreciation) | $ 700,000 | $ 850,000 |
| Depreciation | 200,000 | 50,000 |
|  | $ 900,000 | $ 900,000 |
| Net income | $ 100,000 | $ 100,000 |

### Balance Sheets as of December 31, 1980

|  | *Firm A* | *Firm B* |
|---|---|---|
| Inventory | $ 200,000 | $ 800,000 |
| Fixed assets | 800,000 | 200,000 |
| Total assets | $1,000,000 | $1,000,000 |
| Owners' equity | $1,000,000 | $1,000,000 |

The fixed assets of both firms were acquired in 1976 at a time when the price index was at 144.

Ending inventory was acquired in the fourth quarter of 1980 at a time when the price index was at 178.

It may be assumed that sales and purchases of merchandise were made evenly throughout 1980. The average price index for 1980 was 170.

a. Prepare price-level-adjusted income statements for each of the two companies.

b. Comment on the reason for the differences in price-level adjusted earnings.

**7.** *The price-level-adjusted income statement must articulate (through retained earnings) with the price-level-adjusted balance sheet.*

University Book Store, Inc. comparative balance sheets for the years ending December 31, 1980 and 1979, and an income statement for 1980 are as follows:

## University Book Store, Inc.
## Balance Sheets as of December 31

|  | 1980 | 1979 |
|---|---|---|
| Assets |  |  |
| Cash | $ 15,000 | $ 10,000 |
| Accounts receivable | 36,000 | 40,000 |
| Inventory | 130,000 | 135,000 |
| Plant and equipment | $125,000 | $100,000 |
| Less: Accumulated depreciation | (84,000) | (60,000) |
| Net plant and equipment | $ 41,000 | $ 40,000 |
| Total assets | $222,000 | $225,000 |
| Liabilities and owners' equity |  |  |
| Accounts payable | $ 65,000 | $ 50,000 |
| Notes payable | 70,000 | 100,000 |
| Common stock | 60,000 | 60,000 |
| Retained earnings | 27,000 | 15,000 |
| Total liabilities and owners' equities | $222,000 | $225,000 |

## Income Statement
## for the Year Ending December 31, 1980

| Sales |  | $200,000 |
|---|---|---|
| Cost of goods sold | $115,000 |  |
| Depreciation | 24,000 |  |
| Taxes | 8,000 |  |
| Other expenses | 41,000 | 188,000 |
| Net income |  | $ 12,000 |

Of the plant and equipment, $25,000 was acquired in 1980; the remainder was purchased uniformly throughout 1975. Depreciation charges include $4,000 applicable to the assets purchased in 1980. The company accounts for its inventory on a LIFO basis. The inventory on hand at year end may be assumed to have been acquired evenly throughout 1976. All sales, purchases of both inventory and fixed assets, and other expenses may also be assumed to have occurred evenly throughout 1980. Common stock was issued uniformly throughout 1975.

The value of the dollar is reflected in the following general-purpose price index.

| Year | Average during year | Value at year end |
|------|---------------------|-------------------|
| 1975 | 85  | 90  |
| 1976 | 97  | 104 |
| 1977 | 106 | 108 |
| 1978 | 112 | 115 |
| 1979 | 117 | 120 |
| 1980 | 125 | 130 |

a. Prepare a price-level-adjusted balance sheet for the year ended December 31, 1980, based on current (i.e., year end 1980) dollars. (*Note:* Retained earnings equal $50,890.)

b. Determine any purchasing power gains or losses for 1980. Be sure to take into account all changes in monetary items (i.e., those resulting from purchases of plant and equipment and of inventory as well as from revenues and expenses).

c. Prepare a price-level-adjusted statement of income for 1980. Be sure to take into account the fact that as a result of the reduction in inventory between year-end 1979 and 1980 a portion of the goods sold must be assumed to have been purchased in 1976.

d. Prepare a schedule reconciling, on a price-level-adjusted basis, retained earnings as of December 31, 1980, with those of December 31, 1979. Assume that retained earnings of December 31, 1979 ($15,000) expressed in terms of year-end 1979 dollars would be $38,775.

8. *Use of LIFO may compensate, in part, for failure to adjust for changes in the value of the monetary unit.*

Two companies, the FIFO Co. and the LIFO Co., engage in operations in an identical manner. The former, however, maintains its inventory on a FIFO basis and the latter on a LIFO basis.

As of the start of 1980, each firm had 5,000 units of product on hand. The units of the LIFO Co. were assumed to have been acquired in 1971 and were carried on the books at a value of $170,000 ($34 per unit). Those of the FIFO Co. were assumed to have been acquired in 1979 and were carried on the books at a value of $250,000 ($50 per unit).

In 1980 each company purchased 24,000 units of product as follows:

| | | |
|---|---|---|
| 1st quarter | 6,000 units @ $51 = | $ 306,000 |
| 2nd quarter | 6,000 units @ 52 = | 312,000 |
| 3rd quarter | 6,000 units @ 54 = | 324,000 |
| 4th quarter | 6,000 units @ 56 = | 336,000 |
| | 24,000 | $1,278,000 |

During the year each company sold 21,000 units; at year end each had 8,000 units remaining in inventory.

Relevant values of a general price index are as follows:

| | |
|---|---|
| 1971 | 111 |
| 1979 | 159 |
| 1980: | |
| 1st quarter | 164 |
| 2nd quarter | 167 |
| 3rd quarter | 172 |
| 4th quarter | 178 |

a. Determine cost of goods sold and year-end 1980 inventory for each of the two firms on a historical cost basis. Indicate the differences in amounts between the two firms.

b. Determine cost of goods sold and year-end 1980 inventory for each of the two firms on a price-level-adjusted basis. Indicate the differences in amounts between the two firms.

c. Comment on the use of LIFO as a substitute for price level adjustments insofar as cost of goods sold is concerned.

9. *A decision as to how best to finance a capital investment may be altered by price level adjustments to estimates of earnings.*

A company is planning to construct an addition to its plant. The addition would cost $4 million. The company has under consideration two means of financing the cost of construction. First, it could issue 10-year bonds at an annual interest rate of 10 percent. Second, it could sell an additional 30,000 shares of common stock. The company presently has 300,000 shares of common stock outstanding and in recent years had annual earnings, after taxes, of $2.1 million.

The plant is expected to provide an annual cash inflow of $900,000. Such amount has been determined without regard to financing costs or taxes. Moreover, in determining income, depreciation charges of $400,000 (based on a 10-year useful life, straight-line method) would also have to be deducted.

The applicable income tax rate may be assumed to be 40 percent.

a. Based on a criterion of increase in earnings (unadjusted) per share, do you think the company should finance the construction by issuing additional common stock or bonds?

b. The level of prices is expected to increase at a compound rate of 5 percent per year. The anticipated price level index for the 10-year period is indicated in the following table:

| Year | Index | Year | Index |
|---|---|---|---|
| 1 | 100 | 6 | 128 |
| 2 | 105 | 7 | 134 |
| 3 | 110 | 8 | 141 |
| 4 | 116 | 9 | 148 |
| 5 | 122 | 10 | 155 |

Determine price-level-adjusted earnings per share for year 5 under each of the two alternatives. Express the earnings in current dollars applicable to that year. Assume that the cash inflow as well as earnings will increase proportionately to the rate of inflation. Taking into account the increase in the price level, do you think the company should finance construction by issuing common stock or bonds? (*Note:* Be sure to take into account the purchasing power gain on the bonds between the end of year 4 and the end of year 5. And remember that taxes are levied on unadjusted rather than adjusted earnings.)

10. *Price level adjustments may alter return on investment.*

A state public utilities commission establishes rates such that utilities within its jurisdiction are permitted to earn a return of 7 percent on total invested capital. A condensed balance sheet and an income statement of Atlantic Gas and Electric Co. for the year ending December 31, 1980 appear as follows:

### Atlantic Gas and Electric Co.
### Balance Sheet as of December 31, 1980

| | | |
|---|---:|---:|
| Assets | | |
| Cash and accounts receivable | | $1,500,000 |
| Inventories and supplies | | 160,000 |
| Plant and equipment | $11,000,000 | |
| Less: Accumulated depreciation | 3,000,000 | 8,000,000 |
| Total assets | | $9,660,000 |
| Equities | | |
| Current liabilities | | $1,000,000 |
| Long-term debt | | 5,000,000 |
| Stockholders' equity | | 3,660,000 |
| Total equities | | $9,660,000 |

### Statement of Income
### for the Year Ending December 31, 1980

| | | |
|---|---:|---:|
| Revenues | | $4,026,200 |
| Operating expenses and taxes | $2,500,000 | |
| Depreciation | 500,000 | |
| Interest | 350,000 | 3,350,000 |
| Net income | | $ 676,200 |

Return on investment is defined as net income divided by total assets. Thus, $676,200 divided by $9,660,000 equals 7 percent.

The funds represented by the long-term debt were borrowed in a period in which, on average, the general price index was at 110. The fixed assets were acquired on average, when the price index was at the same level.

Revenues, operating expenses, taxes, and interest were incurred evenly throughout 1980. The average price index value for 1980 was 154.

The company paid dividends in 1980 of $400,000. They may be assumed to have been paid evenly throughout the year.

At the start of 1980, when the price index was at 148, the company had net monetary liabilities (monetary liabilities less monetary assets) of $5,276,200.

Supplies and inventory were acquired at year end. The price index at year end was 159.

a. Determine the actual rate of return for 1980 on a price-level-adjusted basis. Be sure to take into account any gains or losses in purchasing power.

b. Comment on why utility firms are particularly likely to favor the price-level-adjusted "model" of accounting.

11. *Tax rates can increase, even without legislative action.*

Irving Hirsch was generally pleased with the earnings of his office supplies business. Between 1974, when he began operations, and 1979, his with-drawals from the business increased from $25,000 to $45,000. "The im-provement in earnings may not have been spectacular," commented Hirsch, "but at least they're outrunning the rate of inflation."

a. Taking into account the impact of inflation, by how much have the earn-ings of Hirsch increased? The value of a general-purpose price index in 1974 was, on average, 115; in 1979 it was 194. Express earnings of each year in terms of 1979 dollars.

b. The following is an excerpt from the federal individual income tax table:

| Taxable income (A) | Regular tax on amount in (A) (B) | Amount of taxable income in excess of (A) but not in excess of (C) is taxed at rates shown in (D) | |
|---|---|---|---|
| | | (C) | (D) |
| $22,000 | $ 5,990 | $26,000 | 40% |
| 26,000 | 7,590 | 32,000 | 45 |
| 32,000 | 10,290 | 38,000 | 50 |
| 38,000 | 13,290 | 44,000 | 55 |
| 44,000 | 16,590 | 50,000 | 60 |

Assume that Irving Hirsch is not married and had income from other sources in 1974 and 1979 which was just adequate to cover the miscel-laneous deductions and exemptions allowed by the Federal Tax Code. Comment on whether his earnings after *taxes* kept pace with the rate of inflation.

c. It is often pointed out that Congress, by mere inaction, has been legis-lating increases in taxes. In light of the above example, what do you think is meant by such assertion?

12. *Replacement cost statements provide more complete information for making predictions about future earnings than do historical cost statements.*

The income statement of a firm after its first year of operations appeared as follows:

| | | |
|---|---:|---:|
| Sales | | $120,000 |
| Cost of goods sold | $80,000 | |
| Other expenses | 20.000 | 100,000 |
| Income | | $ 20,000 |

Management estimated that during the second year of operations, both costs and selling prices would remain stable but that sales volume could be increased by 10 percent. The increase would have no impact upon other expenses; they are all fixed.

a. What would you expect income of the second year to be?

b. During the first year of the goods sold by the firm had a replacement cost, at time of sale, of $110,000.

   (1) Prepare a statement of income based on replacement costs.

   (2) What would you now expect income of the second year to be?

13. *The limitations of replacement cost information must be recognized.*

The following is an excerpt from the financial report of Eastman Kodak Company for the year ended December 31, 1976:

| Summary, 1976 (in millions) | Per Financial Statements | At Estimated Replacement Cost |
|---|---:|---:|
| Inventories | $1,121.6 | $1,552.1 |
| Cost of goods sold | 3,272.4 | 3,327.0 |
| Gross properties (excluding land) | 4,686.1 | 8,732.4 |
| Depreciated replacement cost | — | 4,663.7 |
| Depreciation expense | 291.9 | 336.4 |

a. If the firm were to prepare its financial statements on the basis of replacement costs, what would be the reported *realized* holding gains on inventories and on gross properties?

b. Is it possible to determine the *unrealized* holding gains for 1976? If not, what other information would be required?

c. Many firms include in their annual reports a comment that they provide information on replacement costs only because it is required; in fact, they believe that it is either meaningless or misleading.

   (1) By how much greater would Kodak Company's expenses be if the firm reported on a replacement rather than a historical cost basis (consider only cost of goods sold and depreciation)? Does this difference necessarily mean that profit margins of the future will probably be lower than those of the past?

   (2) In light of the fact that Kodak is in an industry with rapidly chang-

ing technology, what difficulties do you imagine the firm had in estimating the replacement cost of its plant and equipment?

(3) What conclusions, if any, can be drawn from the information on replacement costs regarding the "economic" value of the firm?

(4) What effect will the difference between historical cost depreciation and replacement cost depreciation have on future cash flows?

14. *Required SEC disclosures enable an analyst to transform statements from a historical to a current value basis.*

Refer to the financial statements of Koppers Co. (and specifically Table 5 in the footnotes) in Chapter 2. Assume that the company were to prepare its financial reports on the basis of replacement costs instead of historical costs.

a. How much greater would depreciation expense be?

b. How much greater would cost of goods sold be?

c. What would be the realized gain from holding machinery, equipment, and buildings?

d. What would be the realized gain from holding inventory?

e. What would be the unrealized gain from holding machinery, equipment, and buildings?

f. What would be the unrealized gain from holding inventory?

g. What would be the difference in net income, assuming that the differences between the replacement and historical costs of other assets are immaterial?

h. How do you account for the fact that realized gain on depreciation is proportionately much greater than that on cost of goods sold?

15. *An increase in reported earnings may not necessarily be reflected in the market price of a firm's common stock.*

The president of a publicly held corporation was considering switching from the FIFO to the LIFO method of accounting for inventory. The shift would enable him to reduce his annual income tax payments. The president was reluctant to authorize the shift, however, because it would result in an immediate decline in reported earnings. Such a decline, he thought, might adversely affect the market price of the company's stock and thereby antagonize the shareholders.

As of January 1, 1980, the company had 1,000 (000s omitted) units of products on hand. They were carried on the books at $20 per unit, and because the company had recently reduced its inventory to zero, they would be valued at $20 regardless of whether the company remained on FIFO or switched to LIFO.

As of January 1, 1980, the president made the following estimate of purchases and sales for the following three years (000s omitted from quantities):

| | |
|---|---|
| 1980 | Purchase 1,000 units @ $22; sell 1,000 units @ $30 |
| 1981 | Purchase 1,000 units @ $24; sell 1,000 units @ $32 |
| 1982 | Purchase 1,000 units @ $26; sell 1,000 units @ $34 |

a. Determine annual earnings after taxes for each of the three years assuming first that the company maintains its inventory on a FIFO basis and second that it shifts to LIFO. The effective rate of taxes is 40 percent. For convenience, disregard all costs other than cost of goods sold and taxes.

b. Determine the annual cash flows after taxes for each of the three years under both FIFO and LIFO. Compare them with annual earnings. Cash flows should represent sales minus purchases and taxes.

c. Assume that the market price of the firm's stock is based on anticipated corporate cash flows. The total market value of all shares outstanding is equal, at any time, to the present value of expected cash flows for a number of years into the future (in this case assume three years). In calculating the present value of expected cash flows assume that stockholders demand a rate of return of 8 percent on their invested capital. Determine the total market value of all shares outsanding assuming first that the company remains on FIFO and second that it shifts to LIFO. (For convenience assume that all cash flows occur at year end.)

d. Suppose that the company has 100,000 shares of stock outstanding. Determine the expected market price per share under both FIFO and LIFO.

e. If the capital markets are "efficient" (if they recognize or are able to distinguish between economic earnings and reported accounting earnings), are the reservations of the president justified?

16. *Problems of accounting for transactions involving foreign currencies with fluctuating exchange rates are similar to those of accounting for transactions in fluctuating domestic currency.*

On December 1, 1980, the New York Co. purchased for $100,000, 100 percent of the common stock of the London Co., a newly organized British corporation. The New York Co. planned to account for its interest in the London Co. as a subsidiary and consolidate its financial statements with its own. At the time of purchase £.50 (British pounds) was the equivalent of $1.00 (U.S.).

At the time of acquisition the balance sheet of the London Co. (in pounds) indicated the following:

**London Co.**
**Balance Sheet as of December 1, 1980**

| | |
|---|---:|
| Assets | |
| Cash | £ 5,000 |
| Accounts receivable | 7,500 |
| Plant and equipment | 47,500 |
| Total assets | £60,000 |
| | |
| Equities | |
| Accounts payable | £10,000 |
| Common stock | 50,000 |
| Total equities | £60,000 |

    a. Express the value of a U.S. dollar to that of a British pound in terms of a ratio. Translate the balance sheet of the London Co. into U.S. dollars (just as in other problems you translated U.S. dollars of a prior period into U.S. dollars of a current period).

    b. Suppose that on December 2, 1980, immediately after the New York Co. had acquired its interest in the London Co., the British government *devalued* the British pound. £.67 (British pounds) was now the equivalent of $1.00 (U.S.). Express the current value of a U.S. dollar to that of a British pound in terms of a ratio. Translate the balance sheet of the London Co. into U.S. dollars at the exchange rate on December 2, 1980.

        a. At what dollar value did you report cash, accounts receivable, and accounts payable? How much gain or loss in purchasing power did the New York Co. realize as the result of the devaluation?

        b. At what value did you report fixed assets? (What conversion factor did you use?) Is there any reason why the fixed assets should be reported at a different value on the postdevaluation balance sheet than they were on the predevaluation balance sheet? Has the value of the fixed assets, expressed in terms of U.S. dollars, changed as a consequence of the devaluation?

    c. Comment on the similarity between adjusting from price level changes and adjusting for foreign currency changes. Refer specifically to why it is important, in both situations, to distinguish between monetary and nonmonetary items (or items denominated in a foreign currency and those that are not).

*solutions to exercise for review and self-testing*

1.

| | Price-level-adjusted statements | Replacement cost statements |
|---|---|---|
| a. Equipment (gross) | $60,000 × 130/110 = $70,909 | $75,000 |
| b. Depreciation | $6,000 × 130/110 = $7,091 (or 1/10th of $70,909) | $7,500 (1/10th of $75,000) |
| c. Equipment (net) | $70,909 – $7,091 = $63,818 | $75,000 – $7,500 = $67,500 |

2.

| | | |
|---|---|---|
| a. Cost of goods sold | $30,000 × 130/120 = $32,500 | $34,000 |
| b. Ending inventory | $10,000 × 130/120 = $10,833 | $12,000 |
| 3. Sales revenue | $50,000 × 130/120 = $54,167 | $50,000 |
| 4. Common stock | $100,000 × 130/110 = $118,812 | $100,000 |

5. Loss on purchasing power

| | Unadjusted amounts | Conversion factor | Adjusted amounts (year-end dollars) |
|---|---|---|---|
| Cash balance, January 1 | $100,000 | 130/110 | $118,182 |
| Add: Sales | 50,000 | 130/120 | 54,167 |
| Deduct: purchase of equipment | (60,000) | 130/110 | (70,909) |
| purchase of inventory | (40,000) | 130/120 | (43,333) |
| Cash balance, December 31 | $ 50,000 | | $ 58,107 |
| Cash balance, December 31 (unadjusted) | | | $ 50,000 |
| Loss on purchasing power | | | $ 8,107 |

6. Holding gains
   *Equipment*

Unrealized gain = Ending balance (net) at replacement cost – Ending Balance (net) at historical cost

= $67,500 – $54,000 = $13,500

(Ending balance at historical cost equals original cost of $60,000 less depreciation of $6,000.)

Realized gain = Replacement cost depreciation – Historical cost depreciation

= $7,500 – $6,000 = $1,500

*Inventory*

Unrealized gain = Ending balance at replacement cost – Ending balance at historical cost

= $12,000 – $10,000 = $2,000

Realized gain = Replacement cost of goods sold – Historical cost of goods sold

= $34,000 – $30,000 = $4,000

*Total unrealized gains* = $15,500
*Total realized gains* = 5,500

7.

## Statement of Income
## for the Year Ending December 31, 1980

|  | Historical costs | Price-level adjusted costs | Replacement costs |
|---|---|---|---|
| Sales | $50,000 | $54,167 | $50,000 |
| Cost of goods sold | $30,000 | $32,500 | $34,000 |
| Depreciation | 6,000 | 7,091 | 7,500 |
| Total expenses | $36,000 | $39,591 | $41,500 |
| Operating income | $14,000 | $14,576 | $ 8,500 |
| Purchasing power loss |  | (8,107) |  |
| Holding gains |  |  |  |
| Realized |  |  | 5,500 |
| Unrealized |  |  | 15,500 |
| Net income | $14,000 | $ 6,469 | $29,500 |

## Balance Sheet
## as of December 31, 1980

|  | Historical costs | Price-level adjusted costs | Replacement costs |
|---|---|---|---|
| *Assets* |  |  |  |
| Cash | $ 50,000 | $ 50,000 | $ 50,000 |
| Inventory | 10,000 | 10,833 | 12,000 |
| Equipment | 54,000 | 63,818 | 67,500 |
| Total assets | $114,000 | $124,651 | $129,500 |
| *Equities* |  |  |  |
| Common stock | $100,000 | $118,182 | $100,000 |
| Retained earnings | 14,000 | 6,469 | 29,500 |
| Total equities | $114,000 | $124,651 | $129,500 |

# Appendix

table 1

**Future Value of $1**     $F_n = P(1 + r)^n$

| No. of periods | 2% | 3% | 4% | 5% | 6% | 7% | 8% |
|---|---|---|---|---|---|---|---|
| 1 | 1.0200 | 1.0300 | 1.0400 | 1.0500 | 1.0600 | 1.0700 | 1.0800 |
| 2 | 1.0404 | 1.0609 | 1.0816 | 1.1025 | 1.1236 | 1.1449 | 1.1664 |
| 3 | 1.0612 | 1.0927 | 1.1249 | 1.1576 | 1.1910 | 1.2250 | 1.2597 |
| 4 | 1.0824 | 1.1255 | 1.1699 | 1.2155 | 1.2625 | 1.3108 | 1.3605 |
| 5 | 1.1041 | 1.1593 | 1.2167 | 1.2763 | 1.3382 | 1.4026 | 1.4693 |
| 6 | 1.1262 | 1.1941 | 1.2653 | 1.3401 | 1.4185 | 1.5007 | 1.5869 |
| 7 | 1.1487 | 1.2299 | 1.3159 | 1.4071 | 1.5036 | 1.6058 | 1.7138 |
| 8 | 1.1717 | 1.2668 | 1.3686 | 1.4775 | 1.5938 | 1.7182 | 1.8509 |
| 9 | 1.1951 | 1.3048 | 1.4233 | 1.5513 | 1.6895 | 1.8385 | 1.9990 |
| 10 | 1.2190 | 1.3439 | 1.4802 | 1.6289 | 1.7908 | 1.9672 | 2.1589 |
| 11 | 1.2434 | 1.3842 | 1.5395 | 1.7103 | 1.8983 | 2.1049 | 2.3316 |
| 12 | 1.2682 | 1.4258 | 1.6010 | 1.7959 | 2.0122 | 2.2522 | 2.5182 |
| 13 | 1.2936 | 1.4685 | 1.6651 | 1.8856 | 2.1329 | 2.4098 | 2.7196 |
| 14 | 1.3195 | 1.5126 | 1.7317 | 1.9799 | 2.2609 | 2.5785 | 2.9372 |
| 15 | 1.3459 | 1.5580 | 1.8009 | 2.0789 | 2.3966 | 2.7590 | 3.1722 |
| 16 | 1.3728 | 1.6047 | 1.8730 | 2.1829 | 2.5404 | 2.9522 | 3.4259 |
| 17 | 1.4002 | 1.6528 | 1.9479 | 2.2920 | 2.6928 | 3.1588 | 3.7000 |
| 18 | 1.4282 | 1.7024 | 2.0258 | 2.4066 | 2.8543 | 3.3799 | 3.9960 |
| 19 | 1.4568 | 1.7535 | 2.1068 | 2.5270 | 3.0256 | 3.6165 | 4.3157 |
| 20 | 1.4859 | 1.8061 | 2.1911 | 2.6533 | 3.2071 | 3.8697 | 4.6610 |
| 21 | 1.5157 | 1.8603 | 2.2788 | 2.7860 | 3.3996 | 4.1406 | 5.0338 |
| 22 | 1.5460 | 1.9161 | 2.3699 | 2.9253 | 3.6035 | 4.4304 | 5.4365 |
| 23 | 1.5769 | 1.9736 | 2.4647 | 3.0715 | 3.8197 | 4.7405 | 5.8715 |
| 24 | 1.6084 | 2.0328 | 2.5633 | 3.2251 | 4.0489 | 5.0724 | 6.3412 |
| 25 | 1.6406 | 2.0938 | 2.6658 | 3.3864 | 4.2919 | 5.4274 | 6.8485 |
| 26 | 1.6734 | 2.1566 | 2.7725 | 3.5557 | 4.5494 | 5.8074 | 7.3964 |
| 27 | 1.7069 | 2.2213 | 2.8834 | 3.7335 | 4.8223 | 6.2139 | 7.9881 |
| 28 | 1.7410 | 2.2879 | 2.9987 | 3.9201 | 5.1117 | 6.6488 | 8.6271 |
| 29 | 1.7758 | 2.3566 | 3.1187 | 4.1161 | 5.4184 | 7.1143 | 9.3173 |
| 30 | 1.8114 | 2.4273 | 3.2434 | 4.3219 | 5.7435 | 7.6123 | 10.0627 |
| 31 | 1.8476 | 2.5001 | 3.3731 | 4.5380 | 6.0881 | 8.1451 | 10.8677 |
| 32 | 1.8845 | 2.5751 | 3.5081 | 4.7649 | 6.4534 | 8.7153 | 11.7371 |
| 33 | 1.9222 | 2.6523 | 3.6484 | 5.0032 | 6.8406 | 9.3253 | 12.6760 |
| 34 | 1.9607 | 2.7319 | 3.7943 | 5.2533 | 7.2510 | 9.9781 | 13.6901 |
| 35 | 1.9999 | 2.8139 | 3.9461 | 5.5160 | 7.6861 | 10.6766 | 14.7853 |
| 36 | 2.0399 | 2.8983 | 4.1039 | 5.7918 | 8.1473 | 11.4239 | 15.9682 |
| 37 | 2.0807 | 2.9852 | 4.2681 | 6.0814 | 8.6361 | 12.2236 | 17.2456 |
| 38 | 2.1223 | 3.0748 | 4.4388 | 6.3855 | 9.1543 | 13.0793 | 18.6253 |
| 39 | 2.1647 | 3.1670 | 4.6164 | 6.7048 | 9.7035 | 13.9948 | 20.1153 |
| 40 | 2.2080 | 3.2620 | 4.8010 | 7.0400 | 10.2857 | 14.9745 | 21.7245 |
| 41 | 2.2522 | 3.3599 | 4.9931 | 7.3920 | 10.9029 | 16.0227 | 23.4625 |
| 42 | 2.2972 | 3.4607 | 5.1928 | 7.7616 | 11.5570 | 17.1443 | 25.3395 |
| 43 | 2.3432 | 3.5645 | 5.4005 | 8.1497 | 12.2505 | 18.3444 | 27.3666 |
| 44 | 2.3901 | 3.6715 | 5.6165 | 8.5572 | 12.9855 | 19.6285 | 29.5560 |
| 45 | 2.4379 | 3.7816 | 5.8412 | 8.9850 | 13.7646 | 21.0025 | 31.9204 |
| 46 | 2.4866 | 3.8950 | 6.0748 | 9.4343 | 14.5905 | 22.4726 | 34.4741 |
| 47 | 2.5363 | 4.0119 | 6.3178 | 9.9060 | 15.4659 | 24.0457 | 37.2320 |
| 48 | 2.5871 | 4.1323 | 6.5705 | 10.4013 | 16.3939 | 25.7289 | 40.2106 |
| 49 | 2.6388 | 4.2562 | 6.8333 | 10.9213 | 17.3775 | 27.5299 | 43.4274 |
| 50 | 2.6916 | 4.3839 | 7.1067 | 11.4674 | 18.4202 | 29.4570 | 46.9016 |

| 9% | 10% | 11% | 12% | 13% | 14% | 15% |
|---|---|---|---|---|---|---|
| 1.0900 | 1.1000 | 1.1100 | 1.1200 | 1.1300 | 1.1400 | 1.1500 |
| 1.1881 | 1.2100 | 1.2321 | 1.2544 | 1.2769 | 1.2996 | 1.3225 |
| 1.2950 | 1.3310 | 1.3676 | 1.4049 | 1.4429 | 1.4815 | 1.5209 |
| 1.4116 | 1.4641 | 1.5181 | 1.5735 | 1.6305 | 1.6890 | 1.7490 |
| 1.5386 | 1.6105 | 1.6851 | 1.7623 | 1.8424 | 1.9254 | 2.0114 |
| 1.6771 | 1.7716 | 1.8704 | 1.9738 | 2.0820 | 2.1950 | 2.3131 |
| 1.8280 | 1.9487 | 2.0762 | 2.2107 | 2.3526 | 2.5023 | 2.6600 |
| 1.9926 | 2.1436 | 2.3045 | 2.4760 | 2.6584 | 2.8526 | 3.0590 |
| 2.1719 | 2.3579 | 2.5580 | 2.7731 | 3.0040 | 3.2519 | 3.5179 |
| 2.3674 | 2.5937 | 2.8394 | 3.1058 | 3.3946 | 3.7072 | 4.0456 |
| 2.5804 | 2.8531 | 3.1518 | 3.4785 | 3.8359 | 4.2262 | 4.6524 |
| 2.8127 | 3.1384 | 3.4985 | 3.8960 | 4.3345 | 4.8179 | 5.3503 |
| 3.0658 | 3.4523 | 3.8833 | 4.3635 | 4.8980 | 5.4924 | 6.1528 |
| 3.3417 | 3.7975 | 4.3104 | 4.8871 | 5.5348 | 6.2613 | 7.0757 |
| 3.6425 | 4.1772 | 4.7846 | 5.4736 | 6.2543 | 7.1379 | 8.1371 |
| 3.9703 | 4.5950 | 5.3109 | 6.1304 | 7.0673 | 8.1372 | 9.3576 |
| 4.3276 | 5.0545 | 5.8951 | 6.8660 | 7.9861 | 9.2765 | 10.7613 |
| 4.7171 | 5.5599 | 6.5436 | 7.6900 | 9.0243 | 10.5752 | 12.3755 |
| 5.1417 | 6.1159 | 7.2633 | 8.6128 | 10.1974 | 12.0557 | 14.2318 |
| 5.6044 | 6.7275 | 8.0623 | 9.6463 | 11.5231 | 13.7435 | 16.3665 |
| 6.1088 | 7.4002 | 8.9492 | 10.8038 | 13.0211 | 15.6676 | 18.8215 |
| 6.6586 | 8.1403 | 9.9336 | 12.1003 | 14.7138 | 17.8610 | 21.6447 |
| 7.2579 | 8.9543 | 11.0263 | 13.5523 | 16.6266 | 20.3616 | 24.8915 |
| 7.9111 | 9.8497 | 12.2392 | 15.1786 | 18.7881 | 23.2122 | 28.6252 |
| 8.6231 | 10.8347 | 13.5855 | 17.0001 | 21.2305 | 26.4619 | 32.9190 |
| 9.3992 | 11.9182 | 15.0799 | 19.0401 | 23.9905 | 30.1666 | 37.8568 |
| 10.2451 | 13.1100 | 16.7386 | 21.3249 | 27.1093 | 34.3899 | 43.5353 |
| 11.1671 | 14.4210 | 18.5799 | 23.8839 | 30.6335 | 39.2045 | 50.0656 |
| 12.1722 | 15.8631 | 20.6237 | 26.7499 | 34.6158 | 44.6931 | 57.5755 |
| 13.2677 | 17.4494 | 22.8923 | 29.9599 | 39.1159 | 50.9502 | 66.2118 |
| 14.4618 | 19.1943 | 25.4104 | 33.5551 | 44.2010 | 58.0832 | 76.1435 |
| 15.7633 | 21.1138 | 28.2056 | 37.5817 | 49.9471 | 66.2148 | 87.5651 |
| 17.1820 | 23.2252 | 31.3082 | 42.0915 | 56.4402 | 75.4849 | 100.6998 |
| 18.7284 | 25.5477 | 34.7521 | 47.1425 | 63.7774 | 86.0528 | 115.8048 |
| 20.4140 | 28.1024 | 38.5749 | 52.7996 | 72.0685 | 98.1002 | 133.1755 |
| 22.2512 | 30.9127 | 42.8181 | 59.1356 | 81.4374 | 111.8342 | 153.1519 |
| 24.2538 | 34.0039 | 47.5281 | 66.2318 | 92.0243 | 127.4910 | 176.1246 |
| 26.4367 | 37.4043 | 52.7562 | 74.1797 | 103.9874 | 145.3397 | 202.5433 |
| 28.8160 | 41.1448 | 58.5593 | 83.0812 | 117.5058 | 165.6873 | 232.9248 |
| 31.4094 | 45.2593 | 65.0009 | 93.0510 | 132.7816 | 188.8835 | 267.8635 |
| 34.2363 | 49.7852 | 72.1510 | 104.2171 | 150.0432 | 215.3272 | 308.0431 |
| 37.3175 | 54.7637 | 80.0876 | 116.7231 | 169.5488 | 245.4730 | 354.2495 |
| 40.6761 | 60.2401 | 88.8972 | 130.7299 | 191.5901 | 279.8392 | 407.3870 |
| 44.3370 | 66.2641 | 98.6759 | 146.4175 | 216.4968 | 319.0167 | 468.4950 |
| 48.3273 | 72.8905 | 109.5302 | 163.9876 | 244.6414 | 363.6791 | 538.7693 |
| 52.6767 | 80.1795 | 121.5786 | 183.6661 | 276.4448 | 414.5941 | 619.5847 |
| 57.4176 | 88.1975 | 134.9522 | 205.7061 | 312.3826 | 472.6373 | 712.5224 |
| 62.5852 | 97.0172 | 149.7970 | 230.3908 | 352.9923 | 538.8065 | 819.4007 |
| 68.2179 | 106.7190 | 166.2746 | 258.0377 | 398.8813 | 614.2395 | 942.3108 |
| 74.3575 | 117.3909 | 184.5648 | 289.0022 | 450.7359 | 700.2330 | 1083.6574 |

*table 2*

**Present Value of $1**

$$P = F_n \frac{1}{(1 + r)^n}$$

| No. of periods | 2% | 3% | 4% | 5% | 6% | 7% | 8% |
|---|---|---|---|---|---|---|---|
| 1 | .9804 | .9709 | .9615 | .9524 | .9434 | .9346 | .9259 |
| 2 | .9612 | .9426 | .9246 | .9070 | .8900 | .8734 | .8573 |
| 3 | .9423 | .9151 | .8890 | .8638 | .8396 | .8163 | .7938 |
| 4 | .9238 | .8885 | .8548 | .8227 | .7921 | .7629 | .7350 |
| 5 | .9057 | .8626 | .8219 | .7835 | .7473 | .7130 | .6806 |
| 6 | .8880 | .8375 | .7903 | .7462 | .7050 | .6663 | .6302 |
| 7 | .8706 | .8131 | .7599 | .7107 | .6651 | .6227 | .5835 |
| 8 | .8535 | .7894 | .7307 | .6768 | .6274 | .5820 | .5403 |
| 9 | .8368 | .7664 | .7026 | .6446 | .5919 | .5439 | .5002 |
| 10 | .8203 | .7441 | .6756 | .6139 | .5584 | .5083 | .4632 |
| 11 | .8043 | .7224 | .6496 | .5847 | .5268 | .4751 | .4289 |
| 12 | .7885 | .7014 | .6246 | .5568 | .4970 | .4440 | .3971 |
| 13 | .7730 | .6810 | .6006 | .5303 | .4688 | .4150 | .3677 |
| 14 | .7579 | .6611 | .5775 | .5051 | .4423 | .3878 | .3405 |
| 15 | .7430 | .6419 | .5553 | .4810 | .4173 | .3624 | .3152 |
| 16 | .7284 | .6232 | .5339 | .4581 | .3936 | .3387 | .2919 |
| 17 | .7142 | .6050 | .5134 | .4363 | .3714 | .3166 | .2703 |
| 18 | .7002 | .5874 | .4936 | .4155 | .3503 | .2959 | .2502 |
| 19 | .6864 | .5703 | .4746 | .3957 | .3305 | .2765 | .2317 |
| 20 | .6730 | .5537 | .4564 | .3769 | .3118 | .2584 | .2145 |
| 21 | .6598 | .5375 | .4388 | .3589 | .2942 | .2415 | .1987 |
| 22 | .6468 | .5219 | .4220 | .3418 | .2775 | .2257 | .1839 |
| 23 | .6342 | .5067 | .4057 | .3256 | .2618 | .2109 | .1703 |
| 24 | .6217 | .4919 | .3901 | .3101 | .2470 | .1971 | .1577 |
| 25 | .6095 | .4776 | .3751 | .2953 | .2330 | .1842 | .1460 |
| 26 | .5976 | .4637 | .3607 | .2812 | .2198 | .1722 | .1352 |
| 27 | .5859 | .4502 | .3468 | .2678 | .2074 | .1609 | .1252 |
| 28 | .5744 | .4371 | .3335 | .2551 | .1956 | .1504 | .1159 |
| 29 | .5631 | .4243 | .3207 | .2429 | .1846 | .1406 | .1073 |
| 30 | .5521 | .4120 | .3083 | .2314 | .1741 | .1314 | .0994 |
| 31 | .5412 | .4000 | .2965 | .2204 | .1643 | .1228 | .0920 |
| 32 | .5306 | .3883 | .2851 | .2099 | .1550 | .1147 | .0852 |
| 33 | .5202 | .3770 | .2741 | .1999 | .1462 | .1072 | .0789 |
| 34 | .5100 | .3660 | .2636 | .1904 | .1379 | .1002 | .0730 |
| 35 | .5000 | .3554 | .2534 | .1813 | .1301 | .0937 | .0676 |
| 36 | .4902 | .3450 | .2437 | .1727 | .1227 | .0875 | .0626 |
| 37 | .4806 | .3350 | .2343 | .1644 | .1158 | .0818 | .0580 |
| 38 | .4712 | .3252 | .2253 | .1566 | .1092 | .0765 | .0537 |
| 39 | .4619 | .3158 | .2166 | .1491 | .1031 | .0715 | .0497 |
| 40 | .4529 | .3066 | .2083 | .1420 | .0972 | .0668 | .0460 |
| 41 | .4440 | .2976 | .2003 | .1353 | .0917 | .0624 | .0426 |
| 42 | .4353 | .2890 | .1926 | .1288 | .0865 | .0583 | .0395 |
| 43 | .4268 | .2805 | .1852 | .1227 | .0816 | .0545 | .0365 |
| 44 | .4184 | .2724 | .1780 | .1169 | .0770 | .0509 | .0338 |
| 45 | .4102 | .2644 | .1712 | .1113 | .0727 | .0476 | .0313 |
| 46 | .4022 | .2567 | .1646 | .1060 | .0685 | .0445 | .0290 |
| 47 | .3943 | .2493 | .1583 | .1009 | .0647 | .0416 | .0269 |
| 48 | .3865 | .2420 | .1522 | .0961 | .0610 | .0389 | .0249 |
| 49 | .3790 | .2350 | .1463 | .0916 | .0575 | .0363 | .0230 |
| 50 | .3715 | .2281 | .1407 | .0872 | .0543 | .0339 | .0213 |

| 9% | 10% | 11% | 12% | 13% | 14% | 15% |
|---|---|---|---|---|---|---|
| .9174 | .9091 | .9009 | .8929 | .8850 | .8772 | .8696 |
| .8417 | .8264 | .8116 | .7972 | .7831 | .7695 | .7561 |
| .7722 | .7513 | .7312 | .7118 | .6931 | .6750 | .6575 |
| .7084 | .6830 | .6587 | .6355 | .6133 | .5921 | .5718 |
| .6499 | .6209 | .5935 | .5674 | .5428 | .5194 | .4972 |
| .5963 | .5645 | .5346 | .5066 | .4803 | .4556 | .4323 |
| .5470 | .5132 | .4817 | .4523 | .4251 | .3996 | .3759 |
| .5019 | .4665 | .4339 | .4039 | .3762 | .3506 | .3269 |
| .4604 | .4241 | .3909 | .3606 | .3329 | .3075 | .2843 |
| .4224 | .3855 | .3522 | .3220 | .2946 | .2697 | .2472 |
| .3875 | .3505 | .3173 | .2875 | .2607 | .2366 | .2149 |
| .3555 | .3186 | .2858 | .2567 | .2307 | .2076 | .1869 |
| .3262 | .2897 | .2575 | .2292 | .2042 | .1821 | .1625 |
| .2992 | .2633 | .2320 | .2046 | .1807 | .1597 | .1413 |
| .2745 | .2394 | .2090 | .1827 | .1599 | .1401 | .1229 |
| .2519 | .2176 | .1883 | .1631 | .1415 | .1229 | .1069 |
| .2311 | .1978 | .1696 | .1456 | .1252 | .1078 | .0929 |
| .2120 | .1799 | .1528 | .1300 | .1108 | .0946 | .0808 |
| .1945 | .1635 | .1377 | .1161 | .0981 | .0829 | .0703 |
| .1784 | .1486 | .1240 | .1037 | .0868 | .0728 | .0611 |
| .1637 | .1351 | .1117 | .0926 | .0768 | .0638 | .0531 |
| .1502 | .1228 | .1007 | .0826 | .0680 | .0560 | .0462 |
| .1378 | .1117 | .0907 | .0738 | .0601 | .0491 | .0402 |
| .1264 | .1015 | .0817 | .0659 | .0532 | .0431 | .0349 |
| .1160 | .0923 | .0736 | .0588 | .0471 | .0378 | .0304 |
| .1064 | .0839 | .0663 | .0525 | .0417 | .0331 | .0264 |
| .0976 | .0763 | .0597 | .0469 | .0369 | .0291 | .0230 |
| .0895 | .0693 | .0538 | .0419 | .0326 | .0255 | .0200 |
| .0822 | .0630 | .0485 | .0374 | .0289 | .0224 | .0174 |
| .0754 | .0573 | .0437 | .0334 | .0256 | .0196 | .0151 |
| .0691 | .0521 | .0394 | .0298 | .0226 | .0172 | .0131 |
| .0634 | .0474 | .0355 | .0266 | .0200 | .0151 | .0114 |
| .0582 | .0431 | .0319 | .0238 | .0177 | .0132 | .0099 |
| .0534 | .0391 | .0288 | .0212 | .0157 | .0116 | .0086 |
| .0490 | .0356 | .0259 | .0189 | .0139 | .0102 | .0075 |
| .0449 | .0323 | .0234 | .0169 | .0123 | .0089 | .0065 |
| .0412 | .0294 | .0210 | .0151 | .0109 | .0078 | .0057 |
| .0378 | .0267 | .0190 | .0135 | .0096 | .0069 | .0049 |
| .0347 | .0243 | .0171 | .0120 | .0085 | .0060 | .0043 |
| .0318 | .0221 | .0154 | .0107 | .0075 | .0053 | .0037 |
| .0292 | .0201 | .0139 | .0096 | .0067 | .0046 | .0032 |
| .0268 | .0183 | .0125 | .0086 | .0059 | .0041 | .0028 |
| .0246 | .0166 | .0112 | .0076 | .0052 | .0036 | .0025 |
| .0226 | .0151 | .0101 | .0068 | .0046 | .0031 | .0021 |
| .0207 | .0137 | .0091 | .0061 | .0041 | .0027 | .0019 |
| .0190 | .0125 | .0082 | .0054 | .0036 | .0024 | .0016 |
| .0174 | .0113 | .0074 | .0049 | .0032 | .0021 | .0014 |
| .0160 | .0103 | .0067 | .0043 | .0028 | .0019 | .0012 |
| .0147 | .0094 | .0060 | .0039 | .0025 | .0016 | .0011 |
| .0134 | .0085 | .0054 | .0035 | .0022 | .0014 | .0009 |

## table 3

**Future Value of an Annuity of $1 in Arrears**

$$F_A = \frac{(1+r)^n - 1}{r}$$

| No. of periods | 2% | 3% | 4% | 5% | 6% | 7% | 8% |
|---|---|---|---|---|---|---|---|
| 1 | 1.0000 | 1.0000 | 1.0000 | 1.0000 | 1.0000 | 1.0000 | 1.0000 |
| 2 | 2.0200 | 2.0300 | 2.0400 | 2.0500 | 2.0600 | 2.0700 | 2.0800 |
| 3 | 3.0604 | 3.0909 | 3.1216 | 3.1525 | 3.1836 | 3.2149 | 3.2464 |
| 4 | 4.1216 | 4.1836 | 4.2465 | 4.3101 | 4.3746 | 4.4399 | 4.5061 |
| 5 | 5.2040 | 5.3091 | 5.4163 | 5.5256 | 5.6371 | 5.7507 | 5.8666 |
| 6 | 6.3081 | 6.4684 | 6.6330 | 6.8019 | 6.9753 | 7.1533 | 7.3359 |
| 7 | 7.4343 | 7.6625 | 7.8983 | 8.1420 | 8.3938 | 8.6540 | 8.9228 |
| 8 | 8.5830 | 8.8923 | 9.2142 | 9.5491 | 9.8975 | 10.2598 | 10.6366 |
| 9 | 9.7546 | 10.1591 | 10.5828 | 11.0266 | 11.4913 | 11.9780 | 12.4876 |
| 10 | 10.9497 | 11.4639 | 12.0061 | 12.5779 | 13.1808 | 13.8164 | 14.4866 |
| 11 | 12.1687 | 12.8078 | 13.4864 | 14.2068 | 14.9716 | 15.7836 | 16.6455 |
| 12 | 13.4121 | 14.1920 | 15.0258 | 15.9171 | 16.8699 | 17.8885 | 18.9771 |
| 13 | 14.6803 | 15.6178 | 16.6268 | 17.7130 | 18.8821 | 20.1406 | 21.4953 |
| 14 | 15.9739 | 17.0863 | 18.2919 | 19.5986 | 21.0151 | 22.5505 | 24.2149 |
| 15 | 17.2934 | 18.5989 | 20.0236 | 21.5786 | 23.2760 | 25.1290 | 27.1521 |
| 16 | 18.6393 | 20.1569 | 21.8245 | 23.6575 | 25.6725 | 27.8881 | 30.3243 |
| 17 | 20.0121 | 21.7616 | 23.6975 | 25.8404 | 28.2129 | 30.8402 | 33.7502 |
| 18 | 21.4123 | 23.4144 | 25.6454 | 28.1324 | 30.9057 | 33.9990 | 37.4502 |
| 19 | 22.8406 | 25.1169 | 27.6712 | 30.5390 | 33.7600 | 37.3790 | 41.4463 |
| 20 | 24.2974 | 26.8704 | 29.7781 | 33.0660 | 36.7856 | 40.9955 | 45.7620 |
| 21 | 25.7833 | 28.6765 | 31.9692 | 35.7193 | 39.9927 | 44.8652 | 50.4229 |
| 22 | 27.2990 | 30.5368 | 34.2480 | 38.5052 | 43.3923 | 49.0057 | 55.4568 |
| 23 | 28.8450 | 32.4529 | 36.6179 | 41.4305 | 46.9958 | 53.4361 | 60.8933 |
| 24 | 30.4219 | 34.4265 | 39.0826 | 44.5020 | 50.8156 | 58.1767 | 66.7648 |
| 25 | 32.0303 | 36.4593 | 41.6459 | 47.7271 | 54.8645 | 63.2490 | 73.1059 |
| 26 | 33.6709 | 38.5530 | 44.3117 | 51.1135 | 59.1564 | 68.6765 | 79.9544 |
| 27 | 35.3443 | 40.7096 | 47.0842 | 54.6691 | 63.7058 | 74.4838 | 87.3508 |
| 28 | 37.0512 | 42.9309 | 49.9676 | 58.4026 | 68.5281 | 80.6977 | 95.3388 |
| 29 | 38.7922 | 45.2189 | 52.9663 | 62.3227 | 73.6398 | 87.3465 | 103.9659 |
| 30 | 40.5681 | 47.5754 | 56.0849 | 66.4388 | 79.0582 | 94.4608 | 113.2832 |
| 31 | 42.3794 | 50.0027 | 59.3283 | 70.7608 | 84.8017 | 102.0730 | 123.3459 |
| 32 | 44.2270 | 52.5028 | 62.7015 | 75.2988 | 90.8898 | 110.2182 | 134.2135 |
| 33 | 46.1116 | 55.0778 | 66.2095 | 80.0638 | 97.3432 | 118.9334 | 145.9506 |
| 34 | 48.0338 | 57.7302 | 69.8579 | 85.0670 | 104.1838 | 128.2588 | 158.6267 |
| 35 | 49.9945 | 60.4621 | 73.6522 | 90.3203 | 111.4348 | 138.2369 | 172.3168 |
| 36 | 51.9944 | 63.2759 | 77.5983 | 95.8363 | 119.1209 | 148.9135 | 187.1021 |
| 37 | 54.0343 | 66.1742 | 81.7022 | 101.6281 | 127.2681 | 160.3374 | 203.0703 |
| 38 | 56.1149 | 69.1594 | 85.9703 | 107.7095 | 135.9042 | 172.5610 | 220.3159 |
| 39 | 58.2372 | 72.2342 | 90.4091 | 114.0950 | 145.0585 | 185.6403 | 238.9412 |
| 40 | 60.4020 | 75.4013 | 95.0255 | 120.7998 | 154.7620 | 199.6351 | 259.0565 |
| 41 | 62.6100 | 78.6633 | 99.8265 | 127.8398 | 165.0477 | 214.6096 | 280.7810 |
| 42 | 64.8622 | 82.0232 | 104.8196 | 135.2318 | 175.9505 | 230.6322 | 304.2435 |
| 43 | 67.1595 | 85.4839 | 110.0124 | 142.9933 | 187.5076 | 247.7765 | 329.5830 |
| 44 | 69.5027 | 89.0484 | 115.4129 | 151.1430 | 199.7580 | 266.1209 | 356.9496 |
| 45 | 71.8927 | 92.7199 | 121.0294 | 159.7002 | 212.7435 | 285.7493 | 386.5056 |
| 46 | 74.3306 | 96.5015 | 126.8706 | 168.6852 | 226.5081 | 306.7518 | 418.4261 |
| 47 | 76.8172 | 100.3965 | 132.9454 | 178.1194 | 241.0986 | 329.2244 | 452.9002 |
| 48 | 79.3535 | 104.4084 | 139.2632 | 188.0254 | 256.5645 | 353.2701 | 490.1322 |
| 49 | 81.9406 | 108.5406 | 145.8337 | 198.4267 | 272.9584 | 378.9990 | 530.3427 |
| 50 | 84.5794 | 112.7969 | 152.6671 | 209.3480 | 290.3359 | 406.5289 | 573.7702 |

670

| 9% | 10% | 11% | 12% | 13% | 14% | 15% |
|---|---|---|---|---|---|---|
| 1.0000 | 1.0000 | 1.0000 | 1.0000 | 1.0000 | 1.0000 | 1.0000 |
| 2.0900 | 2.1000 | 2.1100 | 2.1200 | 2.1300 | 2.1400 | 2.1500 |
| 3.2781 | 3.3100 | 3.3421 | 3.3744 | 3.4069 | 3.4396 | 3.4725 |
| 4.5731 | 4.6410 | 4.7097 | 4.7793 | 4.8498 | 4.9211 | 4.9934 |
| 5.9847 | 6.1051 | 6.2278 | 6.3528 | 6.4803 | 6.6101 | 6.7424 |
| 7.5233 | 7.7156 | 7.9129 | 8.1152 | 8.3227 | 8.5355 | 8.7537 |
| 9.2004 | 9.4872 | 9.7833 | 10.0890 | 10.4047 | 10.7305 | 11.0668 |
| 11.0285 | 11.4359 | 11.8594 | 12.2997 | 12.7573 | 13.2328 | 13.7268 |
| 13.0210 | 13.5795 | 14.1640 | 14.7757 | 15.4157 | 16.0853 | 16.7858 |
| 15.1929 | 15.9374 | 16.7220 | 17.5487 | 18.4197 | 19.3373 | 20.3037 |
| 17.5603 | 18.5312 | 19.5614 | 20.6546 | 21.8143 | 23.0445 | 24.3493 |
| 20.1407 | 21.3843 | 22.7132 | 24.1331 | 25.6502 | 27.2707 | 29.0017 |
| 22.9534 | 24.5227 | 26.2116 | 28.0291 | 29.9847 | 32.0887 | 34.3519 |
| 26.0192 | 27.9750 | 30.0949 | 32.3926 | 34.8827 | 37.5811 | 40.5047 |
| 29.3609 | 31.7725 | 34.4054 | 37.2797 | 40.4175 | 43.8424 | 47.5804 |
| 33.0034 | 35.9497 | 39.1899 | 42.7533 | 46.6717 | 50.9804 | 55.7175 |
| 36.9737 | 40.5447 | 44.5008 | 48.8837 | 53.7391 | 59.1176 | 65.0751 |
| 41.3013 | 45.5992 | 50.3959 | 55.7497 | 61.7251 | 68.3941 | 75.8364 |
| 46.0185 | 51.1591 | 56.9395 | 63.4397 | 70.7494 | 78.9692 | 88.2118 |
| 51.1601 | 57.2750 | 64.2028 | 72.0524 | 80.9468 | 91.0249 | 102.4436 |
| 56.7645 | 64.0025 | 72.2651 | 81.6987 | 92.4699 | 104.7684 | 118.8101 |
| 62.8733 | 71.4027 | 81.2143 | 92.5026 | 105.4910 | 120.4360 | 137.6316 |
| 69.5319 | 79.5430 | 91.1479 | 104.6029 | 120.2048 | 138.2970 | 159.2764 |
| 76.7898 | 88.4973 | 102.1742 | 118.1552 | 136.8315 | 158.6586 | 184.1678 |
| 84.7009 | 98.3471 | 114.4133 | 133.3339 | 155.6196 | 181.8708 | 212.7930 |
| 93.3240 | 109.1818 | 127.9988 | 150.3339 | 176.8501 | 208.3327 | 245.7120 |
| 102.7231 | 121.0999 | 143.0786 | 169.3740 | 200.8406 | 238.4993 | 283.5688 |
| 112.9682 | 134.2099 | 159.8173 | 190.6989 | 227.9499 | 272.8892 | 327.1041 |
| 124.1354 | 148.6309 | 178.3972 | 214.5828 | 258.5834 | 312.0937 | 377.1697 |
| 136.3075 | 164.4940 | 199.0209 | 241.3327 | 293.1992 | 356.7868 | 434.7451 |
| 149.5752 | 181.9434 | 221.9132 | 271.2926 | 332.3151 | 407.7370 | 500.9569 |
| 164.0370 | 201.1378 | 247.3236 | 304.8477 | 376.5161 | 465.8202 | 577.1005 |
| 179.8003 | 222.2515 | 275.5292 | 342.4294 | 426.4632 | 532.0350 | 664.6655 |
| 196.9823 | 245.4767 | 306.8374 | 384.5210 | 482.9034 | 607.5199 | 765.3654 |
| 215.7108 | 271.0244 | 341.5896 | 431.6635 | 546.6808 | 693.5727 | 881.1702 |
| 236.1247 | 299.1268 | 380.1644 | 484.4631 | 618.7493 | 791.6729 | 1014.3457 |
| 258.3759 | 330.0395 | 422.9825 | 543.5987 | 700.1867 | 903.5071 | 1167.4975 |
| 282.6298 | 364.0434 | 470.5106 | 609.8305 | 792.2110 | 1030.9981 | 1343.6222 |
| 309.0665 | 401.4478 | 523.2667 | 684.0102 | 896.1984 | 1176.3378 | 1546.1655 |
| 337.8824 | 442.5926 | 581.8261 | 767.0914 | 1013.7042 | 1342.0251 | 1779.0903 |
| 369.2919 | 487.8518 | 646.8269 | 860.1424 | 1146.4858 | 1530.9086 | 2046.9539 |
| 403.5281 | 537.6370 | 718.9779 | 964.3595 | 1296.5289 | 1746.2358 | 2354.9969 |
| 440.8457 | 592.4007 | 799.0655 | 1081.0826 | 1466.0777 | 1991.7088 | 2709.2465 |
| 481.5218 | 652.6408 | 887.9627 | 1211.8125 | 1657.6678 | 2271.5481 | 3116.6334 |
| 525.8587 | 718.9048 | 986.6386 | 1358.2300 | 1874.1646 | 2590.5648 | 3585.1285 |
| 574.1860 | 791.7953 | 1096.1688 | 1522.2176 | 2118.8060 | 2954.2439 | 4123.8977 |
| 626.8628 | 871.9749 | 1217.7474 | 1705.8838 | 2395.2508 | 3368.8380 | 4743.4824 |
| 684.2804 | 960.1723 | 1352.6996 | 1911.5898 | 2707.6334 | 3841.4753 | 5456.0047 |
| 746.8656 | 1057.1896 | 1502.4965 | 2141.9806 | 3060.6258 | 4380.2819 | 6275.4055 |
| 815.0836 | 1163.9085 | 1668.7712 | 2400.0182 | 3459.5071 | 4994.5213 | 7217.7163 |

*table 4*

**Present Value of an Annuity of $1 in Arrears**

$$P_A \frac{1 - (1 + r)^{-n}}{r}$$

| No. of periods | 2% | 3% | 4% | 5% | 6% | 7% | 8% |
|---|---|---|---|---|---|---|---|
| 1 | .9804 | .9709 | .9615 | .9524 | .9434 | .9346 | .9259 |
| 2 | 1.9416 | 1.9135 | 1.8861 | 1.8594 | 1.8334 | 1.8080 | 1.7833 |
| 3 | 2.8839 | 2.8286 | 2.7751 | 2.7232 | 2.6730 | 2.6243 | 2.5771 |
| 4 | 3.8077 | 3.7171 | 3.6299 | 3.5460 | 3.4651 | 3.3872 | 3.3121 |
| 5 | 4.7135 | 4.5797 | 4.4518 | 4.3295 | 4.2124 | 4.1002 | 3.9927 |
| 6 | 5.6014 | 5.4172 | 5.2421 | 5.0757 | 4.9173 | 4.7665 | 4.6229 |
| 7 | 6.4720 | 6.2303 | 6.0021 | 5.7864 | 5.5824 | 5.3893 | 5.2064 |
| 8 | 7.3255 | 7.0197 | 6.7327 | 6.4632 | 6.2098 | 5.9713 | 5.7466 |
| 9 | 8.1622 | 7.7861 | 7.4353 | 7.1078 | 6.8017 | 6.5152 | 6.2469 |
| 10 | 8.9826 | 8.5302 | 8.1109 | 7.7217 | 7.3601 | 7.0236 | 6.7101 |
| 11 | 9.7868 | 9.2526 | 8.7605 | 8.3064 | 7.8869 | 7.4987 | 7.1390 |
| 12 | 10.5753 | 9.9540 | 9.3851 | 8.8633 | 8.3838 | 7.9427 | 7.5361 |
| 13 | 11.3484 | 10.6350 | 9.9856 | 9.3936 | 8.8527 | 8.3577 | 7.9038 |
| 14 | 12.1062 | 11.2961 | 10.5631 | 9.8986 | 9.2950 | 8.7455 | 8.2442 |
| 15 | 12.8493 | 11.9379 | 11.1184 | 10.3797 | 9.7122 | 9.1079 | 8.5595 |
| 16 | 13.5777 | 12.5611 | 11.6523 | 10.8378 | 10.1059 | 9.4466 | 8.8514 |
| 17 | 14.2919 | 13.1661 | 12.1657 | 11.2741 | 10.4773 | 9.7632 | 9.1216 |
| 18 | 14.9920 | 13.7535 | 12.6593 | 11.6896 | 10.8276 | 10.0591 | 9.3719 |
| 19 | 15.6785 | 14.3238 | 13.1339 | 12.0853 | 11.1581 | 10.3356 | 9.6036 |
| 20 | 16.3514 | 14.8775 | 13.5903 | 12.4622 | 11.4699 | 10.5940 | 9.8181 |
| 21 | 17.0112 | 15.4150 | 14.0292 | 12.8212 | 11.7641 | 10.8355 | 10.0168 |
| 22 | 17.6580 | 15.9369 | 14.4511 | 13.1630 | 12.0416 | 11.0612 | 10.2007 |
| 23 | 18.2922 | 16.4436 | 14.8568 | 13.4886 | 12.3034 | 11.2722 | 10.3711 |
| 24 | 18.9139 | 16.9355 | 15.2470 | 13.7986 | 12.5504 | 11.4693 | 10.5288 |
| 25 | 19.5235 | 17.4131 | 15.6221 | 14.0939 | 12.7834 | 11.6536 | 10.6748 |
| 26 | 20.1210 | 17.8768 | 15.9828 | 14.3752 | 13.0032 | 11.8258 | 10.8100 |
| 27 | 20.7069 | 18.3270 | 16.3296 | 14.6430 | 13.2105 | 11.9867 | 10.9352 |
| 28 | 21.2813 | 18.7641 | 16.6631 | 14.8981 | 13.4062 | 12.1371 | 11.0511 |
| 29 | 21.8444 | 19.1885 | 16.9837 | 15.1411 | 13.5907 | 12.2777 | 11.1584 |
| 30 | 22.3965 | 19.6004 | 17.2920 | 15.3725 | 13.7648 | 12.4090 | 11.2578 |
| 31 | 22.9377 | 20.0004 | 17.5885 | 15.5928 | 13.9291 | 12.5318 | 11.3498 |
| 32 | 23.4683 | 20.3888 | 17.8736 | 15.8027 | 14.0840 | 12.6466 | 11.4350 |
| 33 | 23.9886 | 20.7658 | 18.1476 | 16.0025 | 14.2302 | 12.7538 | 11.5139 |
| 34 | 24.4986 | 21.1318 | 18.4112 | 16.1929 | 14.3681 | 12.8540 | 11.5869 |
| 35 | 24.9986 | 21.4872 | 18.6646 | 16.3742 | 14.4982 | 12.9477 | 11.6546 |
| 36 | 25.4888 | 21.8323 | 18.9083 | 16.5469 | 14.6210 | 13.0352 | 11.7172 |
| 37 | 25.9695 | 22.1672 | 19.1426 | 16.7113 | 14.7368 | 13.1170 | 11.7752 |
| 38 | 26.4406 | 22.4925 | 19.3679 | 16.8679 | 14.8460 | 13.1935 | 11.8289 |
| 39 | 26.9026 | 22.8082 | 19.5845 | 17.0170 | 14.9491 | 13.2649 | 11.8786 |
| 40 | 27.3555 | 23.1148 | 19.7928 | 17.1591 | 15.0463 | 13.3317 | 11.9246 |
| 41 | 27.7995 | 23.4124 | 19.9931 | 17.2944 | 15.1380 | 13.3941 | 11.9672 |
| 42 | 28.2348 | 23.7014 | 20.1856 | 17.4232 | 15.2245 | 13.4524 | 12.0067 |
| 43 | 28.6616 | 23.9819 | 20.3708 | 17.5459 | 15.3062 | 13.5070 | 12.0432 |
| 44 | 29.0800 | 24.2543 | 20.5488 | 17.6628 | 15.3832 | 13.5579 | 12.0771 |
| 45 | 29.4902 | 24.5187 | 20.7200 | 17.7741 | 15.4558 | 13.6055 | 12.1084 |
| 46 | 29.8923 | 24.7754 | 20.8847 | 17.8801 | 15.5244 | 13.6500 | 12.1374 |
| 47 | 30.2866 | 25.0247 | 21.0429 | 17.9810 | 15.5890 | 13.6916 | 12.1643 |
| 48 | 30.6731 | 25.2667 | 21.1951 | 18.0772 | 15.6500 | 13.7305 | 12.1891 |
| 49 | 31.0521 | 25.5017 | 21.3415 | 18.1687 | 15.7076 | 13.7668 | 12.2122 |
| 50 | 31.4236 | 25.7298 | 21.4822 | 18.2559 | 15.7619 | 13.8007 | 12.2335 |

| 9% | 10% | 11% | 12% | 13% | 14% | 15% |
|---|---|---|---|---|---|---|
| .9174 | .9091 | .9009 | .8929 | .8850 | .8772 | .8696 |
| 1.7591 | 1.7355 | 1.7125 | 1.6901 | 1.6681 | 1.6467 | 1.6257 |
| 2.5313 | 2.4869 | 2.4437 | 2.4018 | 2.3612 | 2.3216 | 2.2832 |
| 3.2397 | 3.1699 | 3.1024 | 3.0373 | 2.9745 | 2.9137 | 2.8550 |
| 3.8897 | 3.7908 | 3.6959 | 3.6048 | 3.5172 | 3.4331 | 3.3522 |
| 4.4859 | 4.3553 | 4.2305 | 4.1114 | 3.9975 | 3.8887 | 3.7845 |
| 5.0330 | 4.8684 | 4.7122 | 4.5638 | 4.4226 | 4.2883 | 4.1604 |
| 5.5348 | 5.3349 | 5.1461 | 4.9676 | 4.7988 | 4.6389 | 4.4873 |
| 5.9952 | 5.7590 | 5.5370 | 5.3282 | 5.1317 | 4.9464 | 4.7716 |
| 6.4177 | 6.1446 | 5.8892 | 5.6502 | 5.4262 | 5.2161 | 5.0188 |
| 6.8052 | 6.4951 | 6.2065 | 5.9377 | 5.6869 | 5.4527 | 5.2337 |
| 7.1607 | 6.8137 | 6.4924 | 6.1944 | 5.9176 | 5.6603 | 5.4206 |
| 7.4869 | 7.1034 | 6.7499 | 6.4235 | 6.1218 | 5.8424 | 5.5831 |
| 7.7862 | 7.3667 | 6.9819 | 6.6282 | 6.3025 | 6.0021 | 5.7245 |
| 8.0607 | 7.6061 | 7.1909 | 6.8109 | 6.4624 | 6.1422 | 5.8474 |
| 8.3126 | 7.8237 | 7.3792 | 6.9740 | 6.6039 | 6.2651 | 5.9542 |
| 8.5436 | 8.0216 | 7.5488 | 7.1196 | 6.7291 | 6.3729 | 6.0472 |
| 8.7556 | 8.2014 | 7.7016 | 7.2497 | 6.8399 | 6.4674 | 6.1280 |
| 8.9501 | 8.3649 | 7.8393 | 7.3658 | 6.9380 | 6.5504 | 6.1982 |
| 9.1285 | 8.5136 | 7.9633 | 7.4694 | 7.0248 | 6.6231 | 6.2593 |
| 9.2922 | 8.6487 | 8.0751 | 7.5620 | 7.1016 | 6.6870 | 6.3125 |
| 9.4424 | 8.7715 | 8.1757 | 7.6446 | 7.1695 | 6.7429 | 6.3587 |
| 9.5802 | 8.8832 | 8.2664 | 7.7184 | 7.2297 | 6.7921 | 6.3988 |
| 9.7066 | 8.9847 | 8.3481 | 7.7843 | 7.2829 | 6.8351 | 6.4338 |
| 9.8226 | 9.0770 | 8.4217 | 7.8431 | 7.3300 | 6.8729 | 6.4641 |
| 9.9290 | 9.1609 | 8.4881 | 7.8957 | 7.3717 | 6.9061 | 6.4906 |
| 10.0266 | 9.2372 | 8.5478 | 7.9426 | 7.4086 | 6.9352 | 6.5135 |
| 10.1161 | 9.3066 | 8.6016 | 7.9844 | 7.4412 | 6.9607 | 6.5335 |
| 10.1983 | 9.3696 | 8.6501 | 8.0218 | 7.4701 | 6.9830 | 6.5509 |
| 10.2737 | 9.4269 | 8.6938 | 8.0552 | 7.4957 | 7.0027 | 6.5660 |
| 10.3428 | 9.4790 | 8.7331 | 8.0850 | 7.5183 | 7.0199 | 6.5791 |
| 10.4062 | 9.5264 | 8.7686 | 8.1116 | 7.5383 | 7.0350 | 6.5905 |
| 10.4644 | 9.5694 | 8.8005 | 8.1354 | 7.5560 | 7.0482 | 6.6005 |
| 10.5178 | 9.6086 | 8.8293 | 8.1566 | 7.5717 | 7.0599 | 6.6091 |
| 10.5668 | 9.6442 | 8.8552 | 8.1755 | 7.5856 | 7.0700 | 6.6166 |
| 10.6118 | 9.6765 | 8.8786 | 8.1924 | 7.5979 | 7.0790 | 6.6231 |
| 10.6530 | 9.7059 | 8.8996 | 8.2075 | 7.6087 | 7.0868 | 6.6288 |
| 10.6908 | 9.7327 | 8.9186 | 8.2210 | 7.6183 | 7.0937 | 6.6338 |
| 10.7255 | 9.7570 | 8.9357 | 8.2330 | 7.6268 | 7.0997 | 6.6380 |
| 10.7574 | 9.7791 | 8.9511 | 8.2438 | 7.6344 | 7.1050 | 6.6418 |
| 10.7866 | 9.7991 | 8.9649 | 8.2534 | 7.6410 | 7.1097 | 6.6450 |
| 10.8134 | 9.8174 | 8.9774 | 8.2619 | 7.6469 | 7.1138 | 6.6478 |
| 10.8380 | 9.8340 | 8.9886 | 8.2696 | 7.6522 | 7.1173 | 6.6503 |
| 10.8605 | 9.8491 | 8.9988 | 8.2764 | 7.6568 | 7.1205 | 6.6524 |
| 10.8812 | 9.8628 | 9.0079 | 8.2825 | 7.6609 | 7.1232 | 6.6543 |
| 10.9002 | 9.8753 | 9.0161 | 8.2880 | 7.6645 | 7.1256 | 6.6559 |
| 10.9176 | 9.8866 | 9.0235 | 8.2928 | 7.6677 | 7.1277 | 6.6573 |
| 10.9336 | 9.8969 | 9.0302 | 8.2972 | 7.6705 | 7.1296 | 6.6585 |
| 10.9482 | 9.9063 | 9.0362 | 8.3010 | 7.6730 | 7.1312 | 6.6596 |
| 10.9617 | 9.9148 | 9.0417 | 8.3045 | 7.6752 | 7.1327 | 6.6605 |

# Index

## A

Accelerated depreciation; *see*
    Depreciation
Accountants, 11–17
    auditing, 12
    financial reporting, 12
    in industry, 16
    management advisory services, 16
    in nonprofit organizations, 16
    tax services, 15
Accounting, 2
    accrual basis, 122
    alternative models, 624, 638
    defined, 2
    generally accepted principles, 3, 14
    objectives, 5
    profession, 11–17
Accounting cycle, 74, 94–104
    defined, 74
    demonstrated, 94
Accounting entity, 193, 430
Accounting equation, 27, 28, 430, 534

Accounting "nonstandards," 9–11
Accounting Principles Board (APB),
    15, 189, 267, 269, 342, 377,
    382, 387, 392, 426, 453, 461,
    463, 465, 471, 487, 492, 499,
    514, 532, 556
Accounting profession, 9–17
Accounting series releases, 15
Accounting standards, 6–9
    consistency, 9
    objectivity, 7
    relevancy, 6
    uniformity, 8
Accounts
    control, 150, 248
    ledger, 74, 137
Accounts payable, 37, 78, 246
Accounts receivable
    aging of, 251
    defined, 34, 246
    turnover ratio, 595
    uncollectible, 234, 247, 251

Accounts receivable *(cont.)*
  write-off of, 247, 254
Accrual concept, 122–25, 431
Accrued expenses, 122
Accumulated depreciation, 35, 129, 322,
    339; *see also* Depreciation
Accumulated earnings; *see* Retained
    earnings
Activity ratios, 591, 595, 596
  accounts receivable turnover ratio, 595
  inventory turnover ratio, 595
  plant and equipment turnover ratio, 596
Actuarial cost method (pensions), 393
Actuaries, 393
Additional paid-in capital, 38; *see also*
    Capital in excess of par
Adjusted trial balance, 136, 139
Adjusting entries, 126, 144
Administration costs, 147
Admission of new partners (partnership),
    414–16
Advances from customers, 37
Aging schedule method (accounts
    receivable), 251
AICPA; *see* American Institute of
    Certified Public Accountants
All-inclusive income statement, 462–63
Allocation of costs, 2, 147, 331; *see also*
    Amortization, Depletion,
    Depreciation
Allowance for bad debts (or doubtful
    accounts), 34, 248
Allowance for depreciation; *see*
    Accumulated depreciation
Allowance for sales returns, 255
Allowance for uncollectibles, 248
American Institute of Certified Public
    Accountants (AICPA), 14, 185,
    288, 455
American Telephone & Telegraph
    Company, 428
Amortization, 36, 322, 346, 372, 394, 539
  goodwill, 505
Amounts due from officers, 246
Annuity
  defined, 221
  future value, 221
  ordinary, 221
  present value, 223
Annuity due (or in advance), 221
APB; *see* Accounting Principles Board
Appropriations of retained earnings,
    457–59

Arm's-length transactions, 192
Assets
  accounts, 75
  construction of, 331
  current, 34; *see also* Working capital
  deferred charges, 34
  defined, 26, 27
  determination of useful life, 343
  fixed, 2, 35, 322–50
  intangible, 26, 27, 322, 346, 497
  monetary, 627
  net, 28
  noncurrent, 35, 542
  nonmonetary, 627
  physical obsolescence, 343
  tangible, 26
  valuation of, 173, 190–228, 323
  value to user, 215, 324
Auditing, 12
Auditors' opinion (or report), 13, 194
Authorized stock, 417

## B

Bad debt expense, 247, 249, 252
Bad debts; *see* Uncollectible accounts
    receivable
Balance sheet, 26, 32
  as a statement of residuals, 213
  consolidated, 493
  illustrated, 27, 32, 79, 84, 88, 141
  preparation, 79, 104
  relationship to income statement, 132,
    172
Bank accounts, 228
Bank reconciliation, 229
Bauch & Lomb Corporation, 416, 418
Betterment costs, 333
Bond debentures, 366
Bond indentures, 366
Bonds, 365–79
  amortization of discount and premium,
    372, 376
  call provision, 366, 378
  convertible, 465
  coupon, 366
  defined, 37, 366
  discount (premium) determination, 368
  face (or par) value, 366
  maturity, 366
  municipal, 384
  nature of discount or premium, 371

Bonds *(cont.)*
  negotiable, 366
  principal, 366
  recording of interest payments, 372
  recording of sale, 371
  redemption, 377
  registered, 366
  valuation, 368–72
  versus preferred stock, 419
Book value, 128, 340
Business combinations; *see* Investments in
  other corporations

## C

Call premium, 367, 378
Call provision, 367, 378; *see also* Bonds,
  Preferred stock
Capital contributed by common
  stockholders, 38
Capital in excess of par, 38, 420
Capital markets, 646
Capital received from stock options, 461
Capital stock; *see also* Common stock,
  Preferred stock
  as a source of funds, 542
  characteristics of, 416–20
  common, 38, 416, 420
  defined, 38, 416
  dividends, 28, 96, 125, 416
  issue of, 420, 423
  preferred, 38, 416, 418–20, 423
  retirement of, 426
  treasury, 417, 424–27
Capitalization of costs, 122, 144, 170,
  329, 332; *see also* Intangible assets
Capitalization of interest, 332
Cash, 34, 228–32, 556–59
  in bank, 229
  classification of, 231
  defined, 228
  on hand, 229
  petty (imprest basis of accounting), 229
  sources and uses, 556–59
Cash disbursements (receipts) book, 150
Cash discounts
  defined, 256
  gross method, 257
  inventory cost, 288
  net method, 257
Cash flow, 226, 556–59
Certificates of incorporation, 410

Certified Public Accountant (CPA), 11,
  13, 246, 409
Closely held corporations, 192, 412
Closing entries, 92, 102, 142, 413; *see also*
  Expenses, Revenue
COGS; *see* Cost of goods sold
Combinations; *see* Investments in other
  corporations
Commitments outstanding, 602
Common stock
  authorized, 417
  characteristics of, 416–18
  classes of, 416
  defined, 38, 416
  discount, 420
  dividends, 416, 450
  issuance of, 420–23
  issued, 417
  outstanding, 417
  par (or stated) value, 38, 420
  premium, 420
  retirement of, 426
  treasury, 417, 424–27
Common stock equivalents, 466
Completion of production method of revenue
  recognition; *see* Revenue recognition
Compound interest, 216; *see also* Interest
Concepts underlying accounting, 191
Conglomerate corporations, 606
Conservatism, 195, 303, 582
Consistency principle, 9; *see also*
  Accounting standards
Consolidated financial statements (reports),
  492–514; *see also* Investments in
  other corporations
  balance sheet, 493–500, 507
  defined, 46, 450
  illustrated, 45–51
  income statement, 500–08
  rational for, 192, 492
Construction of assets, 331
Contingencies, 457
Contingent liabilities, 604
Contra accounts, 128, 249, 255, 263, 322
Control accounts, 150, 248
Convertible stock, 465
Copyrights, 346
Corporate capital accounts, 416
Corporate personality, 579–82
Corporations
  certificates, 410
  characteristics, 410, 411
  closely held, 192, 412

Corporations *(cont.)*
  conglomerates, 606
  defined, 410
  formation, 420
  promoters, 420
  versus partnerships, 411
Cost accounting, 289
Cost of goods sold, 37, 143, 286, 589
Cost of sales; *see* Cost of goods sold
Cost method
  investments in other corporations, 487,
    488, 491
  treasury stock, 425
Costs
  accrued, 122
  allocation of, 147, 331, 334
  betterment, 333
  direct, 147
  fixed, 6
  historical, 7, 8, 212, 624
  incremental, 7
  indirect, 147
  input, 214, 307
  joint, 331
  marginal, 7
  opportunity, 214
  overhead, 147, 289
  period, 146, 148, 289
  product, 146, 148, 289
  relevant, 6
  replacement; *see* Replacement cost
  variable, 6
Coupon bond, 366
Coupon interest rate, 368
CPA; *see* Certified Public Accountant
Credit memoranda, 149
Credits, 76
Current assets; *see also* individual asset
    accounts
  accounts receivable, 34
  cash, 34
  defined, 34
  inventories, 34
  marketable securities, 34
  prepaid expenses, 34
Current cash equivalent, 329
Current liabilities
  accounts payable, 37, 78, 246
  advances from customers, 37
  deferred credits, 37
  defined, 36
  revenues received but not yet earned, 37
Current operating performance, 462–63

Current ratio, 53, 597
Current replacement cost; *see* Replacement
    cost
Current value, 305; *see also* Replacement
    cost
Current value approach to accounting,
    638–43

**D**

Date of payment (dividends), 450
Date of record (dividends), 450
Debentures, 366
Debits, 76
Debt to equity ratio, 598
Deferral method (investment tax credit),
    391
Deferred charges (costs), 34, 35, 36, 191
Deferred credits, 37, 127
Deferred income taxes, 386, 540; *see also*
    Income taxes
Demolition costs, 330
Depletion, 322, 344, 539
Deposits receivable, 246
Deposits in transit, 229
Depreciation, 133, 334–39
  accelerated, 335
  accumulated, 35, 128, 339
  airlines, 333
  as a source of funds, 538
  basis, 322
  computer leasing industry, 343
  defined, 3, 322, 334
  double-declining balance method, 336,
    337, 386
  effect on earnings, 589
  nonprofit organizations, 431
  percentage method, 345
  productivity basis, 338
  straight line method, 334
  sum-of-the-year's digits method, 336
  units-of-output method, 338
Direct manufacturing costs, 147
Direct write-off method (bad debts), 247
Disclosure, required, 605
Discount, 368, 371; *see also* Bonds,
    Common stock, Preferred stock
  bonds, 368, 371
  cash, 256
  common stock, 420
  purchase, 258
  sales, 256
  trade, 256, 329

Discount notes, 262
Discount rate, 219, 262
Discounted cash flow, 226
Dividends, 450–59
  cash, 450
  date of payment, 450
  date of record, 450
  declaration of, 125, 450
  defined, 28, 41, 96, 450
  in kind, 452
  intercompany, 489
  payment of, 125
  receivable, 246
  stock, 454
Documents (source), 149
Double-declining balance depreciation,
  336, 337, 386
Double-entry record-keeping process, 12,
  27
Drilling cost in oil industry, 347

**E**

Earned surplus; *see* Retained earnings
Earnings; *see also* Income
  quality of, 301, 582–90
  as a source of working capital, 537
Earnings per share, 52, 464–70
*Eisner* v. *Macomber,* 455
Employee stock options, 460–62
Encumbrances, 431
Entity view of corporation, 429
Entries (journal), 77–83
  adjusting, 126
  closing, 92, 142, 413
  updating, 122
EPS; *see* Earnings per share
Equities
  defined, 26
  liabilities, 26
  owners' equity, 26, 27, 38
Equity method, 487, 489, 491
Equity of owners; *see* Owners' equity
Errors, 142
Estimation of uncollectibles, 251–53
Excess of cost over book value, 496–99
Exchange prices, 191
Executory contracts, 38
Expenses
  accrued, 122
  bad debt, 247, 249, 252
  charging of, 122

Expenses *(cont.)*
  closing entries, 92, 102
  defined, 30, 86
  illustrated, 84–91
  industry practices, 190
  insurance industry, 190
  interest; *see* Interest
  labor, 145
  payroll, 269
  recognition of, 122, 172
    an overview, 190
  retailing industry, 190
  timing, 189
  vacation pay, 269
Expropriation of property, 456
Extraordinary items, 39, 463

**F**

Face value; *see* Par value
Factory overhead costs, 147
Fair (market) value; *see* Market value
FASB; *see* Financial Accounting Standards
  Board
Federal Insurance Contribution Act, 270
FICA; *see* Federal Insurance Contribution
  Act
FIFO; *see* First-in, first-out
Financial accounting defined, 2
Financial Accounting Standards Board
  (FASB), 14, 333, 347, 349, 382,
  384, 457, 459, 488, 624
Financial analysis, 52–55
  corporate personality, 579–82
  objectives, 578
  quality earnings, 582–90
  ratio and percentage analysis, 591–600
Financial leases; *see* Financing leases
Financial reporting
  defined, 12
  interim, 470
  SEC requirements, 604
Financial statements
  analysis of; *see* Financial analysis
  consolidated; *see* Consolidated financial
    statements
  illustrated, 44
  interim, 470
  limitations of, 9
  nonprofit organizatons, 432
  objectives, 532
  price-level adjustments, 624–38

Financial statements *(cont.)*
    ratio and percentage analysis, 591–600
Financing leases, 381
Financing ratios, 592, 598–600
    debt to equity, 598
    times interest earned, 599
First-in, first-out method (inventory), 292
Fixed assets, 2, 35, 322–50; *see also* Assets
    nonprofit organizations, 431
Fixed costs, 6
Flow of costs, 290
Flow-through method (investment tax
    credit), 391
Footnotes, 47–51, 600–05
Ford Motor Co., 451
Franchise industry, 268
Freight-in, 330
Full cost method of accounting for
    drilling costs, 348
Fully diluted EPS, 466, 469
Funds, 42, 533; *see also* Statement of
    changes in financial position
    nonprofit organizations, 430
    pension, 393
    petty cash, 229
    sinking funds, 232
Fungible goods, 290
Future value, 216
Future value of annuity, 221
    nonprofit organizations, 430
    pension, 393

### G

Gains (losses)
    appreciation, 584
    holding, 305
    purchasing power, 630
    realized vs. unrealized, 639
    redemption, 377
    retirement, 339
    as a source (use) of funds, 540
    trading, 305
General Accounting Office (GAO), 17
General ledger, 75, 77, 149
General Mills Company, 579–87
General partners, 411
Generally accepted accounting principles,
    3, 14
GNP (Gross National Product)
    deflator, 626
Going concern, 194

Goodwill, 346, 414, 498
    amortization, 505
Government accounting, 429–32
Gross margin, 595
Gross National Product Implicit Price
    Deflator (GNP deflator), 626

### H

Hand, Learned (Judge), 11
Historical cost, 7, 212, 624
    advantages, 327
Holding gains (losses), 305, 323, 325

### I

Imprest basis of accounting for petty
    cash, 229
Income
    defined, 2, 86
    as a source of working capital, 537
Income statement
    all inclusive, 462
    consolidated, 500–08
    current operating performance, 462
    defined, 30
    illustrated, 39, 101, 140
    preparation of, 90, 100
    relationship to balance sheet, 132, 172
Income taxes, 136, 301, 303, 384–92, 455,
    470; *see also* Investment tax credit
Incremental cost, 7
Indentures, 366; *see also* Bonds
Indirect costs, 147
Inflation, accounting for, 624–38
    adjusting balance sheet, 628
    adjusting income statement, 633
    factors that determine magnitude of
        adjustments, 636
    gains and losses in purchasing power,
        230
    monetary versus nonmonetary items,
        627
    rationale for, 624, 635
    use of index numbers, 626
Input cost (value), 214, 307
Installation cost, 330
Installment basis of revenue recognition,
    171, 176, 184, 387; *see also* Revenue
Installment purchase, 171
Instant earnings, 508, 513

Insurance, 133, 458

Insurance industry, 190

Intangible assets, 26, 346, 497; *see also*
    Assets, Copyrights, Drilling costs,
    Goodwill, Organizational costs,
    Patents, Research and development
    costs

Intercorporate investments and
    transactions; *see* Investments in
    other corporations

Interest; *see also* Bonds
  accrued, 126, 376
  capitalization of, 332
  compound, 216
  computation of, 259
  earned, 135, 259
  expense, 126, 372
  expense versus distribution of earnings,
    427
  intercompany, 501
  prime rate, 267
  receivable, 246
  revenue, 135, 259

Interest-free notes, 265

Interim financial reports, 470

Internal Revenue Service (IRS), 301, 303,
    338, 354

Interperiod tax allocation, 384–90

Inventory, 285–308
  accounting objectives, 286
  defined, 34, 286
  first-in, first-out (FIFO), 292
  included costs, 288
  last-in, first-out (LIFO), 269
  lower of cost or market rule, 303
  periodic method, 131, 143
  perpetual method, 131
  quantities on hand, 289
  retail method, 302
  shortages, 136
  specific identification method, 291
  weighted average method, 293

Inventory turnover, 301, 595

Investment tax credit, 390–92

Investments and other assets, 35

Investments in other corporations, 449–82
  acquisition for stock, 508
  consolidated balance sheet, 493–500, 507
  consolidated income statement, 500–08
  cost and equity methods compared, 491
  cost method, 486, 487, 491
  defined, 486
  degree of influence, 487

Investments in other corporations *(cont.)*
  equity method, 487, 489, 491
  excess of cost over book value, 496–99
  goodwill, 498
  intercompany cost of goods sold, 503
  intercompany debts, 494
  intercompany interests, 501
  intercompany sales, 503
  level of influence, 487
  minority interest, 495
  minority share of consolidated income,
    506
  minority stockholders, 495
  pooling of interests method, 509–14
  principles of consolidation, 492–514
  purchase method, 509

Invoices, 149

IRS; *see* Internal Revenue Service

**J**

Joint cost, 331

Journal
  cash disbursements, 150
  cash receipts, 150
  closing entries, 92, 102, 142, 413
  defined, 77, 149
  general, 149
  sales, 149

Journal entries, 77–83; *see also* Entries

**K**

Kellogg Company, 579–606

Koppers Company, 44

**L**

Labor cost (expense), 145

Land, 330

Last-in, first-out method (inventory),
    296–302
  dollar value basis, 284

Leases
  capitalization of, 383
  defined, 328, 379
  financing, 381
  operating, 383

Ledger
  account, 74, 99
  general, 75, 77, 149
  subsidiary, 150

Legal capital, 420
Legal fees, 330
Liabilities
  accounts, 75
  advances from customers, 37
  bonds, 37, 365–79
  contingent, 604
  current, 36
  deferred income taxes, 386, 540
  deferred revenue, 37
  defined, 26, 27
  leases, 328, 379–83
  long-term, 365–79, 544
  monetary, 627
  noncurrent, 37, 544
  nonmonetary, 627
  notes payable, 78, 246
  payroll, 269
  tax, 384–92
LIFO; *see* Last-in, first-out method
Limited liability, 411
Liquidation value, 194
Liquidity, 42
Liquidity ratios, 597, 598
  current, 597
  quick, 598
Long-lived assets; *see* Fixed assets
Long-term debt; *see also* Bonds, Liabilities
  nonprofit organizations, 431
Losses, 456–57; *see also* Gains
Lower of cost or market rule, 215, 303

**M**

Maintenance cost, 333
Management advisory services, 16
Manufacturing costs, 145
Manufacturing cycle, 145
Marginal cost, 7
Market value, 7, 213, 214, 323; *see also*
    Current value
Marketable securities, 34, 232
Matching principle, 144, 146, 297
Merchandise transactions, 124
Mergers; *see* Investments in other
    corporations
Mineral deposits, 344
Minority interest, 495
Minority share of consolidated income,
    506
Minority stockholders, 495
Modified accrual basis, 431

Monetary items, 627
Monetary unit, 193
Motion picture industry, 188
Municipal bonds, 384, 430
Municipalities, 430

**N**

Natural resources
  defined, 344
  depletion; *see* Depletion
Negotiable bonds, 366
Net assets, 28
Net income; *see* Income
Net realizable value, 214
New York Stock Exchange, 12
Noncurrent assets
  deferred charges, 35
  defined, 35
  fixed assets, 2, 35, 322–50
  investments and other assets, 35
  land, 330
  long-lived (fixed) assets, 322–50
  as sources of funds, 542
Noncurrent liabilities, 37
Nonfund exchanges, 535
Noninterest bearing notes, 265
Nonmonetary items, 627
Nonprofit organizations, 429–32
"Nonstandards;" *see* Accounting
    "nonstandards"
Normal operating cycle, 34
Notes
  defined, 37
  promissory, 256
Notes payable, 78, 246
Notes receivable
  defined, 246
  discount, 261–65
  face-value, 260
  interest included in face value, 261–65
  noninterest bearing, 265
N.S.F. (nonsufficient funds) checks, 231
Number of days sales in accounts
    receivable, 596

**O**

Objectives of accounting, 5; *see also*
    Accounting
Objectivity, 7; *see also* Accounting
    objectives

Offset accounts; *see* Contra accounts
Oil industry, 345, 347, 384
Omissions, 142
Operating cycle of a business, 34, 173
Operating leases, 383
Opportunity cost, 214
Ordinary annuity, 221; *see also* Annuity
Organizational costs, 35, 36, 191, 346
Output price (value), 214, 307
Outstanding stock, 417
Overhead costs, 147, 289
Owners' equity, 26, 27, 38; *see also*
  Stockholders' equity
 components, 38
 defined, 26, 27
Ownership issues, 328

# P

Paciolo, Fr. Luca, 12
Pan American World Airways, 530, 531
Par value, 38, 366, 420; *see also* Bonds,
  Common stock, Preferred stock
Parent company, 493
Participating issues (preferred stock), 418
Partnerships, 38, 408, 411
 accounting for, 412–16
 admission of new members, 414
 agreement, 409
 characteristics of, 408, 409, 411
 formation of, 412
 versus corporation, 411
Patents, 346
Payables, 246
Payroll transactions, 269
P/E ratio; *see* Price/earnings ratio
Pensions, 392–94
Percentage of completion method of
  revenue recognition, 175, 179; *see*
  *also* Revenue
Percentage method of depletion, 345
Percentage of revenue (sales) analysis,
  594; *see also* Profitability ratios
Percentage of sales method (uncollectible
  accounts receivable), 251
Period costs, 146, 148, 289
Periodic adjusting entries, 126–44
Periodic inventory method, 131, 289, 294,
  296
Permanent capital, 428, 455
Perpetual inventory method, 131, 289,
  295, 296

Petty cash (imprest basis of accounting),
  229
Physical inventory, 130, 290
Physical obsolescence, 343
Plant assets, 329
Plant and equipment turnover ratio, 596
Pooling of interests, 509–14
Postclosing trial balance, 98, 103
Posting, 77, 149
Preclosing trial balance, 98, 100
Preemptive rights, 465; *see also* Stock
  rights
Preferred stock
 call provision, 419
 characteristics of, 418–20
 convertible, 419, 465
 defined, 38, 416
 discount, 38, 424
 issue of, 423
 participating issues, 418
 premium, 424
 versus bonds, 419
Premium, 368, 371, 420; *see also* Bonds,
  Common stock
Prepaid expenses, 34, 122; *see also*
  Current assets
Prepaid rent, 78
Present value, 218
Present value of annuity, 223
Prevailing rates of interest, 368
Price/earnings ratio, 52, 508
Price-level adjustments, 624–38; *see also*
  Inflation, accounting for
Primary EPS, 466, 468
Prime interest rate, 267
Prior service costs (pensions), 394
Product cost, 146, 148, 289
Productivity basis of depreciation, 338
Profit; *see* Income
Profitability ratios, 591
 percentage of revenue, 594
 price/earnings ratio, 594
 return on investment, 592
Profit/loss sharing ratio, 415, 416
Profit margin, 595
Promissory notes
 defined, 258
 illustrated, 259
 interest included in face value, 261–65
 noninterest-bearing, 265
 reporting practices, 259
 typical provisions, 258
Promotors (corporation), 420

Property taxes, 135; *see also* Taxes
Proprietary view of corporation, 429
Proprietorships, 38, 408, 412
Public Utility Holding Company Act of
    1935, 15
Purchase discount, 258; *see also* Cash
    discounts
Purchase method (investments in other
    corporations), 509
Purchases, 131, 290
Purchasing power gains (losses), 630

## Q

Quality of earnings, 301, 582–90
Quick ratio, 598

## R

Railroad industry, 328
Ratio analysis, 591–600
Ratios
    activity, 591, 595
    financing, 592
    liquidity, 592, 597, 598
    profitability, 591, 592
Raw materials, 145
Real estate industry, 185
Real estate investment trusts, 253
Realization of revenue; *see* Revenue
    recognition
Receivables, 246, 588; *see also* Accounts
    receivable, Notes receivable
Recognition of expense; *see* Expenses
Recognition of revenue; *see* Revenue
    recognition
Reconciliation of bank balance, 229
Redemption of bonds, 377
Registered bonds, 366
Regulation S-X, 15
Relationships among financial statements,
    30, 31
Relevancy, 6; *see also* Accounting
    standards
Relevant cost, 7
Remittance advices, 149
Rent, 381
Repair cost, 333
Replacement cost (price), 215, 307, 325,
    638–43
Research and development costs, 348

Reserve recognition accounting, 348
Reserves for contingencies, 458
Reserves for encumbrances, 431
Reserves of retained earnings, 458
Retail inventory method, 302
Retail land sales companies, 266
Retailing industry, 190
Retained earnings, 38, 40, 41, 85–94, 101,
    450–59, 537–42
    appropriation of, 457–61
    capitalization of, 454, 455
    contrasted with assets, 41
    as a source of working capital, 537–42
    statement of, 40
Retirement of fixed assets, 339
Retirement gains (losses), 340
Retirement of outstanding stock, 426
Return on investment, 53, 592
Revenue
    closing entries, 92, 102
    deferred, 37
    defined, 30, 86, 170
    illustrated, 84–91
    received in advance, 37
Revenue realization; *see* Revenue
    recognition
Revenue received but not yet earned, 37
Revenue recognition, 122, 170, 584
    analysis of transactions, 177
    at time of sale, 174, 177
    collection of cash method, 176, 184,
        387
    completion of producing method, 175,
        183
    during production, 174, 179, 385
    franchise industry, 268
    guidelines, 174
    impact of timing differences, 172
    motion picture industry, 188
    retail land sales, 266
    selected industry problems, 187–89, 266
    shipping industry, 187
    trading stamps industry, 188
ROI; *see* Return on investment

## S

Salaries, 136, 269, 413
Sales discount, 256; *see* Cash discounts
Sales journal, 149
Sales returns, 255
Salvage value, 3, 34, 337

Securities and Exchange Commission
(SEC), 12, 14, 254, 327, 348, 392,
430, 589, 605, 606
"Self-insurance," 458
Shipping industry, 187
Sinking funds, 232
Social Security; *see* Federal Insurance
Contribution Act
Sole proprietorships, 38; *see also*
Proprietorships
Source documents, 149
Sources and applications of funds; *see*
Statement of changes in financial
position
Specific identification method (inventory),
291
Speculative holding gains (losses); *see*
Holding gains (losses)
Stated capital, 420
Stated value, 38; *see also* Par value
Statement of changes in financial position,
42–44, 524, 594; *see also* Working
capital
  APB's opinion, 532, 556
  cash basis, 556–59
  fund basis, 530, 556
  preparation of, 536–56
Statement of changes in owners' equity;
  *see* Statement of retained earnings
Statement of (financial) position; *see*
  Balance sheet
Statement of income; *see* Income statement
Statement of retained earnings, 40
Statement of sources and application of
  funds; *see* Statement of changes in
  financial position
Sticker price, 191, 341
Stock; *see also* Capital stock
  common, 38
  convertible, 465
  preferred, 38
Stock certificates, 28
Stock dividends, 454
Stock exchanges, 12
Stock options; *see* Employee stock options
Stock rights, 465
Stock splits, 453
Straight-line amortization of bond
  discount or premium, 376, 377; *see*
  *also* Bonds
  APB's opinion, 377
Straight-line depreciation method, 324
Subsidiary companies, 493

Subsidiary ledgers, 150, 226
Successful efforts method of accounting
  for drilling costs, 348
Supplies, 123, 129, 135
Supplies expense, 123
Surplus; *see* Retained earnings

**T**

T-accounts
  defined, 76
Tangible assets, 26, 497; *see also* Assets
Tax services, 15
Taxes; *see also* Internal Revenue Service
  allocation of, 384
  deferred, 384, 540
  income; *see* Income taxes
  on partnerships, 409, 412
  property, 135
Temporary investments; *see* Marketable
  securities
Time value of money, 216
Times interest earned (ratio), 599
Trade discounts, 288
Trade-in allowances, 191
Trade-ins, 340
Trading gains (losses), 305
Trading stamp industry, 188
Transportation costs, 329
Treasury shares (stock), 417, 424–27
  cost method, 425
  par value method, 426
Trial balance
  adjusted, 136, 139
  defined, 98
  illustrated, 100, 134
  postclosing, 98, 103
  preclosing, 98

**U**

Uncollectible accounts receivable
  defined, 247
  estimation of, 251
Uniformity, 8; *see also* Accounting
  standards
Units of output basis of depreciation, 338
Unrealized gains, 234, 639
Unsecured bonds; *see* Debentures
Updating entries, 126, 129
U.S. Treasury Department, 392

## V

Vacation pay expenses, 271
Valuation of assets
  discounted cash flow approach, 226
  historical cost approach, 323
  market value approach, 323
Value
  contrasted with changes in price, 625
  current (fair market), 7, 191, 213, 305,
    323
  defined, 212
  net realizable, 214
  to user, 215, 324
Variable costs, 6
Vouchers payable, 149

## W

Wages, 136, 269; *see also* Salaries
Warranties, 177
Warrants, 465
Wasting assets; *see* Natural resources
Weighted average method (inventory), 293
Working capital, 42, 530–56; *see also*
    Statement of changes in financial
    position
  components of, 534
  computing changes in, 536
W. R. Grace & Co., 647

## Y

Year-end adjustments, 126–44
Yield rate, 369